The Future
of Conflict
in the 1980s

The Future
of Conflict
in the 1980s

Edited by
William J. Taylor, Jr.
The Center for Strategic
and International Studies,
Georgetown University
Steven A. Maaranen
Los Alamos National Laboratory

Foreword by
David M. Abshire

LexingtonBooks
D.C. Heath and Company
Lexington, Massachusetts
Toronto

Library of Congress Cataloging in Publication Data
Main entry under title:

The Future of conflict in the 1980s.

Based on the CSIS Future of Conflict Conference held in Washington,
D.C., in the fall 1981.
Includes index.
1. National security—Addresses, essays, lectures. 2. World politics—1975–
1985—Addresses, essays, lectures.   I. Taylor, William J. (William Jesse),
1933–   II. Maaranen, Steven A.   III. CSIS Future of Conflict
Conference
(1981 : Washington, D.C.)
UA10.5.F87   1982   355′.033′0048   82-48474
ISBN 0-669-06145-x

Published simultaneously in Canada

Printed in the United States of America

International Standard Book Number: 0-669-06145-x

Library of Congress Catalog Card Number: 82-48474

Contents

Foreword

We live in rapidly changing times, and one can safely predict that the pace of change will only accelerate in the years ahead. Challenges to the international-security interests of the United States will grow, and the nature of the United States's world leadership role will be tested repeatedly. Reducing the uncertainties that accompany rapid change will be a monumental task for foreign and defense policy planners and decision makers. The contributors to this book have taken a major step in a continuing effort by The Center for Strategic and International Studies (CSIS) to clarify the challenges of the future and to move the academic world into the world of action.

The main thrust of this book is a forecast of low-intensity-conflict situations that are likely to threaten U.S. national interests in the 1980s. A word about this forward-looking approach may be in order. Forecasting holds both great pitfalls and great opportunities. Although it can be filled with pitfalls for the unwary, forecasting can be useful to those who learn to understand and use it. The timid, afraid of making mistakes or of being proven wrong, are reluctant to risk forecasts. Others denigrate the utility of forecasting, believing that future events are either so capricious or so complex as to defy prediction.

Many people, however, are simply too pressed by daily exigencies to worry about events too far into the future. Herein lies a modern paradox, a product of the frenetic pace and the constraints on time that characterize the system by which the national-security process is managed. Those policy-makers whose decisions potentially will have the widest impact and most-lasting consequences are also those whose attention spans are hardest driven by the daily-operational demands of the present.

In an age where conflict can be manifest in a wide variety of ways, a failure to prepare ahead in appropriate ways may even contribute unwittingly to the potential seriousness of a conflict, particularly if it arises in a totally unexpected manner or takes a totally unfamiliar form. Indeed, the lead time gained by the advance conceptualization of potential problems and conflicts is needed today as never before. On the assumption that the recognition of a problem can be an important first step to its solution, this book examines some of the issues, both functional and regional, that may contribute to conflict in the 1980s and that may influence the forms that conflict may take.

Future events certainly are not predetermined, regardless of the historical roots and antecedents of action that may influence them. Nor are such events ever completely random and arbitrary, despite the surprises that may be involved in a sudden emergence of hitherto unimportant variables.

Skeptics sometimes scoff that events are best predicted in retrospect, but the verity that facts or events can sometimes be explained in retrospect is important; that we can sometimes explain even an extraordinary event after the fact gives some hope that with sufficient experience and insight we may be able to make better predictions about future events. Events in the distant past may be easier to explain than those in the more immediate past. The dust and smoke of irrelevant facts have had a chance to clear. The relationships between occurrences have had a chance to emerge in greater relief. The converse appears to be true when trying to peer into the future. The longer the time frame, the more difficult it is to make predictions. The number of variables increases, and the combinations and permutations of ways that those variables can interact increase geometrically. However, it is precisely the difficulty of looking forward that makes attempts to do so important.

Realizing the difficulties of trying to project too far into a future filled with uncertainties, this study focuses on the future of conflict in this decade, highlighting particularly the low-level forms of conflict that may affect the vital or important interests of the United States in region-, issue-, or function-specific ways. The approach centers on five aspects of the future of conflict in the 1980s: (1) perspectives on the future of conflict and implications for U.S. policies; (2) some of the causes of low-intensity conflict; (3) selected military operations for combating low-intensity conflict, including psychological operations, terrorism, proxy warfare, and rescue operations; (4) the future of conflict in six regional settings, outer space, and the oceans; and (5) the strategic implications of the spectrum of conflict projected for the 1980s.

A word should be added about the conflict scenarios that accompany some of the chapters in this book. It is often easier to develop strategies on the basis of projected specific occurrences, rather than to plan on the basis of general analyses of trends and probabilities. In a sense, the scenario represents a prism that focuses a diversity of information into a specific combination of events, which can then represent a possible occurrence. A scenario can be defined as a set of potential occurrences that: (1) belong to a certain field of relevance; (2) relate to a certain time period; and (3) are connected by various relations in such a way that an approximation of the whole set can be derived from a subset of basic hypotheses taken from it.

It goes without saying that scenario building is a highly subjective task in which the construction of the future is clearly a product of the builder's basic hypotheses. It is best if scenario builders make their starting assumptions explicit; this makes it possible to compare the assumptions of one analyst with those of others. In comparisons of scenarios, both convergence and divergence can be significant. Divergent scenarios produced from similar premises may underline different understandings of the processes that affect the interaction of similar variables. It is worth underscoring that scenario building is not license for wild speculation. A basic assumption must be that of general uniformity of process. This does not mean that new things cannot happen in new ways; rather, scenarios that depict actual trends and represent extrapolations of present conditions are likely to be more accurate than scenarios that do not accept both existing conditions and existing processes of change and continuity. Likewise, convergence can be telling. When independent observers starting from different assumptions about the way possibly different factors may interact develop similar scenarios, this convergence of result strengthens the credibility of the projected outcomes.

Another distinction may be useful. In general, there are two kinds of scenarios. There are those that attempt to paint as likely a landscape of the future as possible. These focus on existing conditions and on the courses of development most likely followed by subsequent events. There is a second kind of scenario, a more speculative one. It also begins by focusing on existing conditions. However, it then postulates that the potentially most dangerous situations or conflicts may be those that have not been conceptualized, let alone anticipated—the ones that come as more or less complete surprises. Such scenarios highlight the dangers of assuming that one lives in a linear world. Every scenario must be carefully rooted in fact or it is merely speculation; at the same time, ideally, each scenario must confront long-term planners with possibilities within the realm of probability that still challenge their conventional ideas about the world to come. Such scenarios do not have to depict either best or worst cases. What they should provide is a sense that anticipates that truth is stranger than fiction and that coping with conflicts in the future real world may be more demanding than expected. Thus, the scenarios in this book will be challenging, stimulating, and, therefore, useful in presenting options that may not necessarily come to pass but that will, in their consideration, prepare us better for the future.

The eternal dilemma remains in the balance of our learning from the past and our learning from our projections of the future. Our efforts in both these directions are, of course, inextricable. As Winston Churchill once observed, the further one would peer into the future, the further he must look into the past. The challenge is to ensure that planners do not prepare to fight the last war or prepare for the last crisis. The challenges and risks posed by conflict in the 1980s will take our best thinking and preparation. And there is real hope that sound thinking and preparation now could become the genesis of a certain amount of the most felicitous kind of self-fulfilling prophecy. To the extent that studies such as this contribute to an awareness of the dangers and difficulties posed by the potential for new types of conflict in the 1980s, they may lead to the containment or defusing of that which they anticipate. If, in the future, some part of this book contributes to disproving itself, whether because crises over resource scarcity were averted or regional threats anticipated and thereby defused, then that would be the greatest contribution for which the authors could hope.

The goal of this collective effort coincides with that of our nation—a foreign policy designed to achieve a stable world peace.

David M. Abshire
President
The Center for Strategic and International Studies

Preface

Represented in this book is the work of a large number of dedicated professionals whose concerted effort was made possible by support from the Los Alamos National Laboratories. The basic ideas for the study were developed by Donald Kerr, director, Los Alamos National Laboratory, and David M. Abshire and Amos A. Jordan, chairman and vice-chairman, respectively, of The Center for Strategic and International Studies (CSIS), Georgetown University. Broad guidance for the study was provided by a CSIS steering committee chaired by Walter Laqueur.

The study was a major undertaking involving working seminars, discussion sessions both in Washington and at Los Alamos, and periodic presentations and reviews of interim findings. The chapters in this book are derived from the efforts of the CSIS staff involved in the project and from the contributions of other scholars invited to prepare and present papers for the CSIS Future of Conflict Conference developed by William J. Taylor, Jr. and Steven A. Maaranen and held in Washington, D.C., in the fall of 1981. The dialogue with panel audiences and the consequent panel reports prepared by CSIS rapporteurs were important in refining the conference papers.

Although many at CSIS and Los Alamos National Laboratory contributed significantly to both the substance of this book and the management and administration of the study and conference, we wish to acknowledge especially the efforts of a few key people. Jeffrey Pierson, Paul M. Cole and Paul R. Ingholt major contributors to the entire effort—substance, coordination, and administration. John Bernard and Mary Park planned and coordinated all the conference functions in the flawless style they have now made traditional at the Center. Kay Batura organized the administrative effort with her usual precision. Shiela Brammer's careful attention to planning and direction was invaluable in anticipating and preempting problems. The rapporteurs' reports were very useful in writing the conclusion; special thanks for these are owed to Martha Bukowski, Gerrit Gong, Steven Hildreth, Elizabeth Kumpa, Todd Leventhal, William McIlhenny, Sophia Miskiewicz, Paula Noonan, and Jonathan Stein. Christa Dantzler, CSIS chief financial officer, kept the project within the confines of budget realities.

Our goal in this entire effort has been to provide a better understanding of the factors likely to lead to conflict situations involving U.S. national interests in the 1980s. This is a large undertaking, leading to a large book. It is our hope that various parts will be useful to students and practitioners of the art of nation-security strategy.

The Future
of Conflict
in the 1980s

1

Introduction

William J. Taylor, Jr.,
and *Steven A. Maaranen*

This book is the culmination of a year-long study on the future of conflict in the 1980s. Leading experts examined likely sources of conflict for the decade and projected ways in which conflict could erupt on land, in the oceans, and in space. A subsequent study is developing and evaluating U.S. strategic options and force postures that might best protect U.S. interests in the turbulent world of the 1980s.

The recent Soviet military buildup of strategic nuclear and theater nuclear forces is well known. It has set in motion a series of U.S. and NATO Alliance force-modernization programs as well as strategic and intermediate nuclear-arms-control negotiations. Both represent approaches to bringing the threat from the Soviet buildup under control, but neither aims, at this point, at more than reestablishing strategic and theater nuclear parity. At best, our response to the Soviet buildup will strengthen mutual deterrence of nuclear-weapon use. The result will be to place a heavier burden on the nonnuclear military forces of both sides.

On the Eurasian land mass, the Soviet Union has, since World War II, exercised conventional-military-force superiority. United States defense policy in the 1980s will have to devise ways to negate Soviet superiority in Europe as its reliance on the threat of nuclear escalation to rectify conventional imbalances declines.

A negation of the political-military utility of strategic and theater nuclear forces of the United States and the Soviet Union will also raise the stakes of this competition in those marginal areas where American and Soviet interests meet and clash. And all this will occur at a time when indigenous challenges to U.S. interests in many areas around the world will be growing, as hostile or unstable regimes exercise power on growing numbers of states and new regional powers and power relationships emerge.

The 1980s thus will confront the United States with an increasing number and diversity of threats to its vital or important national interests worldwide. In his chapter, James Schlesinger suggests that a decline has occurred in both actual and perceived American power, relative to U.S. interests and commitments abroad, which have not undergone any comparable reduction. This decline has contributed to the emergence of new, enlarged, and more urgent challenges to U.S. power and policy. Schlesinger

3

stresses that this "generic change" in U.S. military and economic power, vis-à-vis U.S. interests, combined with a rise in Soviet military strength, has compounded the difficulties of dealing diplomatically with such situations as European opposition to deployment of theater nuclear forces, Arab-Israeli tensions, and Cuban infiltration sponsored by the USSR in Central America and Africa. There is no indication that, for the next several years, the United States will acquire adequate military capabilities (including force mobilization, force strength, and access to bases needed for pre-positioning troops and supplies) to enjoy much freedom of operation (outside Europe) in areas where the likelihood of conflict affecting important U.S. interests appears high. Many future conflicts will not warrant U.S. military responses (or even diplomacy backed up by credible military force). However, repeated failure to respond effectively to those conflicts that do affect significant U.S. interests not only would be damaging but would further erode confidence in U.S. determination and capabilities.

The chapters in this book generally indicate that the most frequent forms of conflict in the 1980s will be in the spectrum of low-intensity engagements (for example, coercive diplomacy, terrorism, subversion, revolutionary war, and limited military actions). These will occur predominantly in the third world. These conflicts may stem directly from changes in U.S. military power. However, actual or perceived decline in U.S. capability or will to act can serve as stimuli to Soviet or Soviet-proxy risk taking.

On the other hand, U.S. concern for the outcome of low-intensity conflicts is not likely to subside. Considering the continuing global reach of U.S. strategic, political, and economic interests (and consequently the need to be able to bring U.S. military strength to bear in the defense of those interests), conflicts occurring in any region of the world almost certainly will affect U.S. national interests to some degree.

Part II focuses on several major sources of potential conflict. Competition for natural resources, especially energy and strategic mineral resources, emerge as a major potential source of conflict for the 1980s. A contributor to the changing character of future conflict, even in the developing world, will be the spread of arms and technology transfers on a global scale. The brief but destructive wars between Israel and its neighbors, and between Britain and Argentina over the Falkland Islands in 1982, testify to the qualitative changes in conventional weaponry and warfare. The special case of possible nuclear-weapon proliferation is considered both as a source of conflict and as a contribution to new directions that conflict may take in the 1980s.

Several chapters survey regions of the world, to anticipate situations in which the various sources of conflict, especially low-intensity conflict, may lead to actual hostilities. Seven regions were chosen: the Middle East, Southwest Asia, Southeast Asia, Northeast Asia, Latin America, Africa, and Europe.

Future conflicts in the third world (regionally defined as Africa, Central America, South America, the Middle East, and Southwest and Southeast Asia) are likely to emerge predominantly because of internal tensions and regime instabilities. Those instabilities and potential conflicts will often fall or be maneuvered into the general East-West competition for political, economic, and strategic advantage. Several likely features of third-world conflicts in the 1980s emerge:

1. The Soviet Union will continue to strive to validate its claims to global power by seeking to gain greater influence in the third world. The relative instability and disintegration of postcolonial, pro-West, third-world regimes will continue to allow access to Soviet or Soviet-sponsored intervention. In effect, as developing nations encourage the import of military assistance needed to satisfy so-called legitimate national-security concerns, Moscow will continue to have the opportunity to exploit its assistance for strategic advantage.

2. The third world has become increasingly susceptible to Soviet-proxy interventions, which, despite some setbacks, serve Soviet national interests effectively without the costs and risks associated with direct Soviet involvement. Intervention in the third world has enabled Soviet proxies to gain greater access to economic markets as well as to gain influence politically. In the long run, Soviet-proxy-state successes in the third world probably will nurture a continued pattern of interventions from which both proxy and Moscow will benefit.

3. General instability caused by economic stringency (for example, continuing increases in oil prices and resulting low rates of growth in developing-nation economies), internal political turmoil, and shifting regional and global power relationships will make the protection of U.S. interests in the third world increasingly difficult, even in the absence of Soviet interest or activity. The need to attend to a series of regional and local troubles, in combination with the need to address East-West tensions, will strain and dilute U.S. diplomatic and military resources.

4. United States resources for responding in regions of the third-world where American interests are threatened are seriously limited by shortages of air and sea lift and by inadequate capabilities for maritime pre-positioning of supplies. Moreover, as recent dilemmas over adequate basing facilities near the Persian Gulf indicate, the United States cannot assume that local support will be forthcoming from host-country governments for direct U.S., or combined, military counterresponses to regional-security threats (and even with an official state endorsement, host-country public reaction may be negative).

5. Beyond the continental land masses, there is potential for conflict on the world's oceans and in space. On the oceans, the United States needs to recognize properly the growing adverse trends between Soviet and U.S.

naval strengths, underscored by mutually competing strategies to secure strategic "chokepoints" and sea lines of communication (especially vital to Western nations). Third-country interests in this realm are also of growing importance. Aside from U.S.-Soviet naval competition, conflicts concerning the merchant marine, oceanography and ocean resources (including oil, gas, and strategic minerals), differences over the jurisdiction of territorial, contiguous, and high seas, and clashes over access to fishery zones will impact substantially on U.S. national interests.

6. Modern technology is carrying the potential for conflict in the 1980s beyond the earth's surface. United States satellite surveillance, communication, and navigation information are vital to the support of the U.S. military (and many satellite systems are becoming increasingly important to the U.S. economy). Soviet development of the antisatellite (ASAT) systems poses a threat to tactical and strategic command-and-control structures, which might seriously affect U.S. military capabilities, both nuclear and conventional, worldwide. United States military research and development efforts on space-based command, control, communications, and intelligence (C^3I), and other more direct military applications in space, as they relate to similar efforts by the Soviet Union, should be viewed as an arena of crucial importance in the 1980s.

Because of the probable importance of low-intensity conflicts in the coming decade, the United States should reevaluate its military capabilities for responding to these types of threats. United States national-security planners are prone to model U.S. general-purpose forces for what is considered the most critical scenario—large-scale combat with the Soviet bloc in Central Europe.

Yet the most common challenges to U.S. interests in the 1980s will develop largely outside the European battlefront. Ambassador Robert W. Komer stresses in chapter 3 that U.S. forces are capable of fighting tomorrow only in the way in which they are sized, configured, equipped, and trained today. For future low-intensity conflicts, which will necessitate unconventional, guerrilla, and counterinsurgency warfare, the United States is noticeably unprepared. Under these circumstances, Komer suggests several changes or improvements in U.S. strategy to deal with low-intensity conflicts:

1. The United States should avoid protracted involvement in situations likely to lead to incremental military buildup and indecisive attrition warfare. A premium should be placed on anticipatory actions (diplomacy, economic and military aid) designed to forestall the outbreak of conflict. After conflict does break out, maintaining escalation control is critically important to conventional (and nuclear) responses to low-intensity conflict. But planning should ensure that acceptable levels of force will bring about a satisfactory result from U.S. involvement.

2. The United States should expand its specially trained, specifically tailored light forces, giving them adaptive command structures and all the other features necessary for low-intensity conflicts. Since the early 1970s, unconventional warfare assets have been badly underemphasized, but it is precisely these types of forces that will be required in the most frequent engagements of the 1980s.

3. The United States should rely to the maximum-possible extent on the forces of its friends and allies. There are many good reasons for this. In many low-intensity conflicts, the United States may not have the capability to intervene alone. Dispatching troops and supplies via U.S. strategic air and sea lift (unless pre-positioning or basing facilities are developed) may prove difficult, if not impossible. Sometimes, U.S. allies or friends may have capabilities (for example, British and Israeli commando units) more efficient and better suited for low-intensity conflicts than those of the United States. Or they might have redundant capabilities, which would permit employment of U.S. resources elsewhere. The introduction of U.S. troops where the Soviet military might be involved (for example, flying Libyan or South Yemeni jets or advising ground units) might entail risks that U.S. decision makers would be unwilling to take but that might be acceptable to allies with more important interests at stake. And finally, intervention by U.S. allies in areas where their colonial and cultural ties remain strong and where their forces may be better received should minimize the risks and improve the prospects for that intervention. Considering their desire to maintain economic relations with developing nations (including many nations where conflict may erupt), our allies often will have interests involved for which they will readily assume responsibility.

Improving U.S. ability to respond to low-intensity conflicts will involve more than improved force design. The handling of atypical missions demands truly innovative and adaptive planning, programming, and execution. This will require extraordinary leadership in many areas. A key need will be to make the optimal use of scarce defense resources. Defense spending must not reflect a feast-or-famine or balance-sheet approach to national defense. In a decade when budgetary and political constraints may frustrate efforts to rebuild U.S. military strength to a level fully capable of supporting our foreign policy, we must be unusually astute in developing and deploying those defense resources that are available. That means creating armed forces able to respond quickly and creatively to unforeseen challenges to U.S. national interests.

Clearly, U.S. military preparedness is incomplete unless it can counter the complete range of threats—from potentially decisive, high-intensity wars to more prevalent, less-decisive, low-intensity conflicts. Strategic planning for low-intensity conflict in the 1980s is only one vital element in an optimal, overall U.S. military strategy. But, in taking into account the full spectrum of U.S. military strategic needs, our grand strategy must take special care to include adequate and appropriate low-intensity forces and strategies.

Part I
Perspectives on the Future of
Conflict and U.S. Policies

2 U.S. National-Security Challenges for the 1980s

James R. Schlesinger

We live today in a period of suspended animation, with the prospects for conflict muted, if ever so briefly. Soviet preoccupation—in both Afghanistan and Poland—is the first reason for this quiet period. The Soviets characteristically avoid taking on too many tasks simultaneously, and, as a consequence, they are not now much interested in any additional ventures that may get them into trouble. Thus, at least for the moment, we are witnessing a slowdown of Soviet activism.

The second reason is the arrival of the Reagan administration. It has now been in power for some ten months. During this period there has been a hold placed overseas on evaluations of U.S. policy to provide time for the new administration to be "calibrated." In the interim the Soviets have withheld judgment of the administration's foreign-policy goals, as have our European and other allies.

Nevertheless, we should recall that the administration came to power with the view that the 1980s were going to be a very dangerous decade for the United States. Despite the present period of suspended animation, little is likely to alter that fundamental judgment. Nature, as we know, does not make leaps. There are too many features of the U.S. position in the world that could not be cured by any administration—even with the best of will, great competency, and total public backing.

President Carter may have been swept out of office in some degree because of perceived or actual failures in foreign policy. (That, no doubt, contributes to the current hiatus while policymakers worldwide evaluate the new administration.) But one widespread belief, when the new administration came into power—that whatever Carter was not, Reagan would be—is basically untenable. This administration will be confronted by the same underlying difficulty in dealing with the world: the decline in American power, a decline only momentarily interrupted by the perception of the new administration and new U.S. will. Our continuing problems will be both generic and specific, and I will deal briefly with some of the specific problems before turning to the generic.

This chapter is taken from a speech delivered by the author to The Future of Conflict Conference held at the Georgetown University Center for Strategic and International Studies (CSIS) in November 1981.

Problem Areas

The first problem area is Europe: the slow disintegration of the Atlantic
Alliance; a spreading distrust of either the strength, and the will or the
wisdom of U.S. policy; a loss of confidence in U.S. leadership somewhat
altered (at least temporarily) by a higher degree of confidence in the
strength of the new administration than in its predecessors. Nonetheless, the
disintegration of the Atlantic Alliance continues. This is not only a result of
specific policy problems we see today, but also a reflection of some of the
generic problems that I shall turn to later.

The administration entered office with great good will in Europe—
largely because the Europeans had "had it" with the Carter administration.
There existed a widespread feeling that the Carter administration was weak,
vacillating, and unpredictable and that the new administration would cure
these ailments. Indeed, it has cured the ailment of being perceived as weak,
or even vacillating—although there is still some feeling that this administration, like its predecessor, is unpredictable. Despite this increased approval,
however, the policies toward the Soviet Union, around which we expected
the European Alliance to rally, were based on an incomplete conception of
the attitudes and the geopolitical position of our European associates.

The European allies indeed do want firmness from the United States.
Yet, at the same time, they are, as they see it, cheek-by-jowl with the Soviet
Union and the Warsaw Pact. They, therefore, want nothing to occur that
will unnecessarily stir up belligerency and dissipate the happy climate of
détente that, whether it exists elsewhere in the world, they believe to exist
on the European continent. What the administration gains by its policy of
greater firmness it loses to a considerable extent through what is perceived
to be unnecessary bellicosity and stridency. It is this image of a rash United
States that regrettably is bringing to an end the ability of European governments to give full support to U.S. policies.

During the course of this decade the tendency toward disintegration of
the NATO alliance will likely continue. It will generate additional tensions
between ourselves and our allies and will force this country to grapple with
problems that would have been unheard of two decades ago. Today the
Europeans question our judgment. Two decades ago they did not, to the
same extent, question our judgment. They then thought us an all-powerful
protector, and one is prepared to put up with a great deal of stupidity from a
protector who one believes to be all-powerful. They no longer believe us to
be the all-powerful protector and, as a consequence, we have sharply altered
relations within the Alliance.

The Middle East is the other primary trouble spot. As in Europe, one
can hypothesize a rapid shift in the balance of power that could be catastrophic for the structure of international politics as it has existed since

World War II. Again, there has been a slow ebbing of U.S. influence in the region and, at the same time, a growth, if not of Soviet influence, of the perception of Soviet power—which has somewhat the same effect.

Some years ago, for example, the Palestinian issue would have been far less critical than it is today in determining attitudes in the region. As long as the United States was viewed as capable of providing unequivocal protection, what was for so long a secondary issue for the region would not have become as prominent. The growing importance of the Palestinian issue in part reflects an accompanying decline in both U.S. power and in the perception of that power.

Yet, perhaps unfortunately, the legacy of the decline remains; it is now useless to attempt to deal effectively with the politics of the Middle East without dealing forthrightly with the Palestinian issue. Perhaps the issue need not have become as important as it has, but under the circumstances, the attempt to disregard it, to create a strategic consensus that is designed to deal with the Soviet problem but does not deal with the internal tensions of the Middle East, is foredoomed to failure.

We certainly did not help achieve our announced goal for the region in the past year. If the United States is to forge consensus within the region, it must be viewed as a reasonably honest broker between Israel and her neighbors. After the attacks on Baghdad and Beirut, the United States was notably mild in rebuking Israel. But more important, when Prime Minister Begin came here in the fall of 1981 and the spring of 1982 he scored, perhaps unintentionally on our part, two great diplomatic coups. During the course of that visit, Israel was declared to be a strategic asset of the United States, and it was announced that a new and still undefined strategic relationship would be developed. Understandably this caused consternation among the moderate Arab states; they simply did not know what that might imply. Simultaneously, it was leaked to the press that no one had bothered to raise explicitly the issue of Palestinian autonomy with Prime Minister Begin during his visit. That, of course, would have reduced the spirit of bonhomie during the meetings, and, apparently, it was therefore felt to be unnecessary. Discussion of the Palestinian autonomy issue simply was avoided, a fact noticed far more in the Middle East than here.

Offsetting that notable omission, to some extent, has been the sale of the Airborne Warning and Control System (AWACS). Yet in light of those prior developments, the AWACS sale (and the accompanying victory of the president in the Congress) was, to a large extent, a damage-limiting operation rather than one that will build great confidence in us among the Arab states.

Of course, we would not be so concerned about the Middle East if it were not the source of the free world's petroleum resources—less ours, of course, than Japan's and Western Europe's. Over the course of the decades ahead, there is no alternative to continued dependence on the Middle East. The politics of the Middle East continue to be as volatile as any in the world. For those interested in the future of conflict, it appears consequently to be a very promising area for study.

The third world will continue to be the source of low-intensity conflicts. Yet, in contrast to major conflict in the Middle East or in Europe, none of these tensions is likely to bring about a serious alteration in the overall balance of power. Included in the third world is, of course, Central America, an area of renewed U.S. interest. The war in El Salvador is not going well. Furthermore, attempts to compel or to induce a change in policy on the part of Nicaragua and Cuba have, to this point, been notable failures.

Unless we are able to improve substantially our capacity to act more vigorously, in all likelihood we can look forward to a further deterioration of our position in Central America. This raises two important points: First, although Central America is close by, and therefore a matter of greater concern to the U.S. people, developments in Central America will not sharply alter the international balance of power. Second, a major problem we face in Central America, as in other third-world areas, is a continuation of the so-called Vietnam syndrome, despite exaggerated reports of its demise. The initial discussion of El Salvador led to a strongly negative, public reaction, not unnoticed at the White House. As a consequence, although it had initially breathed fire regarding the conflict in Central America, the administration was rather muted on the subject in the fall of 1981.

One can be more optimistic in discussing the Far East. In large degree, this reflects the shift of the People's Republic of China to the side of the West, a certain firming up of Japanese policy, and a far better response among the Association of South East Asian Nations (ASEAN) nations after the fall of Vietnam than anybody would have predicted. Generally our position in the Far East has improved. It is not, therefore, a source of immediate concern in terms of conflict. However, if we do not handle our relations with the People's Republic with great care—particularly the Taiwan issue—there could be an estrangement that might lead to future difficulties.

The Basic Problem of Decline in Strength

Let us turn to the generic issue that underlies these specific developments: the relative decline of U.S. power. That decline involves not only our military posture vis-à-vis the Soviets. Perhaps more importantly it also involves the sharp decline of the economic position of the United States in the world. The loss of industrial leadership has sharply reduced our international prestige. The same United States that until the 1960s was clearly the leader in technology and in productivity growth, whose industries dominated world competition, is now in many respects at a disadvantage relative to our competition.

That slow deterioration of our previously advantageous position clearly has sharply reduced our prestige and has also affected our power position. But it is principally the relative decline of the military power of the United States that in the decades ahead will likely be the source of conflict. In the past, both the unity and coherence of the NATO alliance and relative order in the third world reflected the preponderant world position of the United States. The erosion of that position means lessened cohesion in NATO and greater anarchy in the third world.

In this connection, since it is widely believed that present effort at rearmament will restore U.S. strength, it is essential to examine the immediate problem of the budget as it affects prospects for spending on national defense. At present we suffer from a self-inflicted wound affecting our capability to support all public activity, including defense and security assistance. That self-inflicted wound stems from a passing illusion associated with the initial flourishing of supply-side economics. It is, I believe, but one more example of "extraordinary popular delusions and the madness of crowds," doomed to failure from its conception.

I must, however, spell out the implications of these budgetary problems as they affect defense. The deficit for the fiscal year 1983 looks as if it will go well over $100 billion. The deficit for 1985 will be close to $150 billion. In 1984, when the tax effects are completed, the deficit will approach $200 billion.

After 1984, the indexing of taxes will result in a rate reduction corresponding to any further rise in prices. Essentially, U.S. revenues will be frozen at 18.5 percent or 19 percent of the gross national product during a period that spending will be about 23 percent of the gross national product. To this point we have survived the indexation of social programs only through the nonindexation of the tax system. We have now contrived a system that pushes up expenditures while holding revenues stable.

The ultimate impact of such vast deficits is quite clear. Inevitably there will develop unremitting downward pressure on defense spending. We must recognize that now—despite all the fanfare about rearmament. The notion that we will match the Soviet Union in defense spending (let alone achieve so-called superiority), however illusionary as a political promise, has now been overtaken by grim budgetary reality.

We may look back to that period after World War II of U.S. dominance—when we had 60 percent of the world's manufacturing capacity, stable and cheap energy supplies, and a nuclear monopoly. The United States then existed in a kind of Garden of Eden. The fall from this paradise helps to explain the conflicts that we shall face in the decades ahead. Like the aboriginal Garden of Eden, this one also contained a serpent proffering temptation—the overdependence on nuclear deterrence. As the protests in Europe today—and the likely protests in the United States during the summer of 1982—reveal, that overdependence on nuclear weapons, although militarily defensible, implies grave long-run political vulnerabilities.

In 1949 at the Lisbon Conference the NATO alliance had mutually agreed to raise seventy divisions. At the time of the New Look, however, the Eisenhower administration determined that the United States would respond to major conventional aggression with nuclear weapons. (This policy was later enshrined, somewhat briefly, in the policy of massive retaliation.) Although it was initially a United States initiative, that strategy was embraced with even greater fervor by our European allies. Indeed, throughout the last two decades, the effort to correct the weaknesses of NATO conventional forces has been primarily by the United States. In the 1960s, our allies rebuffed attempts to strengthen conventional forces as weakening nuclear deterrence; in the 1980s such efforts were resisted because of budgetary restraints.

It is perhaps poetic justice. In an alliance that depends on the threat of nuclear weapons to offset the conventional superiority of Warsaw Pact forces, and perhaps in the Middle East as well, a serious political problem has now emerged. As understanding of the underlying strategy improves, even the possibility of a nuclear conflict has become increasingly frightening to the Europeans. Much of this risk embodied in the strategy has, quite unjustly, been blamed on the United States.

Just or not, these alarms have now been sounded. We must therefore expect to encounter continued political difficulties in relying on a nuclear response. Indeed, our current strategy may frighten those whom we seek to protect more than it deters those whom we wish to deter. Herein lies a major challenge of the decade ahead. If we are to reinvigorate the NATO alliance, we must start from the premise that the U.S. nuclear umbrella is losing its effectiveness as our principal deterrent against a major conventional military attack.

There are two conclusions to be drawn from this review of temptation and the fall from Paradise. First, quite obviously, we must improve our conventional capability in Europe (and in the Persian Gulf region, as well). A further and most-important conclusion that arises from the generically altered (that is, reduced) position of the United States in the world is that we must now be cleverer than we have been in the past. When the United States was believed to possess overwhelming power, political blunders mattered relatively little. The once-tolerable U.S. propensity to allow international affairs to drift while we tidied up our domestic affairs is no longer tolerable. In the past our allies might have accepted what they saw as U.S. blunders. Now, however, given the decline in the confidence of U.S. protection, they feel there is too much at stake to accept those blunders any longer.

That implies two things. First, we shall have to be more sensitive than we have been in the past, both to substantive developments and to the nuances of feelings in other countries—Europe is but the first example. Second, we shall have to be far more effective in employing diplomatic and political tactics—not relying, as we have in the past, on overwhelming military or economic strength.

Recommendations

These changes in our position bear implications regarding our way of organizing the executive branch. The first point here is rather elementary: either the president must devote sufficient attention to foreign-policy matters or he must clearly and forcefully delegate authority. So far, we have seen neither. I personally prefer that authority be delegated to a secretary of state whom the president trusts totally. Eisenhower made delegation of authority to the secretary of state work; Nixon made delegation to the national security adviser work. In both cases, people at the senior levels of government and within the bureaucracy understood the lines of authority. We thus had a decision-making structure that we do not now have. We must have clear lines of authority if the apparatus is to respond quickly and efficiently.

A second point is that we can no longer afford to treat experience as casually as we have been in the past or as we are at present. The fact is that Secretary Haig is the only senior figure in this administration with considerable experience. It is this lack of experience that adds to my nervousness when I contemplate the fragility of our international position. Secretary Haig, under such conditions, remains almost indispensable in achieving an informed response to what is going on overseas. We should have Secretary Haig's level of experience more widely dispersed throughout the government.

Also, by imposing a pay cap of $50,000 a year, we will not be able to retain foreign-service officers, intelligence officers, or senior civil servants. Nor shall we retain the 80 or 90 percent of senior executives now becoming eligible for retirement and retiring from the federal government—as opposed to 15 percent six or seven years ago. We are now weakening the executive branch and destroying our capacity to respond to the national-security challenges with which the nation will be confronted.

A third point is that we must achieve a better working relationship between the Congress and the president. In the past, under Truman, Eisenhower, and Kennedy, and until Johnson and Nixon to a lesser degree, the president was the ultimate maker of foreign policy. But post-Watergate and post-Vietnam, the division of this responsibility has become a subject of concern. Congress too frequently responds on the basis of short-term political pressures. By accepting the more permanent significance of foreign policy and by looking toward the longer term, Congress could become a more effective participant in the initiation and continuity of foreign policy.

I shall conclude with an anecdote that may provide some cheer. Shortly after the Battle of Saratoga in 1777, Adam Smith was approached on the streets of Edinburgh by an associate, who shouted: "Dr. Smith, Dr. Smith, have you heard the dreadful news?" "No," said Smith, "what is it?" "The news from North America—Burgoyne has been forced to surrender with all of his forces. It's the ruination of the country!" Smith thought for a moment and then responded: "A country can stand a lot of ruining."

3

How to Prepare for Low-Intensity Conflict in the 1980s

Robert W. Komer

Let me approach this subject from the viewpoint of a senior official actually engaged with problems of conflict during the last thirty years in the Central Intelligence Agency (CIA), the White House, Vietnam, and the Department of Defense (DOD). As I reflect on how best to prepare against such contingencies in the next decade, my first response is: "not the way we did it last time."

Last time, of course, was the seven-year (or more accurately, nineteen-year 1956–1975) war in Southeast Asia, which certainly fits the definition of low-intensity conflict. During the bulk of these years conflict was characterized by limited conventional fighting at the most and coercive diplomacy at the least. Despite 550,000 Americans at peak in Vietnam, the war remained one of small-unit actions of brigade size or, usually, smaller. Also remember that Vietnam was two wars—a quasi-conventional conflict superimposed on a rural insurgency. We used to refer to the latter as 44 province wars, 250 separate district wars, or 8,000 hamlet wars. Although each conflict situation is unique, patterns of rural/urban insurgency similar to those encountered in Vietnam are likely to be encountered elsewhere in the 1980s.

So it is instructive to look back at Vietnam for lessons on how to prepare for the next time. I will look at performance rather than policy, because there was an enormous gap between the two. Our operational policy on how to deal with the enemy we confronted had all the right words in it, but our actual performance was quite different. It was so different in my personal experience that I wrote a critique in 1970–1971 (Rand Report R-967) in an attempt to assess why we did what we did the way we did it—with such disastrous results. I called it *Bureaucracy Does Its Thing*, which suggests the nature of my critique.

In essence, we practiced in Vietnam the same U.S. style of war so successful in World Wars I and II and in Korea—large, well-equipped mobile forces employing massive ground/air firepower to crush the enemy. The trouble was that, in the triple-canopy jungle of South Vietnam, it was very hard to find and fix an elusive guerrilla-style enemy so that we could crush him. Not until Hanoi's 1972 and 1975 offensives did the enemy escalate to conventional operations. Indeed the irony is that the war ended the way we thought it would begin—with a conventional-style North Vietnamese invasion of the south.

Why did we fight the Vietnam War this way? Because it was what U.S. forces generally were sized, configured, equipped, and trained to do. We modelled our general-purpose forces (quite correctly in my judgment) for what we saw as the most important (and demanding) scenario—fighting Soviets in Central Europe. This turned out to be more than adequate in Korea too. But when we went to Vietnam, it turned out that the enemy would not stand still for us to clobber him. Unfortunately, we also sized, equipped, and trained our local Vietnamese allies in our own image, to fight U.S.-style, again because it was all we knew how to teach.

The attrition strategy we used in Vietnam was another logical reflection of the U.S. way of war—use our massively superior mobility and firepower to swamp the poorly equipped Vietcong/North Vietnamese army units wherever we could find them. The trouble was, we usually could not find them.

Why was all this? At bottom it was because all big hierarchical organizations (and armed forces are practically archetypes) tend to play out their organizational repertoires—to do what they know best how to do. Why else would General Motors keep building big, gas-guzzling cars for so long?

Bureaucratic inertia is another organizational characteristic. Big institutions tend to change only slowly and incrementally over time. This helps explain why we were so slow to adapt in Vietnam. When we failed to find, fix, and destroy an elusive foe, our natural institutional tendency was to do more of the same—to pour on more coal—rather than to rethink the problem—shades of World War I!

Ergo, the chief lesson I draw from Vietnam is that atypical conflict situations call for specially tailored responses. We cannot afford to play out existing repertoires. As Sam Huntington warned us long ago, Vietnam was unique in many respects, which led him to cite the danger of drawing "mis-lessons" from it. The low-intensity conflicts of the 1980s are unlikely to replicate Vietnam. Thus we must stress adaptability—sizing up each situation on its merits and preparing tailored responses. This is what happened in what I regard as one of the most successful counterinsurgency campaigns in postwar history. As I noted in another Rand Report (R-957: *The Malayan Emergency in Retrospect*, February 1972), in Malaya the British started out just the way we did, with an overwhelmingly military response; but circumstances drew them toward low-cost, innovative police-type solutions, which, although they took twelve years, worked.

Bureaucracy being what it is, designing adaptive responses is easier said than done. When I played a major role in the initial planning for the Rapid Deployment Force (RDF) (aimed primarily at defending Persian Gulf oil), I found many signs that we wanted to defend Persian Gulf oil as if it were being pumped out of Western Europe. I grant that we cannot afford to maintain specialized forces for a wide spectrum of contingencies. The general-purpose-force concept makes a great deal of sense, even though we found in Vietnam that they were not of such general purpose after all.

Nonetheless, given the likelihood of more low-intensity conflicts in the multipolar and volatile world of the 1980s, I see every reason why at least a modest fraction (say 5 to 10 percent) of our general-purpose force should be specially configured and trained for such missions. We badly need more specially trained light forces and more strategic and tactical mobility for them. None of this is high cost, not when compared to what else we buy. Yet, over the past several years, largely in reaction to Vietnam, we have de-emphasized unconventional warfare assets. We have cut back the Green Berets, Air Force, Navy Underwater (UW) units, and the CIA's para-military assets. The stress seems to be on high technology rather than on low intensity. This is a mistake.

But much more is involved than force design. Above all, we must place a premium on adaptive thinking, planning, and execution. To this end I favor creating ad hoc special planning and command structures to handle atypical missions not in conventional organizational repertoires. We tried to do precisely this in creating a separate headquarters for the RDF, and I advo-cated placing it directly under the Joint Chiefs of Staff (JCS) for these purposes (which has now been done). But for the most part, contingency planning for low-intensity conflict is left to unified commands, which are primarily concerned, quite naturally, with high-intensity conflict.

Harking back once again to Vietnam, let me stress another lesson. Historically, small conflicts display a lamentable tendency to grow into big ones—and long ones. No general staff at the outset of World War I, World War II, Korea, or Vietnam planned for a war the size or duration of what actually evolved. This tendency of small, limited wars to expand creates special problems for democracies, which tend to adapt a feast-or-famine approach to their military establishments. In hindsight, perhaps the most important strategic lesson of Vietnam is that its cost grew out of all propor-tion to any strategic gain. The $300 billion (plus another $100 billion in post-Vietnam cutbacks owing largely to the Vietnam syndrome) adds up to perhaps a decade of defense investment, which is one of the key reasons why U.S. military strength has fallen so far behind that of the USSR. It is a major reason why Vietnam turned out to be the wrong war, at the wrong place, at the wrong time, although Korea (to which General Bradley applied this phrase) turned out to have the opposite impact—because it greatly stimu-lated U.S. rearmament.

Thus escalation control, difficult as this is, becomes crucially important in a conventional as well as nuclear sense. We must guard against low-intensity-conflict responses expanding to the point where they cripple our ability to deter or deal with larger conflicts.

To this end, we must also avoid falling prey to what I call the "likelihood fallacy." Minor conflicts, especially in the volatile third world, are much more likely than larger ones. This does not mean, however, that we should posture to deal with the most likely at the expense of our capability to deal with the most important. To employ a reductio ad absurdum, we could afford to "lose" Africa south of the Sahara more than we could afford to "lose" Western Europe or Persian Gulf oil.

Escalation control puts a high premium on such measures as (1) anticipatory actions designed to forestall conflict breaking out in the first place, for example, diplomacy, economic and military aid; (2) tailored efforts to build up friendly capabilities to deter; (3) steps to keep small conflicts small, such as not intervening if others will not; (4) maximum use of our own surrogates; and (5) seeking quick local decisions—avoiding the gradualism that led to expansion of the Vietnam War—especially if we feel compelled to intervene ourselves.

Escalation control also seems to argue against countervailing strategies—going after something of comparable value if we cannot cope locally. I grant that we ought to explore carefully countervailing, conventional options just as we have nuclear ones (in Presidential Directive [PD]-59). There are possibilities at sea, or in areas like Cuba, Nicaragua, or the Horn of Africa, where we have greater access than the Soviets. But escalatory risks and gains, as well as feasibility, need the most careful case-by-case examination. In many instances there would be requirements for the cooperation of reluctant allies. In short, general principles do not decide concrete cases.

These thoughts lead to the third main point: use surrogates and allies to the maximum extent feasible. Somehow the Soviets seem to do a much better job of this than we do. But it does limit escalatory risks. This suggests much higher investment in economic and military aid to strategically important, but needy, allies and friends on a grant basis if necessary (I have long regarded this as cost effective in deterring or coping with high-intensity conflicts too). We should press our rich allies to make parallel investments. Timely assistance of this sort can help forestall conflict. If deterrence fails, aiding the side we favor is generally less escalatory than intervening ourselves, and, almost invariably, it is less expensive too. We also need a U.S. stockpile of items likely to be needed for quick crisis responses. Regular-aid procedures are far too slow.

But the aid we give should be of the right kind as well as amount. We should not create such a huge military burden as to threaten economic stability. We should not provide the wrong kind of equipment, training, and advice. In short, we must not mirror image as we did in Vietnam—to our ultimate great cost. We tend to provide the equipment we use (or have in surplus) whether or not it fits the need. On the other hand, high-technology equipment is no panacea, as seen in the sad performances in the Iraq versus Iran conflict.

A substantial advisory role to local regimes often will be essential; this is less risky than direct intervention. But it is imperative that the advisors and advice be geared to real local needs. We did a poor job of advising our Vietnamese allies, in my judgment. For example, if the conflict is basically an insurgency, focus primarily on counterinsurgency—not on conventional responses. The police are often more useful than the army, as the British discovered in Malaya. Pacification finally worked even in Vietnam, largely because we set up a quasi-autonomous chain of command (Vietnamese as well as U.S.), using military personnel and assets. Gaining or retaining popular support can be crucial (hearts and minds are important!). Regrettably, I doubt that the U.S. military really grasps counterinsurgency even today; nor do we have a counterinsurgency doctrine or assets.

If direct U.S. intervention becomes essential, we should make every effort to secure allied participation. The political gain will generally outweigh the host of problems that mixed interventions invariably entail. But the United States and its allies are poorly prepared to operate alongside each other (even though we think we intend to fight coalition wars). At least some allied participation may be politically indispensable to generating U.S. political support (this was the case in Vietnam and Korea and certainly would be in the Persian Gulf). Moreover, such allies as France, the United Kingdom, Belgium, Portugal, and Pakistan have better units for low-intensity warfare than we do. Often, the U.S. role can be confined mainly to transporting allies to the scene and supporting them logistically (for example, the Belgian/French in Zaire or the Organization of African Unity (OAU) force in Chad).

Nor can we afford to neglect covert action. Despite all the problems it raises, especially for free societies such as ours, it is often the most cost-effective and risk-limiting way to operate. In my experience, the covert-action people usually have proved far more adaptive to the local situation than the conventional military, partly because they "ad hoc" each response.

Finally, the lessons of earlier low-intensity conflicts merit study. We are far too ahistorical in our outlook. We neglected the French experience in the first Indochina war (after all, the French lost, so what did we have to learn from them?); nor did we study Malaya or Algeria. In fact, we do not even analyze systematically what happened in Vietnam. By the same token, we need far more systematic analysis of likely, future low-intensity-conflict scenarios and tailored, adaptive responses.

Part II
Causes and Conditions
of Future Low-Intensity
Conflict

Introduction
to Part II

The five chapters in part II deal with some of the issues that are likely to contribute most powerfully to the development of low-intensity conflict; this analysis includes some of the emerging factors that will help determine the character and course of those conflicts in the 1980s. Chapters by Richard J. Kessler, John Norton Moore, and Robert A. Kilmarx address the large and growing role of resource competition as a source of conflict. Kessler deals with the potential for conflict that flows from the unique reliance of both industrialized and developing nations on energy resources, especially hydrocarbon fuels. Moore considers whether crises similar to those that stemmed from competition for energy in the 1970s may surround access to ocean resources in the 1980s, and Kilmarx examines the problems of access to strategic minerals—an oft-discussed but still unresolved problem for U.S. policy. He identifies a number of possible scenarios to illustrate how needs for access to strategic minerals could lead to conflict.

Both conventional arms transfers and nuclear-weapons proliferation have the potential to cause conflict and to intensify and alter the outcome of conflicts. Michael L. Moodie looks at trends in arms technology and arms transfers to see how they may affect the conduct of conflict in future years, particularly as they impact on U.S. policy. Rodney W. Jones takes up many of the same questions as they relate to the even more volatile and uncertain prospect of nuclear-weapon proliferation. He concludes with an extensive survey of the potential effects of proliferation, in its many possible modes, on the Asian subcontinent.

4 Energy-Resource Competition as a Source of Conflict

Richard J. Kessler

The world seems to have come full circle in about ten years. In the early days of the 1970s, the phrase *energy crisis* was used so frequently that it appeared the world would never recover from continued market upheaval. Now, in the early days of the 1980s, it is possible for a popular magazine to run a lead proclaiming "The Energy Crisis Is Over!" and for a president to begin dismantling the Department of Energy.[1] Have we managed in just a few years to resolve a problem of such global proportions that it surpasses World War II in its impact on everyone's lives?

Although it is no longer fashionable, I would argue that we are in the doldrum days of a phony war. It is clear that these moments of relative tranquility in world oil prices are fleeting. It is still an age of diminishing supplies of petroleum, and the transition to an era of coal, nuclear, and renewables is just beginning.

Worldwide supply-and-demand projections for oil are among the most difficult of predictions to make. For example, Exxon in its December 1980 forecast saw world conventional oil production rising to 71 Tb/d (terabarrels/ day) by 2000, and the U.S. Office of Technology Assessment in October 1980 projected a range of 42–62 Tb/d. Conoco predicts total oil consumption at 52.3 Tb/d by 1990. (The Exxon projections include natural-gas liquids, synthetic liquid fuels, and very heavy oil.) An analysis of ten major oil studies by the Stanford Energy Modeling Forum (April 1981) gave a wide range of projections for 2010 from 38.3 Tb/d in 2010 to 53.3 Tb/d.

The future of world energy can always be predicted with relative confidence: the world will make the transition to new types of fuels. What is uncertain is what this transition will cost—both in an economic sense and in a political sense, that is, the price nations will pay in their relations with each other to ensure access to energy resources.

In 1975, Philip Connelly and Robert Perlman published *The Politics of Scarcity: Resource Conflicts in International Relations*, followed in 1977 by Melvin Conant and Fern Gold's *Geopolitics of Energy*.[2] Both called attention to what Conant described as the "politicization of oil," the increasing importance of control and access to resource supplies as a factor in the quotient of international political power.

Vincent Randazzo provided valuable research assistance for this chapter.

Certainly, resource access and control have been important since time immemorial to the determinance of a state's power. Gaining access to vital resources also has been at issue in a multitude of interstate and intrastate conflicts. What is different about such conflicts today is that they are occurring in an era of interdependence. In modern times, never has the survival of so many states been so dependent for so much on so few.

As an example of the world's dependence, the Organization of Petroleum Exporting Countries (OPEC) contains 434 billion barrels of proved reserves. This represents 77 percent of the noncommunist world's reserves and 67 percent of the world's oil reserves. They also contain 1,000 Tcf (trillion cubic feet) of natural-gas supplies, representing 60 percent of the noncommunist world's supplies and 40 percent of the total world supply. The *primus paribus* in world oil production is, of course, Saudi Arabia.

The Saudis control approximately 165 billion barrels of reserves, accounting for 29.3 percent of the noncommunist world's recoverable reserves and 25.4 percent of the total world supply. They also have the widest discretionary power to produce oil. The Saudis' maximum sustainable production is 11 Tb/d; they are producing at about 10 Tb/d. Their next closest competitor is Iraq which, prior to their war with Iran, could produce at 4 Tb/d. Thus, not only does Saudi Arabia contain the largest number of reserves, it currently has the physical capacity to out-produce any other country. Its minimum physical-production level has been estimated at half that rate: 5.5 Tb/d. But, more important, it is estimated that it requires only 5.8 Tb/d to meet its internal demand and financial requirements.

The significance of all these figures is threefold. First, OPEC will continue to dominate the world oil trade without substantially increasing its present level of production. Second, although oil will contribute a decreasing share of the Western industrial countries' energy mix, it will not be a significant decrease. According to Exxon, by the year 2000, the Organization for Economic Cooperation and Development (OECD) countries will be consuming 35 Tb/d, compared to 40 Tb/d in 1979. Third, the non-oil-producing developing countries will be consuming energy at an average annual rate of 4.8 percent between 1978 and 1990, compared to 1 percent by the United States. Most of this energy will be petroleum.

The political implications of this situation are considerable. The supply of oil for any significant growth in demand will continue to be at the discretion of a few oil-producing countries throughout the rest of the century. Competitors for this oil will be the West and the less developed countries (LDCs). The LDCs are expected to account for much of the growth in world energy demand and virtually all the growth in world oil demand. Unless steps are taken to develop a cooperative framework among these three groups, future relations between the North and the South will be not only acrimonious but also dangerous.

Problems of the developing countries in securing access to oil will be exacerbated by the rising price of oil in real terms. Although the world oil market may remain relatively slack through the early- and middle-1980s, prices will gradually rise (assuming no unforeseen disruptions). By the late 1980s and into the next century, prices will increase more rapidly. Exxon predicts that Middle East crude-oil prices will rise by 50 percent in real terms between 1980 and 2000. Chase Manhattan Bank and Standard Oil of California (SOCAL) both predict that crude-oil prices will rise at a rate that is about 3 percent higher than inflation, with oil reaching $102 a barrel by 1990.

Although the future price of oil is unclear, what is apparent is that the supply of oil is price-driven for only a limited range of circumstances—for example, where the cost of production is close to market prices or where known reserves are viewed as the only national asset able to generate economic development and the rate of development is limited by foreign exchange (Iran and Nigeria). For most of the world production, increases in supply will be determined by geology or political factors.

What and who will decide oil-pricing and production policies will continue to be major issues for the 1980s, as they were for the preceding decade. These issues are not solely the province of oil producers but will also be decided by major oil consumers, including the communist and developing countries. This chapter will examine some of the possible conflicts arising from the struggle to control supplies of energy resources.

What Are Energy-Resource Conflicts?

In his widely discussed piece in *Foreign Policy*, "The Threat is Real," No. 14 (Spring 1974):84–90, C. Fred Bergsten wrote of "One, Two, Three, Many OPECs," predicting a future of resource cartels in the developing world. These cartels did not materialize, but his title illustrates one of the problems of discussing resource conflicts: when are the conflicts just competitive behavior? The oil embargo of 1973–1974 certainly was an example of the use of control over resource access to inflict severe economic damage for political reasons on other states. Should resource control be considered a weapon when it is used for other than just economic ends? The question suggests the extreme difficulty in factoring out energy as an element in conflict. Energy is often only a component of a larger package of problems— often with extensive historical antecedents—which results in interstate or intrastate conflict.

Because of this definitional difficulty, it is useful analytically to describe energy-resource conflicts in terms of their objectives. First, energy conflicts can be viewed as means to other ends or, second, as ends in themselves. Conflicts as means to other ends can be target-specific or diffuse. Target-specific conflicts involve attacks on individual energy installations for any number of reasons—blackmail, economic destruction, publicity, spite, and so on. Energy targets can also be part of a more diffuse conflict situation: for example, riots over high gasoline prices are part of more general economic turbulence.

The history of energy-resource conflict suggests that this form of conflict will be the prevalent mode over the next couple of decades. This is for two reasons: first, energy installations are highly vulnerable to attack, and the effect of damaging them can have immediate and widespread consequences; second, energy has become such a pervasive and critical component of modern and even traditional economies that it can become the focus for other social problems.

An example of the latter is the current conflict in Northern Luzon, Philippines, over construction of a major hydroelectric project on the Chico River, which would flood tribal lands. The Philippine Communist Party's military wing, the New People's Army, is very active in this region, using local opposition to the dams to gain support for its activities. There are other examples: In 1980, in Assam, India, demonstrators—demanding the expulsion of millions of Bengalis—blocked oil installations supplying one-third of India's domestic production for ten months. The Kurdish insurgency in Iraq is partly a result of arguments over revenue from the Kirkuk oil fields.

The vulnerability of energy installations to disruption is well known and is illustrated graphically in the United States by the 1965 Northeast power blackout. This vulnerability will increase as the number of energy installations grows.

The number of nuclear-power stations will increase (table 4–1 lists the number of power stations now operating or under contruction in the third world alone). These installations will be highly susceptible to internal or external attack, as the 1981 Israeli raid on the Iraqi nuclear installation indicates. It would be incorrect to suppose that all countries can develop and support an adequate nuclear-safeguard system. The Iraqi incident illustrates that even a heavily armed country cannot protect its installations.

Other major targets that will increase in number over the next decades will be offshore drilling sites. In 1981, almost five hundred drilling rigs were operating offshore worldwide. These sites, often disparate and far out at sea, are highly susceptible to attack. Although damage to them can to some degree be contained, their destruction could discourage companies from continued field exploitation, particularly in marginal areas. In addition, damage to installations can result in blowouts that may last a long time and cause widespread economic and ecological damage. The blowout at Ixtoc 1 off the Mexican coast burned from 3 June 1979 through 24 March 1980. Kuwait's Burgen field burned for two months in 1978. Nigeria has also had considerable problems with its offshore fields, affecting fishing areas on which the local population is dependent.

Table 4-1
Nuclear-Power Plants in Developing Countries

Country	Total Working Plants	Gross MwE	Total Plants on Order or under Construction	Gross MwE	Total Plants Planned	Gross MwE
Argentina	1	344	2	1,298	2	1,200
Brazil	0	0	3	3,116	6	7,470
Chile	0	0	0	0	1	600
People's Republic of China	0	0	0	0	2	1,800
Cuba	0	0	2	888	3	880[a]
Egypt	0	0	0	0	8	6,900
South Korea	0	0	8	6,828	2	41,100[b]
Libya	0	0	1	440	0	0
Mexico	0	0	2	1,308	2	19,000
Pakistan	1	125	0	0	1	600
Philippines	0	0	1	620	1	620
Thailand	0	0	0	0	2	1,660
Bangladesh	0	0	0	0	1	125
Colombia	0	0	0	0	1	600
Turkey	0	0	0	0	2	1,660
Iraq	0	0	1	900	0	0
Kenya	0	0	0	0	1	200
Venezuela	0	0	0	0	1	na
Total	2	469	20	15,398	35	83,655

Source: Atomic Industrial Forum, "AIF Releases International Survey," *INFO News Release* (March 29, 1982). Reprinted with permission.
Note: MwE = megawatts of energy
[a] Gross MwE for one reactor not available.
[b] May be reduced.

A third major target is the energy transportation and distribution system. This includes both oil and gas-pumping pipeline networks as well as electric-transmission lines. The vulnerability of oil and gas systems is well documented[3] (see table 4-2). The pumping stations are more vulnerable than are the pipes themselves. An explosion on 11 May 1977 at the Saudi Abqaiq pumping station cost $100 million to repair. Electric-transmission lines will also provide more targets as industrial countries develop national power grids and as the developing countries expand their hydroelectric capability. Although industrial states contain and will retain a high degree of flexibility in their transmission capabilities, developing countries will be

Table 4–2
Sample of Recent Worldwide Oil-Well and Gas-Well Fires

Location	Date of Fire	Duration	Type of Installation	Cause of Fire	Geography
Chile	August 1981	Unknown	Oil	Explosion	Offshore
New York	August 1981	26 hours	Oil and Gas	Blowout	Onshore
Singapore	April 1981	Unknown	Oil	Unknown	Onshore
Oklahoma	February 1981	Unknown	Gas	To prevent gas accumulation	Onshore
Gulf of Mexico	January 1981	Immediately extinguished	Oil	Blowout	Offshore
Poland	December 1980	3 weeks	Oil and Gas	Blowout	Onshore
Egypt	October 1980	4 days	Gas	Blowout	Offshore
Texas/ Louisiana	September 1980	2–3 weeks	Gas	Blowout	1 Offshore 3 Onshore
Mexico	September 1980	1 month	Oil	Unknown	Onshore
Gulf of Mexico	August 1980	2–3 weeks	Gas	Blowout	Offshore
Gulf of Mexico	August 1980	Immediately extinguished	Oil	Tanker collision	Offshore
Mexico	August 1980	2 weeks	Gas	Lightning	Onshore
Iran	July 1980	2 days	Oil	Iraqi shelling	Onshore
Peru	July 1980	3 hours	Oil	Explosion	Onshore
China	July 1980	Collapsed into water	Oil	Explosion	Offshore
Brazil	June 1980	Immediately extinguished	Oil	Blowout	Offshore
Indonesia	April 1980	4 months	Gas	Earthquake	Onshore
Texas	March 1980	Unknown	Gas	Explosion	Onshore
USSR	January 1980	2–3 weeks	Gas	Flare melted Rig parts	Offshore

more limited in their capacity to cope with a sudden disruption to electric-power supplies.

It is apparent that the remainder of this century will see a major emphasis on the development of hydro-power resources in the third world. At the same time, hydro supplies are generally located far from demand centers, necessitating construction of extensive transmission lines. Because of the cost of backup systems and the limited availability of other energy resources, many third-world nations will not be able to cope with a breakdown in the transmission lines or at the hydroelectric site. Hydroelectric dams could also be major targets. Destruction of the giant Tarbela facility, the largest earth-rock dam in the world, would flood a large portion of Pakistan.

In none of these examples is energy the principal reason for conflict. As an end in itself, energy has been the cause of several major territorial disputes between states as well as several within states, in recent years. In examining the history of these conflicts, their durability is their most astonishing feature:

> . . . conflicts long dormant have begun to alight all over the globe, as hungry and energy-starved states begin to stake out their claims in disputed areas, especially those in areas where resources are thought to lay. A partial listing for Africa and Asia gives some scope of the potential problem. The Oudalan Border Area, disputed between Mali and Upper Volta, is thought to contain water, oil, natural gas and other minerals. Casualties are already involved. The oil-rich Corisco Bay Islands are disputed between Gabon and Equatorial Guinea. The Somali borders have had adequate ethnic cause to maintain tension with Kenya and Ethiopia, and the suspected presence of oil in some of the disputed zones has intensified the problem. Zambia has a dispute over the hydroelectric power of the Kariba dam with Rhodesia and South Africa. The mineral wealth of Namibia is as much at the heart of the conflict over the territory's future as is the dispute among claimant nationalist groups. Phosphate deposits, as we have seen, have already led to a division of the Spanish Sahara, and Polasario Front Guerrillas, armed by Moscow through Algeria, will increasingly be able to tie Moroccan troops down in the future. Cabinda secessionists would, like those of mineral-rich Katanga-Shaba, like to have their vast oil deposits to themselves, without having to share them with all of Angola.
>
> In Asia, the discovery of new oil deposits at Bombay High had led to a rethinking of naval policy in Delhi and the possibility of increased tension with Pakistan; this on top of the continuing conflict with Bangladesh over water (among other things), and the dispute with Sri Lanka over the boundary in the Palk strait where oil is also thought to lie. Competition between Vietnam, the Philippines and China over the Paracel and Spratly Islands is essentially over potential resources, and in the East China Sea, the PRC, ROC, ROK and Japan have disputes over the control of the continental shelf.[4]

Most of the conflicts mentioned earlier continue in one form or another. Internal disputes over control of energy resources are more quickly resolved (although the 1967–1970 Biafran war lasted much longer, partially because of the interjection of outside forces). Territorial disputes between states are not ended so easily.

This failure to resolve some conflicts, while allowing others to linger, may be a result of the level of forces in the area—either indigenous or external. Although many boundary areas in the world are poorly drawn, states do not precipitously engage in war to redesign borders, even if a critical resource is involved. This may be because of the mystique of rigidity enshrined in the formal structure of the United Nations and the heritage of colonial boundaries in the third world and because of a sense of social fragility among the new nations of the world. One does not want to encourage the first stone to be thrown, for fear the second will be at one's self. Yet, this sense of international ordering may be breaking down.

This breakdown is especially apparent in Africa. During the worst years of Idi Amin's rule in Uganda, the OAU was unwilling to condemn Amin, thereby interfering in internal matters. But recently there have been indications that in recent practice the African states have permitted interference, although in theory the African states still adhere to the sanctity of colonial boundaries. A case in point is the formation of an all-African peace force to replace the Libyans in Chad.

The breakdown (if there ever was an order) is also visible in the Middle East and South Asia. Here again it is difficult to separate out critical variables. The Iran-Iraq conflict is of long standing. Indeed, the dispute over transportation rights on the Shatt al-Arab led both states to develop alternate export facilities (Kharg Island by Iran and Khor el-Amaya by Iraq), but this did not prevent war. Border disputes between Iraq and Kuwait led to the 1977 establishment of demilitarized zones, still an unsettled issue. Kuwait's fear of Iraqi irredentism is one of its reasons for participating in the Gulf Cooperation Council and its Council of Defense Ministers. A factor contributing perhaps to the unsettled nature of Middle East borders is the long dispute with Israel. Calling into question the very existence of one state makes it easier to question the existence of others—thus the resolution of the Arab-Israeli conflict might contribute to regional stability in more ways than one.

In the Mediterranean, border conflicts between Greece and Turkey over the Aegean and between Libya and Tunisia over drilling rights in the Isis field beyond the Gulf of Gabé also contain a strong energy component as well as a heritage of animosity. The Libya-Tunisian dispute is of five years' standing and is now before the World Court. There would probably be no interest in this area if it were not for the estimated reserves of 2 billion barrels of high-quality, low-sulphur, crude oil in the Gulf and Libya's extensive territorial claims (recently contested by the U.S. Sixth Fleet). The Greek-Turkish dispute will continue, probably as long as Cyprus remains an issue. Even so, it would be difficult to resolve legally, since there is no clear demarcation of the continental shelf in the region as there is in other parts of the world where offshore territories are in question, such as the South China Sea.

Offshore territorial disputes have certainly become more difficult to resolve since the problems leading to the Webster-Ashburton Treaty of 8 August 1942. Resources are a prime reason for this: fishing, mineral, and fossil. The South China Sea is another clear case of an area that would not be at issue were it not for interest in potential energy resources and rich fishing areas.

The entire area of the South China Sea is subject to multiple disputes. China, Taiwan, Vietnam, Cambodia, Thailand, Malaysia, Indonesia, and the Philippines all contest areas of the Sea. Claims are made even more complex because several of the states are archipelagos, with claims made from their outermost points. China—and Taiwan in the name of China—claim by historical legacy the entire South China Sea, extending all the way to Indonesia. Nor has the Philippines ever officially renounced its claim to Malaysia's Sabah Province.

Because of the internal regional disputes among the nations of the region—in particular, ones that pit Vietnam against the Association of Southeast Asian Nations (ASEAN), Vietnam against China—the fear China evokes among most of ASEAN, and because of the high level of military forces in the region, the area will continue to be subject to conflict. Such conflict may well draw in the United States. Because the United States has a defense treaty with the Philippines by which the United States guarantees Philippine territorial integrity, the Philippines could well invoke the U.S. obligation should it be attacked while pursuing claims to such islands as the Spratly chain, some of which are already occupied by Taiwanese and Vietnamese forces.

The dependence of all these nations on fish for food and on imported oil for energy ensures that the struggle for control of the South China Sea will continue to be an active and violent one.

Territorial resource conflicts are also important in Latin America. Colombia and Venezuela have long-standing claims over sea rights in the Gulf of Venezuela's entryway to Venezuela's petroleum fields in Lake Maracaibo. Venezuela contests two-thirds of Guyana, which has prospects for oil and gas resources. Argentina and Chile have laid claim to the Beagle Channel. In addition, there continue to be numerous border disputes, which are the results of past wars. On the whole, however, it is unlikely that a flare-up of any of these conflicts would last long or involve the great powers. Latin America shares a social and historical integrity that isolates it from direct military intervention by other powers, and the region is sufficiently advanced in its political links that it would work quickly to resolve any major interstate disputes. Latin America has had extensive experience with regional wars not including external powers.

In general terms, Latin America is a more cohesive region than other parts of the developing world. Africa, Asia, and the Middle East are still more tied to the industrial world—the center countries—than to themselves, the periphery states. External commercial, political, and, in some cases, even social relations are directed outward. This gives the West more influence over events in these areas, and it also tends to involve the West. For this reason, conflict here is more likely to bring great-power participation.

The theme of global interdependence is an overworked one, but it still has meaning and important implications for conflict resolution.

How Energy Conflict May End

The fundamental importance of energy-resource conflict does not come from a threat against specific installations (even nuclear ones), a threat to internal cohesiveness, or a threat of sudden flare-ups in interstate war over poorly conceived borders. The importance of energy conflict comes from a more nebulous area: its impact on stability in world order.

The 1973–1974 oil embargo managed to reveal the fallacy of perpetual good health in the relations between states. Instead, it uncovered the sores between nations, which, if left untreated, could poison all. Problems in the health of the international body became apparent in the relations among industrial states, in the relations between industrial and developing countries, and in communist countries' relations with the rest of the world.

The 1973–1974 embargo fragmented Western Europe, where a generation had been spent trying to establish a strong economic and political union. By selecting Holland as the focus of the embargo while granting other Western European states "friendly status," the Arabs managed to call into question the entire structure of postwar Europe. National interests prevailed over collective security. The concept of "one for all and all for one" was patched up, under U.S. pressure, in a meeting in Washington in February 1974. This conference led to the establishment of the International Energy Agency (IEA) within OECD later that year.

Although the IEA is a U.S. initiative, Europeans remain deeply suspicious of U.S. intentions to abide by the agreement to share oil in another disruption or to cooperate on other energy policies. This suspicion has been strengthened by pronouncements from the Reagan administration.

Although the IEA is in doubt, Europeans have moved in two directions. Economically, they have strengthened the European Economic Community's (EEC's) oil-sharing scheme in the event of another disruption. Politically, Europe has tried to strengthen its ties with the Arab states and to become an integral part of the Middle East peace process. Neither action precludes U.S. involvement. However, they place the onus on the United States to react, and they make it possible for Europe to pursue a track diverging from that of the United States.

The 1973–1974 embargo also had a major impact on the third world. The price paid by these countries for oil increased 800–900 percent from 1973 to 1980, from $3.5 billion to nearly $30 billion.[5] These nations have the fastest-growing rate of energy consumption. Should projections of their current development plans be reached, by 2000 the LDCs will need 35–40 percent of the world's oil supplies. Even if alternative energy sources are developed, oil will still be needed to fulfill 50 percent of their total energy requirements by 2000. If supplies are restricted, developing countries will be forced to bid with rich nations for their share of world oil. In such bidding, they will no doubt lose.

Because of their fears for supplies, most of the developing world moved closer to the Arab sphere of influence following 1973. Diplomatic relations were broken with Israel. Although a cornucopia of aid did not arrive from the Middle East, the basic orientation remains, even as development prospects worsen.

The prospects for a collapse of economic growth and a breakdown of order within third-world countries as a result of high energy prices is one of the most critical issues facing the United States today. Europeans recognize this because of their many ties to former colonies. The United States does not. Yet U.S. relations with the third world have changed dramatically since the 1950s and 1960s. The United States is increasingly dependent on third-world resources and markets to maintain growth. The challenge for the rest of the century, and the next, will be to expand those markets and develop those resources. Without them, the United States cannot survive.

The urgency of the third-world problem is well known and has been the subject of past U.S. policy initiatives. In his speech before the Washington Energy Conference 11 February 1974, Secretary of State Henry Kissinger stated that ". . . the developing countries must quickly be drawn into consultation and collaboration. Their futures are the most profoundly affected of all."

An early—and the only—attempt at consultation with both the oil producers and other third-world countries, the Conference on International Economic Cooperation (1975–1977), resulted in only a limited agreement, partially because OPEC refused to negotiate concessions.[6] Consultation is probably not as important as collaboration. Here the United States has been reticent in discussing proposals for improving third-world energy development or the structural problems of development itself.

Failure to address these problems will make the third world more susceptible to conflict than in the past—precisely at the time that U.S. defense strategy is undergoing a substantial reorientation toward greater dependence on third-world nations to contain the Soviets.

This reorientation is a direct result of Western dependence on imported oil from the Persian Gulf states, North Africa, Latin America, and West Africa. The strategic necessity of maintaining these supplies brings into play a whole host of secondary third-world actors. Bases in the Philippines become even more critical in terms of supporting Indian Ocean operations.

Indeed, the U.S. 7th Fleet now has responsibility for both the Indian and Pacific oceans. Forward-deployment-support areas in Egypt, Somalia, and Kenya, as well as bases in these countries and several others, have become important. The weakness of the chain stretching from the Strait of Hormuz to U.S. shores requires outposts to be established all along the way. It becomes obvious that if the United States is going to sustain a defensive capability in the Gulf, it is going to have to play a much more active role in resolving other third-world problems.

The final major change in the international order has taken place in Eastern Europe and the Soviet Union. Growth in demand, higher prices, and, for the moment, an outlook of declining production are forcing the Soviet Union to choose whether to satisfy domestic demand, export to its satellites, or earn hard currency by exporting oil and gas to Western Europe. Without immediate efforts to develop new fields, the Soviet Union will not be able to bring on stream needed new supplies before 1990. Oil and gas exports to its satellites is one of the principal controls the Soviet Union exercises over these countries. By reducing exports it will be forcing these states to move more onto world markets, both to buy energy supplies and to sell goods to pay for these supplies.

Eastern Europe will be forced to move into the capitalist system, with all its attendant degenerate effects. One expert estimates that Eastern Europe will have to import at least 1 Tb/d from outside the bloc.[7] The Soviet Union will have to develop western Siberian regions if it is going to avoid diminished supplies in this decade. To do so, however, will require Western technology and equipment. Already, both the Carter and Reagan administrations have had to confront this issue—whether to assist the Soviets in energy development—and both have failed to establish a policy. In addition, Western Europe is proceeding with its natural-gas deal with the Soviet Union despite halfhearted U.S. opposition, which will more than double Soviet gas exports to Europe. In West Germany, these supplies would raise West Germany's consumption of Soviet gas from 17 to 30 percent, or about 5 percent of its total energy needs.

All these events give the Soviet Union and its satellites ample justification for greater involvement in the Persian Gulf and third-world energy-producing areas. To date, the communist bloc has not had to develop strong economic ties with any developing country except its few client states. This should change during the next few decades. At the same time, it encourages Western Europe to be more "European" in outlook and less responsive to U.S. leadership.

Thus, the world order is shifting, however slowly, in counter-centrifugal directions. As a result, the United States may end up isolated through no intent of its own. To avoid this situation will require enlightened leadership, not a tunnel vision narrowly focused on the Strait of Hormuz.

Notes

1. See William Tucker, "The Energy Crisis Is Over!," *Harper's* 263 (November 1981).

2. Philip Connelly and Robert Perlman, *The Politics of Scarcity, Resource Conflicts in International Relations* (London: Oxford University Press, 1975), and Melvin A. Conant and Fern R. Gold, *Geopolitics of Energy* (Washington, D.C.: U.S. Senate, Committee on Interior and Insular Affairs, January 1977).

3. See U.S. General Accounting Office, "Key Crude Oil and Products Pipelines Are Vulnerable to Disruptions," EMD-79-63, Washington, D.C., 27 August 1979.

4. Richard Kessler and W. Scott Thompson, " 'Third World' Wars? Resource Scarcity and Conflict Potential in the Coming Ice Age" (Paper prepared at the International Security Studies Conference, The Fletcher School of Law and Diplomacy, Boston, Massachusetts, 4–6 May 1977), p. 19. Reprinted with permission.

5. See Charles K. Ebinger, *Pakistan, Energy Planning in a Strategic Vortex* (Bloomington, Ind.: Indiana University Press, 1981), p. 1.

6. See David M. Adamson, "Oil and North-South Negotiation" Ph.D. diss., The Fletcher School of Law and Diplomacy, Tufts University, 1980.

7. See Tony Scanlan, "Outlook for Soviet Oil" (Paper prepared for Conference on Oil and Money in the Eighties: New Outlooks, September 1981), p. 29. Copyright British Petroleum International, Oxford, England.

5 Ocean-Resource Competition as a Source of Conflict

John Norton Moore

The first purpose of this chapter is to indicate specifically what resources are contained in the oceans; the second is to look at some of the ways in which there may be a significant potential for conflict arising out of competition for these resources. In my judgment, most of this conflict is likely to be political, although intense political conflict in some settings may occasion the outbreak of military hostilities. With a review of ocean resources as a potential source of conflict, it then may be possible to assess U.S. policy in this respect.

From an economic standpoint, the most important ocean resources are the oil and gas of the continental margins. The oil and gas are located primarily in the continental shelf, slope, and rise, which can be thought of as submerged parts of the continental plates associated with the major continents. Although a substantial degree of guesswork is employed in the absence of actual drilling for oil and gas, approximately 40 percent of the entire potential reserves of oil and gas in the world are located under saltwater. Thus oil and gas are extremely important ocean resources.

A second kind of resource, as we move beyond the continental margins of the world to the deep ocean floor, are manganese nodules—accretions resembling lumps of coal—that litter areas of the deep ocean floor. If a television camera were focused on such areas, they would look as if a bucket of coal had been scattered loosely around the ocean floor. These nodules contain what are believed to be commercially attractive quantities of copper, nickel, cobalt, and manganese. A number of international consortia—all begun in the United States—have spent over $100 million in the research-and-development phase for the mining of these nodules. Their potential is very significant in terms of U.S. minerals access. The resource base is staggering: for example, it has been estimated that there are anywhere from 25 to 250 first-generation mine sites for these manganese nodules. A mine site is an area roughly the size of Rhode Island, which could be mined in a fairly large operation for a period of at least some twenty years. With perhaps 2 or 3 of these mine sites operating, the United States would be able to reverse its traditional need to import substantial quantities of nickel, cobalt, manganese, and eliminate the need to import a smaller percentage of our copper. In short, we could shift from a nation that imports very high percentages of these minerals to a nation that would be completely self-sufficient for the foreseeable future in all those minerals. Indeed, if one had few political constraints and were able to operate as many mine sites as desired, there would be few barriers to entering the export trade in these minerals.

In addition to manganese nodules, there may be other deposits on the deep ocean floor. In the fall of 1981, there was a great deal of excitement in the oceans community over the apparent discovery of what have been called poly-metallic sulfides. These deposits are not yet well known, since we only have a few data points. However, there are deposits located at seafloor spreading centers that apparently were formed when mineral-rich hot fluids, rising from rift areas, precipitated out mineral deposits as the fluids cooled on contact with seawater. Current data seem to point to exciting finds of copper, silver, zinc, and other minerals present there. This potential ocean resource is the subject of intense speculation, and it almost certainly will engender a substantial research program. The French, among others, are looking very seriously at these mineral-rich marine sulfides, but it is still too early to have any sense of what the commercial potential might be. These deposits seem to lie along general rift areas and seafloor spreading areas; at this point, nothing has been found in the Atlantic. In any event, this illustrates that there are perhaps a number of valuable resources associated with the deep seabed that are still relatively unknown and that may prove worthy of commercial mining.

In addition to potential hard-mineral deposits on the continental shelf, phosphorite deposits of one kind or another, and fuel and nonfuel minerals, other more obvious kinds of resources exist in the ocean. We should consider fish stocks, direct-ocean-energy potential, and space itself as a resource and a historical source of conflict. Certainly global fish stocks— coastal species, highly migratory species—fall in this category. Too, the thermal gradients in the ocean and the salinity gradients or even wave motion serve to generate energy, which has been useful in supplying electricity to areas, islands, and states such as Guam, Micronesia, Puerto Rico, and even Hawaii. One can talk also of the oceans in terms of sheer space being a resource. For example, offshore nuclear-power plants might be located in a variety of areas; proposals have been made to locate a string of them off, say, the East Coast of the United States. Finally, shipping, which directly utilizes the ocean-space potential, is now and for the foreseeable future will continue to be the largest economic use of the world's oceans. If one needs oil from the Persian Gulf or hard minerals from the southern Africa region, the economic reality almost certainly will require that these resources be moved by ship.

With these ideas in mind, what might some of the potential conflict scenarios originating from competition for ocean resources look like? Broadly speaking, there are four that are most likely to develop, although it is difficult to predict whether all these will necessarily become significant sources of conflict. I reiterate that these conflicts will be predominantly political in nature, but each will have the potential to spill over into some kind of low-intensity military problem. The first of these conflicts is simply the unresolved question of who owns the resources of the deep seabed. Who has the legal right to control the resources—the manganese nodules, the phosphorite deposits, or the metalliferous sulfide deposits—that might be located beyond the continental margin? First, it is relatively clear in ocean law today that the complete continental margins eventually may be under coastal-nation control. In this light, there will probably be no great problem insofar as the seaward area of oil and gas control and ownership are concerned. However, once one proceeds beyond the continential margin to the abyssal plain and the deep ocean floor (the area "beyond national jurisdiction" as it is technically known), competition for control of resources has been fierce since the late 1960s. On the one hand, the Group of 77 developing countries feel very strongly that this area should be available as the common heritage of mankind. On the other, the developed nations, although not opposed to the principal of the common heritage of mankind, have insisted that this principle be worked out through negotiations that would provide for an efficient system of mining the deep seabed and would guarantee access to the mineral resources of the area and protection of the integrity of investments for all countries. This issue has moved through a general phase within the United Nations, specifically in resolutions on the common heritage called the "Principals Resolution," which was supported by the United States, with the understanding that this would be implemented only in an agreement acceptable to the United States. This issue has engendered a substantial period of negotiations, first in the United Nations Seabed Committee and, since 1973, in the Third United Nations Conference on the Law of the Sea (UNCLOS III). There are many other issues at stake in these negotiations, most importantly in regard to access rights through, over, and under straits used for international navigation. However, most of the issues, particularly the straits transit, have been settled to the satisfaction of all concerned parties. Unfortunately, the deep-seabed-mining provisions are in serious disarray. The Reagan administration made exactly the same judgment as it came to office: essentially, negotiation on the part of the United States has come to a halt until U.S. policy is reviewed. This position is a reflection of strong pressure from U.S. industry and from the U.S. Senate, and others in the Congress, arguing that if this treaty were finalized in the form the Carter administration suggested, the treaty would never be passed by the Senate.

Specifically, the problems in the text of the treaty relate first to whether there are stipulations guaranteeing access to resources. Is there any assurance that it will be possible to mine the deep-seabed mineral resources

wherever they may be located? Is the system workable, or hindered with
unrealistic mandatory technology-transfer or production-limitations provisions? Second, there are some concerns about institutional problems. For
example, the present treaty guarantees three seats to the Soviet bloc on the
council of an authority established to regulate deep-seabed mining, a standard UN caucusing arrangement assuring three permanent seats to the
Eastern Socialist bloc. The United States, however, is not provided with any
such guarantee of seats. In addition, there is a review clause providing that,
at the end of a twenty-year period a two-thirds vote of the Group of 77 would
enable them to control and to rewrite completely, if they so desired, the
deep-seabed-mining provision—the only understanding being that the
United States could drop out at the time when the treaty might become
customary international law (making it too late to renegotiate the provision). This issue is under close review at the present time. There are a
number of options going forward to the president in the immediate future.
The Reagan administration in all probability will decide to remain in these
negotiations with a very clear caveat to the negotiators that they must work
for a more agreeable settlement on deep-seabed-mining access and institutional issues.

The deep-seabed-mining issue could become a watershed for political
conflict, since, despite slowed UNCLOS talks, the United States in 1980
pushed the passage of deep-seabed-mining legislation authorizing U.S.
firms to mine the deep seabed. This legislation was considered interim, until
such time as a law-of-the-sea treaty would take effect to work out reciprocal
recognition of these rights with other industrialized nations passing similar
legislation. These negotiations continue at the present time. There are three
possible scenarios in this context. The first is a return to the law-of-the-sea
negotiation with an agreeable resolution of deep-seabed-mining issues. This
is a significant possibility. It certainly would be the optimal outcome and
would be least likely to result in conflict. The second scenario is a drive by
the Soviet Union to finalize a treaty without the presence of the United
States. The principal variable here would be whether our Western European
allies are with us at that point. If our Western European allies and those
involved in the reciprocating-state negotiations follow our lead and do not
accept the new treaty, then I would see operations commencing that probably would serve as a lightning rod, at least for political attacks from the
Group of 77. If these nations were supported strongly by a series of major
maritime powers, I think it likely that conflict would be confined to the
political realm.

The last probable scenario is conclusion of the treaty over U.S. objec-
tions in a setting in which our allies do not support us and sign the treaty
themselves. Clearly, a ratified law-of-the-sea treaty that excluded the
United States from state negotiations could place the United States in an

extremely poor position. If such a situation were to arise, we might feel compelled to take measures to protect our interests in ocean resources in a fashion that possibly could engender more intense conflicts between the United States and others.

Three additional potential sources of conflict require examination. The first involves lateral, adjacent, and opposite ocean-boundary disputes. These conflicts have been most likely to emerge over issues concerning arbitrary separation of potential oil and gas areas. Based on heightened controversy involving the extension of fishery zones to 200-mile limits and jurisdiction of ocean littorals over the continental-shelf seabed, there are now over two hundred potential unresolved ocean-boundary disputes. Many of these are in the process of negotiation; others have already become significant areas of conflict. The most important dispute that involves U.S. strategic interests is the conflict between Greece and Turkey over the control of the continental shelf in the Aegean Sea. Since apparently there are significant oil and gas resources at stake, many have argued that this issue, over time, could foment serious conflict between allies of the United States.

Another possible source of conflict concerns the offshore resources, and, indeed, the entire continent of Antarctica, which has been claimed by a number of different states since 1959. The Antarctic Treaty governing the continent basically has prohibited any nation from exploiting onshore and offshore resources, especially along the continental margins, in areas other than those designated for that nation specifically. The United States has never made a claim for additional territory, but, were it to make a claim, its right to claim is as great as that of any other nation in the world, including any of the claimant states that already have made such claims. Today, there is disagreement between the claimant states concerning the unresolved sovereignty over Antarctica, and there is uncertainty whether Antarctica in fact will be claimed by these states or whether the territory should be recognized as another example of the common heritage of mankind. A number of countries within the United Nations are pushing the latter principle, and a number of claimant states have, of course, resisted strongly. If current interests in Antarctica are any indication, it is my opinion that this area will not become another example of the common heritage of mankind. The reality is that Antarctica is simply an area of disputed sovereignty among Antarctic Treaty participants.

Finally, the potential of terrorism could be directed not only against a resource installation but also against shipping, which, in terms of overall mineral policy, is even more important than the installations themselves.

The importance our nation should assign to access to the mineral resources of the oceans—and, in essence, what we might consider frontier areas in general—must be emphasized. This should apply to the continent of

Antarctica as well as to Antarctic offshore areas. These regions may appear to be far down the line in terms of development, but I do not believe we can afford to take the kind of shortsighted view that some took, for example, at the time of the acquisition of Alaska, which, of course, history branded "Seward's Folly." By taking a long-range view, we may come to understand that some very important resources are at stake. Some of these, such as manganese nodules, would be ready for immediate exploitation were it not for particular market conditions or political and legal uncertainties. It is particularly important that we hold firm to a model that emphasizes assured U.S. access to these areas. The institutions that are created must have good precedents for future negotiations that guarantee the same kind of access to the United States as other nations and that do not include one-sided provisions working to the advantage of the Soviet bloc or the Group of 77.

6

Strategic-Minerals Competition as a Source of Conflict

Robert A. Kilmarx

In this chapter I limit the concept of resource competition to competition for access to or control over the sources of supply of strategic raw materials, not including oil. In a broader sense, the concept of resource competition could even be extended to include competition for markets for the sale of goods and services. This whole basket of trade issues related to the General Agreements on Tariffs and Trade (GATT) agreements and codes, discrimination, and growing trends toward protectionism are worthy of separate treatment. The driving forces that lead a nation to adopt protectionist measures and the forces that lead to potential conflict over sources of raw materials are not unrelated.

The importance of this topic needs to be emphasized repeatedly to opinion molders, planners, and decision makers, even in an administration that understands the Soviet threat. The threat of resource war advanced by conservative interests prior to and early in the Reagan administration is now confronted by an articulate covey of liberal academics and their political counterparts. According to their philosophy, in effect it does not matter what kind of government controls the minerals resources on which U.S. economic viability and security depends. In their view, any future government of any type in a resource-rich source country will be compelled to sell to us in any case, to earn essential foreign exchange for economic development and political stability. Such apolitical views lead to accommodation to radical political change in the third world, supported by the Soviet Union and its communist allies.

Strategic minerals should now be viewed as a central factor in possible scenarios of conflict in some form, especially in the Middle East and Southern Africa. They could also play a part in causing or contributing to conflicts in a number of other areas, for example, North Africa and Southwest Asia.

Source of conflict can take many forms:

1. Aggressive policies of acquisition as a direct national objective for reasons of security of supply, to obtain control over external sources of raw material to increase the economic strength of the aggressive power.
2. National (or multinational) policies of denial of a resource to potential adversaries to erode their economic or political stability, evoking a conflict response.

3. Conflict that results from a national strategy of political or ideological expansionism or from opportunistic adventurism to increase political leverage, radicalize foreign leadership, and change foreign policies of targeted states. Resource aspects in such cases contribute to priorities and strategy but are not central.
4. Internal conflict or civil war based on demands for resource control.

Potential conflicts thus could be between superpowers, between a superpower and a nonsuperpower, between regional states that may or may not be states supported by superpowers, or even between regions within a state.

A number of exogenous variables would, of course, affect conflict probability. These would include the capabilities and intentions of foreign powers; their interests in, dependence on, or proximity to the area at issue; their influence over contending powers; the value of the minerals and the availability of alternative supplies or substitutes; state of world markets; new technological applications of the resources; and so on. In a number of the scenarios to be discussed, a key variable could be U.S. power and resolve and the policies and priorities of the U.S. administration in power at the time of crisis.

Scenario I—North Africa

The long-festering conflict between the government of Morocco and the Polisario guerrillas escalates after periods of varying intensity. Increasingly, the guerrillas—backed by the Palestine Liberation Organization (PLO) and the USSR and using sophisticated military equipment including ground-to-air missiles, tanks, and other equipment—threaten established Moroccan positions.

There is a serious danger that the conflict will escalate to higher levels of intensity, with the use of even more sophisticated weaponry (following the recent defeat at Guelta Zemmour of a Moroccan batallion by Polisario forces armed with T-54 tanks and possibly SA-6 surface-to-air missiles). As a result, the Moroccans asked a recent visiting U.S. military team for more advanced weapons, possibly including aircraft like the A-10 or A-7. This development threatens both the outlook for a cease-fire and a referendum in the Sahara that was agreed to at last June's Organization of African Unity (OAU) conference in Nairobi.

Although the contested area is barren and sparsely populated, it contains rich reserves of phosphates—the demand for which has grown since 1975. The USSR and other Eastern European countries are particularly anxious to ensure sources of supply. Although the USSR in the early 1980s assisted the government of Morocco in developing its phosphate reserves, it has since ceased to rely on Morocco for political reasons, including Morocco's close Western ties and conflicts with two of the USSR's allies—Libya and Algeria—both of which back the Polisario. In addition, Mauritania is providing a base and safe haven for Polisario combat units.

The protracted conflict, which took almost 40 percent of Moroccan gross national product (GNP) in 1981, has so weakened the existing pro-West government that its continued existence is in doubt. The government and territory are threatened by both internal political opposition and external forces. The military continues to back the monarchy, but opposition leftist forces, supplied by Libya and Algeria, are poised to overthrow the weakened government. The provision of military equipment and supplies by the United States and Western Europe has not been sufficient.

It may be that only direct military intervention can save Morocco and its vast minerals resources, including phosphates (of which it is the world's largest producer and exporter), coal, lead, zinc, copper, and others. The fall of Morocco would mean access by hostile states to phosphate deposits in the disputed territory as well.

Scenario II—Southern Africa

The West continues to be dependent on southern Africa for certain critical minerals—especially for chromium, cobalt, manganese, and platinum. Substantial production capacity in South Africa, Zimbabwe, and Zaire has maintained adequate supplies of these minerals since the Korean War. The black government of Zimbabwe and the government of South Africa will continue to support mineral policies conducive to meeting the mineral supply needs of the West. However, internal strife could very likely disrupt the production of strategic minerals over the short and long terms. The same statement applies to southern Africa's other two major mineral suppliers— Zaire and Zambia—as well. All four of these countries are vulnerable to resource conflicts in the decade of the 1980s.

Apartheid in South Africa shows no signs of reform, and a swelling of radical activism is on the horizon. Since the rise of the black-consciousness movement and mysterious death of Steve Biko thereafter, blacks in South Africa have coalesced into underground and nationalist groups. Local black groups, seeing no redress through established institutions, may develop well-organized, externally supported military organizations. They have the support of blacks throughout Africa and many parts of the world.

Because blacks are unable to confront the South African military directly, they will probably seek to force change by bringing internal pressure on the government. This is accomplished by sabotage of mining processing and transportation facilities in South Africa. An example of this type of conflict scenario occurred when a South African government-owned coal, oil, and gas corporation (SASOL) plant was destroyed by guerrillas. There are a number of attractive targets for subversive forces to attack, because they strike at the heart of South Africa's economy and the country's role as a vital raw-material supplier to the West. The railway lines that connect South Africa to its northern neighbors are easy targets in remote, unguarded areas of the country. Not only can South Africa's mineral production be delayed from reaching the market, but Zimbabwe output can be cut off. Zimbabwe also sends the bulk of its exports to markets through South African ports via South Africa's rail network.

Similarly Zimbabwe, Zaire, and Zambia depend on mineral exports as their primary source of foreign exchange and the mainstay of their economy. Zambia depends on copper for 95 percent of its foreign revenue. Zambia's striking mine workers have a stranglehold on the country, which they have exercised effectively to the dismay of President Kaunda. Strikes that shut down the mines in the summer of 1981 caused political chaos and the most significant threat to the rule of Kaunda.

In Zaire, internal pressures are reaching explosive proportions, but the greatest threat to the minerals industry remains guerrilla invaders from neighboring Angola. Incursions into the copper- and cobalt-producing Shaba province in March 1977 and May 1978 shut down mining operations and caused severe worldwide cobalt shortages. Soviet- and Cuban-dominated Angola was the staging area for invading forces. The USSR supplied weapons, and Cuba trained the intruding Katangese rebels. The continued presence of 16,000 Cuban troops in Angola and the weakening of internal and external support for President Mobutu make this scenario increasingly more plausible. Unlike the 1978 invasion, France and Belgium may not be as willing to rescue Mobutu's corrupt regime by driving out the rebels. The Belgian Parliament could be reluctant to approve sending paratroopers into the conflict. France's Prime Minister François Mitterrand is not disposed to supporting Mobutu and could pull out of the U.S.-Belgian-French agreement.

The most frightening scenario one can imagine is Soviet domination over the entire region of southern Africa. This would result in communist control of over 50 percent of global output of about fifteen of the most strategic minerals, including chrome, platinum, gold, cobalt, and manganese. The correlation of forces in southern Africa today is such that there is nothing absurd in the hypothesis of Zaire, Zambia, and Zimbabwe being brought into the Council for Mutual Economic Assistance (COMECON) sphere of influence.

Developing this scenario, pressure has increased to the point where black African countries finally plan military intervention in support of indigenous black elements—with Soviet-Cuban backing. Military equipment and supplies, as well as technicians, are being supplied by the USSR and Cuba. This raises a major dilemma for U.S. policymakers as to whether some military support of South Africa could be made politically palatable. The dilemma for U.S. and European policymakers would be far worse than Vietnam.

Scenario III—Latin America

Bolivia, which has continued to undergo frequent coups and changes during the 1980s, continues to suffer from political instability and economic stagnation. Minerals production has become increasingly noncompetitive, but export earnings from the sale of tin, zinc, lead, antimony, and tungsten are essential for economic survival. There is some upward movement in prices in the later 1980s and therefore brightened prospects for increased export earnings and economic recovery.

Bolivia, however, is encountering difficulties in transporting the minerals products to third markets. It has relied on rail transportation to the Chilean ports of Arica and Antofagasta, across territory that Chile seized from Peru in an earlier war. Efforts by Bolivia, with the cooperation of Peru, to obtain assured access to the sea in the late 1970s led nowhere. Since that time, Bolivia has had no diplomatic relations with Chile. But use of railways has continued through the 1980s.

More recently, there have been disputes between Bolivia and Chile and Chile and Peru over a common Andean policy. Also, Chilean railroads have increased the rates, so that Bolivian minerals products become less competitive in third countries. Labor instability in Chile has resulted in sporadic rail strikes, which have delayed Bolivian shipments. The government of Chile seems either unwilling or unable to take measures to ensure access to the ocean of Bolivian goods.

Bolivian sensitivity to its vulnerable geographic position is heightened by an array of economic and political developments. Peru, perceiving itself stronger than Chile militarily, joins with Bolivia in pressing Chile—hoping for restoration of lost lands. The failure of negotiations leads to armed intervention in the Arica area by Peruvian and Bolivian military units, with the United States caught in a position of trying to be friends of both sides and unwilling to exert force to resolve the dispute.

Scenario IV—Central America

Panama is of great strategic importance to the United States for the movement of goods, including raw materials, through the Panama Canal and soon across the isthmus. The importance of this territory, from a resource stand-point, is likely to increase when the Cerro Colorado copper mine comes on stream.

Panama today, a little over one hundred days after the death of strong man Omar Torrijos, is becoming a much less stable place. The trend is developing at a time when forces of radical leftist revolution, backed by Cuba and the USSR, consolidate an emerging Marxist state in Nicaragua and threaten to defeat the U.S.-supported military junta in Salvador. Royo is believed to be a weak, figurehead president. It is not clear who will be the military successor from the ranks of the dominant National Guard. Mean-time, the communists are busy expanding their influence in labor unions, schools, and farm groups.

In the case of Panama, a variety of conflict scenarios could emerge that have a considerable chance of involving the United States. One is that the present head of the National Guard, Colonel Florencio Florez, is over-thrown after a barracks power struggle. A charismatic military leader with radical leftist leaning gains control over the National Guard and turns Panama into another Nicaragua. A second, possibly related scenario is that external revolutionary forces support a civil war in Panama and infiltrate the country from a destabilized Costa Rica with Soviet and Cuban armed military forces—of course in defense of a claimant to political power in Panama. A third scenario is that free elections are held in 1984, and a leftist, procommunist wins: also a prescription for civil war or foreign intervention.

Embargoes or major denials of strategic minerals could cause policy responses by a future U.S. administration that could have conflict implica-tions, for example, stimulating activity by friendly opposition forces in southern Africa to ensure access to, and security of, the supply of chrome.

Scenario V—Papua New Guinea

A little-known area of potential conflict, with resources as the causal factor, is in Papua New Guinea. The economic health of the country largely depends on the output of copper and gold from the Bougainville Copper Mine. Bougainville, an island lying off the shore of the mainland of Papua New Guinea and its neighbor, Irian Jaya, has long sought autonomous status. In fact, there was a strong secessionist movement in the 1970s, which failed. A compromise was reached, and a provincial-government system was established, giving the individual provinces like Bougainville a great deal of autonomy. This autonomy, however, did not include the power of taxation, and only a small percentage of the royalties from the mineral operation were turned over to the government of Bougainville. During 1981, the issue again flared up, and the provincial government of Bougainville sought a higher percentage of royalties from the government centered in Port Moresby.

They threatened to close down the mine. This situation has not yet been resolved.

A scenario of conflict in the 1980s, involving Bougainville Island, might run along the following lines. The provincial government of Bougainville again falls into the hands of a radical activist like Father Momis. They demand secession from the central government, backed this time by foreign support. The Indonesian government at that time (possibly a leftist government), seeks control of all Papua New Guinea—an ambition long held by Indonesians, who covet the economic resources of Papua New Guinea and resent the financial drain of backward Irian Jaya compared to Papua New Guinea. The Bougainville government invites the presence of Indonesian forces (the behavior of Indonesia in the case of Timor shows their willingness to intervene in local situations if risks of major conflict are considered to be low).

As the scenario unfolds, Indonesian forces position themselves in Bougainville and bring the Bougainville mine to a standstill. The Papua New Guinea government, backed up by the Australian armed forces, sends in paratroopers to open up the mine. The battle is joined, risking escalation into a war between Australia and Indonesia.

The significance of this scenario, from a resource standpoint, would be if such a conflict escalated—perhaps bringing in a superpower. It could jeopardize the short-term supply of minerals from a number of mines in Australia, not necessarily because of an unlikely invasion of Australian territory but because of hazards to the sea transport of mineral cargoes from Australia, particularly to Japan.

Bougainville Copper Limited, at a time of high copper and gold prices, is a particularly rich mine—one of the largest copper mines in the world. In 1980, the net pretax earnings of Bougainville Copper Limited were over 130 million *kina*, with a *kina* worth almost $1.45.

Returning especially to the southern Africa scenario, let us see how serious, economically, a shortfall of one major strategic mineral—chrome—could be, turning to the work done by Charles River Associates (CRA) and the Heritage Foundation.[1] In case of a 26 percent supply disruption, real prices for chromium would rise as much as 950 percent. Annual economic losses, from this event alone, would range between $378–438 million per year over a ten-year period, for a total of about $4.2 billion.

According to the Heritage Foundation analysis of the CRA research, careful examination of the assumptions used by CRA shows that they are on the optimistic side. According to the Heritage Foundation, if we assume that the likelihood of a disruption lasting for a period of, say, five years, is very high, a five-year economic loss with a 26-percent disruption would reach the astronomical figure of $38.1 billion. This output loss of $38.1 billion in the U.S. economy implies a loss of 2.1 million man-years of employment.

The loss could be considerably greater if the embargo decreases supplies even more. The Heritage Foundation concludes that if political unrest or instability produces major dislocation in the economy of South Africa that resulted in halting all shipments of chromium and other minerals, it would reduce the world supply of chromite about 35 percent. The percentage could be even higher if the USSR did not come to the rescue of the United States by exporting its chrome. The Soviet Union is a major producer of chromite, but none has been sold in free world markets recently. The cutoff of South African production and one-half the Zimbabwe production—with no Soviet chrome exports and the inability of the West to utilize refractory-grade Philippine chrome production for important applications—could cause a decline of approximately 65 percent in the available supplies.

Surely, this may not be enough to lead to war, but enough perhaps to cause policy actions that could create major regional friction, instabilities, and even local conflict in the interest of the economic security of the United States—especially if a concurrent defense buildup is required because of events in an area like the Middle East.

As we look ahead, we can predict increasing uses for minerals and metals with unique properties that were, until recently, unimportant—some perhaps not yet discovered—as a result of technological advances. Although the United States is a source of some, it will continue to rely on imports for others. For example: today, columbium (nobium) and tantalum are being used in the production of high-strength, low-alloy steels and electronic parts. Rapid advances in data processing and communications portend new requirements for materials such as platinum, palladium, rhodium, and osmium. Iridium, a platinum-group metal, is considered the most corrosion-resistant element, suggesting uses in systems operating under rugged industrial conditions or in outer space. These and other exotic minerals and metals could play a part in a conflict situation.

If we let our imaginations run amok, we can even conceive of a major mineral discovery in the late 1980s—perhaps a new element from Antarctica or under the ocean—that contains such unusual properties that it could change the strategic balance. Perhaps it will be "stealthiam," a rare and exotic mineral that, when applied to the external fuselage of a long-range bomber, renders it totally invisible to radar, if not to the naked eye! Would a future world leader risk war to control such an invaluable resource that could contribute to world domination?

The prospect that resource competition could become a source of conflict for major industrialized nations could be significantly reduced if more serious attention were given to industrial-base mobilization planning, but little is being done in this most important area.

For example, only the United States has a significant strategic stockpile of critical raw materials; a few countries like Japan and France maintain very small stockpiles. The adequacy of our stockpile in times of national emergency, however, is greatly reduced by major shortfalls in stocks below target levels and the decline of minerals-processing industries in the United States, for example, ferrochromium and other ferro alloys, zinc, and now copper. The stockpiles are not to be used as economic stockpiles in times of shortages or soaring prices. Also, tax laws and accounting principles could be more helpful in encouraging a buildup of privately held inventories of minerals and metals.

Our vulnerability could also be further reduced if higher priority were placed on developing technologies to reduce the need for critical minerals, through systems design and engineering or substitution and if recycling and conservation were given higher priority. So far, no effective substitutes have been found for such critical minerals as chromium. With minerals prices lower and availability high at this time, incentives are presently not strong.

Furthermore, vulnerabilities could be reduced if the governments of major powers did more to encourage direct investment in mining—especially in countries in their geopolitical orbit and even in their own territories. Under present budgetary pressures, little is being done to stimulate mining of limited resources of critical minerals in the United States under the Defense Production Act or in Alaska, following the Alaskan Claims Settlement Act.

Although this administration—and the country—is more aware than before of the issue of strategic-mineral vulnerability from a security standpoint, remedial measures are difficult to pursue economically and politically. Unlike oil, the shortage of a critical alloy does not cause immediate pain to the body politic; but, like undiscovered hypertension, it can nevertheless contribute to a terminal condition.

Note

1. See: National Bureau of Standards, Experimental Technology Incentive Program, *Policy Implications of Producer Country Supply Restrictions: Overview and Summary.* (NBS-JCR-ETIP-77-36, volume one of nine volumes, February 1977).

7 Arms Transfers and Future Conflict

Michael Moodie

From the time early man first picked up a heavy stick and wielded it as a club against another, the connection between arms and conflict has been obvious. Almost as apparent has been the importance of the transfer of arms from one key actor to another in determining the outcome of a given conflict. Thucydides makes clear the importance of military assistance during the Peloponnesian war. The role played by French arms in the U.S. Revolution was underscored by the comment of a diplomatic historian who observed that " . . . without the munitions sent (by France) to America in 1776 and 1777 the revolt would have collapsed."[1] The importance of the resupply effort of the United States to Israel during the Yom Kippur War in 1973 is well known.

In one sense, then, analyses of conflict and arms transfers are nothing new. In another sense, however, the problems involved are very new. This novelty stems from several factors. First, the present diffusion of military capabilities is unprecedented. More countries have more weapons with greater destructive capabilities than ever before. That diffusion will condition the environment within which the business of international affairs will be conducted. The new environment will have important repercussions for the ways nations will manage their differences and, since force remains the final arbiter in the resolution of disputes, for how they will perceive the role of force and their willingness to resort to force. In short, the diffusion of power will continually change the calculations of the trade-offs, the costs and benefits, of the exercise of military power.

Second, the diffusion of military power is transpiring at an unprecedented rate. The phenomenon is not only a function of the speed with which nations, especially third-world nations, are procuring arms from abroad. It also results from the growing number of countries capable of producing an increasingly wide range of military equipment. The accelerated rate of the diffusion of military power is tied also to the growing sophistication of arms being procured to include, ultimately perhaps, the most destructive armaments yet devised by man—nuclear weapons. The list of countries hovering at the nuclear threshold is growing. Although this chapter will deal with conventional arms, the link to nuclear weapons cannot be ignored.

Third, the diffusion of military power will demand of industrialized nations new ways of conceptualizing the problems associated with developing coherent arms-transfers policies. As more countries improve indigenous production, focus will shift from transferring finished systems to providing sensitive military technologies. Competition in the arms market will increase, creating pressures for greater alliance coordination if competition is not to divide the allies. The United States's decisions about the utility and exercise of military power will have to be reconsidered. These are only some of the new problems the United States will be confronting regarding arms transfers in the years ahead.

Clearly, there is a need to examine the relationship between arms transfers and the future of conflict in the international system, especially in the third world, where conflict is likely to characterize the interaction of key actors for much of the next two decades. The impact of arms and the arms trade will be particularly important in regard to potential stimulus to conflict, the manner in which a conflict is conducted, and prospects for a conflict's resolution.

The Postwar Experience

In the years since the end of World War II, the world has witnessed a transformation in the global trade in arms and military-related equipment. Both the quantitative and qualitative dimensions of the arms trade have accelerated enormously. The broad trend has been one of continuous growth. For example, between 1963 and 1972, the average annual world-growth rate in arms transferred was $400 million in constant dollars, translating into an increase of almost 100 percent over the decade. By 1974, the world arms trade was ten times what it had been fifteen years before. The United States alone transferred approximately $110 billion in arms between 1950 and 1976.[2] The pace of arms transfers has not slackened since the mid-1970s. In the five years between 1974 and 1979, transfers to the third world grew by almost 30 percent.[3]

Four trends characterized the postwar diffusion of military power. First, the terms of transfer have changed from aid to trade. In large part, this change reflects the fact that many of the primary importers of military equipment during the last decade—the states of the Middle East—had large oil revenues with which to pay for their arms and military equipment.

Second, the focus on recipients of arms shifted from close, traditional allies of the United States and the Soviet Union to the third world. A recent UN survey estimates that the third world accounted for 75 percent of all arms imports during the 1970s.[4] The Middle East—especially Saudi Arabia, Jordan, Syria, Iran, and Iraq—consumed almost one-third of all major weapons imported by developing countries during the last decade. The U.S. Arms Control and Disarmament Agency estimates that the level of imports in the Middle East grew fivefold in the decade between 1969 and 1978. Although this increase was substantial, the situation in Africa was even more dramatic. Arms imports in Africa in 1978 were twenty-one times the level of imports in 1969.[5]

The shift in the postwar focus of arms-trade recipients should not be surprising. As Geoffrey Kemp notes, "The direction of the flow of arms is as volatile as world politics."[6] Many of the postwar arms increases in the third world represented symbols of national sovereignty to new nations or reflected the aftereffects of decolonization, including the growing professionalization of the armed forces in developing countries. Most recently, the acquisition of advanced weaponry is serving, to some extent, as a similar symbol. At the same time, most postwar international conflict has occurred in the developing world, thereby generating a continual orientation within these countries toward national security, the probability of conflict, and the need to possess the tools by which national interests and integrity can be maintained.

A third significant trend in the postwar arms trade has been the increasing sophistication of arms transferred to the third world. The U.S. decision to sell F-16s to Pakistan (and perhaps Venezuela) and the French push to provide the Mirage 2000 to India are only the latest developments in a trend that has seen developing countries procure more and more top-of-the-line equipment. Today, many of the arms procured by third-world countries are at the frontier of technological development. In the Middle East, one need only note that the states of the region maintain a roster of combat aircraft that includes F-15s, F-16s, A-4s, MiG 23s, MiG 25s, MiG 21s, Mirage F-1s, F-14s, and Jaguars.[7]

It is not only in the Middle East, however, nor just in the area of combat aircraft, that the trend can be seen toward the procurement of increasingly sophisticated arms. The market for light armored vehicles, for example, seems insatiable in the Middle East, Africa, and Asia. The publication *Strategy Week* has pointed out that the market for light military vehicles (LMVs), the backbone of many third-world states' land forces, will grow during the next decade since the present generation, most notably the Panhard AML and British Ferret, are aging. Continuing external threats and ever-present potential for internal disorder will intensify the demand. Moreover, the trend has begun toward improving the punch of armored units, demonstrated by the popularity of Britain's Scorpion and the Brazilian Urutu and Cascavel.[8] Although most developing countries outside the Middle East are unlikely to procure large numbers of main battle tanks, their armored vehicles are likely to become increasingly potent.

On the opposite end of the spectrum from combat aircraft and armored vehicles are small arms. Even in this area, third-world states are attempting to exploit the latest technological developments. By and large, these countries take their lead from the industrial producers, demonstrated by the trend in third-world procurements of smaller-caliber assault rifles in the wake of NATO's movement in that direction. However, there are also reports of a slow but steady move toward acquisition of the military shotgun, since many conflict engagements in third-world environments demand an initial burst of firepower over a large area at very short ranges. This shift seems to be part of an overall increase in the demand for police weapons.[9]

Other systems attractive to developing countries for improving their firepower are barrage systems, or light, mobile rocket launchers. Increasingly popular in industrializing countries with maritime concerns is the tactical cruise missile mounted on fast attack craft. This system is sophisticated, effective, and relatively cheap. The proliferation of missile-armed, fast patrol boats reflects the emphasis of developing countries on securing more "bang for the buck" through greater use of advanced technology.

The area in which this trend is most noticeable is the field of defense electronics and precision guided munitions. The battlefields of Vietnam and the Middle East demonstrated the growing need for defense electronics and spurred an interest in developing countries that could dominate their procurement habits for the next decade. Some analysts have predicted that the purchase of electronic equipment by the third world over the next decade could exceed the amount spent on conventional arms during the past two decades.[10] The emphasis in the third world on defense electronics will extend well beyond just weapons such as antitank and antiaircraft missiles to include the procurement of communications, radar, and other surveillance systems as well as electronic countermeasure equipment.

The development of an electronic-defense environment is already well underway in the Middle East; the American-Saudi AWACs deal is only the latest step. Some Asian nations have also procured or developed indigenously an above-average level of defense electronics, particularly Japan, Australia (although neither can truly be considered a developing country), South Korea, and Taiwan, and, to a lesser extent, the Philippines, Singapore, and New Zealand.

Africa, especially south of the Sahara, appears to be the one region that has lagged in the evolution of an increasingly dense electronic-defense environment. The one exception, of course, is South Africa, whose Silvermine complex is one of the most sophisticated monitoring facilities in the world. Although Africa lags behind other regions, many countries in black Africa currently are examining a number of alternatives for improved air-defense, communications, and electronic countermeasures (ECM) equipment.

The situation in Africa suggests that the level of sophistication of military equipment, in and of itself, is not the critical factor in addressing the relationship between arms and conflict. Rather, in assessing the impact of advanced technology, the key concern is the regional context in which more- or less-sophisticated weapons are introduced and, most important, the relative levels of sophistication of the arms inventories of potential combatants. At the battle of Crecy, the English longbow (hardly high technology) was relatively more advanced than the military hardware available to the French and played a decisive role in determining the outcome of the engagement. Similarly, the fact that the arsenal of a black African country today is less advanced technologically than that of a Middle East state says very little about the prospects of either of those countries becoming involved in a conflict or the possible outcome of hostilities. What matters is the regional context in which the states exist and their relative military capabilities compared to those nations with which they might find themselves in armed conflict.

This observation leads to the further conclusion that the impact of a particular arms transfer, especially during an ongoing conflict, is highly dependent on the regional context. The arms transferred by the Soviet Union to Angola during its civil war were neither as numerous nor as advanced as arms Moscow supplied to the Middle East during the 1973 War. Yet, from the Soviet perspective, the arms in Angola contributed to a successful outcome, and the arms shipped to Egypt and Syria did not. It is again a question of the relative quantitative and qualitative balance of the combatants.

This trend, however, must be put into perspective. Third-world states know that sophisticated technology exists and is available. They want it, and this demand has been the driving factor in the trend just described. At the same time, these states continue to procure less-sophisticated arms as well, often in significant numbers. These simpler technologies will frequently play a more important role in determining the outcome of a particular conflict than will the level of sophistication of the combatants' weapons. One should not assume that because the trend has been toward increased sophistication, the third world in general has achieved a high level of technological development in the military sphere. The trend only shows that arms inventories in industrializing countries are improving. After all, the level at which most third-world states began was relatively low.

One final trend must be noted in the postwar environment characterized by the diffusion of military power. In short, a growing number of countries are increasingly able to produce military-related systems. Today, more than thirty industrializing countries produce weapons of some sort, from munitions in Nepal to the wide range of weapons produced by Israel. The weapons most widely produced include small arms, ordnance, naval-patrol craft, armored fighting vehicles, some electronics, and a few aircraft. A few third-world defense industries predate World War II, such as Argentina's Fabrica Militar de Aviones or India's Hindustan Aeronautics Limited.

Most were established, however, in the postwar period as the age of colonialism came to an end and nationalism and national sovereignty became the hallmarks of third-world attitudes. This trend, in particular, is likely to accelerate during the next two decades.

The reasons for greater third-world emphasis on indigenous defense production are complex, stemming from political, military, and economic concerns, and they have been considered in detail elsewhere.[11] The incentives, however, can be reduced to the desire of developing nations to decrease their dependence on traditional arms suppliers of the industrialized world. Whether or not this goal is immediately achieved, over time a third-world state can learn to use available technology, steadily decreasing its need for external advice and direction. When one considers that most third-world defense producers are limited to less-sophisticated technologies—and most consider that sufficient—the trend takes on heightened importance. Most third-world states remain concerned with achieving success in a conflict through firepower and numbers rather than through reliance on high-technology arms. Less-sophisticated systems produced indigenously by third-world countries will, therefore, affect specific conflicts in the future.

The one exception, of course, is the Middle East. Even there, however, it has been forcefully argued that the

> Threat of less advanced arms . . . remains very much a part of the Arab-Israeli scene, serving as a central dynamic of the overall conflict and as a contributing factor to the current military buildup. At lower levels of violence . . . Arab unsophisticated weapons systems can still impose unacceptable cumulative costs in Israeli casualties. Attrition by means of unsophisticated Arab arms can trigger an escalation in an Arab-Israeli conflict both in terms of strategies pursued and force structures used in support of such strategies.[12]

Another dimension of this trend is the growth of arms exports from third-world defense producers. According to an Arms Control and Disarmament Agency (ACDA) study published in December 1980, the average annual value of all arms sales, including the reexport of arms by major suppliers in the third world, has increased almost fifteenfold on an annual basis during the last four years. Over 80 percent of all developing-country arms sales over the last decade have occurred during the same four-year period.[13]

Israel and Brazil are the leading arms exporters of the third world. Israel, for example, was estimated to be earning $500 million to $1.3 billion per year in arms sales.[14] Brazil, too, is approaching the $1-billion mark. Both countries rank among the world's top-ten arms exporters. Israel's success has derived from the high quality of equipment produced. Most appealing have been Israel's Uzi submachine gun, Gabriel maritime surface-to-surface missile, and Reshef/class fast attack craft. Brazil also makes good equipment, especially armored vehicles, which have found major markets in Latin America and the Middle East. More so than Israel, Brazil enjoys an attractiveness among third-world countries because it shares a common experience as a developing country. Both countries complement the third-world desire to reduce dependence on traditional arms suppliers, and both produce systems ideal for third-world environments because they are simple to operate and easy to maintain. Israel can point also to the fact that much of its equipment is combat-tested.

What are the implications of this trend for the relationship between arms and conflict? In some cases, particularly the Middle East, where the regional military balance is at a relatively high technological level, third-world arms production and arms trade are unlikely to have a significant impact. In other regions such as Africa, however, particularly later in this century, arms produced by industrializing countries could alter military balances. Moreover, growth of third-world defense industries will further choke an already crowded market and may well reduce the ability of major arms suppliers to limit a given conflict in scope, duration, or intensity. In the area of long-range, surface-to-surface missiles, for example, if industrializing countries produce the systems in quantity, the impact could be severe.

One final point: in the shadows of the analysis of conventional-arms transfers and third-world defense production looms the specter of nuclear proliferation. It is ironic that those industrializing states with the most advanced conventional-arms industries—Israel, India, Brazil, and South Africa—are also states that top the list of candidates for crossing the nuclear threshold. Pressure on these states for restrictions in all areas is unlikely to achieve great success. Those interested in keeping the lid on nuclear proliferation, therefore, may find that trade-offs must be made, perhaps in easing efforts to limit indigenous defense production and conventional-arms transfers.

Arms Transfers and the Future of Conflict

We turn now to an analysis of the impact of the burgeoning arms trade on the initiation, conduct, and termination of conflict in the 1980s.

In announcing his arms trade policy in 1977, President Jimmy Carter stated, "The virtually unrestrained spread of conventional weaponry threatens stability in every region of the world." His observation is repeated frequently in discussions of the pros and cons of arms transfers. There is an assumption among a significant segment of the population, not to mention defense analysts, that traffic in arms fosters conflict and is often a direct cause of the outbreak of violence.

Is this assumption correct? Is the arms trade a destabilizing factor in international affairs that breeds war and violence? Like most issues in international politics, this one cannot be resolved with a definitive yes or no.[15]

It is difficult to accept the argument that arms are inherently destabilizing and cause conflict. If one argues that high levels of arms inventories and/or more sophisticated arms increase the probability of conflict, then one must conclude that Europe is a more volatile region and more prone to conflict than Africa, the Middle East, or Southeast Asia. Yet, this has not proven to be the case in the post–World War II world, and there is little evidence to suggest that it will be the case in the future.

Notwithstanding the potential for conflict erupting as a result of miscalculation, instability in a particular region often reflects pressure for change desired by at least one key actor. To the degree that arms transfers foster that desire or alter the actor's perceptions of the costs and benefits associated with action designed to precipitate change (through the resort to military power, for example), arms transfers can be said to be destabilizing. But, arms transfers are not the sole factor at work in these situations. They interact with a host of other variables influencing both the actor's desire for change and his perception of his capability to achieve the desired result. Arms transfers do not create the desire for change; they interact with and play on it. In many parts of the world, the prospects for armed conflict remain high irrespective of the level of arms inventories or the magnitude of the arms flow. Moreover, procurement of arms is often a response to existing conflict (albeit not in a military form) or potential instability. This can be seen in Shahram Chubia's description of the attitude behind Iran's military buildup in the 1970s: "In the absence of a cohesive defense arrangement and similar perspectives among neighboring states on the threats to the region, Iran should not be deterred from looking to its own defenses, nor should it give other states a veto over its security program."[16]

Arms transfers may exacerbate incipient or existing instability and make a region more volatile as a result, but they do not directly cause instability or the conflicts that result from it. The existence of other elements interacting with the arms factor makes it particularly difficult to identify precisely the contribution of arms to the initiation of conflict. As Richard Betts points out, assessing the impact of arms transfers "must include a stipulation 'all else being equal,' and all else is rarely equal."[17] Arms transfers can in fact be stabilizing, because they can redress the inequitable balance of other factors. Israel, for example, is heavily outweighed by its potential Arab adversaries in manpower and economic resources. The arms Israel has received from the United States have helped to offset these disadvantages.

To say that arms transfers inherently do not create instability or conflict is not to argue that arms procurements have not contributed to the outbreak of conflict in the past and will not do so in the future. As indicated, arms transfers can exacerbate instability. One way is by fueling a country's concerns over the growing military capabilities of a potential adversary, thereby leading the concerned state to initiate a preemptive attack before the arms recipient is able to exploit its new acquisitions. The massive Soviet arms deliveries to Libya, for example, clearly have generated intense anxiety among Libya's neighbors. A state such as Egypt may decide that, before Libya gets too strong, it should take some form of preemptive action.

Arms transfers also may change a state's calculations of the effectiveness of a military option by altering the perception of the state's ability to undertake action successfully. In the early 1970s, Egypt did not feel it could successfully initiate any military action against Israel until it had adequate air-defense capabilities. The Soviets provided the necessary systems, thereby creating the milieu in which Egypt decided the balance between potential costs and benefits of a military move was positive enough to proceed. Iraq clearly believed in late 1980 that it had received sufficient numbers of the proper kinds of arms to secure quickly its military goals against Iran. In Egypt's case, the perceptions proved largely to be correct. In the case of Iraq, it was the opposite.

Looking to the future, the weapons most frequently debated as to their impact on stability are precision guided munitions (PGMs). On one hand, the argument has been made that because of the so-called defensive qualities of PGMs, they will be a stabilizing factor. By improving the defensive capabilities of third-world states, PGMs will raise the cost of military aggression and deter potential attackers. On the other hand, there are those who argue that the transfers of PGMs to the third world will be destabilizing because the acquisition of those systems will not proceed in a balanced manner, thus giving some states at least a temporary great increase in firepower that could upset existing regional military balances.[18]

As with many issues associated with this general topic, the response to opposing points of view depends on the specific environment into which PGMs are introduced. In the Middle East, for example, the procurement of advanced equipment in one state generates pressures in other nations to procure new systems as a counter. Although the AWACs are not PGMs, the U.S. promise of additional aircraft to Israel in the wake of the sale of the radar planes to Saudi Arabia exemplifies this process. Moreover, there is an additional possibility that weaker states in the Middle East could, through the acquisition of PGMs and other advanced military technology, become bolder in their stance toward a stronger state (that is, Israel) and even initiate, or at least participate in, a military action against the stronger state.[19] For its part, Israel or a strong Arab state would then have to procure additional capabilities to overcome the increasing capabilities of surrounding weaker states, whether or not they are allied in some form.

The dynamics of the Middle Eastern situation underline the fact that the preconditions for conflict among states exist before arms are introduced into the equation. The fundamental causes of any conflict are not rooted in arms races or military technology. Rather they stem from historical, cultural, ideological, and other factors. Of course, accidents can happen. There have been, and are likely to be, conflicts between nations that both sides preferred to avoid. Even in these cases, however, the potential for conflict already exists. The balance of arms between combatants is one factor determining whether that potential is realized.

The same dynamics are at work in other third-world regions, albeit to a lesser degree, since for some time the procurement of PGMs and other advanced technology will not reach the level it has in the Middle East. Although one can question the rate at which such technologies will be introduced into sub-Saharan Africa, Latin America, or East Asia, for example, nevertheless, there is little doubt that such a diffusion will occur in the years ahead. The arms inventories of the states in these regions are currently at a comparatively low level of technological sophistication; this suggests that the marginal impact of even a few such systems will be greater than it is in the Middle East. If this is the case, pressures generated by the cost of war on countries that can ill afford to pay high prices for advanced technology will inhibit PGM procurements. At the same time, there will be growing pressures on many states to respond in some way to the PGM procurements that do occur in their respective regions. Of course, PGMs and advanced technology are not relevant to many kinds of conflict likely to occur in the third world, including at times, the Middle East. Much of the terrain in the third world, for example, does not provide environments conducive to the use of such systems. More important, sophisticated anti-air defenses are useless against guerrilla activity, internal subversion, or revolution.

This point leads to a final issue in considering the impact of arms transfers on stability, that is, the destabilizing impact of arms transfers on domestic political and social structures of industrializing countries. Iran is frequently cited as the case in point. The argument has been made that large-scale procurements of advanced arms by the Shah strained a rigid political structure and fragile economic system that also had to meet enormous development demands. As a consequence, the system collapsed. Barry Rubin argues somewhat differently, however, noting that: "the overall importance of the [Shah's weapons procurement] program should not be overestimated in assessing the contributing factors to the revolution, and it may well be that these purchases were more significant in undermining the Shah's legitimacy than they were in terms of the economic damage they did to Iran."[20] Again, the issue is not clear cut. Arms acquisitions probably played a role in fostering a domestic situation in Iran that led to the revolution. This role, however, must be judged in the context of other factors in Iran—repression, corruption, religious differences, political rigidity, and so on. More over, one cannot ignore the positive direct and indirect development effects that modernizing the military establishment can have in a developing country. In Turkey, for example, the military has played largely a progressive role since Ataturk created the Turkish Republic. There are convincing arguments about the double-edged nature of the impact of arms acquisitions on the domestic milieu of industrializing states.[21]

There is also the question of the degree to which Iran is representative of situations elsewhere. To be sure, one can find parallels between Iran and other countries. However, one is also apt to discover as many divergencies. In most third-world countries, the introduction of enormous amounts of sophisticated technology at very high rates of acquisition are sure to stimulate a reaction. The key factors appear to be the speed of the buildup and the specific nature of the acquisitions. There are few countries in the world, however, with the resources or the desire to modernize their armed forces at the rate the Shah attempted. Even in Saudi Arabia, for example, there has been greater emphasis on infrastructure and less on finished systems, grounded on the logic of providing a reasonable base from which to develop the country's military forces. This emphasis has led some analysts to conclude that, although the military buildup in Saudi Arabia has had some disruptive effects on Saudi society, these have been manageable to date. As Saudi Arabia shifts toward increased procurement of finished military systems of relatively high sophistication, it will be instructive to discern whether those pressures become more stressful.

It is difficult to generalize about the relationship between arms and military-technology transfers and the outbreak of conflict in the developing world. The interactions between arms and other factors that promote or inhibit the resort to military force by a third-world state are too complex outside an environment-specific analysis. There is a relationship; that much is sure. However, the nature of that relationship in any given situation will depend on the interplay of arms and other factors.

Conduct of Conflict

Three trends depict the evolution of conventional warfare: (1) the mechanization of armies, which emphasizes increasing firepower through capital rather than manpower inputs; (2) increasing force mobility designed to concentrate firepower; and (3) growing rates of material consumption.[22] These trends characterize the evolution of third-world conflict as much as they do warfare in Europe. Similarly, they are the factors currently emphasized in shaping force structures and arms inventories for the future in both

Europe and industrializing countries. An important difference, however, is that most third-world armed forces are not as far along these particular paths as are the forces confronting one another in Central Europe.

How is the continuing transfer of arms and associated equipment likely to affect the conduct of third-world conflicts? What, in particular, will be the impact of the growing diffusion of more sophisticated military hardware? The easy answer is that it will intensify the trends noted. The difficult answer is that the impact will be confusing and, to some extent, unpredictable. In comparison to the 1973 Yom Kippur War, for example, who would have predicted that the Iran-Iraq conflict—a war between two states presumed to be the most highly advanced military powers in the Persian Gulf—would have evolved into a static conflict with indecisive engagements drawn out interminably.

The following observations about arms and the conduct of conflict in the third world are offered more as hypotheses than as definitive answers. Research is extremely limited on the relationship between military technology, its use in more recent third-world conflicts, and its impact on the course of those conflicts. Significant data are not available, and further research on this important issue would be extremely useful.

In assessing modern warfare between industrialized countries, Martin van Creveld has argued: "When states go to war . . . the duration, intensity and often the outcome of the struggle are governed by political factors. The factors that determine the outcome of wars are changing—during the last eighty years they have moved progressively away from the battlefield to the smoke filled room."[23] One might argue to the contrary that, in the third world, for the most part this is not the case, because armed forces are in an earlier stage of development. Rather than a smoke-filled room, the battlefield between Tanzania and Uganda, such as it was, determined the outcome of that conflict. At the very least, military developments in the third world will create the "facts" with which politicans in smoke-filled rooms must deal. This implies that future third-world conflicts could remain relatively less limited than potential conflict between the superpowers. The ultimate impact on global stability might not be as great as a limited superpower conflict, but for the third-world combatants, the impact could well be a case of all or nothing.

In this context, how will the past, present, and future transfer of arms and military technology to third-world countries affect their conduct of conflict? Two general points must be made. First, with the exception of states in the Middle East (a special case), developing countries will continue to opt for firepower through numbers rather than technology. There are many reasons for this, including the relatively high cost of advanced equipment and the lack of skilled manpower. As mentioned earlier, therefore, the bulk of their arms acquisitions will be less-sophisticated systems. An additional result will be emphasis on large standing armies. Second, some advanced technology will also be procured, most likely in the form of surface-to-surface missiles and air-defense systems. The sales of F-16s to Venezuela and Pakistan may reflect the beginnings of a trend toward the diffusion of extremely advanced aircraft; at the very least the next generation of aircraft flowing to the third world will be a step beyond the F-5.

The combination of simple and sophisticated arms can be devastating. According to Charles Perry:

> It has been the composite threat posed by advanced and less advanced arms (and the prospect of their *concurrent exploitation* in a mode similar to that of October 1973)—*not* the threat of advanced arms alone—that has had such a formative impact on Israeli casualty expectations and, by extension, on Israeli strategic alternatives and force structure preferences.[24]

The interaction of these two trends will make future conflict between nations of the third world an unusual phenomenon. At times, it will resemble the high-technology wars of the future envisioned for Central Europe. At other times, it will parallel warfare as it was conceived in the first fifteen years of the twentieth century with conscript armies engaging in decisive battles. At still other times, it will be not unlike World War I, in which "commanders willy-nilly resorted to a prolonged process of attrition."[25] Although any given third-world conflict may have elements of all these modes of warfare, the dominant motif will be determined by a number of factors, including the nature of the military hardware employed by each side, the balance between the two sides, the quality of the manpower, and the terrain over which the conflict is fought.

Third-world battlefields, then, will be characterized by the simultaneous use of sophisticated arms and of simpler weapons systems. They will be less automated than battlefields in Western Europe. Numbers will continue to count, but the kinds of equipment now being procured also indicate an emphasis on mobility of forces for both offense and defense (hence the continual heavy trade in armored vehicles), increased firepower (the growth in the trade of missiles and combat aircraft), and command, control, and communications matériel.

Given these patterns, some generalizations might be offered about the nature of conflict between developing countries. First, the human factor will remain paramount. Whether it is in terms of the ability of third-world recruits to use advanced arms effectively in combat or in the personal quality of commanders, there will be no substitute for quality personnel. Despite all the advanced arms in the inventory of Iran and Iraq, for example, evidence provided by their current conflict suggests that "the effectiveness of forces . . . is far more dependent upon the capabilities of a few key officers and NCOs who can catalyze a particular unit or operation. . . . The human element is likely to dominate."[26]

Second, the element of surprise will continue to be a premium, and many conflicts will be characterized by a maximal effort of the combatants from the outset with the aim of forcing a decision quickly. No third-world nation had the indigenous industrial power to sustain an intensive conflict over an extended period. Few also enjoy a totally reliable relationship with an arms supplier that would, in essence, replace that indigenous industrial capability. As a consequence, conflicts will often be fought with forces in being and a quick outcome will be sought.

The exception, of course, is conflict in the form of civil or guerilla war, which is likely to be protracted. The other exception is an interstate conflict in which the initial objective is not quickly attained and there are sufficient arms supplies to sustain the confrontation at a low level. The Iran-Iraq war provides an example. If the pace of military operations between Iran and Iraq were to quicken appreciably as a result of a change in one or the other's strategy, consumption rates would rise rapidly, and an early decision would then likely be the goal of one side if not both. A mitigating factor, however, would be the level of arms resupply by the superpowers or other major arms suppliers.

As arms inventories of third-world countries are upgraded and their military establishments modernized, a third characteristic of interstate conflicts in the third world could be the expansion of the conflict theaters and increases in the number of potential targets to include second-echelon forces and rear areas. To some extent this is a function of, on one hand, the emphasis on mobility and, on the other, the greater ranges of some systems such as attack aircraft and surface-to-surface missiles. In the Middle East, for example, the geographic spread of the conflict has expanded with each successive war. During the 1973 conflict, there was even some reported concern that both Cairo and Tel Aviv were being targeted by long-range, surface-to-surface missiles.

Moreover, to the extent that the modernization of armed forces in the third world makes it more difficult to resolve conflicts on the front line of the battlefield (as has happened in Europe and the Middle East), combatants could seek a decisive advantage through threatening, or perhaps attacking directly, other targets in the rear. These may include second-echelon forces, logistics or communications centers, or, in extreme cases, population centers. The acquisition of long-range capabilities, then, serves as a potential hedge against defeat at the front.[27]

A fourth factor to consider is the growing appreciation for "back-end" problems, or "those activities that . . . include not only the initial support for a new program (training, infrastructure, etc.), but follow-on support, including maintenance and logistics."[28] Once weapons are used in combat, the demands on the support services increase geometrically.[29] The demand skyrockets for fuel for forces on the move, ammunition, and stores. Simple maintenance gives way to the need for major repairs (often in the field), a need that intensifies as a conflict continues. The logistics-and-support dimension of military operations in some ways becomes the dominant concern. This concern will be heightened further as these services become increasingly vulnerable to attack from long-range systems.

As developing countries continue to import the vast majority of their military equipment, they will require foreign back-end support. To a large extent, then, the successful exercise of military power in the third world will depend on the ability and willingness of foreign powers to underwrite it. In the absence of foreign support, training, maintenance and support limitations, if not actual shortages of matériel, will constitute significant barriers to successful operations. This suggests that the pace of conflict may be slower than otherwise anticipated. Moreover, the presence of foreign advisors may serve to increase the risks of targeting rear areas.

The impact of the diffusion of military power and arms transfers on the conduct of interstate conflict in the third world is difficult to assess. The issue is again scenario-dependent. The Middle East, for example, is a special case because of its unique technological development in the military sphere. Yet, as the Iraq-Iran War demonstrates, presumed technological implications can be undercut by other factors. Clearly, this issue is in need of considerably more study. A combination of case studies and functional analyses would serve as a starting point from which insights could be developed and eventually translated into effective policy.

Termination of Conflict

A fundamental issue centers on (1) the relationship between arms transfers and the resolution of conflict in the third world and (2) whether arms suppliers can manipulate the arms pipeline to force combatants to cease hostilities and negotiate a settlement. There is certainly evidence to suggest that a shut-off of arms supplies can create a situation in which hostilities cease. The U.S. and British arms embargo on India and Pakistan in 1965 reduced their war-waging capabilities considerably (especially Pakistan's) and forced the combatants toward resolution. In the wake of the U.S. refusal to supply the necessary matériel, the war between El Salvador and Honduras in 1971 ended in one week. The impact of the U.S. and Soviet resupply policies on the course, duration, and outcome of the Yom Kippur War in 1973 is well known. In fact, according to Geoffrey Kemp: " . . . it is difficult to think of an example of protracted, high intensity war in less industrialized regions that has not ultimately been dependent upon the industrial powers to sustain it."[30] This conclusion is supported by William Quandt's analysis of the relationship between arms supply and influence in the Middle East. He concludes that: " . . . decisions on military operations or policy concerning war and peace are the categories most likely to be influenced by an arms supplier if he chooses to make the attempt. Arms recipients are more vulnerable to influence attempts in the midst of crises that pose serious threats to their security than in more normal times."[31]

The key to Kemp's assertion, however, is his description of the conflicts as protracted and of high intensity. For many conflicts in the third world, these adjectives would not be applicable. In some cases, conflicts will be of short duration because the objectives are either limited and quickly reached or easy to achieve (for example, Tanzania in Uganda). In others, a conflict may persist over time at relatively low levels of intensity, as has happened in the Iran-Iraq War. Although resupply has a part to play in these conflicts, the leverage or influence of the arms supplier is somewhat diminished.

Civil wars or guerilla conflicts are likely to be protracted, but at fairly low levels. In most recent guerilla activities and in potential civil wars in third-world countries, at least one side, and probably both, will be supplied by external sources who have decided to provide that support for political reasons. Ultimately, the suppliers will decide the success or failure of the side they are supporting. In many cases, however, that support is low cost, thus representing little risk to the supplier, who will often find the price acceptable. Obviously, in such cases, there is little interest in ending the violence.

Control of the weapons pipeline to nations at war can be a significant factor in bringing armed hostilities to an end. It is not likely, however, that shutting the arms tap will terminate the conflict, because the underlying causes of enmity between the combatants will continue to exist. The measure, therefore, is a short-term one and of limited utility. It may bring the immediate fighting to a stop, but it does nothing to determine the long-term military balance of the adversaries or the stability of their region.

The Diffusion of Military Power, The Future of Conflict, and U.S. Policy

On 8 July 1981, President Reagan signed a directive on U.S. conventional-arms-transfers policy that signalled an approach far different from that of his predecessor. Rather than emphasizing restrictions on U.S. arms flows, the Reagan administration's statement emphasized that it viewed: ". . . the transfer of conventional arms and other defense articles and services as an essential element of its global defense posture and an indispensable component of its foreign policy."[32] Differing from the Carter administration's focus on broad guidelines to direct U.S. arms-transfer policy, the Reagan policy stressed its intention to "tailor its approach to arms transfer requests to specific situations," and consider requests "on a case-by-case basis."[33]

In its own way, the arms-transfer policies of both the Reagan and Carter administrations reflected the problems confronting the United States in developing a coherent arms-transfers policy that is sensitive to U.S. policy needs and goals on one hand and regional implications on the other. In light of the preceding analysis of the relationship between arms and the future of conflict, what are the general implications for U.S. policy?

First, U.S. policymakers must realize that the growing militarization of the third world is a reflection, albeit a dangerous one, of a broader diffusion of power in the international system. Assertion of political power, for example is also on the rise—for example, in the Group of 77 at the United Nations. Third-world demands for a redistribution of economic wealth, and thus power, through a new international economic order is a somewhat parallel trend in the economic sphere. To some extent that diffuse power in the industrializing world is truncated with some states enjoying economic but not military power (for example, Saudi Arabia) or the reverse (Cuba). Despite this split, the general trend is greater influence and assertiveness throughout the third world in general. Many people in the United States had come to believe that the U.S. ascendance in global affairs after World War II was the natural order of international politics. History, however, demonstrates otherwise. The kind of international system that is now emerging, one that is more nonpolar than multipolar (certainly not bipolar), is closer to the traditional nature of international politics. U.S. policymakers and the public must adapt to a reality of the changing distribution of international power. Fundamental questions must be answered: How should and will U.S. relationships with other countries be changed in this fluctuating environment? How can the United States take advantage of these trends? How can the positive impact of arms transfers be maximized in this situation?

Second, U.S. decision makers must understand that neither the transfer of a particular system nor the development of a system indigenously automatically confers a new military capability on the recipient or developer. It may be the intention, but it is not always the result. A host of other factors—strategy and tactics, logistics support, training levels, and so on—must also be considered in assessing the effectiveness of a nation's armed forces and the impact of a particular military procurement. Although U.S. policymakers cannot assume that industrializing states will be unable to use the weapons systems they import or build, especially less-sophisticated arms, they cannot view the issue in simplistic terms and solely on the basis of technology.

Third, U.S. policymakers must realize that not selling arms in a given situation is as much a decision as transferring military equipment. Just as a positive decision, the decision not to transfer has both benefits and costs. Failure to transfer arms, for example, may upset a regional arms balance fostering instability that eventuates in a conflict. The stability of the Middle East, for example, would be upset drastically if the arms balance shifted significantly as a result of a shut-off of the flow of arms to Israel. A similar argument might be made with respect to the Persian Gulf and Saudi Arabia, or Northeast Asia and South Korea.

For U.S. policymakers, the decision to transfer or not to transfer arms must be based on a complex matrix of the costs and benefits of many political, economic, and military factors. These advantages and disadvantages have been categorized and discussed in detail elsewhere.[34] Suffice it to say that an arms-transfer decision based on only one set of these factors, let alone a single factor, will be shortsighted at best and disastrous at worst. The factors must be assessed in combination; there is no simple solution. The dangers inherent in basing policy on a simplistic set of guidelines were demonstrated by the failure of the Carter arms-transfer policy. The complexity of any arms-transfer decision militates for a disaggregated case-by-case approach, as has been adopted by the Reagan administration. One should recognize, however, that there are dangers with this approach as well. In most individual cases, the pressures to proceed with a transfer are almost always irresistible, and the arguments for going ahead are almost always persuasive. In such a situation, will policymakers recognize when it is really in their interests to say no?

Fourth, the complexity of the arms trade will intensify in the next two decades and will make decisions about U.S. arms transfers more difficult. As third-world arms inventories are built up and the level of sophistication increases, regional military balances will become more difficult to assess. Moreover, one nation's buildup may be in response to a perceived threat from one direction, but it could have important repercussions in another. Pakistan's current desire to bolster its military forces, for example, is in response to the Soviet move into Afghanistan, but it has prompted India to seek to add to its own arsenal. Although this has always been the case with arms transfers, the problem will become more acute in light of the improvements in weapons systems. Saudi Arabia was a marginal participant in past Arab conflicts with Israel. Today, in light of the military forces and politics in the Middle East, the Saudis are likely to find themselves on the front lines.

Another factor adding to the complexity of the problem is the growing intricacy of the arms market. More sellers will continue to enter the market. They may not pose a direct threat to U.S. arms industries, but they may create problems for U.S. allies whose defense industries now depend for their health on exports. Brazilian success in selling armored vehicles in what had been a traditional market for the British and French may be a precursor. The result might eventually be greater specialization of producers with respect either to markets or to products. If the competition becomes too great, the allies might press the United States to make accommodations of some sort for the sake of their industrial health, an action that could have a potentially negative impact on U.S. domestic defense industries.

A further complication in the arms market will be the changing nature of demand. With more and more countries producing at least some arms indigenously, the nature of their demands on traditional-arms suppliers will shift from requests for finished systems to demands for technology. The United States will have to develop a policy, therefore, that is sensitive to these changes on one hand but does not jeopardize U.S. interests, especially its technological advantage, on the other.

Fifth, although generalizing about arms-transfers decisions outside a regional and scenario-specific context is risky, the preceding analysis suggests that one key factor is the impact of a given transfer on the cost-benefit calculi of the recipient, its potential adversaries, and other concerned actors with respect to the effective use of military power. Those perceptions determine whether force would be an appropriate instrument to resolve disputes that already exist as well as whether military exports would be successful. An obvious conclusion is that the United States should not rush into an arms transaction that either reduces the perceived costs or raises the expected benefits of a resort to military force. The prescription is easy; the practice obviously is very difficult, not only because perceptions are difficult to assess accurately but also because the number of actors whose perceptions must be taken into account and the number of factors that contribute to those perceptions are so numerous.

Finally, it must be realized that there is no magic formula to determine whether a sale should be made. This reality is made more depressing by another reality confronting policymakers; that is, try as those policymakers might, conflict will continue to be a prominent characteristic of international relations, and arms, some of them from the United States, will be used in those conflicts.

U.S. policymakers can deal with these problems best by approaching decisions with a clear understanding of what arms transfers are and what they can and cannot do. They are neither good nor bad. Ultimately, they are only a tool that cannot be used in isolation from other diplomatic, economic, and political instruments that must be exploited to serve the goals of U.S. policy. As such their impact will vary directly with the wisdom with which they are used.

Notes

1. Robert Jewell, *American Diplomacy* (New York: W.W. Norton, 1969), p. 34, cited in Geoffrey Kemp with Stephen Miller, "The Arms Transfer Phenomenon," in *Arms Transfers and American Foreign Policy*,

ed. Andrew J. Pierce (New York: New York University Press, 1979), p. 16.

2. Kemp with Miller, "Arms Transfer Phenomenon," p. 26.

3. *New York Times*, 21 June 1981.

4. *The Financial Times*, 27 October 1981.

5. U.S. Arms Control and Disarmament Agency (ACDA), *World Military Expenditures and Arms Transfers, 1969–1978* (Washington, D.C., "Arms Transfer Phenomenon," December 1980), p. 10.

6. Kemp with Miller, p. 36.

7. *The Military Balance, 1981–82* (London: The International Institute for Strategic Studies, 1981), pp. 49–59.

8. John Burton, "No End in Sight to Market for Light Armor, " *Strategy Week*, 9–15 June 1980, pp. 8–9.

9. "Changing Trends in Small Arms Buying," *Strategy Week*, May 12–18, 1980, pp. 6–7.

10. John Burton, "Electronics Change the Third World Balance," *Strategy Week*, 23–29 June 1980, p. 8.

11. See, for example, Michael Moodie, *Sovereignty, Security and Arms* (Beverly Hills, Calif.: Sage Publications, 1979), Washington Paper 67.

12. Charles M. Perry, "The Threat of Less Advanced Arms: The Arab-Israeli Case," in *Arms Transfers to the Third World*, ed. Uri Ra'anan, Robert Pfaltzgraff, and Geoffrey Kemp (Boulder, Colo.: Westview Press, 1978), p. 2.

13. ACDA, *World Military Expenditures*, p. 20.

14. *New York Times*, 24 August 1981.

15. This discussion is based primarily on ideas from Richard K. Betts, The Tragicomedy of Arms Trade Control," *International Security*, Vol. 5. No. 1 (Summer 1980): 80–110.

16. Shahram Chubin, "Implications of the Military Buildup in Less Industrial States: The Case of Iran," in Ra'anan, Pfaltzgraff, and Kemp, *Arms Transfers*, p. 272.

17. Betts, "Tragicomedy," p. 89.

18. Richard Burt, "New Conventional Weapons Technologies," *Arms Control Today*, Vol. 5, No. 1 (January 1975): 2.

19. James L. Foster, "New Conventional Weapons Technologies: Duplications for the Third World," in Ra'anan, Pfaltzgraff, and Kemp, *Arms Transfers*, p. 80.

20. Barry Rubin, *Paved with Good Intentions: The American Experience and Iran* (New York: Penguin Books, 1980), p. 261.

21. Janne E. Nolan, "Arms and Technology Transfers as a (Potential) Source of Conflict" (Paper prepared from the conference on the Future of Conflict, at the Georgetown Center for Strategic and International Studies, Washington, D.C., November 23–24, 1981), pp. 4–8.

22. Foster, "New Conventional Weapons Technologies," p. 67.

23. Martin van Creveld, "Turning Points in Twentieth Century War," *The Washington Quarterly* 4 (Summer 1981): 7.

24. Perry, "Threat," pp. 299–300.

25. Van Creveld, "Turning Points," pp. 3–4.

26. Abdul Karim Mansur, "The Military Balance in the Persian Gulf: Who Will Guard the Gulf States from Their Guardians," *Armed Forces Journal International* Vol. 118. No. 3 (November 1980): 50–51.

27. Carried to its extreme, this trend would result in the procurement of nuclear weapons.

28. These problems are discussed in detail in Geoffrey Kemp, "Arms Transfers and the 'Back-end' Problem in Developing Countries," in *Arms Transfers in the Modern World*, ed. Stephanie Neuman and Robert Harkavy (New York: Praeger, 1979), pp. 264–275.

29. Ibid., p. 269.

30. Ibid., p. 270.

31. William B. Quandt, "Influence through Arms Supply: The U.S. Experience in the Middle East," in Ra'anan, Pfaltzgraff, and Kemp, *Arms Transfers*, p. 129.

32. Statement issued by the Office of the Press Secretary, the White House, 9 July 1981.

33. Ibid.

34. See, for example, Kemp with Miller, "Arms Transfer Phenomenon," pp. 45–86.

8

Nuclear-Weapons Proliferation and Future Conflict

Rodney W. Jones

By far the largest number of industrialized and less developed countries have abstained from nuclear-weapons and support nonproliferation. Nonproliferation policies and institutions no doubt have helped to check the spread of nuclear weapons in the postwar world.[1] Yet proliferation trends undoubtedly surged in the 1970s, especially in third-world regions. We can expect the 1980s to crystallize these trends and confront us with the beginnings of a more proliferated world. Nuclear proliferation will interact with other aspects of the political and military turbulence of developing areas to face the United States and its allies with novel forms of conflict and unprecedented challenges.

The only surety of the future is that it will surprise us, but we should be better prepared to cope with the unforeseen if we probe current conditions and trends to narrow the range of uncertainty and clarify the limits on choice. Thus the purpose of his chapter is to assess the impact of proliferation trends on prospective international conflict over the next decade, evaluate the implications for U.S. foreign and national-security policy, and indicate the different approaches available for response.[2]

Proliferation Effects

The Cosmic View of Proliferation

Speculation about the consequences of nuclear proliferation goes back to the start of the nuclear-weapons era in the 1940s. A U.S. consensus existed then that the consequences of proliferation would be dangerous, indeed, that they could be catastrophic. The early, extreme judgment feared eventual nuclear war with the Soviet Union, an emerging superpower protagonist, or alternately, the prospect of atomic warfare in a reconstructed, multipolar balance-of-power system of nuclear-armed states. It was not surprising then that the United States sought to preserve its nuclear monopoly (or when monopoly perished, to conserve its nuclear predominance) and

I am especially indebted to Dr. Thomas Blau, senior associate of Jeffrey Cooper Associates, for his comments on an earlier draft of this chapter.

also worked to promote a system of international nuclear cooperation to keep the genie in peaceful channels. Nor is it surprising that the overwhelming emphasis in the literature on proliferation was on preventive measures and that essentially the same condition prevails today.

Reevaluation of Proliferation Threat

Analysts began in the 1950s and 1960s to examine more closely the effects of nuclear proliferation, coinciding partly with its incidence in Western Europe and China and partly with refinement of strategic nuclear analysis. Confidence increased in the stability of mutual nuclear deterrence in a postwar system that was essentially bipolar in structure; anxiety that French or Chinese proliferation would disrupt systemic stability seemed in retrospect to be exaggerated.

Herman Kahn led his charge on the prevailing assumption that atomic warfare inevitably was unsurvivable, and, although few became true converts of the converse proposition, many became more conscious of the gradations of nuclear effects and, implicitly, of limits on the potency of threats from new proliferants.[3] Kahn's colleague, Albert Wohlstetter, and his associates, provided a corrective to another prevailing strategic notion that deterrence was automatic or easy merely by virtue of the possession of nuclear weapons.[4] Thomas Schelling provided elegant and comprehensive frameworks for strategic analysis that demonstrated the many facets of rationality in strategic interaction.[5]

The theories of General Gallois supporting the French *force de frappe*[6] and its descendants down to the recent work of Kenneth Waltz have contributed to the respectability of the presumption that such nuclear decisional traits as rationality and prudence need not be confined to the original nuclear powers.[7]

Managing Proliferation

The cumulative effect of this new thinking was not to reverse the general belief that proliferation effects would be dangerous but rather to cast doubt on the assumption that they necessarily would be catastrophic. By the 1970s, discussion opened on how to cope with new proliferation—or how to manage its effects with the least sacrifice to other interests. This new perspective was essentially one of damage limitation; it squarely faced what seemed inevitable, that some additional proliferation would occur and that its repercussions should be prepared for and "managed."[8] As the Wohlstetter-Rowen group's studies make plain, however, there are wide differences in strategic perspective and attitude regarding the policy implications of additional proliferation among experts on that subject.[9]

Adopting a perspective that some additional proliferation might be manageable should not imply that preventive (antiproliferation) policy should be relaxed or treated casually. This point deserves emphasis both because some otherwise may be tempted to draw such an inference and because policies designed to cope with or manage proliferation admittedly could create certain tensions with nonproliferation policy in particular cases.

If additional proliferation is to be managed and new instrumentalities are to be developed for that purpose, the threats and other effects of such proliferation have to be understood. Elucidating such threats and effects, especially in the domain of U.S. defense policy, has been a major concern of such recent studies as those of the Hudson Institute. These studies tend to follow demonstrable near-term threats to U.S. defense interests from new proliferation in certain specific regional settings. Whether those regional threats are the most consequential effects of additional proliferation, however, is an unresolved question.

Future of Proliferation Issues

The literature on the future of proliferation has advanced the discussion of U.S. defense planning along a range of possible contingencies. It has only begun to provide some measure of discrimination among contingencies according to relative importance (a function of consequentiality, as well as probability) and likely distribution (in time, as well as space). Such analysis is difficult and will take time.

Until future nuclear trends and events provide empirical answers, controversy will persist over two fundamental and interrelated sets of issues concerning future proliferation. The first set of issues is about the scope and pace of proliferation. The second set of issues concerns the nature, gravity, and direction of the dangers posed by proliferation: where will the impact be felt? Whose interests will be threatened, and to what degree? Different schools of thought about these issues have led to divergent approaches to policy.

Scope and Pace of Proliferation

With respect to the issues about the scope and pace of proliferation, the controversy today comes down to a difference of views about the relative importance of technical capabilities, existing national and international organizational commitments, and political decisions in determining proliferation phenomena. The traditional perspective, associated with so-called atoms-for-peace policies and the development of an international system of peaceful nuclear cooperation, emphasizes legal criteria for identifying proliferation (for example, diversion of material from peaceful uses) and thus construes the scope of proliferation narrowly. Traditionalists emphasize that although technical capabilities admittedly are prerequisites for proliferation, they are not sufficient conditions and normally are not even incentives for proliferation. Proliferation occurs only when political decisions are made to acquire nuclear weapons, and proliferation need not be expected where conditions of state insecurity of ambition provide the motives for nuclear-weapons decisions.

More recently, an alternate perspective that attributes inherent proliferation risk to nuclear technical capabilities, even to safeguarded nuclear-fuel-cycle facilities, gained currency and strongly influenced Carter administration policies and concurrent U.S. legislation. Albert Wohlstetter, Henry Rowen, and other proponents of the proliferation-risk perspective focused attention on the potential for weapons diversion in the geographical spread of civilian fuel-cycle technologies, especially spent-fuel reprocessing and plutonium separation. They suggested that past economic rationales for closing the nuclear-fuel cycle by recycling plutonium were misleading and that nuclear suppliers could for the foreseeable future refrain from sale of such sensitive technology without impeding either the use of uranium for nuclear energy or peaceful nuclear-cooperation obligations under the Nuclear Nonproliferation Treaty (NPT). This perspective left the implication that technical capabilities could be regarded as a cause of proliferation (hence the concept of latent proliferation) and, in turn, as one of the criteria for identifying proliferation.[10]

These alternate perspectives implied different estimates of the scope and pace of proliferation and different policy approaches to the problem. The traditional perspective finds a very low incidence of proliferation, using legal criteria (apart from the five traditional weapons powers, perhaps India and Pakistan) and a larger but still restricted class of cases where some capabilities exist and proliferant motivations are indicated or widely suspected (Libya, Israel, Iraq, Taiwan, South Korea, and South Africa). In the proliferation-risk perspective, the list of logical candidates—for technical as well as political reasons—is much longer, more emphasis is placed on contingencies that could unfavorably alter nuclear motivations or policy, and estimates of the scope and rate of future proliferation are correspondingly pessimistic.

To contain proliferation, the traditionalists place greater confidence in what they see as the incentives of interdependence in peaceful measures designed to minimize policy motivations for nuclear weapons. Proponents of the proliferation-risk perspective regard the tools of peaceful nuclear cooperation, diplomacy, and security assistance as important but insufficient. To make those approaches more effective, they have to be strengthened, thus calling for (in the sphere of peaceful nuclear cooperation) restriction of transfer of sensitive technology—an approach their critics have dubbed "technical denial."

Although they differ in emphasis on the determinants and criteria of proliferation, these views are not far apart on which countries and regions merit priority attention. Both perspectives acknowledge that the scope and rate of proliferation will be influenced by various intersecting factors, including security, economics, and energy-supply conditions, and that the recent trends in these conditions have been unfavorable for a nonproliferation climate. Most would recognize the usefulness of distinguishing stages of the proliferation process, which can take different forms or have a long elapsed time in particular countries. Most would acknowledge that proliferation in a particular country has repercussions on neighbors and even on calculations by states outside the immediate region. But divergence in views, not necessarily along the same lines, occurs in speculation about proliferation effects.

Effects of Additional Proliferation

One perspective, a mainstream view, regards additional proliferation as profoundly destabilizing for regional security and forecasts intensification of threat perceptions, the aggravation of crises that occur for other reasons, fairly high probabilities of local nuclear conflict, and serious risks of escalation via regional entanglement to superpower nuclear confrontation. An alternative set of hypotheses and arguments has been put forward by those who are more optimistic about the manageability of nuclear spread. An academic expression of this revisionist viewpoint is offered by Kenneth Waltz's theoretical exposition of international politics.[11] Another expression of this view comes from certain policy analysts in near-nuclear states.

Waltz bases his analysis of proliferation effects on his theory about international politics, which posits a durable, bipolar structure and the normality of rational decisionmaking. He believes that the awesome power of nuclear weapons will impose circumspection and restraint on the policymakers of new nuclear states and therefore reproduce local conditions of deterrent stability. Then, he believes, nuclear warfare among proliferants becomes unlikely and thus the possession of nuclear weapons reduces their scope for adventure. Moreover, he finds the enormous military-capability gap between the superpowers and new nuclear states to be too large to be significantly narrowed, and thus additional proliferation would not threaten the stability of the central, nuclear strategic balance. Nuclear minipowers will not only remain fundamentally dependent on the superpowers for their ultimate security but they will also become more dependent on the outside world to compensate for their reduced room for local maneuver. In short, Waltz concludes not that proliferation is beneficial but that its dangers have been exaggerated and that the structure of international politics will make it tolerable by disciplining proliferants and limiting the risks they can afford to take.

Policy analysts from some near-proliferant states are even more sanguine about the prospective benefits of proliferation. Writing from an Israeli perspective, Shai Feldman advocates explicit adoption of a nuclear-defense posture because he thinks that it would deter further armed conflict and favor a peace settlement in the Arab-Israeli context.[12] K. Subrahmanyam, a leading Indian defense analyst, contends that nuclear weapons are militarily unusable for rational objectives against a similarly armed opponent, but their possession is imperative for new owners as a deterrent and shield against political intimidation in a world where a few nuclear-armed powers have special privileges by virtue of their nuclear status.[13]

It may be impossible to resolve a priori the issues that divide the pessimists and the revisionists. Perhaps each side grasps part of the truth, but only part, because the truth is context dependent and therefore variable. This would explain why, as we observed earlier, proliferation effects are more demonstrable in regional contexts. To aid examination of the different schools of thought the rest of this chapter focuses on the effects of proliferation on U.S. interests in regional settings, specifically those in the developing areas. We may find in these regional contexts that Waltz's view of stability through his notions either of the permanence of a bipolar international structure or the prevention of global nuclear warfare is oversimplified or not well grounded in empirical reality. As for the views of third-world publicists, discussion would be helped by recognition that the United States too has interests, such as access to vital resources, protection of allies and friends, and the promotion of democratic values, which cannot be aided by the spread of nuclear weapons. Similarly, we may find that proliferation both increases U.S. leverage over some countries and reduces it over others, an ambiguous outcome, but one that overall tends to reduce U.S. capacity to manage regional crises, a decidedly unattractive prospect.

Before proceeding to regional analyses, nuclear terrorism and the fate of the nonproliferation regime should be mentioned. The framework of analysis in this chapter emphasizes national proliferation, not that among subnational entities or terrorist organizations. There are those who view nuclear terrorist potentials as more worrisome than national proliferation. But the conditions and motives for nuclear terrorist activities can best be assessed with a different form of analysis, and they have distinct implications for policy response. These problems would overburden this chapter and therefore are omitted.

The second point to note is that a number of near-nuclear states seem to exploit nuclear policies of ambiguity for diplomatic leverage. This approach extracts influence by threatening the nonproliferation regime. Some observers believe that this may be the most common near-term proliferation threat in developing areas. Defending the nonproliferation regime against such threats, of course, presupposes that proliferation is dangerous but begs the question of how dangerous. Naturally, it would be foolhardy not to defend the nonproliferation regime merely to satisfy one's curiosity about this question. But it is worth noting that the threats posed by policies of nuclear ambiguity to the nonproliferation regime represent a different order of dangers than the effects of outright proliferation. Obviously, the former could lead to the latter.

Regional Analysis of Proliferation Effects

Our proliferation assessment by region emphasizes what is likely or could happen over the next ten years, taking technical capabilities into account. The degree to which vital and primary U.S. interests are at stake differs among regions, but we assume that distribution will remain virtually constant in the next decade.

Vital U.S. interests on which regional proliferation could impinge include the safety of U.S. and allied territories and assets, deterrence stability in the central balance, solidarity of North Atlantic and Pacific alliance relations, assured access to vital natural resources, and regional defense against Soviet or other hostile encroachment or subversion. Primary U.S. interests include prevention of intraregional warfare, steady economic growth, and legitimate self-government.

The effects of proliferation on these interests can be both direct and indirect. They can range from the destruction produced by outright nuclear attack to changes in perception, risk, calculation, or diplomatic behavior produced by tacit nuclear threats. As a general rule, proliferation introduces novel elements of uncertainty into military planning and diplomatic objectives.

Most would agree by any measure that the Middle East region is where the effects of proliferation on U.S. interests are likely to be most consequential in the next decade. South Asia probably is next in importance because proliferation there is so pregnant with Middle East implications. Beginning in that order, we then take up in succession the Far East, sub-Saharan Africa, and Latin America. A brief section on Europe follows, not as a region of likely proliferation but rather because it is crucial to broader coordination of nuclear-supplier and nonproliferation policy and happens to be subject to new domestic political and economic pressures on nuclear policy.

The Middle East

United States strategic and diplomatic interests are deeply engaged in the Middle East because of the commitment to Israel's acceptance in the region, the region's central importance in international oil exports, and the threatening geopolitical implications of Soviet proximity, ambitions, and military power. Soviet military predominance in the Mediterranean would not only isolate Israel but also outflank NATO defenses, and Soviet domination of regional oil supplies would expose U.S. allies to economic jeopardy that could compel accommodation of Soviet demands and vitiate the Western alliance system.

The Middle East harbors many neighborhood conflicts over territory, population, regional leadership, and religion that intersect with, aggravate, and complicate strategies for ameliorating the U.S.-Soviet and Arab-Israeli conflicts. Imperialism and aggrandizement by several local states represent active forces in this region. The effects of proliferation on layered conflicts in this region may be exceptionally far reaching and complex as well as risk-laden for the United States in terms of potential nuclear confrontations with the Soviet Union.

To the extent that the superpowers stay immune from direct nuclear confrontation, the intensity of conflicts and high incidence of political instability in the region suggest that proliferation could threaten not only the social and economic survival of smaller members of the region but also the delivery of the oil on which so much of the rest of the world depends.

Local nuclear forces in the Middle East, to note the asymmetry of threat, would not present the continental United States with active military threats (weapons delivered by unconventional means could be a threat, but not a so-called military one) but could pose military threats to parts of the Soviet homeland, several NATO countries, and U.S. assets based in those NATO countries.

Scope and Rate of Proliferation. Middle East proliferation may not proceed as far in the next decade as the last remarks suggest, but there are several reasons for concern that within two or three decades the situation would become much more threatening. First, the nuclear-weapons intentions of several states in the region are either manifest or highly plausible. Second, oil revenues and overlapping identities, either Islamic or Arabic, provide capabilities and incentives for regional cooperation in developing nuclear technology and armament industries. Third, affirmation as well as consciousness of the political and diplomatic utility of nuclear-weapons possession is spreading in this region. Finally, the pressures on nuclear suppliers, particularly those most dependent on imported oil, but also on the Soviet Union, for access to nuclear technology are growing and can be expected to increase.

Israel is the only regional state that presently has actual nuclear-weapons-production capabilities. Reputedly, it also has a stockpile of nuclear-weapons components that could be assembled and deployed on fairly short notice, and they may have reached this threshold over a decade ago. Former Israeli officials have advocated adoption in Israel of nuclear defense. In the perceptions of Israel's rivals, proliferation in the region is a fact.

Two recent events, the Iranian Revolution in 1979 and the Israeli air strike on the OSIRAK research reactor in June 1981, have postponed for at least three years and probably longer the appearance of other indigenous nuclear-weapons-production capabilities in the region. In the interim, some danger will remain that a regional power may purchase one or more nuclear weapons, as Libya apparently tried to do, or that weapons-grade material may be brought into the region from Pakistan or black-market sources.

By the end of the decade, several states, including Iraq, Libya, Egypt, Syria, and, perhaps, Iran, Kuwait, and Saudi Arabia, may actively be developing a nuclear infrastructure. France has promised to rebuild OSIRAK; the Soviet Union is providing Libya with extensive research assistance and at least two large reactors; Egypt has begun procurement for a major nuclear-power program; and Syria is conducting feasibility studies. Conceivably Iran, after settling her domestic political problems, could reactivate parts of the former ambitious nuclear-research and power program.

Although lately Libya and Iraq have been the chief sources of concern, Egypt's nuclear-research program, which dates back to the early Nasser period and is the most sophisticated in the Arab world, could turn out to be more significant for military purposes. Now that Sadat has been assassinated, his successors may renew close ties with other Arab states and could consider nuclear-weapons development as part of a new foreign-policy posture.

Aborting Embryonic Proliferation. As NPT members, several potentially nuclear-capable Arab states could build civilian nuclear programs and expertise, eventually renounce their NPT obligations, and develop nuclear weapons to employ in the Arab-Israeli or other regional conflicts. Israel, suspecting Iraq of such designs, struck and destroyed OSIRAK as a preventive measure. Iran, earlier and for more obscure reasons, also tried to disable Iraq's research reactor during the escalatory initial stage of its conventional war.[14]

These precedents suggest that preventive uses of force against nuclear facilities, possibly quite innocent ones, are likely to become a more common phenomenon during the early stages of nuclear development in this region—unless the region becomes much more stable, which is conceivable should a nuclear-free zone take firm root. Preventive strikes can buy time against a threat. Conceivably, they might convince the state so struck to pursue other priorities. On the other hand, preventive strikes are rather likely to provoke retaliatory measures and thus escalate violence, probably exacerbating existing conflicts.

Other costs may result from repetition of preventive strikes. If they are all Israeli in origin, Arab states will have no stronger incentives to cooperate in nuclear development, and such development with military motives may be driven underground. Air defense and other measures for protecting nuclear facilities will be a growing concern, and exposed states may seek greater levels of outside assistance, turning in some cases to the Soviet Union or Soviet friends, as Libya already does for other reasons, to supply combat and operational personnel to man the defense of sensitive facilities. Oil supply could be affected if a preventive strike induces retaliation against oil facilities. Excessive tightening of nuclear-export controls by suppliers, if perceived as discrimination against the Arab world, could also have effects on the price and other terms of oil delivery.

In general, these costs will place periodic and sometimes severe strains on efforts to strengthen the nonproliferation regime as well as on Western cooperation in alliance matters, energy supply, and diplomatic efforts to promote an Arab-Israeli peace settlement. They do not necessarily imply an abrupt departure from currently familiar conditions, but they probably do mean continued, gradual erosion of regional security and U.S. political influence.

Effects of Additional Proliferation. By the end of the decade, rudimentary nuclear military capabilities could appear in the possession of one or a few additional states in the region. The effects on U.S. interests could vary somewhat according to the identity, location, and interests of the proliferant and the reactions of neighboring countries. The most likely proliferants (assuming Israel is one already) are Iraq, Libya, and Egypt.

Proliferation success in any one of these countries probably would stimulate or accelerate nuclear development in its immediate neighbors, presenting two possible proliferation chains, one to the north between the Mediterranean and the Persian Gulf, and the second to the south along North Africa. Proliferation in Iraq probably would stimulate matching efforts at least in Iran and Syria, and quite possibly in Saudi Arabia, and initial success by either Libya or Egypt would be reacted to by the other, and would therefore stimulate development in Algeria.

Northern Proliferation Chain. Both proliferation chains could seriously endanger U.S. interests, most obviously because of the implied threats to Israeli security and the Middle East peace efforts from either direction. But the more critical of the two chains almost certainly is the northern one for several reasons: first, it means proliferation close to Soviet borders; second, it could put added pressure on Saudi Arabia and the concentration of other oil producers in the gulf and jeopardize international oil supply. Finally, since it could not be ignored by Turkey, this might reopen the prospect of further proliferation within NATO and probably would draw this NATO member into intra-Arab and Arab-Israeli conflicts.

The effects of the Iranian revolution and Iran-Iraq war have already demonstrated the vulnerability of Persian Gulf oil to disruption. Use of nuclear rather than conventional weapons in the latter conflict could have totally disabled Gulf oil-delivery facilities. Nuclear weapons specially designed for prolonged contamination of large stretches of territory could, if detonated over the oil producing areas, prevent repair and recovery indefinitely.

Although nearby proliferation could not mortally threaten the Soviet Union, it could present the Soviet Union with nasty contingencies. Contemplating these, the Soviet Union can be expected to become even more deeply involved in the affairs of its neighbors, to prevent or mitigate proliferation in some cases, and to help deter conventional preventive attacks or even nuclear threats to a client in other cases, as adjuncts to its traditional objectives in the region. Insofar as Israel, Iraq, or other regional states could pose plausible nuclear threats to Soviet population centers in the Caucasus or to Soviet military forces deployed in the Middle East itself, the chances of mistaken identity and hasty decisions on the one hand or of defense commitments to local states on the other would increase the risks of U.S.-Soviet military and even nuclear confrontation in a regional crisis.

Southern Proliferation Chain. Crises evolving from a proliferation chain linking Libya and Egypt in North Africa could also be extremely serious, but they would probably be somewhat less consequential overall than in the region adjacent to the Soviet Union. The potential jeopardy from proliferation to Soviet interests in North Africa would not be so vital, implying that U.S.-Soviet confrontations there would be less likely or of lower intensity. Threats to Persian Gulf oil supply would be at least one step removed, except in the worst-case scenarios. However, assuming Sadat's successors wish to preserve close security cooperation with the United States, including a staging area in Egypt for U.S. rapid-deployment forces in the event of Persian Gulf emergencies, proliferation in Libya could jeopardize that access and reduce the credibility of U.S. emergency response in the Gulf.

Israeli anxieties about threats to its security from proliferation in either Egypt or Libya would be profound. Israel almost certainly would conduct military operations, even at considerable cost, in efforts to prevent the consummation under Qaddafi's rule of weapons-capable nuclear facilities in Libya, and this could entail confrontation with Soviet air or naval forces in the Mediterranean. The prospects for success of preventive operations may depend on Egypt's disposition. Conceivably, Egypt would conduct its own operations, or use nuclear threats from Libya as a cause for preemptive invasion and even annexation. But Israel's worst fears would materialize in the alternate case of rapprochement between Libya and Egypt, followed by close nuclear cooperation and joint military planning against Israel.

How additional proliferation would affect the Arab-Israeli peace-settlement negotiations is difficult to predict. Presumably it would increase the sense of urgency among many that a settlement be achieved, but flexibility in negotiating objectives and style might or might not follow. Confrontation states newly equipped with nuclear arms might have greater negotiating confidence but less tractable objectives. External guarantors, particularly the major nuclear powers, might find that the placement of some of their forces at risk within the territories of regional states would become an indispensable but unappealing condition for progress toward settlement.

If the present conflicts persist or intensify, the leverage of small nuclear-armed states may increase in proportion to their willingness to pursue high-risk actions. Pressures on oil-import-dependent states to take sides in one or another conflict, or their vulnerability to blackmail, could exacerbate the already divisive trends in alliance relations and international energy cooperation and jeopardize the East-West military balance in Europe. Controversy over appropriate U.S. or allied military response, under proliferated conditions, to Persian Gulf emergencies could be exceptionally disruptive of North Atlantic security. Such difficulties may overload U.S. decisional and crisis-management capacities.

Studies conducted by the Hudson Institute have anticipated a variety of implications for U.S. defense planning of additional proliferation in the Middle East, speculating about the impact of small nuclear forces on the projection of U.S. military power.[15] Additional requirements that may be expected for intervention forces include preparation for operations in nuclear battlefields, detailed threat assessments and real-time intelligence concerning the numbers, location, and deployment of small nuclear forces, and newly designed weapons for suppression, deterrence, or active defense against local nuclear forces. It is clear from these analyses that additional proliferation could escalate the cost and increase the operational complexity of U.S. force deployments for regional contingencies. These added future costs alone make the present price of preventing proliferation more attractive and place a premium on determining realistic priorities in planning the use of U.S. emergency forces.

South Asia

Proliferation in South Asia is accelerating and probably will be established there before new thresholds are crossed in the Middle East. The Indo-

Pakistan nuclear rivalry has Middle East implications, certainly in demonstration effects and possibly in spillovers of nuclear technology or other effects of deteriorating subcontinental security. Proliferation in the subcontinent could influence the strategic interaction of the United States, Soviet Union, and China over developments in the Persian Gulf, Afghanistan, and continental Asia. South Asia also presents what are commonly viewed as test cases for nonproliferation policies.

India's so-called peaceful nuclear explosion of 1974 indicated development of nuclear-weapons capability as a hedge against a potential nuclear threat from China. Although that threat in Western perceptions appears remote, the Chinese invasion of India in 1962, disputes over bordering territories, and Chinese security support for Pakistan make the China threat tangible for Indian strategic planners. By 1970, India had launched a long-haul program for the development of a strategic-missile-delivery capability as a foundation for the nuclear military option.

Decisions in India to undertake advanced development and manufacture of nuclear weapons were deferred in the 1970s for several reasons, including counterpressure from nuclear suppliers, a shortage of unconstrained plutonium, shortfalls in the space program, competing claims on budgetary resources, and the absence, until recently, of additional nuclear threats on India's borders. Since 1979, however, disclosure that Pakistan could be on the verge of testing nuclear explosive devices has visibly disturbed India and may precipitate decisions to manufacture and deploy air-deliverable nuclear weapons for defense against Pakistan.

Should India take this step overtly, the near-term threat from Pakistan will provide the rationale. India may for this reason await a Pakistani nuclear detonation. Even so, Indian planning for a nuclear force almost certainly will be geared to military-threat assessments of China and perhaps other geopolitical contingencies. India will resist the suggestion that the scope or pace of its own weapons program should be dictated by, or coupled with, nuclear capabilities in Pakistan. India can be expected to aim for a nuclear arsenal big enough to be viewed in Pakistan as overwhelming; it would be something much larger, therefore, than a token force. Unless India diverts plutonium from safeguarded power-reactor spent fuel (for example, the CANDU reactor, Rajasthan), this would not be feasible today, but it may become feasible by the end of the decade if India's indigenous-reactor-construction plans are fulfilled.

Evidence that Pakistan is pursuing a military nuclear capability has become overwhelming over the last two or three years. The most compelling evidence is the clandestine acquisition under military auspices of gas-centrifuge, uranium-enrichment technology; nuclear-power plants able to use enriched fuel neither exist nor are under construction in Pakistan. In addition, Pakistan is developing plutonium reprocessing facilities.

Pakistan is estimated to be capable of exploding a nuclear device within a year or two. The fissile material probably would be plutonium in this case, but enriched uranium might also be available. There is some doubt whether Pakistan will succeed in efficiently operating the enrichment machinery being assembled. If Pakistan does succeed, it conceivably could accumulate a stockpile of material sufficient for several dozen weapons by 1990. Perhaps more likely, however, Pakistan may accumulate only enough material for a dozen or so warheads in the next decade.

Prior to the Iranian revolution and Soviet invasion of Afghanistan, the conventional U.S. view of South Asia accorded it limited strategic importance. The Indian subcontinent was too heavily populated, resource-poor, and inaccessible to be intrinsically appealing to expansionist powers. Its distance from the main flashpoints of East-West and Sino-Soviet conflict also removed it from the more intense forms of geopolitical competition. United States policies, accordingly, aimed to strengthen the economic and political self-reliance of countries in the region. The principal impediment was the tragic and debilitating rivalry between India and Pakistan. The conflict afflicted both countries with seemingly permanent mutual insecurity, had destabilizing effects on their political institutions and economic performance, and provided entry points for rival Soviet and Chinese influence in regional affairs.

Proliferation is making headway in South Asia just when that region's strategic value to the United States has appreciated. The sudden gain in strategic importance of South Asia is a function of the increased vulnerability of Persian Gulf oil sources, which in turn is due to the weakened condition of Iran, Soviet military encroachment through Afghanistan, and obstacles facing development of credible U.S. defense measures for the new regional requirements.

Proliferation in South Asia can be expected to affect traditional U.S. interests in the stability of the subcontinent and the security of its members, both in their local relations and in their capacity to resist outside pressures or intrusions. Proliferation there may also affect U.S. interests in the security of the Persian Gulf and the United States itself. Proliferation steps in India and Pakistan have already complicated U.S. efforts to achieve Soviet withdrawal from Afghanistan and to improve the security of Pakistan. Fresh proliferation events in the subcontinent may further reduce U.S. leverage on the Afghanistan issues.

A pivotal issue in the next ten years will be how India and Pakistan conduct their mutual relations. The development of nuclear weapons by both conceivably could lead them to pursue détente and possibly even submerge their rivalry in the interests of coordinated subcontinental defense. Alternatively, proliferation could overwhelm incentives for détente and exacerbate the rivalry, by driving nuclear and conventional-arms competition, increasing the frequency and intensity of crises, and compelling consideration of preemptive warfare. Both countries would seek to improve unilateral capabilities for deterrence, but there are grave risks, especially in the early stages of nuclear-weapons development and deployment, that neither could be confident that conditions of stable mutual deterrence had been achieved. These risks will be pronounced throughout the next decade.

In the next year or two, moreover, there will be strong temptation in India to conduct a preemptive bombing attack on Pakistan's uranium-enrichment and perhaps -reprocessing facilities. This temptation could be reduced if Pakistan fails for technical reasons to separate significant amounts of fissile material and India's intelligence information is on the mark. India might also be deterred from a preemptive attack by the possibility of Pakistani retaliation against India's main nuclear-research center, which is on the west coast and relatively difficult to defend. An Indian preemptive attack might be more likely if armed hostilities break out in Kashmir or on their mutual frontier. An admittedly remote but technically plausible possibility is Soviet or joint Indo-Soviet surgical air strikes on Pakistani nuclear facilities under the cover of punitive attacks on Afghan refugee sites; the fact that much of the Indian Air Force is Soviet-equipped raises the theoretical possibility that the identity of the originators of such an attack could not be firmly established. A successful attack by India would be a serious setback to Pakistani nuclear-weapons capabilities and could provoke a limited conventional war. An unsuccessful attack would lessen the potential for future stability in the relationship.

Pakistan may detonate a nuclear explosive device once it has surmounted the technical barriers (although such a test might be conducted outside Pakistan, in the wilderness of a friendly state or on the high seas), but Pakistan could also defer explosive testing or conceivably avoid it altogether and rely like Israel on a nuclear posture of ambiguity. More likely, Pakistan will attempt at some point to detonate what it will describe as a "peaceful explosion" in emulation of India and then seek to persuade India that the new status quo is in their mutual interest so that further overt proliferation on either side can be resisted.

Detection of further detonations attributable to either Pakistan or India could stimulate near-nuclear or aspirant states in other regions, particularly the Middle East. Beyond that, the emerging nuclear-supplier and technical-training capabilities of both India and Pakistan will have added interest to other states and possibly strengthen the temptations in South Asia to compete for outside support of influence through nuclear exports or cooperation.

Intensification of military and nuclear competition or the outbreak of war between Pakistan and India could affect the perceptions and strategic initiatives of China and the Soviet Union, drawing both more deeply into the political and security affairs of the subcontinent. Most likely, such initiatives would be designed to contain regional proliferation, but they could inadvertently exacerbate it. Eventually both might find reasons to consider exploiting nuclear trends in the subcontinent as potential means of complicating the nuclear-threat environment, and possibly the geopolitical reach, of the other in the Asian context. Nuclear-proxy relationships by these major powers could also have destabilizing effects on the principal strategic balances and thus introduce new risks in U.S. and Western security arrangements.

Based on current trends, it is conceivable that nuclear military forces will appear in the subcontinent before the end of the decade. An Indian nuclear military force may well be large enough to influence U.S. defense planning for Persian Gulf security, particularly if Indo-Soviet military cooperation becomes explicit or more extensive. It could, for instance, pose potential threats to Indian Ocean sea lines of communication, U.S. installations based at Diego Garcia, or naval deployments and facilities in the Arabian Sea. United States emergency-force deployments to assist Pakistan in the event of major Soviet military encroachment on Pakistan could also be affected by Indian military threats. Similarly, cooperation between a nuclear-armed Pakistan and one or more Persian Gulf allies to dissuade or resist U.S. military intervention should not be regarded as implausible under all contingencies.

Far East

Compared to the Middle East and South Asia, the region of Northeast Asia encompassing China, Taiwan, Japan, and the two Koreas is relatively stable, largely because of U.S. security commitments to South Korea and the insular states and the process of normalizing relations with China. Insular Southeast Asia is also relatively stable, but the mainland portion (including the former states of Indochina) is not. For the next decade, major steps in nuclear proliferation are conceivable in Taiwan, the Korean peninsula, and, of course, Japan, but they are improbable in Southeast Asia.

Japan has impressive nuclear capabilities and could, technically speaking, develop both nuclear weapons (on fairly short notice) and also sophisticated delivery capabilities (within a matter of years). Given its strongly antinuclear disposition, however, Japan remains unlikely to develop independent nuclear forces, provided the principal military balances among the United States, the USSR, and China remain stable. Proliferation in neighboring countries, especially Korea, might provoke reconsideration, but even then a nuclear-weapons decision in Japan would not be a foregone conclusion.

Taiwan and South Korea have smaller nuclear programs than Japan, but their programs are very substantial when compared with other LDCs. The technical training and proficiencies of personnel are of very high quality, especially in Taiwan. There is little doubt that either could develop nuclear weapons in the next decade if decisions were made to bear the political costs. Both have strong incentives to consider nuclear defense, but counterincentives and foreseeable risks prevent an easy decision. In both cases, it is conceivable that development of nuclear military options short of outright weaponization, declaration, or deployment would be of interest for diplomatic or political purposes integral to their overall security calculations. Both would take into consideration the rather interesting factor that their likely principal adversary in the event of nuclear hostilities would be part of the same national self.

For Taiwan, the main fulcrum of future security calculation undoubtedly is whether to aim for separate national status or seek reconciliation with mainland China, and, in the latter case, what its preferences regarding the modalities of reconciliation would be. The perceived utility for Taiwan of nuclear weapons might be their deterrent effect on military initiatives China might take to coerce Taiwan's reintegration into China and the preservation of Taiwan's bargaining power until satisfactory terms of peaceful reconciliation are forthcoming. The appearance of nuclear weapons in Taiwan could also signify either that it had lost confidence in the residual security support that the United States provides or that it perceived in nuclear weapons a tool to revive stronger U.S. support.

If the region is otherwise stable, proliferation in Taiwan could still have destabilizing effects on the perceptions of neighbors and potential proliferants; it might stimulate South Korea, for example, to move in the same direction. But such disturbances probably could be countered without serious difficulty. The principal related threat to U.S. interests might come from Chinese perceptions of the significance of and reactions to nuclear arms in Taiwan. First, supposition of U.S. complicity in Taiwan's nuclear-weapons decisions is conceivable and would strain U.S.-China relations. Second, China would be disturbed to find Taiwan developing weapons of great destruction if their number or character indicated potentially offensive use against key cities on the mainland or if their possession by Taiwan became a seemingly insurmountable barrier to peaceful reconciliation.

If Taiwan does not move toward reconciliation but rather acquires so-called international pariah status, although the United States and China might share sufficient interests to keep their normalized relations intact, Taiwan's nuclear policies could have other destabilizing effects. Taiwan might, for example, seek to cope with the pariah predicament by engaging in sensitive and presumably covert nuclear cooperation and exports with developing countries, particularly with some of those that remain outside the

NPT framework. China would find this worrisome mainly to the extent that it occurred in South or Southeast Asia, but it could affect U.S. interests in other regions as well.

It seems most improbable that nuclear warfare would actually materialize between China and Taiwan. It would be suicidal for Taiwan to initiate such hostilities, and China's interests in restoring political as well as physical control over Taiwan would be undermined by nuclear contamination. But the slim chance that China-Taiwan confrontation could lead in this direction would affect U.S. defense-operations planning in the Pacific insofar as de facto security commitments to Taiwan exist or U.S. forces or citizens might be in the affected area.

Proliferation in the present decade is more plausible in South Korea (ROK) than in the North on technical grounds and because of the steady, high-level conventional threat to the South from the North. There has been strong evidence in the previous decade of ROK interest in sensitive nuclear technology, nuclear explosives, and, potentially, nuclear-ballistic-missile delivery systems. Actual ROK proliferation is unlikely as long as the U.S. defense commitment to South Korea retains high ROK confidence and U.S. opposition to proliferation remains firm.

ROK interest in nuclear-weapons development is not surprising, however, in view of its precarious security situation. The conventional military forces deployed by North Korea are impressive. Seoul, the ROK capital and primary concentration of industrial assets, is only 30 miles from the demilitarized zone (DMZ), immediately vulnerable to bombardment, and only hours away from envelopment by successfully penetrating invasion forces. It is not lost on ROK military officials that the United States reputedly deploys tactical nuclear weapons in South Korea as a means of deterring and, if need be, resisting an invasion. Removal of the U.S. military-defense presence would greatly increase ROK incentives for the provision of comparable means of self-defense.

The Korean peninsula is a relatively small area and connects both with China and a strategically important extension of Soviet territory. It is also close to southern Japan. Proliferation in either part of Korea, then, would have direct security implications for each of these states. Successful ROK development and deployment of nuclear weapons would push the North into acquiring its own nuclear capability and, in the interim, into a more dependent security relationship with either China or the Soviet Union. The latter choice might produce new frictions in the Sino-Soviet relationship, with potential repercussions on Japan and complications for U.S. relations with each.

The danger of nuclear proliferation in Korea might be much further removed if the country could be peacefully reunified. But practical prospects for this in the near term do not seem to exist. Moreover, Northern political conditions for negotiating such a settlement seem to imply U.S. military withdrawal and this, as we have seen, could drive proliferation in the South.

If U.S. military forces entirely disengage from ROK defense (which now seems unlikely), both Koreas might take steps toward nuclear weapons, perhaps more rapidly in the South. There could be great instability in this process, especially at early stages; North Korea might attempt preventive strikes or even invasion. The same could be true in reverse when North Korea approaches the nuclear-weapons threshold. In between, the South might seek psychologically to exploit nuclear asymmetry for reunification negotiations.

As in some other dyadic nuclear relationships, some measure of deterrent stability might ensue, should both countries succeed in developing nuclear forces, but the history of the relationship leaves room for uncertainty. Perhaps a more important source of uncertainty would be the interaction of two nuclear-armed Koreas with rival, nuclear-armed giants on the mainland. China and the Soviet Union might respond by greatly augmenting their own military forces in this neighborhood, with escalative effects on U.S. and Japanese defense requirements in the Pacific.

Sub-Saharan Africa

The Republic of South Africa is the only state of this region capable of developing nuclear weapons in the near term. Many experts have concluded that South Africa already has nuclear-weapons capability; some believe that the December 1979 flash detected in the South Atlantic was a test detonation possibly attributable to South Africa. Most other states in the region face resource constraints, and all lack the technical personnel to take major strides in nuclear development in the next decade. Nigeria is a possible exception, and a few instances of interest in nuclear leverage have appeared there. But the informed consensus in Nigeria's case is that insufficient incentives exist for it to take a nuclear course in the foreseeable future.

South Africa's nuclear weapons capability is based on indigenous uranium-enrichment technology. It is unclear how much weapons-grade uranium the Velindaba facility can produce, but competing internal demands on the output apparently exist. There seems like doubt, however, that South Africa could produce at least a handful and perhaps several dozen nuclear weapons from enriched uranium over the next ten years.

South Africa is a besieged state with powerful incentives to improve both its security and standing in the world community. The usual question asked in the nuclear-policy context is, against whom or what could South Africa practically use nuclear weapons? The presumption is that South

Africa is militarily superior to any combination of its neighbors, so that the chief threat to South Africa's security is from guerrilla or irregular warfare and ultimately therefore internal. Against this threat, nuclear weapons seem pointless. This reasoning has some force, but it probably overlooks various South African security perceptions.

A South African rationale for nuclear weapons could have military as well as political dimensions. The principal military dimension would be the capacity to threaten those military forces that a hostile foreign power (for example, the Soviet Union or Cuba) might deploy in nearby territories or coastal waters, to increase the risks of such deployment and to deter military engagement. Such a capability also attracts the attention of other powers and can stimulate efforts on their part to dissuade further buildup of the foreign military forces, increasing South Africa's indirect leverage. Presumably, a nuclear capability could also be used to hold the main cities of neighboring states hostage against active support for insurgencies within South Africa, although admittedly there could be difficulties in making such threats credible.

South African proliferation could threaten U.S. interests in several ways. First, nuclear-weapons possession could create false confidence in South Africa that it could defer or avoid political reforms that may be indispensable to its security in the long run. Second, it could be counterproductive by provoking higher levels of hostile foreign-military involvement in neighboring states. Third, it could force the United States and other Western countries to adopt postures that are even more antagonistic to South Africa and perhaps less conducive to a durable political settlement in the area.

Latin America

This region overall is probably the most stable in the less-developed world. Deference to domestic and international law is well established. Boundary and territorial disputes are comparatively few and far between. Outside of the Caribbean, the propensity for interstate warfare seems quite rare. The Tlatelolco Treaty, which prescribes a nuclear-weapons-free zone, is not yet universally adhered to in the region but is remarkably inclusive nonetheless and a substantial instrument for nonproliferation goals.

Potential interest in nuclear weapons appears to be limited mainly to Argentina and Brazil. Both these countries are developing sensitive nuclear technology and could develop nuclear weapons within the next decade, although Argentina is further along in this respect than Brazil. Cuba's exclusive partner in nuclear development is the Soviet Union, which seems likely to insist on stringent nonproliferation conditions in Cuba as a basis for nuclear-technology supply.

If stable conditions persist in Latin America throughout the decade, nuclear weapons are not likely to appear in the region. Brazil and Argentina will develop the basic capabilities for nuclear weapons but probably will refrain from weaponizing those capabilities. Both seem eager to avoid perceptions by the other of nuclear provocation; they have even agreed to bilateral nuclear-energy cooperation in several specific areas, and the effects of this could be mutually reassuring.

Proliferation in the region could affect U.S. interests in several ways, particularly if there is a deterioration in regional international relations. Nuclear-weapons capabilities could produce mutual insecurity and increased polarization between various pairs of states in the region. Such polarization in turn could lead states to look to major external powers for protection or support, and this could open new opportunities for the extension of Soviet political and military influence in the region. Soviet involvement could produce additional insecurity, cause deterioration of international stability in the region, and break down the factors that have thus far permitted Latin America to remain largely insulated from the deeper conflicts of other developing regions or of world politics at large. Proliferation in countries neighboring the United States, to date an extremely remote possibility, could threaten the continental United States (CONUS) directly and thus would be of great U.S. concern.

The ambiguous but assertive nuclear policies of such Latin American countries as Brazil and Argentina are already injurious to the international nonproliferation regime. Both will also be capable of entering commercial markets as suppliers of nuclear technology and material and could enter into nuclear-supply relationships with sensitive countries in other regions. A potential relationship of this kind between Brazil and Iraq has been publicized recently, and Argentinian nuclear technicians played a key role in the development of Iran's nuclear infrastructure before the revolution there altered the picture.

Western Europe

Western Europe is faced with growing transnationally organized and increasingly strident antinuclear movements. Moreover, there appear to be novel elements of coordination between groups opposed to nuclear energy and those that oppose nuclear weapons, specifically, augmented NATO theater nuclear-force deployments (GLCM, Pershing II, and enhanced radiation warheads for artillery). The nuclear-energy opposition tends to focus on grass-roots obstruction at nuclear-power-plant construction sites, and the opposition to tactical nuclear weapon (TNW) deployments is relatively important also in parliamentary and party-leadership circles. The movements are particularly strong in West Germany, the low countries, and

Scandinavia, but they are not inconsiderable in the United Kingdom and even in France.

Against the background of Europe's high levels of energy-import dependence and growing reliance on energy supplies from the Soviet Union, the joint opposition to nuclear energy and TNW has profound threat implications for NATO cohesion and vitality, undermining energy and economic security as well as military security. Orderly development of nuclear energy in Europe could mitigate—but not completely relieve—the energy-security pressures.

In this context it is also worth asking how the antinuclear opposition will affect the external nuclear cooperation and export policies of West European states and what the implications will be for the future of the nonproliferation regime. On one hand, the slowdown in nuclear energy in Western Europe (which must be accounted for by economic factors as well as political opposition) could be a further propulsive factor in nuclear exports and commercial competition for third-world nuclear markets—a tendency already evident in the 1970s. On the other hand, the antinuclear movement could also have inhibiting effects on nuclear exports by demanding more restrictive policies.

The links between domestic antinuclear pressures and nuclear export and cooperation policies are complex. External considerations such as market demand for nuclear services, proliferation events, regional-security issues, and potential reciprocity in other produce areas (for example, oil supply) are also factors in the equation and possibly are more important than the influence of antinuclear forces, whose primary attention is focused on what happens within Europe or NATO. Moreover, significant changes in external nuclear policy can be subtle and are usually esoteric, for example, in safeguards conditions and applications.

Through the late 1970s, there was increasing convergence among the advanced nuclear-supplier countries on sensitive nuclear-exports and safeguards conditions. Progress continues to be made even now. Recently elected French President François Mitterrand's response to the Israeli strike on Iraq, for example, suggests that more restrictive nuclear-export policies are likely in France. But patterns of change in policies of international nuclear cooperation and nonproliferation become evident slowly and incrementally. The results of the antinuclear activities in Western Europe have yet to mature—a problem that deserves extensive analysis.

Policy Implications and Conclusions

Some additional nuclear proliferation seems bound to occur, but there are quite different future paths possible. Proliferation in a gradualist scenario could continue at a relatively slow pace, often marked by ambiguity, for example, where the detonation threshold is not crossed, and self-contained with primarily regional implications for the most part. Alternately, a burst-in-the-dike scenario could be visualized where visible and aggressive nuclear proliferation in one spot triggers corresponding surges in overt proliferation not only in the neighboring region but in other regions, swamping developing areas in nuclear crises with sweeping implications for the superpowers and central strategic balance. The gradualist scenario is more in accord with the preceding regional analyses and seems by far the more probable, and it is the basis on which future U.S. policy considerations are discussed. It should not be overlooked, however, that there are at least remote dangers in the Middle East nuclear situation that could bring about something closer to the second scenario, not in the present decade but conceivably in the 1990s.

A U.S. strategy for coping with some additional proliferation would not be radically different from—but would be somewhat more demanding than—that relied on in the past. It would, as before, continue to emphasize attainable nonproliferation, supporting and improving the institutions and procedures of the existing nonproliferation regime. It would require greater attention, however, to diplomatic and security instruments designed to manage proliferation where its occurrence turns out to be ineluctable.

International Nuclear Cooperation and the
Nonproliferation Regime

Continuity and evolutionary innovations are critical to the viability of the international system of peaceful nuclear cooperation and its nonproliferation adjuncts. Certain initiatives of the Carter administration seemed to break with important principles of this system, particularly in the way they collided with Allied interests and bruised perceptions of the United States either as a reliable supplier or as a leader in technological development. The present administration intends to remove such sources of irritation but otherwise appears ready to maintain continuity in the basic structure of U.S. policy and cooperation, about which there is overall consensus, and to restore momentum to U.S. leadership in nuclear technological development.

Improvements of the nonproliferation regime are going to be necessary, however, in several key areas, including nuclear-supplier consensus on dual-use exports; improved safeguards (including more efficient use of personnel, more effective procedures, and new technology); assured nuclear supply and cooperation, especially with developing countries; institutions and procedures for the management and storage of surplus plutonium, including consensus about where and when plutonium can be used; and development of physical-security arrangements for transportation. Proposals for multinational or international institutional arrangements for sensitive facilities, spent-fuel management, and radioactive-waste disposal will undergo further examination and some may need development.

Justification exists for renewed attention to related arms-control proposals that require negotiations between the superpowers or among the nuclear-weapons powers, particularly those started in the Strategic Arms Limitation Talks (SALT), Mutual and Balanced Force Reductions (MBFR), and Comprehensive Test Ban (CTB) contexts. Efforts to give the Tlatelolco system comprehensive effect in Latin America should be maintained. The current development of proposals for a nuclear-free zone in the Middle East is heartening. Any proposal undoubtedly will have to negotiate many pitfalls, but now that both Egypt and Israel have expressed support in principle for such a concept, it must be regarded as sufficiently promising to attach a high, sustained priority—although this by no means should be confused by excessive or inept public diplomacy.

Diplomatic- and Security-Policy Considerations

Proliferation is driven primarily by insecurity. Provision of security is the most important antidote. The slippage that has occurred in Western strategic security as a result of failure to dissuade or counter the continued Soviet buildup of its military forces and increasing resort to long-distance or proxy military interventions, is a condition that has to be rectified for nonproliferation as well as traditional strategic and national-security purposes. The resolve demonstrated by the new administration on this broader issue is encouraging, because it is the first step in turning around worldwide apprehensions about the state of the strategic balance, likelihood of Soviet or proxy involvement in regional conflict, and consistency of U.S. international security policy. This is not to say proliferation can be solved only with military means, merely that it cannot be effectively addressed without the perceived stability of critical military balances.

As suggested in the regional analyses, a variety of new costs and dangers to U.S. interests will be associated with additional proliferation. The most consequential seem to be region-specific. Threats to the stability of the central strategic balance, the future of oil supply, and the solidarity of alliance relationships, for example, are much more likely to originate in the Middle East or Southwest Asia than in other regions in this decade. Only in South Asia, in a similar vein, is a regional nuclear military exchange or war a foreseeable contingency in the next decade. Additional proliferation in any region where both superpowers are engaged will put additional strains on crisis management. Diplomatic bargaining with new proliferants and some of their neighbors will become much more difficult over a wide range of issues, including security assistance. The requirements for maintaining international security and perceived confidence in security response to evidence of deterioration will become more formidable.

Additional proliferation by its nature challenges the nonproliferation regime, although more so in some forms than others. Policies of nuclear ambiguity are erosive, as are most of those nuclear-supplier relationships that fall outside the NPT and major-suppliers-group framework. Certain proliferation events, particularly new nuclear detonations, tend to be erosive, but other possibilities—such as an actual nuclear strike or exchange — might energize measures to strengthen the nonproliferation regime. The sanctions area of policy is critical in this regard and needs to be developed much more imaginatively.

In the next decade, there is little danger that new proliferants will directly threaten CONUS at a military level, but such threats to U.S. allies or U.S. citizens or forces they host are not entirely implausible. Insofar as such threats drive Soviet augmentation of military forces or consideration of anti-ballistic-missile defenses, they could also require adjustments in U.S. strategic planning. But the main proliferant threat to U.S. citizens or military forces in the foreseeable future is likely to be regional and is more readily visualized in the Middle East and Southwest Asia. Threats by small nuclear forces to U.S. intervention forces deployed to cope with an emergency are conceivable in the next decade.

Proliferant threats to U.S. forces and citizens, and to those of allies and friends, will require a broad range of technical, intelligence, planning, and decision-making innovations. Augmented intelligence capabilities will be needed to monitor nuclear technical developments, force dispositions, and local decision making. Naval assets and overseas basing facilities may need more effective early warning or detection systems and more sophisticated defenses. Contingency planning and analysis will require elaboration, and decision makers will need increased exposure through gaming and simulation techniques to crisis management under proliferated conditions. Intervention planning will have to take account of nuclear effects and may require operational capabilities for preemption or suppression of small nuclear forces.

Notes

1. Those who prefer to distinguish horizontal and vertical proliferation may wish to qualify this statement, but the primary concern of this chapter is with the classical concept of nuclear weapons spread to additional nations and, in that context, the statement holds.

2. This chapter draws on a series of specialized working papers prepared at the Center for Strategic and International Studies or commissioned to outside experts and on the discussions in a small conference held at the Center on 25 September 1981 to critique those papers. The authors and titles of the working papers are: Debra Van Opstal, "Review of Literature on a Proliferated World"; Thomas Blau, "Nuclear Proliferation in the Middle East"; John Oseth and Richard Dunn, "Proliferation and the Future of East Asian Conflict"; Rodney W. Jones, "Nuclear Scenarios in Southern Asia"; Kenneth Steuer and Robert McDonald, "Africa and Nuclear Proliferation"; Steven Hildreth, "What Price Proliferation? The Politics, Problems and Prospects of Latin America's Search for Prestige in Nuclearization"; Nancy Ambrose, "Nuclear Power and Nuclear Weapons Proliferation Connection."

3. *On Thermonuclear War* (Princeton, N.J.: Princeton, 1961); *Thinking about the Unthinkable* (New York: Horizon, 1962).

4. "The Delicate Balance of Terror," *Foreign Affairs* 37 (January 1959): 211–234.

5. *The Strategy of Conflict* (Cambridge, Mass.: Harvard, 1960); *Arms and Influence* (New Haven, Conn.: Yale, 1966).

6. *The Balance of Terror: Strategy for the Nuclear Age* (Boston: Houghton Mifflin, 1961).

7. Waltz, "What Will the Spread of Nuclear Weapons Do to the World," in *International Political Effects of the Spread of Nuclear Weapons*, ed. John Kerry King (Washington, D.C.: U.S. Government Printing Office, April 1979), pp. 165–196; and *Theory of International Politics* (Reading, Mass.: Addison-Wesley, 1979), chap. 8, pp. 180–183.

8. The pioneers of this proliferation-management analysis were Herman Kahn et al., *Trends in Nuclear Proliferation* (Philadelphia: Hudson Institute, 1976); Lewis Dunn and William Overholt, "The Next Phase in Nuclear Proliferation Research," *Orbis* 20 (Summer 1976): 35–39; Lewis Dunn et al., *U.S. Defense Planning for a More Proliferated World* (Philadelphia: Hudson Institute, 1979). More recent works that are influenced by or adopt the same perspective include: from the Council on Foreign Relations, David G. Gompert et al., *Nuclear Weapons and World Politics* (New York: McGraw Hill, 1977); from the Brookings Institution: Joseph Yager, ed., *Nuclear Proliferation and Foreign Policy* (Washington, D.C., 1980); and for the Central Intelligence Agency: John Kerry King, ed., *International Political Effects of the Spread of Nuclear Weapons* (National Foreign Assessment Center, 1979). See also Rodney W. Jones, *Nuclear Proliferation: Islam, the Bomb and South Asia*, The Washington Papers, no. 82 (Washington, D.C.: Center for Strategic and International Studies, Georgetown University, 1981).

9. Albert Wohlstetter, "Spreading the Bomb without Quite Breaking

the Rules" *Foreign Policy* 25 (Winter 1976–1977):88–96, 145–179; *Swords from Plowshares: The Military Potential of Civilian Nuclear Energy* (Chicago: University of Chicago, 1979).

10. It should be noted that the Wohlstetter-Rowen group had long been sensitive to the security dimension as an incentive to acquire nuclear weapons and critical of what they regarded as the weakening of U.S. commitments and capabilities to defend others. The availability of civilian nuclear facilities, however, seemed to them to be an additional issue whose importance was underscored by what they saw as U.S. strategic decline and resulting global instability. At the same time, many who supported the Wohlstetter-Rowen nonproliferation perspective, such as some of the members of the Carter administration in its early years, did not share their strategic perspective.

11. See note 7.

12. "A Nuclear Middle East," *Survival* 23 (May/June 1981): 107–115.

13. See, for example, his *Self-Reliance and National Resilience* (New Delhi: Abhinav, 1975).

14. James P. Wooten and Warren H. Donnelly, "Israeli Raid into Iraq," IB 81103, Library of Congress, Congressional Research Service, 1 October 1981.

Part III
Military Operations for
Low-Intensity Conflict

Introduction
to Part III

To apply force effectively in low-intensity conflicts, a nation must operate flexibly and discriminatingly. In particular, it will need to conduct military operations at the lower end of the conflict spectrum. For such politicomilitary operations, U.S. forces typically are not well prepared.

The four chapters in part III treat the features of and needs for some of these low-intensity politicomilitary operations. William J. Taylor, Jr. addresses psychological operations—one of the least understood but most useful ways to apply force, but one for which democracies seem to be especially unsuited. Terrorism, on the other hand, is at least widely known as a threat, even if preparations to deal with it have not until now gone very far toward decreasing its menace. Yonah Alexander assesses what form technological and strategic aspects of terrorism will assume in the 1980s.

The last two chapters deal with somewhat more conventional military operations. Christopher Lamb details the characteristics of proxy warfare, one of the novel and very troubling forms of conflict that emerged in the 1970s, which may dominate much of U.S. military conduct in the 1980s. Finally, Michael C. Ryan evaluates U.S. performance in rescue operations, a most demanding but almost sure-to-be-repeated form of special military operation.

9

Psychological Operations in the Spectrum of Conflict in the 1980s

William J. Taylor, Jr.

Willy Brandt, former chancellor of West Germany, returned recently from the Soviet Union, where he had conferred with Soviet President Leonid Brezhnev. According to the 24 August 1981 issue of *Time*, the trip represented a triumph for the Soviets. They succeeded in getting Brandt, still a powerful political figure, although no longer in the government, to advance the proposition that the United States not deploy the Pershing II missile in Europe in return for vague promises to "begin negotiations about the removal of the 250 SS-20s already in place." At the same time, Brandt was influenced to push for a nuclear-free zone in Scandinavia, where NATO would agree not to install any weapons in the region without a concomitant guarantee on the part of the Soviets. Brandt's trip was characterized by the conservative Franz Josef Strauss as being part of "Brezhnev's psychological warfare aimed at intimidating the West."

Indeed, the Soviet psychological warfare (PSYWAR) program may be the most powerful weapon in that nation's arsenal. To date, the program has prevented the deployment and assembly of the neutron bomb in Western Europe, thus robbing the West of an extremely potent and persuasive means of projecting power. This move cost the Soviets nothing but words and allowed them to concentrate still further their buildup of armed forces. The program also has cost the United States a loss of prestige in the pursuit of improving its defense posture in Europe.

As opposed to the Soviet Union, the United States has today no viable coordinated or comprehensive psychological operations (PSYOPS) program. There is in the United States a general distrust of anything even intimating PSYWAR and an even greater misunderstanding. For example, a bare minimum of cooperation exists between the military and civilian agencies concerned with such matters. In the past, the civilian government agencies have hesitated to associate themselves with the military PSYOPS community; today, there is still no regular liaison between the two. Representative John LeBoutillier has called for a more aggressive program from the U.S. International Communication Agency (ICA), which runs the Voice of America. Yet the agency operates without any formal contact with the few military experts in PSYOPS.

The most telling example of the atrophy of the U.S. ability to wage

113

successful PSYOPS is in the military establishment. In tactical command-post exercises, commanders shun the use of PSYOPS tools, such as loud-speakers simulating armored-track-vehicle movement in conjunction with electronic means representing normal armored-unit communications. The problem with this is that armed forces fight they way they train. Without training, there cannot be a wartime PSYOPS capability. The army, the executive military agency responsible for PSYOPS, has only one individual on its staff dedicated to such endeavors. The army PSYWAR representative on the staff of the Joint Chiefs of Staff (JCS) works only part-time at the task. The active army units, of which there are four very small ones, lack many of the required qualified officers and noncommissioned officers. Almost the entire military PSYWAR capability of the United States rests in the U.S. Army Reserve, yet reserve units are burdened with administrative levels of command that neither understand the importance of PSYOPS nor assist the reserve units to become combat-ready.

The baseline for PSYOPS at present is near zero; that is, the potential is unlimited. There is a compelling need to exploit immediately the advantages accruing from the use of PSYOPS. The squeamishness that U.S. policy-makers now display must be overcome and a hard line taken in developing a coherent and coordinated effort to develop a successful strategy and launch effective PSYOPS campaigns.

Targets

There are many aspects of PSYOPS related to high-level civilian-propa-ganda efforts of various U.S. agencies that have both foreign and domestic targets. These arenas, however, are not the subject of this chapter. We are interested here in the external targets of PSYOPS in which the military has an appropriate role.

A major target set consists of those foreign nations or foreign political-action groups that are not necessarily enemies of the United States but that often differ with U.S. policies and take public stands in opposition to U.S. national interests. The ICA and the Department of State could be more effective in this arena; the military has largely avoided it, principally because military involvement might be viewed as inappropriate or counterproduc-tive. Considering the distinct possibility of the countries in this target swing-ing into the enemy's camp, however, it is an important question whether the military should become more involved even if only for planning purposes. Angola, Ethiopia, the Yemens, El Salvador, Nicaragua, Iran, and Afghani-stan all might be considered PSYOPS targets where a military role is legitimate. The rationale is simple; U.S. forces could be committed in these nations.

The second major target group is the so-called enemy, targeted by the U.S. Department of Defense, the State department, the Department of Commerce, and various other agencies. The enemy includes the Soviet Union and its allies and proxies. The extent of the enemy "without" is not well defined. There are elements of it working in allied countries, and some of these elements are, unknowingly, working for Soviet causes. The Soviet Union has a whispered disinformation program, that is, the use of rumor, insinuation, and distortion of facts to discredit foreign governments, leaders, and international organizations.

The United States has an enormous task ahead of it with a wide range of targets and very limited means. It appears that the U.S. PSYOPS effort should be greatly expanded in the future and that military roles and capabilities deserve serious study. The question, then, is how in the 1980s this is to be accomplished.

Means

Before promulgating PSYOPS campaigns involving military capabilities directed against the various targets mentioned, it is necessary to examine the tools, or means, that are at present in the inventory or that need to be developed. Once having determined what resources are or should be made available, so-called psywarriors can develop plans to employ PSYOPS through the entire spectrum of conflict.

There are essentially three basic tools the psywarrior can use: the spoken word, the written word, and image projection—both visual and audio. Each can be used singly or in combination, depending on the circumstances. The limitations on their employment are time, expense, and bulk, but these vary in proportion according to how, when, and where they are used.

Of the three tools, the written word is the most easily disseminated. In its simplest form, a pencil and a few pieces of paper are all that are needed to get across the appropriate message. At the other end of the spectrum are high-quality, well-illustrated, and professionally produced books, pamphlets, and magazines. The primitive items would most likely be passed from hand to hand, having been initially delivered by air, artillery gun, balloon, or courier. The more sophisticated items would be placed in the hands of the target audience most likely by government mail or private handling systems.

How the written word is to be used must be carefully examined before it is applied, for there is a danger that it may backfire. A safe-conduct pass, for example, must be written in such a way that it accomplishes several objectives. The pass must not incriminate the person carrying it; on the other hand, it must contain sufficient information so that the individual to whom the bearer surrenders understands what the document is. At the same time, the pass would invalidate the PSYOPS campaign if the terms-of-surrender document clearly could not be carried out.

On a different level, any high-quality publication about the United States failing to show a balance between what is good about America and what is not would lack credibility. Although not responsible for a life-or-death situation in this instance, a noncredible item could be counterproductive. Credibility is best gained by looking at the product through the eyes of the intended audience and presenting it in a manner that is acceptable to its recipients. A book filled with stilted translations of U.S. polemics would only elicit contempt and would not produce desired results.

The second tool, the spoken word, is relatively easy to employ, but its success depends on many variables. The type of audience, for example, can have numerous configurations. It can be a huge mass—the kind Hitler addressed. Such an audience facilitates wide impact as well as manipulation. Today's equivalent of such an audience might be a revival meeting. A more subtle equivalent, however, would be that of a rock concert, where the message is transmitted through words in popular songs. Political nuances, which are impossible to censor, rather than obvious rhetoric can thus be projected. And there is little difficulty in attracting this kind of audience as U.S. experiences have shown. Such events, however, take great organization, must be held at the appropriate time and place, and generally require extensive sound-projecting equipment.

Another audience configuration is large numbers of small groups assembled at different locations around television sets or radios. During World War II, many citizens in occupied countries used to assemble to listen to special programs broadcast especially to them. Still a third audience would be widely dispersed individuals who could be reached only with the spoken word, requiring radios, tape cassettes, and loudspeakers mounted on vehicles and aircraft. Range, however, currently limits the effectiveness of radios and loudspeakers.

Range extension of transmitting devices is an area that will advance in the 1980s. Satellites offer particularly great potential for broadcasting. Today, for example, Soviet Central Asia cannot be reached by radio, but technology will soon be available to make it possible for U.S. radio communicators to reach every corner of the earth from North America. It will no longer be necessary to depend on vulnerable stationary transmitting posts located in isolated parts of the world. Satellites used in conjunction with advanced FM equipment offer great potential savings in terms of effort, funding, and staffing.

Communications satellites may be able to extend the range of radio and television, but such extension would be for naught if no receivers picked up the signals. One might look forward to inexpensive but powerful miniature receivers resembling wristwatches or earrings implanted with tiny receivers. Available modes of distribution of such receivers, which would have to be mass-produced, must be considered.

Electronics have recently made available the cassette tape recorder, another means of dissemination. In Iran, verbal tapes condemning the regime of the Ayatollah Khomeini are being distributed clandestinely, just as tapes with other messages were in the time of the Shah. Since the cassette need not bear a particular signature (that is, label) like a leaflet does, it is virtually impossible to detect its origin unless it is played. All that is required to camouflage a cassette is to give it a false label or none at all. Further, since the proliferation of tapes in the world is so great it is also nearly impossible to prevent their distribution.

Another step forward with the cassette idea is the mass production and distribution of the videotape. Although it may be many years before propaganda can be distributed in the poorer regions of the world using video cassettes, the situation is different in Western Europe and the United States, as well as in oil-rich countries such as Libya and Saudi Arabia. In the 1980s, wide distribution of video cassettes is well within the realm of the possible.

Video cassettes introduce the third tool—image projection, both audio and visual. The former is actually a means of deception that the military finds particularly effective, by way of tape recordings of armored vehicles that simulate the presence of mechanized formations in the area. Through the adroit use of loudspeakers, a scenario that includes reconnoitering an area, moving into the area, digging in, consolidating the position, expanding it, and firing from it can all be simulated. In conjunction with fake radio traffic, the illusion can be created by the sounds from a couple of light trucks with speakers and radios simulating the presence of a large and powerful armored organization.

The more common, and more sophisticated, means of projecting images, however, is through the medium of television. United States television producers conducted a very successful PSYOPS campaign that redounded to the benefit of the enemy during the Vietnam War. There is little doubt that the pictures of returning "body bags" shown on television, coupled with the constant reiteration of questions about U.S. interests in Vietnam during that time, had a deteriorating effect on public morale and, eventually, on soldiers in combat.[1] This psychological victory for the enemy was gained, probably unwittingly, by competing media groups that were interested primarily in the money to be made and less concerned about the damage that might be done to the nation. As it turned out, one riot perpetrated by the left-wing Weathermen may have had more impact on U.S. viewers than did many successful battles against the North Vietnamese and Viet Cong. The Vietnam War coverage is vivid evidence of the effectiveness of visual-image projection, and one can look to its continued effectiveness.

As with radio transmissions, it should be possible in the 1980s to develop low-cost receivers that could be distributed on a random basis to target audiences throughout the world. Although not as small as earring or watch-size radio receivers, television receivers the size of tennis-ball cans possibly could be cheaply produced and distributed by courier, balloon, or aircraft. Made of high-impact material with solid-state circuitry, the device would be able to receive several channels to reduce the possibility of losing them to electronic jamming. Programs would be sent via satellite, which would make it possible for those in even the most remote areas of the world to receive messages.

The means described only scratch the surface of possibilities. Modern communications technology is expanding so fast that the psywarrior must constantly watch for new and fast ways to reach the target audience. This search must also be directed toward new concepts in PSYOPS, such as the use of mechanical devices that suggest ideas and implant them in a person's subconscious. Extrasensory means of waging PSYWAR are already being experimented with by the Soviet Union. Allegedly, great amounts of money are being directed to Soviet institutes researching what is known as parapsychology, which includes extrasensory perception (ESP). United States intelligence agencies, according to the National Broadcasting Company (NBC), have not taken the Soviet effort too seriously, but the military uses of parapsychology cannot be overlooked, even if they do not seem to comply with the Western attitude of fair play. With the state of U.S. technology as high as it is, the transmission of extrasensory messages is certainly possible. Technology provides the technical means for background mixing of secondary, subliminal messages into ostensibly routine broadcasts. The target audience "hears" messages without knowing it.

Developing Programs

Inventors will come up with the mechanical devices, but thinkers will have to develop programs that make use of the devices. Although different agencies have different methods, there are a few essential common steps. The military probably has the simplest procedure, consisting of three steps: performing research and analysis; integrating current intelligence into the product; and producing propaganda.

Research and analysis is the most involved. Once the general target area is identified (for example, a country such as Albania), a decision has to be reached concerning the best means to attack it. This is done through exhaustive study of the country's demography, geography, linguistics, history, economic and political structure, and sociological composition, to name but a few substantive areas. The idea is to determine the vulnerabilities and strengths of the target. Once the vulnerabilities are determined, it must then be decided whether they can be exploited.

If the target is determined exploitable, the next step is taken—intelligence is incorporated into the research. Timeliness is critical; current intelligence is dependent on time-sensitive material. In combat, this material comes from finding documents on the battlefield, intercepting enemy communications, and interviewing recently captured enemy prisoners. The intelligence gained is exploited best by swift military action, which may include a PSYOPS ploy. Normally, however, the current intelligence is integrated into the studies done by the research and analysis teams, who dispatch the entire integrated package to the propaganda teams for implementation.

The propaganda team determines how to use the material coming from the research and analysis and intelligence teams. It examines the target, its susceptibility to different types of propaganda, and how best to reach the target. The team then develops a program of attack. The team might decide that an ethnic minority serving at a certain part of the front can be reached by a leaflet suggesting that members of the minority in the armed forces are being used unfairly by their government. This is a simplistic example, but it illustrates the most basic function of a propaganda team.

At a different level, it may be decided that a series of broadcasts on a certain theme should be beamed at a potentially receptive target group. Because of the amount of required coordination, the money involved, the lead time required, and expertise demanded, the campaign could take a long time to prepare and might extend over a long period. Such campaigns can be very involved as, for example, targeting an ethnic group in the Soviet Union with little access to reception means such as radios. It might be necessary to produce and distribute radio receivers that are simple to operate, easily distributed, sturdy, and easily concealed. The answer might be a receiver built into an earring. The earrings would have to be of a type popular with the natives, could be produced in many colors, would work on only one frequency, and would have only one switch—to turn the receiver on and off and adjust the volume.

Psychological Operations in the Context of Changing Applications of Force

Although it is difficult to identify psychological aspects within the functions of the conflict spectrum, it is easiest to do so at the lower levels of intensity. This is because "words should talk louder than actions," that is, it is better to talk an issue out than to fight over it. Nevertheless, PSYOPS play an important role throughout the entire spectrum.

If one accepts that threats of force are at the lowest end of the conflict spectrum, then one is dealing exclusively in the realm of PSYOPS. Threats play on the mind. They are designed to compel a person, a group of people, a nation to bend to the will of another. Effectiveness of the threat depends on this credibility, and credibility varies widely, since it is dependent on many factors.

In Europe, for example, a credible threat may be to assassinate a key leader in a democratic country. It is credible because it would be relatively easy to accomplish. Freedom of movement is extensive in Western Europe; crossing national boundaries is simple. In addition, people in Western Europe place a great deal of value on their democratically elected leaders. On the other hand, European peoples are not receptive to giving up individual freedoms, which makes population control difficult. Western Europeans also know what the application of force can accomplish—Hitler is still remembered. Thus the population is relatively well conditioned to reacting in the manner desired when an opponent uses the threat of force.

On the other hand, threats of force in other parts of the world have less psychological impact. Iraq, for example, could be expected to scoff at threats of force by Iran or by Syria. There are many reasons for this. First, the government is conditioned to the threats of force. Prior to 1979 and the war with Iran, there was considerable threatening of force (as there is between Israel and its neighbors). Second, the use of language that implies the use of force is common in that area: "death to the infidel" and similar epithets are used frequently. Even the shooting of guns into the air in celebrations in North Africa, a terrifying act to the uninitiated, is part of the language. Third, since force is an accepted way of life to many, its mere threat is considered relatively commonplace. Leaders are accustomed to threats against their lives, but they also have the resources to prevent comparatively easily the actual application of force. Bodyguards complement any important person's entourage. At the same time, control over the population is much greater than in the Western democracies. Since many of these countries are also ruled by authoritarian governments, the secret police have broad powers to exercise such control.

The conditions mitigating against the effectiveness of PSYOPS aspects of the threat of force exist in most of Africa and Latin America as well. Again, such threats are not uncommon, and since most countries cannot be classified as democracies, the same physical restraints to carrying out threats also apply. Threats of force are not viewed as being as effective as the application of force itself. Consequently, there is a greater propensity to use force—for example, terrorism.

The situation in Southwest Asia, Asia, and the Pacific varies widely. Muslim countries such as Indonesia and, to a certain extent, the Philippines, have experienced levels of violence known in Mideast Muslim countries. To be sure, disaffected Moluccans have brought their violence to the Netherlands in a most vicious manner. In other countries, however, such as China, Vietnam, Korea, and Japan, threats of force have a different connotation. They tend to become matters of honor and are couched in terms that almost demand action. Even today, when a family's name is besmirched in Japan, the ceremonial sword or dagger takes the place of rhetoric.

Terrorism

Where the propensity to use the threat of force to undermine an opponent psychologically varies throughout the world, terrorism is a different matter. In terms of application of force, it is absolute. By definition, *terrorism* is the act of doing bodily or psychological injury or, more exactly, terrorism is a psychological act of violence. Such an act does not have to be large in scale; it need only be conducted to have a psychological effect far out of proportion to the act itself. The shooting of the pope had a devastating effect worldwide; but had the pope been a simple priest, the news of the shooting would not have made more than a few lines on the back page of a local newspaper.

Given modern, extensive media coverage and the difficulty of covering up terrorist incidents, terrorism is an exceptionally effective application of force. No matter where the act takes place, it is capable of exploitation around the world. In fact, the effect of the act is not necessarily the greatest at the place it happens. It is more a function of media interest and media competition. With all the deaths of innocent people in El Salvador, perhaps the deaths with the greatest psychological impact were those of the four U.S. nuns. Although the act undoubtedly affected people in El Salvador, it had a tremendous psychological impact on the people of the United States. United States newspapers and television saw a great opportunity to publicize an abysmal act, and, because it was "good news," the coverage in the United States was widespread. The media competed for the best shots of the slain victims, and in the process gave the U.S. public an extensive view of the whole morbid affair.

Such exploitation is possible in countries such as the United States where the Constitution guarantees the rights of the press. The public can be informed, and it can simultaneously be manipulated. For example, in North Vietnam during the war, only a few correspondents were allowed to view the so-called glorious efforts of the Vietnamese people. These newscasters generally could be counted on to provide a favorable account of what they saw, because what they saw were carefully chosen pseudo-images that their sponsors wanted projected to the outside world. Since the information was relatively sparse, it was snapped up eagerly by news services around the world. The view the Western public got was that the North Vietnamese were prevailing despite the barbarous acts of the United States. On the other hand, our media coverage in South Vietnam focused on what made news, which more often than not was U.S. and South Vietnamese casualties (bringing one close to the war) or weapons firing at some unseen enemy (an impersonal, seemingly unproductive act). The combination had a great adverse psychological impact on people in the United States and anyone else who had a television set. The coverage is an excellent example of what could be termed "controlled terrorism" through psychological manipulation of the media.

Manipulation of people in countries such as the Soviet Union is both easier and harder. In many cases, the psychological effects of terrorism can carefully be controlled in totalitarian societies. This is accomplished by censoring material. For example, it is conceivable (although not probable) that the Soviet people in large cities surrounded by large jammers did not learn for some time that the Pope had been shot. If, however, the Soviet government could quickly have used that act of terrorism to its advantage in a propaganda campaign, the Soviet news media easily could have shaped its presentations to achieve such an effect. At the same time, the Soviet government can shield (although only partially) the Soviet people from the effects of Western propaganda by jamming broadcasts from the West. Unfortunately for the Soviets, as transmission of imagery becomes more sophisticated, the Soviet task becomes more complicated. Indeed, in the occupied Baltic states, more television sets today are tuned to Western stations. Education renders manipulation more difficult as people eventually learn that they are being manipulated. They discredit and discount what they hear and see their own governments produce, unless the government appeal to the people has a special compulsion, such as defending the homeland. What the people hear from other sources then becomes all the more important and credible, which means that they are increasingly susceptible to outside manipulation.

Terrorism then depends on the psychological effect it can stimulate. The psychological impact depends less on where the act is carried out than on the sophistication of the media exploiting the terror. In the 1980s, terrorism will have a psychological effect that increases in proportion to the number of people who hear of it. The more sophisticated the means become, the more effective PSYOPS exploitation of terrorism will be.

Surgical Operations

The next level of intensity in the application of force, surgical operations, also makes use of PSYOPS, but that application requires a different function for the use of psychology. Surgical operations are best conducted surrounded by a PSYOPS cloak. That is, the public must be well prepared psychologically for both the success and the defeat of a surgical operation. The 1981 fiasco in Iran vividly demonstrates the latter contention. People in the United States were prepared for a successful operation; the need for it had been well established through media coverage of the condition of the hostages. Whether this was a deliberate psychological ploy is not known, but judging from subsequent events, it appears that the entire psychological cover, as well as rescue plan, was botched.

President Carter had a national consensus when he decided to send the rescue team into Iran, even if Secretary of State Vance was opposed. Had the operation been a success, there is little doubt that the media would have spread the appropriate acclamations and compliments. Evidently, no preparations were made for dealing with a possible failure, which is a serious PSYOPS failure. Considering the very poor U.S. record in executing hostage-seizure operations, the area will need special attention in the 1980s. This is especially important given the apparent shift of national mood in the United States toward more military assertiveness and the very slow pace of U.S. counterterrorism plans and programs at home and abroad.

The use of PSYOPS in surgical operations is threefold: to prepare the public and the enemy for the operation; to exploit the operation's success; and to explain or exploit, the best way possible, an operation's failure. It is generally accepted that a surgical operation needs a good cover or deception plan. This is accomplished by concealing preparations for the operation while conditioning the public for its execution. A deception plan may be employed or secrecy imposed that limits access to information on the operation.

It is equally important that preparations be made to exploit a successful surgical operation. This might include a PSYOPS plan to minimize side effects or to justify the operation. It is easier to justify success than failure, but adequate planning is nonetheless required. Such planning should take into account the possibility of exploiting any positive spin-off that might result from the operation.

New emphasis must be placed on dealing with failed operations. A surgical operation must be war-gamed for failure as well as for success. The PSYOPS goal should be to explain the failure as quickly and completely as possible. The agony will, under any circumstances, be intense. Recognizing this, all efforts must be made to have a credible explanation for the failure immediately available, even if the specific reason is not or should not be made known. The explanation must contain all facts that do not reveal operational secrets. It must be straightforward, concise, and devoid of self-flagellation. Answers to logical questions leading from the failure must be anticipated and prepared. Those asking the questions of the government must not be given the impression that anything is being withheld from them, even if it is. Action must be taken to curtail any attempt to prolong the crisis. In these ways, psychological function in surgical operations are always required.

Military Advisors

The introduction of military advisors normally comes after diplomacy has proven inadequate to the task; that is, other instruments of diplomacy are insufficient, and preparations for physical action are necessary. In a sense, having advisors on the scene would seem to indicate that PSYOPS are less important, but that is not the case. As with surgical operations, PSYOPS can greatly benefit advisors. Before advisors enter a country, the introduction should be carefully explained both in the host country and in the country from which they came. Credible justification for their presence must be established in advance; this may be done by analysis and exposition of a credible threat. How the host country as a whole, not only the military, is to benefit should be explained. The need for advisors must be clearly and consisely explained so that probable attacks on the advisors' presence can be thwarted.

Once advisors are in the country, their activities must be exploited. How well they integrate themselves into the country's fabric, handle their charges, demonstrate concern for local customs, and mix with the populace should be advertised in the best light possible. Again, this is as important in the United States as it is in the country being aided. Whereas little along these lines has been done in the past, the nature of future conflict will make it mandatory. In the long run, the psychological impact may be more important than the actual training the advisors impart to foreign military establishments.

The integration of PSYOPS with the deployment of military advisors, similar to surgical operations, really is not dependent on the region where advisors operate, since psychological operations are an integral component of the use of advisors. The region, however, will influence the type and level of psychological activity. In El Salvador, for example, the type of PSYOPS employed depends on the sophistication of the people, the government, and the military. The military lacks the effectiveness to bring peace to the country. It does not have much experience with modern weapons such as helicopter gunships. The military establishment is not sophisticated, however, the civilian communities in urban areas are. At the same time, the peasants in the countryside and small towns are not well educated. How these diverse elements will be reached could tax the best psywarriors in their attempts to exploit the situation to the benefit of the United States. At present, however, there appears to be no coordinated PSYOPS effort in El Salvador to justify the deployment of military advisors.

Special-Forces Training and Operations

If it is important to explain the presence of military advisors in a country and to protect them through a PSYOPS campaign, then it is imperative that the introduction of special-forces units be accompanied by adequate PSYOPS preparation. Such introduction intimates the initiation of U.S. participation in combat operations. Although the employment of noncombatant advisors may be accepted fairly easily in the United States today, U.S. troops, however few, fighting on foreign soil could be a different matter. The U.S. people must be conditioned psychologically for such intervention.

This raises the question of conducting formal PSYOPS targeted at the people in the United States. Certainly, the campaign could be considered sound public relations, but the degree of coordination and sophistication required means, in essence, that the public will be subjected to what are, in effect, PSYOPS. No civilian apparatus exists today to conduct such operations, but there can be little doubt that in the 1980s there will be increasing pressure for one.

Historically, U.S. presidents have been ill-served when confronted by the necessity to introduce troops into combat. Repeatedly, a cataclysmic event has been necessary to commit U.S. citizens to war. The United States being unprepared militarily in 1939 aside, President Roosevelt had to wait until Pearl Harbor was bombed in 1941 to enter World War II. Had the nation been prepared psychologically (and materially) to enter in 1939, when Japan was preoccupied in China and Germany had not yet invaded Western Europe, the terrible death and destruction worldwide might have been unnecessary.

The Korean War is another example of a psychologically unprepared United States. World War II had been won and, in the absence of a serious, sustained effort to prepare the U.S. public to shoulder the military responsibilities of world leadership, the prevailing mood was to "bring the boys home." Caught again unprepared, U.S. units, when committed to battle, had to fall back to a perimeter around Pusan until hastily mobilized reservists and troops in the United States could be sent to Korea. The reaction of a psychologically unprepared United States took the form of scapegoatism and the excesses of the McCarthy era.

The Vietnam War, however, was a different matter. The gradual introduction of troops into the country met initially with little resistance in the United States. Although there was frustration with the topsy-turvy political situation in Vietnam from 1962 to 1966, the U.S. public gave its tacit approval to U.S. participation in advisory and special-forces operations. This was PSYOPS more by default than through a coordinated effort, but it was nonetheless relatively successful.

President Reagan hardly wants to be known as the initiator of another U.S. intervention disaster. His best course of action is to establish an apparatus that will prepare the U.S. public psychologically not only for such actions as direct intervention in El Salvador but wherever it might be in the nation's interests. The matter becomes all the more critical when one contemplates commitment of the Rapid-Deployment Joint Task Force (RDJTF) in far-flung regions of Southwest Asia or Africa. The U.S. public has not even begun to contemplate seriously that the force actually might be required to fight.

PSYOPS has an integral relationship with special-forces deployment. Whereas a friendly government requesting foreign advisors can justify their presence to the population in a variety of ways, it is more difficult to justify the introduction of soldiers who may fight as well as advise. In effect, the foreign government is admitting that the situation is getting out of control. The introduction of U.S. special-forces soldiers means that they probably will encounter a hostile environment. Under these conditions, it is imperative to both the survival and effectiveness of special-forces elements that they be accepted and supported by the host government. The military or paramilitary groups that the special forces are to assist must be psychologically prepared to receive the U.S. elements. The host group must understand why the special forces are there, what they are expected to do, and how they are going to do it. Once on the ground, the group must be motivated to accomplish its mission or conduct the appropriate training. This is primarily a function of the special-forces element, but it must receive PSYOPS backup.

One of the potential difficulties that special-forces elements might encounter is PSYOPS planning for disengagement from or termination of their commitment. In this case, there must be measures of progress toward clearly established and perceived objectives. As a political-military endeavor, the move should involve planning at the National Security Council (NSC) staff level, which integrates PSYOPS efforts involving the departments of State and Defense, the Central Intelligence Agency (CIA), the Joint Chiefs of Staff (JCS), and a PSYOPS plan to convince those being aided that it is time for U.S. special forces to terminate their involvement.

The very nature of special-forces operations presents a particular challenge to PSYOPS support. Distance from viable logistical support is a major factor. Whereas psywarriors may accompany the special forces into an area of operations, many aspects of support operations have to be administered from afar. Leaflet drops, for example, might have to be made deep in hostile territory. Depending on the volume needed, it might entail a major operation to penetrate enemy airspace with large aircraft such as the C-130 or C-141. Advanced technology, however, offers many possibilities. The special-forces elements on the ground might be able to distribute, on a selective basis, the exotic receivers described earlier. Special forces, through their own communications net, should have a capability of broadcasting via satellite to the target audience, making broadcasts more timely, geographically relevant, more credible, and thus more effective.

Small, Conventional-Unit Commitments

In future conflicts, special-forces units will most likely be the first to cross the brink of war. Operating behind the lines, they will draw the fire first, most likely from internal-security troops. Whether or not the United States wants to admit the presence of special-forces units in an enemy's rear area, it can reasonably be assumed that the special forces will be the first to fight, even if they do not get credit for it.

There is another operation short of war, however, which also must be considered. Whereas special forces might be training foreign dissidents, or fighting alongside them, they will not be fighting as self-contained U.S. units, such as conventional ranger batallions, marine amphibious units, or infantry battalions. The latter, the small conventional units committed to combat, also need the assistance of PSYOPS elements.

A recent example of small-unit commitment where PSYOPS were involved occurred in the August 1981 air engagement with Libya. It is an interesting case of a successful PSYOPS ploy preventing a major confrontation, or war, between the United States and the Soviet Union. Ironically, the ploy does not appear to be the result of a carefully planned PSYOPS program. Nonetheless, what happened is valid as an example of what should occur in the future.

First, the animosity between the United States and Libya has been long-standing (the no-real-surprise factor). The most recent incident prior to the destruction of two Libyan SU-22s was the 6 May 1981 closing of the Libyan People's Bureau (embassy in Washington, D.C.). Preceding that by little more than a year was the burning of the U.S. embassy in Libya. If violence were to erupt it would hardly qualify as a major surprise. The threshold for escalation into full-scale war, therefore, was set relatively high.

Second, the U.S. public had been prepared psychologically to accept combat between the two countries. The Reagan administration had raised U.S. consciousness and sensitivity to those nations who would "step on the toes of the United States." It is not that the U.S. public was spoiling for battle; rather, after the Iranian hostage situation, there were few people in the country willing to see the United States humiliated again.

Third, the United States psychologically prepared the rest of the world, including the Soviet Union, for any confrontation. This was done through the media, through military channels, and by economic means. The United States let other countries know that it would obey international law but would not be intimidated by bombastic measures.

Fourth, the Sixth Fleet maneuvers were conducted within strict guidelines. The commander of the U.S. task force reviewed the rules of engagement covering the circumstances under which a pilot could fire at an adversary: shoot only if attacked. By following the script exactly, one could document—and justify—every action involved in any provocative act. This was a form of immunity against PSYOPS. When the results of the aerial encounter were made known to the world, there was little protest. Even Libya did not react violently. There were few gray areas that could lead to factual distortions constituting a propaganda weapon against the United States.

Fifth, after an initial uproar, the matter was closed for most of the world. Libya was still smarting, but the United States simply focused on different issues. Through PSYOPS efforts, the air battle was downgraded on the conflict spectrum from the higher-intensity-unit commitment to that of a surgical operation.

War

PSYOPS in any kind of war serve as multipliers. Whether war be limited conventional war or general nuclear conflict, there is an important place for PSYWAR across the entire spectrum. The employment of PSYOPS, although not generally recognized as such, can be as decisive as many of the most significant new weapons now in the U.S. and Soviet arsenals. One of the most important uses is to prepare the public for the hardships and losses of war, which can be done by appealing to such concepts as patriotism and self-sacrifice. United States participation in both world wars was accompanied by extensive sloganeering and pamphleteering. All nations, indeed, used psychological operations to gain backing for their war efforts.

PSYOPS can be used to weaken the will of the enemy. Army PSYOPS units are trained to exploit enemy weaknesses. Targeting ethnic differences, for example, can cause dissension and strain within the enemy's ranks, especially when morale is low. This in turn seriously degrades combat capability. Alexis De Tocqueville told us that "democracies go to war at their own peril." He meant that armies of democracies must have the support of their republics or their morale becomes degraded. PSYOPS can be used to undermine public support and, thus, to demoralize the enemy's fighting forces.

PSYOPS can be employed to coax others to come to one's aid. Great Britain was especially successful in bringing the United States in on its side in both world wars. This can be achieved by exploiting enemy PSYOPS failures such as the German U-boat campaign. An operational success, the campaign had the opposite effect by enraging, not demoralizing or intimidating, the U.S. public.

The use of deception, an important combat multiplier, serves as a form of PSYOPS. Whereas loudspeakers have present and future tactical-deception uses, satellites and multimedia-dissemination means have present and future strategic-deception uses.

The prognosis for the use of PSYOPS in potential conflicts in the 1980s is high. The Soviets are masters in its employment. The United States and its allies are bombarded daily with hostile PSYOPS weapons, many of which we are unable to recognize. The United States cannot help but lose any war in which it fails to exploit its PSYOPS.

What If?

Proper utilization of U.S. PSYWAR assets in the 1980s requires increasing relevant U.S. capability. The following is a list of requirements for the PSYOPS community that will improve that capability:

1. An expansion of U.S. civilian and military PSYOPS forces. A civilian PSYWAR agency is required. Whatever its name, it would conduct PSYOPS as an independent U.S. agency in time of peace and subsume the military effort during war. Further, the active army should greatly expand its PSYOPS assets. The reserve forces need to be equipped with modern training devices. Probably a tenfold increase in military PSYOPS manpower is required.

2. The development of inexpensive high-technology items such as radio and television receivers. If the chip can revolutionize the computer industry, it certainly can revolutionize the image-reception business as well.

3. The exploitation of communication networks for PSYOPS purposes. The expanded use of communications satellites is particularly needed to extend the range and scope of radio and television. The state of the art is such that this is possible, and the necessity dictates development.

4. The expansion of data banks and word-processing equipment. This could permit accurate and swift compilation of the data needed to formulate PSYOPS programs. Fleeting targets of opportunity cannot be engaged, for example, because the necessary data cannot be accumulated and processed fast enough to exploit such targets. The automated battlefield is as important to psywarriors as it is to artillerymen and tankers.

5. Most of what is required lies within the realm of the possible. With appropriate emphasis by the government on PSYOPS, all should be obtainable.

Scenario: PSYOPS
in West Germany

The date is 16 July 1988. The Soviet psychological campaign against Western Europe and NATO has succeeded in driving a deep wedge into the alliance. West German confidence in the combat effectiveness of U.S. ground forces has been eroded through a subtle campaign of playing up the capability of Germany and downgrading that of the United States. Competitions in tank gunnery, for example, where U.S. troops scored poorly against other NATO tank gunners, have been used by high Western European government officials to intimate the inability of the U.S. Army to perform effectively in combat. Press reports of poor use of camouflage, cover, and concealment by U.S. Reforger units deployed yearly from the United States to Germany have been cited as examples of poor training at all echelons. Routine incidents involving misconduct of U.S. soldiers off duty have been blown out of proportion in the left-socialist newspapers in Germany. The Soviets have discreetly fanned any antagonisms that have emerged among the various NATO allies. There has developed a pervasive feeling that, if war were to come, the United States would disengage rapidly, cut its losses, retreat to "Fortress America," and rely totally on strategic nuclear options.

The Soviets have seen their campaign produce dramatic results. NATO forces have been weakened by a long series of decisions by European parliaments forcing the withdrawal of U.S. tactical nuclear forces. Countries have excluded the storing of U.S. nuclear weapons on their own soil; they have gone to a nonnuclear territorial-defense system designed to wear down the enemy in the event of an attack. Many of the NATO troops from Britain, Belgium, and the Netherlands have been withdrawn to their respective homelands.

West Germany, confident in its own ability to defend its territory against unlikely attack while reducing spending, has maintained a standing army of twelve divisions at reduced unit strengths and now relies heavily on its reserves. It has become more closely aligned with the Soviet Union in economic matters and is cooperating in joint projects with the East German government.

The U.S. government, none too happy with Western European attitudes, has stopped its POMCUS program (Prepositioned Matériel Configured in Unit Sets or equipment overseas to be used by soldiers moved to its location quickly by air transport) and has begun using equipment formerly stored in West Germany for foreign military sales. It has withdrawn a mechanized infantry division as well as its tactical nuclear weapons as part of

a budget-cutting move. The U.S. public, disgruntled over European attitudes, has pressed Congress to reduce defense spending after it became
obvious that other NATO countries, including Japan, were not reinforcing
their own defense establishments.

The United States, however, had made an important decision in early
1982 about improving its PSYWAR capability. Congress encouraged the
expansion of the effort by appropriating funds to PSYOPS activities. Civilian government agencies developed new PSYOPS programs that were integrated into a national defense strategy, and the military establishment
increased its PSYWAR capability tenfold while commanders actively prepared to employ PSYWAR techniques on the battlefield.

Such was the situation on 16 July when the Soviets, determining that
they could finally add part of Western Europe to their empire through a
quick, limited acquisition of territory, struck across the East German/West
German border. In the U.S. zone, they struck through the Fulda Gap with
motorized and tank divisions. The advancing troops punched through U.S.
defenses east of the Fulda River and are now entering the Wetterauer
corridor, a so-called bowling alley leading from Alsfeld straight through
Frankfort to the Rhine River. United States forces are falling back fast, but
in good order, as the Soviets advance down the autobahn, trying to avoid
entrapment in the Vogelsberg Mountains to the east of the Soviet invasion
route. Soviet intelligence has it on good authority that there is no threat
remaining in the Vogelsbergs but that the West Germans are moving to
attack the Soviet north flank. The Soviets can deal with the German threat,
provided that their southern flank in the Vogelsbergs remains secure. The
Soviets are confident that the U.S. forces will continue to move down the
autobahn.

The West Germans appear to be maneuvering slowly. Their two divisions, however, are being watched closely. If the Soviets get overextended,
that north flank would be in jeopardy of being smashed and the U.S. forces
would gain time to turn around to counterattack. The key remains the exposed south flank, which rests on the fringes of the Vogelsberg Mountains
and which, if the Germans are to be crushed, must be guarded.

Night falls and Soviet radio-security troops begin to pick up U.S. radio
traffic in the Vogelsbergs. Visual-imagery monitors in Soviet command
posts turn their remote electronic cameras toward the mountains. On the
survey screens appear images of U.S. attack helicopters and moving armored fighting vehicles. Soviet reconnaissance aircraft equipped with heat
sensors pick up unusually high heat readings in the extensive forests, indicat-
ing the presence of large groups of people. Then Soviet patrols report
hearing moving tanks, troops digging in, people moving about speaking
English, and sounds of firing. They also report that their forward surveillance radars are jammed.

Reports of all this activity begin to accumulate rapidly at the Soviet army front headquarters. All indications point to a U.S. armored threat, estimated at more than a reinforced brigade, assembling in the Begelsberg Mountains. That exposed Soviet flank will have to be reinforced. A rapid decision must be made because time lost will accrue to the advantage of the West Germans and U.S. forces.

The Soviets decide to launch a division attack into the Vogelsberg Mountains at dawn, drawing forces from the north flank and slowing the advance down the bowling alley. Victorious up to this point, the Soviets are confident they can destroy the threat on the southern flank, fend off the Germans to the north, and easily regain any lost momentum.

At dawn the attack is launched. Those on the Soviet north flank are on their guard, but the Germans appear far away. All eyes are focused on destroying the U.S. armored units massing on the other flank. Soviet electronic cameras mounted on drones send back images of tanks and armored personnel carriers in position and moving into attack locations. At 7 o'clock, the sun is well up but no contact has been made, although tanks have been heard and Soviet survey screens show them in large numbers. Physical evidence of U.S. troops is also found. Candy wrappers, milk cartons, message forms, and C-ration cans are picked up. Tracks of wheeled vehicles are all around, but no tank tracks are located. By 8 o'clock, the attack echelons are fully committed but nothing actually is spotted except attack helicopters firing from long range. Yet the intensity of radio transmissions among vehicles increases and large numbers of moving tracked vehicles are heard and counted on electronic detectors.

At 9 o'clock, the West Germans strike the Soviet north flank hard. The Soviets, concentrating on the events to the south, are surprised. They withdraw from their positions on the fringes of the Wetterauer corridor onto the undulating terrain. Allied aircraft appear and batter the now-exposed Soviets. The U.S. forces, having conducted a fighting withdrawal, turn around on the autobahn and reinforce the West German attack that emanates from the Taunus Mountains east of Frankfort and on the Soviet north flank.

The Soviet attack into the Begelsbergs loses direction and purpose, like a prizefighter's punch that fails to connect. The attack bogs down in confusion because there are no U.S. forces to destroy. There are no combat troops in the area because none were ever intended to be there. Instead, on that flank were a platoon of attack helicopters that engaged, harassed, and destroyed Soviet reconnaissance elements; loudspeakers that broadcast the sounds of moving vehicles, troops digging in, and other customary troop activity; signal troops with equipment to generate radio traffic and impose on Soviet surveillance equipment visual images of moving vehicles and personnel; and a deception team that brought with it battle litter and heat-generating equipment.

This new equipment was the result of applying U.S. technological talent in the PSYWAR field. The loudspeakers employed were expendable re-mote-controlled transmitters placed in various concealed locations on appropriate terrain features. Others were carried on light trucks that moved from place to place. Manipulation of the remote and mobile speakers made it possible to simulate very credible maneuvering by troops and vehicles. The signal elements carried radio-deception modules that broad-casted and received prerecorded scenarios of various levels and types of armored radio communications over a number of different frequencies. The U.S. PSYWAR troops also carried electronic visual projectors that could transmit visual images of moving vehicles, troops, and equipment. Using laser intercept equipment, it was possible to block out actual images being received by Soviet visual-survey equipment; then visual projectors superimposed movements on the Soviet receivers. The deception team distributed items that U.S. troops often discard around likely battle positions to indicate the presence of troops. They also employed a ropelike device that could be laid out over a large area and then activated to emit signals that translated into readings on heat-sensing detectors. Used particularly in wooded areas and hamlets, heating-detection equipment received a distorted view of what was actually on the ground.

These U.S. PSYOPS troops had concocted an elaborate, yet simple, scheme. When tied in with the West German counterattack plan, this PSYOP slowed down and diverted the Soviet attack for just the right amount of time. Essentially, the U.S. psywarriors were conducting an economy-of-force operation. With such PSYWAR assets integrated into a battle plan, the commander gains a potential combat multiplier that can hardly be ignored in any future conflict.

Note

1. See Peter Braestrup, *Big Story: How the American Press and Television Reported and Interpreted the Crises of Tet 1968 in Vietnam and Washington*, 2 vols. (Boulder, Colorado: Westview Press, 1977); see also Don Oberdorfer, *Tet* (New York: Avon Books, 1971).

10 Technological and Strategic Aspects of Terrorism

Yonah Alexander

Terrorism, as an expedient tactical and strategic tool of politics in the struggle for power within and among nations, is not new. From time immemorial both established regimes and opposition groups, functioning under varying degrees of stress, have intentionally used instruments of psychological and physical force, including intimidation, coercion, repression, and, ultimately, destruction of lives and property, for the purpose of attaining real or imaginary ideological and political goals.

During the past two decades, pragmatic and symbolic terrorist acts, including arson, bombing, hostage taking, kidnapping, and murder, undertaken by extremist groups for the purpose of producing pressures on governments and peoples to concede to the demands of the perpetrators, have victimized, killed, and maimed thousands of innocent civilians. These casualties include government officials, politicians, judges, diplomats, military personnel, police officers, business executives, labor leaders, university professors, college students, school children, travelers, pilgrims, and Olympic athletes.

Terrorist acts have also inflicted considerable damage on nonhuman targets. Terrorists have already attacked government offices and police stations, pubs, restaurants, hotels, banks, supermarkets, department stores, oil pipelines, storage tanks, refineries, railroad stations, air terminals, jetliners, broadcast stations, computer and data centers, and electric-power facilities.

In sum, from 1970 to 1980, 10,748 domestic and international terrorist operations have occurred, with a toll of 9,713 individuals killed, 10,177 wounded, and property damage of $701,839,542.[1] In submitting a policy statement to the Senate Foreign Relations Committee, Richard T. Kennedy, undersecretary of state for management, emphasized the worldwide menace of terrorism. The year 1980 was a record year for international terrorism; 642 persons were killed and 1,078 wounded. Among the dead were 10 U.S. citizens; 95 others were injured. Of the 760 acts of terrorism last year, 278 were directed against the U.S. people or U.S. property.[2]

So far in 1981, the high frequency of terrorism has continued. During the first eleven months of this year a total of 2,346 acts of ideological and political violence occurred throughout the world. The resurgence of German terrorist activity directed against U.S. military targets, the warning by

Armenian "suicide commando" spokesmen that their squads will strike again at Turkish interests "by any means possible," the assassination of President Sadat, and the recent Brinks robbery in Rockland County illustrate the persistence of modern terrorism.

It is safe to assume that ideological and political violence is now an established mode of conflict. Terrorism will continue and probably intensify because many of the roots of contemporary violence will remain unsolved and new causes will arise in the coming months and years of this decade. Moreover, the advances of science and technology are slowly turning the entire modern society into a potential victim of terrorism, with no immunity to the noncombatant segment of the world population or to those nations and peoples who have no direct connection to particular conflicts or to specific grievances that motivate acts of violence. This development was succinctly assessed by Justice Arthur J. Goldberg: "Modern terrorism, with sophisticated technological means at its disposal and the future possibility of access to biological, chemical, and nuclear weapons, presents a clear and present danger to the very existence of civilization itself."[3] Such an awesome eventuality forces us to think about the unthinkable with grave concern.

Technological Terrorism's Weapons, Targets, Motivation

Although, at least thus far, no catastrophic disruptions and casualties have resulted from a single and subrevolutionary terrorist attack, experts suggest that future incidents could be much more costly. First, there is the extremely difficult problem of protecting people and property. The security of a state depends on the goodwill of the people within its borders. The terrorist, however, has the advantage of surprise. Police and citizenry cannot check everyone and every place.

Second, new technology is creating new dangers. Among weapons that provide terrorists with an increasing capacity to do damage, explosives are the most reliable and popular; bombs have been used to cause property damage and occasionally to cause limited casualties. Terrorists have not used fire against people, although they have used incendiary devices to cause property damage. Terrorists have also used whatever portable and concealable weapons they have been able to obtain, suggesting that such exotic infantry weapons as antitank missiles, mortars, and flamethrowers eventually may be acquired and used by terrorists bent on mass murder and destruction. Although the historical records provide no evidence that terrorists have ever been involved in serious plots to use chemical, biological, and nuclear weapons, their future use should not be ruled out. These instruments of massive death and destruction are capable of producing from several thousand to several million casualties in a single incident and of causing governmental disruption of major proportions and widespread public panic.

To be sure, there are inherent differences among weapons of high technology with regard to their characteristics and modes of action. The resort to chemical and biological weapons is considered more achievable than the use of nuclear explosives. More specifically, there are no insurmountable technological impediments to the use of chemical agents (for example, fluoroacetates, organophosphorous compounds, and botulinum toxin). They are relatively easy to obtain; their delivery systems are manageable; and their dispersal techniques are efficient. For example, it has been reported recently that "terrorists wanting to make deadly nerve gases can still find the formulas at the British Library despite attempts by the Government to remove them from public access."[4]

Once in possession of such information, a terrorist with some technical know-how could synthesize toxic-chemical agents from raw materials or intermediates. In fact, many chemical toxins (for instance, Cobalt-60 and TEPP insecticides) are commercially available. They could be either bought or stolen.

Also, covert and overt options for dispersing chemical agents are virtually limitless, including contamination of food supplies, generation of gases in enclosed spaces with volatile agents, generation of aerosols in enclosed spaces with nonvolatile agents, and dispersal with explosives.

Notwithstanding the assumption that in the short-term future chemical and biological terrorism is more feasible technologically, nuclear terrorism—the explosion of a nuclear bomb, the use of fissionable material as a radioactive poison, and the seizure and sabotage of nuclear facilities—has received far greater public attention. As one observer remarked, "It cannot be assumed that these possibilities have been ignored by existing or potential terrorists or that they will not be considered in the future."[5]

Discussing some of the technological dimensions of the nuclear option, Theodore B. Taylor asserted that "given access to less than ten kilograms of commercial or military grade plutonium or less than 20 kilograms of highly enriched uranium . . . terrorists, or conceivably, one person working alone, could build a nuclear device with a yield likely to be greater than one kiloton of high explosive equivalent." He further stated that "the required information and materials" to make such devices "could be transportable in a small automobile or possibly by hand." He estimated that under a variety of different types of circumstances, explosion of such a device could "kill more than 50,000 people, destroy facilities worth more than one billion dollars, or force the decontamination of many square miles of land area to make it suitable for permanent human occupancy." The dangers of damage resultant from "automatically dispersing radiation and radioactive materials" should also be considered, he pointed out.[6]

Three considerations suggest the probable development of more destructive forms of violence. First, bringing terrorism under substantial control in the foreseeable future through national and international legislation as well as through increased security and enforcement measures might, in fact, hasten the advent of more daring types of terrorism. Terrorist groups tend, whenever possible, to attack so-called soft targets—those without security or the appearances thereof. This worldwide trend has been noted clearly over the 1970–1980 time span and accounts for an evolution in terrorist targeting from concentrating attacks on police and military facilities (1970–1972), to a shift toward assaulting diplomatic personnel and related activities (1973–1975), to an emphasis on business targets (1976–1980). In each stage, the primary target group selected for assault was less secure, and thus easier to attack, than the previous one. Today, however, many business firms are following the lead of police and diplomatic establishments by upgrading their security. As a result of this trend, other vulnerable targets created by technological advances of contemporary society are likely to become more attractive to terrorists.

For example, the disruptive potential manifest in attacks within the maritime environment—the navy, the merchant marine, and shipbuilding and energy industries—makes them increasingly attractive to terrorists. As Robert H. Kupperman observed: "Whether oil rigs are attacked by zealous environmental groups, or modern versions of piracy occur, ocean liners are taken hostage, or supertankers are destroyed all hell would break loose. A great deal of thought needs to be given to this subject."[7] Moreover, there is growing evidence that training for such attacks is being developed and refined by terrorist organizations. Some governments have contingency-response plans, trained personnel, and dedicated equipment. Many, including the United States, do not. In the absence of a credible response capability, the terrorists have a far better chance for success and for meeting their prime objectives of political turmoil and economic disruption. Thus, the lack of a credible response capability serves as a stimulant in the terrorist process of selecting targets of greatest vulnerability.

A second consideration for the probable shift to more destructive forms of violence is the propaganda and psychological-warfare value of such operations to terrorist groups. Since the strategy of terrorism does not prescribe instant victories over adversaries, an extension of the duration and impact of violence is indispensable. As a keen observer stated, "The media are the terrorist's best friends. The terrorist's act by itself is nothing; publicity is all."[8] It is because of this realization that terrorist operations have been broadly symbolic rather than physically oriented. In relying on immediate and extensive coverage by television, radio, and the press for the maximum amount of propagandizing and publicizing, terrorists can rapidly and effectively reach watching, listening, and reading audiences at home and abroad and thereby hope to attain essentially one of the following communications purposes: First, they can try to increase the effectiveness of their violence by creating an emotional state of extreme fear in target groups, and, thereby, ultimately alter their behavior and dispositions, or bring about a general or particular change in the structure of government or society. Second, they can try to draw the attention of the whole world to themselves forcibly and instantaneously in the expectation that these audiences will be prepared to act or, in some cases, to refrain from acting in a manner that will promote the cause the terrorists presumably represent.[9] Thus, should effective governmental and intergovernmental attempts to impose media blackouts deny terrorists their publicity objectives, they are likely to change tactics, increase their audacity, and escalate their symbol-oriented acts through high-technology weapons, if available.

Another distinct consideration that might encourage escalated terrorism is the fact that, since ideological and political violence is usually a means to an end, it progresses in proportion to the aims envisioned. If the goals are higher, then the level of terrorism must necessarily be higher. It is possible, therefore, that certain conditions could provide terrorists with an incentive to escalate their attacks dramatically. Relevant examples could include, inter alia, ethnic differences that might allow dehumanization of intended victims; religious fanaticism that might in the view of the terrorists be sanctioned by God; brutalizing effects of a lengthy struggle; and perceptions that the cause is lost and hence recourse to the so-called ultimate weapon is justified.

If these precipitating factors motivate desperate terrorist groups with technological and financial assets, they would attempt to improve its bargaining leverage by resorting to a major disruptive form of violence. Because the confrontation would be seen by them as an all-or-nothing struggle, in case of failure the terrorists would be prepared to bring devastation and destruction to many lives, including their own. Surely these terrorists would not fear deterrence or retaliation as would states.

It is obvious that the prospects of success for such a group would be improved if it had previously demonstrated high technological capabilities and a willingness to incur high risks involved in similar ventures. No rational government would lightly risk an incident with a mass-destruction potential even if it were skeptical about the credibility of the threat. The danger here is that if one subnational body succeeds in achieving its goals, then the temptation for other terrorist groups to escalate their operations may become irresistible.

In sum, having achieved considerable tactical success at least thus far, terrorists found it politically and morally expedient to restrain the level of violence. Assuming that these self-imposed restraints of terrorist groups will not persist indefinitely, we can therefore expect future incidents to be more

costly in terms of human lives and property and to have important consequences to the political, economic, and military interests of the United
States and its allies. Since more ideological and political violence can be
anticipated in the 1980s, terrorism poses many threats to contemporary
society and is likely to have a serious impact on the quality of life and on
orderly civilized existence. Perhaps the most significant dangers are those
relating to the safety, welfare, and rights of ordinary people; the stability of
the state system; the health and pace of economic development; and the
expansion or even the survival of democracy.

Strategic Aspects of Terrorism

Recognizing this menace posed by terrorism, Western nations have adopted
various approaches in their opposition to it.[10] Noncommunist countries
spend billions of dollars every year on improving security and increasing
protection for ordinary civilians and civilian facilities. Special measures have
been developed for ensuring the safety of diplomats and government officials. More than a dozen nations have set up commando units designed to
fight terrorists and rescue hostages from their grasp. Big corporations provide their top executives with instruction in protecting themselves and their
families and spend huge sums on safeguarding their investments.[11]

Despite all efforts at control, the level of terrorist violence remains high.
There are many reasons for this, including foreign support of terrorism. For
example, some terrorist groups are able to survive simply because they
enjoy the support of thousands of sympathizers within their own country and
abroad, as well as assistance from foreign states. As Brian Jenkins explained
this phenomenon, "Relatively few terrorist movements are entirely homegrown and self-sufficient, although it is equally true to say that unless a
group has roots in its home territory, it is unlikely to flourish, regardless of
foreign support. This point, however, is that foreign support does enable
such groups in many cases to increase their effectiveness and pursue their
efforts until final victory."[12]

More specifically, the key factor contributing to the high level of terrorism is the toleration, encouragement, and even the support of ideological
and political violence by some states. It is becoming increasingly clear that
ideological and political violence is, to paraphrase Karl von Clausewitz, a
continuation of policy by other means for the purpose of compelling an
adversary to submit to specific or general demands.[13] Indeed, terrorism is
escalating into a form of surrogate warfare, whereby small groups as proxies
of states are able to conduct political warfare at the national level, and
ultimately they may even succeed in altering the balance of power on the
international scale. For example, the dramatic takeover of the U.S. Em-

bassy in Tehran and its tragic consequences have illustrated that a ninth-rate nation could humiliate a superpower without an outbreak of conventional military hostilities.[14] And, more recently, the United States has been concerned with a Libyan plot to assassinate the president and other high government officials.[15]

Whereas these and similar acts of terrorism sanctioned by Middle Eastern states are generally self-evident, there is a considerable dispute among experts whether, and to what extent, terrorism is used by the Soviet Union. One school of thought asserts that the strategic thinking of Moscow calls for the manipulation of terrorism as a suitable substitute for traditional warfare, which has become too expensive and too hazardous to be waged on the battlefield. By overtly and covertly resorting to nonmilitary techniques and by exploiting low-intensity operations around the world, the Soviet Union can continue its revolutionary process against the democratic pluralism of the free world, as well as against a wider target area.[16] Another school of thought is more skeptical about direct or indirect Soviet support for terrorist groups. Although admitting that Moscow approves what it considers legitimate liberation movements, or struggles of people for their independence, the proponents of this view point out that the dynamics of modern terrorism indicate that the Soviets are ambivalent about the utility of this form of warfare.[17]

Clearly, the Reagan administration subscribes to Soviet involvement in ideological and political violence. For instance, former Secretary of State Haig charged that "Moscow continues to support terrorism and war by proxy," and "with a conscious policy, programs if you will, which foster, support, and expand international terrorism."[18] Elaborating on these assertions State Department former spokesman William Dyess listed examples of Soviet backing, including financial support, training, and arms to groups such as the Palestine Liberation Organization (PLO); surrogate use of Cuba and Libya to assist terrorist organizations; Moscow's propaganda effort aimed at national liberation movements; propaganda supportive of the hostage taking of U.S. citizens in Iran; and "general Soviet advocacy for armed struggle as a solution to regional problems" (El Salvador, Namibia), which promotes the use of terrorism and impedes peaceful resolution of conflicts. Finally, possible Soviet sponsorship of terrorism is a subject of consideration on Capitol Hill, where Senator Jeremiah Denton's Subcommittee on Security and Terrorism has held hearings.

Any analysis of this phenomenon should consider three facts: first, the scope and nature of Soviet involvement in terrorist activity—ranging from the political legitimization of violence to the supply of funds, training, arms, and other operational support—have fluctuated over the years in accordance with Moscow's changing appreciation of its vital interests. Second, the promotion of specific terrorist operations has often been no more than the

largely unintended by-product of Soviet behavior at particular stages of its
history. And finally, because of the USSR's position as an undisputed
superpower controlling, or influencing to a greater or lesser extent, the
foreign-policy conduct of other socialist countries that subscribe to its ideological line, it is not always easy to determine whether a particular terrorist
action or series of actions in one of these countries is, so to speak, homegrown, or whether it is Moscow-inspired. In this context, Bulgaria, Cuba,
Czechoslovakia, East Germany, North Korea, and Vietnam spring to mind.
The support provided by these countries to various communist and noncommunist terrorist movements in both developed and developing countries
is generally attributed to the decision makers in the Kremlin. Socialist states,
then, serve both as intermediaries between the Soviet Union and terrorists
and as essential actors in assisting, or aiding and abetting, the promotion of
ideological and political violence throughout the world.[19]

In sum, terrorism, whether backed directly or indirectly by the Soviet
Union or independently initiated, is an indispensable tactical tool in the
Soviet struggle for power and influence within and among nations. In relying
on this supplementary instrument, Moscow aims at achieving strategic ends
when the use of armed might is deemed either inappropriate or ineffective.

The broad goals that the Soviet Union hopes to achieve from terrorism
include the following:

1. Influencing developments in neighboring countries. For instance,
Moscow planted subversive communist seeds in Iran for decades, contributed by proxy to the fall of the pro-Western Shah, and is currently helping
local Marxist-Leninist factions in Iran to prepare the requisite conditions for
the overthrow of the revolutionary Islamic government.[20]

2. Drawing noncommunist states into the Soviet alliance system or at
least into the Soviet sphere of influence. For example, Moscow's activities in
Portugal—ranging from subsidizing the Communist Party to infiltrating the
administrative machinery of the country—culminated in chaos and almost
enabled the revolutionaries to seize power.[21]

3. Helping to create new states in which it will have considerable
influence as a result of its support of those countries' claims at self-determination. The Soviet assistance rendered to the PLO aims at this end.[22]

4. Weakening the political, economic, and military infrastructure of
anti-Soviet alliances such as NATO. A case in point is the Soviet support of
the Irish Republican Army (IRA). Moscow hopes that if the violence in
Ulster continues, Britain, a member of NATO, will be neutralized as a
potential adversary.[23]

5. Frustrating efforts of non-NATO countries to joining the alliance.
For instance, the Spanish government accused Moscow of fomenting Basque
terrorism, apparently for the purpose of forcing a military coup in the
country, as a reaction to this form of political violence. The assumption is

that Spain, under a dictatorial government, would not be accepted as a full-fledged member of the European community.[24]

6. Destabilizing prosperous Europe because stabilization of the West is an attraction to East Europeans and, hence, a real threat to the consolidation of the Soviet alliance system. The recent events in Poland illustrate the tangible dangers that East Europe faces, thus destabilization in West Europe will neutralize the temptation of the inhabitants of the Soviet realm.[25]

7. Initiating proxy operations in distant geographic locations where direct conventional military activities requiring long-distance logistics are impracticable, where direct United States–USSR confrontation is too risky. For instance, the Kremlin's manipulation of the South West Africa People's Organization (SWAPO) aims at setting up a Marxist regime with a pro-Soviet orientation, thus gaining vital strategic and economic advantages in this region.[26]

Russia's justification of the use of terrorism as a legitimate political tool has its ideological roots in the works of the founders of orthodox Marxism-Leninism and other prominent communist authors. To a greater or lesser extent they all advocated the employment of confrontation tactics, including terrorism, for achieving communist aims.

In *Das Kapital* Karl Marx asserted: "Force (*Gewalt*) is the midwife of an old society which is pregnant with a new one. *Gewalt* is an economic factor (Potenz)."[27] Writing in 1848, Marx expressed a strong belief in the necessity for political violence: ". . . only one means exists to shorten the bloody death pangs of the old society and the birth pains of the new society, to simplify and concentrate them—revolutionary terrorism." A year later, he predicted that "when it is our turn, we shall not hide our terrorism."[28]

This conviction persisted not only in Marx's later writings but also, with some modifications, in the works of Nikolai Lenin. He too held that the revolutionary struggle might appropriately include terrorism. Lenin and the Bolsheviks saw, for instance, the usefulness of terrorism as a tactic of disorganization of the Tsarist enemy and as a means of acquiring experience and military training.

Writing in 1906, Lenin responded to critics of this approach by asserting that "no Marxist should consider partisan warfare (including political assassination) . . . as abnormal and demoralizing."[29] Indeed, terrorism was regarded by Lenin and his successors as a part of the "proletarian revolution," but to be employed only under the direction of "the Party" and only where conditions existed for its success.

Thus, from the first Marxist-Leninist revolution against Tsarism, when more than a thousand terrorist acts were perpetrated in Transcaucasia, to the present, Moscow-oriented communism has encouraged and assisted terrorist groups that follow a strict Party line and are highly centralized.

Terrorist movements with less Party discipline and control, including
the New Left and even Trotskyists (working for the furtherance of international communism but generally hostile to the Soviet Union), have also
received some kind of support. Moreover, from considerations of political
expediency rather than ideological solidarity, a greater variety of extremist
groups that are, for example, sectarian, nationalist, separatist, or anarchist,
have frequently been supported by the Soviet Union.

True, many of these movements have adopted Marxist ideologies as a
flag of convenience. They reasoned that Marxism provides a model for
revolution against the state; denies the legal authority of the government;
establishes a successful historical example of revolution; grants some sort of
respectable international status; affords a sense of affinity with other revolutionary movements; and guarantees some assurance of direct and indirect
support by like-minded groups and socialist states. With the adoption of a
Marxist philosophy, however, some of these terrorist movements have
fallen victim to internal ideological debate, division, and conflict.[30]

Notwithstanding such ideological differences, the Soviet Union does
not hesitate to provide assistance to a multitude of groups, holding that
social discord and political turmoil in enemy territory is likely to advance
Moscow's cause. On the other hand, it would be a gross exaggeration to
assert that most terrorist operations are Soviet-sponsored. As Lord Chalfont observed correctly: "I do not believe that the forces of international
terrorism are centrally inspired or centrally controlled, but I do suggest that
when it suits their purposes, the forces of international communism will
support terror groups throughout the world."[31]

It is equally true that practical considerations have dictated that Soviet
policy toward terrorism must necessarily be adapted to changing circumstances. More specifically, Moscow has long recognized that it, too, is
vulnerable to various forms of terrorism. In fact, as early as the 1920s the
USSR was the object of terrorist attacks by White Guard émigrés, who used
neighboring countries as an operational base. Exercising its right of self-
defense, the Soviet Union sent troops into Mongolia and China to liquidate
these bands.[32] During the interwar period, Moscow supported various international efforts to eliminate certain kinds of terrorism, particularly armed
attacks.

More recently, as a superpower with political, diplomatic, economic,
and military interests all over the world, the Soviet Union has become
increasingly vulnerable to various forms of terrorism. One need only mention the hijacking of Soviet aircraft, the kidnapping and assassination of
Soviet officials and diplomats, and the bombing of Soviet embassies and
trade missions.

It is for these reasons that Moscow has adopted a more cautious and
restrained stand. Indeed, the activities of various terrorist groups, including
some that proclaim Marxist revolution to be their objective, have even been

branded as "adventurism." At times the Soviet Union has also acted in concert with capitalistic states in condemning subnational violence. It supported, for example, the U.N. Declaration on Principles of International Law Concerning Friendly Relations and Cooperation among States in accordance with the Charter of the United Nations, adopted by the General Assembly as Resolution 2625 (XXV) on 24 October 1970. This document asserts, inter alia, that terrorist and other subversive activities organized and supported by one state against another are a form of unlawful use of force.

Also, as a country with dissidents who sometimes perceive aerial hijacking as the only means of escaping to the West, the Soviet Union became a party to the 1970 Hague Convention for the Suppression of Unlawful Seizure of Aircraft and to the 1971 Montreal Convention for the Suppression of Unlawful Acts against the Safety of Civil Aviation. In addition, it has concluded bilateral agreements with Iran and Finland that provide for the return of hijackers to the state that registered the aircraft.[33]

Clearly, the Soviet Union has attempted to achieve a balance between opposition to terrorist activities to which it is itself vulnerable and support for operations that attempt to tear down the fabric of Western society and weaken other nonsocialist governments. For example, subtle psychopolitical encouragement of nonstate violence was provided by the Kremlin when it frustrated efforts by others to obtain UN backing for a comprehensive international convention for the prevention of terrorism. Admittedly, the Soviet Union stated that it opposed "acts of terrorism . . . such as the murder and kidnapping of foreign citizens and aerial hijacking,"[34] but it opposed the attempt by Western powers to give a broad interpretation to the term "international terrorism" and to extend it to cover national-liberation movements.[35]

Notwithstanding the discrepancy between the apparently antiterrorist public stance of the Soviet Union and its actions, Moscow's support of ideological and political violence in the post-Krushchev era expanded. Two major factors contributed to the Kremlin's determination to play a more active role. First, the turbulent 1960s saw some surprising developments in different quarters of the globe: the failure of the rural guerrilla movements in Latin America and the resort to urban guerrilla warfare and terrorism; the defeat of the Arabs in the June 1967 war and the subsequent rise of Palestinian terrorism; the Vietnam War and the widespread demonstrations against it; and the French students' revolt of 1968. Second, many subnational movements adopted a certain comradeship in their struggle against imperialism, capitalism, and so-called international Zionism and for the liberation of dependent peoples. As Ulrike Meinhof's "Manifesto" puts it clearly, "We must learn from the revolutionary movements of the world— the Vietcong, the Palestine Liberation Front, the Tupamaros, the Black Panthers."[36]

Capitalizing on these welcome developments on the world scene, Moscow became intimately involved with a substantial number of terrorist groups, however misguided their operations might be designated officially. Of course, as a respected member of the family of nations, the Kremlin could not openly support these movements, lest it jeopardize its peaceful relations with various countries. The policy of détente which has brought the Soviet Union considerable benefits also dictated clandestine activities.[37]

However, despite the often circumstantial nature of the evidence, it is obvious that there exists a carefully developed terrorist infrastructure that serves Moscow's foreign-policy objectives. The International Department of the Central Committee of the Communist Party of the Soviet Union (CPSU), the Soviet Security Police (KGB), and the Soviet Military Intelligence (GRU) have played a major role in this process.[38] The first of these organizations, for some time headed by Boris Ponomarev, has been the most important Soviet agency for the support of terrorism. For example, it established in Moscow the Lenin Institute (also known as the Institute of Social Studies, the Institute of Social Sciences, and the International School of Marxism-Leninism), directed by F.D. Ryshenko, with G.P. Chernikov and V.G. Pribytov as his deputies responsible for supervision of the curriculum and liaison with the Central Committee of the Party. Selected members of Western and third-world communist parties following the Soviet line have been trained there in propaganda and psychological warfare as well as in armed and unarmed combat and guerrilla warfare.

The CPSU also built Moscow's Patrice Lumumba Friendship University to serve as a base for the indoctrination and training of potential freedom fighters from the third world who are not Communist Party members. More specialized training in terrorism is provided in Baku, Odessa, Simferopol, and Tashkent.[39]

In addition, the CPSU has been involved in setting up terrorist groups for its own purposes. There is evidence, for example, that it had a hand in the establishment of the *Solidarité* and *Aide et Amitié* terrorist network. Directed by Henri Curiel, a communist Egyptian Jew who died in 1978, this organization has connections with some seventeen illegal groups, including the Popular Revolutionary Vanguard (VPR) in Brazil, the Movement of the Revolutionary Left (MTR) in Uruguay and Chile, the Quebec Liberation Front (FLQ), and the African National Congress (ANC) in South Africa.[40]

Moreover, the KGB has established at its Moscow headquarters a special section for recruiting and training terrorists. According to many sources, Carlos the "international jackal" is a product of the KGB. Originally recruited in Venezuela, Carlos studied under Colonel Victor Simonov at Camp Mantanzas outside Havana and was later sent to the Soviet Union for further training at the Patrice Lumumba Friendship University and other specialist institutions run by the KGB. It was Carlos who established liaison between Dr. Wadi Haddad, chief of Operations for the Popular Front for the Liberation of Palestine (PFLP) and the German Red Army Faction (RAF), the Japanese United Red Army (URA), the Turkish Peoples' Liberation Army (TPLA), and the Italian Red Brigades and enabled him to receive support from these bodies.[41]

Like the CPSU, both the KGB and GRU have tried to establish various terrorist movements or to gain control of existing ones. V.N. Sakharov, a defecting KGB officer, has revealed that the KGB sought to form terrorist cells in Saudi Arabia, the smaller Arab states in the Persian Gulf, and in Turkey. Similarly, there were clandestine Soviet efforts in the early 1970s to penetrate and control the Palestinian movement.[42]

Attempts have been made by KGB members to establish links with the IRA through the British and Irish communist parties and the Marxist wing of the IRA. Moreover, since the KGB is believed to control the Cuban Intelligence Service (*Direction General de Intelligencia*, or *DGI*), it is probably able to influence the activities of a number of Latin American and African Castroite terrorist groups.[43]

The work of the KGB has been greatly facilitated by Soviet client states in Africa and Asia, including Algeria, Angola, Iraq, Libya, Mozambique, South Yemen, and Syria, to name a few. In their view, ideological and political violence is a legitimate tool used by oppressed people in their struggle against tyranny, colonialism, capitalism, and Zionism. These countries have been suppliers of foods, weapons, medicine, communication facilities, intelligence information, and fake identification and passports. They have also provided terrorists with training, transit privileges, and havens. Thus, these countries have become centers for promoting terrorism in and beyond the Middle East, and thus they serve the aims of Moscow.[44]

Conclusions

In light of the foregoing, the following preliminary conclusions are offered:

1. The problem of expanding terrorism is serious and poorly understood. Furthermore, terrorism's implications, both domestic and international, have scarcely been explored. Answers to terrorist problems are elusive and need much greater attention.

2. Although predictions are hazardous, it is safe to assume that terrorism is now an established mode of conflict. It will continue to persist through the 1980s because many of the causes that motivate terrorists will remain unresolved, and new ideological and political confrontations will emerge within and among nations.

3. Terrorist operations have so far been limited in scope and have not been indiscriminate. Terrorists have desired to demonstrate their tactical capabilities rather than to commit a major violent act for its own sake.

However, technological developments offer new targets and new capabilities. Future incidents could be much more costly in terms of human lives and property.

4. The advances of science and technology are slowly turning the entire modern society into a potential victim of terrorism, with no immunity for the noncombatant segment of the world population or for those nations and peoples who have no direct connection to particular conflicts or to specific grievances that motivate acts of violence. Terrorists operating today are better organized, more professional, and better equipped than were their counterparts in the 1970s. They are likely to take greater operational risks in the 1980s, particularly if certain precipitating factors such as resurgence of religious fanaticism are present.

5. It is an established fact that terrorist groups within the direct and indirect support of the Soviet Union are becoming increasingly potent. Indeed, they are even helping to change the balance of power in the struggle between the West and the USSR. Since the lip service paid to détente and peaceful coexistence has not been accompanied by any manifest weakening of the Soviet ambition to achieve regional and global hegemony, the exploitation of terrorism as a tactical tool to disturb the status quo calls for a realistic Western strategy to deal effectively with this challenge.

6. The oceans and their related infrastructures, including critical ports, terminals, offshore facilities, vessels, and inland waterways contain significant economic and military assets. Because of their commercial, strategic, and symbolic value they are becoming increasingly vulnerable to terrorist attacks. If the maritime environment becomes a future soft target, it will have an adverse effect on the vital interests of democratic industrial countries.

7. The energy industry, its personnel, facilities, and operations are other attractive targets of terrorists. Although small-scale targeting of the system has characterized the past, vulnerability will increase as the energy-supply sources of the United States (such as oil, gas, and nuclear plants) become more concentrated.

8. Preventive and reactive programs at home and abroad are not the exclusive responsibility of either industry or government but rather a joint obligation of both. A successful antiterrorist strategy must be based on cooperation, coordination, and communication between the private and public sectors.

References

Alexander, Yonah, ed. *International Terrorism: National, Regional and Global Perspectives*. New York: Praeger, 1976.

Alexander, Yonah, Marjorie Ann Browne, and Allan S. Nanes, eds. *Control of Terrorism: International Documents*. New York: Crane Russak, 1979.

Alexander, Yonah, David Carlton, and Paul Wilkinson, eds. *Terrorism: Theory and Practice*. Boulder, Colo.: Westview Press, 1979.

Alexander, Yonah, and Charles Ebinger, eds. *Political Terrorism and Energy: The Threat and Response*. New York: Praeger, 1981.

Alexander, Yonah, and Seymour M. Fingers, eds. *Terrorism: Interdisciplinary Perspectives*. New York and London: John Jay Press and McGraw Hill, 1977.

Alexander, Yonah, and Robert Friedlande, eds. *Self Determination: National, Regional, and Global Perspectives*. Boulder, Colo.: Westview Press, 1980.

Alexander, Yonah, and John Gleason, eds. *Behavioral and Quantitative Perspectives on Terrorism*. Elmsford, N.Y.: Pergamon Press, 1981.

Alexander, Yonah, and Allan S. Nanes, eds. *The United States and Iran: A Documentary History*. Washington, D.C.: University Publications of America, 1980.

Bell, J. Boyer. *Terror out of Zion*. New York: St. Martin's, 1976.

———. *On Revolt*. Cambridge, Mass.: Harvard University Press, 1976.

Carlton, David, and Carlo Schaerf, eds. *International Terrorism and World Security*. London: Croom Helm, 1975.

Clutterbuck, Richard. *Kidnap and Ransom: The Response*. London and Boston: Faber and Faber, 1978.

Crelinsten, Ronald D., and Denis Szabo, eds. *Terrorism and Criminal Justice*. Lexington: Lexington Books, D.C. Heath and Company, 1978.

Elliot, John D., and Leslie K. Gibson, eds. *Contemporary Terrorism: Selected Readings*. Gaithersburg, Md.: International Association of Chiefs of Police, 1978.

Kupperman, Robert H., and Darrell Trent. *Terrorism: Threat, Reality, Response*. Stanford: Hoover Institution Press, 1979.

Laqueur, Walter. *Terrorism*. Boston: Little, Brown and Co., 1977.

Livingston, Maurius H., Lee Bruce Kress, and Marie G. Wanek, eds. *International Terrorism in the Contemporary World*. Westport: Greenwood Press, 1978.

Possony, Stefan T., and Francis Bouchey. *International Terrorism—the Communist Connection*. Washington, D.C.: American Council for Freedom, 1978.

Rapoport, David C., and Yonah Alexander., eds. *The Morality of Terrorism: Religious and Secular Justifications*. Elmsford, N.Y.: Pergamon Press, 1981.

———. *The Rationalization of Terrorism*. Washington, D.C.: University Publications of America, 1981.

Wilkinson, Paul. *Political Terrorism*. London: Macmillan Press, 1974.
———. *Terrorism and the Liberal State*. New York: John Wiley and Sons, 1977.

Notes

1. These statistics are derived from the information provided by Risks International, a private consulting firm. The 10,748 terrorist incidents are based on the following categories: (1) kidnapping, (2) hijacking, (3) assassination, (4) maiming, (5) attacks against facilities, and (6) bombing. Information contained in this data base is derived from foreign and U.S. government reports, police records, and the foreign and English language press. Data relating to damages, persons killed and wounded, and hostages taken are dependent on the accuracy of such reporting. In many nations, governmental policies preclude the publication of such data. Accordingly, the figures cited for these categories can give only a relative approximation of actual human and material losses.

2. "International Terrorism," *Current Policy*, no. 285, U.S. Department of State, 10 June 1981.

3. Foreword in Yonah Alexander, *International Terrorism: National, Regional and Global Perspectives* (New York: Praeger, 1976).

4. *The Observer* (London), 19 November 1978.

5. Brian Jenkins, "The Potential for Nuclear Terrorism" (Santa Monica, Calif.: Rand Corporation, May 1977) and "Will Terrorists Go Nuclear?" (Santa Monica, Calif.: Rand Corporation, 1975), p. 541.

6. Theodore B. Taylor, "Weapons of Mass Destruction as Possible Tools for Terrorism," May 21, 1981, mimeo. unpublished.

7. "Comments on Technological Vulnerabilities" (Paper read at the International Conference on Legal Aspects of Terrorism), (Washington, D.C.: Department of State, December 1978), p. 104.

8. Walter Laqueur, "The Futility of Terrorism," *Harper's* 252 (March 1976): 104.

9. For detailed discussions on this subject see Yonah Alexander, "Terrorism, the Media and the Police," *Police Studies* (June 1978): 45–62, and "Communication Aspects of International Terrorism," *International Problems* 16, (spring 1977): 55–60; and Yonah Alexander and Seymour Maxwell Finger, *Terrorism: Interdisciplinary Perspectives*, (New York: McGraw Hill, 1977), pp. 141–208: and "Terrorism and the Media," *Terrorism: An International Journal* 12 (1979): 55–137.

10. See, for instance, Yonah Alexander, Marjorie Ann Browne, and Allan S. Nanes, eds., *Control of Terrorism: International Documents* (New

Technological and Strategic Aspects of Terrorism 151

York: Crane, Russak, 1979), and Robert H. Kupperman, *Facing Tomorrow's Terrorist Incident Today* (Washington, D.C.: Law Enforcement Assistance Administration, 1977).

11. *Terrorism and Business: Conference Report* (Washington, D.C.: Center for Strategic and International Studies, July 1978). See also, Yonah Alexander and Robert A. Kilmarx, eds., *Political Terrorism and Business: The Threat and Response* (New York: Praeger, 1979).

12. See Brian Jenkins, *High Technology Terrorism and Surrogate War: The Impact of New Technology on Low-Level Violence* (Santa Monica, Calif.: Rand Corporation, November 1975), p. 2.

13. Karl von Clausewitz, *On War* (London and Boston: Routledge and Kegan Paul, 1968), 1: 2,23.

14. See John Collins, "Definitional Aspects" in *Political Terrorism and Energy: The Threat and Response*, Yonah Alexander and Charles Ebinger, eds., (New York: Praeger, 1981), p. 6; and Ray S. Cline's Foreword, in *Behavioral and Quantitative Perspectives on Terrorism*, Yonah Alexander and John Gleason, eds., (Elmsford, N.Y.: Pergamon, 1981).

15. *Washington Post*, 13 October 1981.

16. The major recent study representing this view is Claire Sterling, *The Terror Network* (New York: Reader's Digest Press/Holt, Rinehart and Winston, 1981).

17. See, for instance, *Washington Post* 23 September 1981.

18. *Washington Star*, 29 January 1980, and 30 January 1980. See also, *Washington Post*, 7 February 1981 and 15 April 1981.

19. For some details on assistance given to terrorists by various governments in recent years see, for instance, *Congressional Record* 123 (9 May 1977): S7253.

20. *New York Times*, 16 June 1979. See also James A. Bill, *The Politics of Iran* (Columbus, Ohio: Charles E. Merrill, 1972) and Marvin Zonis, *The Political Elites of Iran* (Princeton, N.J.: Princeton University Press, 1971).

21. On recent developments see "Europe," *Risks International Report*, Alexandria, Va., February 1979, pp. 85–87. See also Michael Harsgor, *Portugal in Revolution*, Washington Paper #32 (Beverly Hills, Calif.: Sage, 1976).

22. *New York Times*, 11 June 1979.

23. See, for instance, Bowyer J. Bell, *The Secret Army: A History of the IRA* (Cambridge, Mass.: Harvard University Press, 1976).

24. Ernest Halperin, "Patron States and State-Sponsored Terrorism," May 1981, mimeo.

25. Ibid.

26. See, for example, Muriel Horrell, *Terrorism in Southern Africa* (Johannesburg: South Africa Institute of Race Relations, 1968).

27. Karl Marx, *Das Kapital* (Berlin: Dietz Verlag, 1962), reprint, p. 779.

28. Arnold Kunzli, *Karl Marx, Eine Psychographie* (Vienna, Frankfurt, Zurich: Europa Verlag, 1966), pp. 703, 712 and 715.

29. V.I. Lenin, "Partisan Warfare," reproduced in F.M. Osanka, ed., *Modern Guerilla Warfare* (New York: Free Press 1966), p. 68. See also, V.I. Lenin, *Selected Works, vol. 3, Left-Wing Communism—An Infantile Disorder* (Moscow: Progress Publishers, 1975), p. 301.

30. Yonah Alexander, "The Various Ideologies and Forms of International Terrorism" (Paper prepared for the International Scientific Conference on Terrorism, Berlin 14–18 November 1978).

31. Lord Chalfont, "Freedom in Danger: The External and Internal Threat," *Atlantic Community Quarterly*, 14 (fall 1976): 234–235.

32. See, for example, I. Brownlie, *International Law and the Use of Force by States* (Oxford: Oxford University Press, 1963), pp. 241–242.

33. For text, see Yonah Alexander, Marjorie Ann Browne, and Allan S. Nanes, eds., *Control of Terrorism: International and Local Control* (Dobbs Ferry, N.Y.: Oceana Publications, 1979).

34. United Nations General Assembly, 27th Session (A/C 6/SR 1389), 13 December 1972, pp. 4–5.

35. United Nations General Assembly, (A/AC 160/I Addendum 1), 12 June 1973, Ad Hoc Committee on International Terrorism, 16 July- 10 August 1973, p. 26.

36. See, for example, Ray S. Cline, *"Soviet Policy in a Global Perspective: Implications for Western Policy"* (Washington, D.C.: Center for Strategic and International Studies, Monograph, 25 March 1975).

37. Brian Crozier, *Testimony before the Subcommittee to Investigate the Administration of the Internal Security Act of the Committee on the Judiciary*, U.S. Senate, 94th Cong. 1st session, part 4, 14 May 1975; *Daily Telegraph* (London), 16 July 1979; *New York Times* 2 November 1980 and 8 March 1981; unpublished statement to the Senate Subcommittee on Security and Terrorism by Arnaud de Borchgrave (23 April 1981); and Israeli Defense Force (IDF) "PLO Ties with the U.S.S.R. and other Eastern Bloc Countries," *Israeli Defense Forces Journal*, September 1981.

38. *Annual of Power and Conflict 1973–1974* (London: Institute for the Study of Conflict, 1974), pp. 230–258.

39. *Le Point*, 21 June 1976. See also, John Barron, *KGB: The Secret Work of Soviet Secret Agents* (New York: Bantam Books, 1974), pp. 76–77.

40. See, for example, Colin Smith, *Carlos: Portrait of a Terrorist* (London: Sphere Books Limited, 1976), *Baltimore Sun*, 14 March 1980.

41. The Russian Connection (film by the Canadian Broadcasting Corporation and the Public Broadcasting Service, 1979); and *Wall Street Journal*, 4 January 1980; Sterling, *The Terror Network*.

42. *Christian Science Monitor*, 14–15 March 1977; *Washington Post*, 26 March 1980; and *Wall Street Journal* 15 April 1980.

43. For details, see Lester A. Sobel, *Palestinian Impasse: Arab Guerillas and International Terror* (New York: Facts on File, 1977).

Scenario I: Maritime Terrorism

Maritime terrorism is not new in the history of man's inhumanity to man. Piracy, for instance, was practiced by the ancient maritime nations of Greece, Rome, and Carthage. The Vikings and the Moors terrorized the high seas. The European maritime states, between the sixteenth and late eighteenth centuries, found it expedient to employ pirates, or privateers, as instruments of national policy. And in the early 1800s, the United States and maritime European states operating in the Mediterranean paid tribute to the piratical Barbary states of North Africa to prevent their commercial shipping from being plundered.

Although piracy ended in the aftermath of the War of 1812, it has reemerged in the past decade.[1] The historical record of the 1970s and the first twenty months of this decade contain only isolated terrorist incidents in the maritime environment. For example, in July 1979 pirates took over a Thai tanker after it left Bangkok and siphoned 80,000 gallons of diesel fuel into a waiting pirate tanker. Similarly, in 1980, a U.S.-flagged very large cargo container (VLCC) at anchorage in the Singapore Straits was boarded via the anchor chain by two assailants who accosted the master in his cabin.

Also, in 1981, Mobil, Shell, and British Petroleum have confirmed that some of their oil tankers have been targets of pirates in the Phillips Channel off Singapore. The seriousness of the problem is underscored by the fact that the General Council of British Shippers asked the Singapore government for assistance. The latter, in turn, has appealed to Interpol for help.

It is noteworthy that only recently it became known that the Thai Navy, with U.S. aid, began a program of air and sea operations in efforts to seize Thai pirates said to be robbing and raping large numbers of Vietnamese boat people in the Gulf of Thailand.

Commenting on the implications of modern piracy, one reporter suggested that the chances to conduct raids on cargo vessels in Southeast Asia may illuminate the consequences of a more serious development—"the hijacking of an oil tanker by an organization with political, rather than commercial motivations."[2]

Indeed, those charged with the security of maritime assets at home and abroad face a growing list of adversaries, from modern pirates to foreign agents to ideological and political groups. Although the practice of domestic and international terrorism has become all too familiar, acts against maritime objects are relatively few and usually not well publicized.

However, some one hundred planned and actual attacks directed against maritime objects or activities have been recorded in the past two decades.[3]

All sections of the industry, including personnel, facilities and operations, the navy, and other related maritime interests have been affected. The spectrum of incidents, both successful and unsuccessful, covers ten areas of activities:

1. smuggling of arms via seas
2. threats
3. plots
4. attacks on maritime facilities and operations onshore and offshore, including inland waters and rivers
5. political mutiny at sea
6. hijacking
7. sea-launched attacks on civilian populations and property bombing, and sinking of merchant marine ships
8. disappearance of supertankers in mysterious circumstances
9. attacks on naval personnel and property

In sum, the variety of tactics utilized by revolutionary and subrevolutionary groups is, indeed, impressive and is cause for concern. Most merchant vessels operate in international waters with little or no protection from potential terrorist attacks. Shipping companies obviously do not wish to publicize these vulnerabilities, but the likelihood of such terrorist or hijacking incidents will increase in the 1980s.

Palestinian Tactical Capabilities

Since the 1970s, a number of terrorist organizations (namely Fatah and the Popular Front for the Liberation of Palestine) have established naval units whose purpose was to impart the necessary know-how for the perpetration of terrorist infiltration and the smuggling of arms into Israel from the sea. These naval units consisted of Palestinians who had been employed as fishermen and divers. The Fatah is the largest and most prominent terrorist organization in the field of naval activity. It possesses a naval unit established in the 1970s. Also, the Black September group was active overseas.

The terrorist naval units are equipped with a wide variety of material. Most of their equipment comes from Arab states. However, some of it is acquired on the world market. An additional source of acquisition is self-production, and for this purpose the various terrorist organizations maintain workshops. This equipment includes speedboats (which are capable of attaining a speed of more than 20 knots per hour), a large number of rubber dinghies, surfboards, and even inflated air mattresses. Their naval material likewise contains 500–600 mother ships, diving equipment, and sea mines. Infiltrators from the sea are armed with standard ground-force weapons. There have been some attempts to improve the material at their disposal, and there have been cases in which terrorist vessels were equipped with antitank weapons. There has likewise been a case in which terrorists attempted to launch Katyusha rockets at the Israeli coast via vessels equipped with timing devices. The attempt was thwarted. The terrorists are instructed in the naval arts in Syria, Lebanon, and Iraq. However, most training in this domain takes place in Lebanon.

The following discussion describes in some detail how several Palestinian groups have attempted to exploit the maritime environment to achieve limited or broad goals.

Fatah

In September 1978, the sinking by the Israeli Navy of an explosive-laden freighter foiled a sensational Al Fatah terrorist scheme. The terrorists planned to sail the vessel into the port of Eilat, fire forty-two 122mm rockets at the port's tank facilities, and then ram the 660-ton boat, crammed with more than 3 tons of explosives, onto the crowded beach.

Similarly, in April 1979, the Navy seized a cargo ship carrying six Fatah terrorists headed for a mission in Israeli population centers. Although the vessel flew a Cypriot flag, it was owned by the Fatah.

Finally, in June 1980, the Israeli Navy thwarted a terrorist attack off the coast of Achziv. When the Israeli patrol vessel came within 200 meters of the fiberglass boat, one of the three terrorists aboard fired a RPG rocket at the Israeli craft, whose crew immediately returned the fire. The three Fatah members were killed.

Black September Organization

On 5 August 1972 the Black September Organization set afire an oil-storage facility in Trieste because it supplied oil to West Germany and Austria, both of which supported Israel. The fire caused an estimated $7 million in damage. A statement distributed by the Palestinian News Agency reported:

> This operation was carried out in accordance with the Black September organization's policy of dealing blows to the enemies of the Palestinian revolution, in continuation of the operations carried out by the organization to strike at the imperialists' interests which support Zionism—most important of which were operations carried out against West Germany and

other European countries—and in confirmation of the Palestinian masses' ability to challenge and strike at the imperialist interests effectively.

The Trieste oil facility received oil from the Middle East and repumped it to West Germany and Austria through the Trans-Alpine pipeline. Warrants were issued for the arrests of Mohammed Boudia, who led the attack, another Algerian, two French women, and Ludovico Codella, an Italian who was ultimately arrested. The rest escaped to France. Italy was never able to produce enough evidence to back an extradition request.

Popular Front for the Liberation of Palestine

In May 1969, members of the Popular Front for the Liberation of Palestine (PFLP) placed an explosive charge in the Baniyas River, heavily damaging a section of the Trans-Arabian Pipeline, which is owned by ARAMCO, in the Golan Heights. The pipeline provides millions of dollars in royalties and transit fees to Saudi Arabia, Jordan, Syria, and Lebanon. The flow of oil through the 1,000-mile pipeline, which connects Dharan, Saudi Arabia to Sidon, Lebanon, was blocked because of the resultant fire. A PFLP spokesman claimed that his group had intended to pollute water supplied to Israeli settlements and fisheries in Hutch Valley. Oil was reported to be seeping into the northern part of the Sea of Galilee, and oil slicks were seen on the Jordan River. The Israelites managed to contain the blaze. In August of that year, another squad of the PFLP threw a hand grenade into a London office of Israel's Zim Line, wounding an employee and damaging property. In June 1971, PFLP terrorists carried out an assault on the Liberian-registered oil tanker *Coral Sea*. Terrorists on a speedboat fired ten bazooka shells at the tanker, causing some damage but no casualties. The attack occurred in the Strait of Bab el Mandeb at the entrance to the Red Sea. It was intended to deter tankers from using the Israeli port of Eilat on the Red Sea.

In January 1974, two Japanese belonging to the radical United Red Army (URA) and two Arabs of the PFLP tried to blow up a Shell Oil Company refinery in Singapore, then seized eight hostages aboard a ferry-boat and threatened to kill themselves and the hostages unless they were given safe passage to an Arab country. The terrorists had tried to blow up three oil-storage tanks belonging to Shell Eastern Petroleum, a Shell International company, but only succeeded in setting one on fire.

Background to Scenario I

It is April 1982. Having succeeded in reestablishing control over the whole of Sinai in line with the Camp David accords, Egypt again pressed her counterpart to address the Palestinian issue. This demonstrated to the world that Egypt's concerns were not totally self-centered and, to a large extent, coincided with common Arab interests. The United States backed Mubarak's insistence that new Israeli West Bank settlements, harsh policies by Israel against the Palestinians, and continued military intervention in Lebanon could only intensify Palestinian antagonism of the Israeli state.

Nonetheless, obstacles to further compromise could not help but mount. President Reagan's May invitation for mediation produced no more than a reiteration of earlier positions. An escalating cycle of violence and counter-violence between West Bank militants led to the postponement of autonomy talks in June and their suspension by Cairo in mid-August. Despite a cursory resumption of talks fostered by U.S. representatives, it remained clear that unless the United States further pressured Israel to relax its policies vis-à-vis the West Bank, the diplomatic impasse would continue. This problem was illustrated once again when Prime Minister Begin, in a Jewish New Year interview in September, asserted that Israel's intention is "not to create a state for a stateless people, because the Palestinians have their state and their country is now called Jordan."

Clearly, this disposition of Israel reinforced in the Palestine Liberation Organization (PLO) a growing feeling of desperation. Despite the fact that, on the diplomatic level, recognition of the PLO as worthy of international status was gaining momentum, radical groups once again intensified their attacks against Israeli targets at home and abroad. Moreover, an abortive assassination attempt was directed against Arafat, "who left the proper course of the armed struggle," in October. The Al-Assifa extremist group, led by Abu-Nidal, who split from the PLO and accused Arafat of being too moderate in his stand against Israel, claimed responsibility for the attack.

A new extremist coalition of Palestinian revolutionaries, disappointed that Saudi Arabia was unwilling to use the oil-embargo weapon against Western interests because of gratitude to the United States for approving the AWACS sale in the previous year, has emerged. Their target is Western oil interests in the Persian Gulf.

The Incident

On the night of 29 November 1982, the thirty-fifth anniversary of the U.S. partition resolution in Palestine, several maritime squads calling themselves the Secret Army for the Liberation of Palestine (a previously unknown group), seize "X" and "Y," two Liberian-registered loaded supertankers of 350,000 tons each. Both ships are hijacked in the Persian Gulf between Oman's Musandam Peninsula and the Iranian coast in the Strait of Hormuz.

Once on board, the hijackers—possibly with the help of some collaborators among the crews—ring the ships with explosives equipped with time-delay fuses. In their communication the attackers threaten to blow up the "X" and "Y" if their demands are not met within forty-eight hours. They also threaten to sink the ships if they are approached by sea or overflown.

The hijackers are not responding to any attempts to communicate with them. The PLO disclaims any responsibility for the incident.

The Demands

The Secret Army for the Liberation of Palestine communicates press releases to major news agencies at UN Headquarters in New York City, which include the following messages:

> Members of the United Nations—We, the Secret Army for the Liberation of Palestine, speak for ourselves only, but since the PLO embodies the institutionalization of the hopes and aspirations of Palestinians for self-determination, statehood, and human dignity, any Palestinian who shares in these aspirations can, in a sense, be said to be a representative of the PLO.
>
> Let us underscore the following points:
>   1. Palestinian reality is defined by three facts: dispossession, exile, and occupation.
>   2. After 35 years, Palestinians are a cohesive, well-organized, determined group. Clearly, they will not just disappear as some have hoped.
>   3. Israel is not the homeland of the Jews or of Zionism which, along with Nazism, is regarded as a threat to mankind.
>   4. Palestinian demands are identical with those of all peoples seeking liberation. These demands consist of the right to self-determination, including the right to independent political existence, and the right to repatriation or compensation as internationally prescribed by consecutive UN resolutions since 1949.
>   5. The right of self-determination, in the nationalist Arab sense, means total liberation and the restoration of all the national and historic rights of the Palestinian people in their country. The right of the Palestinian people to self-determination, in its overall meaning, is manifested in the exposure and destruction of the Zionist idea and of Israel, which is a product of this idea.
>   6. The Camp David Accords, concluded without the Palestinians' agreement or participation, have incorporated the Zionist aggressors' demeaning autonomy plan, which the Palestinians reject out of hand. At the present stage, the imperialist offensive against the region has intensified by presenting a variety of settlement schemes. We believe that resistance to these schemes is the duty of all Arab Liberation forces.
>   7. The creation of a mini-Palestinian state including the West Bank and the Gaza Strip will solve the problem of only one million Palestinians out of three million. The only solution for these people is to return to their country and not to the West Bank.

8. The only way to achieve our aim is through the armed popular revolution. The armed revolution of the Palestinian Arab people is a decisive factor in the battle of liberation and the liquidation of the Zionist presence. This struggle will not stop until the Zionist entity is liquidated and Palestine is liberated.

9. The liberation of Palestine and putting an end to Zionist penetration—political, economic, military, and propaganda—into Moslem states is one of the duties of the Moslem world. We must fight a Holy War (*Jihad*) against the Zionist enemy, who covets not only Palestinians but the whole Arab region.

10. We take a firm and clear stand against imperialism and its interests in the region, and affirm that imperialism—primarily U.S. imperialism—is our principal enemy. Therefore the interests of the United States in the area should be crushed, and any thought that that country could be neutral in our conflict with the Zionist enemy should be abolished and rejected.

It is against this background and aims of the Palestinian revolutionary forces that we threaten to blow up the two vessels in the Strait of Hormuz if our demands are not met within forty-eight hours. The demands are two: first, that Israel recognize the PLO as "the sole representative of the Palestinian people," and second, that the UN General Assembly revoke its 29 November 1947 Partition Resolution and recommend the establishment of a secular democratic state in Palestine in which Moslems, Christians, and Jews will live in peace side by side.

There is no room for negotiation and compromise because this would mean concessions to the enemy of mankind. If our demands are met, control of the supertankers will be returned to their owners. Let us conclude with our slogan:

YES to the prolonged battle of the nation;

YES to retaining the Arab rifle;

YES to opening the borders for Arab revolutionaries to wage battle against the Zionist entity;

YES to the unification of the progressive Arab forces and the Palestinians.

Notes

1. For a recent article on this subject see Alfred P. Rubin, "Terrorism and Piracy: A Legal View," *Terrorism: An International Journal* 3 (1979): 117–130. See, also, Jeffrey St. John, "History and the High Seas: Moral Defenses for a Maritime Civilization," 22 September 1981 (mimeo).

2. *Christian Science Monitor*, 18 September 1981.

3. Sources for information on piracy, as well as on maritime-related terrorist incidents, are derived from various data bases including the Center for Strategic and International Studies, the State University of New York's Institute for Studies in International Terrorism, the Rand Corporation,

various studies—for example, Edward F. Mickolus, *Transnational Terror-ism: A Chronology of Events 1969–1979* (Westport, Conn.: Greenwood, 1980)—and different media reports.

Scenario II:
Electric-Utilities
Terrorism

Private and state entities engaged in the energy effort have been particularly exposed to terrorist attacks. As one observer explained, "Utilities are a highly symbolic target because they represent the capitalist system. A point-by-point defense of utilities is difficult, and they do provide a simple way to disrupt a large part of modern life. In addition, their public image is poor and they are highly vulnerable, especially during a recession."[1]

Since 1970, there have been over 150 attacks directed against electrical utilities in the United States and abroad. Power lines, electric-power substations, electrical-control systems, transmission towers, power facilities, electrical-transmission lines, electrical installations, utility towers, and power-line poles have been targeted from California to the Philippines, from France to Colombia. Approximately 40 percent of all utilities attacked from 1970 to 1980 were electrical. Transmission-line structures, for instance, are particularly vulnerable because they are often located in isolated areas where terrorist groups can attack them with ease.

The threat in the United States was assessed recently by an energy analyst who observed that "the development of a [U.S.] national power grid [connecting eastern, central, and western transmission systems] may simplify the terrorist's objective of identifying the critical transmission links and destroying them. . . . A key terrorist target would be to identify the transmission line interconnecting points which now enhance the system's power transfer capability."[2]

One of the most active groups in the United States involved in attacking electrical utilities is the New World Liberation Front. For example, in March 1978 it bombed a Pacific Gas and Electrical Company substation in a San Francisco suburb, causing more than $1 million in damage. More recently, in September 1980, the group exploded a bomb outside the same utility in Berkeley.

Although no major disruptions to the electrical industry have occurred so far, incidents abroad have been more costly. One dramatic example of the industry's vulnerability was the September 1978 terrorist operation in the Philippines. The Moro National Liberation Front blacked out almost one-half of Mindoro as a result of attacks on ten power facilities owned by the government. And, in November 1980, elements of the Movement of the Revolutionary Left (MIR) or the newer Militias of Popular Resistance bombed nine high-tension towers carrying power between Santiago, Valparaiso, and Vina del Mar and other high-tension towers near San Bernardo

(Chile). These bombings were particularly significant: they cut off power to a substantial portion of Santiago, Valparaiso, and Vina del Mar. According to police reports, an estimated thirty terrorists participated in the operations. As a tactic, the destruction of electrical-power lines and substations appears to be gaining favor among Latin American revolutionary groups, with similar activities in El Salvador, Colombia, Guatemala, and Peru.

Damage to utilities and their transmission systems does not necessarily result in long-run reduction in electric-power generation. But damage to any part of the system can be extremely costly to repair. Moreover, the psychological costs of terrorist propaganda are even higher. Consider, for example, the April 1980 Puerto Rican blackout. An explosion in the Palo Seco electrical plant knocked out the island's entire electrical-distribution system. It cost millions of dollars in damage-repair and business losses. Puerto Rican separatists claimed credit for this incident.

Background

It is the summer of 1983. For the past several years, it has been evident that the United States is becoming more terrorist-prone. This is in part because the U.S. public has been disillusioned about the effectiveness of the system in meeting its needs, more burdened by economic and social strains, more distrustful of authority and leadership, and less committed to civic responsibility and public duty.

As early as 1981, there were many symptoms of the increasing fragility of the social fabric of the United States. For example, there were signs of erosion of the coalitions of groups and interests that had contributed to compromise, stability, and tranquility. There developed powerful grassroots opposition to high taxes that were appropriated to meet the needs of the less advantaged. The requirements of larger defense budgets, justified by the burgeoning Soviet military threat and resurgent Soviet expansionism, came at a time when antiinflation policy dictated fiscal constraint. Other programs thus were faced with larger cutbacks. Work stoppages and strikes by increasingly organized and more militant worker groups were already on the rise. Growing prospects of insolvency of urban centers were countered by the growing unwillingness of Congress to assume the added burden.

Writing in *The Washington Post* on 30 October 1981, Carl T. Rowan predicted that the social and economic policies of the Reagan administration would, out of growing public desperation, "create more radicals and terrorists, of every race, than anyone ever dreamed possible in [The United States]."

It is not surprising, therefore, that highly militant groups intensified their attacks against the U.S. establishment. Indeed, a poll commissioned by

The New York Times in spring 1983 reveals that 48 percent of unemployed youth believe that violence is sometimes justified to bring about political and economic change.

In brief, conditions were merging and taking root that led to more explosive forms of illegal and terrorist activity by individuals or groups in response to several crises including uncontrolled inflation, a deep recession, and serious Soviet military challenges abroad. Tears in the social fabric seemed to provide perhaps unprecedented challenges to the stability of the U.S. political system. It has become increasingly difficult for the U.S. government to cope with such threats without violating its fundamental principles and values. But the U.S. public has become less tolerant of extralegal intrusions and constraints since the Vietnam war and the Watergate crisis.

One of the most active groups in the United States during this period is the New World Liberation Front (NWLF). Based in the San Francisco area since August 1974, it grew from a predecessor organization known as the Americans for Justice. The NWLF, a leftist organization, has adopted techniques similar to those of the Weather Underground—bombings accompanied by warnings and communiques. Its operations over the years have been directed against public utilities, business firms, foreign diplomatic establishments, and federal, state, and local facilities.

As a radical Marxist organization, it published in its formative years the popular *Minimanual of the Urban Guerrilla* by the late Brazilian revolutionary Carlos Marighella. Adopting the ideology of its revolutionary mentors, NWLF is committed to the destruction of the U.S. capitalist system and dedicated to support "oppressed peoples" and a "class war toward a classless society that is firmly controlled by the people." Because it advocates the use of violence to achieve political and economic goals, NWLF supports the activities of other U.S. revolutionary movements. It also expresses its support for foreign revolutionaries, including the Vietnamese and the Palestinians. For many years NWLF has acted as an umbrella organization for other terrorist movements in California, such as the remnants of the Symbionese Liberation Army (SLA), the Chicano Liberation Army, and the Red Guerrilla Family. It has also maintained contact with the Black Liberation Army and the Weather Underground.

Organizationally, the NWLF functions on two levels. First, its combat units, or "peoples forces," are small quasi-military covert squads acting under direction from a central command. Its overt propaganda and administrative structure, the People's Information Relay (PIR-1), is involved in agitational, press, and publication activities.

Although its membership in the 1970s was estimated to consist of not more than several dozen hard-core activists, by 1983 it has successfully recruited many more operatives. Apparently, because of the deep economic and political disappointment in the Reagan administration, a growing number of well-educated left-wing (for example, anticorporate and antinuclear) environmentalist individuals have joined NWLF. As a result, its bombing operations have been over 95 percent successful, whereas in the 1970s the rate of success was only 83 percent.

This sophistication and expertise can be attributed to other factors. First, more elaborate and accurate information on explosive use of dynamite and Tovex Gel is provided in NWLF publications and covert-training courses. For example, instruction is given on how to achieve the electrical detonation of a device even when using a fuse-type blasting cap or on how a few dozen pounds of high explosives can be placed at structurally critical points of major government buildings. A second factor is the infiltration by NWLF members of various target-facility staffs and the presence of former employees among the group's membership. For instance, several of the attacks for which NWLF claimed responsibility clearly demonstrated inside knowledge of the target system at different levels.

Indeed, during June and July of 1983, dozens of bombings of Pacific Gas and Electric (PG&E) and other utilities have been hit in California, Colorado, Nevada, Oregon, and Washington State. High-tension power lines and electrical substations have been destroyed, resulting in blacking out sections of cities and towns for short periods and causing damage exceeding several million dollars.

The Incident

On 5 August 1983 at 10 A.M., President Reagan arrives at San Francisco International Airport. He is scheduled to deliver several campaign speeches at the University of California at Berkeley at noon and, later, at other locations in the Bay area.

During the previous night in the Oakland vicinity, some twenty PG&E power poles are cut partway through and power cables are severed. A communique from NWLF is received by major television networks and press offices in California that morning as the president's jet is landing. The communique reads:

> To the capitalist president, the corporate vampires, and the oppressed people of the United States.
>
> The capitalist president is in the Bay area to deliver major campaign speeches for his reelection. He is seeking a second term in office at a time when our social programs have been cut to the bone, when unemployment is already 10 percent, inflation has reached 20 percent, and interest rates are a staggering 22 percent.

We are determined that this intolerable situation will be reversed. For many years we have served the needs of the poor and oppressed of the United States as well as those "have nots" in Latin America, the Middle East, Asia, and Africa. We shall continue to conduct a class war toward a free, classless society that is controlled firmly by the people. We will not submit to the corporate vampires, who loot and plunder in the name of justice, who feed their greed addiction with billions of more dollars of blood money for their coffers.

Last night we initiated a number of operations directed against PG&E, the parasite corporation that feeds off the misery of the poor, constantly raising utility rates. Tonight at midnight we threaten to cause a total blackout in the San Francisco metropolitan area by destroying a number of vital substations. Attached is a detailed map of the San Francisco power grid. As all know, we have demonstrated our technical capabilities over the past twenty years. Have no doubt about our determination and know-how.

We are prepared, however, to cancel our most sophisticated operation if only one demand is accepted by 11:30 P.M., namely, that the capitalist president, together with the moguls and barons of PG&E and other major utilities in the West, appear on the major television network to make the following joint announcement: "The U.S. government and all U.S. utilities in the West are committed to provide free utilities for senior citizens, unemployed, and poor people as of 12:01 A.M. 6 August 1983."

If this justified and humanitarian demand is not accepted, we will carry out our sacred mission. If our demand should be accepted by 11:30 P.M. today, but in the future the commitment for free utilities is reneged, we shall escalate our attacks against facilities throughout the United States until such a time as our demand is fully observed.

Notes

1. Economic Regulatory Administration, Office of Utility Systems, *The National Power Grid Study,* volume 2, *Technical Study Reports* (Washington, D.C.: Department of Energy, September 1979) (DOE/ERA-0056-2), p. 135.

2. Remarks made by Richard J. Kessler at the State University of New York's conference on Terrorism, Business, and Hostage Negotiations, 20 November 1980. For more extensive details, see Economic Regulatory Administration, Office of Utility Systems, *The National Power Grid Study,* volume 2, *Technical Study Reports* (Washington, D.C.: Department of Energy, September 1979) (DOE/ERA-0056-2).

11 The Nature of Proxy Warfare

Christopher Lamb

Proxy is a recent addition to the lexicon of international relations. Although it is used with increasing regularity, the term still has no generally recognized definition. Much of the confusion and ambiguity surrounding the term's usage could be cleared up if analysts would differentiate between proxy as a classification of interstate relationships (*x* is a proxy of *y*) and proxy as a mode of strategic maneuver (*x* intervenes in *y* by proxy).

An example of the former is provided in an editorial by Joseph Kraft calling on the United States to "keep pressure on Khadafy and all Soviet proxies"; he identifies Libya, South Yemen, Vietnam, and Cuba as Soviet proxies.[1] Kraft categorizes these states by virtue of their relationship with the Soviet Union. Other analysts do not use the term, however, to categorize a particular type of bilateral (proxy-patron) relationship but rather to identify a specific form of strategic maneuver, such as when South African journalists called the civil war in Angola "a spreading war by proxy between China and Russia."[2] At first it might appear that differentiating between these two usages is specious, since it might be assumed that a proxy-patron relationship is defined by what a proxy in fact does. This, however, has not been the case.

The importance in the distinction between proxy as classification and proxy as mode of strategic operation is that the uses of the term tend to lead to two different definitions of proxy. For example, when using proxy as a classification, several criteria are relevant. A proxy is a state that substitutes for another in some role, and as the concern here is with conflict, this means intervention. In doing so, it serves the national interests of that state (the patron). But these two criteria, intervention and interests of a third party, are not sufficiently discriminating.

For example, using just these two criteria, Turkey would have to be considered a proxy of the Soviet Union during its military intervention in Cyprus, since the result of that intervention was to weaken substantially the southern flank of NATO (eventually leading to Greek withdrawal from NATO and the termination of U.S. access to electronic listening posts in Turkey), which certainly was in the Soviet Union's national interest. Considering Turkey as a proxy of the Soviet Union, however, violates an intuitive understanding of what a proxy constitutes. The missing element in this definition is collusion between the patron and proxy, whether it be simply consultation and approval or outright logistical cooperation. Without the element of collusion, the perpetrator of almost any intervention would have to be considered a proxy of one of the two superpowers, because the international system is still essentially bipolar and a shift in power anywhere will likely be in one of the superpower's interests, depending on how the deposed power or intervening state was aligned.

How, then, does a proxy differ from an ally? An ally, because it acts at least as much in its own interest as in its ally's, joins a cooperative venture voluntarily. A proxy, even though it may serve some of its own interests by cooperating with its patron, is subject to powerful coercion by the patron and thus often has little or no choice about whether it will act as an agent on behalf of its patron. (Some observers have implicitly acknowledged the importance of control by a patron as a criterion for classifying proxies by arguing that an alleged proxy is not in fact a proxy because it is not controlled by the supposed patron.[3]) Thus, when one state is subject to substantial coercion by another state and regularly intervenes or operates on behalf of that state, particularly if this is at cost to its own interests, it would seem to merit classification as a proxy.

Considering a proxy as a means of strategic maneuver shifts the emphasis behind the inquiry and usually leads to a less restrictive definition. It retains the elements of intervention, collusion, and service of the patron's interests, but it would not require that the patron control the proxy. Because such a definition is unconcerned with classification, it would not need to differentiate between proxy and client, ally, satellite, and so on. Such a definition would allow for all of these to act as proxies at a given time for a given operation.

Gavriel Ra'anan's attempt to define proxy illustrates the problems that arise from a failure to distinguish between these two perspectives on proxies. In classifying Cuba, North Korea, and North Vietnam as Soviet proxies, he maintains that "the key element is *leverage*" (his emphasis). He states that "thus, the surrogates (i.e. proxies) are *compelled* to cooperate with the USSR, regardless of their policy preferences" (my emphasis).[4] On the other hand, and in contradiction, his study concentrates on proxies as a mode of operation, and so he states that proxies need to operate exclusively at the behest of their patrons, adding that just because proxies operate on their own initiative "does not exempt them from the label" of proxy.[5]

Both methods for studying the proxy phenomena—as a means of classification and as a means of strategic maneuver—have disadvantages. The classification definition of a proxy requires that a proxy be identified in part by its substantial control by a patron. This leads to a tortuous and often sterile debate over how much influence a patron has over a proxy and when a proxy acts in its own interests as opposed to those of its patron; this in turn leads to yet another endless debate: what are a nation's real national interests? The disadvantage of an operational definition of proxy is the difficulty in establishing collusion, and the definition can become so general as to be of little interest to analysts and social scientists.

Reasonable judgments can be made on control, collusion, and national interests, so both proxy perspectives can be used for analysis. Since this chapter is primarily concerned with conflict, however, the concentration here will be on proxies as a mode of strategic maneuver, since this allows for a more general definition and, thus, a broader spectrum of empirical investigation. In short, for the purposes of this chapter, x will be considered as a proxy for y when (1) x intervenes in another state's affairs, (2) in doing so serves y's interests, and (3) does so in collusion with y. It should be noted that by dropping the element of patron control from the definition as only necessary for a classification of a relatively static bilateral interstate relationship, the motives of any proxy in question become largely irrelevant. Motives are interesting only when they shed light on which patron a proxy is cooperating with. Similarly, the element of patron control is important only when it helps substantiate a patron's collusion with its proxy.

Nature and Form of Proxy Warfare

It can be argued that proxy warfare is not a historically unique phenomenon, but it undoubtedly began to flourish in the post–World War II international environment. Three characteristics of the consequent system make proxy conflict an attractive alternative for patron states. First, the system is essentially bipolar; second, the onset of nuclear weapons makes direct super-power confrontation extremely unattractive; and third, the world today consists almost exclusively of nominally independent nation-states, which for the most part guard their sovereignty closely, a reflection of the global importance of nationalism and popular public opinion.

The bipolar nature of the current international system, whether tight, loose, or otherwise, lends a certain zero-sum-game condition to international affairs and contributes two important elements to the development of proxy conflict. First, usually only superpowers have the means (will and resources) to cultivate and use proxies; and second, a surrogate is defined, in part, as a proxy because its gains are readily transformed into the patron state's gains, a situation that reflects the bipolar system—a gain for one superpower is measured, to some degree, by the loss it dictates for the other superpower.

The Chinese experience in the third world illustrates the difficulty lesser powers have in recruiting proxies. The People's Republic of China (PRC) has enjoyed a reputation and influence in the third world, but because of limited resources, the PRC has had difficulty using proxies beyond immediately contiguous areas. On the same day (6 June 1977) the Sudan expelled

172 The Future of Conflict in the 1980s

the Soviets from Khartoum, Sudanese President Nimeiri arrived in Beijing for a ten-day visit to discuss future cooperation between the two countries. The relationship was stillborn, however, since the P.R.C. could not afford major assistance nor could it offer technological expertise. The Chinese have met similar results in Mozambique and elsewhere. Only in Cambodia, where the P.R.C. enjoys the advantages of proximity, have the Chinese approached anything resembling a patron-proxy relationship. Prior to the 1979 Vietnamese invasion, the Chinese trained, financed, and led Khmer Rouge raids into Vietnam to destabilize the new revolutionary Vietnamese regime.[6]

Other regional examples can be found, such as the Syrian use of Abu Nidal's Palestinian faction to coerce Yasir Arafat and the Palestine Liberation Organization (PLO), but they are the exceptions that prove the general rule that most states functioning as proxies prefer to cooperate with superpowers, since they have more significant benefits to offer.[7]

Proxies also provide a means for strategic competition without the undue risk of nuclear conflagration, an omnipresent post–World War II threat. The seemingly detached nature of the superpowers' involvement minimizes the deleterious effects military disasters would have on their images of invulnerability, such as the Soviets are now beginning to suffer in Afghanistan. They greatly reduce the risk of an escalatory superpower confrontation. The superpowers have abandoned surrogates when circumstances have demanded, even though it would have been difficult, if not impossible, to have done so if their own forces had been committed. For example, the Soviets left the North Koreans to their own resources in 1952 and acquiesced to the bombing and mining of North Vietnamese harbors in 1972 and the Chinese invasion of Vietnam in 1979. Similarly, the United States stood by while Nationalist Chinese forces were crushed in an invasion of mainland China in 1952 and abandoned Union Nationale pour L'Independence Totale d'Angola (UNITA) forces in Angola in 1975.[8]

It is for the sake of preserving this option of retreat with honor that the Soviet Union has refused to guarantee Cuba's defense, despite Fidel Castro's alternately insisting and importuning for just such a public guarantee for twenty years. Proxies are expensive but expendable, and the Soviet Union can stomach the defeat of Cuban troops or Cuba itself where it could not accept similar damage to its own forces.

Finally, the post–World War II surge in nationalism and public sensitivity of young states to manipulation and foreign control has been a primary impetus behind the use of proxy forces. In the past, colonial powers could set up puppet regimes to pacify their colonial subjects and accordingly use their resources, including manpower. Today, such a situation is virtually certain to elicit worldwide outrage, as the Soviet installation of a puppet regime in Afghanistan illustrated. The result is a need for at least a façade of independence, and hence we see the reluctance of superpowers to unilaterally intervene abroad with a high profile. One way to circumvent the problem is to use proxy forces, which, for a variety of reasons, may seem more palatable to those nations directly concerned.

Limited use of proxies on a small scale allows a superpower to deny responsibility for their actions. Thus, throughout the Nicaraguan revolution, Castro repeatedly denied he was supplying the Sandinistas with weapons, and although some accepted his assurances and others did not, virtually no one held the Soviet Union responsible.

Use of proxies on a larger scale may be less deniable, but it still can prove confusing when accompanied by disinformation and propaganda. The most prestigious newspaper in the United States saw fit to publish an apolegetica by Michael Manley (former prime minister of Jamaica, a proclaimed Marxist, albeit not so identified) for Cuban-Soviet interventionism. Manley declared, "Common sense and my own extensive conversations with Fidel Castro on the matter satisfy me that the Soviet Union did not order Cuba into Angola," and he claimed that it was also a myth that Cuba "spends its time plotting revolution throughout Latin America."[9]

Communist disinformation reaches more select audiences as well. Castro reportedly told visiting U.S. legislators that "the United States should not blame the Soviet Union for Central America. Russia has nothing to do with Central America. The United States should blame me. I have been supporting change in Central America for 21 years."[10]

Proxies may seem less obtrusive for purely ideological reasons. Socialism's popularity may have been eclipsed among intellectuals and even some of the more practical third-world leaders, but it is still a most effective propaganda tool, one to which many governments around the world are obliged to pay lip service. When Castro explains that his troops are protecting socialist revolution, many third-world observers refuse to ridicule that explanation, even if they do not personally find it convincing. Even in the West there is significant support for socialist revolution, both public and governmental. Sweden, for example, was willing to tarnish its reputation for pacifism by announcing in 1974 that it was tripling its aid to Front for the Liberation of Mozambique (FRELIMO) guerrillas fighting the Portuguese in Mozambique.

Even in those cases where plausible denial is virtually impossible, conflict by proxy still may seem less intrusive than would be the case with more active superpower participation. This is particularly true of the Soviet-Cuban relationship in Africa. The presence in Africa of Cubans with African ancestry is much less offensive to Africans. The Cubans are also notably less abrasive than the arrogant Russians, or so their reputation goes. In short, proxies can tread where superpowers would have to pay substantial political costs to do so.

These features of the postwar international system may condition the general use of proxies, but more immediate circumstances determine the form of proxy intervention—for example, the priority a patron assigns to an intervention and the amount of force required to intervene effectively. Although there are a multitude of specific options for using proxies, the following categories reflect the most salient forms of intervention: (1) provision of weapons, training, and even combat advisors through a proxy for a third party, (2) actual introduction of proxy forces in a direct combat role in a limited fashion, particularly to fill positions demanding technical expertise, for example, pilots and missile command-and-control technicians, and (3) large-scale intervention by proxy combat forces.

The Soviets have made use of proxies for transporting arms and providing military training and advisors throughout the world, but to date their use of proxy forces in combat has been limited. The Soviet use of proxies in Africa, however, provides examples of all three levels of proxy intervention. The Nigerian civil war marked the first time Soviet proxy forces were used in combat as Egyptian, East German, and other Eastern European pilots flew for the Nigerian air force. Succeeding with active participation in the Nigerian conflict, Soviet pilots flew for the Egyptians in the 1970 "War of Attrition" with Israel. Three years later in the 1973 Arab-Israeli War, the Soviet Union not only provided North Korean, North Vietnamese, and Soviet pilots but also reportedly used Cuban tank crews in Syria, where they performed less than satisfactorily against Israeli armor. Palestinian paramilitary units trained in Cuba served as interpreters.[11]

The very next year, tens of thousands of Cuban troops were transported to Angola by the Soviets. Today, Cuba has over 40,000 troops in Angola and Ethiopia and a civilian or military presence in thirteen other African countries. In addition to such chores as ferrying guerrillas into the Rhodesian civil war with Soviet helicopters, the Cubans have taken on palace-guard duties for shaky regimes.[12]

The Soviets have been careful not to overtax Cuban capabilities. East Germans are used extensively in the Middle East and Africa, particularly in Mozambique, where they "constitute the personal body guard and secret police of President Machel," and in the Malagasy Republic and the Marxist People's Democratic Republic of Yemen (PDRY).[13] The East Germans have even been credited with masterminding the 1978 incursion from Angola into the Shaba province of Zaire as well as the assassination of North Yemen's president that same year.[14]

In fact, one observer believes that the East German presence in southern Africa "is now so extensive that it has begun to challenge the Cuban presence both quantitatively and in terms of influence," for example, "in the course of periodic offensives against UNITA strongholds in the south East German pilots have gradually taken the place of their Cuban opposite numbers in flying MIG-21 sorties." [15] The PDRY is at present crawling with Soviets, East Germans, and Cubans (over 3,000). It has donated 3,000 troops to the cause in Ethiopia and attacked Oman and North Yemen with Soviet cooperation and encouragement. The current training in Cuba of 400 Afar students from the strategically located Djibouti region (located on the Bab el Mandeb straits guarding access to the Red Sea) suggests it may be the next target of Soviet aggression. [16]

Frequency, Scope, and Intensity

Any attempt at a detailed frequency count of proxy conflicts would soon become mired in lengthy discussion of when is a proxy a proxy? Still, many observers believe that the use of proxies is on the upswing, fueled by changes in the international environment that augment those features of the postwar international system reviewed above.

First, the balance of power is shifting. Throughout the 1950s and early 1960s, when the United States was undisputably the world's greatest military power, there was no need to rely on proxies; the CIA (in Guatemala in 1953 and Iran in 1954, for example) or the Marines (Lebanon in 1958, the Dominican Republic in 1965) were more dependable tools for intervention. As James Schlesinger has noted, however, the breakdown of the Pax Americana in the late 1960s and 1970s and the gradual growth of Soviet military might have encouraged the Soviet Union to intervene more frequently in third-world conflict. [17]

This shift in the geopolitical balance of power from a clear U.S. superiority to a questionable equilibrium has directly influenced the use of proxies by encouraging the Soviet Union to intervene with them in an increasingly unrestrained fashion. It is not merely a coincidence that Soviet proxies have graduated from covert gun running to large-scale combat concurrently with the growth of Soviet power vis-à-vis the United States. Soviet use of proxies has proven quite sensitive to Western responses as, for example, the timing of Cuban offensives in Angola has demonstrated. [18]

Just as the shifting balance of military power encouraged Soviet adventurism, it forced the United States to search for alternatives to its previous role of solitary global police officer. The result was Richard Nixon and Henry Kissinger's policy of building up local clients for use as regional proxies. The use of 5,000 Iranian soldiers in 1972 to squash a communist insurgency in Oman—backed by the Soviet proxy, the PDRY—may have been the first successful case of the new policy.

The U.S. public and Congress, however, were in no mood for potentially entangling foreign commitments, as events in Angola soon proved. When the Congress forced the administration to withdraw support from

pro-Western forces in Angola, Kissinger urged South Africans to intervene.[19] He was unable to provide any support for the South Africans,
however, and their presence simply lent legitimacy to the massive Cuban
intervention.

If the Nixon/Kissinger policy of using proxies (an outgrowth of the
Nixon Doctrine) ran into trouble with the domestic political climate of the
times, the Carter administration's policy was the embodiment of that political climate.[20] Unwillingness to encourage the use of force at all and complications with the human-rights policy agitated against the use of proxies and
helped to destroy one: Iran. "With the coming of the Reagan administration, though, proxies may once again have found their place in U.S. policy,"
reports Jack Anderson. He states that the administration is allegedly using
or intending to use the CIA to "cooperate with Egypt, Israel, Turkey,
Pakistan, Guatemala, South Africa, and South Korea in foreign intervention."[21] The Reagan veto of the UN resolution condemning South Africa's
recent incursion into Angola may be the first signal of just such a shift in
policy.

Although the U.S. use of proxies has been intermittent and interrupted
by domestic political changes, the Soviets have not been similarly constrained. As Barry Blackman has noted, the USSR is not deterred in the use
of force in the third world by public opinion.[22] Although the Soviet use of
proxies has been encouraged by the shifting balance of power, the effects of
a U.S. military buildup may not necessarily reverse that trend. If Soviet/
Cuban behavior in Angola is illustrative, Western policy is more likely to
affect the level (or intensity) of proxy conflict supported by the Soviets.

Conditions were highly favorable when the Soviet Union began to
escalate its proxy presence in Angola during 1975. The United States was in
disorder over the fall of Indochina and congressional intransigence, and
NATO was in disarray caused by communist election victories, Turkish-
Greek hostility, and Portuguese instability. The chances of a united front
and firm reaction from the West must have appeared slight. Even so, the
Soviets began cautiously, and Cuban forces were delivered in small contin-
gents with Cuban planes. In January of 1976, however, one month after the
passage of the Clark amendment, which cut off all U.S. aid to Angola, the
Soviets started airlifting troops directly from Cuba on Soviet transports.
United Nations Ambassador Andrew Young's remark that the Cuban presence was a "stabilizing influence" certainly was not construed as the definitive U.S. position on the matter, but it must have helped convince the
Soviets that the United States was too confused to mount an effective
response. From Angola and the nonreaction in the West, the decision to
intervene similarly in Ethiopia was easy.

Conditions of Inception

Like all calculated state-sponsored activity, the decision to commit proxy forces reflects a basic cost-benefit analysis. The higher the anticipated costs are, the higher the potential gains must be to make the venture an attractive option. The potential costs include financial consideration and resource allocation, the embarrassment of failure and attendant reduction in prestige, and the risk of alienating or alarming previously neutral nations. Benefits include the substantiation of Soviet willingness to intercede decisively on behalf of its interests and the control over strategically important territories and resources.

Most Soviet use of proxy forces is low level, low risk, and of modest benefit. Dispatches of Czech, North Korean, Vietnamese, East German, and Cuban pilots have not entailed much in the way of costs or benefits. The commitment of internal proxy security forces produces more noticeable advantages in that it ties a particular elite to Soviet security assurances and provides the Soviet Union with influence and leverage at modest cost.

The Soviets have proved parsimonious toward their clients and proxies when additional output seemed unlikely to produce commensurate input to Soviet interests. This is true both on financial and political counts. For example, during the past year, delegations from Grenada, Guyana, and Nicaragua went to Moscow seeking economic aid and returned home empty-handed.[23] They were unable to offer the Soviets advantages not already available from Cuba, and aid from the West could be expected to ensure that they do not collapse, thereby threatening Soviet influence already established in these countries. Consequently, there was no reason for the USSR to provide the economic assistance. Vietnam ($3 million a day) and Cuba (over $3 million a day) already constitute a serious drain on Moscow's resources.

In Angola, the same situation exists politically and militarily. UNITA guerrillas, led by Joseph Savimbi, control approximately one-third of the most desolate countryside. Although Czech, East German, and Cuban pilots periodically fly sorties against UNITA forces, the Soviets refuse to engage their proxies in major combat. Recently, when Savimbi's troops were overrunning the town of Mavinga and destroying Popular Movement for the Liberation of Angola (MPLA) relief forces in an ambush, nearby Cuban troops refused to come to the MPLA's rescue.[24] For the past two years, Soviet proxies in Angola have satisfied themselves with protecting major towns and economically important areas. Thus, the Soviets keep the MPLA in power, control the ports they need for fishing and military reasons, and keep the major threat to MPLA rule alive—which keeps Angola in

Moscow's back pocket at minimum cost. (The Soviets have evidently adopted the enclave strategy that the United States rejected in Vietnam, another illustration of the differences between the United States and the USSR. The United States sought victory in Vietnam and an independent, self-sufficient South Vietnam, and the Soviets seek control in Angola at minimum expense.)

Beyond a balance between anticipated costs and benefits, two other conditions are necessary: a local opportunity and an available proxy. Opportunities, to reassess an old Vietnam cliché, are not necessarily like street cops, that is, they do not come along only if one waits long enough. On the contrary, opportunity can be helped along. The most obvious type of opportunity for proxy intervention is domestic armed conflict. By training, arming, and advising guerrillas, the Soviets help create their own opportunities for proxy intervention. The third-world conditions that contribute to such a situation of instability—fragmentation along lines of nationality, development realities and rising expectations, cultural clashes between traditional and modern social mores, and liberation struggles—seem likely to continue and grow throughout the 1980s.

If proxy support of popular uprisings is successful when working from the bottom up, it is also possible to work from the top down. The Soviets began to realize in the late 1960s and early 1970s that, to quote Boris Ponomarev, "Experience confirms that the position adopted by the army largely determines whether a particular regime can remain in power or not."[25] Consequently, the Soviets have been courting the military as a method of influencing elite power groups. Even such an ideologically incompatible country as Argentina has entered into agreements with Moscow to have military personnel trained in the Soviet Union.[26] This strategy has met with success (for example, in Peru, in the dissolution of the Portuguese African colonies, and in the removal of Salim Rubai Ali in the PDRY), but it has also failed miserably.

Along with arms sales come training programs and some ideological penetration, which, together with Soviet and proxy intelligence officers, provide a lethal trojan horse. Yet, if the gamble fails, the horse is quickly slaughtered. Such was the case in Iraq in 1978. Iraqi leader Saddem Hussein discovered that East German and Soviet intelligence officers were organizing a coup with the aid of Iraqi security personnel they had trained. Hussein launched a massive purge of his military and security forces to flush out and destroy the underground cells the Soviets and East Germans had created. Soviet, East German, and Cuban commando and intelligence experts moved to the PDRY, Libya, and Uganda, and Soviet-Iraqi relations cooled considerably.[27]

In addition to a local opportunity for proxy intervention, a willing proxy must also be found. Proxies can cooperate with a patron for a variety of reasons. In some cases, such as Cuba, there is little chance for the proxy to refuse its role even if it were to so desire.[28] Other proxies may demonstrate just a confluence of interests and a quid pro quo arrangement for services. For example, the PLO receives training, weapons, and diplomatic support from the Soviet Union and in turn has offered its services to Soviet-backed clients and other proxies, such as Idi Amin and leftist groups in Iran.[29] Ideological compatibility may be yet another reason for service as a proxy. Such is at least partially true in the case of the PDRY.

A proxy usually operates as such for a combination of reasons, which can reflect the idiosyncracies of individual leaders. For example, the activities of Libyan General Muammar Qaddafi suggest his motives stem, at least in part, from ambition and perhaps are even a consequence of megalomania. He has attempted to expand Libyan influence through federations with Egypt, Tunisia, Sudan, Chad, and Syria, all of which fell through and were usually followed by Libyan coup and assassination plots against the leaders of these countries.[30]

A list of Qaddafi's activities reads like a Soviet wish list: direct assistance to Idi Amin; an invasion of Chad; and military aid to guerrillas in the Philippines, the Irish Republican Army (IRA), the Sandinistas, PLO terrorists, liberation movements in Angola and Mozambique, black Moslems in the United States, leftists in Lebanon, and Basque, Corsican, and other separatists in Europe. At times he seems particularly amenable to Soviet interests, as when he switched support from Muslim Somalia and Eritrean irredentists to Ethiopia, as the USSR did, and when he funneled money to the government of Mauritius in the Indian Ocean, where the Soviets are working on establishing a naval base.[31]

On the other hand, the Soviets appear wary of Qaddafi, who in April of this year told Moscow to withdraw from Afghanistan and that "Poland should be free." The Soviets have also resisted Libyan requests for consulates in their Central Asian republics, where large numbers of Moslems live.[32] In addition, Qaddafi's threats to allow Warsaw Pact bases in Libya have never materialized, and he is not dependent on the Soviet Union economically. His planes are reportedly piloted by Pakistanis, Palestinians, and Syrians as well as Soviets and East Europeans, so he does have alternatives to dependency on Soviet military assistance.[33] Nevertheless, the $12 billion worth of Soviet military equipment and 12,000 Soviet and 4,000–5,000 Polish, Czech, and Bulgarian advisors in Libya (compared to a Libyan army of 40,000) represent a substantial commitment to Soviet goodwill.[34] In fact, the late President Sadat claimed that a 1976 arms pact between Libya and the Soviet Union gives the USSR access to Libyan air bases, and the 1980 closing of Banghazi Airport to all foreign civilian air traffic may presage the fruition of such an agreement.

For whatever reasons (and as the case of Libya suggests, they may be a complex combination), Libya has proven to be a highly effective proxy for the Soviet Union and, as noted earlier, it is results and not motives that are most important. The results of Libyan intervention in Africa, as will be discussed, have worked to the Soviet advantage.

Regional Potential for Proxy Conflict

All the aforementioned conditions of inception—a favorable cost-benefit ratio, the opportunity for proxy conflict, and the availability of proxies—combine to make possible some calculations about the regional likelihood of future proxy conflict.

Africa

It is difficult to generalize about proxy conflict in a regional context, but some estimations of susceptibility can be tendered. Africa is by far the region most prone to proxy intervention. The prizes to be won there are significant and will become increasingly so as the world grows ever more dependent on African minerals. Although some African countries are strategically less than important, others are geographically vital to Western security, especially those countries situated for interdiction of Western oil routes. The most important factor contributing to Africa's salience as a tempting target for proxy intervention is its instability and military weakness. A brief but forceful infusion of well-trained troops with technologically superior weapons can quickly and decisively affect the outcome of a conflict. The prospect of a fait accompli by proxy is enticing.

Just how easily African governments can be toppled was demonstrated somewhat ironically by a U.S. attempt to counter a proxy threat. In 1979, a special-forces detachment was sent to Liberia—America's most consistent and enthusiastic ally in Africa—to train a Liberian army battalion and demonstrably counter the presence of 40 Cuban advisors in Sierra Leone and 100 Soviet and 200 Cuban advisors in Guinea. The United States trained the Liberians well. Several months after the U.S. advisors had left, one particularly outstanding student, Samuel K. Doe, overthrew the Liberian government and executed the president and all his top generals. United States interests may not have suffered lasting damage, since 102 Green Berets were back for joint exercises this past April. Nevertheless, the incident highlights a couple of points. First, it underscores just how fragile many African regimes are, and, second, it illustrates one of the disadvantages the United States encounters in comparison with Soviet proxies. The United States, in seeking self-sufficiency for its allies and clients, never attains the control over their domestic environment that the Soviets can manage with a continuing proxy presence.

For not only are proxies used to expand Soviet influence through interstate intervention, such as when the PDRY invades North Yemen, but they can also increase a regime's dependence on Soviet auspices by providing internal-security services. After the Soviets were expelled from Egypt and Sudan, they helplessly watched leftists such as Lumumba of the Congo (1960), Ben Bella of Algeria (June 1965), Sukarno of Indonesia (September 1965), Nkrumah of Ghana (February 1966), and Keita of Mali (November 1968) fall prey to coups and assassinations. The Soviets then decided that they needed a better method of securing their clients in power. A relatively modest number of proxy troops and internal-security personnel can prove highly effective at just that, as Cuban and Eastern bloc forces are now proving in the Malaguay Republic, the PDRY, and Mozambique. Since changes in third-world leadership come about more often by the bullet than the ballot, the ability of a patron to guarantee a regime's survival with proxy forces is a major advantage.

As Shai Feldman has observed, it is difficult for the United States to guarantee domestic security.[35] At best it is possible to counter low-level threats, such as coup plots. Potential U.S. proxies, however, have been able to make more substantial contributions to regime stability in Africa, for example, the French and the Moroccans. Morocco has proven especially willing to counter Soviet-inspired top-level intervention. Morocco sent troops to Equatorial Guinea in 1979 to help topple a pro-Soviet leader and stayed on as a praetorian guard. When the Soviets countered with their own coup attempt recently, the Moroccans helped defeat it and saw to a substantial reduction of the Soviet presence in that country (from 195 to 15 embassy personnel).[36]

Middle East

One of the more important but less publicized proxy conflicts in Africa and the Middle East has been waged between, on one side, Egypt and Sudan, supported by the United States and, on the other side, Ethiopia and Libya supported by the Soviet Union. The isolation of Egypt has been an ongoing policy objective since 1974 of the Soviet Union, and its strategy has been to pressure those states sympathetic and contiguous to Egypt. In Moscow on 22 February 1979, plans were finalized for an Ethiopian attack on Sudan, but they were brought to a halt by a defensive line consisting primarily of Egyptian paratroopers. Egypt also moved most of its naval craft to Port Sudan, and at the same time the U.S. 6th Fleet moved to fill the void off the Egyptian Mediterranean coast. The United States also flew reconnaissance flights along the Sudanese-Ethiopian border, reporting its findings back to Cairo.[37] Soon thereafter, the Arab League moved to settle the South and North Yemeni conflict, and the Tanzanian-Ugandan war began to sour on the Soviets. The Libyans moved to support Amin, but once again they were quickly countered by Egypt, which sent arms and advisors to Tanzania (perhaps pilots for their MiG-19s as well). Egypt also warned Libya that if its combat planes entered the fray in Uganda, Egyptian planes operating out of Sudan would aid Tanzanian forces. The Soviet Union, fearing an Egyptian attack on Libya while it was engaged in Uganda, sent several Cuban battalions to Libya along with seventy-five North Korean pilots.[38]

As the preceding suggests, all the conditions for proxy conflict in Africa remain ripe. It is too difficult for regimes that are inherently unstable to remain neutral; they need outside support, and if competition between the East and West continues to heat up in Africa, those African countries involved will have to choose one patron or another, clearing the way for proxy war. Qaddafi's pledge to fight at the side of Angola to "repulse the racist and imperialist aggression" of South Africa is an appropriate harbinger for the future of proxy conflict in Africa.[39] As long as Africa remains strategically important and inherently unstable, the Soviets will find no lack of opportunity or availability of proxies for their goals, and the West will have to either respond directly or with its own proxies or cede the field to the Soviets.

The Middle East is more important than Africa, both for its resources (oil) and strategic location. Unlike Africa, however, it is not a prime area for large-scale proxy conflict. Most Middle Eastern countries are very well armed, thanks to copious oil dollars, and are not prone to destabilization or defeat by proxy forces. It would take an extremely large component of proxy forces to decisively affect a conflict, and even then the intervention would probably be self-defeating, since it would most likely elicit a retaliatory or counterresponse from the United States or, even more likely, a nearby opponent of the proxy's beneficiary. Barring an Arab-Israeli war, major use of Soviet proxies in the Middle East is unlikely.

There are exceptions to this conclusion, notably the smaller but strategically rich countries such as Oman, Kuwait, and the Yemens. Even in these cases, however, there lies reason to doubt the effectiveness of proxy forces. All Middle Eastern countries consider so-called godless communism anathema, especially following recent events in Afghanistan, and would probably not accept a communist-inspired intervention in any of these countries. The Marxist PDRY may be the exception that proves the rule. The Arab League ostracized the PDRY for its professed communism, and the Saudis moved quickly and forcefully to squelch growing Soviet influence in neighboring North Yemen. On 4 March 1980, the Saudis occupied a North Yemeni position at Al Quba where the Saudi, North Yemen, and PDRY borders meet. In the ensuing clash at least five North Yemeni soldiers were killed. After commanding North Yemen's attention the Saudis sat down for high-level talks with North Yemen. Consequently, Saudi forces left North Yemen's territory, and North Yemen agreed to accept no more Soviet military advisors and eventually to see to the withdrawal of 100 currently there.

However, most Middle Eastern countries have not been willing to tolerate a renewed U.S. military presence either. Egypt is the exception to this, and may be the principal U.S. proxy (especially now that Iran is lost) for the future in responding to any new Soviet proxy thrusts, such as a renewed PDRY challenge to North Yemen or Oman. On the whole, however, the Middle East is not likely to see a large-scale proxy conflict, although the constant and ongoing bickering and plotting of the Arab nations against one another will provide numerous opportunities for small-scale proxy intervention with arms, training, and advisors.

Southeast Asia

Southeast Asia does not appear a likely area for large-scale proxy war either, at least not for the immediate future, principally because of the lack of targets. Weak governments rule in the area, but none can offer advantages that Vietnam does not already supply the Soviets. In addition, the USSR appears to be having some problems consolidating its hold on Vietnam. Popular resentment of the Soviet presence is growing in Vietnam and, apparently, there is some friction with Vietnamese authorities over Kampuchea as well. Some reports indicate that a growing Soviet presence in Phnom Penh has alarmed the Vietnamese and has led to competition for influence.[40] Furthermore, Vietnam, the Soviet Union's most promising prospect for proxy status in the area, is tied down in Kampuchea and must constantly be on guard against the Chinese, who have demonstrated their willingness to punish Vietnam for its indiscretions. In fact, it appears that one reason the Chinese did not support the Association of Southeast Asian Nations (ASEAN) proposal for a special worldwide conference on Kampuchea recently was their desire to continue bleeding the Vietnamese a while longer with the assistance of their Khmer Rouge clients.

Finally, the Chinese have a virtual monopoly on ties to guerrilla movements outside Laos, Kampuchea, and Vietnam. Since the Chinese have accepted resistance to Soviet hegemony as their top priority, they have sought the aid of ASEAN. The federation, in turn, has loudly demanded that the PRC suspend support for the indigenous communist guerrilla movements afflicting ASEAN countries. The PRC has sought to reassure the ASEAN nations, but they remain skeptical. They reject Chinese assertions that a complete severance of Chinese ties with the guerrillas would provide the necessary entrée for the Soviets and Vietnamese to step in and take over, citing that many communist guerrilla leaders are ethnic Chinese (all are in Malaysia) and would not be responsive to Hanoi or Moscow. Despite such concrete Chinese overtures as a major reduction in aid to Thai communists and pressure on the same for a united front against Vietnam, ASEAN remains convinced that the PRC will continue to use its links with guerrilla movements as a method of coercing ASEAN into cooperation with Chinese interests.[41]

As long as all these circumstances remain static, Southeast Asia will most likely not witness any proxy conflicts. If the Soviets and Vietnamese consolidate their position in Kampuchea, if Chinese pressure on Vietnam is deflected, and if the Vietnamese elite succumbs to Soviet control, chances for proxy intervention, on a small scale at least, will improve dramatically. The same can be said for the use of U.S. proxies as long as the ASEAN countries continue to fear the PRC as much as Vietnam. Continuing warnings from ASEAN leaders concerning the Chinese threat and ASEAN unwillingness to serve as a conduit for U.S. arms to the Khmer People's National Liberation Front suggest that this will remain the case for the near future.[42]

Latin America

Latin America has never been an easy target for proxy intervention. Even though some governments in the region turn over with tragicomic regularity, the area has been adept at crushing leftist insurgencies (with substantial U.S. support, it should be added). Cuba, Moscow's local proxy, exists in the U.S. shadow and is pinned down by its own security needs. Any large commitment of Cuban troops to a conflict in the area would most surely invite retaliation from the United States.

On the other hand, there is a growing willingness to embrace the socialist alternative in the area. In addition, the Soviets—in a change of heart that probably reflects the shift in the superpower balance of power and amusement over President Carter's vacillating foreign policy and acquiescence elsewhere—have apparently decided that the potential benefits of limited proxy ventures in Latin America outweigh the risks. Whereas Moscow once bitterly feuded with Castro over his support for guerrilla movements in the area, it is now willing to back such ventures, if they are pursued at a low-risk level. Taking advantage of Nicaraguan domestic turmoil and considerable Latin American support for the Sandinista cause, the Cubans supplied the rebels with weapons, advisors, and logistical support. Now the Soviet Union is moving to create a client state out of Nicaragua. Sandinista pilots are training in Soviet MiGs in Bulgaria; Libyan money flows into the government coffers; the Sandinista army is being expanded to double—40,000—the size of Somoza's old National Guard (plus an additional 70,000 militia, aiming for 200,000); U.S. labor representatives are being expelled and replaced by East German experts; Eastern bloc or Soviet technicians are overseeing the enlargement of airfields to accommodate Soviet planes; Cuban troops are being integrated into the army; and Soviet automatic weapons, SAMs and T-55 tanks, are now in use by the Sandinistas.[43]

The Cubans have also moved to destabilize El Salvador, Costa Rica, Guatemala, and Colombia (at least El Salvador, with Sandinista help). Panama, under the enigmatic General Omar Torrijos, aided the Cubans by allowing Panamanian territory to be used as a transit point for troops and arms bound for El Salvador and Nicaragua and for M-19 guerrillas trained in Cuba on their way to Colombia via Ecuador.[44] Cuba has paid a price for its efforts; both Costa Rica and Colombia have severed relations with Cuba, and many observers in the area who were previously sympathetic to Cuban support of popular movements were more than a little concerned over Cuba's attempts to undermine two of the area's rare democracies. (There are mixed reports on the probable future for the large Soviet/Cuban presence in Guyana. Other observers, however, have reported Guyana as cooling toward the Soviets and Cubans.[45]) The benefits to the Soviet Union, however, are clear: The United States is on the defensive in its own backyard, and Soviet weapons are very near the Panama Canal—all at minimal costs and risks to the USSR. Some believe that it may be the next opportunity for a major Cuban military intervention.

Outcome of Proxy Conflict

The outcome of any given client or proxy conflict essentially rests on two sets of factors, one military and the other political. Of obvious importance militarily is the condition of the opposition (to proxy) forces. The greater the disparity between the proxy and the opposition (that is, the more poorly trained and ill equipped the opposition is, the better the chance for a decisive input by the proxy). Beyond that elementary observation, three other conditions are important.

First, how long and intensive are the histories of military cooperation of the patron-proxy and patron-proxy-client (those the proxy and patron are assisting)? If the proxy forces are familiar with the patron's military organization, procedures, techniques, and weapons, as they most likely will be, they will be able to take quick advantage of the benefits the patron can offer. The same can be said for the indigenous (client) forces; if they are familiar with Soviet tactics and weapons, they will be able to work smoothly and immediately with the proxy forces.

Second, what sources of assistance does the opposition have? If it already has lines of communication open to outside powers, and established procedures for assimilating aid from those sources to their best advantage, the intrusion of proxy forces might be matched by aid from other sources. It still may not be enough, but the better the opposition's ties to powers with means to supply significant assistance, the greater its chances are at holding off the proxy and preventing a fait accompli that will eventually be accepted by other nations.

Finally, terrain and geography are of major importance. Are they conducive to guerrilla-style warfare, a factor that can agitate against a quick victory by proxy? Similarly, is the terrain likely to assist or prevent the technological superiority transferred from patron to proxy from being brought to bear on the opposition forces? For example, is the terrain open, with few hiding places from helicopter gunships and warplanes and few obstacles for tanks? Perhaps most important, can contiguous areas be used as sanctuaries for beleaguered opposition forces? If so, the opposition will hold out longer and probably live to fight another day, which may not reduce the immediate effectiveness of the proxy influx but bodes ill for the long run.

Political factors influencing proxy conflicts revolve around the support proxy/client and opposition forces can expect from various sources. How much popular support exists for the client or the opposition? Is the population, long excluded from the political process, essentially apolitical? If so, this will be to the proxy's advantage, as the inhabitants will be more easily pacified. If the area of conflict is ethnically homogeneous and/or intensely nationalistic, the presence of the proxy on a large scale may engender resentment—perhaps even discredit the client—thereby eroding popular support.

Just as important, what are the attitudes in the area toward benefactors of the opposition? If the proxy and patron enjoy a good reputation in the area, their intrusion may be more tolerable—even palatable—and there will be less risk of a backlash, and vice versa. The same can be said of the opposition's supporters. Nigeria's attitudes toward the Soviet/Cuban intervention in Angola exemplify this; in part because the odious South Africans were assisting UNITA, Nigeria sent 5,000 troops to fight side by side with the Cubans against the UNITA guerrillas.[46]

The Cuban experiences in Angola and those of the Vietnamese in Cambodia are cases in which military and political factors, although a mixed slate, were in conflict with one another. In Angola, military factors favored the Cubans. The UNITA forces were no match for the Soviet-supplied Cubans, and they had no immediate means of assistance from comparable sources. Political factors, however, were more favorable. UNITA represents Angola's largest political faction because its ranks are primarily filled from the country's largest ethnic group, the Ovimbundu; UNITA also sought and received a quick rapprochement with South Africa, which, along with other nations such as Morocco, has provided Savimbi with steady assistance.

In Kampuchea, Vietnam met opposite circumstances. As in Angola, the opposition forces could not hope to match the Soviet enemy, but other military conditions were better. The terrain is suitable to guerrilla tactics, and the Khmer Rouge fighters were battle-hardened veterans of such conflict—probably the only group that can lay claim to exceeding the Vietnamese in ruthlessness. They also had the benefit of close ties to the PRC for assistance. On the other hand, political factors were less favorable. Traditional Kampuchean animosity toward the Vietnamese was subdued by the dread with which most Kampucheans (the survivors) viewed the Khmer Rouge. The barbarous reputation of the Khmer Rouge also made it difficult for outside sources to support its resistance to Vietnam.

Proxy Activities and Superpower Relations

Proxies and Soviet Strategy

Proxies afford the Soviet Union a very convenient and effective method of moving the world stage out of the era of the encirclement of socialism by capitalism to a new era of capitalist encirclement. The Soviets have suffered numerous setbacks even in their own immediate sphere of influence, namely, in Afghanistan and Poland. These are manageable though and, in the long run, are part of the confusion natural for a world in transition. In the Soviet view, there is more good news than bad when seen from a historical perspective.

From a post–World War II paper tiger, the Soviet Union has evolved into a bona fide superpower commanding worldwide attention, fear, and respect. The Soviets have expanded their influence in Southeast Asia at Western expense; they have helped transform the Middle East from a Western serfdom into a fragile collection of states capable of toying with vital Western oil resources; they have made numerous inroads into Africa and tightened the noose around South Africa, a linchpin in the anti-Soviet league controlling critical supplies of minerals; they have made great progress toward pacifying Europe; and they have succeeded in bringing Soviet influence to the United States' very doorstep in Central America. Clients or proxies have been instrumental in all these gains.

Analysts often debate whether Soviet policy is best understood in terms of ideology or pragmatism, but there need be no conflict between the two. Soviet strategy is defined by pragmatic tactics and short-term decisions within an ideological framework that outlines long-term goals. If freedom were to run rampant through Eastern Europe, or the Soviet empire is similarly destabilized, or if a new Soviet leadership were to evolve with no respect for communism as a guiding light, Soviet strategy might change. Until then the USSR will continue to seek the demise of pro-Western governments, broad guarantees of its security, and a general expansion of its influence. In doing so, the USSR will continue to use clients and proxies, and Soviet propaganda will continue to camouflage client and proxy ties to the Soviet Union, thereby sustaining their images of independence and thus their utility.

Within the bounds of this general strategy, the Soviet Union has made an ominous shift in its objectives during the last decade. As Francis Fuka-yama argues, whereas the Soviets were once content to groom and recruit clients who were ostensibly nonaligned but, in fact, usually supported the Soviet policy line, the Soviet Union now seems more determined to demand total obedience. It has installed "slavishly pro-Soviet" governments in Ethiopia, Afghanistan, and the PDRY and attempted to do so in Iraq but failed. And as Fukuyama notes, what makes these actions so significant is that each country was pro-Soviet to begin with. They did, however, insist on independence and occasionally disagreed with Soviet foreign-policy initia-tives, which, according to Fukuyama, is what precipitated their demise.[47]

Naturally, the Soviet Union prefers as much control over its proxies and clients as possible and now seems willing to risk moving very forcefully to secure such control. Returning to the introductory discussion, it is here that categorization of Soviet proxies becomes important. Those proxies that are substantially controlled by the Soviet Union (for example, Cuba, the PDRY, and Afghanistan) must be dealt with differently from other proxies who are more independent. With controlled proxies, neither carrots not sticks are likely to be effective, since the firm control a patron exercises over the proxy will probably make it impossible to either cajole or coerce the proxy away from cooperating with its patron state. If this is correct, the Mexican policy toward Cuba, for example, is futile. The Mexicans are seeking to reduce Cuba's dependence on the Soviet Union by entering into trade agreements and assisting the Cubans in oil exploration. It is an unrealistic policy. Mexican support has only relieved pressure on Cuba, making its task of destabilizing the area easier. Likewise, however, threatening Cuba will have little effect.

U.S. Policy

Several years ago, Robert Osgood took account of the new Soviet threat, which he believes to be "the Soviet willingness and ability to project arms and combat units to non-contiguous territory where neither material Soviet interests, security, or commitments are at stake."[48] He then made a simple observation: In the face of such a Soviet offensive, the United States will have to either meet the challenge or drastically devalue the nature and scope of its security interests.[49]

If security interests are not to be devalued, the United States will have several options to consider. One is to build up U.S. limited-war capability, especially the logistical support necessary for moving large numbers of troops and large amounts of equipment quickly and far, that is, its power-projection capability. However, with the U.S. public still very wary of fighting limited foreign wars, the only immediate U.S. response to Soviet-sponsored proxy wars is the use of U.S. proxies. Indeed, this is precisely what a growing number of analysts are suggesting, at least in effect. Lawrence Grenter makes a typical case. He recommends that the United States (1) multilateralize Western responses to Soviet interventions, (2) in doing so, build on British, French, and local military facilities in the area, and (3) cultivate and bolster the most reliable friends in the area, such as Egypt, Israel, Saudi Arabia, Sudan, Kenya, Oman, and Turkey.

This is not an unrealistic set of options. More and more nations are showing a willingness to forcefully counter Soviet clients and proxies. In Latin America, for example, the Colombians have executed a volte-face. After supporting the revolution in Nicaragua, Colombia was distressed to discover that its democratic credentials did not immunize it from Cuban conspiracy. No sooner had the Sandinistas won in Nicaragua than the Cubans were financing, training, and exporting guerrillas for revolution in Colombia. This past month, Colombian President Julio Cesar Turbay Ayala announced the discovery of the Cuban activity, claiming that it "was a kind of Pearl Harbor for us." He then gathered all his ambassadors from the Caribbean basin to formulate a plan of resistance, signed an agreement with Chile (previously eschewed) to "combat Cuban expansionism," declaring that the Cubans had replaced the U.S. Marines as the consummate symbol of intervention, and proclaimed that "Central America and the Caribbean are now our number one priority."[50]

In Africa and the Middle East, Western European nations have demonstrated a willingness to intervene, particularly in areas of previous colonial experience where ties are still strong. In the early 1970s, the British dispatched Special Air Service (SAS) personnel to help the Iranians quell the Dhufar revolution in Oman and reportedly performed effectively.[51] Just this past August, while Gambia's pro-Western President Dawda Jawara was attending the royal wedding, a local communist, Kukli Samba Sanyang, led a revolt supplied with Soviet rifles. The British SAS and 1,500 Senegalese troops squashed the coup attempt and saved one of Africa's multiparty democracies.[52] The French have been especially determined to resist Soviet expansion and preserve French influence in traditionally Francophone Africa.

France currently has 14,000 troops in twenty African countries. Between 1960 and 1964, French forces intervened in the Cameroon, Congo, Gabon, Chad, Niger, and Mauritania. They did so again in 1967 in the Central African Republic and in Chad between 1968 and 1974.[53] Following the Soviet-Cuban success in Angola, the French reassessed their relations in Africa and launched into a flurry of diplomatic activity culminating in twenty-two new agreements with African nations, six of which provide for the use of French troops in the event of external aggression.[54] President Giscard d'Estaing tried to secure U.S. financing for a "Franco-African Solidarity Fund" in 1976 to no avail. After two successful Western defenses of Zaire's Shaba province from Cuban- and East German-inspired invasions of Angola, the French began to build up their conventional forces.[55]

More recently, the French have assisted Morocco and Mauritania against Polisario guerrillas and, a year ago, moved to support Tunisia against Libyan-sponsored guerrillas (for which the Libyans burned their French embassy). There were even reports—denied by the Saudis—that French antiterrorist commandos assisted in the retaking of the Grand Mosque in Mecca in November of 1979. (Future French policy is admittedly contingent on the new Mitterrand government, however, and foreign-policy changes are likely.)

In 1977 and 1978, Western and pro-Western powers were able to launch a multilateral defense of Zaire's Shaba province when it came under attack from separatists operating out of Angola. The 1977 attack was turned back with Moroccan troops, French logistical support, and Saudi finances.[56] The 1978 attack was similarly defeated with 700 French and 1,700 Belgian paratroopers, transported into battle with U.S. Air Force (USAF) C-141s. This time the West followed up with U.S. and Saudi financial aid to Zaire and transported 1,500 Moroccans, 600 Senegalese, and smaller forces from Togo, Gabon, and the Ivory Coast to Zaire to deter future aggression. In 1979, Belgium sent 250 troops to a base at Kitena, Zaire, to signal its continuing determination to support Zaire.[57]

The PRC is another potential ally for active containment of Soviet proxies. Its behavior over the last decade demonstrates that it can be more anti-Soviet than prorevolution. The PRC terminated aid to the Dhofar revolutionaries in 1971 and 1972, in deference to Iran, whose military buildup the Chinese publicly applauded.[58] During the Angolan civil war, Beijing authorized Zaire to release sizeable quantities of Chinese weapons being held by Zaire for the anti-MPLA forces in Angola at the same time that U.S. covert assistance to those groups began.[59] The PRC is also cooperating with the West in ensuring Zaire's security by training its small navy.[60] As noted earlier, the PRC used the Khmer Rouge to raid Vietnam and provide anticommunist guerrilla groups (Buddhists, Christians, and the Hoa

Hoa and Cao Dai sects) with weapons and supplies.[61] Thomas Bellows believes that the PRC incursion into northern Vietnam following the Vietnamese invasion of Kampuchea was an attempt not only to recoup some lost prestige but also to demonstrate to the West that the PRC could be a reliable ally, was worth supporting, and could punish a Soviet client and get away with it.[62]

Beyond cooperating with proxies whenever possible, the United States will want to develop weapons and logistical capabilities that enable it to quickly counter Soviet proxies. Technology has an important role to play in this regard. To counter proxies, the United States must see to it that they are thwarted in the field. Proxies usually have two advantages over indigenous forces—training and equipment. The former can be offset with U.S. and allied training programs (although this must be done with caution, lest a repetition of the aforementioned Liberian episode occur), the latter with applied technology.

In guerrilla conflict, the principal advantage the Soviet and Cuban troops accrue from superior technology is improved mobility. Helicopters and close air support take a devastating toll among the Afghan rebels and, to a lesser extent, Savimbi's guerrillas. They also undermine morale, since they allow the communists to wreak havoc while remaining practically invulnerable. The United States could counter by supplying resistance movements with lightweight (perhaps even remote-controlled) surface-to-air missiles. Similar antitank devices would be helpful also. Supplying the antiproxy guerrillas with reliable lightweight radar units and communication devices would enable early warning of impending air attack and make defensive measures more effective. The more rugged and inexpensive such items are, of course, the more utility they will have.

Conclusion

The task of tying down and exhausting Soviet proxies will require some finesse and certainly an eclectic set of methods. In some cases the United States will want to press harder to enlist assistance, working through proxies and with those allies that are willing—sometimes covertly, sometimes overtly. The choice is to enlist proxies and allies or acquiesce to Soviet proxy interventions, which certainly will continue.

Notes

1. Joseph Kraft, editorial, *Miami Herald*, 24 August 1981.
2. Robin Hallett, "The South African Intervention in Angola, 1975–76," *African Affairs* 77 (July 1978): 357.

3. See, for example, Christopher Coker, "East Germany and Southern Africa" *Journal of Social and Political Studies* 5 (Fall 1980).

4. Gavriel Ra'anan, "The Evolution of the Soviet Use of Surrogates in Military Relations in the Third World, with Particular Emphasis on Cuban Participation in Africa," p.75. *The Rand Paper Series* (The Rand Corporation, 1979).

5. Ibid.

6. Martin James and Peter Vanneman, "The Soviet Intervention in Angola," p. 98; and Thomas J. Bellocus, "Proxy War in Indochina," p. 21 *Strategic Review* 4 (Summer 1976).

7. *Washington Post*, 13 September 1981.

8. Thomas Powers, *The Men Who Kept the Secrets*, p. 102. (New York: Simon and Schuster) 1979.

9. *New York Times*, 13 August 1981.

10. U.S. News and World Report, p. 28 by Carl J. Migdail. "Inside Cuba: Castro Thumbs His Nose at Reagan," vol. XCI, no. 5. 3 August 1981.

11. Ra'anan, "Soviet Use of Surrogates," pp. 12–13, 36–37.

12. Powers, *Secrets*, p. 181.

13. Ra'anan, "Soviet Surrogates," p. 54.

14. Ibid.

15. Coker, "East Germany and Southern Africa," p. 239.

16. Ra'anan, "Soviet Use of Surrogates," pp. 56, 92.

17. James R. Schlesinger, "The International Implications of Third World Conflict: An American Perspective" in "Third World Conflict and International Security" *Adelphi Papers* no. 166, 1981. International Strategic Seminar, London.

18. *Foreign Report*, no. 1560, 15 November 1978. Economist Newspapers, Ltd., London.

19. *Foreign Report*, no. 1554, 4 October 1978. Economist Newspapers, Ltd., London.

20. See Melvin Gurtor, "Security by Proxy." The Nixon Doctrine and Southeast Asia" in March Zacher and R. Stephen Milne, eds. *Conflict and Stability in Southeast Asia*. (Garden City, 1974).

21. Jack Anderson, "CIA Gearing up for Operations with Foreigners," *Washington Post*, 27 August 1981.

22. Barry Blechman, "Outside Military Forces in Third World Conflicts," *Adelphi Papers*, no. 166, 1981.

23. *Business Week*, 29 June 1981. "Latin America: The Soviets Find Trade Partners on the Right," p. 64, no. 2694.

24. *Washington Post*, 29, 20, 21 July 1981.

25. Boris Ponomarev, quoted in John J. Dziak, "Soviet Intelligence

and Security Services in the Eighties: The Paramilitary Dimension," *Orbis* 24 (Winter 1981): 771–786.

27. Francis Fukayama, "A New Soviet Strategy," and *Foreign Report*, no. 1545 (2 August 1978).

28. For a detailed account of Soviet penetration of Cuba's communist party, military and intelligence service, as well as Cuban military and economic dependence on the USSR, see Maurice Halperin, *The Taming of Castro*. (Berkeley: University of California Press, 1981).

29. *Foreign Report*, no. 1582, 16 May 1979. Economist Newspapers, Ltd., London.

30. John K. Cooley, "The Libyan Menace," and Nathan Alexander, "The Foreign Policy of Libya." *Foreign Policy* (Spring 1981).

31. Cooley, "Libyan Menace," and *Miami Herald*, 20 August 1981.

32. *New York Times*, 23 August 1981.

33. *New York Times*, 20 August 1981.

34. Brian Crozier, "The Surrogate Forces of the Soviet Union." *Conflict Studies*, no. 92, p. 4, February 1978. Great Britain: Eastern Press, Ltd.

35. Shai Feldman, "Superpower Security Guarantees in the 1980s."

36. *Foreign Report*, no. 1679, 14 May 1981. Economist Newspapers Ltd., London.

37. *Foreign Report*, no. 1576, 21 March 1979. Economist Newspapers, Ltd., London.

38. *Foreign Report*, no. 1578, 4 April 1979. Economist Newspapers, Ltd., London.

39. General Muammar Qaddafi, quoted in the *Wall Street Journal*, 28 August 1981.

40. *Christian Science Monitor*, 12 August 1981.

41. *Christian Science Monitor*, 17 August 1981.

42. *New York Times*, 23 August 1981.

43. For Sandinista army size, see *Miami Herald*, 7 August 1981; for replacement of U.S. labor representatives, see *Washington Star*, 18 July 1981; for integration of Cuban troops, see *Miami Herald*, 2 August 1981; and for Soviet weapons, see *New York Times*, 13 August 1981.

44. *Miami Herald*, 21 June 1981.

45. See, for example, Leiken, "Eastern Winds," *Foreign Policy* (Spring 1981): 94–113.

46. Ra'anan, "Soviet Use of Surrogates," pp. 12, 62, 73. n.68.

47. Fukayama, "Soviet Strategy." *Commentary* (October 1977).

48. Robert Osgood, *Limited War Revisited*, p. 72.

49. Ibid., p. 85.

50. *New York Times*, 13 August 1981.

51. J.E. Peterson, "The Rebellion in Dhufar," p. 287. *World Affairs* 149 (September 1979).

52. *New York Times*, 9 August 1981.

53. Pierre Lellouche and Dominique Moisi, "French Policy in Africa: A Lonely Battle Against Destabilization," *International Security* 3 (Spring 1979).

54. Hallett, "South African Intervention."

55. Lellouche and Moisi, "French Policy," p. 126.

56. Roger W. Fontaine, "Cuban Strategy in Africa: The Long Road of Ambition," *Strategic Review* 9 (Summer 1978): 21.

57. Peter Mangold, "Shaba I and Shaba II." *Survival* 21 (May-June 1979): 107–115.

58. Thomas J. Bellows, "Proxy War in Indochina," *Asian Affairs* 7 (September-October 1979): 13–30.

59. Charles K. Ebinger, "External Intervention in Internal War," *Orbis* 20 (Fall 1976): 669.

60. Mangold, "Shaba I and Shaba II," *Survival* 21 (May-June 1979): 107–115.

61. Bellows, "Proxy War in Indochina," *Asian Affairs* 7 (September-October 1979): 13–30.

62. Ibid., p. 27.

12 Combat Rescue Operations

Michael C. Ryan

Except in the Civil War, despite scores of tries, there had never been a successful rescue of prisoners . . . during all the years of America's military history.
—Benjamin F. Schemmer, *The Raid*

This statement reflects the surprising and disappointing performance of the United States in the conduct of combat rescue operations.[1] The proud military tradition of the U.S. armed forces is somewhat tarnished by the lack of even a single success in the rescue of hostages from foreign captors. Why? What have we learned from these failures?

This chapter examines the cases of recent history related to the U.S. military response to prisoner/hostage situations. The purpose of such a comparative case-study approach is to explore the operational aspects of combat rescue operations conducted by the United States from 1970 to 1980 to discover whether recurring phenomena or causal factors influenced the outcomes. The results are relevant to defense analyses and studies because the identification of recurring, measurable, and causal variables can benefit decision makers, planners, and participants. The knowledge of the existence and importance of these phenomena can directly influence decisions whose ultimate purpose is to maximize the probability of success (and, conversely, to minimize the probability of failure).

The major cases examined are the Son Tay prisoner-of-war rescue attempt in North Vietnam in 1970; The S.S. *Mayaguez* crew rescue attempt off the coast of Cambodia in 1975; and the Iran rescue attempt in 1980 (see appendix 12A for case scripts). These three cases are unique in many respects, but the critical variables transcend the superficial differences among the cases and help to explain the outcomes of these operations.

A major criticism encountered in researching and examining the cases in a comparative fashion is reflected in the following statement: "There are no similarities whatsoever between Iran and Entebbe, or between any of these combat rescue operations if you really look closely. . . . It is like comparing horses and cows or apples and oranges—they are not comparable."[2] At first glance, the conclusion appears to be true. If the issue is profitability, however, the comparison of horses and cows becomes an economic choice, constrained by measurable criteria. If the question is nutritional value as measured by vitamin content, the comparison of apples and oranges becomes a chemical comparison, based on the scientifically measurable comparison of the vitamin content of the two fruits. In both these analogies, as in this chapter, the approach dictates whether the cases can be compared. The method of "structured and focused" comparison, suggested by Alexander George, is a useful method of analysis through which the cases can be compared and common causal factors identified and examined.[3]

The methodology employed in this analysis is organized around the answers to two central questions: (1) What hypotheses can be generated for success and failure? (2) How can these hypotheses be tested within the format of a structured comparative analysis? The answers to these questions considered in the following discussions of hypotheses generation and hypotheses testing.

Hypothesis Generation and Testing

Ten important variables are important to the outcomes of rescue operations: assessment, speed, surprise, security, command, control, communications, transportation, force selection, and force training. These variables were derived from the study and analysis of several foreign experiences, most notably the Israeli rescue at Entebbe and the German rescue at Mogadishu. In addition, U.S. service manuals and military doctrinal publications provided the theoretical framework for the identification of the variables. A detailed analysis of how these were developed is beyond the scope of this chapter; however, the variables were developed independently of the three cases examined here.

These ten variables appear to have a great impact on the outcomes of the operations. The causal link to ultimate favorable results and the interrelationships among the variables are not known, but in the Entebbe and Mogadishu cases the highly favorable outcomes were critically dependent on these variables. To approach the problem of applying the variables to three U.S. cases, the first step was to group similar and apparently related variables into a single hypothesis with multiple parts. For example, it is simpler to discuss command, control, and communications (C^3) within the context of a three-part hypothesis, and the artificial grouping does not degrade the independence of the variables. The ten variables were then grouped by this method into five hypotheses. For example, in the C^3 hypothesis, it is stated that if the operations were successful, then their success was critically dependent on effective command, control, and communications. (The definitions are contained within the hypothesis statement.)

Each hypothesis is followed by a brief discussion of the concept and meaning of the variable as they apply to the combat rescue operation in general.[4] In short, the five hypotheses state that success and failure can be accounted for by the level of performance of the key functional variables.

The concept of hypotheses testing follows three distinct steps. The first step is to construct a model in tabular form through an analysis of the appropriateness and performance of each hypothesis to each of the three cases, considered in chronological order. The format is reflected in table 12–1. The distinguishable aspects of each hypothesis will be assigned a rating based on an analysis of its application and function in each of the three cases; the ratings are high, medium, or low. The perspective in time for rating the performance is after the act—hindsight with the benefit of detailed knowledge. A high rating reflects the conclusions that the variable was operative and functioned in a highly favorable and beneficial manner to the performance of the operation. A medium rating shows a performance in a less beneficial manner. A low rating is based on the conclusion that the variable was operative but the performance was poor.[5] (These ratings could be viewed probabilistically. A high rating might correspond to a .98 chance of success, a medium to a .80 chance, and a low to a .65 chance.[6])

The second step is to develop a definition of success and failure, independent of the hypotheses and variables, according to which the three cases can be rank-ordered into relative positions of the most successful to the least successful.

The third step is to rearrange and rank-order the cases vertically and horizontally and to rearrange the ratings from high to low in an array that is basically a rearrangement of table 12–1. The model can then be examined for any evidence of Guttman-type scaling, and relevant conclusions can be derived.[7] The combination of testing, ranking, and rearranging yields interesting results, which are presented in the third section of this chapter.

There are distorting factors inherent in a study of this nature: oversimplification of inherently complex operations; the role of unidentified variables and imponderables such as luck and "Murphy's Law"; and the ease of criticism facilitated by hindsight. Much caution has been exercised to minimize their impact.

Finally, the implied purpose of this chapter is not to criticize the historical record. Rather, it is to analyze the cases of recent U.S. experience with the intention of deriving conclusions that will be of benefit in future, similar operations. The men and women associated with these operations were, and are, dedicated, courageous, and self-sacrificing. Any criticisms of these

Table 12–1
Table Format for Hypotheses Testing

	HI	*HII*	*HIII*	*HIV*	*HV*
Case one					
Case two					
Case three					

operations are not directed at them nor in any way intended to detract from their heroic efforts.

Hypotheses and Cases

A discussion will follow the statement and definition of each of the five hypotheses to be tested. The discussion will serve as an introduction to the cases and relate each hypothesis to combat rescue operations. The hypothesis will then be tested against each of the three cases. The results and ratings will be summarized as the analysis progresses, and the results will be tabulated at the end of this section.

Hypothesis I

The first hypothesis is that success is critically dependent on assessment (the collection, evaluation, and dissemination of information), which drives the planning, training, and execution of the operation. Assessment requires: (1) the continual modification of planning, training, and execution based on the latest intelligence; (2) centralized, integrated, and coordinated assessment efforts; and (3) the maximum use of the widest range of assessment assets.

In a combat rescue situation, the intelligence community must support the necessary preparations from the first moments the military option is considered. Unlike most conventional operations, the combat rescue is generally a one-shot opportunity in which the role of assessment is greatly magnified. The key aspects of this hypothesis, as expressed, are critically important to the outcome of the operation.

Hypothesis I: Son Tay. The discovery of U.S. prisoners of war (POWs) at Son Tay was a dramatic tribute to U.S. assessment efforts.[8] As early as 1968, Son Tay had been identified as a possible prison compound, but no conclusive evidence of its occupation by U.S. POWs had been discovered. Reconnaissance photographs were the primary means of intelligence for the initial confirmation of U.S. prisoners at Son Tay.[9] An analyst discovered on 9 May 1970 that there were two POW camps west of Hanoi, at Son Tay. A message at Son Tay was communicated through a code deciphered from a photograph of rocks piled in unique patterns, saying "There are U.S. prisoners here and a rescue is possible."

By May 25, the information had been passed through a series of official and unofficial channels and the chairman of the JCS was briefed. Given the fairly remote location of the compound and the strength of corroborating photographic evidence, the military option for a rescue became a viable consideration, and the order was issued to proceed with more detailed planning, to organize supporting intelligence, and to establish a core of personnel with supporting communications. The information about Son Tay was collected, evaluated, and disseminated to the highest authorities in the Pentagon in a relatively short time. The plan was conceived from this initial assessment process and involved further evaluations by other experts and military leaders.

As the plan evolved, the problem became how to get to and from the compound, surprise the enemy, rescue the POWs before they could be killed or removed (and avoid casualties in the initial assault), and then extract the force—all with confidence of a high degree of success. Nearly every detail of the planning depended directly on the assessments of the weather, the North Vietnamese defenses, the situation at the camp and general vicinity, and other variables. Thus, the role of assessment was paramount.

During the preparations and training of the joint task force (JTF), the plans and requisite training requirements were continually modified to reflect the latest changes and updates in assessment. By this time, the coordination among the various intelligence agencies had been accomplished and included the priority and assets from the Defense Intelligence Agency (DIA), the CIA, the National Security Agency (NSA), and the National Reconnaissance Office (NRO). Preparations and changes in training proceeded to the very last minute and were dictated by such factors as the forces they expected to encounter at the camp in North Vietnam and environs.

Although the assessment generally functioned well throughout the Son Tay operation, there were faults in the system and in some procedures—especially, but not exclusively, the failure to confirm the presence or absence of the POWs.[10] The clarity of hindsight was not lost on the Son Tay participants, who recognized the failure for what it was—a failure to use the necessary means, procedures, and organizations in a centralized, organized, and coordinated fashion to ensure that the mosaic painted in the assessment process was a picture of reality. There were at least three reasons for this failure.

The most serious problem resulted from the incorrect assessment that the prisoners were at Son Tay prison. Photographs confirmed that the U.S. POWs were there until around mid-July, when the compound was apparently abandoned. Around October, the compound was reoccupied, but every effort to determine who had reoccupied it was frustrated by some other problem.[11] Secretary of Defense Melvin Laird recommended proceeding despite the doubts and disagreements.[12] The operation was conducted and the rescue then confirmed that U.S. prisoners had been removed. In the face of uncertainty, a more coordinated and intense intelligence collection and evaluation effort would have revealed the true situation at Son Tay.

The second area of failures was related to the first requirement for assessment: continual modification of plan according to latest intelligence. An H-3 helicopter, which was supposed to fake a crash landing in the interior of the prison compound, almost truly crashed when it hit the trees around the compound. The intelligence assessments had failed to account for the growth of the trees over time, which in that climate was substantial. The analysts had further failed to assess properly a compound near the prison, which was heavily armed and well defended—it had been mis-identified as a secondary school. Only the accidental, albeit fortuitous, landing of the ground-force commander and the assault force next to the so-called school prevented that error from turning into a disaster.[13]

A final point in the assessment considerations of Son Tay is the question of means. At no time was a reliable human source tapped for direct intelligence on Son Tay. The information received from a North Vietnamese official regarding the move of the POWs was a remarkable piece of intelligence, but it was not completely reliable. A variety of other means was available and included remote ground sensors, reconnaissance teams, controlled U.S. sources, and so on. The tendency to rely on photographs created the conditions for ultimate failure and could have spelled disaster for the raid into North Vietnam.[14]

Does the hypothesis fit? There were major problems with the accuracy and completeness of the intelligence, with the organization of the assessment effort, and with the use, or nonuse, of the widest range of assets. All three aspects of hypothesis I contributed to the ultimate failure of the assessment—no POWs. Surveyed from a broader perspective, however, the mission produced major success as well—the discovery of POWs in the first place; the assessment of North Vietnamese air-defense capabilities; and a correct assessment of the necessary forces, equipment, and plans. Considered in total, and with the benefit of hindsight, the outcome of the Son Tay raid was greatly affected by the assessment variable. A low-to-medium rating is assigned to this variable in light of the overriding problems identified.

Hypothesis I: S.S. *Mayaguez*. Assessment was the driving force in the reaction to the Cambodian seizure of the S.S. *Mayaguez*.[15] General Jones's first order as acting chairman of the JCS was to dispatch a P-3 reconnaissance aircraft from Thailand, and later the Philippines, to gather information on the location of the ship and confirm its seizure.[16] Subsequent flights and intelligence-gathering efforts were somewhat limited by time constraints imposed by the decisions of the president, and real problems developed. The photographs taken by the reconnaissance aircraft were slow in reaching Washington, and analysts and interpreters were not immediately available to ensure the correct evaluation and timely dissemination of the intelligence on the crew's location.[17]

The in-theater intelligence assets of PACOM (Pacific Command) provided the initial analyses and interpretation of the photographs, debriefings, and observer reports. The assessments provided to the on-scene commander and his planners indicated that Koh Tang was lightly defended. The DIA analysts in the area and in Washington concluded that there were 150 to 200 well-equipped soldiers on the island. But the DIA was operating in a different assessment chain of communications. The DIA assessment was made available to the JTF intelligence staff, but it was not integrated and reconciled with the "lightly defended" assessment; it was therefore not made known in time to the key planners and the task-force commander (TFC).[18] The impact of the error soon became clear.

Does the hypothesis fit? The assessment effort was not centralized in Washington, nor in the local area of the Gulf of Thailand. The information available to the National Security Council (NSC) and the local decision makers was not fully coordinated, including the best use of assets for confirming the location of the crew. The unintegrated assessment effort locally contributed to the discounting of the DIA report. A fully integrated effort, coordinated at the highest level and centralized at the NSC and/or the task force headquarters very likely would have precluded the problem of assessing the threat on Koh Tang Island. The acceptance of the assessment of a strong force on the island would at least have generated contingency planning, which would have made close air support available.

In a very short period, a complex and detailed operation was prepared, planned, and executed. Both the crew and ship were recovered intact. Assessment weaknesses, however, contributed to the failure of the rescue operation in a very significant and avoidable fashion. Given the brute-force nature of the assault on Koh Tang, it is difficult to imagine the rescue of the prisoners without the incurrence of severe casualties among them. The crew's release was apparently a result of the air strikes and had little to do with the rescue attempt.[19] It was simply good fortune for the crew that they were not held captive on Koh Tang Island.

In summary, the hypothesis is relevant to the performance of the *Mayaguez* assessment operation. Despite the severe constraints imposed by time and distance, certain problems could have been avoided. The two most important assessment failures were the estimation of the forces on Koh Tang and the true location of the crew. These two problems combined to make the rescue precarious and unfruitful. For these reasons, the assessment rating is low.

Hypothesis I: Iran. The president and his assistants recognized from the start that any rescue operation into Iran would be very complex and that a maximum assessment effort would have to be made.[20] Not only was the distance an overriding problem, but there was also a complicated refueling problem, an air-space-penetration problem, and many others—all of which depended on the best possible intelligence. The sources, means, and assets dedicated to the effort were impressive and emphasized the recognition that assessment would drive the complex Iran rescue operation.[21]

President Carter felt that the operation in its final form was based on the best possible information, was well conceived, and had an excellent chance of success. This subsection will focus on the assessment effort in general and its function in the operation as it was conducted (without speculating on the outcome that could have been expected beyond Desert One).

The importance of this variable and the need for the continual revision and modification of plans and training was recognized and was reflected in numerous evolutionary changes to the plan and in the conduct of the training. The detailed planning for the assault on the embassy was continually revised, especially regarding the choice of weapons and equipment, as the picture of the situation at the embassy became clearer. Contingency plans were developed to deal with difficult problems such as how and at what phase the rescue force would be extracted should the attempt falter. The plan was continually modified to reflect the latest assessments of the Iranian ground and air forces and any potential outside interference. The assessment was very detailed and accurate, and U.S. forces were selected to match the perceived threat. United States planners apparently knew the location, capability, condition, and readiness of the entire Iranian air force.

Despite the recognition of the importance of assessment, and the extent of the effort, there were many problems and some obvious failures. The dust-storm phenomenon was known to occur but was not predicted by the weather-intelligence experts. In fact, its importance was discounted twice. First, a decision was made not to fly the route with a weather-evaluating aircraft prior to the actual launch of the rescue, because of security considerations. Second, the pilots were not briefed on the possibility of encountering dust clouds or storms, nor were any contingency plans developed to cope with the problem should it occur.[22] The weather problem had a tremendous impact on the mission and directly contributed to its failure.[23]

A second major problem was the choice of location for Desert One. Other sites were considered, but they were ruled out for a variety of reasons. The threat to security at Desert One presented by a road that ran nearby was a consideration and was hedged against by adding an additional security element to the orginal rescue force. In the actual operation, three Iranian vehicles passed on that road almost simultaneously with the arrival of the force at Desert One. The security element rounded up all but one Iranian, who escaped. Some decision makers discounted his importance, but he was considered a potential compromise of the entire operation by others.[24] In any case, it is clear that the traffic on the road was not expected, nor was the security-team force capable of ensuring that unfriendly traffic and personnel could be controlled.

The third major problem was the assessment of security requirements for the penetration to Desert One. Difficult choices were faced, for example, in the trade-off between total security en route and the need to communicate in case unforeseen problems arose. The choice for radio silence was influenced by the assessments of the Iranian air-defense system and of the Soviet capability to detect the flight and react.[25] These assessments were apparently very serious and led to a choice for more security at the expense of radio-use flexibility. The serious command-and-control problem that occurred during the flight was caused mostly by the prohibition against radio communications.[26]

The intelligence capability for the JTF was slow in developing and neither well organized nor integrated with the intelligence agencies.[27] Unlike an operation in which one of the intelligence agencies becomes the focal point for the management of the assessment effort in direct support of the JTF, in this operation the JTF intelligence staff attempted to manage the effort internally. This caused a wide range of severe problems, including severe delays, cases of raw data flowing directly to the planners, and failure to capitalize on a wider range of exterior agency personnel and equipment assets. By the end of the planning period, however, most of the problems encountered had been solved, and the necessary personnel and communications augmentations had been completed. The effort was centralized, as the hypothesis suggests; but it was centralized in the wrong place—in the Intelligence Staff (J-2), of the JTF.

In summary, assessment played an important role in the events leading to the cancellation of the rescue attempt at Desert One. The emphasis on intelligence, organization, and utilization of assets was clearly operative and influential on the outcome. In retrospect, despite many positive aspects (most of which are relevant to the planned operation beyond Desert One), the three most serious problems in assessment directly contributed to the failure: choosing the rendezvous site, discounting the dust problem, and overemphasizing security en route. In the latter case, the assessment may have been absolutely correct, but the excessive security reaction to the assessment was problematic. Overall, this variable rates a medium.

Hypothesis II

The second hypothesis is that success is critically dependent on effective speed, surprise, and security: (1) Speed is the degree to which existing or ad hoc organizations facilitate the effective management of time constraints for organizing, planning, training, and executing the operation. (2) Surprise is the act of catching the enemy unaware or presenting him with a fait accompli, frustrating his ability to respond effectively, and utilizing various means of diversion, deception, weather terrain, and time to create the conditions for success. (3) Security is the prevention of the compromise of the operation during any phase prior to the actual rescue (often referred to as operations security, or OPSEC).

Speed is an important element in every operation. From the crisis to its termination, time constraints operate on the decision makers, the planners, the trainers, the participants, and the adversary. Time constraints affecting combat rescue operations are particularly restrictive. It takes time to organize, train, and equip the forces necessary to the mission. The use of existing conventional forces drastically reduces the time, as in the *Mayaguez* case, but the inherent complexity of this type of operation generally demands a more specialized selection and training of forces. It also takes time to establish the necessary command-and-control elements and procedures unless contingency plans, routines, and systems capabilities already exist and are available and appropriate.

Surprise is a principle of war in nearly every modern army's doctrine. In a conventional conflict, surprise is a multiplier that can change not only the outcome of the battle but the direction of the war. It is one of the most important aspects of combat rescue operations. The successful rescue of hostages or prisoners from an armed and hostile force is predicated on overwhelming the enemy before he has a chance to injure the hostages or stop the progress of the rescue force. On some occasions, surprise may not be possible. The adversary may expect a rescue attempt and take extensive precautionary measures. In that case, the element of surprise must be created through a variety of means: deceiving, diverting, infiltrating, or simply presenting the enemy with a situation where he is overwhelmed (even if not surprised).

Security is also a principle of war and entails the use of all necessary means to prevent the enemy from discovering the existence and plans of the operation. It includes active and passive means to frustrate the adversaries' ability to discover the impending operation, as well as internal protection to prevent compromise through accident or mistake. Articulated by Napoleon Bonaparte and Carl von Clausewitz, security considerations are not new. Their importance in combat rescue operations is magnified, however, and deserves special emphasis throughout planning, training, and execution.

Hypothesis II: Son Tay. Considering the element of speed in the Son Tay operation, over two months elapsed from the first awareness of the presence of POWs to the appointment of the TFC. The Son Tay planners were constrained by a number of time factors, including "weather windows," political considerations (especially simultaneous negotiations for the release of the POWs), organizing and training the forces, logistical preparations, and so forth. The chairman of the JCS chose to create a force from "scratch," which made it a necessarily slow operation. The choice was deliberate, based on a calculation of risks and chances of success.[28] The absence of some key and required organizations, forces, and equipment exacerbated the slowness of the process. The preparation effort, as a result, took five months, and the rescue opportunity passed—an existing capability launched quickly at least would have had a chance. Because the POWs were permanently moved from the camp on 13 July 1970, any rescue attempt after that date had no chance (against Son Tay). The variable of speed is assigned a rating of low for these reasons.

There is little doubt that the Son Tay force achieved surprise. There were no U.S. fatalities and only two minor injuries. The surprise was achieved through no simple means and was created by excellent pre-operation security, successful penetration of the North Vietnamese air defenses, crash-landing the shock team of the assault force in the center of the prison compound, deceiving the air-defense forces and creating deception through "flare drops" over Haiphong, F-105s to draw SA-2 fire from air defense gunners near Son Tay, and diversionary air strikes to the south. Further, the surprise created by the rapid, violent, and lethal arrival of the ground force overwhelmed the North Vietnamese and other forces encountered. Son Tay was an excellent example of the operation of surprise and gets a high rating.

The great emphasis on security was illustrated by the attention to training security at Eglin Air Force Base (AFB), Florida, where the forces were training.[29] Only the four key leaders in the rescue force knew of the raid's true purpose and destination—even up to the final deployment to Thailand. In the operation itself, the team exercised excellent radio security in the flight across Laos to Son Tay. The OPSEC, however, was not so inflexible as to preclude breaking radio silence or to restrict the occasions for open-communications conversations (by the task force) that were felt to be necessary. A good balance was attained between security requirements and the need to reduce security for some greater purpose. Security and surprise reinforced each other in this operation. In short, Son Tay was an excellent example of how security can be achieved and contribute to success, and it gets a high rating in this case.

Hypothesis II: S.S. Mayaguez. In the case of the *Mayaguez*, a crisis-management team was activated at the White House and the Pentagon, and the National Security Council oversaw the organization with command-and-control authority through existing lines of command. The nonavailability of a specially tailored force for the *Mayaguez* rescue led the key decision makers to direct the relocation of Marine Corps combat troops to Thailand for possible employment in the operation. It is not known whether a special rescue force would have been used, even if it had existed, because it appears that a somewhat conventional operation was envisioned at the time.[30] Along with rapid speed, however, came problems related to assessment and planning, which created severe problems for the rescue-mission planners.[31]

In this case, the decision makers reacted quickly and used available forces. The Marine elements were trained and deployed as units, rather than serving an ad hoc function. Their combination with other service elements in a JTF was ad hoc, however, and differed from the organization of a typical Marine assault operation.

The operation was extremely rapid; however, the ad hoc nature of the organization was weak, and the consequent problems surfaced in action. Speed therefore receives a rating of medium.

Surprise was achieved in the initial attacks by U.S. warplanes on the Cambodian gunboats. This alerted the Cambodians, however, to the probability of more action against the remaining ships and possibly the island or the mainland. When the assault was launched, the helicopters were exposed for several minutes during their approach to the island and did not surprise the defenders. Evidence of the lack of surprise was apparent when the defenders opened fire with machine guns and rocket fire almost simultaneously with the approach of the first wave of helicopters to the two designated landing zones on the beaches.[32] Three helicopters were shot down and several others damaged in the first few minutes. It is not difficult to imagine what would have happened to the crew of the *Mayaguez* had they been held captive on the island. Surprise was almost nonexistent and the *Mayaguez* operation receives a low rating.

Security for the *Mayaguez* operation from the president down through the ground troops was provided by routine measures within the existing structures of the crisis action system (CAS). On the operational level, however, it was very difficult to conceal the deployment of the Marines, the redirection of naval forces, and other indicators of an impending operation.[33] The *Mayaguez* crew rescue presented a difficult situation. After the first gunboat was destroyed, the attainment of surprise and the preservation of security were difficult. Avoiding a variety of mistakes, however, could have reduced the difficulty of the situation. Movements, communications, and reconnaissance were not conducted in secrecy adequate to ensure a high degree of security. In fact, the perceptions of the Cambodians, as demonstrated through their reinforcement of the island and the coordinated fires that were placed on the assault force, indicated that security was not achieved. The rescue therefore receives a low rating.

Hypothesis II: Iran. According to the *Holloway Report*, it took from 4 November until 29 November 1979 for the United States to develop a reasonable rescue capability with a high confidence of achieving success. The plan was developed under the auspices of an ad hoc group that was similar to the organization that undertook the Son Tay operation—that is, under the control of the JCS.

The ad hoc approach led to a number of delays and problems, the most notable of which included the difficulties in coordinating the effort; the lack of proper standard operating procedures for security; and the failure to call on the widest possible range of active and retired experts (especially those accomplished in long-range helicopter operations) and submit the plan to a thorough review. Not only was the slowness, attributable in large measure to the ad hoc nature of the effort, a major problem, but the final operational plan reflected some of the weaknesses caused by the approach. For these reasons, the speed of the Iran operation is given a low rating.

The arrival of the force at Desert One was apparently achieved without the knowledge of the Iranian government, and the Iranian defensive forces were not activated.[34] The surprise was quickly lost, however, and the operation endangered by the arrival of Iranian civilians and the escape of one Iranian. How this compromise might have affected the remaining phases is subject to conjecture, but the risk of a loose eyewitness was real.[35]

It is a tribute to the personnel involved that a force of this size and composition could have been trained, deployed, and launched halfway around the world without detection. Surprise was achieved at least initially at Desert One and the operation deserves a high rating.[36] How the surprise would have paid off at the embassy is speculative, but the alleged confidence in the operation was so great that the president felt that the Desert One phase was the most difficult. If the surprise had been transferred to the embassy phase of the operation, it would have greatly aided the operation there.

The security throughout the Iran rescue operation was excellent. It was based on a concept of minimal knowledge of the operation. Few knew the entire plan. A complete plan was not even compiled until after the operation was over. All those involved were generally limited to their specific areas of involvement, and every facet of the plan, including training, was rigidly compartmentalized. Yet, the *Holloway Report* concluded that the excessive security was at the center of the failure—there is such a thing as too much security. The overriding concern with operation security created problems in several other areas: the number of helicopters, limited rehearsals, contingency preparations (especially communications), the selection of the Desert One location, and a number of equipment and training considerations. The balance between operations security and other requirements leaned heavily in the favor of security. The evidence suggests that the high level of security was attained at the cost of other variables such as force training and control.

In summary, the Iran case was an excellent example of how a high degree of surprise and security can be attained. The speed of preparation was slow and the ad hoc nature of the effort created numerous time-consuming and unnecessary problems. The ratings of high for surprise and security and low for speed are assigned for these reasons.

Hypothesis III

The third hypothesis is that success is critically dependent on effective command, control, and communications (C^3): (1) command that is unified (with clear lines of authority), qualified, and properly positioned; (2) control that is adequate to regulate the performance of the mission, including contingencies; and (3) communications that use the most advanced equipment and that are based on effective techniques, procedures, and redundant systems.

These three variables (C^3) are critical to every operation, but their importance in combat-rescue operations is magnified for several reasons. First, the rescue force generally does not possess the capability (by virtue of its purpose) to operate independently.[37] Second, the sensitive nature of these operations necessitates their control by the highest authorities of government.[38] Third, during the execution of the operation, the critical aspects of speed and timing necessitate the best possible C^3.[39]

In all three cases, the effectiveness of the C^3 contributed in identifiable ways to the success or failure of the operations. The command orders; the control regulates; and the communications provide the central nervous system. A failure in any one of these can jeopardize the entire effort. In the Son Tay and *Mayaguez* cases, command and control were so intertwined as to be difficult to separate. As such, they will be discussed together. In the Iran case, communications were also very interrelated, and all three variables will be discussed together.

Hypothesis III: Son Tay. In the Son Tay case, the chain of command extended from the president to the JCS to the TFC to the unit commanders (air and ground). This case was unique in that it was the first military operation in U.S. history coordinated under the direct control of the Office of the Chairman of JCS.[40] With few exceptions, the unified and specified commands (PACOM and theater service) in Southeast Asia were not informed of the nature of the operation. They exercised no command or control authority over the force, except for particular elements that were designated within their commands to support the rescue, such as air strikes. (The efficacy of this structure is debatable in theoretical as well as practical terms.)

The commanders and leaders in this case were well trained and well qualified. Every member of the force was well briefed and prepared for a wide range of contingencies. For example, the written plan's annex contained an 8-page section on hand-and-arm, flare, and light signals.[41] The force was tested to the utmost, in fact, when the ground commander (CO) landed in the wrong location during the first few minutes of the raid. The assistant commander, and second in line, automatically took over and executed "Plan Green" (CO killed or lost, wrong location, and so on). The operation continued successfully despite the major error. Command and control remained excellent throughout the ground operation and broke down only once near the end of the operation, when one helicopter was almost left behind.

The TFC was located at Da Nang and was exercising C^3 below with the rescue force and above with the National Military Command Center (NMCC) at the Pentagon. Once the operation was launched from Thailand, however, the TFC's control was weak and tenuous. His communications system failed and left him with after-the-fact information and little control over the situation at Son Tay. Events were so unclear, in fact, that he was forced to abandon his position at Da Nang and fly to Thailand to meet the returning rescue force and confirm the results of the raid. Meanwhile, above him at the Pentagon, the confusion and delays were incapacitating. Had a major problem developed at Son Tay, the decision makers would have known about it only well after the fact.[42]

Overall, the excellent C^3 within the rescue force facilitated the relatively smooth rescue attempt. The TFC, however, was neither in the best position nor properly equipped to ensure positive control. Rating command and control is difficult because of the disparity of performances within and above the rescue force, but they are rated high, based on the function of these variables at Son Tay.

The communications plan for the Son Tay rescue was very complex. The confusion that was experienced in establishing links with the Air Weather Service at Takhli Royal AFB foretold the problems this complexity would cause.[43] Brigadier General Manor's headquarters near Da Nang was set up to monitor the transmissions of the rescue force via a linkup with two EC-121 aircraft orbiting over the Tonkin Gulf along with a visual display of the progress of the concurrent air diversions. The original communications concept was to monitor the radio transmissions at Son Tay and observe the progress, with minimal interference from higher headquarters. The plan and the system failed in practice. The TFC could not speak to the rescue-team leaders, and his ability to monitor their transmissions was fragmented and weak.

On the ground at Son Tay, ninety-two radios on five different frequencies operated successfully at Son Tay and assured the rapid and successful assault. The coordination of the operation, especially in-flight communications, across a wide range of different frequencies and radios was excellent. The near-perfect insertion, assault, and return were facilitated by the effective communications planning, equipment, procedures, and techniques. Despite the problems above the level of the rescue force, the excellent plan and execution rate a high score.

Hypothesis III: S.S. *Mayaguez*. Command and control in the *Mayaguez* case were established under more self-constrained circumstances than in the other two cases. Consequently, the president used existing units and structures and operated through the existing unified and specified commanders. The chain of command extended from the president to the JCS to the commander in chief of the Pacific (CINCPAC) to the U.S. Support Activity Group (USSAG) 7th Air Force (the USSAG Thailand Commander wore two hats, being designated the TFC and on-scene commander). The rescue operation entailed the use of navy, air force, army (air), and Marine Corps units. Modern sophisticated communications enabled the president to speak almost instantly with anyone he desired. The existence of similar excellent communications in the theater of operations should have enabled the TFC to establish effective communications and through that system exercise his direct command and control of the operation. There were serious problems, however, as a result of communications difficulties. The inability to communicate properly and evaluate the assessment of enemy positions and strength on Koh Tang Island has already been mentioned, but other equally serious command and control problems arose as well.

The TFC and the pilots flying the mission were criticized in several postoperation reports—not for their judgment but rather for their lack of specialized experiences required for operations of this type. The air-force helicopter and pilots designated to fly the Marines to Koh Tang were not assault trained or oriented. Discussions and disagreements arose in the planning as a result of the service difference.[44] The problems that were encountered underscore the importance of experience, especially in time-constrained situations.

The command and control within the theater were generally well structured and tactically sound. The communications coordination problem, however, coupled with the lack of preparations for contingencies, quickly weakened the command and control over events at Koh Tang Island. The direction of the air strikes against the mainland and the control of the assault on the *Mayaguez* were executed without significant difficulty. The focus here, rather, is on events on the island.

In the actual assault, the importance of command and control was clearly demonstrated in several ways. During the lead assault wave, three helicopters were lost and approximately fifteen soldiers were killed before the first Marine landed on the beaches. The commander of the ground force was landed at the wrong location and was separated from the other two units, which were themselves pinned down on opposite sides of the island. The separation of the commander from the main forces and the loss of most of the communications capability on the two beachheads led to a severe state of confusion among the U.S. forces. As might be expected, the TFC airborne command post was also confused, as was the crisis-management team at the Pentagon. The situation on the island was desperate. The loss of command and control reduced the ability of the TFC to evaluate what was needed to improve the situation and then to provide it. Air observation efforts eventually produced a picture of events, and communications were reestablished through a series of communications patches and links. In short, severe problems with command and control had an unfavorable impact on the outcome of the operation. For these reasons stated, these variables are rated low.

Communications are rated low. The preparation for the operation was characterized by a large number of unsecured communications—attributable to both the status of the equipment and the planning for its use. The equipment and the plan did not permit rapid and easy communication among the airborne headquarters, and tactical aircraft, and the ground forces because of the variety of unintegrated radio—FM, UHF, and VHF. In addition to radio incompatibility, the lack of coordinated frequencies compounded the difficulty, even when the radios were compatible. The complexity of an operation with multichannel and multitype communications equipment necessitates a well-coordinated plan. Such had not been accomplished. On the ground, the CO eventually fought his way to one of the beachheads and began to reestablish control of his forces. The fortuitous availability of an Army Forward Air Control aircraft, equipped with a variety of communications capabilities, aided the situation by establishing communications with the air and ground elements and coordinated the supporting air strikes.

In summary, the C^3 situation proved itself to be poor because of the lack of prior planning for coordination of existing systems and of contingencies and the identification and preparation of potentially useful equipment. There was no evidence of any breakdown in communications above the task-force level. The communications problems contributed to the serious command-and-control problems as well. The combination of problems rates the performance of all three variables as low.

Hypothesis III: Iran. In the Iran case, the chain of command extended from the president to the JCS to the JTF commander to the subordinate TFC (air and ground refueling site). The force was organized through an independent task-force organization with channels of the C^3 outside the normal existing route, similar to the Son Tay scheme. This ad hoc organization created severe difficulties for the operation and hindered the success of the mission.

Above the JTF level, the command-and-control channels were clearly established and understood. The president was in direct communication with the JTF commander throughout the operation, and the various aircraft pilots had the capability to link up with the JTF commander (or even the president), were it deemed desirable or necessary.[45] The same clear command and control did not exist, however, within the JTF.[46] This problem is clearly illustrated in two distinct phases—the penetration to Desert One and the refueling operation there.

First, problems began for the helicopter force about two hours into the flight. The helicopters had taken off from the S.S. *Nimitz* in a loose formation (in pairs, with four pairs staggered), and they were to follow a complex, dangerous, and highly demanding route. Since the dust problem had not been anticipated, there were no provisions for communications in such a situation—even though a sophisticated system of light signals between aircraft had been designated and rehearsed. The authorized procedures allowed only for the flight commander to speak to the JTF commander; for internal contingencies, only visual signals were authorized. The security was so strict that radio silence was not to be broken even if helicopters were to abort. The combination of dust and maintenance problems caused the flight commander to lose control of the mission. Further, these problems became obvious only on arrival at Desert One, hours later.[47] The overriding concern for OPSEC led to the severe restrictions on communications—for many very good reasons; however, the sacrifice of communications flexibility and control cost the operation severely.[48]

The second illustration of command-and-control failure was at Desert One. Confusion existed at the site because of the delayed and staggered arrival of the helicopters. The flight commander was the last to arrive. The deputy commander had returned to the *Nimitz*. The air-force officer designated Desert One commander had very little warning of his appointment and had very limited means for dealing with the situation that developed. Even under the best of circumstances managing the situation would have been difficult: darkness, noise from twelve helicopter and twenty-four C-130 engines, swirling dust, and no alternate means of C^3 for coordinating the refueling operation. There was no designated command post, no clear identification of those authorized to give orders and relay messages, and no alternate means—runners, prearranged codes, and so on—to deal with contingencies.

The late arrival of the helicopter commander and the late assessment of the helicopter situation left the leaders with little darkness in which to react. Darkness was believed essential to cover the move to the so-called Mountain

Hideout. Even after the decision to abort was made, a future attempt at rescue was not completely ruled out. Provisions were made to destroy evidence of the U.S. presence and even to fly the Iranian so-called detainees out of the country. After the collision of the helicopter and C-130 at the site, however, any second attempt the following night was out of the question.[49]

Throughout the operation, and at all levels, the best communications equipment was utilized. Other systems, however, could have been employed: an advance weather mission; a pathfinder to lead the helicopter flight; and secure, special-communications (for within the flight) capabilities. The technology that was used performed well, but the techniques and procedures in the use of that technology were, in some cases, lacking—especially as it affected command and control en route to and at Desert One.

In summary, the technical means of communications and the exisiting capabilities were excellent and receive a high rating. The restrictions on the use of the communications, however, were part of the command-and-control plan; and the problems in those cases are clear. Overall, command and control receive a medium rating.

Hypothesis IV

The fourth hypothesis is that success is critically dependent on transportation, which includes travel to and from the objective with reliable and tested systems. This transportation problem is simple as stated, but it is complicated in reality. In all three cases, helicopters and fixed-wing aircraft were employed in transporting the rescue forces to and from the objective or in supporting the moves with logistical or tactical functions. There are several problems associated with the use of helicopters and aircraft on this kind of operation. First, secretly penetrating foreign airspace is difficult, especially when sophisticated detection means are available. Second, aircraft, particularly helicopters, are highly vulnerable to rocket fire and gunfire. Third, the long distances typically associated with these missions can tax the maximum capabilities of the pilots and fuel and maintenance systems.[50] These problems and considerations make the transportation variable extremely important. The hypothesis states that if the transportation systems are not tested and reliable, then the performance of the operation will be degraded. In the following three cases, the transportation problem was addressed in entirely different ways.

Hypothesis IV: Son Tay. In the case of Son Tay, the transportation aspect of the operation served as a near-perfect planning and execution model. The TFC, an air-force pilot, had hundreds of hours of flying experience with all kinds of aircraft. He handpicked the crew, support team, and equipment based on their dependability and reliability and the demands that the mission would require.[51] The only significant problems in the actual operation were related to command and control. The command helicopter landed at the wrong location, and one helicopter was almost left behind. Overall, however, the transportation was excellent and receives a high rating.

Hypothesis IV: S.S. *Mayaguez*. In the *Mayaguez* case, the natural choice of the means of transportation, helicopters, was necessitated by the order for a quick capability to assault the island and the nonavailability of other means of transport.[52] The number of helicopters and the location of friendly bases, however, were also limited. The TFC was therefore restricted in his choices for a scheme of operations. He chose to fly the Marines from bases in Thailand and to assault in two waves with all available helicopters. The second wave would be inserted after a turnaround flight of over three hours.

The concept posed several problems. First, if the first wave were to encounter serious opposition, reinforcements were over three hours away. Second, if any helicopters were lost in the first wave, the ability to extract the forces quickly or reinforce the island would be proportionately degraded.

In addition to conceptual problems, there were practical problems associated with the tactics of the employment of the transportation systems. There was some discussion before the operation regarding insertion tactics. A combat insertion called for either a low-level concealed approach or a drop-out-of-the-sky quick insertion—both accomplished with as much surprise as possible. In addition, either tactic called for direct naval and aerial fires to support the insertion. Finally, insertion required a quick landing, a rapid offload of the troops, and a speedy departure and the requisite skills, for these are very different from normal takeoffs and landings.[53] Over complaints by Marine Corps personnel, air-force pilots were designated to fly the mission. The pilots lacked the combat-insertion experience to adhere to doctrine or the polished skills associated with the art of insertion.

In the actual operation, the helicopters approached in clear view of Koh Tang Island, and three were shot down within a few seconds of the beginning of the assault; two others were damaged. In the smoke and confusion, the ground commander was inserted farther down the beach and became isolated from his units. After much confusion on the ground and in the air, the situation was finally brought under control (sufficient to cover the withdrawal).

The transportation performance in the case of *Mayaguez* was poor for these reasons and receives a low rating. The issue in this type of operation is much more than a simple ticket to and from the objective. It requires an adequate number of aircraft (or vehicles) with appropriate backups, special training to insure the reliable utilization of the systems, and well-established command-and-control means.

Hypothesis IV: Iran. In the Iran case, the planners recognized the seriousness of the transportation problem from the start.[54] To their credit, the planners developed a plausible, however complex, plan. Helicopters and C-130 transports were again chosen for the transportation means.

Without speculating on the plan beyond Desert One, the transportation concept up to that point was flawed in two ways. The first issue was the choice of the number of helicopters and the margins of safety built into the operation. A *Time* report claimed that a JTF study of the flight records of the particular helicopter used served as a basis for the decision to send eight and to expect no more than 25 percent loss.[55] Hindsight is of course very clear, and the debate will continue in and out of military circles, but the 25 percent margin is risky by any standard in light of the risk and complexity of this type of operation; high confidence is attained through systems redundancy and wider margins of safety. The second issue concerns the method chosen for navigation to the Desert One site. The C-130 pathfinder had proved itself a navigational method for leading helicopters on exactly this type of mission, as was demonstrated at Son Tay. The decision not to use it was apparently based primarily on security considerations and on confidence in the sophisticated navigational aids installed in the helicopters.[56]

There were many positive aspects to the transportation variable as well as serious problems. The pilots and crews were well-trained, experienced, and proved their capabilities despite the dust problem. The failure of the equipment, which was beyond their control, caused the cancellation of the mission.

Overall, the transportation hypothesis had great relevance and applicability to the performance of the rescue operation. Severe, mostly avoidable problems degraded the outcome and lead to an assignment of a rating of between low and medium for transportation.

Hypothesis V

The fifth hypothesis is that success is critically dependent on the rescue force, including: (1) the selection of adequate forces and the use of state-of-the-art technology and equipment; and (2) the proper training of the forces, which consists of integrated training for all operational elements, full rehearsals, comprehensive evaluations, and retraining.

The arrival of the force at the prescribed location is critical, but the performance of the force is the final measure in the completion of the mission. In all three cases, the quality of the forces was excellent. The motivation, courage, discipline, and dedication of the people involved were clearly demonstrated throughout the operations. The questions raised in this hypothesis concern the manner in which the forces were organized and trained. The focus here is primarily on the ground forces, since the pilots were discussed as part of the transportation issue.

Hypothesis V: Son Tay. In the Son Tay case, the ground force was composed entirely of special-forces experts and volunteers. Team members were trained individually, and then small teams and groups were integrated into more comprehensive exercises. A final comprehensive rehearsal and evaluation led to several major modifications in the plan (the addition of a helicopter gunship, the use of F-105 fighter airplanes for diversions, and so on) as well as preventing certain problems from surfacing during the operation. The rescue force performed almost flawlessly. The team had spent hundreds of hours preparing for the mission and were ready for nearly any conceivable situation. The equipment accumulated for the operation included specialized visual aids that were not even in the military-supply system. The combination of personnel, equipment, integrated training, and a full evaluation and retraining resulted in an outstanding performance at Son Tay. Force selection and training in this case clearly deserve a high rating.

Hypothesis V: S.S. *Mayaguez*. In the *Mayaguez* case, the operation was compressed in time and therefore afforded no opportunity for handpicking people or for specialized training, the assembly of specialized advanced equipment, or fully integrated training. The use of an existing unit of trained and capable Marines, however, avoided many of the problems encountered when a unit is created from scratch—especially unit integrity. The Marine units were disciplined and had good leadership and training, as well as functional equipment. The units were briefed; they had planned a rapid assault on the suspected hostage compound and even had time to conduct limited dry-run rehearsals on the insertion and subsequent actions. The problems on Koh Tang Island were in fact more a mismatch of forces than problems with the Marine forces themselves. Because the enemy forces were much stronger than expected, the assault rapidly converted into a hasty defense. Once the notification of the release of the prisoners was received, the operation turned into a withdrawal under fire.

It is not suggested here that only specialized forces can or should be used in these operations. All units conduct specialized training beyond basic soldiering, and the Marines committed to the rescue operation were fully capable of performing the mission. The lack of adequate time to conduct fully integrated training was the most severe shortcoming, particularly regarding the tactical insertion. A comprehensive review of the plan would likely have revealed the vulnerability of the force to unforeseen contingencies and other plans or alternatives considered. For these reasons, the force selection receives a high rating, and the force training one of high to medium.

Hypothesis V: Iran. In the case of the Iran rescue, a full evaluation of the performance of the ground forces cannot be made. The force was specially trained, however, and in a high state of readiness for the rescue. Problems at the Desert One site resulted from other failures discussed in previous hypotheses, but the ground forces were not really involved. (A full-scale dress rehearsal would likely have revealed the problems that would be encountered at the site, and appropriate corrective measures would have been adopted.)

The ground forces were well prepared for the operation. Although the units were not tested during the actual conduct of a rescue, the team and the decision makers shared a high confidence in their capabilities. For this reason, the force selection and training receive a high rating.

Tabulation of Results

Table 12–2 reflects the results of the five hypotheses tested. With the possible exception of hypothesis V in the Iran case (because the operation was not completed), all the hypotheses are relevant to these operations as a class of phenomena, and certain variables cut across and through the unique and distinguished characteristics of the individual cases. The results of the hypotheses testing are summarized in the following section.

Analyses and Conclusions

The first issue to be addressed is the formation of a workable definition of success and failure in combat rescue operations. The second issue will be to apply the definition to the three cases and determine a rank order for the cases, from the most successful to the least successful. The third issue

Table 12–2
Hypothesis Ratings for Each Case

		Hypothesis						
		II			*III*			*V*
Case	*I*	*1*	*2*	*3*	*1*	*2*	*3*	*IV*	*1*	*2*
Son Tay	L—M	L	X	X	X	X	X	X	X	X
S.S. *Mayaguez*	L	M	L	L	L	L	L	L	X	M—X
Iran	M	L	X	X	M	M	X	L—M	X	X

Note: X = high; M = medium; L = low. Numbers under hypotheses refer to numbered elements in hypotheses II, III, and V.

will be to combine the analyses of the variables and hypotheses with the definition and case-ranking analysis in this section to derive conclusions.

Success and Failure

A workable, widely applicable, and generally acceptable definition of success and failure is an evasive creature. Many different studies have wrestled with this problem.[57] Here the challenge is not to measure success or failure precisely but rather to propose a definition that establishes a relative order of success among the cases. The definition must also be independent of the hypotheses tested, otherwise the Guttman-type scaling would be invalid. The following comparative two-part definition is offered: A combat rescue operation is the most *successful* if: (1) the primary objective is accomplished, that is, the hostages/prisoners are rescued with minimum casualties to the force and the rescued; and (2) certain operational steps are completed in the best manner. These steps are arbitrarily established as bench marks, or major phases, in the operation and are (1) deployment from staging areas to the objective; (2) activities at the objective; and (3) redeployment from the objective. *Best* is evaluated by examining the number of serious problems and challenges encountered, how the forces reacted to the problems, and how the resolution or nonresolution of the problem affected the next phase. This is not intended to be a formal evaluation but rather a relative comparison and evaluation of the cases.

Rank Order of Cases

According to the first part of the definition of success, none of the cases accomplished their primary objective and, hence, all three were failures. In terms of completion of operational steps, the ranking of the cases is as follows:

Steps	*Best*	*2d Best*	*3d Best*
Deployment to the objective	Son Tay	Iran	*Mayaguez*
Activities at the objective	Son Tay	Iran	*Mayaguez*
Redeployment	Son Tay	*Mayaguez*	Iran

These rankings are then consolidated into an overall ranking that yields: Son Tay—most successful (all three steps); Iran—second most successful (better than *Mayaguez* in two out of three steps); and *Mayaguez* —third most successful.

Conclusions

In this section, the ratings and the case-ranking results will be combined and analyzed, followed by a discussion of the conclusions.

Table 12–3 reflects the rearrangement of the variables according to their ratings in each case. First, note that this horizontal rearrangement is a manipulation of the hypotheses only to the extent that the variables that were discussed within the context of a specific hypothesis are now separated and in a different order. Speed, for example, is completely disassociated from surprise and security. (Also, recall that the association of the variables originally was an artificial arrangement to facilitate the discussion and analysis and that it did not detract from their hypothesized independence.) Second, note that the variables are grouped from left to right according to the high to low ratings that were assigned for each variable and in each case. Third, the curve drawn in the table outlines the apparent increase in number of high-performing variables as the degree of success of the overall operation increases. It shows a very positive relationship between the increasing success and the identity and number of high-rating variables. Fourth, the box drawn around the variables and ratings highlights the variables that appear to be most sensitive to success and failure.

To draw conclusions, first consider the variables within the box in table 12–3. As the degree of success of the cases increases, the number of higher-performing variables increases. This is what might logically be expected if the correct variables are identified, and, in these cases, they are operative. The scaling effect shown by the curve seems to demonstrate that there are important variables associated with success and that surprise, security, communications, command, control, and transportation are positively related to increased success. No concrete conclusions can be derived, however, about the weights or relationships among the variables; nor can it be concluded that the variables constitute the sufficient conditions for accounting for success. In the analysis in the previous section, several relationships were suggested and might form the basis for further hypotheses formation and testing. For example, surprise and security are very closely related and show a positive correlation.

A second observation is that if the X (or high rating) in table 12–3 is viewed probabilistically, then the variables assume a meaning in terms of the outcome that reflects the effects of multiple probabilities. Assuming, for example, that in Son Tay all ten variables explained the outcome, the expected probability of success would be .51 or $P_s = (.98)^8 * (.85) * (.7)$. Viewed from hindsight, this suggests that these operations are very risky even under the best circumstances. Because of so many potential unforeseen circumstances, these operations are perhaps, at best, 50:50 odds. The

Table 12-3
Rated Variables for All Cases

	V, 1: Force Selection	V, 2: Force Training	II, 3: Surprise	II, 3: Security	III, 3: Communications	II, 1: Command	III, 2: Control	IV: Transport	II, 1: Speed	I: Assessment
Success										
Son Tay	X	X	X	X	X	X	X	X	L	L—M
Iran	X	X	X	X	X	M	M	L—M	L	M
S.S. *Mayaguez*	X	M—X	L	L	L	L	L	L	M	L
Failure										

Hypotheses

Note: X = high; M = medium; L = low.

implications of this conclusion (perhaps, in fact, more like 60:40 in a really successful case) should be obvious to the decision maker or planner: (1) the results of these operations are very sensitive to the performance of a single variable, and a lack of attention to any one drastically affects the outcome; and (2) a hedge against the degradation problem is to build as much redundancy as is reasonably possible into the operation (especially regarding equipment) and to plan extensively for Murphy's Law effects. Planning for every conceivable contingency is impossible, but certain means can simplify the problem. Lieutenant Colonel Robert Costa, an expert on special forces and operations, stated that there are literally hundreds of contingencies prepared for in the course of intensive and specialized training of individuals and units. In Son Tay, the execution of Plan Green was very easy because of the high degree of training. Routine standard-operating procedures and a so-called sharing of the mind of the participants through the unit-training process minimize the impact on contingencies. This realization is a strong argument for the preparation of an existing capability that would require only minor tuning for the unique requirements of the impending operation.

Turning to the least successful case, could the probability of success, $(.98)^* (.85)^2 * (.92) * (.65)^6 = .05$, have been so low in the case of the *Mayaguez*? Did the *Mayaguez* have about a one-in-twenty chance of success? Viewing the operation from hindsight and detailed knowledge, this author would argue that the answer is yes. The poor assessment, planning, and execution endangered the operation from the start. There were very few helicopters, which made the time gap between insertions of troops on the island too wide. What few there were were extremely vulnerable and needed more protection and support. There was little or no coordination for supporting fires. It is easy to be critical, and this author is not an expert. Yet the awareness of such a performance, coupled with the debilitating effect of multiple probabilities, should encourage decision makers and planners to look closely at the requirements for success in these operations.

Second, consider the two variables to the right of the box, assessment and speed. They are apparent anomalies because they are inconsistent with the pattern displayed in the table.

The importance of assessment to the outcomes of these operations has been well established, at least subjectively, in the analysis of hypothesis I. The fact that all three cases had major assessment problems (none rated high) may indicate that the poor performance of assessment explains, in part, why none of the cases fulfilled the requirements of the mission. (As defined, a first-order success entails the successful rescue of the prisoners/hostages.) In future studies that incorporate more cases (including more successful ones), it is likely that the curve will continue upward through the assessment if the hypothesis is correct. The conclusions therefore are: (1) the Guttman-type scaling used here has not enabled the derivation of solid conclusions regarding assessment; and (2) future studies will likely confirm the applicability of that variable to successful outcomes.

The essence of the variable of speed is that success is critically dependent on the degree to which existing or ad hoc organizations facilitate the effective management of time constraints for organizing, planning, training, and executing the operation. The degree to which speed played a critical part in the outcomes of these cases is not clear from this study; it appears to be very important, however, based on the analysis in the second section of this chapter. The addition of more cases to the study may also demonstrate the role of speed relative to the outcomes.

The inherent applicability and function of both of these variables was stated in the hypotheses and tested subjectively in the analysis of each case. The fact that the results did not confirm the relevance of the variables is not to imply that they are irrelevant. On the contrary, the analysis substantially supports the effect of these variables on planning, organizing, training, and conducting these operations—even though the relationship has not empirically been demonstrated.

Last, consider the final conclusion, by looking to the left of the box in table 12–3. The scaling effect in the table, along with the peculiarities of the variables, suggests that perhaps some of the variables are more controllable than others. Force selection and training are two variables over which the decision makers, planners, and trainers exercised a great deal of control, demonstrated by the high (except one medium-to-high) rating of these variables. Even in the least successful case, the variables performed well. One would also expect C^3 by this reasoning to be better because it is more controllable; but this is not the case, according to the results in the table. Perhaps the suggestion of controllability would be useful in a future, more detailed study of the variables themselves with implications for those concerned with the operations. A verification of the hypothesis, for example, that six of the ten variables are very controllable, two are somewhat controllable, and one is almost uncontrollable, would assist in several ways. It would aid in setting priorities when allocating time and resources for addressing problems. The classification of variables in such categories would assist the planners who (before a situation arises) must design the organizations and procedures to overcome the problems associated with controllability. Finally, if this knowledge could be combined with a knowledge of the weight of the variables, the information would be very useful in allocating resources.

This chapter was motivated by the puzzling dearth of success the United States has enjoyed in more than a hundred years of trying. In all fairness, Admiral James L. Holloway III might have been right when he remarked that "perhaps this is so because we frequently attempt the impossible" where others fear to go. Our attempts, however, and the likelihood that we will face the need in the future to conduct these operations suggest that we must prepare for them as best we can.

Many more questions were raised in this chapter than were answered. The effort was an initial approach, however, to cutting through the morass and confusion of "horses and cows," and its value lies in its usefulness for rejudging our efforts and decisions in expending lives and resources. This chapter demonstrated in an empirical way that there are indeed independent causal factors (variables), or groups of them, that operate across combat rescues. Hopefully, by understanding their meanings, functions, and relationships, we can more effectively manage them to produce successful outcomes.

Notes

1. Combat rescue operations are distinguished from other types of rescue, police, and special operations in that they generally: (1) are conducted across the borders of unfriendly nations and involve rescues within those nations; (2) are extremely complex, with multiphased plans and numerous problem areas; and (3) are conducted under hostile fire or combat conditions. This typology is my own, based on my analysis of the key distinguishing characteristics of this type of operation. The typology deliberately allows for the inclusion of a wide range of military rescues, from commando raids to larger conventional operations.

2. Interview with anonymous military planner for the Iran rescue attempt. The sentiment reflected in the quotation was encountered frequently in interviews and in the literature on comparisons of this type of operation, especially in comparisons of Iran to Entebbe.

3. Alexander George, "Case Studies and Theory Development: The Method of Structure, Focused Comparison, " in Paul G. Lauren, ed., *Diplomacy*, (New York: The Free Press, 1979), pp. 43–68.

4. A sixth hypothesis was generated but not listed. It was based on an eleventh variable—planning. Instead of developing the variable separately, the concept was incorporated into the other five hypotheses, especially contingency planning.

5. A fourth rating is implied here, which is "not applicable." All were found to apply without exception.

6. A planner might view this rating from the standpoint of calculations of probabilities of success based on the likelihood of successful outcomes for particular cases and variables. A variable with a high probability of success might serve as a guide for planning or training in a future operation. More important, such a probabilistic rating might encourage planners to hedge

strongly against contingencies by building redundant systems and flexibility for contingencies into the operation.

7. A conclusion based on this author's analysis and evaluation, evidence in the public record, and evidence presented in the chapter's second section. In this simplified version, the analysis is nonstatistical. The arrangement of the cases and variables on vertical and horizontal axes in the form of a tabular array might yield meaningful results if patterns exist across cases and a rising curve cuts across the cases—thereby identifying the most relevant variables in the cases examined.

8. Facts used throughout the remainder of the Son Tay discussions are based on information from Benjamin F. Schemmer, *The Raid* (New York: Harper & Row, 1976); congressional hearings; transcripts of briefings; periodicals; official reports; and interviews. Contested or controversial points are cited individually.

9. Extensive use was made of sophisticated equipment, experts, and techniques, including SR 71 "big bird," "Buffalo Hunter" drones, RF4 reconnaissance jets, weather and special-intelligence experts, and experts who knew how to "thread the needle" and penetrate air defenses.

10. These issues were raised in Schemmer, *The Raid*, and in Brigadier General Leroy J. Manor, "Report on the Son Tay Prisoner of War Rescue Operation," (Office, Joint Chiefs of Staff, Washington, D.C., 1971). The organization and emphasis here is based on my own evaluation of those and other issues.

11. A special drone photographic mission flew over the compound, but it maneuvered a moment too soon, and the clouds above the compound were the closest the photographers came to viewing the compound.

12. This is a somewhat controversial issue. Henry Kissinger stated in *The White House Years* that he was not informed that there was doubt about the status of the POWs at Son Tay. Others, including the key participants, did not share in the discussions. The failure to coordinate the mission and allay the doubts meant that the mission was riding on the hope that the prisoners were still at Son Tay.

13. Only 400 yards away, the compound's machine guns would have been able to place effective fire on the rescue force and helicopters.

14. The misinterpretation of photographic evidence (location and deployment of local enemy forces and tree height at the compound) along with the lack of evidence (drone photo of the clouds) clearly illustrate the risks and dangers of relying almost exclusively on photographic services.

15. U.S. Congress, House, Committee on International Relations, Subcommittee on International Political and Military Affairs, *The Seizure of the Mayaguez*, page 61. (Washington, D.C.: U.S. Government Printing Office, May 1975, herein after referred to as "Hearings-I"). Also, facts utilized throughout the remainder of the *Mayaguez* case study are supported

by other congressional hearings, transcripts of briefings and interviews, periodicals, official reports, and investigations. Contested or controversial points are cited individually.

16. See: U.S. Congress, House, Committee on International Relations, Subcommittee on International Political and Military Affairs, *The Seizure of the Mayaguez*, Comptroller General's Report. Part 4, October 1976, pp. 100–101.

17. Ibid., pp. 18–60.

18. There is little doubt that the ground commander would have demanded a change in the plan had he known of the DIA assessment.

19. Conclusion based on evidence from Hearings-I. See also chronologies in: Roy Rowan, *The Four Days of the Mayaguez*, (New York: W.W. Norton, Inc., 1975), and Richard G. Head, et al., *Presidential Decision Making in the Mayaguez and Korean Confrontations* (Boulder, Colo.: Westview Press, 1978).

20. Facts used throughout the remainder of the Iran discussions are based primarily on information from: hearings before Congress; periodicals; interviews; and James C. Holloway et al., *Rescue Mission Report*, (Washington, D.C.: Joint Chiefs of Staff Special Operations Review Group, 1980).

21. Evidence of this recognition can be found in the variety and intensity of assessment efforts: infiltrated agents contact with in-country agents, use of international organizations (Red Cross), and use of third-nation contacts.

22. Further, the compartmentalized-training concept did not permit a face-to-face briefing between pilots and weathermen (the normal procedure was the opposite), and therefore there was no opportunity for the problem to surface. Professional pilots are very sensitive to weather conditions and there was a good chance that the issue would have been raised.

23. Holloway, *Rescue Mission Report*, pp. 57–60.

24. Since the actual rescue would not take place until the following night, the escapee had twenty-four hours to pass on his experience to Iranian authorities, who would have had time to investigate the report. Perhaps he was a bandit, or was engaged in some illegal activity in the middle of the desert in the middle of the night; but perhaps not. Would he have reported the incident or not? Would it have made any difference? The answer is debatable.

25. Interview with Lieutenant Colonel Hugh Shaw, Iran rescue planner, March 1981.

26. The judgments involving trade-offs between security, control, communications, and the Iranian (and Soviet) electronic and visual air-defense capabilities are much clearer in hindsight. But it illustrates the importance of balance in the assessment process. Buying security at the expense of

flexibility (and based on assessments of the adversary and possible contingencies) is another illustration of the existence of dilemmas and trade-offs among some of the variables.

27. See Holloway, *Rescue Mission Report.*

28. A conventional force in Southeast Asia could have been hastily assembled and launched, but an initial review determined that the use of local forces was very risky.

29. It was known that Soviet Cosmos reconnaissance satellites flew regularly over Eglin, so special efforts were made to conceal the training during periods when the satellite was overhead. Also, wary of the Soviet electronics capability in the Gulf of Mexico, the training was conducted under a well-disguised communications program.

30. Interview with Admiral James R. Holloway, March 1981.

31. There were several other factors that could have contributed to a more successful operation: (1) the use of existing contingency plans, (2) the availability of a specially trained unit with its own transport capability, and so forth.

32. See House Committee on International Relations, *Seizure of the Mayaguez*.

33. Ibid.

34. *New York Times*, 25 April 1980.

35. Interview with Major General Alfred M. Gray, April 1981.

36. The Iran case is a good example of how artificial conditions of surprise can be created through deliberate means. According to an analysis in *Time* 5 May 1980, the president pursued a deliberate deception plan to help create the necessary conditions for surprise.

37. The rescue force is dependent on outside reaction and support in case of major contingencies, such as transportation, failures, and ambush. A small unit with limited capabilities in hostile territory has a vital need for reliable communications and effective command and control by the higher authority.

38. The detailed control of the operation, generally over great distances, is facilitated through the establishment of clear and unified lines of authority and decision making and the provision of the necessary means to exercise it.

39. In a larger sense, the political and diplomatic implications of the operation are heavily dependent on communications as well. For example, the lack of an ability to communicate with the Khmer Republic during the *Mayaguez* crisis created a number of problems that had a direct bearing on the operation itself.

40. See Schemmer, *The Raid*, p. 133.

41. Ibid., p. 110.

42. To illustrate the tenuous control, the TFC had added a flight of

escort F-105 jets to the mission as a diversion, one of which was shot down. The JCS level of the operation was completely unaware of a significant augmentation to the plan.

43. The task force relied on communications support from within the theater. Because some of the equipment was not available where expected, extensive efforts were required to assemble and operate the equipment for last-minute communications. With the NMCC dependent on Manor in turn, the communications problems contributed to the command-and-control problems.

44. See House Committee on International Relations, *Seizure of the Mayaguez.*

45. *Aviation Week and Space Technology*, 1 September 1980, p. 37.

46. Holloway, *Rescue Mission Report*, pp. 50–52.

47. Helicopter 6 aborted after a warning light and visual inspection revealed a cracked rotor blade. Helicopter 5 aborted after an electrical failure and concerns for safety in the dust cloud. The deputy flight commander was on helicopter 5 and could not notify the flight commander of his decision to return to the *Nimitz*. Upon arrival at Desert One, helicopter 1 was confirmed as having an irreparable hydraulic leak. With only five helicopters available to continue the mission (a minimum of six was required, according to the plan), the president authorized the decision to terminate the mission.

48. Gray interview.

49. The degree to which the C^3 problem contributed to the accident itself is unclear, but C^3 problems after the accident reflected poor conditions at Desert One: intact helicopters were abandoned without executing destruction plans; and sensitive and classified equipment, plans, maps, and even money were not removed from abandoned aircraft. See Holloway, *Rescue Mission Report*.

50. There are a multitude of other considerations for each situation, but there does seem to be a pattern in that transportation decisions contribute to the outcomes in a very significant manner. The rescue force must get to the objective without being discovered. The force must be extracted along with any rescued prisoners/hostages and must include the capability to handle casualties. The group must then return to friendly territory.

51. See Holloway, *Rescue Mission Report*, for interesting contrasts and comparisons regarding the transportation aspects.

52. Amphibious landing craft were not immediately available. Helicopters may have been the preferred choice in any case, but there was very little flexibility to choose an alternate transportation means.

53. Gray interview.

54. Iran is thousands of miles from the nearest U.S. base, adjacent to the Soviet Union, and Tehran itself is over 550 miles from the Persian Gulf.

The embassy is located in the middle of a densely populated and unfriendly city. The guards and the general population were well armed. The situation presented a seemingly impossible task of transporting to and from the embassy successfully.

55. Reprint of the Holloway Report in *Aviation Week and Space Technology*, September 22, 1980, p. 143.

56. The use of the C-130 would have provided some protection against four potentially serious contingencies: (1) it would have led the flight through unforeseen and difficult weather conditions; (2) a single lead aircraft with extensive electronic capabilities would have provided quicker and more unified movement to prevent delays, which would impact on the daylight problem; (3) the lead aircraft would arrive first, assuring the arrival of the key leader (helicopters) and the necessary equipment for critical operations at the site; (4) a lead aircraft would have been able to aid an organized withdrawal from Iranian airspace in the event of detection or cancellation of the mission.

57. See, for example, Barry M. Blechman and Stephen S. Kaplan, *Force Without War*, (Washington, D.C.: The Brookings Institution, 1978). The nature of the definition problem was illustrated by Stephen M. Walt's cogent critique of that work in " . . . A Critique of Force without War," *Professional Paper 279*, (Washington, D.C.: Center for Naval Analyses, May 1980).

Appendix 12A
Scripts

Son Tay

On 9 May 1970 an intelligence analyst with the Air Force 1127 Field Activities Group, Fort Belvoir, Virginia, indentified a North Vietnamese prison camp—Son Tay—that appeared to be holding U.S. prisoners of war. Information was disseminated from the intelligence community to the office of the chairman of the JCS at the Pentagon and eventually to an organization called SACSA (Special Assistant for Counterinsurgency and Special Activities), which eventually became the organization managing the operation for the JCS. By 23 May, the chairman (General Earl Wheeler) had made the decision to study the feasibility of a rescue operation and to organize and proceed with the effort.

In phase one of the operation beginning around 10 June a fifteen-person feasibility-study group was authorized by the JCS. (Phases are artificially designated for organizational purposes.) The group began serious planning to prepare the tentative rescue plan and was directed to select the appropriate leaders, forces, equipment, and training sites. (Tragically, the U.S. POWs were moved out of the Son Tay prison camp on 14 July. Ironically, this was the day after the ground-force commander, Colonel Arthur D. Simons, had been chosen to lead the rescue mission and months before the rescue attempt.) By 28 August the plan had been finalized, subject to improvements and changes necessitated by continually incoming intelligence. Phase two began about 9 September and included the completion of the selection of the forces, intensive training, preparation of equipment and briefings, and comprehensive evaluation of the force's readiness. By 10 October the force was ready. The launch was slated for 21–25 November since a failure to launch in this period would probably incur a delay until spring—after the monsoon rains and poor weather conditions had subsided. The secretary of defense gave tentative approval to the chairman for deployment and final preparations. The force was deployed to Thailand; equipment was readied; and the final go-ahead was received on 18 November. In phase three, the rescue team assaulted the prison compound at Son Tay, accompanied by diversionary missions of naval and air-force aircraft. The compound was indeed occupied as the reconnaissance photographs had revealed, but there were no U.S. POWs. The rescue force completed a reorganization and consolidation after a brief, but explosive, firefight with local enemy forces, and the U.S. force departed the area without a single rescued prisoner of war.

S.S. *Mayaguez*

The S.S. *Mayaguez* was a thirty-one-year-old U.S. registered cargo ship, with a crew of thirty-nine U.S. citizens. It was sailing from Hong Kong to Sattahip, Thailand, with a containerized cargo of commercial items. On the morning of 12 May 1975, Cambodian gunboats fired on the *Mayaguez*, and it was seized by Khmer Rouge coastal forces near Poulo Wai Island, approximately 60 miles west of the Cambodian mainland and about 6 miles south of Koh Tang Island. During the seizure, the captain had sent an S.O.S. and a report, which was received in Jakarta, Indonesia. The notification of the seizure was passed on to the U.S. embassy in Jakarta and forwarded to the White House through embassy channels. The *Mayaguez* was led to the island of Poulo Wai, where it anchored and spent the night. The Cambodians attempted to move the ship into the port of Kompong Som, but the captain's delaying tactics successfully prevented the move.

In phase one, notification of the seizure was received at the State Department and forwarded to the NMCC at the Pentagon and to the Situation Room at the White House. The acting chairman of the JCS, General David Jones, ordered reconnaissance efforts to locate the ship and confirm the report. The president and secretary of state were notified of the situation early that morning—12 May 1975. President Ford met with the NSC at noon to discuss the crisis. A consensus of opinion was reached at the first meeting. The first objective was to recover the ship and crew; the second was to do so in such a way as to demonstrate firmly to the international community that the United States could and would act with firmness to protect its interests. During the remainder of phase one, the ship was being located by reconnaissance aircraft and was tracked in its move from Poulo Wai to Koh Tang Island. By early Tuesday morning, 13 May (phase two), intelligence reports confirmed that Cambodian gunboats were escorting the ship to the mainland. As reports flowed into the White House, the president and his advisers became concerned with the means to prevent the movement of the crew and ship to the mainland. Assets were identified, and U.S. aircraft were authorized limited demonstrations of force—firing across the bow of the *Mayaguez* and the gunboats. Eventually, the Cambodian gunboats disregarded the warnings and the president authorized the sinking of any gunboats attempting to sail to the mainland. A fishing boat was allowed to move into Kompong Som only after warning shots across the bow and gassing the boat with riot agents failed to stop its movement. From this point forward, no U.S. decision maker knew with great reliability the location of the entire crew. Later reports revealed that four gunboats had been sunk by this time. The NSC met for the second and third times during this phase. Between the third meeting that night and the fourth held the next afternoon, the evolution of events confirmed the opinion of the president and his advisors of the need for the rescue. Phase three began with the fourth NSC meeting and the order to begin the rescue operation. The plan of operation consisted basically of three simultaneous actions. First, one element would seize the *Mayaguez*. Second, aircraft from the Coral Sea would strike the Cambodian mainland and support the other operations. Third, a Marine battalion would conduct a heliborne assault on Koh Tang Island in two waves to rescue the crew believed held there. In the actual operation, the ship was seized without a shot being fired—it had been abandoned. The strike aircraft bombed the mainland with little opposition. The Koh Tang Island assault, however, quickly became a major problem. The expected resistance was greatly exceeded by strong defenders on the island. Overall, the operation was considered a success by the president, most of the Congress, and the U.S. public. The rescue operation at Koh Tang Island, however, was clearly not a good operation, and it merits further study to determine why.

Iran

On 4 November 1979, Iranian student militants stormed the U.S. embassy in Tehran, Iran, and seized U.S. embassy personnel, visitors, and some Iranian workers. Shortly thereafter, a small group of prisoners was released, but fifty-three U.S. citizens remained in captivity until a negotiated settlement was finally reached and the hostages released on 20 January 1981. President Carter was notified of the seizure on 4 November, and before the full implications of the Iranian government's role were known, the United States denounced the act and demanded the return of the embassy and the freedom of the embassy personnel. In the days that followed, the president utilized the NSC and, later, a modified crisis-action group to deal with the situation on a continuing basis. The president renounced direct military action as a viable option the day after the embassy was taken. The receipt of a series of demands through unofficial channels heightened the seriousness of the situation, and the United States denounced the seizure as criminal international blackmail.

   In phase one, from 4 November 1979 to 29 March 1980, the JCS activated an ad hoc organization to plan, organize, and train for a rescue operation in the utmost secrecy. The forces and equipment were assembled and trained, and many serious problems were discovered before Christmas 1979. During successive fits and starts in training, planners and leaders of the rescue force became more and more confident in their capability. By 29 March 1980, the key decision makers shared that confidence. In phase two, lasting roughly until 23 April the plan was finalized and late-developing changes incorporated into it. On 16 April the JCS approved the plan and briefed the president, who gave the order to go ahead with a target date of 24 April. The mission (the third phase) began with the launch of helicopters from the U.S. carrier *Nimitz* and C-130 aircraft from Egypt on 24 April. The two elements were to rendezvous at a refueling site called "Desert One." Because of an excessive number of helicopter problems, the mission had an insufficient number of vehicles with which to continue, and it was cancelled. Shortly thereafter, an accident occurred at Desert One in which two aircraft caught fire, eight servicemen were killed, and the mission was hopelessly compromised. The decision was made by the leaders at Desert One to quickly evacuate the area. (Had the plan been executed in full, two phases would follow. From Desert One, the force would move under cover of darkness to a "mountain hideout," link up with agents, infiltrate the following night into Tehran, overcome security and resistance at the embassy, call for the helicopters, extract the force and hostages, and then fly to a second desert site. In the final phase the entire group would transfer to C-130s and fly out of Iran.) The failure of the mission at Desert One makes a critical analysis of subsequent planning somewhat speculative.

The rescue attempt was a courageous effort, and there were many very positive aspects to the operation in the areas of assessment, training, and execution. The failure of the operation, however, was a severe embarrassment to the president and to the military capability of the United States. The subsequent JCS Special Operations Review Group Report identified twenty-three issues of significance that were worthy of criticism.

**Part IV
The Future of
Regional Conflict**

Introduction
to Part IV

The chapters in part IV survey likely developments in the regions of the developing world, in Europe, and in space and the oceans that are likely to lead them toward or away from violence and to shape the form of conflict that will occur in those regions during the 1980s. The Middle East, a perennially volatile region, central to U.S. security interests, is reviewed by M. Thomas Davis. The peripheral regions of the Asian continent are reviewed in three chapters: Rodney W. Jones addresses the future of Southwest Asia, W. Scott Thompson that of Southeast Asia, and Gerrit W. Gong that of Northeast Asia. In chapter 17 Robert S. Leiken considers the trends and prospects for Central America, which now promises to surpass even Southwest Asia as the focus of U.S. security concern. Bruce E. Arlinghaus looks at developments in Africa, and Paul M. Cole and William J. Taylor, Jr. examine prospects for European security. Finally, Gilven M. Slonim, Thomas H. Johnson, Jeffrey R. Cooper, Lowell Wood, and Richard L. Garwin remind us of the new dimensions of future conflict that may be created by our increased expansion into space and exploitation of ocean resources.

13 Another Decade of Confrontation in the Middle East

M. Thomas Davis

The record of the past three decades, as compiled by seven U.S. administrations, clearly demonstrates that U.S. interests in the Middle East are considered vital. Former Assistant Secretary of State for Near Eastern Affairs Harold Saunders, has observed that more significant U.S. interests come together in the Middle East than in any other region.[1] Henry Kissinger noted in his memoirs that, in the past few years, the Middle East has become "the vortex of global politics."[2] No other area of the world has captured the attention of U.S. policymakers so completely and so continuously as has the Middle East. This situation will continue in the 1980s. If there is one thing more obvious than U.S. interests in the region, it is that endemic conflicts there will certainly place those interests in jeopardy.

Although clear, U.S. interests in the Middle East are difficult to rank in importance. Containment of Soviet power and influence is always at or near the top. The Kremlin has distinct interests of its own in the region, interests that fall into the broad categories of historical attraction, regional proximity, third-world competition, geopolitics, and oil.[3] So important are these interests to the USSR that is is unlikely that any U.S. policy can eliminate the Soviet presence from the area within acceptable costs, but well-conceived policies can serve to limit the latitude of Moscow's initiatives. The Soviet effort in the region cannot be stopped, but it can be narrowed, curtailed, and its adverse impact on U.S. interests reduced.

A second U.S. interest, in reality a derivative of the first, is reduction of the likelihood of a superpower confrontation in the region. In particular, Washington is eager to avoid a repetition of circumstances such as those in 1975 when it appeared for a brief period that there would be a clash of U.S. and Soviet forces over the settlement of a regional conflict. The geographical relationship of the Middle East to the Soviet heartland and the recently demonstrated power-projection capability of the Kremlin's armed forces, mark the area as a location where direct superpower confrontation certainly is possible if not probable.

Another regional U.S. interest is the survival and prosperity of Israel. Since the declaration of Israel's existence in 1948, the United States has committed itself firmly to the survival of the modern Jewish state. Even as other U.S. allies have distanced themselves from Jerusalem, the United States has steadfastly maintained its position as the ultimate guarantor of

Israeli security. The recent erosion of the U.S.-Israeli relationship has not changed the fundamental nature of the U.S. commitment. Whether the United States has accepted this role out of self-interest or because of domestic political considerations is irrelevant; the fact is that the U.S. position on Israel is widely recognized and must be assumed as effectively constant despite occasional exchanges of unflattering rhetoric.

The next U.S. interest in the Middle East is the maintenance of cordial relations with moderate Arab regimes. This creates a dilemma because the service of this interest is a direct disservice to the interest concerning Israel. It is an exceptionally difficult diplomatic task to be friendly simultaneously with hostile governments; nonetheless, this has been a fixture of the U.S. Middle Eastern experience in the recent past. To diminish the difficulty of the situation, the United States has invested enormous energy over the past decade in the quest for a solution to the Palestinian problem, which is widely recognized, at last, as the core of the Arab-Israeli dispute. Although the returns have yet to be proportionate to the investment, the centrality of this issue to other U.S. regional interests is such that persistent efforts to solve the Palestinian question are highly likely.

The final U.S. interest is the continued flow of Middle Eastern oil from the region's vast petroliferous areas. The major U.S. oil corporations were instrumental in both finding and developing this resource, which has so dramatically served to change the face of Middle Eastern life—especially since the tremendous price rise of 1974. This interest is, however, one that is in flux. Whereas the other interests are quite direct in their implications for U.S. foreign policy, oil is becoming more indirect as the quantity of U.S. oil imports continue to fall. The United States does import significant amounts of Middle Eastern crude, but the major concern is the extensive imports required by the major Western allies.[4] Conservation efforts have reduced the demand for oil, but it still remains the single major fuel source of modern industrial economies, and a significant change in the energy profile of Europe and Japan is in the distant future. Even if the level of U.S. oil imports from the Middle East dropped to zero, the heavy dependence of the allies (effectively a total dependence in the case of Japan) will dictate that U.S. concerns remain on the nature of the Middle Eastern oil trade.[5]

The interests of the United States in the Middle East are easily documented as both extensive and intensive. Even events that occur outside the region's commonly accepted boundaries can create reactions in Washington if there is the possibility that the effects will spill over into the Middle East proper. The Soviet invasion of Afghanistan in December 1979, which triggered the announcement of the Carter doctrine the following month, stands as testimony to the existence of this U.S. sensitivity. Because of this sensitivity, the United States undoubtedly will suffer through some apprehensive and perhaps trying times in the years ahead, for if there is one certainty about this extraordinarily dynamic and complex area, it is that conflict is endemic.

Conflict in Historical Perspective

The Middle East contains conflicts that persist on almost every level of analysis. There are clashes between rival groups within established regional states. Over the last five years, Lebanon and Iran have served as case studies for this type of upheaval. Large groups in both countries have banded together to seek radical restructure of the existing political system because they believed it to be misguided, unresponsive, corrupt, or simply unrepresentative of the true national will. Lebanon had descended into virtual anarchy as the national government lost control to other internal forces seeking adjustments of a political system that has undergone extensive demographic changes. In 1958, the United States landed forces in Lebanon pursuant to the Eisenhower Doctrine when it appeared that the established governmental structure was in danger of collapse. In 1975, when chaos again became the mark of Lebanese internal affairs, Syrian forces intervened to restore a semblance of order in the midst of an escalating fratricidal war.[6]

In Iran the changes were not so much demographic as they were economic and spiritual. The clash between the programs of modernizing, secular elites and the traditional theological orientation of the Shi'ite clergy has marked the internal politics of Iran for centuries. In this century alone, there have been significant developments in this struggle in 1905, 1924, 1953, and most recently in 1979. Even as the clerics came to power in the person of Ayatollah Khomeini following the last clash, the secular opposition was forming to counterattack when the opportunity developed.[7]

The Middle East has been center-stage for the clash of ideologies. The landscape is dotted with governments of dramatically different character. The spectrum of political ideologies goes from feudal monarchy—the governmental form of most Persian Gulf states, notably Saudi Arabia—to totalitarian Marxism as found in South Yemen, the only admittedly Marxist state in the region. In between are several versions of homegrown progressive socialism, best illustrated by Colonel Qaddafi's regime in Libya, which blends a complete socialist state with Islamic zealotry, and the Baathist regimes in Syria and Iraq, which emphasize economic centralization and the merits of Arab nationalism.

The clash of ideologies (and Islam itself can be viewed as ideology) has produced several confrontations. The five-year struggle over Yemen between socialist Egypt and monarchical Arabia stands as the most obvious example. Dramatically divergent political ideas certainly are no absolute requirement for conflict; however, even those of similar persuasion, such as

Syria and Iraq, can find ample evidence of divergence to justify cries of heresy against those who would appear to be philosophical brethren.

The struggles between those who are cut from the same political cloth indicate that there can be conflicts reflecting regional rivalries. Iraq and Egypt have been traditional rivals for regional leadership, and this condition remained unchanged even after the 1958 Iraqi revolution when the Hashemite monarchy in Baghdad was toppled in a leftist military coup. Despite the similarities between this development and the Egyptian experience of 1952, the two states and their leaders, Nasser in Egypt and Kassim in Iraq, were unable to achieve regional cooperation. In 1961, when Kassim announced his intention to annex Kuwait, Nasser joined forces with Saudi Arabia and Jordan to defend Kuwait from Iraqi attempts at hegemony. In a bizarre twist, the three Arab countries sent military forces to Kuwait, which relieved British troops providing defense, until an Arab response to the Iraqi design was coordinated.[8]

Obviously, the most fundamental and persistent struggle in the Middle East is the clash between Arabs and Israelis. Whether this is, as some have suggested, a clash of two nationalist groups[9] or a struggle created by misunderstanding and circumstance, the result is the same—persistent tension occasionally yielding to violent conflict.[10] Since the founding of Israel, there have been four open, conventional wars between the Jewish state and its surrounding neighbors. In addition, there have been static wars such as the so-called War of Attrition fought along the Suez Canal by Egypt and Israel from 1969–1970 and unconventional wars such as the guerrilla campaigns of the Palestinian Liberation movements and the inevitable Israeli responses. Ever since the first major guerrilla action against Israel in 1954, and the reactive Israeli attack into Gaza in February 1955, this condition has existed as a regional fixture. Evidently it is chronic.

A final historical dimension of conflict has been in the realm of the superpowers. In this regard, the powers themselves have changed with the British and French presence of the past yielding to the U.S. position of the present. The Western proclivity for intricate involvement in Middle Eastern affairs has a long history, but the period of intense association with the region's fortunes is most directly traceable to the British occupation of Egypt in 1882.[11]

The last gasp of British and French intrigue was the ill-advised Suez War of 1956, which saw the United States and the Soviet Union emerge as the major forces operating regionally.[12] Since Khruschev's conscious decision in 1955 to enter the Middle East in greater scale, and his simultaneous effort to compete with the United States for the hearts and minds of the third world, the two superpowers have jostled for position all across the Arab world. So far this has not resulted in a catastrophic confrontation, although there have been some reasonably close calls. The Soviets' clumsy efforts leading to the

1967 war, a classic example of misperception and disinformation creating conditions that soon careened wildly out of control, could have excited a superpower confrontation had it not been for the unexpected swiftness and decisiveness of the Israeli victory.[13] The 1973 experience provided another example of the dangerous potentials present when world powers become the servants of regional clients.[14]

Conflict in Present Perspective

A survey of the Middle East (moving geographically from west to east) is a survey of conflict. On the Atlantic coast one finds the clash between Morocco and the *Polisario* guerrilla movement. This struggle, which pits an established government against an indigenous (although externally based and supported) guerrilla force, has existed at various levels of intensity since Spain relinquished control of the Western Sahara in 1975. Morocco claims the region as its thirty-seventh province and asserts that public-opinion polls support that position. The *Polisario*, on the other hand, claims to represent a legitimate nationalist movement and has stated that its goal is the establishment of a new state. Morocco has enjoyed a lengthy and constructive relationship with the United States and has requested U.S. assistance in the form of foreign military sales to secure its border areas and crush the *Polisario*. The *Polisario* is widely reported to have support from Libya, Algeria, and possibly the Soviet Union. This association with radical forces has allowed the Moroccans to claim that they are not seeking the destruction of a liberation movement but are merely attempting to defend their country against a Soviet-backed invasion.

As the war has moved northward along the international border between Morocco and Algeria, there has been concern that a local conventional war might erupt. This fear has been complicated by a somewhat controversial decision made by the Carter administration in its last months to sell counterguerrilla equipment to King Hassan's army. Many have argued that such a move would alienate the United States from Algeria, which has been seeking improved relations with the West in general and the United States in particular. Others feel, however, that such a sale would give Washington some leverage over Moroccan policy and could induce progress toward a negotiated settlement. The entire issue is unclear largely because of uncertainty about the actual composition of the *Polisario* leadership and the precise nature of the outside support it has managed to secure.[15]

One of the most disturbing factors in the *Polisario* issue is the alleged connection with Libyan leader Muammar Qaddafi. The air engagement that occurred in the Gulf of Sidra in August 1981 was but the latest in a long series of grievances that the United States holds against the Libyan revolutionary government headed by Qaddafi. With a disproportionately large armed force, expansively equipped with some $12 billion of Soviet military hardware, Libya has become increasingly bold in its involvement with its neighboring states.[16]

In mid-1980, the Qaddafi government supported a large raid into Tunisia. Apparently, this was the warm-up for his next adventure, the December 1980 invasion of Chad in support of General Goukouni Oueddei, who was engaged in a civil war. In January 1981, Radio Tripoli announced that Chad and Libya would merge, although the actual result was an eventual Libyan withdrawal from the country and a seeming reorientation by Oueddei toward the West. Several members of the Organization of African Unity (OAU), including Gambia and Ghana, severed diplomatic relations with Libya; other such as Niger and Senegal, concerned over further Libyan meddling south of the Sahara, hinted at the desirability of French troops to keep the Libyans under control.[17]

Concerns about Libyan terrorist activities were greatly heightened in the wake of the assassination of Egypt's President Sadat in October 1981. Whether there was Libyan involvement in the murder remains unclear, but some of the credit was claimed by expatriate Egyptians, such as former chief of staff of the armed forces, General Saad El Shazli, who resides in Tripoli. Regardless of the nature of the assassins' external support (if there was any), the result is an uncertain future for the new government led by Sadat's chosen successor, Housni Mubarak.

Beyond real political questions concerning the decade of the 1980s are the long-term economic realities that face Egypt. It is clear that the economic revival the peace with Israel was supposed to bring as Egypt shifted funds from the military to capital investment is slow in developing. Many former policies such as food subsidies and guaranteed employment for college graduates have proven difficult to reverse. This has greatly retarded the government's plans to control public spending. In addition, the population continues to grow at the rate of one million per year, putting continued pressure on the available arable land, much of which is lost to urban sprawl. The economic infrastructure remains one of the region's worst—even though the United States has transferred more money to Egypt since 1975 on a per-capita basis than it did to Europe during the days of the Marshall Plan.[18]

The fact that Sadat had failed to make economic progress commensurate with societal expectations may have been reflected in the lack of public grief at his passing. President Mubarak can expect a reasonable honeymoon period, but if there are no significant signs of progress after the expected return of the Sinai in April 1982, then he will find himself in deep trouble, particularly if the Islamic opposition further expands its base and penetrates the armed forces.

To the east, the Arab-Israeli conflict drones on even in the absence of Egypt. In spring 1981, another crisis occurred over Lebanon as Syria moved ground-to-air missiles into the Bekaa valley of southern Lebanon following the downing of a helicopter by the Israeli air force. Israeli Prime Minister Begin demanded the removal of the missiles and stated that uninhibited access to the airspace of Lebanon was vital to Israel's security. The sensitive nature of the situation caused President Reagan to dispatch Ambassador Philip Habib on a special mission to head off another general conflict over Lebanon.[19]

Just as the dust was settling over this altercation came the attack by Israel on the Iraqi nuclear reactor. Israel insisted that such action was necessitated by the announced plans of the Iraqi Baathist regime to use the facility to produce weapons aimed against "the Zionist entity." Unfortunately, the Israelis were unable to produce the exact quotes referenced, and the perception grew that the attack may have been designed for domestic political impact.[20]

On 30 June, the Israeli electorate returned to power the government of Prime Minister Begin by a very slim majority. The election results reflected emerging fissures within the Israeli body politic, manifested by the appointment in August of a more ideologically doctrinaire cabinet.[21] This was preceded, however, by a massive Israeli air raid on downtown Beirut that left hundreds dead and again flamed the passions of the Palestinian resistance.[22]

In Syria, the regime of President Haffez Assad struggled to maintain power while confronting Israel and maintaining a peacekeeping force in Lebanon. Because of this large external burden as well as concerns over the narrow base of the ruling regime internally, Assad spent much of his time on the road drumming up support. He courted Libya's Qaddafi briefly, even going so far as to issue a statement about the eventual merger of Libya with Syria, and he signed a Treaty of Friendship and Cooperation with the Soviet Union. By summer 1981, Syria and the Soviet Union were conducting joint military operations in the eastern Mediterranean, a development that caused considerable alarm in both Israel and Turkey.[23]

Another dimension of the Syrian condition was its continued antagonistic relationship with its brother Baathist regime in Iraq. Although these two governments represented different wings of the same party, the ideological affinity was not close enough to prevent a regular exchange of insulting innuendo. From the start of the Iraq-Iran war in September 1980, Syria sided with Persian Iran and at one time underscored its rejection of Iraqi calls for support based on Arab brotherhood, by massing troops along its Jordanian border where King Hussein was actively supporting Baghdad with a line of communications running through his only port at Aqaba.

In Baghdad, meanwhile, efforts to capitalize on the turmoil in Iran and simultaneously to halt the apparent meddling of Iranian clerics in the predominantly Shi'a provinces of southern Iraq resulted in stalemate along the Shatt-al-Arab war zone. As both countries took turns attacking each other's oil installations, fears mounted in the West that the oil flow from the Gulf could be interrupted, creating a new price spiral similar to the one that played havoc with the international economy in 1979. There was also concern that the war would spread to the neighboring Gulf states, placing the entire world in a crisis situation of indefinite duration.[24] The United States responded to this possibility by stationing advanced Airborne Warning and Control System (AWACS) radar aircraft in Saudi Arabia in an effort to bolster that country's air defense, thereby protecting its oil facilities from nuisance attacks that either combatant might mount.[25] But through it all, the war stumbled along, both sides unable to afford the costs of either victory or defeat.

Conflict Analysis for the Future

This brief survey across the Middle East illustrates the types of conflicts that have prevailed and are likely to continue throughout the 1980s, for reasons that are as complex as the region itself. It is difficult to reduce the sources of conflict into a simple paradigm, but there appear to be three fundamental variables that cause and contribute to the region's traumas. First is the simple fact of the region's geographic location. As the crossroads of a tricontinental area, the Middle East has strategic importance to both of the major alliances. The West's strategic interests were central to the disastrous decision of France and Britain to go to war with Nasser over the Suez Canal in 1956. As for the Soviet Union, the Middle East remains its only border area that is neither neutralized nor communized. In addition, the growing Islamic fervor of the region has implications for the Soviets that are quite disturbing. As the fifth largest Muslim country in the world, and with the bulk of this internal Muslim population located in areas bordering on the Middle East, Moscow has to be concerned about a possible spillover effect of Islamic fundamentalism. These conditions combine to guarantee great-power interest and intrigue unlikely to diminish in the foreseeable future.

The second variable is closely associated with the first—the nature of the region's oil trade and the geopolitical implications of the control, disruption, or interruption of that trade. Although the United States has reduced its oil imports significantly since 1979 and has also managed to diversify its sources, the major allies in Europe and Japan have been unable to follow suit. As long as this condition continues, the Middle East will remain a sensitive area.

But perhaps the single most important variable contributing to regional conflict is the nature of the Middle Eastern state system. It is paradoxical that despite the states' demonstrated resilience (the borders have remained essentially unchanged since the mid-1920s), they are nonetheless artificial in design and fragile in structure. Because of this condition, the states are the targets of numerous groups motivated by various causes and stimulated by diverse interests both internal and external to the region.

Regime Instabilities

The states are artificial creations largely because their borders were drawn by colonial powers that had a greater interest in administrative necessity than geographic, demographic, or ethnic reality. The nations of the Levant, in particular, reflect the arbitrary nature of the local border histories. In general, Saudi Arabia is the only modern state that totally escaped a colonial experience. Not only do the regimes reflect philosophical divergences, but the existence of ideologically incompatible governments in adjoining states sharing both common historical experiences and ethnic compositions is at once remarkable and dangerous. It creates inevitable frictions that can be controlled and managed only through continuous attention.

The states of the region have become fixtures withstanding all calls for their dismemberment or absorption into greater regional entities. The very purpose of both the Pan-Arab and Pan-Islamic movements has been the collapse of existing states into a greater nation, but neither of these efforts has produced anything beyond the loosely structured organizations represented by the Arab League and the Islamic Conference. Nevertheless, despite their continued survival, the states are destined to serve as lightning rods that attract regional trouble.

Control of an established state is the goal that most of the challenge groups in the Middle East seek. This goal exists in part because the apparatus of a state, particularly its communications capability, gives competing factions the capability of spreading and furthering their messages. Control of an established military machine is another purpose, but this is apparently less important in light of the Iranian experience.

The most easily documented evidence of weak internal conditions in the local states is their general failure to develop institutionalized procedures for leadership succession. To be sure, Egypt, Algeria, and Saudi Arabia have witnessed leadership successions without accompanying violence; but in all these cases succession followed the death of an established ruler, and in no case was there an assumption of power by a rival political movement. No Middle Eastern country, with the exceptions of Israel and Turkey, has yet seen a peaceful transfer of real power to a group previously in opposition to the established order.[26]

The internal condition of the states and the existence of serious domestic challengers will continue to make political stability difficult to maintain for several reasons. First are the pressures of modernization. Most Middle Eastern states are attempting to transform essentially feudal societies into modern, progressive entities within a couple of decades. The same process in the established industrial states took several generations. The process of modernization has been most rapid in the oil-producing countries, where the tremendous influx of petroleum wealth has financed expansive development projects. Unfortunately, these same states are the ones that must start from the lowest level of economic, social, and political development. The effects of educating whole new segments of society that were formerly outside the cultural mainstream and of creating entirely new administrative and technocratic elites are not even partially understood. If there is one message from the Iranian revolution that is totally unambiguous, it is that the consequences of economic development in traditional societies are unknown.[27]

A second condition that will retard political stability is the supposed transitory nature of the states' regimes.[28] In many, such as Iraq, Syria, Libya, and even Egypt, the official dogma is that current conditions reflect only a temporary way-station to the next stage of development. One might argue that this condition (as well as the one concerning the lack of institutionalized vehicles for succession) is similar to the so-called official position of the Soviet Union—not normally considered an unstable state. But the Middle Eastern states, despite great effort, do not have the centralized internal security apparatus enjoyed by the Kremlin and do have serious internal opponents. If the illusion of power is often as useful as power itself, then the illusion of weakness is just as dangerous as real vulnerability.

A third source of state weakness likely to persist is the maldistribution of wealth both within the countries of the region and among them. A serious problem is the gap that clearly exists between the haves and the have nots. In the oil-rich states, the affluence of ruling classes often stands in sharp contrast to the conditions of the masses. Where there is sufficient money to go around, as in Saudi Arabia and Kuwait, even an inefficient trickle-down policy can achieve satisfactory results.[29] However, where resources are more constrained, as they were in Iran, the failure to spread recognizable benefits across the society will be disastrous.

This situation can have an external component as well. It is clearly recognized that the distribution of the region's petroleum resources ironically is skewed. The countries with substantial oil deposits are generally the ones with the smallest populations and the least potential for significant development outside the energy sector.[30] Iran (and Iraq to a lesser extent) are the only countries possessing substantial oil reserves in conjunction with a significant internal market, other resources, and a substantial agricultural base. Those states in need of foreign exchange to feed large, underdeveloped and underprivileged populations clearly would like access to the oil producers' surplus wealth. Indeed, some have even claimed that the oil treasure is not the inheritance of any particular state but of the Arab people as a whole. Such claims, formerly pressed by the Pan-Arabists, have found little official sympathy from the producing governments.

A fourth source of challenge to some regimes will continue to reside in the ethnic fissures existing within modern state boundaries. This reflects the unstructured history of the border decisions previously referenced. Some groups with close ethnic identity have been scattered across several state boundaries. The dispersion of the Kurds in eastern Turkey, northern Iraq, and northwestern Iran is the most obvious but hardly the only example (Kurds can also be found in the south-central Soviet Union). Other prominent ethnic groups with grievances include Berbers, Baluchis, and Palestinians. When these ethnic distinctions are further reflected in class and political asymmetries, contentious possibilities become violent certainties.

Such conflicts need not be wholly a function of ethnicity; religion also can serve the same purpose. In Lebanon, the importance of religion, so central to the country's society that it finds codification in the national constitution, has served as the general rallying point of the fratricidal struggle that has crushed the fabric of Lebanese society over the last six years. Syria also has the potential for such violence, since the ruling elite surrounding President Assad are drawn from his Alawite sect, which comprises only 5 percent of the national population.[31]

Nothing in the international political system is so traumatic as the collapse of a state; it sends ripples across the whole system. Because of the extreme fragility of the Middle Eastern regimes, and because of the region's acknowledged strategic and geopolitical importance, challenges to the regional governments from either purely internal forces or from internal forces operating with external support are the most likely causes of Middle Eastern conflict in the 1980s.

The Soviet Threat

Much has been written about the possibility of a direct Soviet invasion of the Middle East in the coming years. After the twin shocks of 1979—the collapse of the shah of Iran and the invasion of Afghanistan—the fear was that the Soviets would move to establish some type of hegemony in the Persian Gulf area.[32] Much of this concern was fed by the 1977 Central Intelligence Agency (CIA) estimate that the domestic Soviet oil industry soon would be incapable of meeting the energy demands of both the Soviet Union and its Council on Mutual Economic Assistance (COMECON) satellites. Although the

CIA report has been extensively revised, the fear exists that an ultimate Soviet goal is access to or control of shipments of Middle Eastern oil.[33]

The problems and risks associated with a direct Soviet move into the Middle East are enormous—perhaps not forbidding, but close to it. The terrain over which combat forces of the Red Army would travel is difficult and lends itself to relatively easy interdiction by either air attack or spirited local resistance. The experience in Afghanistan should hardly whet the Soviet appetite for additional international adventures. But should the situation arise where the Soviets need quantities of imported oil to service either their own needs or those of their allies, their interest in the Middle East should be expected to increase proportionately.[34]

The actions of the Kremlin since the end of the 1967 war (and perhaps more significantly since the end of the 1969–1970 war of attrition along the Suez Canal) indicates that the Soviets prefer indirect, circumscribed efforts in furthering their interests. Soviet activity using proxy forces around the periphery of the Arabian peninsula is an ominous development. It is also very difficult to address in terms of foreign policy options available to the West.[35]

Soviet efforts through proxy, regional challenge groups contain several distinct advantages. First, the movement can appear to be totally indigenous, giving efforts to deal with it by external powers the appearance of illegitimacy. The scope of justifiable criticisms to which state regimes will be susceptible will provide oppositions extensive opportunity for success in searching for the responsive chord that will raise the multitudes. Once this is achieved, once the cause that rallies mass support has been identified, it will be almost impossible to still the tide and reverse the direction of events. It seems clear that the days when a Kermit Roosevelt could restore a friendly government to power for a few thousand dollars are gone.

The Arab-Israeli Conflict

It would be misleading to see the Arab-Israeli conflict as a mere interstate or boundary dispute, for it has far deeper and wider implications—perceived as it is by both sides as a battle for survival. The two fundamental ideologies in Arab politics—Islam and Pan-Arabism—hold that Israel is an illegitimate phenomenon against which all good Muslims and Arabs must fight and whose very existence is living testimony to the failure of the Arab governments to fulfill their missions. Ideologies do not change quickly; one can expect these two to be major forces throughout the 1980s.

In the case of Egypt, the burden of the thirty-year battle—with its heavy losses in lives and wealth—convinced President Sadat that there must be a major break with the past. He went to Jerusalem and agreed to the Camp David accords. But Egypt is strong enough and located properly to be partly insulated from inter-Arab pressures. Other Arab states are not so fortunate—or have suffered fewer losses—and cannot take this major step. The death of President Anwar Sadat and the position of the Begin government on the territories do not offer them added incentives.

There are a wide variety of possible developments in the Arab-Israeli conflict involving both moves toward political solutions and steps toward increased tension. Another major war remains a real possibility. Sadat's withdrawal from confrontation made this seem far less likely; the will or ability of post-Sadat Egypt to maintain this position will be pivotal.

In a future conflict the Arab states most directly involved would be Egypt, Jordan, and Syria. Others would send military and financial aid. Jordan learned a lesson in 1967, when it lost the richest part of its territory, and would probably try to avoid involvement in a new conflict. Syria, to end its own isolation and to rally Arab support, is the most eager to renew the conflict, and the Palestine Liberation Organization (PLO) also has some stake in such an enterprise.

A distinction should be made between a new war and a simple increase in tension to levels seen in the past. Under sufficient threats, verbal or involving troop movements, Israel might stage a preemptive attack. Nevertheless, an Egyptian swing toward heightened criticism of Israeli policy, combined with Cairo's attempts to mend fences with the Arab world, would not necessarily presage a conflict. The Egyptians probably would be careful to send signals to both Israel and the United States explaining its wish to avoid military confrontation.

An important feature in any new Arab-Israeli war could be the introduction of Saudi Arabia as a full confrontation state. In the short run, this could involve Israeli attacks against Saudi military installations capable of supporting aircraft against Israel as well as attempts to shoot down Saudi AWACS planes, which may or may not include U.S. crew members.

In the longer run, as Saudi Arabia integrates the large amount of military hardware it has been buying and becomes stronger militarily, there will be increased pressure from within and without to use this weaponry against Israel in any new conflict. An all-out war could threaten Saudi stability and even possibly inflict damage on oil installations.

The result of any renewed warfare would be difficult to predict and would also depend on what point during the 1980s it did break out. One might suggest that any Arab effort against Israel lacking full Egyptian cooperation probably would be doomed to failure.

While in 1981 war seemed unlikely for the short to medium run, it would be hard to project forward to the end of the decade without seeing any new conflict in the absence of progress on the diplomatic front. Even progress toward a political solution would not guarantee peace, for each proposed outcome will bring with it different problems.

A so-called Jordanian solution might well create severe internal problems for Amman and encourage alliances between the PLO and Syria in particular, designed to overthrow the Jordanian monarchy.

If a Palestinian state were created, it probably would be dominated by the PLO. There would then develop a two-level conflict for control over the state. On the domestic level, Yasir Arafat and most of Al-Fatah (although it might itself split) would battle the smaller groups that want a revolutionary state. The likelihood is that both sides will be friendly toward the USSR, both because of their past close relations and because any deviation by Arafat would encourage Soviet support of his rivals as true revolutionaries.

The second conflict would be among the Arab states for influence on the new regime. Certainly, the Saudis would use their money to try to shape its policies, but the Palestinians would be well aware that the Saudis and other oil producers would have little choice in supporting them no matter what they did at home and in terms of foreign policy. On the other hand, Syria, Iraq, and Libya probably would have relatively little influence on the new state unless they managed to back the winning parties in the probable civil war.

What makes this scenario difficult to imagine is that the Israelis also would be well aware of the likely outcome and therefore will be most reluctant to agree to such a state. If they were to do so, conditions over boundaries and such things as demilitarization would be advanced and probably would not be acceptable to the Arabs.

It is probably not true that the Arabs—with the exception of the Jordanians and Egyptians (and in those two cases the governments more likely than the people)—will be against a Palestinian state. Despite the probable radicalism of a Palestinian state, so much is at stake for the conservative Arab regimes that they certainly would go along with it. As rationalization, the Saudis would argue that they would be able to control the new government, although this is highly debatable.

If the Palestinian state were established, there is a good chance that it would be revanchist. There would be strong internal pressures to continue the struggle until Israel were destroyed. This might, in fact, be a major issue in a Palestinian civil war. Either way, such an eventuality would not be particularly stabilizing for the region. This is not to argue against such a state under the proper conditions, for it would be the only solution that could truly defuse the issue. The problem is that it will be extremely difficult to achieve, and such an outcome would furnish new dangers for all involved. There should be no illusions that there is any easy way out.

The Soviets have a variety of options in dealing with the matter. Of course, they will try to take advantage of U.S. involvement with Israel and

with the Camp David peace accords, but this has been surprisingly unsuccessful so far. If the Arabs mistrust the United States they also tend to distrust the Soviets, who have not furnished them with the amount of support
they wanted on more than one occasion.

Furthermore, although the Soviets could enjoy some gains by heating
up the situation, they also would be in danger of having to prop up a
client—Syria—that might drag them into significant difficulties. A low
profile, coupled with persistent statements in favor of the Arabs, might help
them secure better relations with the Gulf countries—most notably Saudi
Arabia—and that appears to be Soviet strategy for the near term. It should
be noted that, although involvement in the Arab-Israeli conflict and arms
supplies for the Arabs have yielded many financial advantages for Moscow,
few lasting political advantages have ensued. Since the mid-1950s, the
Soviets have invested a great deal of time, effort, and money in the Middle
East. Their period of alliance with the radical nationalist forces in Egypt,
Iraq, Sudan, and Syria appeared for a while to give them a strong regional
position. Ultimately, however, the first three regimes broke with Moscow,
and two of them—Egypt and Sudan—became friendly with the United
States.

The lesson taken from this, in Moscow, was to concentrate on the
periphery instead of the core area of the region. Rather than spend capital
on such relatively strong and organized countries, it became preferable to
wield greater influence in the more marginal, undeveloped (economically,
culturally, and ideologically) nations such as Afghanistan, South Yemen,
Ethiopia, and Libya. Naturally, this was in large part a response to opportunities. Still, these states are much less able to resist increasing degrees of
Soviet influence, exercised principally through army and secret-police advisors, that might provide Moscow leverage in determining future leaders and
turning client states into satellites.

However, it does not appear that there will be much more mileage for
the USSR in the Arab-Israeli dispute. Certainly, the supply of arms to Syria
and other countries and the opening of relations with the Gulf may be aided
by this situation. However, since Soviet aid has failed to help the Arabs win a
decisive victory in the past, Moscow's involvement has not been without its
discrediting features. Indeed, the disillusion with the USSR has paralleled
the wearing out of other hopes and beliefs. The patent failure of radical
Arab nationalism to win the conflict and to solve the problems of development have been major factors in the rise of Islamic radicalism.

Conclusion

The number of variables—domestic upheaval, the death or assassination of
leaders, the interplay of Arab states and of the great powers, and the

Arab-Israeli conflict—make it extremely difficult to predict Middle Eastern conflicts in the 1980s. Basically, however, the Pan-Arab and Islamic dreams will not be fulfilled. The area will see the continued existence of the present states. Current patterns of political alignment and rivalry also will be sustained. Even in the best case, the Arab states will not have reconciled themselves to Israel; Egypt will still face serious economic problems; Syria will be a state without a firm and stable identity; the PLO and Syria will be friendly toward the Soviet Union; and Lebanon will be unable to restore formal unity and real stability.

Notes

1. See the testimony of Harold Saunders in U.S., Congress, House, Committee on Foreign Affairs, Subcommittee on Europe and the Middle East, *Hearings: U.S. Interests in, and Policies toward, the Persian Gulf, 1980*, 96th Cong., 2d sess., 1980, p. 2.

2. Henry A. Kissinger, *The White House Years* (New York: Little, Brown, 1979), p. 346.

3. This listing of Soviet goals and interests was drawn largely from four sources: John C. Campbell, "The Soviet Union in the Middle East," *The Middle East Journal* 32 (Winter 1978): 3–4. Mohamad Heikal, *Sphinx and Commisar* (London: Williams Collins, 1978); Lincoln Landis, *Politics and Oil: Moscow in the Middle East* (New York: Dunellen, 1973); and Ivo J. Lederer and Wayne S. Vucinich, eds., *The Soviet Union and the Middle East* (Stanford, Calif.: Hoover Institute, 1973).

4. For some current data, see National Foreign Assessment Center, *International Energy Statistical Review* (CIA Document, 24 November 1981): CI-IESR-81-011: 6–14.

5. This compilation of U.S. interests is derived largely from George Ball, "The Coming Crisis in Israeli-American Relations," *Foreign Affairs* 58 (Winter 1979–1980): 231–256. Benedict F. Fitzgerald, "U.S. Strategic Interests in the Middle East in the 1980s," Strategic Studies Institute, The Army War College, Carlisle Barracks, Pa. and Harold Saunders, "The Middle East and Southwest Asia: What Strategies for the U.S.?" (Paper presented at the National Security Affairs Conference of the National Defense University, Ft. McNair, Washington, D.C., 13–15 July, 1981.

6. Walid Khalidi, *Conflict and Violence in Lebanon* (Cambridge, Mass.: Center for International Affairs, Harvard University, 1979).

7. For a good discussion of the events leading to the collapse of the shah, see Michael Ledeen and William Lewis, *Debacle: The American Failure in Iran* (New York: Knopf, 1981).

8. The best discussion of the phenomenon of Arab rivalry is contained in Malcolm H. Kerr, *The Arab Cold War* (London: Oxford University

Press, 1971). For information on the Kuwait episode, see pp. 20–33.

9. Nadav Safran, *Israel: The Embattled Ally* (Cambridge, Mass.: Harvard University Press, 1978), see chap. 1–3.

10. An excellent history is Fred J. Khouri, *The Arab-Israeli Dilemma* (Syracuse, N.Y.: Syracuse University Press, 1976).

11. An excellent treatment of the relationships and antagonism of the big powers with the Middle Eastern states is contained in Safran's *Israel: Embattled Ally*. See, in particular, chaps. 16 and 22.

12. A recent book dealing with the Suez crisis that is quite informative (but quite journalistic) is Donald Neff, *Warriors at Suez* (New York: Linden Press, 1981).

13. The Soviet role in the 1967 war is highly confused. In addition to Haikal, see Anwar Sadat, *In Search of Identity* (New York: Harper and Row, 1978), and Abba Eban, *Abba Eban: An Autobiography* (New York: Random House, 1977).

14. See the narrative of William B. Quandt, *Decade of Decisions* (Los Angeles: University of California Press, 1977), chap. 6.

15. For a detailed discussion of the *Polisario* movement and its implications for U.S. foreign policy, see U.S., Congress, House, Committee on Foreign Affairs, Subcommittee on Africa, *Hearings: Current Situation in the Western Sahara—1980*, 96th Cong., 2d sess., 1980; see also Stephen Solarz, "Arms for Morocco?," *Foreign Affairs* 58 (Summer 1980): 278–299.

16. John K. Cooley, "The Libyan Menace," *Foreign Policy*, no. 42 (Spring 1981): 74–93.

17. Ibid., p. 76.

18. See Henry F. Jackson, "Sadat's Peril," *Foreign Policy*, no. 42 (Spring 1981): 60.

19. See John Yemma, "Begin Tells U.S. 'Get Syria's SAM Missiles out . . . or Else'," *The Christian Science Monitor*, 12 May 1981.

20. See "Israel Stung by Erroneous Quotations, Cites Others to Depict Peril," *New York Times*, 21 June 1981, p. 3. Also see the editorial by Flora Lewis, "Decision for Israelis," *New York Times*, 22 June 1981, p. A17.

21. For an informative analysis of the election, see Don Peretz and Sammy Smooha, "Israel's Tenth Knesset Election," *The Middle East Journal* 35 (Autumn 1981): 506–526.

22. "Escalating the Savagery," *Time*, 27 July 1981, pp. 36–46.

23. See Jay La Monica, "Soviet Exercises off Syria Raise Tensions," *Journal of Commerce*, 10 July 1981, p. 4; see also "Syrian President Arrives in Libya for Talks on Merger," *New York Times*, 9 September 1980, p. A1.

24. Claudia Wright, "Iraq-Iran War," *Foreign Affairs* 59 (Winter 1980–1981): 275–303.

25. See Center for Strategic and International Studies, *An American*

Imperative: The Defense of Saudi Arabia (Washington, D.C.: Georgetown University, September 1981).

26. Constant exceptions are made to Israel and Turkey throughout this discussion. Both countries to some extent are unique in the Middle East. Israel, because of its direct evolution from the old Zionist political organization, reflects numerous European traits in its political structure. Turkey has made a conscious effort to break with the past and adopt modern Western methods of government. Hence, neither country fits the norm of Middle Eastern state behavior.

27. These comments are very similar to those expressed in September 1979 by Henry Kissinger on an NBC News White Paper, "No More Vietnams, but Oil and American Power."

28. See the introduction in Majid Khadduri, *Arab Personalities in Politics* (Washington, D.C.: The Middle East Institute, 1981).

29. Robert Lacey, "How Stable Are the Saudis?" *New York Times Magazine*, 8 November 1981, pp. 35–38, 118.

30. See the essay by John Waterbury in John Waterbury and Ragaei El Mallakh, *The Middle East in the Coming Decade* (New York: McGraw Hill, 1978).

31. For a thorough discussion of the Syrian situation see Hanna Batatu, "Some Observations on the Social Roots of Syria's Ruling, Military Group and the Causes for Its Dominance," *The Middle East Journal* 35 (Autumn 1981): 331–344.

32. For examples, see Jeffrey Record, *The Rapid Deployment Force* (Cambridge, Mass.: Tufts University, 1981); Geoffrey Kemp, "Military Force and Middle Eastern Oil," in *Energy and Security*, ed. Joseph S. Nye and David Deese (Cambridge, Mass.; Ballinger Pub. Co., 1981); and Christopher Van Hollen, "Don't Engulf the Gulf," *Foreign Affairs* 59 (Summer 1981): 1064–1078.

33. See, for examples, Marshall I. Goldman, "The Role of Communist Countries," in Nye and Deese, *Energy and Security*; and Bernard Swertzman, "CIA Revises Estimate, Sees Soviets as Oil Independent through 80s," *New York Times*, 18 May 1981, p. A1.

34. See the testimony of Dr. James Moose in U.S., Congress, House, Committee on Foreign Affairs, Subcommittee on Europe and the Middle East, *U.S. Interests in Persian Gulf*, p. 197.

35. See Gary Samore, "The Persian Gulf," in Nye and Deese, *Energy and Security*; for an excellent analysis of the vulnerabilities in Soviet proxy relations and U.S. foreign-policy options in the 1980s, see William J. Taylor, Jr., "Responding to Soviet-Proxy Interventions in the Third World" (Paper presented at the Foreign Policy Research Institute Conference on Military Interventions in the Third World,Washington, D.C., 14 December 1981).

Scenario: Conflict and Crisis in Egypt

By early 1986, the internal conditions in Egypt had deteriorated greatly. Although the government of President Housni Mubarak endured (despite its initial repressiveness) after the shock of Anwar Sadat's assassination in October 1981, Egypt went through several pronounced periods of domestic unrest, which were increasing both in their severity and frequency.

Poverty and a growing population were the fundamental problems that faced Egypt. Despite intensive population-control efforts by the government, Egypt's birth rate remained constant at 3 percent, and the historical problem of feeding the people (estimated at over 500 million) was now overwhelming. The agricultural sector, which had been deteriorating for two generations, was further weakened by the effects of the population explosion. In addition, large tracts of arable land were lost to urban sprawl, particularly around Cairo and Alexandria. Government plans to resettle people in the desert regions beyond the Nile met with little success. Moreover, farming increasingly was more difficult. For over twenty years the Aswan High Dam prevented the flooding of farmlands and effectively stopped the periodic replenishment of the land. Although farmlands were triple-cropped, the money spent on vast amounts of fertilizer affected adversely the profit of the small farmer and Egypt's balance of payments.

By 1985, Egypt imported nearly 60 percent of its food. Even though the United States provided most of this quantity at subsidized prices, the monetary and social costs to Egypt were too high. In March 1985, food riots erupted in several locations. These riots, unlike those of January 1977 that were caused by the high price of bread, resulted this time from the lack of bread. President Mubarak reacted forcefully to the riots and arrested several opponents of his regime, whom he charged with inciting the disturbances and attempting to use the riots to further their ends.

The U.S. government grew increasingly alarmed at the persistence of the Egyptian crisis. Since President Carter involved the United States in Egyptian affairs in the mid-1970s, the U.S. aid program expanded greatly—from less than $1 billion in the late 1970s to over $1.5 billion per year (excluding military aid) under the Reagan administration. Nevertheless, progress was difficult to discern in the lives of the Egyptian people.

The infrastructure weaknesses of Egypt remained. Major efforts by U.S. engineers, for example, to redesign Cairo's transportation system resulted in only marginal improvements. Public transportation and traffic were inadequate for Cairo's needs, and the national communications network remained poor. Businessmen continued to find it easier to fly to

Athens or Rome to telephone than to try to use the Egyptian service. Egypt's gross national product ceased to grow after 1980, and the rising international debt threatened the economy. These economic and social conditions created a vast potential for domestic revolution. In particular, the largely uneducated and unemployed population posed the most explosive threat to the stability of the government.

After Mubarak succeeded to the presidency in 1981, he conducted a nationwide crackdown on opposition groups of all types. In particular, he pursued the demise of several religious fundamentalist groups—some extremist members of which were believed responsible for Sadat's death—and succeeded in eliminating their public presence. However, many observers remained unconvinced that the absence of such groups indicated either their long-term defeat or their subjugation. The brief but violent war with Libya in 1982 distracted Egyptian public opinion from their usual domestic problems, and several analysts felt that international events in no small way accounted for the fairly docile period that existed through the second and third years of Mubarak's rule, which enabled him to carry out the crackdown.

In early 1982, Mubarak announced several new domestic-policy initiatives that he believed would pave the way to a more representative government. In a speech before the National Assembly, President Mubarak declared that political parties in opposition to the ruling National Democratic Party would be sanctioned and allowed to field candidates for the upcoming national elections. In addition, the press was liberalized, and officially registered parties were allowed to operate their own publications. Many felt that these steps were premature; succeeding events proved them correct.

It became obvious that the basis for the opposition parties, which emerged quickly, was Islamic fundamentalism. Many organizations—at least those described as "neo-Islamic"—sought to influence the government through political actions. But other groups—those who desired more immediate and sweeping change in the tradition of Muslim brotherhood—resorted quickly to violence. The latter fundamentalist factions found willing adherents among the unemployed and hungry masses, and, to the surprise of many, these militants recruited extensively and successfully in the upper middle classes and among college graduates. Dissatisfaction with the economy under Sadat and with his peace initiatives toward Israel, coupled with the memory of disappointment under Soviet tutelage, led the more radical factions to conclude that the only correct course for Egypt lay in the abandonment of Western concepts of representative, secular government as well as Eastern concepts of centralized control. Islam was to be Egypt's redemption. In July 1982, while celebrating the anniversary of the 1952 revolution, which brought Gamal Nasser to power, massive riots broke out in Cairo. President Mubarak, temporarily detained by a mob of demonstrators on his way to the National Assembly, was forced to rely on trigger-happy security forces to extricate himself from the situation, and order broke down quickly as a result. Before order was restored temporarily, the army was called in to patrol the streets of Cairo.

Washington viewed this new situation with alarm. After several days of top-level consultations, the president decided to dispatch a special envoy to Cairo to discuss the Egyptian dilemma with the Mubarak government. Recalling the 1978 Iranian situation, the United States advised the Egyptians to take a firm stance on law and order. Subsequently, President Mubarak announced the suspension of earlier reforms and reinstituted martial law by a decree of national emergency.

For a few days, calm appeared to prevail throughout Egypt, but the peace was uneasy. A few weeks later, on 8 August, an enormous explosion in the residential area of Heliopolis killed the prime minister, Mustafa Ghazli, as he prepared to leave for his office. Shortly thereafter, a group calling itself *Talibi Rasul* claimed responsibility for the bombing.

The following day, several broadcasts calling for the overthrow of the Mubarak regime and the creation of a new state based on so-called Islamic socialism were beamed from Libya. These broadcasts caused great concern in Cairo and Washington. The Libyans had remained relatively quiet since the border war with Egypt and the consequent replacement of Colonel Qaddafi by his long-time, moderate associate Abdul Salam Jalloud. Jalloud was believed to be more cautious than Qaddafi, and his actions since taking power reflected as much—he terminated Libyan support of certain terrorist groups and established some distance between Tripoli and Moscow. The inference in Washington was that if Jalloud sought to take advantage of the situation in Egypt, then either he and/or Moscow would feel that the odds were in their favor.

For the next three days, massive pressure on the government continued, but peaceful demonstrations were staged by various fundamentalist groups in the major Egyptian cities. President Mubarak, increasingly concerned, called his senior officers together in Aswan for two days of intensive discussions. Several reports circulated widely in the Cairo diplomatic community that the government also held unofficial meetings with several opposition leaders in an attempt to find a compromise formula for reconciling the major points of disagreement. Evidently, these sessions were not successful, and at least one religious leader commented to the Algerian ambassador that "there could be no compromise where the word of God is concerned." Nonetheless, the message coming from Aswan appeared that the senior Egyptian leadership believed a significant act (on the scale of those for which Sadat became famous) might diffuse substantially the situation—or at least divide the opposition by splitting the moderates with the zealots.

In late August, Mubarak unexpectedly called a press conference and announced that he was requesting the United States to withdraw its forces, those stationed at the pre-position facility of Ras Banas as well as those assigned to the multinational force supervising the Sinai buffer zone between Egypt and Israel. Both Washington and Tel Aviv were thunderstruck. A second special envoy was dispatched from Washington to Cairo to get Mubarak to reconsider his decision. The Egyptian president listened politely but reaffirmed his position with the now-famous rejoinder: "You have your domestic limitations and I have mine."

Obviously, Mubarak intended this gesture to be symbolically important to the fundamentalist opposition. Unfortunately, they were less impressed with the implications of Mubarak's decision than was the United States. Two weeks after the meeting between the envoy and Mubarak, another bomb exploded, killing the Egyptian foreign minister. Having failed to find a suitable replacement for the prime minister after his assassination, Mubarak was forced to assume the role of the foreign minister as well as the premiership. Clearly, his authority and support eroded even among those classes that normally supported his regime.

In early September, an army unit stationed along the Canal near Ismailia revolted. The leaders of the revolt declared themselves members of *Talibi Rasul* and called for a general uprising by the people and by the military. An army brigade stationed north of Suez City moved into put down the rebellion, but the insurgents fortified heavily their positions, and the commander on the scene elected to lay siege to the town rather than attack the rebel garrison. After ten days, the army brigade began to receive sporadic sniper fire from supporters of *Talibi Rasul*, who were located apparently in small Canal villages. Shortly thereafter, the insurgency became an international media event, with coverage that encouraged the fundamentalists and discouraged the Egyptian government. Finally, after more than a month, Mubarak decided that he had to act more forcefully, and he ordered a massive assault against the fortified garrison. The battle was televised around the world, and, after the smoke cleared, the global audience learned that there were no survivors in the rebel compound.

The government claimed that the fanatics killed themselves rather than surrender to the army. But the streets of Egypt soon filled with masses declaring the rebels martyrs and demanding the resignations of Mubarak and his generals. An attempt by the army to restore order led to more rioting and bloodshed. Soon, the disturbances spread to Alexandria and then to Port Said. Reports circulated back to Cairo that mobs attacked the offices of the Suez Canal Company, and consequently the canal was closed to traffic. This fact was verified when a U.S. destroyer was prevented from transit through the canal from the Arabian Sea.

As riots spread across Egypt, the leadership of *Talibi Rasul* announced the organization of a committee of fundamentalist groups that was to provide national leadership after the collapse of Mubarak's government. This committee was to abolish immediately all vestiges of (1) foreign domination, including the banking institutions, (2) the representative government, and (3) any agreements or commitments with Israel.

The following day, Washington announced that it viewed the Egyptian crisis with utmost alarm, but that the U.S. government had no intention of interfering in the domestic affairs of Egypt. The Pentagon announced that both the 6th and 5th fleets, and the rapid-deployment joint task force, were placed on full alert.

14 Regional Conflict and Strategic Challenge in Southwest Asia

Rodney W. Jones

Southwest Asia is a region defined by geopolitics, not by the conventions of scholarship. It corresponds to what the British once called "east of Suez," a sprawling, heterogeneous region stretching from the Red Sea to the Indian subcontinent on the rim of continental Asia. It is Asia west of China, south of the modern Soviet Union. Historically, it has been a collision zone of great empires and civilizations. Each left imprints, although the dominant political and cultural forces today are Islamic, Arabic, and Persian. Persia, whose modern political expression is Iran, occupies a central location overlooking the Gulf.[1] Across the Gulf and to the west, the region merges with the Arab world and Turkey. To the east, it merges with Afghanistan, Pakistan, and the Indian subcontinent, where Arabic, Persian, and Islamic influences also diffused. Afghanistan is the Switzerland of this region, the transmontane crossroads of several cultures, although its principal languages are variants of Persian.

Southwest Asia is nearly devoid of geographically unifying or protective features. The main exceptions are the Himalayan and Pamir ranges in the east, the Alborz and Caucasus mountains in the north, and the Arabian Sea in the south. Among the major states of the region, only Saudi Arabia and India possess, by virtue of peninsular location, a measure of physical protection from neighborhood threats, and even in these cases it is a matter of degree.

Conflict of all sorts has been an almost constant theme in the region's history. On the plane of superpower relations, the postwar U.S. containment strategy and the relative stability of Pahlevi Iran afforded a respite, until recently, from major military conflicts in the Gulf. Intraregional relations, on the other hand, were plagued by chronic low-intensity conflicts and political instability throughout that period. The Gulf itself, however, was insulated for the most part from the warfare between Israel and the Arab confrontation states as well as from the wars between India and Pakistan. In retrospect, we may find that postwar freedom from major military conflict around the Gulf was a luxurious interlude and that what we have witnessed since 1979 is the reversion to a historically more normal, turbulent state of affairs. A major war is now in progress in the Gulf. The Gulf is no longer so detached from the Arab-Israeli or Indo-Pakistani rivalries as it once was. The susceptibility of the region to Soviet pressure is dramatically increased.

Fortunately, there are few any longer who subscribe to any illusions about either the high geopolitical stakes or the precariousness of Western interests in this region. The shah's overthrow and Iran's revolutionary turbulence, followed by the Soviet invasion of Afghanistan, made regional vulnerabilities all too painfully obvious. The hostage seizure in Iran brought the message home to the public more profoundly than successive oil-price shocks have. Soviet self-indulgent calculations about Afghanistan and the inception of the Iraq-Iran war convincingly show how revolutionary upheaval in one part of this region is prone to reverberate, as in an echo chamber, with effects that unravel security in the region at large.

Southwest Asia then is a critical region, not only because of oil. Unlike other developing regions, moreover, it is simultaneously adjacent to the USSR, far from the United States and weakly defended. Southwest Asia is, after all, where NATO (North Atlantic Treaty Organization) stops. It contains no local great power that, like China and Japan in the Far East, promises sufficient local resistance against Soviet military threats to enable the addition of marginal U.S. military power to produce credible deterrence. Southwest Asia is where high stakes, profound vulnerabilities, and poor defense opportunities coincide.

This region also possesses in abundance the various kinds of local rivalries and internal sources of political instability that are characteristic of developing regions. In some third-world regions, local instabilities normally overwhelm the East-West dimension of conflict. In Southwest Asia, conflicts that originate indigenously may have analytic distinctiveness, but it is not clear that they can be so separated in practical terms. Partly by local state choice, partly because of the local animosities toward Israel, and increasingly because of energy, local conflicts involve the superpowers; there is a corresponding tendency for the East-West rivalry to play itself out through those local conflicts.

Superpower Interests and the Geopolitics of Southwest Asia

U.S. Interests

United States interests in Southwest Asia are geostrategic. They are derived from the vital importance of Southwest Asia as a source of critical Western energy supply and as a political barrier to potential Soviet domination of the Eurasian landmass and connecting seas.[2] The strategic balance in the region already has been altered suddenly and adversely by the neutralization of Iran, and further erosion is likely. Preventing any further precipitously adverse shift is imperative for strategic stability. The problem is complex because the conflicts that threaten to upset this balance may originate locally, in the turbulence of the region, but the potential seriousness of local conflicts largely arises from the proximity of great Soviet military power and its imperial effects on political developments in key states of the region.[3]

Reliable Western access to Persian Gulf oil reserves is the issue of the moment and an inescapable strategic priority beyond the 1980s.[4] Oil delivery could be interrupted in various ways, by local actions as well as Soviet intervention, as the Iraq-Iran war testifies. The physical vulnerability of the international oil-delivery installations and oil-transport systems to damage from acts of sabotage or war is manifest. These physical threats are secondary, however, to those that would be posed by Soviet political control over Western oil supply.[5]

Should the Soviet Union ever be in a position to determine or even substantially influence the allocation of Persian Gulf oil among Western customers, it could use that leverage to neutralize U.S. allies in Europe and the Far East and thus dismantle Western security arrangements that underpin the geostrategic balance. It is in the U.S. interest not only to prevent such an outcome but to head off fatalistic perceptions in allied and friendly states that could have the effect of a self-fulfilling prophecy.[6]

It follows from these observations that it is misleading to construe the threat to Western oil security in exclusively military terms. But it is equally misleading either to divorce the Soviet political threat to Persian Gulf oil from its military underpinnings or to misunderstand the potential impact on Western military-defense arrangements of Soviet influence over Persian Gulf oil supply.

Southwest Asia's geopolitical importance is amplified by the oil factor, but it is crucial in other respects. The independent states of the region also constitute political and territorial barriers against the projection of Soviet power into the Indian Ocean and Africa. The region thus limits the scope of both Soviet geopolitical competition in other developing regions and Soviet operational military threats to U.S. or allied forces in the Mediterranean and the Pacific. It represents an obstacle to potential Soviet encirclement of China, the materialization of which could jeopardize the Sino-Soviet equilibrium in Asia. By the same token, Southwest Asia faces the Soviet Union with extensive defense requirements along its southern flank, where the future loyalty of the inhabitants could be unreliable, and thus probably serves as a constraint against Soviet military adventurism on its European and Pacific fronts.

Soviet Interests

Soviet interests in Southwest Asia are also couched in a geostrategic perspective, are defined primarily in the context of the perceived hostility of the

United States and its allies, and can be characterized as both defensive and expansionist in nature. As a practical matter, Soviet defensive and expansionist aims are imperfectly distinct, and even the Soviet pursuit of defensive goals frequently clashes with Western interests. It is crucial therefore to avoid the popular error of assuming that because certain Soviet interests or objectives can be traced to defensive motivations they are ipso facto non-threatening or harmless to Western interests.[7]

The assessment of threats must be based in the first instance not on the perceived motivations of an adversary but rather on its capabilities and the potential consequences of exercising those capabilities in plausible circumstances. Planned U.S. responses, however, face inherent resource limits and necessarily take into account estimates of the probability of threats of different magnitude. In this connection, discriminating judgments about Soviet interests and motivations are both necessary and useful; in view of the intrinsic uncertainties in subjective assessments, however, a respectable margin for error remains advisable in estimating related defense requirements.

Objective Soviet defensive interests minimally include (1) the preservation of domestic order in boundary territories that are contiguous with Southwest Asia; (2) the avoidance of political instability in or military hostilities among adjoining nations that could spill over into the Soviet Union itself; (3) the maintenance of diplomatic and commercial intercourse with regional states; and (4) the limitation of military capabilities of regional states or external powers that could tax Soviet territorial military defenses or threaten its strategic-nuclear-deterrent system in unexpected ways.[8] An additional Soviet defense interest in Persian Gulf energy supply may materialize in the 1980s if domestic Soviet energy production falls far short of growing Soviet and East European energy requirements, which various studies consider likely.[9] Increased Soviet interest in imported energy, however, illustrates the more fundamental point that defensive interests may lead to or become indistinguishable from policies of expansionism or aggrandizement in the region.

Actually, the Soviet and East European interest in Persian Gulf energy has been in evidence for some time. Prior to the war with Iran, Iraq was a major supplier of oil to Eastern Europe, enabling the Soviet Union to export a corresponding amount to Western Europe for hard currency. Similarly Iran, prior to the revolution, supplied large quantities of gas to the Soviet Union by pipeline, offsetting Soviet gas exports to Western Europe. Apart from the hard-currency earnings, the Soviet defensive interest in energy is a strategic matter, that is, it enables the Soviet Union to perpetuate the energy and economic dependency of its Warsaw Pact allies.[10] Domestic energy shortfalls will increase Soviet external-procurement efforts. Thus far, external sources of energy have been commercially available to the Soviet Union and Eastern Europe. But in the event that the Soviets face domestic short-falls, external commercial arrangements become insecure (or are disrupted, as in the Iraq-Iran war), or the price is driven too high, the Soviets may seek to guarantee supply at affordable rates by expanded political influence or military coercion, leading them on an expansionist course.

Soviet policies designed to secure oil supply by political or military means would be hard to distinguish from policies of energy denial aimed at the West, and the consequences in any case might be quite similar. Whether the opportunity to squeeze Western oil supplies for political leverage arises by design or accident, it seems unlikely that the Soviets would shy from it. That such a tempting objective could itself weigh heavily on the benefit side of any calculus of the costs and risks of overt intervention cannot be ruled out.

A similar expansionist logic is inherent in the Soviet political and military-defense posture as it relates to Southwest Asia. To seal out from the Soviet Central Asian republics the influences of Islamic fundamentalism, the Soviets attempt to exert countervailing influence in neighboring Islamic states. Defense of earlier Tsarist and prewar Bolshevik annexations today drives further imperial inroads, as the Soviet invasion of Afghanistan illustrates.[11] Likewise in the East-West dimension, to deny to the United States listening posts, potential launch pads for strategic air power, or the availability of well-armed local allies that could tie down Soviet defense forces on its southern flank, the Soviet Union at minimum strives to disengage any U.S. or Western military presence from Southwest Asia by exerting a variety of pressures on states in the region. Normally, however, the Soviets seek more than the exclusion of Western influence from the region, they seek to displace that influence by entrenching their own.

Soviet Revolutionary Objectives and Practices

The maintenance of international stability and security would be somewhat easier even in turbulent regions like Southwest Asia if Soviet external goals were essentially conservative, that is, confined to the defense of the postwar political and territorial status quo. In fact, the inspiration for long-term Soviet international objectives remains at least in part revolutionary and messianic in origin. Recognition in some quarters of this elemental fact has been confounded by the complexity of international developments, the academic and media repudiation of outdated clichés, and the hopes in the détente era for reform of Soviet behavior. It also has been obscured by the increasing sophistication of Soviet foreign-policy conduct, and its pragmatic flexibility in dealing with short-term objectives. It is discounted by some as irrelevant in view of the declining appeal of Marxist-Leninist orthodoxy in developing areas.

No doubt there has been change over the years in the Soviet conduct of foreign policy. Respect for the resilience of modern capitalism and Western technological progress is now imprinted in Soviet perspectives. Ideological tenets have been subordinated so often to necessities of state that they have lost much of their original mystique. Most Soviet foreign-policy practitioners today seem to subscribe to a relatively instrumental, as opposed to theological, interpretation of official ideology. Contemporary Soviet foreign policy is not addicted in a singleminded way to the export of revolution. Yet none of these caveats alters either the underlying Soviet commitment to the long-term propagation of a socialist world in the Soviet image or the conviction that historical change inexorably rearranges the correlation of forces to Moscow's advantage as fundamental premises of the Soviet approach to foreign affairs.[12] Furthermore, there exists a natural tendency in the politics of policymaking for competing players to evoke ideological tenets either as standards for assessing the performance of incumbents or as part of the justification for a preferred policy option.[13]

Where political circumstances are congenial, other strategic objectives would not be compromised, and the risks of embarassment or failure seem manageable, the Soviet Union pursues revolutionary political transformation as a matter of course and by a variety of means, although usually weighted with military instruments of one kind or another. To be satisfactory, results need not be orthodox, merely in the right direction, which usually means disengagement from, or the souring of relations with, Western countries and countries oriented to the West. Part of the new sophistication of Soviet foreign policy, of course, is the increased resort to surrogates, which themselves are a proliferating feature of contemporary world politics.[14] The irony is that Soviet success in producing or capturing revolutionary change to establish client states in the 1970s has been most durable in comparatively underdeveloped states; in Southwest Asia, such clients fortunately are also strategically peripheral, including, for example, South Yemen, first Somalia and then Ethiopia in the Horn of Africa, and most recently Afghanistan.

The character of these states suggests a hypothesis that deserves more detailed study. The hypothesis is that the contemporary appeal of Marxist-Leninist constructs and associated Soviet paternalism, if one leaves liberation movements aside, tends to be strongest in weak, underdeveloped, and internally disorganized states, less because of deep convictions about social justice (although these motivations may coexist and operate in parallel) than because those constructs and the modalities of Soviet assistance provide putatively effective authoritarian antidotes to the conditions of weakness and internal disorganization. That the proponents of this communist version of a so-called quick fix may represent only a fraction of sentiment in a country or might be instigators of internal disorder prior to seizure of power, is not inconsistent with the position.

The potential in most of Southwest Asia for internal political disorder providing a point of entry for Soviet power by collaboration with internal political groups, by the use of surrogates or through direct military intervention, are extremely troublesome in the decade ahead. Some of the most strategically important states, particularly Iran, Saudi Arabia, Iraq, and the smaller Arab states along the Persian Gulf are also either the more vulnerable today or potentially vulnerable in the near future to externally exploited internal unrest.

Regional Potentials for Superpower
Confrontation or Conflict

The dangers of direct superpower confrontation and warfare are present in Southwest Asia in the 1980s in several forms; U.S.-Soviet hostilities would be a logical consequence of preplanned Soviet military moves against vulnerable targets in Southwest Asia that jeopardize the Persian Gulf. They also could be the result of domestic upheavals or wars within the region that provide pretexts or opportunities for Soviet intervention threatening the security of oil flow.

Partly because Soviet military decision making tends toward caution we need not assume that the most dangerous and most probable Soviet military threats are identical. But a preplanned strategic Soviet military drive for control over Persian Gulf oil should not be superficially discounted. The anarchy in Iran, the local military preponderance of the Soviet Union, and the possible energy crunch in the Soviet Union all make it plausible. The fact that the United States expects by the end of the decade to close certain strategic and conventional military vulnerabilities in the superpower balance suggests that a Soviet move, if it is to come, might well be in the near term.[15]

Soviet moves could come for strategic or political reasons other than oil, as seems to have been the case in Afghanistan. However, as the Soviet invasion of Afghanistan makes clear, the repercussions of a strategic move in one country of the region is profoundly disturbing to neighbors and almost inevitably increases the threat to oil in two ways.[16] First, it adds greater variety and capacity to immediate military threats to the oil or to the forces that may be deployed to defend the oil (for example, the use of Afghan airfields for Soviet air-power projections over the Arabian Sea and Hormuz Strait). Second, it puts the Soviet Union in a position to exert additional pressures on states that produce or could help defend oil (for example, Iran and Pakistan) or states that otherwise might provide more effective means of resisting Soviet encroachment on the independence of the region in general (for example, India).

Although it is clear that Soviet initiatives are likely in most cases to be the occasion for U.S.-Soviet confrontation or warfare in this region, for the sake of completeness, we should not overlook the possibility that U.S. moves, even if invited by legitimate governments of the region, could trigger a hostile Soviet counterintervention response in the same theater (or, perhaps, in another region, although the latter possibility is outside the scope of this chapter). Such a threat is implicit in Soviet warnings about counter-moves over Afghanistan and was explicit in Soviet warnings against U.S. military intervention in Iran to forestall the downfall of the shah or, later, to extricate the hostages. The 1921 Soviet-Iran Treaty of Cooperation, despite the Iranian denunciation of the relevant clause, provides in Soviet eyes legal justification for its own military intervention in the event that foreign military forces are introduced into Iran.[17] Similarly, it is conceivable that the Soviets might attempt to obstruct U.S. military intervention requested by the Kingdom of Saudi Arabia to secure the oil fields or help suppress a domestic uprising against the monarch.

Plausible Soviet-initiated Southwest Asian contingencies that could lead to U.S.-Soviet confrontation or armed conflict in the 1980s would include the following. In the context of direct Soviet military moves against oil, the contingencies are:

1. Military drive for the oil fields through Iran.
2. Long-range bombing of oil-delivery facilities.
3. Mining of the Hormuz straits by air or sea action.

Soviet military moves to enhance strategic position in the region would include:

4. Occupation as a prelude to annexation of northern provinces or creation of a client state in Iran.
5. Punitive invasion of Pakistan.
6. Dismemberment of Pakistan via Baluchistan.

The contingencies involving indirect Soviet military moves including surrogates would be:

7. Promotion of overthrow of Saudi ruling family, for example, by invasion from South Yemen.
8. Establishment of client state and naval facilities overlooking tanker routes in the Gulf or along Hormuz strait.
9. Combat participation on one side in a war between Gulf states (Iraq-Iran war, for instance).
10. Instigation of terrorist sabotage of oil facilities.

Permutations of the options in this list are conceivable, but the list covers the main contingencies. These are discussed below with minor variations in sequence. The last category, however, is deferred to the chapter's second section.

Soviet Moves against Oil. Soviet long-range bombing of the Gulf oil facilities could, as a technical matter, effectively put the oil facilities out of operation and could be repeated to prevent recovery and repair. But the Soviets are most unlikely to destroy the oil facilities physically by air attack in peacetime for several compelling reasons. First, this would risk U.S. reprisal and escalation to general war. Second, it would permanently alienate the governments of the targeted countries. Third, it would be pointless to destroy what would be highly valuable under Soviet control. After the outbreak of general war, of course, the probability of Soviet air action against the oil facilities would rise but, because the advantage of surprise would be missing, that air action possibly would be less effective.

Mining of the Hormuz Strait by a long-range air drop or naval action is also technically feasible and could be repeated at intervals, but it seems highly unlikely. Mine-clearing operations, for one thing, would easily negate the effectiveness of this option (except for its effects on oil-tanker insurance rates). Moreover, it would be an act of war, and might possibly be resisted on the spot by U.S. military forces. Mining carried out by Soviet surrogates could be more difficult to deter but probably would be easier to counter by mine sweeping.

The serious peacetime threat is a surprise Soviet military drive to seize and occupy the oil fields of one or more Gulf states. Iran is the most plausible target, but Iraq could be another, and success in either might be followed by moves against Kuwait or other states in the Gulf. This danger is serious, because Soviet military capabilities make it theoretically feasible against local armed resistance and possibly even against U.S. resistance.[18] Since it would entail Soviet sacrifices and high risks of war escalation, it may be less likely as long as Soviet decision making remains characteristically cautious, but the probability could rise if after Brezhnev's demise a succession struggle produces greater risk-taking propensities in the Kremlin.[19]

Carter administration planning for the development of the rapid-deployment force (RDF) had as an objective deterrence of just such a Soviet military thrust for the oil fields, presumably through Iran.[20] Reagan administration initiatives seem to imply upgrading RDF capabilities to perform a more demanding defense mission. Although it is doubtful that it could be ready for a defense mission before the late 1980s, the recent emphasis on augmentation should also strengthen the deterrent value of that force in the near term.[21]

Despite well-publicized weaknesses, U.S. military capabilities for a

Persian Gulf contingency may even have some defense value at the present time. Such an argument is made by Joshua Epstein, who explores the feasibility of staging U.S. forces to defend Khuzistan (Iran's oil province) while using air power to slow Soviet southward progress through the Alborz and Zagros topographical obstacles, thus buying time for the long-distance buildup of U.S. forces.[22] Epstein concludes that available Soviet assault forces deployable at that distance under those conditions could be confidently denied Khuzistan by the U.S. blocking force fighting in a defense mode. But this analysis implicitly concedes northern Iran to Soviet invasion forces, a premise that is hardly encouraging.[23] If taken seriously, it could invite an invasion of Iran ostensibly for more limited objectives. Moreover, the implication of trading territory for oil could have a demoralizing effect on perceptions in Saudi Arabia and other Gulf states.[24] It raises the more fundamental question of how reliable U.S. deterrence based on the RDF or any other emergency preparations can be unless the scope of implied U.S. defense objectives includes the territorial boundaries of the states in question as well as the oil fields they contain.

Soviet Moves to Improve Strategic Position. Iran's current internal weakness and political unrest together with historical Russian (and Soviet) imperial interests in Persia make it likely that the Soviet Union will attempt to expand its influence in that country, perhaps by stages, as manipulative opportunities arise. Soviet encroachment, if it materializes, would take one of two forms either of which would serve strategic purposes. One pattern, for which there are World War II antecedents, would be to instigate or provide military support for the creation of separatist, pro-Soviet regimes in Iran's ethnically distinct northern provinces of Azerbaijan, Kurdistan, or even Turkmenistan, followed by annexation and integration with Soviet republics of similar ethnic and linguistic composition. The alternative to dismemberment would be to bring to power in Iran a client regime, capable of governing Iran as a whole but predisposed to friendly and close association with its northern neighbor. Pursuit of either approach to conclusion of course would tend to preclude the alternative, but prior to that time the Soviet Union might speculate in both directions by perpetuating a policy of ambiguity. Indeed, separatist tendencies could be instigated as a form of pressure on Iran to compel accommodation and eventually a client-state condition.

There seems to be no current evidence that the Kurd, Azerbaijan, or Turkoman minorities of Iran would be hospitable to Soviet incorporation. But their appetites for political autonomy have been excited by the revolution in Iran even as certain centralizing and sectarian features of that revolution have precipitated sporadic regional military resistance and incipient forms of civil war. Prolonged low-intensity military conflict between the provinces and Tehran could harden regional sentiment and strengthen local organizations receptive to Soviet overtures, but Soviet military intervention probably would follow rather than precede regional declarations of independence and calls for external assistance.

Although postrevolutionary anti-U.S. sentiment in Iran has been broadcast to the world and is unmistakably widespread in the urban areas of the country, there seems little popular pro-Soviet sentiment in the country either. Anti-Soviet expressions by the Khomeini regime or public at large are comparatively low-key but are also unmistakable, particularly in opposition to the Soviet invasion of Afghanistan. The revolution was as much an expression of xenophobia as anti-U.S. sentiment. Most of the political-party or partylike organizations in Iran appear to be antagonistic to and suspicious of Soviet encroachment, although they are not hostile to normal economic, and political relations with the Soviet Union. Declaratory and informal Soviet support of the Khomeini revolution paid the Soviet Union rich dividends in this respect.

The Soviet opportunity to intervene to establish a client regime would come from a continuation of the fratricidal conflict in Iran among the groups that coalesced to produce the revolution, with a bid for power by some new constellation of groups. An ostensibly national but essentially leftist coalition eventually could form in opposition to clerical rule (the Islamic Republican Party and Revolutionary Guards), possibly including the small but disciplined Tudeh (communist) party and Marxist factions of the National Front, Mujaheddin-e-Khalq (for example, Paykar), and Fedayeen-e-Khalq. A leftist coalition would be the most likely source of an appeal for Soviet fraternal assistance and intervention. But it is also conceivable that a more ideologically heterogeneous coalition of centrist as well as leftist parties, perhaps including even sections of the Iranian armed forces, would seek Soviet support to construct a social democratic government, finding in due course that the effective power was increasingly in the hands of groups allied with the Soviet Union.

The death of Ayatollah Khomeini could be a near-term signal event for a shifting balance of forces and even more intense power struggle within Iran, producing opportunities for Soviet manipulation. Soviet opportunities to exploit Iran's low-intensity internal conflict, although speculative in some respects, provides incentives for Soviet policymakers to put their emphasis on incremental change rather than uninvited, overt military intervention; an explicit invitation for limited military intervention could come by this route anyway in due course. The subsequent pressure on Iran's oil policy and on the orientation of neighboring Persian Gulf governments would then be extraordinary. It is this incremental-intervention option that is most likely to bring a significant Soviet military presence directly into the Persian Gulf.

A final point about incremental Soviet encroachment is in order. Although gradual improvement in Soviet influence in the Gulf would be injurious in its own right to Western interests, it could also interact with or provide a foundation for the Soviets at some point to resort to the more naked invasion option, under circumstances where the means of deterrence or denial were no longer meaningfully available.

After the Soviet invasion of Afghanistan, it was apparent that Soviet military moves to improve strategic position could be launched against Pakistan. Pakistan is vulnerable to direct military attacks by Soviet or Soviet-supported Afghan forces and also to dismemberment in Baluchistan.[25] The likelihood of Soviet exercise of major military power to assault Pakistan probably depends on what Soviet objectives in that vicinity and in Afghanistan will be in the 1980s.

Soviet objectives in invading Afghanistan in the first place do not appear to have been based on a conscious game plan to seize the oil fields, control Hormuz, or establish warm-water ports and naval bases on the Arabian Sea. Such aspirations in some form may exist, but it is doubtful that Afghanistan was considered the first step. The main reason for the invasion was to purge and bolster a pro-Soviet and essentially communist regime that was faltering in the face of growing rebellion against its inept policies. These policies were too radical for the overwhelmingly traditional, preindustrial setting; likely to discredit the Soviet relationship as well as the Marxist-Leninist approach they were based on; and almost bound to produce a successor conservative regime open not only to Western influence but potentially to the introduction of new Western and perhaps Chinese military influence. The invasion, in short, was to prevent the possible reversal of gains in the Soviet position, some of long standing and others achieved as recently as the 1978 Saur Revolution, which first brought the communists to power in Afghanistan.[26]

Yet it should be clear that pre-Afghanistan Soviet objectives are not necessarily constraints; they can be expected to change in light of experience and subsequent developments. The opportunities at least to nudge Pakistan and even India into positions more receptive to Soviet geopolitical interests may be difficult to resist, especially if, as now appears to be the case, the Soviets are settling down for indefinite military occupation of Afghanistan and relentless prosecution against the *mujaheddin* (resistance) of a war of suppression. In this connection, low-intensity warfare (hot pursuit of refugees, helicopter attacks on border posts) will be pursued sporadically against Pakistan.

An examination of regional geography and of the Soviet force and logistical requirements for a significant solo invasion through Afghanistan of Pakistan suggests that it would be a large and costly undertaking, probably entailing forces at least three times as large as those used to occupy Afghanistan (a so-called friendly neighbor), with a corresponding logistical effort at least five times as large because of the distance involved.[27] Even this assumes tacit Indian neutrality, which would tie down major Pakistani forces in the east. If hostile Indian military forces invaded simultaneously, Pakistan's resistance would be focused on the eastern front, and the required Soviet effort could be smaller. Indo-Pakistan military collaboration against a Soviet invasion, on the other hand, although seemingly unlikely now, is conceivable later in the 1980s, and such a combination probably would tax Soviet capabilities beyond the point of expected gain.

A Soviet military invasion of Pakistan from Afghanistan would have to come through high mountain passes, principally the Khyber Pass opening on Peshawar in the Northwest Frontier Province (NWFP), or the openings on Quetta in Baluchistan. A punitive invasion designed to produce a submissive posture in Pakistan to insulate Afghanistan, or perhaps to act as a catalyst for the overthrow of the government in Islamabad, would be more likely than one designed to seize Baluchistan and dismember Pakistan. A punitive invasion could be carried out quickly and probably with relatively low casualties and might, by early withdrawal, escape retaliation from other powers responding to Pakistani appeals for assistance. An invasion would be most punitive if carried out in the NWFP and fringes of Punjab adjacent to Islamabad. But a punitive invasion probably would gain little of strategic value for the Soviets.

Seizure of Baluchistan, in contrast, could have considerable strategic value but would require military occupation. This would be a much more formidable task, particularly against continued Pakistani or U.S. augmented resistance. To accomplish this objective, the Soviet Union would for instance have to take Karachi and other points to the northeast (for example, Sukkur) on Pakistan's internal lines of communication. Soviet airborne forces landed near Karachi would be vulnerable to U.S. sea-based air power, and the staging of Soviet mechanized forces beyond Quetta would be difficult logistically to mount, reinforce, and defend. Baluchistan's rugged, arid terrain would be difficult to traverse given its dearth of metalled roads and single railway.

Pakistani officials themselves discount the likelihood of a major Soviet military invasion, on motivational as well as feasibility grounds, although they concede a punitive invasion is conceivable. More worrisome from their standpoint, and in any case a highly likely low-intensity Soviet threat in the 1980s, is Soviet instigation and arms assistance to the Baluch for guerrilla warfare against Pakistan's central governing authority. A protracted Soviet-supported guerrilla war in Baluchistan eventually would become a Baluch war for independence, but successful Baluch secession from Pakistan by military means almost certainly would produce a Soviet client state on the Arabian Sea. A Soviet attempt to experiment with this scenario is highly probable, but not inevitable, and a determined effort to accomplish it is by no means a foregone conclusion. Soviet calculations about Baluchistan probably will be contingent on developments in Afghanistan and Pakistan, including, for example, whether the war in Afghanistan is going well or badly, whether Pakistan becomes directly involved in support of the Mujahedeen, or whether external powers escalate arms supplies to the Mujahedeen.

For the Soviets to play the so-called Baluch card, moreover, does not guarantee its success. As a low-intensity form of conflict, it would be protracted, and various countermeasures would be employed. The ethnic Baluch population of Iran and Pakistan combined probably is less than 4 million, is spread over a vast territory where communications and mobility are poor (good for guerrilla concealment and sporadic combat, but poor for effective displacement of Pakistani forces or construction of an alternative government), and is tribally subdivided in ways that make wholesale Baluch resistance improbable.

Regional Conflicts and Low-Intensity Soviet Threats

Indigenous sources of conflict would present troublesome threats to oil, regional security and Western interests whether or not Soviet military power and related influence were present in the region. The Soviet presence magnifies the dangers and the difficulties of coping with regional security problems. Inappropriate as it would be to ignore this fundamental point, it is also important to recognize that Western responses to the conflict problems of Southwest Asia must fail if they are not cognizant of the distinctive, historically embedded interests, cultural perspectives, and political dilemmas of this region and of the manner in which they engender and shape conflict.

United States planners will be concerned with at least four levels of regional conflict in Southwest Asia in the 1980s: (1) regional hostility to alien influence, Western as well as Soviet, inspired by Islamic or Arabic identity; (2) national rivalries reflected in competitive arms acquisition, in certain low-intensity threats to neighbors, and occasionally in full-fledged conventional wars; (3) interstate conflicts involving overt foreign participation via surrogate relationships; and (4) violent intrastate political instability arising from internal social heterogeneity, transnational forces, the tensions of modernization, and clandestine foreign influence.

Regional Resistance to Alien Influence

Underlying the obvious national and subnational pluralism of Southwest Asia are strong currents of resistance to alien influence. In India, these currents are manifest in the well-articulated doctrine of nonalignment, a doctrine that has broad appeal elsewhere in the area. The rest of Southwest Asia shares with most of the Middle East the traditions of Islam, the memories of empire, and, in the Arabic-speaking regions, certain additional cultural propensities toward a common world view. The Islamic and Arabic bases of identity provide opportunities for regional coalescence on political issues that affect the region and for definition of Europe and non-Islamic parts of Asia as alien spheres. Anticolonial sentiment is an added, widely shared, reinforcement for older currents of regional identity.

The Arab-Israeli conflict and difficulties in achieving peaceful acceptance of the state of Israel have been the principal postwar rallying points for regional sentiment. Western commitments to Israel's security and acceptance in the region are viewed by most other states of the region not only as the source of Western opportunities for imperial encroachment on the area but also as the explanation for Soviet appeals, as a balancing factor in the region. Since it seems unlikely that complete reconciliation of Israel with its neighbors will be feasible in the 1980s, this source of tension will continue to influence conflict propensities in Southwest Asia. Indeed, the radical shift in Iran's orientation on this issue following the 1979 revolution geographically expands the scope of the conflict over Israel.

The principal significance to Western interests of Southwest Asian regional resistance to alien influence is twofold: On one hand, it represents a sufficient barrier neither to Soviet encroachment nor to intraregional threats posed by intense national rivalries. On the other hand, it operates to limit the effectiveness of those Western security responses to intraregional as well as externally induced conflicts that depend on the cooperation of local states.

National Rivalries

Most of the states of Southwest Asia are locked into one or more conflictual relationships with neighbors. The Iraq-Iran war is only the most recent of a number of postwar conventional wars and more numerous low-intensity conflicts precipitated by political threats or unsettled territorial claims. There are at least four main clusters of such national conflict that are likely to persist in the 1980s: (1) the rivalry between Iraq and Saudi Arabia for Arab leadership; (2) the contest between Iran and the Arab Gulf states over stakes in the Gulf; (3) the Indo-Pakistan conflict; and (4) the attempts by smaller states, particularly the two Yemens, to chart their own courses in regional affairs, usually at the expense of Saudi Arabia or Oman. The Horn of Africa conflicts also have a bearing on Arabian peninsular and Gulf affairs, but these can be considered here only in passing.

There are also certain strands of cooperation that tend either to moderate or to reinforce these national rivalries. The most salient, despite certain lasting suspicions and tensions, has been the pattern of cooperation between Saudi Arabia and the smaller Gulf states, especially Kuwait, Bahrain, Abu Dhabi, Qatar, and the United Arab Emirates, recently formalized in the Gulf Cooperation Council. Closer political and military cooperation between Saudi Arabia and Pakistan has emerged, and tacit Oman-Pakistan cooperation has been reinforced since the destabilizing developments in Iran and Afghanistan of the last three years. Relations between Iran and Pakistan have remained cordial despite the revolution, although material cooperation has deteriorated along with Iran's capabilities. Iraq's war with Iran has produced tension-reducing adjustments and new elements of cooperation in Iraq's relations with Saudi Arabia and other Arab Gulf states.

In its early stages the Iraq-Iran war caused considerable damage to oil facilities and production in both states and threatened to escalate into a broader Gulf war. The escalation potential now appears to be largely under control, and the experience probably will prove a sobering one for both combatants as well as their neighbors. Iraq's expectations for a quick and conclusive result were dashed. A crucial political benefit for Iraq, however, may be the at least temporarily dampened Iranian attempts to incite Shi'a rebellion within Iraq. The revolution in Iran and results of the Iraq war thus far have also diminished the military reputations and possibly the perceived urgency of military threats either from Iran to the smaller Gulf states or from Iraq to Kuwait and Saudi Arabia. Iraq has also ceased to instigate low-intensity conflict in Baluchistan. Saudi Arabia's influence in Arab circles is not based on military power but rather on its prestige as the origin of Arab culture, guardianship of the Islamic holy places, oil power, and political acumen; the setbacks to Iraq and Iran, however, have increased relative Saudi regional influence. By the mid-1980s, Iran and Iraq may have begun to rebuild their power, with potentials for replay of the same conflicts.

India and Pakistan have been at war three times since 1947, nearly once each decade. The probability of renewed conventional (perhaps nuclear-tinged) warfare between them within the decade is quite high. Chronic tension, border conflicts, and conventional warfare have characterized the Yemeni relationships with each other, Saudi Arabia, and Oman. These conflicts probably will escalate in frequency and intensity in the 1980s. An Arab-Israeli war might seem somewhat less likely after the Israeli-Egyptian peace treaty than before, but the recent Israeli annexation of the Golan Heights certainly suggests that it is conceivable. A fifth Arab-Israeli war might have much deeper repercussions on Southwest Asia than its predecessors.

Thus far the Soviet Union has refrained from direct involvement or openly siding with either Iraq or Iran in their war. The potential for the

Soviet Union to join either side is there and will increase in the event that there are future replays of this conflict or future conflicts in the Gulf or on the subcontinent. The introduction of extensive Soviet and Cuban military support for Ethiopia by air and sea in 1977–1978 fundamentally altered the outcome of the war with Somalia and demonstrated Soviet commitment to engage in such a fashion where the circumstances are propitious and strategic gains are possible.

Surrogate Relationships

Surrogate relationships have been anticipated by earlier discussion in some cases. It appeared for some time in the 1970s that the Soviet military-supply relationship with Iraq was so intimate and extensive (including, for example, the provision of Soviet naval facilities at Um Qasr, at the head of the Gulf) that Iraq might be used as a Soviet surrogate against Iran, Kuwait, or even Saudi Arabia. Iraq never became a true-Soviet surrogate (except in the sense that a certain parallelism of interests may have existed), partly because the Ba'ath political strategy has been to preempt the political ground usually inhabited by communists and partly because the oil revenues freed it from excessive financial dependency.

Soviet surrogate success in Southwest Asia thus far has been exclusively with small states—a fact that has its bright side. But North and especially South Yemen, the states in question, are strategically situated in two respects. First, their contiguity and social ties with Saudi Arabia and (in South Yemen's case) with Oman make them useful for staging destabilization efforts against the Saudi and Omani monarchies; several past unsuccessful instances of such efforts have occurred, and more are certain in the coming decade. Second, Soviet naval bases provided by South Yemen in Aden and Socotra, when combined with those in Ethiopia on the Red Sea, possess maritime strategic significance either as threats to oil lifelines or as counters to the U.S. naval power in the Indian Ocean, on which emergency response will so heavily depend.

The principal new Soviet surrogate potential for the 1980s in Southwest Asia seems to be in the use of access from Afghanistan to foment Baluch nationalism under Marxist auspices, in the hopes of creating a client state on the Arabian sea. In that case, the Soviets would gain primitive but uninterrupted land access directly to the Indian Ocean, a position overlooking Hormuz and a new vantage point for direct pressure on the Persian Gulf and Pakistan. Although unlikely in the 1980s, there is some potential that radical revolutions or political instability would increase Soviet influence in smaller Gulf states. An objective already pursued, for example, is the Soviet- and South Yemen-supported Dhofar rebellion against Oman.

Finally, there is the technically conceivable Soviet surrogate threat of organizing Palestinians or other dissident Arab groups, or their counterparts in Iran, to attempt sabotage of oil facilities. It is technically unlikely that terrorist threats to oil facilities could effectively disable the flow of much oil for long. Although the Soviets might be responsible for the general training of terrorists in such missions, it is doubtful that they would direct a comprehensive sabotage effort against Gulf oil. They might utilize surrogates in specific, limited acts of sabotage against some act they deplored by a Gulf state or to produce a sense of uncertainty or intimidation. But this would not be a basic threat to oil supply. The threats of political control over or military occupation of oil-producing areas are the ones to worry about in the 1980s.

Conflict Implications of Military Technological Change

Military technological change in Southwest Asia in the 1980s, with a few important exceptions, will come largely from imports from advanced countries. The superpowers may introduce new weapons and detection and combat-management systems into the forces they earmark for or deploy in the region. Some new technologies will be incorporated in arms transfers from the major supplier countries to recipients in the area. Of the regional states concerned, only India and to a lesser extent Pakistan have indigenous weapons-production capabilities that could have a significant impact on regional conflicts in the 1980s; in their cases, the principal technological innovations in this decade are likely to be in nuclear-weapons capabilities, a matter of profound importance.

Innovations in Superpower Military Technologies

The principal U.S. military effort for the next five years will stress not so much technological innovation as contingency-force availability, readiness, and rapid employment and reinforcement capability. Equipment pre-positioning and airlift and sealift capabilities require the greatest attention. Technological innovation will probably play a modest role in these areas in the development of new long-range air transports (the CX requirement to supplement C-5s and earlier transport aircraft) and refinement of logistics ships. Early warning and command and control are already seeing improvements, as the recent U.S. deployment of AWACS aircraft to Saudi Arabia implicitly indicates. A likely area of future development will be nonnuclear standoff systems, including cruise missiles, with precision-guided munitions for long-range attack of ground targets such as airfield, Petroleum, Oil and Lubricants (POL) storage facilities, and railroad-staging

centers. Some consideration almost certainly will be given to the supple-
mental deterrent and potential combat utility of theater nuclear weapons
(TNW), including enhanced radiation warheads (ERW), but the political
controversy such weapons tend to generate in allied or friendly states would
argue against disclosure of or excessive reliance on TNW, particularly
land-based systems.

Soviet military improvements will probably emphasize the upgrading of
equipment and manpower readiness of ground forces stationed in the Trans-
caucasus and Turkestan military districts; augmentation of airborne units,
air-transport capabilities, and mobile air defenses; and improvements in the
combat range, remote-target acquisition, and standoff firepower of the air
forces. Soviet naval improvements will center on the attack mission against
U.S. naval assets—which means increasing at-sea sustainability and ship-to-
ship missile range and firepower—primarily to put U.S. aircraft carriers at
risk and complicate U.S. reinforcement by sea.

Arms Transfers

The 1970s brought a significant escalation in the introduction of sophisticated weaponry, especially aircraft, to key Southwest Asian states. The
provision of F-14s with Phoenix air-to-air missiles and promise of AWACS
aircraft to Iran was followed by the sale of F-15s and commitment of
AWACS aircraft to Saudi Arabia and the recent agreement to supply F-16s
to Pakistan. India has begun a major air-force modernization program,
procuring the Anglo-French Jaguar and Soviet MIG-23 and exploring the
availability of the French Mirage 2000 and Soviet MIG-27. Improvements in
ground-combat capabilities and naval equipment, although technically less
impressive, are also underway, including increasing submarine procurement.

The 1980s will almost certainly see a continuation and possibly some
acceleration of sophisticated-arms transfers, although several years will be
required to absorb as yet undelivered equipment. The implications for
regional conflict are several. First, there will be some intensification of arms
competition, notably between India and Pakistan but also in the Gulf area,
especially after the Iraq-Iran war is terminated. Second, future conventional
conflicts will show somewhat greater intensity of ordnance-consumption
rates and equipment attrition—a trend in southwest Asia prefigured by the
1973 Arab-Israeli War and the Soviet/Cuban-supported Ethiopian counter-
offensive of 1978–1979 and at least partly borne out in the slower-paced
experience of the Iraq-Iran war. Third, the advanced-equipment transfers in
certain cases may be regarded as a form of equipment pre-positioning for
superpower engagement in regional conflict. Finally, the sophisticated-arms

transfers pose increased dangers to U.S. intervention forces in the event that local states equipped with such arms decide to oppose U.S. intervention. The Soviet Union, of course, faces a similar problem in those cases where it is the principal supplier, Iraq potentially being a prime example.

Regional Defense Production

India is the only state in Southwest Asia that currently possesses the diversified, heavy industrial base and extensive scientific and engineering resources needed to support indigenous defense-production industries. Pakistan's related capabilities are far more limited; although efforts to expand them are underway, they will not, except in the nuclear area, have much impact on the 1980s. The Southwest Asian oil-producing countries have been investing in industrial development and manufacturing as well, but they remain heavily dependent on foreign technical assistance and will not in the 1980s have much defense-production capacity. Oil revenues from Southwest Asian countries could be used, however, to support defense production under sympathetic auspices in Egypt or Pakistan. But both Iraq and Iran, if they invest in defense industries, are more likely to concentrate on developing internal capabilities.

Defense production in India is not particularly innovative, despite official rhetoric, but it has made steady progress in the use or adaptation of foreign technical assistance, designs, and licensed technology in its own public-sector industrial setting. India has also stimulated private-sector technology acquisition and manufacturing in key defense-related areas such as electronics and data processing. Actual defense production is fairly self-sufficient in conventional-ordnance light arms and military transport. India also produces light tanks and armored personnel carriers.

Efforts have been made, with only partial success, to acquire an independent, high-performance aircraft development and manufacturing capability, and MIG-21s are produced in India under license. India's space program is ostensibly for peaceful purposes, but defense applications are assiduously explored. By the end of the 1980s, India conceivably might be able to produce and deploy short- or medium-range battlefield missiles against Pakistan and eventually will have a long-range ballistic-missile capability relevant to the perceived threat from China (but not before the 1990s).

A potentially growing factor in regional conventional conflicts in the 1980s will be third-country weapons transfers among Southwest Asian states. Another could be direct military supply from less developed countries (LDCs), with India a potential local supplier of indigenously produced equipment and ordnance. Both India and Pakistan are potential suppliers of military training, equipment-repair facilities, and other technical military expertise. Pakistan is also, of course, a potential source of assistance with manpower or even military units, as its current relationships with Oman and Saudi Arabia suggest.

Nuclear Proliferation

The most significant military-technology innovation now materializing in some Southwest Asian countries that could have major effects on regional conflicts in the 1980s is in the nuclear area.[28] With India a possible exception, nuclear-weapons-delivery systems in regional states will be aircraft-based and probably unsophisticated. The countries of greatest concern are India and Pakistan. Potentially worrisome nuclear developments in Iran have been abandoned, at least for the time being, as a result of the 1979 revolution. In Iraq's case, the Israeli bombing attack in June 1981 destroyed the near-term technical potential. Iraq is likely to rebuild the bombed facility and perhaps develop others, but development of a nuclear-weapons capability in Iraq is now improbable before the end of the decade.

Nuclear-weapons proliferation is incipient both in India and Pakistan, and the development of limited nuclear military capabilities probably will occur in both countries during the decade. The probability of a limited nuclear conflict between the two within the decade is not negligible. Other threats posed by nuclear proliferation in the subcontinent include those that arise from possible transfers of nuclear technology or assistance to other states in the region, the adverse impact of nuclear insecurity on domestic political stability and perceptions of conventional defense needs (proliferation is likely, for instance, to accelerate rather than dampen conventional-arms competition); the complications that local nuclear armaments will pose for U.S. emergency military deployments and operations in the region; and the increased opportunities for nuclear terrorism by criminal, subnational, or international terrorist organizations.

Policy Implications

United States strategy for coping with Southwest Asian conflict in the 1980s will be based at a minimum on the following objectives: assuring the secure flow of energy resources from the region; checking the growth of Soviet political power and deterring Soviet military expansion in the region; limiting risks to the stability of the central strategic balance from regional confrontation or conflict; amelioration of causes and resolution of conflicts among states in the region; and furtherance of conditions favorable for orderly regional political and economic development.

A fundamental question that should be raised is whether the United States ought to adhere not just to these traditional objectives but also to forward objectives with much more activist implications, or should the United States trim its containment strategy to conform to drastically changed power realities and political trends.

A forward objective that sometimes is suggested, for example, would be to exploit Soviet domestic sociopolitical vulnerabilities to shrink rather than merely contain Soviet influence in Southwest Asia. Another would be to press for the demise of the Organization of Petroleum Exporting Countries (OPEC). The first of these objectives would be fraught with additional dangers. For practical reasons, probably neither would be feasible in the near term. A strategy based on either objective would be hard to sustain.

Similarly, accommodationist strategies could be visualized, for example, the tacit parcelling out of spheres of influence, perhaps accepting greater Soviet influence in the Indian subcontinent for abstinence from interference in Iran and the Persian Gulf. So-called Finlandization proposals for an Afghanistan settlement, incidentally, could easily work in this direction.

Major shifts in strategic approach of either sort would be much less productive in the 1980s than would upgrading the regional approaches that already have a measure of acceptance. Forward strategies against either the Soviet Union or OPEC probably would be perceived by the allies as highly risky and thus could take a heavy toll on North Atlantic and Pacific alliance relations. Accommodationist strategies, on the other hand, would be regarded by allies as failures of commitment and eventually would cause an even more severe strategic deterioration in Western influence in the region.

Upgrading existing approaches, however, requires a great deal of specific work on the solidification of political and security cooperation between the West and Southwest Asian countries, and among the regional countries themselves, based on a much more sensitive understanding of how those countries are evolving. It requires, in addition, completion of those improvements in U.S. military-power-projection capabilities, which are already planned; here the difficulties lie partly in conceptualization, but equally important, in resources, lead times, and management.

Integrating Political and Military Responses

Political responses to the problems of Southwest Asian conflict cannot be divorced from military considerations any more than military responses can be applied in a political vacuum. Diplomatic and military measures are interdependent elements of any realistic strategy for coping with conflict whether in peacetime conditions or in war. The proper question is not which should have precedence over the other, but rather how they should be integrated (or what is the appropriate mix) for the spectrum of threats faced.

It is true, of course, that resort to the actual use of force in peacetime should be rare and normally only where other means do not suffice.[29] But the common tendency to confuse all military measures of foreign policy with the use of force must be resisted. Military measures including readiness to use force may serve the purposes of deterrence and political reassurance; indeed, in peacetime, this is their primary utility. Deterrence forestalls temptations by opponents to resort to force. Political reassurance relieves friends and allies of the full weight of their individual vulnerabilities and improves collective security. Military measures with these purposes are integral to political diplomacy. Either, when effective, tends to lower the frequency of actual uses of force.

Devising well-integrated responses serving deterrence and political-reassurance purposes is difficult for several reasons. First, the spectrum of actual and likely forms of conflict is wide, and the means of deterrence or resistance to some can be ill-suited to others. Second, the states of the region differ radically among themselves as well as with the United States over which are the salient threats, whether their origin be internal or external. This thwarts intraregional security cooperation, and impedes security cooperation with the United States even by regional states that share close relations. It also produces great tension between country-specific and broader regional policies of the United States. Third, even where close cooperation with the United States is welcome, Islamic and nationalist sensitivities pose obstacles to the objective identification or most efficient implementation of specific security measures, whether in the types of weapons systems procured or in granting foreign access to local military facilities. Fourth, the introduction of foreign security assistance can become a focus of domestic political controversy with destabilizing implications. Finally, effective responses also require cooperation between the United States and its Western allies, yet impediments to cooperation result from differences of interest and perspective in the West with respect to Southwest Asia. What is urgently needed for the 1980s is a strategy that not only integrates objectives and tasks coherently but also takes each of these factors into practical account.

Regional and Country-Specific Priorities

There has been a running debate since the events of the Iranian revolution, Soviet invasion of Afghanistan, and Iraq-Iran war over whether high-intensity-conflict or low-intensity-conflict potentials are the dominant threat to Western interests in Southwest Asia. Similarly, these events have raised the issue whether conflicts of local origin are more salient than threats of Soviet origin. No totally satisfactory a priori resolution of these issues is possible.

What can be said is the following: Conflicts of local origin are prolific. In that sense they are the most common, indeed the prevalent, threats to Western interests in the region. But they are much less likely to be permanently damaging, or to fundamentally alter the strategic balance, than Soviet high-intensity military threats. Conflicts of local origin in general are much more difficult to prevent, but they are more susceptible to amelioration once they materialize. In comparison, Soviet high-intensity military initiatives probably are more susceptible to deterrence, but they are more likely, when deterrence fails, to be strategically decisive. Conflicts of local origin intrinsically are less salient threats.

However, a general rule that local conflicts are less threatening is misleading on two grounds. First, the exceptions that prove the rule may be the cases that matter. The Iranian revolution, for example, has drastically altered the perceived global as well as regional balance of power, yet it is unique among numerous postwar cases of local instability in having that effect. Second, more important than the intrinsic threats to Western interests are the regional vulnerabilities to Soviet exploitation that conflicts of local origin entail. Given the abundance in this region of such opportunities, Soviet threats to Western interests are likely to materialize most frequently in low-intensity rather than high-intensity conflicts. As suggested before, low-intensity threats may be more common, but whether Soviet or non-Soviet in origin, they are unlikely in most cases to prevail in a decisive way. Yet there could be decisive exceptions, and a series of cumulative lesser setbacks could also prove injurious. Since the more common, albeit normally more manageable, threats to Western interests arise from domestic instability and local conflict in the region, it follows that measures to cope with low-intensity conflict ought to have high policy priority, especially in the day-to-day management of political and economic relations prior to crises.

It does not follow, however, that a sophisticated strategy for low-intensity conflicts precludes the need to prepare a combat capability for high-intensity conflicts. Not only is there a need for a deterrent to offset any Soviet inclination to resort to high-intensity conflict, it is important to bear in mind the interdependence that exists in countermeasures for high- and low-intensity conflict: local determination to resist Soviet low-intensity moves will become unsteady if there is disbelief in the credibility of deterrence against high-intensity threats. Ultimately, there is no escape from either the potential decisiveness of the high-intensity threat or the prevalence of the low-intensity threats. Which is dominant is less important—what is salient is the connection between them. Both will have to be addressed as critical tasks for the 1980s, despite the extraordinary defense-budget considerations.

The salience of indigenous and Soviet threats, and high- and low-intensity conflict potentials, differs geographically and by country. So does the relative capacity of the United States to respond in practical terms to high- and low-intensity threats. Policy priorities will have to take these factors into account, along with the relative importance of the real estate or local resources that may be at stake. Today Iran, for example, is far more accessible politically as well as geographically to a Soviet high-intensity threat than Saudi Arabia, but the prospects for receptivity to U.S. assistance in coping with such a threat are far more favorable in Saudi Arabia than in Iran. Iran, on the other hand, has the manpower to be a more effective partner, theoretically, in a combined-arms approach to high-intensity conflict than does Saudi Arabia.

The two countries in Southwest Asia that will have unique importance in U.S. strategy in the 1980s will continue to be Iran and Saudi Arabia—this remains geopolitically inescapable. Iraq and Pakistan will also be important, but they must, on the same scale, be ranked several notches below. There should be no illusions about the strategic intersubstitutability of these countries.

Little can be done for the time being to repair U.S.-Iran relations, but a process of rapprochement eventually is to be expected if Iran's independence is not first subverted. Iran probably will look more to Europe and Japan than the United States initially, but Western influence in some fashion will return. It is important not to seem overly eager to draw Iran back to the fold—this tends to feed countercurrents and grandiose presuppositions that Iran's strategic importance is a shield against its vulnerabilities. Rather, the latent incentives for reconstruction, normalized relations, and defense reinsurance should be left for the most part to reassert themselves naturally. This does not preclude U.S. readiness to extend spontaneous support to a friendly regime, should the present one be superseded, or to help resist the insinuation of Soviet influence if the present situation degenerates into civil war.

Saudi Arabia's singular importance as the largest international oil supplier and source of moderating influence in Middle East affairs is objectively independent of the recent crises in the area, but those crises have highlighted how vital Saudi decisions and capacities are to the economies of the West and much of the developing world. The resulting competition for Saudi attention has greatly increased its diplomatic influence; however, this has also put the spotlight on Saudi vulnerabilities, thereby increasing them in certain respects. Saudi Arabia is potentially vulnerable to almost the entire spectrum of regional conflict and is least able among the principal states of the region to counter high-intensity conflicts by itself. Although it is better equipped to cope with low-intensity conflicts, this is a relative matter, by no means certain, and properly the overriding source of Western concern about Saudi Arabia.

Although Saudi Arabia objectively is highly vulnerable to high-intensity conflict, the probability of such threats materializing from the Soviet Union in peacetime is low, because they would be deterred by U.S. security commitments. The probability of regional high-intensity threats materializing is considerably higher but still likely to be contained by U.S. commitments. This was underscored by the dispatch of AWACS and other elements of U.S. air-force presence to deflect further spread of the Iraq-Iran war. Confidence in the U.S. defense commitment to Saudi Arabia is subject to one important qualification. Serious damage by surprise air attack to oil-field installations is difficult to protect against, and it is not fully clear that an Israeli threat of this sort would be deterred under all circumstances. It should be a high priority for U.S. policy in the 1980s to make the intolerability of such action unmistakably binding.

Saudi Arabia is not likely to suffer a revolutionary crisis analogous to that of Iran because of differences in politics and society, including the extensive reach in Saudi Arabia of the large ruling family, its Islamic modalities of government, and its distributionist approach to the domestic oil wealth. But it is potentially vulnerable to sudden political change resulting from discord in ruling circles, commoner dissatisfaction, unrest from Shi'ite population in the eastern province, and destabilizing pressures from immigrant laborers, particularly Yemenis and Arab groups from neighboring countries. The royal family is especially sensitive to the potentially divisive domestic effects of radical forces, whether communist inspired or Arab in origin, that emanate from other sources in the region. Modernization is bound to intensify cross-pressures in conservative Saudi society, despite the pragmatic flexibility of its political system.

It will continue to be a priority in the 1980s to provide political and security reassurance to Saudi Arabia against regional threats from Iraq and the two Yemens, especially the Soviet/Cuban/East German proxy threats from South Yemen. Local conflicts with these countries are unlikely to swallow territory so much as to sow seeds of internal unrest or to overthrow the monarchy. Saudi leadership of the smaller Gulf states, now somewhat better organized for security coordination in the Gulf Cooperation Council, should be encouraged. United States training and equipment for the Saudi military forces is extensive and crucial to security reassurance and provides the infrastructure to make cooperative U.S. military use of Saudi facilities plausible for certain contingencies.

Saudi Arabia also draws on regional military assistance, particularly from Pakistan. Although ostensibly for training, implicit in the latter relationship is the emergency provision to Saudi Arabia of military manpower by Pakistan from its more substantial armed forces to stiffen smaller Saudi forces. This is another form of regional-security interdependence that the United States should favor, even though informal multilateral relationships for security purposes add to the management burdens faced by the United States.

Since the primary Saudi vulnerabilities to be offset involve threats to domestic political stability, it is crucial to manage the U.S. security relationship in a way that minimizes its own abrasive impact on Saudi politics. Too large or too visible a U.S. presence tends to offend local sensibilities and become a target for local dissidents. The same is true of U.S. access that might be interpreted as constraining on Saudi sovereignty. Sensitivities of this sort preclude Saudi authorization of military-base rights. It will remain prudent to defer in such cases to Saudi preferences in the interest of keeping the risks to domestic stability low.

The extraordinary stakes in the preservation of Saudi security and stability also require sensitivity in the United States to Saudi interests in the development of policies for other countries or the region as a whole, especially in those matters that pertain to the Arab-Israeli conflict or the special relationship with Israel. Saudi involvement in Arab diplomacy vastly expanded after 1973, and Saudi Arabia consequently is much more internally susceptible to divisive Arab pressures as well as potentially exposed, in the event of renewed hostilities, to Israeli military retaliation. Balance in U.S. Middle East policy is an imperative for Saudi and Gulf security in the 1980s.

The gradual opening of a rift between Iraq and the Soviet Union, which was accelerated by the Soviet tilt to Iran in the Iraq-Iran war, has opened opportunities to restore some Western influence in Baghdad. This opening should be cautiously explored, and the nascent Saudi-Iraq and Jordan-Iraq cooperation should be encouraged. But care should be taken not to further embitter or alienate Iran needlessly.

A revitalization of the security relationship with Pakistan became imperative after the invasion of Afghanistan because of the destabilizing implications of that event for the Persian Gulf and because Pakistan's support is indispensable for any effective response to the Soviet invasion as well as to any new Soviet pressures on Pakistan borders. Modern defense equipment is essential to Pakistan's borders. Modern defense equipment is essential to Pakistani confidence in its own self-defense capacity. In this case, it also symbolizes a U.S. commitment that can be viewed as a deterrent against high-intensity Soviet threats to Pakistan. Without such U.S. support, Pakistan could not withstand Soviet diplomatic intimidation. It is much less valuable as a counter to low-intensity subversion in Baluchistan, where political and economic measures are more likely to be decisive. The U.S.-Pakistan security relationship could be jeopardized by domestic political unrest within Pakistan (to which it could also be a contributing cause), by the tragic rivalry with India, and by the nuclear-defense element in Pakistan's foreign policy.

Notes

1. By historical convention it is the Persian Gulf, but it could as easily be thought of as the Arabian Gulf connecting with the Arabian Sea. For a useful multidisciplinary survey of the states surrounding the Gulf, see Alvin J. Cottrell et al., *The Gulf States: A General Survey* (Baltimore: Johns Hopkins University, 1980).

2. James R. Schlesinger, "The International Implications of Third World Conflict: An American Perspective in Third World Conflict and International Security, Part I," Adelphi Papers, no. 166 (London: International Institute of Strategic Studies, Summer 1981), pp. 5–13.

3. Robert W. Tucker, "America in Decline: The Foreign Policy of 'Maturity'" *Foreign Affairs* 58 (1980): 449–484.

4. Melvin Conant, "Resources and Conflict: Oil—The Likely Contingencies, Third World Conflict and International Security, Part II," Adelphi Papers, no. 167 (London: International Institute of Strategic Studies, Summer 1981), pp. 45–50; Herman T. Franssen, "World Economic and Energy Trends, Implications for Energy Security" (Paper prepared for Conference on the Future of Nuclear Power, Bonn, West Germany, December 1981).

5. "Defending the Gulf: A Survey," *The Economist*, 6 June 1981, pp. 1–38.

6. There are some who are skeptical that this is any longer feasible; see, for instance, Walter J. Levy, "Oil and the Decline of the West," *Foreign Affairs* 58 (Summer 1980): 999–1015.

7. A similar conclusion is sometimes reached by investing geopolitical competition with the spirit of a game, as though the destiny of states in Asia should be determined by great powers playing musical chairs. See David Fromkin, "The Great Game in Asia," *Foreign Affairs* 58 (Spring 1980): 936–951.

8. For a sophisticated analysis, see Shahram Chubin, "Soviet Policy Towards Iran and the Gulf," Adelphi Papers, no. 157 (London: International Institute of Strategic Studies, Spring 1980).

9. For a recent assessment, see John P. Hardt, "Soviet and East European Energy Policy: Security Implications" (Paper prepared for Conference on the Future of Nuclear Power, Bonn, West Germany. December 1981). The point was brought to public attention by National Foreign Assessment Center, *The World Oil Market in the Years Ahead: A Research*

Paper, ER79-10327U (Washington, D.C.: Central Intelligence Agency, August 1979). A comprehensive study of the Soviet energy situation may be found in Leslie Dienes and Theodore Shabad, *The Soviet Energy System: Resource Use and Policies* (New York: John Wiley & Sons, 1979).

10. Soviet energy-supply capacities also threaten to bring about the dependency of Western Europe. See Thomas Blau and Joseph Kirchheimer, "European Dependence and Soviet Leverage: The Yamal Pipeline," *Survival* 23 (September/October 1981): 209–214.

11. Hugh Seton-Watson, "The Last of the Empires," *The Washington Quarterly* 3 (Spring 1980): 41–46; William E. Griffith, "Superpower Relations after Afghanistan," *Survival* 22 (July/August 1980): 146–150; Zalmay Khalilzad, "Afghanistan and the Crisis in American Foreign Policy," *Survival* 22 (July/August 1980): 151–160.

12. Seweryn Bialer, *Stalin's Successors: Leadership, Stability, and Change in the Soviet Union* (Cambridge: University of Cambridge Press, 1980).

13. Dennis Ross, "Considering Soviet Threats to the Persian Gulf," *International Security* 6 (Fall 1981): 159–180.

14. For a perceptive analysis, see Donald Zagoria, "Into the Breach: New Soviet Alliances in the Third World," *Foreign Affairs* 57 (Spring 1979): 733–754.

15. Tucker, "America in Decline."

16. Jiri Valenta, "From Prague to Kabul: The Soviet Style of Invasion," *International Security* 5 (Fall 1980): 114–141.

17. Barry M. Blechman and Douglas M. Hart, "Afghanistan and the 1946 Iran Analogy," *Survival* 22 (November/December 1980): 248–252.

18. Carnegie Endowment for International Peace, *Challenges for U.S. National Security, Assessing the Balance: Defense Spending and Conventional Forces, A Preliminary Report*, part II (Washington, D.C., 1981).

19. Bialer, *Stalin's Successors*.

20. It was inevitable that the RDF be conceived of as a force with other potential emergency missions as well. For confusion over the difference between missions and strategy, the latter concept being inappropriately applied to the RDF, see Kenneth Waltz, "A Strategy for the Rapid Deployment Force," *International Security* 5 (Spring 1981): 49–73.

21. Jeffrey Record, *The Rapid Deployment Force and U.S. Military Intervention in the Persian Gulf* (Cambridge, Mass.: Institute for Foreign Policy Analysis, February. 1981); Sir John Hackett, "Protecting Oil Supplies: The Military Requirements" in *Third World Conflict and International Security, Part I*, Adelphi Papers, no. 166 (London: International Institute of Strategic Studies, Summer 1981), pp. 5–13. Congressional Budget Office, *U.S. Airlift Forces: Enhancement Alternatives for NATO and Non-NATO Contingencies* (Washington, D.C.: U.S. Government

Printing Office, April 1979); Congressional Budget Office, *U.S. Projection Forces: Requirements, Scenarios, and Options* (Washington, D.C.: U.S. Government Printing Office, April 1978).

22. Joshua M. Epstein, "Soviet Vulnerabilities in Iran and the RDF Deterrent," *International Security* 6 (Fall 1981): 126–158.

23. Epstein's article contains various other difficulties. Although Epstein does not fall into the trap of strictly worse-case analysis (that is, one that assumes the Soviets in fact make optimum use of their capabilities, and U.S. forces in contrast cannot because they suffer from a series of known deficiencies), he does make some startling leaps of faith about the scenario, including that: (1) the requisite Soviet preparatory buildup not only would be detected but recognized for what it is; (2) U.S. advance preparations would be promptly initiated and proceed in tandem; and (3) once the Soviet invasion began, the United States would be politically capable of making the decisions to fight the Soviet Union in this theater, to initiate the air strikes required to slow and degrade the Soviet invasion thrusts, and to commit the several divisions of ground forces that would be needed for the defense of Khuzistan to emplacement in that zone. (These assumptions would not be so breathtaking if U.S. military forces were assured of local superiority or capable of defending Iran as a whole.) Epstein also omits from his analysis any of the complications that could arise from the hostility or active resistance of Iranian or other national military forces in the vicinity. Moreover, he does not address the implications of the Soviet augmentation and upgrading of military forces that might be feasible over the next five to ten years.

24. For an assessment of Saudi foreign-policy perceptions, see Adeed Dawisha, *Saudi Arabia's Search for Security*, Adelphi Papers, no. 158 (London: International Institute of Strategic Studies, Spring 1980).

25. "South and Southwest Asia" IISS *Strategic Survey 1980–81* (London: International Institute of Strategic Studies, 1981), pp. 63–72; Selig S. Harrison, *In Afghanistan's Shadow: Baluch Nationalism and Soviet Temptations* (Washington, D.C.: Carnegie Endowment for International Peace, 1981).

26. Anthony Arnold, *Afghanistan: The Soviet Invasion in Perspective* (Stanford, Calif.: Hoover Institution Press, 1981).

27. This judgment assumes Pakistan's armed forces would vigorously resist a Soviet invasion—an assumption that may be open to question, but not one that Soviet military planners would necessarily discount.

28. Rodney W. Jones, *Nuclear Proliferation: Islam, the Bomb, and South Asia*, Washington Papers, no. 82 (Washington, D.C.: Center for Strategic and International Studies, Georgetown University, 1981).

29. In fast-breaking crises, this parsimony condition is intrinsically difficult and sometimes impossible rigorously to satisfy, i.e., what can be accomplished by alternative means may be highly uncertain. But this does not negate the presumptive validity of the condition.

15 Invasion and Instability in Southeast Asia

W. Scott Thompson

Southeast Asia is the regional theater of the greatest internal and international conflict today and has been such for almost thirty years. If greater attention is currently focused on Southwest Asia and the Persian Gulf, it is because of the way such incipient conflict therein bears on regions of, arguably, intrinsically greater importance like Europe or East and Southeast Asia. And, if Iran and Iraq are at war, it must be remembered that, only two years ago, the People's Republic of China (P.R.C.) invaded Vietnam, after Vietnam had invaded—and occupied—Kampuchea. Moreover, the interests of all the superpowers and great powers in fact intersect in Southeast and East Asia.

It is also the area in which the greatest single postwar conflict occurred, the consequences of which have yet to be fully absorbed by either losers or winners. Both the character of the U.S. entry to the Vietnamese land war and of its withdrawal continue to have consequences for the future of conflict in the region. It can be argued, for example, that the move toward harsher internal order in several states—for example the martial-law periods in the Philippines and Korea—was a response to the uncertainties set in motion by the U.S. withdrawal from Vietnam in the early 1970s. And these internal crackdowns have had tangible results in the regions as internal opponents have sharpened their opposition to the regimes in power.

Southeast Asia's status as an area of continued conflict thus seems guaranteed. An analysis by a Thai official succinctly foreshadows much of our argument as to why this should be so. In addition to the U.S. withdrawal and "the extension of Soviet power" in the region ("to serve its strategy of global expansion"), the Thai study cites "the ambitious objectives and aggressive policies of . . . Vietnam" as the basic changes underlying conflict in the region. Thus, it is argued, national interests have transcended ideological interests in the struggle for influence among communists in Southeast Asia. The "current struggle for influence," however, is "derived basically from the geopolitical importance of the region to the strategic confrontations between first, the Soviet Union and the United States, and secondly, between the Soviet Union and the P.R.C., with the immediate focal point of conflict and external involvement being the aggressive ambitions and intransigent policies pursued by [Vietnam]."

Despite, and in part because of, the U.S. withdrawal from Vietnam and the ensuing drawdown throughout the region, Southeast Asia remains of immense importance to the United States. The United States' future engagements in the region derive from this tangled past and the alliances and relationships that issued from it; they will also affect engagements elsewhere. The character of the conflict projected for this region affects in considerable measure that elsewhere as well. Perhaps for historical and ethnic reasons Western Europe remains the theater of greatest U.S. involvement abroad; yet Asia, by dint of trade in the same order of magnitude as that between the United States and Europe, growing ethnic ties, and, surprisingly, more assured power-projection access rivals Europe in its relative importance to the United States; a rearrangement of the variables might produce a product of greater importance. There is no way the United States can swing its forces—military, political, or economic—away from Asia without the gravest of risks.[3] In short, conflict in Southeast Asia must continue to engage U.S. attention.

Great Powers and Systemic Instability in Southeast Asia

By definition, Asia has been destabilized by the enormous military buildup of the Soviet Union in the region—to whatever motive one attributes it. The buildup began, of course, in the late 1960s as a response to the deepening conflict with the P.R.C. In a second phase, it would seem to have progressed simply as a response to the partial strategic vacuum that developed with the withdrawal of U.S. forces.

Yet the Soviet buildup seems to have more of an objective than a mere replacement of the United States as the preeminent military force of the Southeast/East Asian theater. From within official sources, and on the basis of hard but highly esoteric sources, it can be argued that the buildup in this third phase has occurred in response to yet another substantive fear.[4] This fear is that, for all the withdrawal of U.S. forces, Asia has remained, at least relatively, the soft or weak spot of the Soviet perimeter. According to this argument, the European theater hardened in the Soviet favor once the strategic balance had either stabilized or tilted in Moscow's favor (depending on whether one considers quantitative and qualitative indicators relevant). Such hardening made it impossible for the North Atlantic Treaty Organization (NATO) to compensate for its conventional inferiority with U.S. strategic superiority. West Central Asia had become a Soviet geopolitical salient with the occupation of Afghanistan, with the indirectly related anarchy in Iran, and with the return of Indira Gandhi to power in India. Moscow's power in East-Southeast Asia is a function of one highly vulnerable rail line and the slow movement of ships from vulnerable northern European or Black Sea ports a distance equal to halfway around the world;

Asia had thus become a place where, in a war, the United States might probe, bottle up the Soviet fleet in the Sea of Okhotsk, and thus establish a U.S. bastion of regional supremacy in Northeast Asia from which to batter Soviet forces and interests.

Thus Soviet power has poured into Asia on all fronts. Although this has ample diplomatic precedent in the continuing Soviet attempt to establish a so-called Asian collective security system (and even if a Soviet presence was intended originally for purposes of outflanking the P.R.C.), it has become clear through some channels that the Soviet intentions include shoring up the empire's perimeter.

The Soviets have rationalized this as a response to the remarkable change in the balance of forces in the region occasioned by the Japanese-Chinese entente and the increase in the size of the Japanese defense budget. The argument is buttressed neither by the absolute size of the numbers involved nor by the intangible nature of Japanese-Chinese cooperation, even given Soviet phobias about the P.R.C. Soviet frontal aviation in the region is now almost double that of the U.S. Pacific Command (PACOM); SS-20s cover virtually the entire region. The twenty-one surface combatants compare with eighty-five Soviet ships; U.S. attack submarines, outnumbered everywhere, face odds of 14 to 1 in Asian waters. To say, as is so often said, that U.S. naval forces control the seas makes little sense when the Soviet navy can cut the control in so vital a region as East Asia. Admiral Elmo Zumwalt has further argued that in a general war, Washington would have to write off all its Asian allies to keep the sea lanes open to Western Europe. Small wonder that the 1978 Japanese White Paper called the Soviet Union the premier naval power in the Western Pacific. Nor is the threat confined to the sea lanes. According to a British military expert, the deployment of the Backfire bomber and other new strike aircraft "presents a formidable threat to Japan's airfields and logistic support facilities," not to mention the threat to South Korea and other countries.

The perceived threat to Southeast Asia has grown apace as well. From their bases in Cam Ranh Bay and Danang, Soviet Anti-Submarine Warfare (ASW) missions have flown against regional targets, establishing a wholly new calculus and balance of power as seen by such leaders as the Thai foreign minister, the entire Singapore leadership, and of course President Marcos in the Philippines. The Soviet establishment of a client relationship with each of the Indochinese states as their economies falter and as the security position in Kampuchea deteriorates has created a capability useful in any regional contingency, whatever the original motivation for involvement. In this subregion, however, it is probably fair to say that the possibilities of a Soviet exacerbation of conflict depend at least in part on systemic (world) factors, since the relative balance remains less unfavorable (other than along the Thai-Kampuchean border) to the Association of Southeast

Asian Nations (ASEAN) states and their great-power ally than do the
balances in Southwest Asia and Europe to the noncommunist states.

The P.R.C. contributes to regional stability at the superpower level only
insofar as its weakness is provocative to the Soviet Union, as was seen in the
contemplated 1969 takeout of its nuclear capability. However, Chinese
perceptions of the depth of the Soviet threat are such as to require, in the
Chinese mind, daring and risky behavior to deter Moscow and its clients
from further upsetting the regional balance. The invasion of Vietnam in
1979 must be seen in this light; however much it revealed Chinese weakness, it demonstrated Chinese resolve above all else. Thus, to the question
of what the P.R.C. would do in the event that Vietnam probed 25 kilometers
into Thailand in a second invasion, as compared with 3 on the first, a Chinese
diplomat ventured that the P.R.C. "might probe 25 km into Vietnam."[12]

Indeed, the extent to which the P.R.C.'s posture has changed both
toward guerrilla "people's" war and, derivatively, her neighbors, can be
seen in the very case of its relations with the Royal Thai government.
Despite the narrowness of the buffer between Thailand and Vietnam,
despite the intensity of animosity between those two Southeast Asian rivals
(an intensity inflamed by U.S. use of Thai airfields for bombing North
Vietnam), and despite the access Vietnam had to internal Thai politics
through the refugees who arrived in the 1950s from North Vietnam, it was
always the P.R.C. that posed the more serious threat to Thailand. The
reasons, derived from history and the ease of penetration of certain northern
Thai ethnic groups, need not be discussed here. What is important is that in
1979–1980, as the P.R.C. concluded its reassessment of its strategic position, the Chinese found it prudent to cut off support to their clients in
Thailand—with dramatic and measurable consequences for the continuing
rebellion. The P.R.C. had always defended residual assistance to Thai
guerrillas, along with continued broadcasts of the "Voice of the People of
Thailand" from Kimming, by claiming that it could not prevent certain party
elements from sustaining such aid.[13] Yet when the incentives were sufficient,
it was easily managed.

The extent of the P.R.C.'s volte-face can be seen in the astonishing fact
that the P.R.C. initiated antiguerrilla support to Thailand in early 1980. This
occurred as a delayed consequence of increased Soviet assistance to Vietnam and Kampuchea and of continued Soviet buildup at Cam Ranh Bay,
which Beijing of course saw as a flanking move against itself.[14]

To assess the future of U.S. involvement in conflict in Asia one must
remember how much the U.S. military presence has changed in the region since Vietnam. Following promulgation of the Nixon doctrine, 26,000
troops left Japan, 17,000 left Korea; the Pacific fleet in 1964 had eleven
carriers, today the total is six. For the past year and a half, most of the
fleet's deployable power has been in the Indian Ocean; U.S. sealift has

shrunk. "The residue of dry cargo ships and tankers at this stage would be able to support a sizeable contingency only if optimistic planning factors all panned out," an authoritative net assessment by *Aviation Week* points out.[15]

The shift in base rights in the region is more dramatic. The United States negotiated itself out of its base rights in Thailand gratuitously and forfeited its access in Taiwan. Hanoi in effect chased the United States out of South Vietnam and granted increasingly wide access to the Soviet Union at the former U.S. bases. Such changes have made our tenure at remaining bases less secure; but they have also made the remaining bases indispensable. The uncertain fortunes of President Marcos do not augur well for Subic Bay or Clark Air Base, even though his most probable successors probably will try to design a formula for keeping the United States in the Philippines. There are too many explosive forces at work in that country, however, for Washington to rest well about such critical bases.

In sum, there is reason to doubt the future stability of this region on grounds of shifts of great-power involvement, without questioning the designs of powers. At their best, the designs look foreboding—at least in relation to the conflict potential elsewhere in the world.

Regionally Derived Conflict

Conflict is more present today in the Philippines than in any Asian state other than Kampuchea in the dry season. It exists at three levels, which are increasingly interconnected: the Moro secessionist war in Mindanao and the Sulu Peninsula, the New People's Army (NPA) Marxist guerrilla struggle, and the largely incipient urban-guerrilla struggle in Manila.

Most conspicuous, but least dangerous to regional or national stability, is the nine-year-old conflict in the southern Philippines (with roots going back centuries). It seems to "defy all efforts to bring it to an end," a *Far Eastern Economic Review* study argues.[16] Sparked in the first instance by the insistence in the new martial-law administration that all private firearms be given up, it had deeper roots in the immigration of non-Moslems into Mindanao—these non-Moslems had long since composed the island's majority and used land titles and other legal action to deprive Moslems of ancestral rights.

The military arm of the Moro Liberation Front (MNLF) has 6–12,000 troops armed largely from outside—Libya is the principal external supplier. The level of fighting has gone down from the high of 1973–1975, but it is now localized in hard-core areas into which the Philippine armed forces (AFP) have uncertain access. Every tactic from bribery (free trips to Mecca for guerrillas turning in their rifles) to attrition has been tried, but casualties remain high enough to cause the regime a continuing political and security problem. And although the AFP has become increasingly skilled in counter-insurgency, the Moro fighters are increasingly clever at avoiding confrontation.

The NPA was formed in the late 1960s as the military arm of the Philippine Communist Party, but it never in fact coordinated strategy with the party; its intimate links with Peking in those days precluded such. Originally localized in a historic province of rebellion, Pampanga, the NPA forces have by now reached out throughout the archipelago to find support. Defense Minister Juan Ponce-Enrile puts NPA strength at 3–5,000 armed men plus a support base of 130–150,000, figures confirmed by Eduardo Lachica, the authority on Philippine rebellion.[17]

Originally a doctrinaire guerrilla force applying imported ideology to indigenous conditions, the NPA has, in effect "gone local." Foreign arms are no longer the threat to the regime, nor is Maoism; the NPA feeds on discontent with the Marcos regime, wherever it is greatest. The NPA is a greater threat than the MNLF precisely because of its radical appeal to the whole strata of the nation. The more the regime tries to delegitimize the traditional opposition that had functioned prior to martial law, the more the NPA comes to symbolize, in many ways, opposition to Marcos. Its broadly populist and agriculturally based program has little of the esoteric appearance of the group's predecessor leaders, most of whom are now in jail.

The NPA threatens even more by its attempts to link its efforts to those of the MNLF. So far, such cooperation has been problematic: the NPA considers the Moros romantics, "adventurers who [talk] too much," and "the traditionalist leaders who still predominate in the MNLF dislike almost everything the NPA stands for. At times, they suspect that the communists are out to subvert their movement."[18] Indeed, they will be successful insofar as they continue to share a common enemy who is unable to build a sounder mass base for his rule.

Ironically, the gravest threat to Philippine stability may well be a force that has barely been tested—the hitherto legitimate opposition to regime rule. The premartial-law dukes and earls of Philippine provinces and industry have, with conspicuous exceptions, done well enough economically in the martial-law republic not to protest the new order. In any event, the most effective of their number were incarcerated; Senator Aquino, the most prominent, was detained for almost eight years. Few are romantic visionaries (such as absent former Senator Manglapus), and all know how canny their old colleague Marcos is.

In 1979, however, frustrated by their lack of political access and by Marcos's continued stifling of all opposition, they began to show a capability to cooperate, where need be, to organize urban terrorism. The major instance of this—a bomb in an international tourism conference (designed to show the Philippines as a tourist Mecca)—did considerable damage to the country's image and served a critical warning. The timing, however, in the minds of many was off; Marcos still had cards to play, and the terrorism campaign was turned off for the time being. The maneuvering of both sides in the ensuing year and a half leading to the new constitution and elections of 16 June 1981 deferred the problem further.

Marcos, however, has failed to coopt the opposition, failing even to prevent their boycott of his election to a regular term, detracting substantially from the perceived constitutionality of the new dispensation. As usual, moreover, Marcos also overreacted to his own generosity. Having ended martial law and softened censorship he passed a retroactive law disallowing opposition by any person who had changed parties—a blatant sledgehammer tactic to smash those who had maneuvered party affiliation to oppose the regime from within the law. From a technical point of view, he is well ensconced in office for a six-year term, but he may have now ended, in the minds of the "legitimate" opposition, the possibility that roles or outlets can ever exist for them, much less that democratic procedures will ever return.

If that is the case, then possibly within the year of the new constitution's proclamation there will be a return to urban terrorism on a wholly new scale. It would bring together elements of each of the three strands of opposition discussed herein. The opposition has used the interval to inform itself on the techniques of urban struggle, and it has a network of leaders, the passion of the young, who provide cannon fodder, and the experience in working with different ideological milieux.

The deteriorating economic scene makes this scenario more likely. Inertia in the private sector, a current-account deficit twice that of last year, continued low prices for most export commodities, and continued dependence on expensive foreign oil all make the scene less hopeful.

There is a final point with respect to the Philippines. Subic and Clark are not only the largest U.S. bases of their kind outside the United States, they are among the few remaining that are under full (if de facto) U.S. control, and the threat to them comes not from the will of the host government but from the threat to that same government from within national ranks. The geostrategic criticality of the Philippines to the United States may make it imperative to hold onto the bases at all costs—something that Senator Aquino has conceded the possibility of in a hostile environment. "If Castro couldn't get you out of Guantanamo, we certainly couldn't get you out of Subic," he commented, while affirming his own intention to keep the bases there, were he to come to power. As the U.S. military presence has declined precipitously around the globe, the remaining assets have become all the more important. The United States must consider the possibility of far more substantial involvement in the internal-security arrangement of the Philippines.

Thailand is the front-line state within the ASEAN alliance, mostly because of the Vietnamese threat on its borders; but an internal threat has long existed and is not wholly distinct from the external one. Even despite the cut that the P.R.C. has made in its support to communist forces within Thailand, there is every reason to expect that conflict will continue within Thailand for the foreseeable future.[20]

The insurgency as a formal movement surfaced in late 1965 after years of dormancy. Although it grew steadily, it was from so small a base that as such it did not threaten Thai society. A repression of student demonstrations in 1976, however, caused some several thousand of their number to make their way to the jungle, temporarily invigorating the insurgency. But it was the Vietnamese invasion of Kampuchea that affected it the most.

At the time, Communist Party of Thailand (CPT) units operated in half of the nation's provinces and were growing at an annual rate of 6 to 10 percent. With the Vietnamese occupation of Laos, that rear base was of course cut off to the CPT, forcing it to move headquarters back into Thailand. The Chinese cut forced a full rethinking of strategy, not all of which has worked to the benefit of the insurgency; indeed, in 1979, insurgent defections tripled while government casualties fell almost 30 percent.[21]

It would be premature, however, to assume that the insurgency will continue to decline in efficacy; the changes of the past few years reflect the one-time gain of the RTG (Royal Thai Government), thanks to the Chinese cutoff, and they do not reflect the new opportunity the Vietnamese have to supplant the Chinese. In fact, in March 1979, CPT adherents of the Vietnamese line joined the newly formed Indochinese Communist Party, which brings together communist elements from Vietnam, Laos, and northeastern Thailand. Pro-Soviet members of the CPT also formed a new communist party, the Thai Northeastern National Liberation Party. As Sean Randolph and W. Scott Thompson have argued: "The CPT, though at present on the defensive, is far from defeated. . . . Although the number and intensity of military contacts [mostly Chinese] has declined, attacks on Thai government outposts and road construction sites have continued, as have assassinations, mining of roads, and attacks on moving vehicles."[22] It presumably also is only a matter of time before Vietnam can initiate guerrilla activity of its own in Thailand, unless some brake is applied to Vietnamese interference more generally.

Certainly, from the inception of the insurgency, the stability of the Thai state was always a given, against which any challenge must be calculated. Despite student protests, army factional infighting, or labor unrest, there was no threat to the inherent stability of the nation and its monarchical head. That situation has changed, opening for the first time the possibility of regime instability, which, linked with rural instability, alters the prospects for the entire region. The problem began in the palace, where an adventurous queen has intervened beyond all precedent in the domestic political scene. Since 1932, the palace has been politically neutral, and it is not clear if this new factor can be absorbed. "There is actual talk of assassinating Her Majesty," an old Thai hand commented. "In twenty-three years of following Thai affairs, I have never seen so grave a crisis," the same former official commented.[23]

The economy is likewise in grave crisis: this year has witnessed the first two postwar devaluations of the currency, and the problem seems to have no immediate solution, least of all with the political scene so increasingly turbulent. Whether Prime Minister Prem can rebuild a more stable regime is at best problematic.

Malaysia first defeated a major communist insurgency a generation ago and then broke the back of its remnants in more recent years. Malaysia has suffered acute communalism that erupted in riots in 1969—but the country has in recent years gone from strength to strength. Still, the potential for communal violence remains Malaysia's darkest cloud.

The fragments of the Communist Party of Malaysia have scored few successes in the past two years. Movement between these and the guerrillas in southern Thailand has been substantially inhibited by the completion (in late 1979) of a 27-mile security fence along the Thai border and the establishment of an infantry brigade in the border town of Kroh. Moreover, Malaysia is planning a $675-million air base on the northeastern coast, which ties in with a national expansion of defense infrastructure, long put aside while the insurgency was fought and mopped up. Thus Malaysia has ordered ten A-4M Skyhawk fighters and five F-5Es; substantial additional purchases are envisaged, thanks to Malaysian prosperity.[24] Thanks also to Malaysian security perceptions, Malaysian leaders have been at the forefront within ASEAN pressing for closer security coordination as its leaders have watched Vietnam move into Kampuchea and to the Thai border.

Little needs to be said about Singapore, where instability is unthinkable within the present framework of law and regime; and Kuan Yu Lee means to keep it that way. Indonesia at the moment is also stable, thanks to the surge of oil revenues in the last two years, which has enabled the regime in effect to buy off discontent that had long been festering and was often breaking out—into riots (as in 1974) and, more tragically, in the communal-ideological wars of the late 1960s. As recently as five years ago, it should be remembered, it was possible for experts on this vast country to pronounce the gloomiest possible prognostications for the regime's future, thanks to corruption, inefficiency, and declining popularity. Nothing has changed—but for the moment there appears to be little alternative in the popular mind to the present regime. There is enough existing conflict in Southeast Asia, and enough whose present configuration is plain enough for recurrence in the future, to dissuade one from dealing with such hypothetical conflict; on the other hand, the problems of Indonesia are so grave, and the manner in which societal change has occurred is so dramatic, that it behooves the United States to pay due regard to the potential instability there. The word *amok* is not of Indonesian origin by accident. The possibility of massive upheaval is an acknowledged fear among Indonesian elites. For example, in the spring of 1979, newspaper editors were warned by government officials not to "overplay" the events of the Iranian revolution. Indeed, there are similarities between prerevolution Iran and Indonesia, especially in regard to their oil-based economies and their military regimes. To the Indonesian leaders, the overthrow of the shah appeared as a warning of what could become their own fate.[25]

Vietnam—and Indochina more broadly—present a great paradox. On the one hand, theirs are the economies on verge of collapse—"1980 was for Hanoi a year of crushing economic defeat," as Douglas Pike put it. Indeed there was an "extraordinary pessimism . . . discontent . . . disillusionment and a sense of hopelessness among intellectuals. . . . The sense of it was that the country was being overwhelmed by economic and security problems with which an aging leadership was unable to cope."[26]

On the other hand, when one considers the possibility of conflict in Southeast Asia, the principal variable is Hanoi's intentions. Whether Hanoi would really wish to conquer and occupy Thailand, for example, is not only hypothetical, it may be problematical. Thailand is a largely homogeneous country with an illustrious history and indigenous institutions enjoying the overwhelming support of its people, all of which would make it a far less digestible bite for Hanoi than Laos or Cambodia. Yet the threat can hardly be dismissed idly; the resounding argument that Hanoi was far too bogged down by its previous conquests of South Vietnam and Laos to threaten seriously, let alone invade, Cambodia was the formal judgment of the senior U.S. government intelligence and political analysts in November 1978, on the eve of the Vietnamese invasion of the former buffer state.[27]

Yet invade Cambodia (hereafter referred to as Kampuchea) Hanoi did. And if devouring this ancient rival has proved more difficult than envisaged, Vietnam has nonetheless given no sign whatsoever of an intention to relinquish its control there under any guise. As with the illusions of many seeking to provide a face-saving cover for a Soviet withdrawal from Afghanistan, those who see only Hanoi's difficulties in Kampuchea without seeing the strategic advantage such occupation gives her, talk of neutralization anew. It will not happen unless Vietnam itself were to feel threatened.

The conflict will go on within Kampuchea, however, in the considered opinion of various experts. There is a more-than-adequate supply of arms to supply the 30,000-odd troops of the so-called legitimate government of Pol Pot's successors, this even if Vietnam were suddenly able to seal the borders. Geography favors rebellion, and it is unlikely that Hanoi will be able to prevent continued support to various sets of rebels from Thailand and the

P.R.C. This will continue to destabilize the region and provides Hanoi with an excuse in its growing conflict with Thailand. The issue regarding Thailand, however, is broader.

For if Vietnam would be chary of invading Thailand, it may well wish to humiliate the latter sufficiently to throw off balance the kingdom, and thence ASEAN, one of the world's most dynamic alliances. This may be at the base of Hanoi's policy and hence a key variable in whether Hanoi will push on beyond its present overstretched limits.

With roots going back to 1961, the ASEAN organization did not really take off until the reality of the U.S. withdrawal from Vietnam, and thence South Vietnam's defeat, was manifest. By 1980, however, ASEAN had become an organization with both regional and international influence. Its representatives work together intimately at the UN and other fora, probably more closely than any other regional grouping save the five Nordic states. There is an alliancewide style in popular culture and tastes and a visa-free passage of peoples between the five member states (Indonesia, Malaysia, Philippines, Singapore, and Thailand). The regular summit meetings are a great annual event. Hanoi must realize that it is in competition. And with its dynamic economies, ASEAN looks good beside the stagnant Indochinese lands, with their declining growth rates, their boat people, prison camps, food shortages, and martial ethic.

Perhaps the purest Vietnamese view of ASEAN is seen in its own party theoretical journal, *Communist Study*. It makes plain its conviction that ASEAN states are not independent: they are colonial; their people demand that their rulers drop all ties with the United States and win true independence by disposing of capitalism and demanding "mutual assistance" with Indochina. As a Thai official sees it, "mutual assistance" in practice means "the exchange of the country's resources for the privilege of being protected by the Vietnamese army."

Thus a probe 5 kilometers inside Thailand would send proportionately larger shudders down the ASEAN spine than the 3-kilometer incursion did in June 1980; ASEAN members know the military balance, and they know that all together they are no match for Vietnam. They know that, without substantial and swift U.S. military support and probably Chinese support as well in the form of diversionary activity on Vietnam's northern border, Thailand could be dealt a massive blow by the world's fourth-largest armed forces, those of Vietnam. This could knock the self-confidence right out of ASEAN and press each state to consider separate alternatives in dealing with Hanoi.

Some analysts have even thought it opportune to disinter the long-unfashionable domino theory, according to which, by some mechanical inevitability, Thailand and the rest of Southeast Asia would ultimately fall to communism if South Vietnam did not survive. In its essence, the domino

theory was an otherwise mundane hypothesis claiming that actions in one
country of sufficient scope would influence actions in neighboring countries.
It came to represent, however, an inflexible mind set of historical determin-
ism that failed to take into account the differing national histories and
vulnerabilities.

Great events in one nation—like the fall of South Vietnam—do mani-
festly affect events in others in proportion to the shared links of history,
culture, and, of course, geography. It is the other side of the interdependence coin. And Southeast Asia's nations surely exhibit some of the vulnerabilities that Laos and Kampuchea (then Cambodia) showed before their
conquest—at least to the extent that they could be overwhelmed militarily,
forcing them to parlay on Hanoi's terms. In such circumstances not only
would the ASEAN nations' spirits be dampened, perhaps fatally, but dissident radical elements within would be encouraged to play for power in each
ASEAN state more openly. Some would presumably win their internal
fights, as governments sought to accommodate Hanoi. So it perhaps is not
unreasonable that the domino theory has found a new standing in some
Southeast Asian circles.

The Nature of Conflict in the 1980s

There is scarcely any dimension of conflict that cannot be envisaged for
Southeast Asia during the 1980s, on the basis of existing capabilities of the
powers, precedents, and unresolved issues. One starts with the coercive use
of diplomacy and the projection of power—defined in terms of creating
anxiety, rather than of effecting specific deeds—one step short of peaceable
compulsion. Southeast Asia is indeed ripe territory for such demonstration
of power. The superpowers—the Soviet Union and the United States—are
not so deeply ensconced as to work their will forceably (as the United States
all too painfully demonstrated in Vietnam), but there is a more-than-
sufficient military presence on the part of both and a sufficiency of interest in
its maintenance (on the U.S. part) and expansion (on the Soviet part) to
make for much power-projection activity, especially in one or two years, by
which time Moscow's rights at Vietnam's bases will by all logic have expanded considerably.

The kind of activity envisaged herein is of the sort already demonstrated
by Moscow in September 1980, when the 43,000-ton aircraft carrier *Minsk*
ventured out of Cam Ranh Bay to within 100 miles of the Thai naval
base at Sattahip, precisely as the Thai prime minister returned from a
visit to the P.R.C.[30] Coming so soon after Vietnam's incursion and on top
of other naval movements in the Gulf of Siam, the threat understandably
unnerved the Royal Thai leadership—just as intended by Moscow, one

presumes. Precisely because so much of the interplay of forces between the superpowers will be accomplished through clients and allies, power projection will be relevant. As Moscow tries to improve its posture by way of its continued utility to Vietnam, the United States will eventually be forced to make countermoves; the P.R.C. has already begun within its limited—but growing—capabilities. And precisely because Vietnam's fighting capability is so formidable, giving it a comparative advantage therein, it will be using real military probes, and possibly larger military moves, to accomplish its objectives—in contrast to the shadow play in which its great-power protector will indulge. Of course, Chinese policy is to discourage Vietnamese mischief making by refusing to settle the border conflict. "We don't want stability on that border," a Chinese diplomat put it. "For then Vietnam would be free to turn elsewhere with more forces."

Terrorism

Already an omnipresent dimension of Southeast Asia's political scene, terrorism has been present in most of its international and internal forms. Red Guards and Palestine Liberation Organization (PLO) factions alike have been involved in international terrorist incidents in the region, for example, in Bangkok in 1977. So far, the ASEAN states have shown skill and courage in dealing with both the threat and the reality of this dimension of terrorism, which diminishes it as a threat for the future. Indigenously derived terrorism, however, appears to have a bountiful future in the region. This will be of two sorts. First, there is the organized terrorism that comes as a first stage of a revolutionary movement—as occurred in Vietnam in the 1950s. It is practiced today in the Philippines and, to an extent, in southern Thailand. Second, there is the organized terrorism in its fully flowered urban form, a product of political distress but a function of modern urban demographic conditions. A foretaste of this in Manila shows what could happen in Jakarta if the government there declined in efficiency. There is, in any event, little margin.

In sum, terrorism of the international/transnational sort is a low-order threat to Southeast Asia, of nuisance value alone. Terrorism as a function of low-intensity warfare is now prevalent in Southeast Asia and will continue to be so in the 1980s. Urban terrorism almost assuredly has a large future in Manila and could become an important factor in Jakarta or in Kuala Lumpur, if the racial equation were radically to change in the latter.

Surgical Operations

Very little conflict has had a so-called surgical character in Southeast Asia; the region has a tendency to prolong commitments, to dull the knife, but forever to spawn illusions. It was as true for the United States in Vietnam as for Vietnam in Kampuchea—what were thought to be quick, brief interventions that would change the equation to their favor permanently and swiftly simply did not work that way. There are reasons for this. Most theaters of conflict are distant from military bases; the annual cycle of monsoon and dry seasons alternately gives "surgeon" and "patient" opportunities; and the ethnically plural nature of most of the societies muddles the black-and-white character of the intended move.

Security Assistance

In the past, the great powers have offered security assistance as the first avenue of involvement prior to open commitment to clients, as with the United States in Vietnam and, increasingly, the Soviet Union in Indochina. Although U.S. personnel involvement today is quite small (37 advisors in Thailand in connection with the security-assistance program, 53 in Indonesia, and 32 in the Philippines) the security assistance itself is high and growing, as shown in table 15–1. For 1982, the commitment of over $90 million to Thailand in foreign military sales (FMS) and Economic Support Fund (ESF) commitments, or over $100 million to the Philippines, gives an indication of the commitment at stake.

Moscow's stake, of course, is far greater in psychological terms; for its personnel involvement is of a larger magnitude. Although it is impossible to obtain precise figures, there certainly are at least 1,500 Soviet advisors in both Laos and Kampuchea and of course far more in Vietnam. It is still harder to disentangle Soviet financial disbursements in the military field, but it is clear that Moscow's commitment is advisor intensive, as it were—long on personnel and relatively short on money—compared to Washington's involvement. This is, of course, as one would expect, so long as Washington continues to react to the Vietnamese war in every case of security assistance.

Yet what is striking about the U.S. figures is their global amount and what they symbolize—a far greater commitment than the country perhaps grasps, although the commitment is not at all out of proportion to the size and scale of U.S. interests. The threshold for U.S. involvement in actual fighting is consequently raised, that of the Soviet Union is proportionately lower. As table 15–1 suggests, the U.S. role will continue to increase.

One side-effect of security assistance is the opportunity the importation of weapons from a great power provides to the insurgents, against whom the weapons were intended to be used. This is sufficiently significant in the Philippines to warrant special mention. For Filipinos have something of a comparative advantage in pilferage from military arsenals, and much of the rebellions in the past have been supplied from official matériel. The

Table 15–1
East Asia and Pacific: Security-Assistance-Program Summary
(dollars in thousands)

	Foreign-Military-Sales Financing Program					Economic Support Fund			Military-Assistance Program			International Military Education and Training Program		
	Actual FY1980	Estimated FY1981	Proposed FY 1982 Direct	Guarantee	Total	Actual FY1980	Estimated FY1981	Proposed FY 1982	Actual FY1980	Estimated FY1981	Proposed FY1982	Actual FY1980	Estimated FY1981	Proposed FY1982
Burma												30	31	150
Indonesia	30,000	30,000		45,000	45,000							1,639	1,630	2,950
Korea	129,000	160,000		167,500	167,500				1,451[a]	342[a]	130[a]	1,028	1,200	1,800
Malaysia	7,000	10,000		12,500	12,500				532[a]	360[a]	80[a]	258	300	650
Papua New Guinea												11		20
Philippines	50,000	50,000		50,000	50,000	20,000	30,000	50,000	25,000	25,000	1,466[a]	539	580	1,300
Singapore														
Taiwan									45[b]	10[b]	10[b]			50
Thailand	36,000	50,000	50,000	30,000	80,000	2,000	2,000	10,000	1,683[c]	95[a]	50[a]	764	770	2,000
Regional Total	252,000	300,000	50,000	305,000	355,000	22,000	32,000	60,000	28,711	25,807	1,736	4,267	4,511	8,920

Source: Congressional Presentation Document, Security Assistance Programs FY 1982, Defense Security Assistance Agency, Office of International Security Affairs, U.S. Department of Defense, Washington, D.C.

Note: Totals may not add due to rounding.

[a] Wind-up costs under section 516(b) of the Foreign Assistance Act, including supply operations.

[b] Supply operations only for delivery of previously MAP-funded matériel. The grant Military Assistance Program for Taiwan ended in FY 1975.

[c] A Military Assistance Program under Section 506(a) drawdown authority was implemented for Thailand in FY 1980 in the amount of $1.1 million.

problem goes beyond weapons; in 1979 the United States was embarrassed by the theft of a U.S. naval manual on what to do in the event of a nuclear-weapons accident in the Philippines—a subject that the U.S. government has never gone into and, in the past, has paid a high price to avoid.

The other dimension of security assistance that must be mentioned is that of Vietnam in Laos and Kampuchea, where Hanoi has approximately 50,000 and 200,000 troops respectively. The two cases are different—the presence in Laos was the result of a gradual supplanting of local influences and that in Kampuchea resulted from an outright invasion. In the most massive sense, however, this guarantees a continued Vietnamese role in the internal affairs of both states, with the future of conflict—especially in Kampuchea—very bright.

Conventional War

I have already discussed the possibility of a Vietnamese invasion of Thailand in another context. In looking at the region as a whole, one sees that the possibilities for a conventional war are functions of Indochinese borders. The broad international context of conflict in Southeast Asia must, however, be stressed.

One possibility has occurred to both Thai and U.S. strategists—that a Vietnamese invasion of Thailand might be prompted by the Soviet Union. In this scenario, the Soviet Union would wish to exercise its new international strategic superiority by permitting the engendering of a conflict with the P.R.C. A Vietnamese probe deep into Thailand might well prompt another Chinese invasion of Vietnam. The last time the Soviet Union was content to demonstrate its own forebearance and study Chinese inefficiencies and weaknesses; this time it could not afford, and might not wish, to forbear. It might, for example, knock out Chinese nuclear installations as a retaliatory measure, which would in all likelihood not become a world war, given the probable perception that the P.R.C. "had asked for it" and the muddling of the question of who had prompted the war in the first place.

A war between Thailand and Vietnam, or between Vietnam and the P.R.C., could of course begin without Soviet scheming. But it is difficult to envisage a state whose clientage goes so far—$3 million a day in subsidies and membership in the Council for Mutual Economic Assistance (COMECON)—allowing itself to move too far down the road to war without Soviet knowledge and approval. With the order of battle as it is on the Thai-Kampuchean border, however, the possibility of conventional war exists independently of great-power collusion.

Indeed, Vietnam could easily match whatever forces all ASEAN nations could muster, with its million-troop-plus under arms, compared with the roughly 700,000 in ASEAN as a whole. And geography, to understate massively, works in Vietnam's favor. Hanoi, in other words, could be expected to hold back anything but a full-scale Chinese assault while occupying Kampuchea and invading Thailand. Such realities have prompted exceedingly serious thoughts about security in ASEAN. If there are substantial differences in emphasis as to the relative danger of the P.R.C. and the Soviet Union among the alliance members, they are in far more agreement on the scale of the Vietnamese threat. The very scope of Vietnam's economic catastrophe augurs for more diversionary military expeditions, not the reverse.

A Vietnamese invasion of Thailand is not the only scenario that must worry ASEAN and Western defense planners. In the event of civil war in the Philippines, further outbreaks of communalism in Malaysia, or another round of Indonesian struggles between outer islands and Java, Vietnam could use its massive surplus of manpower (and, to a lesser extent, matériel) to aid one side, in the form of either guerrilla or conventional war.

Theater and Strategic Conflict

It follows from the preceding that, although the likelihood of conventional war in Southeast Asia is quite high—indeed, maybe the highest in the world—the likelihood of nuclear war in the region is quite low. Vietnam can fight on its own, or it can fight as a client of Moscow, but it is unlikely that the Soviet Union would get directly involved in conflict, given the advantages for conventional war that adhere to its Vietnamese ally. What is more pertinent is the possibility of world war starting as a result of conflict in Southeast Asia, which is arguably the second most likely location for such, after the Persian Gulf, during the 1980s. Horizontal escalation—escalation, that is, from state to state in the scope of the war rather than up the ladder toward strategic nuclear war—would result, since the Southeast Asian theater conduces toward conventional and guerrilla war. None of the powers there has either the incentive or the near-term capability (through the 1980s) to "go nuclear."

In the final analysis, the ultimate variable for conflict in Southeast Asia during the 1980s will be the strategic and theater balance between the Soviet Union and the United States. However much local conflicts are the so-called cash flow of instability, the bankers are still the external powers who instigate, reinforce, and rearm their clients and allies. If the strategic balance on virtually every indicator has tilted to the Soviet Union's advantage, there are still theaters where advantages continued to adhere to the United States and its allies. Is the Pacific—and hence the medium of Southeast Asia—one of those? Given PACOM advantages in some conventional dimensions, it was still possible, as of last year, for assessments to be made in which a rough parity was seen in Soviet and free-world forces in the Far East. "Present U.S. force levels," an *Aviation Week* anthology put it, "which seem sufficient to deny the Kremlin quick success in any limited conflict, should stand as a strong deterrent as long as 'best case' conditions pertain." It warned, however, that no reinforcements could be expected if the conflict were likely to spread beyond the Pacific—as if it were possible to conceptualize Soviet strategy as not calling for actions to tie down U.S. forces in other theaters.

There is a much-practiced tendency in U.S. official military writing of recent years to insist, year in and year out, despite all the Soviet gains often honestly reported in the interval, that parity continues to exist in any given theater or at any given weapons level. Logically, either assessments were too gloomy at earlier dates, or they are too optimistic today. With respect to the Far Eastern balance in late 1980, however, there could no longer be any rationalization. The commander in chief of the Pacific Command (CINCPAC) had already told the Pentagon that his forces were only "marginally" able to carry out the tasks assigned to them prior to the fall of the shah and the seizure of the hostages. The movement to the Indian Ocean of the two carrier-battle groups assigned to Northeast Asia dramatically and decisively shifted the balance against the West, ironically (but not accidentally) just as the Soviet carrier *Minsk* entered the area. True, the U.S. carriers went to the new theater in part to protect Japan's oil supplies, as U.S. officials frequently reminded Japanese audiences. But the swing— even if within and largely from CINCPAC's command area—reassured few. It is to be doubted that Moscow would hesitate to take advantage of the position just because it was caused by purported U.S. philanthropy toward Japan. What was apparent to naval observers was the increased interest Moscow began showing in the newly depleted areas. In sum, if the United States' relative strength in the theater itself and the credibility of its resolve in the past could not preserve the stability of the region, and if the societies of the region have numerous structural defects conducing toward further instability, then it must be the sober tentative conclusion of this overview that in an era of Soviet superiority worldwide and regionally, the prospects for stability in Southeast Asia are diminished. But then, it is a region full of wild cards and thus surprises; more conflict is not inevitable, it is only what the trends suggest.

Notes

1. Kim Kyung-won, interview by the author. Kyung-won, a Korean scholar and statesman, made this point while national-security advisor to the president of Korea. President Marcos has made the same argument for the Philippines, in interviews with the author. In both cases, a self-serving dimension is present to the argument, but the point stands on its own nonetheless.

2. "Vietnamese Objectives and Strategy in Indochina and Noncommunist Southeast Asia" (Paper given to the author by the office of the prime minister, Royal Thai government), pp. 2, 3.

3. For an expansion of this argument, see "The Indivisibility of World Politics," in *Comparative Power Projectional Capabilities: the Soviet Union and the United States, 1980–85,* ed. W. Scott Thompson, U.S. Navy, OP-965. Thompson was the principal investigator of this study for the U.S. Navy.

4. Reported in discussions with senior naval and state department persons, on the basis of still highly classified sources.

5. The so-called Asian Collective Security Proposal is customarily discounted in the U.S. literature; for example, Arnold L. Horelick, "The Soviet Union's Asian Collective Security Proposal; A Club in Search of Members," *Pacific Affairs* 47 (Fall 1974): 269–285. It is worth remembering the patience with which Moscow pressed the case for a European collective-security system, however—which in any event it obtained. For more elaboration of this argument, see W. Scott Thompson, "Regional Instability in Northeast Asia: Soviet Policy and the World Power Balance," *Conflict* 1 p. 47.

6. For example, in discussions between members of the Institute for the Study of the U.S.A. and Canada and the Foreign Policy Research Institute, December 1980, in Philadelphia, in which the author participated.

7. See "U.S.-Soviet Military Balance: Concepts and Capabilities 1960–80," Aviation Week and Space Technology (1980).

8. Elmo Zumwalt, Presentation, Fletcher School of Law and Diplomacy, September 1978.

9. *Defense of Japan 1979,* White Paper, trans. *Mainichi Daily News.*

10. Air Vice-Marshal Steward Menaul, *Japanese Defence Policy,* London: Foreign Affairs Research Institute 13 (1978).

11. Interview, in particular, with Air Chief Marshal Sihhdi Savetsila, foreign minister of Thailand, September 1980.

12. Interview, 1981.

13. See Sean Randolph and W. Scott Thompson, "Thai Insurgency:

Contemporary Developments," *Washington Papers*, no. 81, 1981.

14. Interviews with intelligence experts on Thailand, Washington, D.C.

15. "U.S.-Soviet Military Balance," *op. cit*, p. 350.

16. Richard Vokey, "Islands under the Gun," *Far Eastern Economic Review*, vol. 112 No. 20 (8 May 1981): 40.

17. Vokey, "Islands under the Gun," and discussion, Eduardo Lachica, 1981.

18. Richard Vokey, "Cooperation Is the Password for the Rebels," *Far Eastern Economic Review*, 112 (May 8, 1981).

19. Discussions with Senator Aquino, 1979–1981.

20. See Randolph and Thompson, "Thai Insurgency," pp. 61–68.

21. Ibid.

22. Ibid.

23. Interview, Washington, D.C., 1981.

24. See Hans H. Indorf, "Malaysia 1979: A Preoccupation with Security," *Asian Survey* 20 (February 1980): 139.

25. See Henry Kamm, "Striking Similarities to Situation in Iran Causing Concern to Indonesian Regime," *New York Times*, 4 June 1979.

26. Douglas Pike, "Vietnam in 1980: The Gathering Storm?" *Asian Survey* 21 (January 1981): 85.

27. Interviews with the CIA, November 1978.

28. Cited in "Vietnamese Objectives," pp. 3, 5.

29. Ibid.

30. See Institute for International and Strategic Studies, *Strategic Survey, 1980–81* (London: IISS, 1981) p. 100.

31. See Clark Neher, "The Philippines, 1979: Cracks in the Fortress," *Asian Survey* 20, 166. See also W. Scott Thompson, *Unequal Partners: Philippine and Thai Relations with the United States, 1965–75*, pp. 66–67.

32. See Paul H. Nitze, "Strategy in the Decade of the 1980s," *Foreign Affairs*, Fall 1979. See also Daniel Arnold and W. Scott Thompson, "On the Thai-Cambodian Border," Draft Manuscript, (Cambridge, Mass.: Tufts University, 1980).

33. "U.S.-Soviet Military Balance," p. 359.

34. See Robert Hanks, "The Swinging Debate," *U.S. Naval Institute Proceedings*, (Annapolis, Md.: U.S. Naval Institute, June 1980).

16 The Potential for Conflict in Northeast Asia in an Era of Change

Gerrit W. Gong

If there is a strategic melting pot where the vital interests of the major powers brew in uncertainty together, it is in Northeast Asia. In Northeast Asia the political, economic, military, cultural, and ideological concerns—including those of national security deriving from geographical propinquity—of the Soviet Union, People's Republic of China (P.R.C.), Japan, and the United States converge as nowhere else. Further, the developments in Korea and the intricacies of the situation on the Korean Peninsula are also integral factors in the Northeast Asian power equilibrium.

A combination of human and natural resources and geopolitical position make the direction and development paths of the countries in Northeast Asia of great importance to the potential for stability or conflict in the international system as a whole. During the decade of the 1980s, stresses will arise within the region as a natural outgrowth of the current dynamism of the countries within it. This potential for tension and conflict will also be exacerbated by the shifting strategic positions of China, the United States, and the Soviet Union.

U.S. Interests in Northeast Asia

In assessing the future of conflict, it is essential to consider the national interests for which the United States would be willing to contemplate the use of military force. For political, economic, military, and ideological reasons, U.S. interests in East Asia in the 1980s can be categorized in two main ways: (1) systemic or functional interests; and (2) specific-country interests. Systemic or functional interests are those that derive from the international framework in which U.S. foreign policy in general will be conducted. Specific-country interests are those that pertain to the bilateral or multilateral interests that the United States shares with particular countries in the region.

The interests of the United States in Northeast Asia have historically been described under the rubric of the "Open Door." Enunciated at the turn of the last century, the "Open Door" policy was founded on two fundamental systemic premises. The continued fulfillment of these two conditions will remain in the U.S. interest through the 1980s.

The first premise was that the power equilibrium in the region would be maintained. In the nineteenth and early twentieth centuries the "Open Door" was to guarantee that China in particular not be carved up like a melon among the different imperialist powers, that its market not be monopolized by a single power, and that, therefore, its territorial and administrative integrity (and open access to its market) would be guaranteed by all. The forces vying for political paramountcy in Northeast Asia have changed, but the guiding principle remains the same. The stationing of U.S. ground troops in Korea (along with the whole trip-wire concept they symbolize); the U.S.-Japanese defense treaty and security arrangement; and the recent announcement that for the first time the United States would consider selling lethal weapons to the P.R.C. on a case-by-case basis all symbolize the commitment of the United States to the maintenance of the power equilibrium in Northeast Asia.

This principle will be challenged in the coming decade by (1) the dynamism of the region, for example, growth in Japan, Korea, China; (2) the possibility that solutions to Poland and Afghanistan could lead to greater Soviet emphasis eastward, with an eye both to the encirclement of China and to increasing Soviet strength and presence in the Indian Ocean by means of its Pacific fleet; and (3) the vacillations in U.S. mood between isolationism and overcommitment and the difficult choices posed by the ongoing questions of the U.S. role in Japan's rearmament, in China's development, or in the stationing of U.S. ground forces in East Asia.

Maintenance of the power equilibrium in East Asia will also be complicated if Sino-Soviet confrontation extends into the region as a whole. Moscow will seek to contain China by furthering its alliances and relations with Beijing's neighbors, and Beijing will seek to develop a coalition of antihegemonist countries. Particularly if some understanding is maintained between the Soviet Union and Vietnam (not a point to be assumed), stresses and tensions on the Sino-Soviet border (including those in the region of the Pamirs), on the Sino-Vietnamese border, and on the Thai borders could mean the interlinking of events in Southeast, Southwest, and Northeast Asia.

The second premise of the "Open Door" was that all countries should have equal and uninhibited access to free trade. Projections of U.S. trade in East Asia over the coming ten years suggest increases even beyond the current one-fourth of all U.S. trade, a volume that already exceeds U.S. trade with Europe. In the coming ten years, as now, U.S. commercial interests in Northeast Asia will depend in part on U.S. ability to maintain the supply and communication lines that contribute to the stability necessary for unimpeded long-term economic and commercial growth.

In an age of so-called resource diplomacy, where access to strategic minerals and supplies of energy is crucial to economic survival, the line between the two premises of the "Open Door" is increasingly blurred. The United States has declared that threatened compromise of the Persian Gulf area could be sufficient reason for the United States to take strong and forceful action. In the course of the next ten years, the question will almost inevitably arise: Under what circumstances would threats to Japan's, Taiwan's, or Korea's economic lifelines—by whatever forces—be similarly construed as threats to U.S. vital interests? The potential for instability, tension, and conflict will remain until (1) the scope for adventurism is appropriately circumscribed by clear delineation of mutual policies and country roles and (2) an appropriate negotiating modus vivendi is developed to help settle peacefully any disputes that might arise.

Potential for Conflict: Country Analyses

It is possible that the major potential for conflict in Northeast Asia in the coming ten years will derive from the internal changes faced by the countries in the region. Internal changes could easily cause dramatic shifts in the power equilibrium, either because other powers may attempt to exploit internal instability for their own causes, as will be discussed in the cases of Soviet probing into North Korean affairs, or where internal changes naturally lead to the reorientation of a country, as will be discussed in the case of Japan. Indeed, rather than external pressure acting against internal resistance, the most likely possibilities leading to conflict in Northeast Asia are those that begin with internal shifts; result in instability and the appearance of troubled waters; and thereby invite "fishing" from outside powers and internal power struggles among groups looking for external support.

It is also important to realize that internal changes will occur naturally as the result of increasing domestic stresses and strains associated with, among other things, accelerated modernization. Conversely, failures or difficulties in modernization, particularly in the case of China, could bring tremendous pressure for change when the regime in power has made economic progress and a rising standard of living a major focus of its program. In the cases of Japan, Korea, and Taiwan, difficulties in maintaining sustained growth could lead to reexamination of orientations and policies. Also, since the economies of the countries in this region are largely export oriented and competitive with one another, fluctuations in the world economic situation will have exaggerated potential for contributing to both inter- and intra-regional conflict. Further, economic competition with the United States and Western Europe may well increase the self-conscious sense of the countries of Northeast Asia in being Asian. A burgeoning sense of culturalism could manifest itself in neonationalism, particularly if protectionism and continued economic difficulties within the West were to cause a backlash against what some perceive as a Western model and order.

China

Although China's plans to modernize agriculture, industry, science and technology, and the military are generally referred to in the West as "the four modernizations," the Chinese use the term as a shorthand expression for goals that are much more comprehensive in scope. The Chinese make quite clear that their efforts are more than merely those of a backward China struggling to catch up. What China has embarked on is a wide-reaching program aimed at fundamental construction in all sectors of its polity, the primary objective being the building of a "modern and powerful socialist country, which is prosperous, highly democratic and culturally advanced."

China's policy planners have noted with concern the potential effects of industrialization and modernization on their country. Accordingly, they are developing plans to make China powerful and modern without compromising its socialist, democratic, or cultural ideals. China's proposed solution to the dilemma of providing both rapid growth and long-term stability focuses on the need to find the proper synthesis of the general principles of Marxism-Leninism and the "concrete reality of the Chinese situation" (what is called Mao Zedong Thought). In this sense, China may develop relatively gradually over the coming years, and therefore that development will less likely be at the expense of its traditional social and cultural bases. In a decade that may well see China's East Asian neighbors questioning their social and cultural identities, China's sense of cultural integrity will remain more certain.

By emphasizing its historical position and by appealing to the character of its people, China will seek to foster its gradual but full emergence as a regional great power. Eventually, it hopes to take a place among the leading countries of the world. However, over the coming decade, China's task is more specific. It must strengthen what it recognizes as a relatively backward and weak position in the face of two major challenges. First, there is the threat to its national security posed by its somewhat paranoid neighbor to the north and its Vietnamese ally to the south. Second, there is the more fundamental challenge to modernize its society without compromising either economic construction or socialist revolution. In a sense, the objective exigencies of the first challenge will gradually diminish with the solution to the second. For this reason, China will continue to seek a double benefit from the course of action it will pursue over the coming ten years: bolstered security, on the one hand, and technology and capital transfers needed for modernization on the other. Its present alignment and policy offer both and could well continue to do so through the 1980s.

China's present alignment is characterized by four main factors: China's new and friendly relations with the United States; the relative stabilization of relations between China and the Soviet Union; the continuing political and military isolation of Taiwan; and the commitment of its present regime to domestic construction.[6] Its present policy priority on domestic construction suggests that China will pursue three supporting objectives or conditions over the coming ten years: (1) to establish, both domestically and internationally, a period of peace and stability sufficiently long for successful continuity of domestic construction; (2) to guarantee its national security against the Soviet Union (and its allies, Vietnam for example), the country with the power and proclivity necessary to pose genuine immediate and long-term military threats to China; and (3) to facilitate the transfers of the technology, capital, and skills from the West needed for modernization.

These three supporting objectives are directly related. Continued use of "parallel strategic concerns" with the West will help China underwrite its own national security, thus helping to preserve a period of peace and potential stability while the technology, capital, and skills necessary for domestic construction are secured from the West. In turn, the West will provide these resources more readily and on better terms as China is able to portray itself as an active and indispensable part of an anti-Soviet coalition.

Although China would desire a convergence of its three supporting objectives, it also realizes that international realities may force a choice among them. For this reason, it is necessary to emphasize China's recognition that the objectives of domestic and international peace, national security against the so-called forces of hegemonism, and transfer of Western technology and capital are only means to a greater end, not an end in themselves. Particularly in a discussion of the future of conflict in the 1980s, this distinction between means and ends is important, because it offers a key to differentiating China's short- and long-term objectives.

Although the need for domestic construction has been clearly recognized since the founding of the P.R.C., China has elected to divert sorely needed resources to meeting perceived external dangers with military force on five main occasions since 1949. These were in Korea in October 1950; on the Sino-Indian border in 1962; on the Sino-Soviet border in 1969; in capturing the Paracel Islands held by South Vietnamese forces in 1974 (for both political and strategic reasons); and on the Sino-Vietnamese border in February 1979.[7] And, although they did not result in an actual conflict, the Taiwan Straits crises must also be considered in our analysis. Of these confrontations, Korea is a marked exception, an extended conflict that began without China's prior knowledge or consent, in which China found itself involved only very reluctantly when its other options were foreclosed by circumstances beyond its control. The other confrontations, especially the 1979 Sino-Vietnamese border clashes, are in an altogether different category.

As in the martial arts, where unexpected moves can cause an otherwise formidable opponent to lose his confidence and balance, so China has developed a strategem of feint and thrust in an effort to parry its relatively backward economic and military situation into a credible deterrent. This kind of approach leads to a somewhat paradoxical position. China has been willing to engage in skirmishes (as in 1969 along the Sino-Soviet border) when it has been in her perceived interests to keep her enemies off-balance. Likewise, despite obvious risks after the conclusion of the 1978 Soviet-Vietnamese alliance, China undertook to teach Vietnam a lesson in February 1979. What lesson did China seek to teach? It was not so much the military lesson, which from all accounts was costly and relatively indecisive. A more important lesson was for China to show the utility and resilience of the emerging Sino-U.S. relation and to underscore that it was willing to defend its perceived long-term interests with military force if necessary. In this sense, one of China's main lessons was that controlled demonstrations of limited military force in the present may defuse the need for extended military operations in the future. China's campaigns were not preemptive attacks in the conventional military sense of the word; they were designed, however, to be psychologically preemptive. Therein was also one of the lessons China wanted to teach India in 1962.

It would be wrong to see such expressions of political will as merely bluffs. It would be equally wrong to think that China, which had Sun Tzu long before we in the West had Karl von Clausewitz, will not continue to see military operations as a means to fulfill political ends. And China will remain an astute judge as to the limits of those political aims, whether in the Korean peninsula, in Taiwan, in Vietnam and potentially, if necessary, in the Sino-Soviet border regions (although China will be extremely wary not to give the Soviets the least excuse for preemptive strikes).

Taiwan

It remains highly improbable that the P.R.C. would contemplate, except as a last resort, an actual invasion of Taiwan. Outright aggression would cost the P.R.C. much and offer little in return. It would mean risking the destabilization of the Northeast Asian region; the damaging of the P.R.C.'s relations with the United States (even if they were already poor) and with its Pacific rim neighbors; and the draining of its economy while possibly destroying whatever industrial infrastructure it might hope to gain in Taiwan. A military victory would be a Pyrrhic victory. Continuation of civil war by military means would be anathema to Chinese on both sides of the Taiwan Straits. And, in the coming decade, only the costliest of extended campaigns of attrition could hope to settle the Taiwan question by military means.

Would Taiwan's declaration of nuclear-weapons capability change this picture? Presumably Taiwan's nuclear-research facilities and technology are already sufficiently advanced to produce nuclear weapons. Reports also circulate that Taiwan is continuing work on missiles with sufficient range and accuracy to strike cities on the Chinese mainland. But two major factors militate against the ultimate utility of Taiwan's nuclear option.

The first is the aforementioned reluctance of Beijing to seek a military solution to the Taiwan question. True, Beijing has not precluded the use of military force against Taiwan. But this is more to maintain its diplomatic freedom of maneuver and arsenal of psychological pressure than its military options. Beijing would not be so foolish as to give Taipei an excuse to use nuclear weapons, assuming it had them.

Second is Beijing's adamant declaration that it will not be the first to use nuclear weapons in a confrontation. While this no-first-use position is generally seen as Beijing's way to strengthen a weak position vis-à-vis the Soviets, it also has profound implications as a way to forestall or at least circumscribe Taiwan's nuclear option. Taipei could hardly hope to maintain legitimacy should it be the first to use nuclear weapons in what would be characterized as a crime against the Chinese people as a whole. Even in the event of armed confrontation, Taipei would have to consider very carefully before crossing the nuclear threshold, even in the name of self-defense.

But, precisely because no one knows the exact role the military will play in the solution to the Taiwan question, active military pressure may play an important role in the evolution of P.R.C.-Taiwan relations. Some senior Chinese officials have suggested that the Chinese bombardment of the offshore islands in 1958, that is, the Taiwan Straits crisis, was not so much for the benefit of the United States as for the making of a point with the Soviets. Likewise, resumed heavy shelling of the islands could be used for any number of psychological reasons. Assuming the unlikely case that present Sino-U.S. relations change dramatically, the P.R.C. could, if it so choose, pressure Taiwan by initiating the mobilization of the kinds of large conventional amphibious and naval forces needed to take the Taiwan-held offshore islands through military force.

Indeed, if Beijing is successful in isolating Taiwan completely and in instilling the feeling that unification, forcible or otherwise, is only a matter of time, then such threats could be psychologically devastating. No doubt a highly sophisticated dose of both carrot and stick would be applied at the same time. In addition to declaring that the military force would be used only as an undesirable and unwanted last alternative, the P.R.C. would hold out the kinds of enticements that appear in its recent unification proposals. These would offer Taiwan some governmental role and autonomy; domestic trade (the tantalizing effect and allure of the China market is not lost on Taiwan's business community); uniting of families; and so on. Should carrot and stick become sufficiently persuasive, it is possible—according to certain scenarios—that some groups within Taiwan, fearing the inevitable and wanting to make the best of a bad situation, may be open to manipulation, internally and externally.

Should Taiwan be isolated, and desperate to the point of willingness to consider any measure necessary to maintain its existence, would some kind of accommodation with the Soviet Union be an option? No doubt the rumors that periodically circulate about Soviet willingness and ability to assist Taiwan reflect Soviet wishful thinking as much as anything. It is possible but unlikely that some of these rumors have been sent up by Taiwan as trial balloons or as efforts to develop a Soviet card. Although cooperation between the Soviet Union and Taiwan is theoretically possible, nothing would galvanize Sino-U.S. resolve against Taiwan faster, nor destroy any credibility there was in Taiwan's anticommunist arguments, than for Taiwan to be seduced into a Soviet embrace. Taiwan's proclaimed raison d'etre would ring hollow if such a move were effected, even if done in the name of self-preservation. Indeed, given such circumstances, the P.R.C. has threatened a violent response, which would likely gain at least the tacit support of Japan, Korea, and possibly the United States, all of which would see a Soviet presence in Taiwan as a worst possible case. But, to repeat, given the present and projected orientations of the P.R.C. and Taiwan, the most likely scenario in the coming ten years will be one of slow evolution in their mutual relations, whatever the pressures and official rhetoric.

So long as a policy of one China retains general acceptance, support for Taiwan by sources external to China—political, military, or otherwise—will be condemned by Beijing as a violation of China's sovereignty. The P.R.C. will persist in its position that the United States agreed at the time of normalization that relations between the People's Republic of China and Taiwan were strictly an internal matter, intrusion into which violates sovereignty. Still, with time apparently on the P.R.C.'s side and unification with Taiwan a lower priority than modernization (although Taiwan could provide much-needed help in modernization), it is unlikely that the coming ten years will see any dramatic changes in the P.R.C.'s view regarding the political status of Taiwan or in Taiwan's view of the Chinese mainland. However, the official policy of the P.R.C. for expanded ties with Taiwan will seek to bring about peaceful unification by an increasingly complex tapestry of mutual relations, which could evolve to include burgeoning trade (initially by way of Hong Kong if necessary), exchange of mail, electronic communications (radio and television), family visits, and other forms of communication on the German model.

Although the interpersonal aspects of this exchange process will be emphasized, what will not follow the German model is the trend toward mutual recognition of separate governments and independent sovereignties. It is impossible to predict the outcome of the coming transition in power in Taiwan after Chiang Ching-kuo, already over 70 and suffering from diabetes, but it is no secret that the P.R.C. worries that he may be the last leader in Taiwan with sufficient stature and commitment to bring about peaceful unification in the near future.

Also difficult to predict is the eventual strength of the groups favoring Taiwan's independence. Much will depend on the finesse, sensitivity, and political acumen used by the Taiwan authorities in maintaining domestic political harmony in a period of rising political expectations. The uncertainty of Taiwan's strategic position and its dependence on external trade make room for sharp political disagreements as to its best course of action. Increasing numbers of outspoken dissidents in favor of an independent Taiwan and increasing numbers of native Taiwanese winning legislative seats in recent years mean that Taiwan's internal situation will be monitored carefully by all concerned. It is facile to suggest that changing percentages in the legislature of those born in and out of Taiwan ipso facto mean increasing or decreasing stability. However, what is clear is that domestic stability and confidence (or lack thereof) will be a primary factor in determining both Taiwan's role in Northeast Asia over the coming decade and whether it contributes to the conflict potential of the region.

As demonstrated by the difficulties the Reagan administration recently faced in deciding whether or not to sell advanced fighters to Taiwan, the uncertainty of the U.S. position toward Taiwan will be a factor of diplomatic instability over the coming decade in Northeast Asia. Present U.S. interests in Taiwan include (1) the strategic importance of Taiwan's geographic positioning and industrial infrastructure; (2) U.S. involvement with Taiwan's security, for reasons of historic commitment, ideological principle, and moral honor; (3) substantial economic investments. These are juxtaposed in an apparently irreconcilable manner against the U.S. desire to forge closer ties with the P.R.C.

At this time, it appears that the United States is letting the flow of events decide its position regarding Taiwan, since precedent and the principle of *opinio juris* in diplomacy and international law can lead to the crystallization of a position. For this reason, skillful propaganda on the part of the P.R.C. and the generation change over the coming ten years may contribute to a gradual shift until the U.S. attitude toward P.R.C.-Taiwan relations is not dissimilar to that of Europe. Whether this is in the U.S. interest will remain a policy decision of the first order. And the extent of U.S. willingness to defend (diplomatically or militarily) its interests in Taiwan will continue to be a determining if not decisive factor in relations among the three countries and, therefore, an important factor in the potential for conflict in Northeast Asia in the 1980s.

Japan

It is somewhat paradoxical that Japan, which is constitutionally permitted to maintain only the forces necessary for defense and which has limited its primary foreign-policy interests to the economic sphere, will play such an important role in the stability or instability of Northeast Asia, including the regional power equilibrium, in the coming decade. But Japan is at a cross-roads, and the events of the coming decade will determine her future direction. Domestically, four major trends could singly or in aggregate lead to significant shifts in Japanese perceptions and policy and possibly thereby to an increased potential for conflict (or to changing stabilities) in Northeast Asia in the 1980s.

First is the ongoing debate over what kinds of defense forces Japan should maintain. Under persistent U.S. pressure and despite intense domestic debate, the Suzuki cabinet approved a plan to increase the defense budget by 9.7 percent, bringing it to 0.91–0.93 percent of Japan's estimated gross national product (GNP), while holding budget increases in other areas to around 7.9 percent. Japanese sentiment covers a spectrum from the extreme nationalism associated with Tetsuya Kataoka, which calls for sweeping revision of the Japanese constitution and the acquisition of independent defense capacity—including nuclear capability, to the more moderate but no less insistent calls for a reexamination of U.S.-Japanese relations with an eye to placing them on a more equal footing.

It is too little realized in the West that the personality traits once symbolized by the chrysanthemum and the sword remain at odds within the Japanese psyche and character. One must take seriously the Japanese concern for their so-called nuclear allergy. It stems in part from the real Japanese concern that an emotional public demand for rearmament could potentially lead toward remilitarism of Japanese society in general. Once started, some Japanese warn, it might be difficult to stop such a process. There is also genuine uncertainty as to the consequences should Japan be pushed unwillingly to nuclear capability. The potential for rapid shift within the Japanese personality, and therefore within Japanese society as a whole, causes some to warn that nothing must be permitted that might undermine the present stringent civilian control over the military. The memory of the 1920s and 1930s remains.

A second and related trend is the generational shift now occurring in Japan. Those born in the generation that witnessed Japan's rise, its defeat, and its postwar reconstruction and reemergence are slowly being replaced by a generation somewhat skeptical of the West's values and orientation. Although the relative decline in Japan's birthrate in past years may increase the percentage of older citizens over the coming years (many of whom have supported more traditional Japanese values toward the military) the pendulum is also currently swinging toward a younger generation of Japanese leaders, who bring a different ethos to the positions of authority they will assume in greater proportions in the coming decade.

A third pressure within Japan comes from the Hokkaido fishermen, businessmen eager for trade and for Siberian resource development, and certain segments of the Japanese left who are prime targets for potential Soviet influence. Although the China market is Japan's first preference, a notable depression occurred among Japanese businessmen after the unpromising beginnings of various Sino-Japanese joint ventures, the most notable being the Baoshan steel mills. Couple a rising demand for new resource and trade markets close to home with a general economic slump or energy crunch, and the allure of a Siberian pipeline may become as appealing to the Japanese as the German one seems to be to the Europeans. Should the Soviet Union be able to put aside some of its arrogance and heavy-handedness in its negotiations with Japan, then special-interest pressures within Japan for a return to more omnidirectional diplomacy may well increase over the coming decade. Although such pressures would in no way constitute a frontal attack on the U.S.-Japanese security treaty, they could undermine the perception of common interests on which it rests.

A fourth potentially disrupting undercurrent that may surface in different ways over the coming few years is the Japanese concern that the United States does not treat Japan on an equal and balanced footing, despite the official rhetoric. Rooted in the Japanese sense of ethnic and cultural self-consciousness and thereby reflected in Japan's historical and psychological perceptions of international affairs, this concern for equality of relations results in a Japanese hypersensitivity to the perception of unfair or unequal treatment. This is especially true if some kind of racial discrimination is perceived to be the cause of the slight to Japan's dignity. Articles entitled "Dolphinisms—Ragtag Remnant of 'Imperial Isms' " and subtitled "Self-Righteous Westerns Should Analyze Own Violent History before Imposing Values," and letters to the editor in the Japanese press citing the clubbing to death of rabbits by U.S. farmers evidence the Japanese tendency to take even the concerns of conservationists very personally. In short, this emerging sense that Japan's economic strength and world position merit more equal treatment is merely one manifestation of a strong and possibly rising tide of Japanese neonationalism, which could well result in a fundamental reexamination of U.S.-Japanese political, diplomatic, commercial, and even security relations during the course of the 1980s.

The ongoing Japanese reconsideration of its relations with the United States suggests that disagreements over trade policy; intensified competition in, for example, the computer and electronics field where Japanese research and development is already being strategically invested with an eye to challenging the United States in the coming decades; backlash to U.S. pressure over defense spending; and failure of the China market might act as triggering mechanisms for a new and intense policy debate within Japan. Although it is unlikely that Japan would fall into the orbit of the Soviet Union (the intentions of which Japan views with deep-seated suspicion), it is possible that Japan may deliberately opt for a return to a more omnidirectional foreign policy and thereby increase its relations with the Soviets without totally renouncing existing ties with China or the United States.[14] At the same time, there is also the chance that rising neonationalism could cause Japan to loosen and to lessen its security dependence on the United States. Such a reorientation could lead in one of two major directions: either toward Japanese neutralism (perhaps on the European model, which Japan scrutinizes carefully) or to Japanese rearmament. Either case would necessitate a new East Asian power equilibrium.

The conventional wisdom is that the northern-territories issue more or less permanently divides the Soviet Union and Japan, for four reasons. First is the obvious strategic value of the islands to the Soviets, who have already invested heavily in military facilities and whose potential control of the sea-lanes in the area would be drastically compromised by a surrender of the islands and the resultant need to develop new bases much further north. Second is the Soviet perception that the unequal-treaties controversy is indivisible, that is, that concessions to one country might be demanded by all. In this view, what is at stake in the Soviet viewpoint is not the boundary delimitation of only the Kuriles but also of the Sino-Soviet frontier and possibly of the borders with Eastern European countries such as Poland, which too might demand revision of unequal treaties should a precedent be provided. Paralleling this is a third line of reasoning, the ideological argument that would make surrender of territory vociferously claimed as Soviet an unacceptable setback for the irrevocable progress of socialism, particularly in light of the Brezhnev doctrine. Fourth is the practical argument that the Soviets are too stubborn and proud to give the Japanese (a colored people after all) the satisfaction of claiming victory, no matter the size of the area.

However, the Soviets could gain great credence and bargaining position merely by floating the possibility of being willing to negotiate on the northern-territories issue. Some sources suggest that feelers in this area have already been extended. Although a negotiated settlement may not be found for the northern-territories issue, Soviet accommodation on other contentious issues, such as fishing rights, may earn them a certain amount of

Japanese goodwill. At a minimum, it will help to maintain the current Japanese perception that the chance of overt Soviet military attack is minimal.

It is in the perceived Soviet interest for Japan to remain demilitarized. Indeed, a Soviet best case calls for a neutralized Japan. This argues for Soviet efforts to downplay the military threat to Japan, to offer economic enticements of joint exploration and exploitation ventures in Siberia and in the Russia market, and thereby to wean Japan from dependence on the United States and China. Accordingly, the Soviets have tried to emphasize that the military buildup on the Sino-Soviet frontier is aimed at a single potential enemy—China. Japan is not to worry. Thus far there has been a tendency for Japanese elite sentiment to reflect a relatively limited concern with the Soviet threat to Japan, particularly as regards Soviet adventurism in the third world and the dangers to the flow of Middle East oil. It is simplistic to equate Japanese attitudes with those of an ostrich burying its head in the sand; at the same time, some analysts suggest that this Japanese emphasis on nonmilitary means for protecting Japan's national security derives from the psychological downplaying of the Soviet threat until it more or less coincides with the perceived levels of Japanese defense capability.

Whatever the case, it is almost certain that the debate about Japan's rearmament will remain extremely controversial throughout the 1980s. Advocates for the strengthening of Japan's military capabilities may well point to the declining protection offered by the U.S. nuclear umbrella in an age where the vulnerability of U.S. cities and military installations to Soviet attack is feared. Further, such critics of Japanese dependence on U.S. forces may argue that even a conventional attack against Japan would be difficult to repel, in part because a theater nuclear option would exist only against North Korea, and even there with severe restrictions. Indeed it is argued that the changes over time in U.S.-Japanese relations; the decline of U.S. military and economic strength and the rise of Japan's economic success; the systemic changes in the world economic situation from 1945; the U.S. encouragement for Japan to increase its independence; and the rising tide of Japanese neonationalism discussed earlier may all contribute to the distinct possibility that those who argue along Gaullist lines may well prevail. Their arguments are that the United States may lack either or both the will and capacity to honor its commitments and to defend Japan and that Japan's own historic role and position merit a greater independence of foreign policy and the concomitant prestige that would accrue therefrom.

If this occurs, it is likely that Japan would increase its capabilities incrementally, just as it is now accepting responsibility gradually for safeguarding the sea-lanes surrounding the Japanese home islands. The Japanese decision over whether to acquire nuclear capability would certainly engender intense domestic debate. Indeed, the destabilization of Japanese society likely to result from such an extended and emotional controversy may pose one of the greatest challenges to the peaceful status quo in Northeast Asia over the coming decade.

There is strong evidence that particularly the countries in Southeast Asia would view an emerging Japanese military presence with great concern. Nor has China forgotten the last war. Even in resource diplomacy Japanese aggressiveness continues to be resented, despite careful (and in some cases, successful) Japanese efforts to remake their image. The mere presence of increased Japanese armaments may not make their use more likely, but they would certainly increase tension in Northeast and Southeast Asia in the short term and possibly in the longer term if Soviet fears and ambitions were activated. If an increasing Japanese military capability comes to symbolize decreasing U.S. commitment or ability to honor its commitments in East Asia, then such would constitute a fundamental change and a fundamental cause for concern in the region in the 1980s.

Korea

It could well be that Korean domestic instabilities with the potential for leading to tension and perhaps to conflict (with or without Soviet adventurism) will be greatest in the 1980s. Should Kim Il-sung gradually lose control of his senses while retaining a modicum of political power, it is still possible that he may be tempted to attack the South in a preemptive now-or-never blitzkrieg. Support to this pessimistic view is given by the widely publicized report that the North Koreans were allegedly digging secret infiltration tunnels even while engaging in dialogue with the South in the early 1970s. Even if Kim Il-sung does not give the fateful marching orders, conflict could arise in his passing.

Stiff domestic opposition is expected as Kim Il-sung seeks to make his son Kim Chong-il his successor in an unprecedented effort to establish a hereditary succession in what some have called a "communist dynasty." It was only after the Sixth Party Congress of the Korean Workers Party (KWP) in October 1980 that a "subtle system of code words, slogans, and symbols were used to refer to Kim Chong-il and his achievements" and thereby to groom him as a likely successor to his father. The use of such terms as the "party center," "comrade leader," and "ray of guidance" made direct mention of young Kim unnecessary. Kim Chong-il has further been described not only as the "sun of the nation," but also as the "future sun of communism." Yet by referring to him in a manner befitting deity, his future role is made clear to all though without opening him to personal or political attack and without compromising Kim Il-sung's own political status or position.

Nevertheless, a downturn in the North Korean economy, stiff domestic opposition, or internal power struggles with the passing of Kim Il-song could easily create openings for Soviet influence. Particularly if the Taiwan situation takes on a sour note for the P.R.C., the Soviets may try to argue that North Korean ambitions—particularly those for unification—would be better served under Soviet direction and tutelage. In the event of intense domestic infighting, various groups may call on the Soviet Union for inspiration and support. Still, a shift toward the Soviet Union would require something of an adjustment, since North Korea has tended in some ways, excepting the years of China's Cultural Revolution, to lean more to Beijing than to Moscow.

The Koreas are generally pointed to as a sensitive area over which P.R.C. and U.S. policy sharply divide. According to this logic, Soviet-backed North Korean aggression against South Korea would present the P.R.C. the dilemma of abandoning its North Korean ally (either in actuality or de facto through neutrality) or of alienating the United States, which would presumably support South Korea. The possibility of driving a wedge between Beijing and Washington arguably increases the likelihood of Moscow's willingness to fish in troubled waters. Whether Moscow will be given such opportunities is another matter. Despite the P.R.C.'s success in influencing North Korea thus far, Foreign Minister Huang Hua has tried to maintain some room in which Beijing can maneuver by stating that the door to relations with South Korea is closed but not necessarily locked. If conflict over the Koreas does arise, the manner in which it begins will be of great importance. Clear-cut North Korean aggression could give China options this time around that it did not have when it was forced reluctantly to enter the last Korean war.

It is unlikely, however, that clear-cut North Korean aggression will occur. Guerrilla and commando operations, "spontaneous uprisings," and other forms of low-level and unconventional warfare behind South Korean lines not only will be more difficult to resist but could create panic and disruption, especially if combined with an element of surprise. Rather than giving South Korea and her allies and friends a chance to react solidly and unitedly against a flagrant attack perceived to threaten the security of all, it is more likely that any deliberate attack would attempt to keep South Korea off balance by opening with quickness on many fronts.

In the event of aggression against South Korea in whatever form, it is difficult to believe that the traditional aphorism that "Korea is the dagger aimed at Japan's heart" would not hold true. In the highly unlikely event that South Korea's overthrow occurred with sufficient alacrity almost so as to present a fait accompli, it is possible that Japan might adopt a nonprovocative posture and try to establish a working relationship with her new neighbor. More likely is the scenario that presents Japan using all available economic and diplomatic means (and in a last resort, limited military ones) to mobilize support for South Korea, whose defense Japan considers vital to her own.

There is also the possibility that conflict could be accidentally triggered, for example by North Korea shooting down a plane over international waters or, to take another example, by a South Korean plane mistakenly overflying sensitive areas. It is currently true that it would be in the interests of the major powers to contain the tension. The correlation of forces would need to change dramatically in the coming decade for the Soviet Union to risk outright military confrontation for a temporary or tactical advantage in Northeast Asia. But targets of opportunity to be had by other means will remain in order.

Should conflict arise in Korea, refugee problems could heighten tension, whatever its cause; any sizeable exodus of Korean boat people could bring strong international pressure on Japan, which, if previous reactions are any guide, would equally strongly resist such pressures. Japan might feel that its sensitivities to the problems that could arise from adding a potentially disruptive minority to an otherwise basically homogenous population were not properly understood. Further, the Korean population within Japan could also be expected to be violently divided in their loyalties north and south. What might happen, in that case, would depend on how the Japanese authorities handled the situation.

Soviet Union

Something must be said of Soviet intentions and capabilities in assessing the potential for conflict in Northeast Asia. It is generally recognized that strategic, territorial, and historical interests make the Soviet Union an Asian power as well as a European one. Indeed, at least from the times of Sergei Witte, whose efforts led to an increased focus on Asia in the nineteenth century, there has been something of a pendulum effect in the Soviet Union's turning between east and west. These shifts parallel in a rough way the swings in U.S. interest between Europe and East Asia. However, a fundamental difference is that the Soviet Union's interests from Europe to East Asia are little affected by questions of isolationism and over-commitment; for Moscow, it is more an issue of where, not whether or not, to focus its attention and commitment.

It is plausibly argued that "the Soviet leadership sees the strategic centre of gravity moving slowly but inexorably in the direction of East Asia, the source of a potentially critical challenge to Soviet power and prestige."[18] The natural and human resources of the area and the strategic and economic importance of sea-lanes and communication lines make any potential inroads into the region extremely valuable. The dynamism current in the area will almost magnetically pull additional wealth, influence, and power to the East Asian region, and the Soviet Union will seek to fortify its position there. The anecdote is told that the Soviet people could bear the loss of Minsk or Smolensk (cities once lost to invading German armies) "but the loss of Vladivostok—never."[19] Be that as it may, Soviet interests and opportunities in the 1980s will depend in large measure on how the power equilibrium in Northeast Asia develops.

China is generally perceived as the Soviet Union's primary long-term enemy.[20] For this reason, the primary thrust of Soviet policy in East Asia over the coming decade will be the encirclement and neutralization of China. Even those who recognize that China is not currently a military threat still suffer from what is described as a "visceral fear of the Chinese arising from deep racial, ethnic, ideological and historical animosities."[21] These deep-seated fears are manifest in various ways, in everything from popular Soviet literature to the nickel peep shows depicting the perils of the yellow hordes.

The coming ten years will do little to dissipate this near-paranoia. From the Soviet point of view, little could be worse than continued indirect Western help in China's modernization and direct aid in armament (even the offers of which have caused great distress in the Kremlin), if such military efforts are directed specifically at the Soviet motherland. Soviet technological superiority can do little to ease the psychological dimensions of Soviet frustration at having apparently limited means to curb the growth (and menace) of Chinese power. If Moscow solves its problems in Poland and Afghanistan in the coming years, the Soviet Union may well turn greater attention eastward. The continued presence of troops in Afghanistan (ostensibly to inhibit counterrevolutionaries) could be used as much to pressure China's traditional ally, Pakistan, and India, as China itself.[22] Further links will also likely develop between the perceived necessity to contain China and the possibility of furthering Soviet ambitions related to military or political domination of the Persian Gulf States.[23] Vietnam offers a useful point from which to project Soviet power in both the Pacific and Indian oceans and potentially from which to interdict the sea-lanes in those areas. The Soviet merchant marine may also play a role in increasing Soviet presence and capabilities.

The body of literature that discusses internal or systemic weaknesses in the Soviet system rightly emphasizes that the next generation of Soviet leaders will face difficult choices. The probable Soviet responses to these policy dilemmas are as uncertain as who will succeed Leonid Brezhnev.[24] Just how wide the West's window of vulnerability is perceived to be and how the Soviets choose to assess their opportunities will contribute greatly to whether Soviet adventurism is likely to occur before possible targets of opportunity fade and the pull of domestic concerns turns Moscow's attention inward again. Internal developments within the Soviet bureaucracy and in Soviet politicomilitary relations could also influence Soviet Asian policy over the coming ten years. One trend suggests an increased role for foreign policymakers in the overall decision-making process: the need for their input on the technical or military aspects of foreign policy may make them indispensable.

The claim to 13–15 percent of the Soviet GNP is another element of bureaucratic influence now enjoyed by the military. Military membership on senior commissions and key Party organizations through the minister and the Ministry of Defense also offer opportunity to influence policy. Further, influence also accrues to the military because of the direction the military gives, directly and indirectly, to other bureaucratic and scientific mechanisms and to the industrial and agricultural sectors, where expert talent and spin-off developments are largely beholden to military-related budgets.[25]

Whether these trends will influence overall Soviet foreign-policy objectives remains to be seen. That they will influence Soviet military doctrine and—on the more operational level—Soviet strategy and tactics, is clear. Soviet efforts to establish coordinated deployment of forces through joint and integrated command-and-control systems now focus on predetermined theaters of potential combat. This is in marked contrast to Western strategies that suggest bringing forces from Asia in the event of a Soviet-U.S. confrontation in Europe or to the use of rapid-deployment forces (RDF) designed for wide-ranging missions. The extent to which the logistic snarls inherent in the Soviet theater commands can be overcome bears careful watching over the 1980s. China will be watching carefully as always and will perhaps feel somewhat vulnerable in Sinkiang and Manchuria.

Conclusions

The primary U.S. interest in Northeast Asia will be to help guarantee the continued maintenance of the power equilibrium and of open and equal access to free trade. This task will be made difficult by the shifts inherent in the gradual emergence of a modernizing China, the vulnerability of an uncertain Japan, the likely succession and related transition in North Korea, and the probable assertiveness of a cautious but confident Soviet Union. Further, other systemic challenges will also require the United States to help make adjustments in the political, military, and economic orders in East Asia. The leading role traditionally played by the United States in the region may well change over the coming decade.

The most likely causes of instability, tension, or perhaps conflict are those arising from potential domestic changes. A sudden or dramatic shift, whether a severe economic slump, a rough leadership transition, a rapidly changing public sentiment, or even internal political-military rivalries could presage the reorientation of a country's direction and policy in a region where the equilibrium is already precariously balanced. Hence, triggering mechanisms such as remilitarism or neutralism in Japan; Soviet meddling in North Korean domestic politics; insurgencies within Thailand; conflicts along the Sino-Vietnamese border; tensions in the strategic region of the Pamirs in the aftermath of Afghanistan; or severe refugee problems—singly or in an interacting manner—could precipitate shifts affecting the stability and thereby the potential for conflict in Northeast Asia.

It is assumed that South Korea, Japan, and Taiwan could acquire nuclear capability in a short time, should they so choose. Geographical proximity to potential enemies reduces the problem of developing effective delivery systems. And, indeed, rumors suggest that Taiwan has already developed surface-to-surface (presumably nuclear-capable) missiles with sufficient range and accuracy to strike cities within the P.R.C. However, geographical proximity and size (or lack thereof) also work to make South Korea, Japan, and Taiwan vulnerable in the event of a showdown with their larger neighbors. Should confrontation occur, their larger neighbors could call on decisively larger conventional forces, thereby keeping the conflict far below the nuclear threshold while severely circumscribing the utility of even theater nuclear deterrents. The use of unconventional methods of warfare would also place the smaller countries in Northeast Asia at a distinct disadvantage. Particularly in the case of Taiwan, any tendencies toward a Masada complex will be carefully assuaged by seeking political solutions to political problems.

Still, concern for stability will leave some utility in threats or limited demonstrations of military force, if the aims they purport to advance are perceived not to merit the risk of upsetting the general power equilibrium. Limited engagements could occur along the Korean demilitarized zone, the Sino-Soviet or Sino-Vietnamese frontiers, or in Southwest Asia. China might choose to teach another lesson to Vietnam either directly or against Vietnamese-held offshore islands. Similarly, the offshore islands in the Taiwan Straits could come under bombardment.

The general state of the world economy will play an important role in the stability or instability of Northeast Asia in the coming decade. Some rough spots are anticipated and will be weathered, not necessarily without substantial difficulty. However, stringent protectionism in Western Europe or the United States, severe energy crises, or sudden and stubborn economic slumps could destabilize the domestic polities of certain countries in Northeast Asia, not unlike the way the Great Depression did in the 1930s.

In terms of specific countries, China's primary objective is to build the internal infrastructure necessary to make it powerful and modern without compromising its socialist, democratic, or cultural ideals. The debate over specific priorities and implementation policies will continue. Some twists and turns are likely in the years ahead, although these will presumably be moderated by the declining effect of individual personalities. Should economic take-off fail or radical trends reemerge, China could withdraw into a period of isolationism and defiant self-reliance.

The long-term trend will be for China to increase in independence as its relative power and prestige grow and as it assumes a place as a regional great power. In the coming decade this suggests P.R.C. efforts at good relations with its neighbors, particularly with the association of Southeast Asian nations (ASEAN) countries (where official government-to-government relations may contribute to the downplaying of the potentially explosive issue of Chinese ethnic minorities). The P.R.C. will continue its efforts to break the Soviet encirclement by mending fences with India. In Northeast Asia, including Taiwan, China will remain persistent but will be likely to continue to place a premium on stability.

Japan is at a crossroads and faces difficult decisions ahead as to its place in the global and regional economic and political order. Internal psychological perceptions and trends may increase the debate within Japan over how to resolve the issues of defense expenditures, of developing a more equal relation with the United States, and of maintaining her security in light of shifting power balances in Northeast Asia. Japan will continue to tread softly in Southeast Asia; the coming ten years will do little to dim fears there of a remilitarized Japan. The Chinese and Russia-Siberia markets will continue to beckon, although the latter will remain circumscribed so long as the antihegemony clause of the Sino-Japanese treaty is taken seriously.

The Koreas will remain a sensitive area. The propaganda war and the clandestine efforts at mutual subversion will continue. Unconventional or guerrilla operations may occur. North Korean belligerence could lead directly to tension if, for example, the United States decided to take its Libyan air-attack experience as a precedent in case of North Korean attack on a U.S. plane (as has occurred). Beijing and Moscow will continue to compete for North Korean favor through arms supplies and political support. A potential trouble area not generally mentioned is that of Korean minorities in Japan—trouble because of the unknowns of their presumably divided loyalties (to Seoul and Pyongyang) and because an exodus of Korean boat people could raise the question of refugee policy and bring international pressure to bear on Japan on what is a sensitive and emotional issue.

Notes

1. A. Doak Barnett, *China and the Major Powers in East Asia* (Washington, D.C.: Brookings Institution, 1977) remains one of the more interesting and helpful discussions of this region.

2. This theme is analyzed in Richard H. Solomon, ed., *Asian Security in the 1980s* (Cambridge, Mass.: Oelgeschlagger, Gunn, & Hain, Publishers, Inc.,: Rand Corporation, 1980).

3. The historical background for such perceptions is discussed in Christopher Thorne, *Allies of a Kind* (New York: Oxford University Press, 1978).

4. Hu Yaobang, speech celebrating the 60th Anniversary of the founding of the Communist Party of China, 1 July 1981, text in *Beijing Review*, 13 July 1981, p. 24.

5. See "On Questions of Party History," adopted by the 6th Plenum of the 11th Central Committee of the CCP on 27 June 1981, text in *Beijing Review*, 6 July 1981, pp. 29–35.

6. Leo Yueh-Yun Liu "The Modernization of the Chinese Military," *Current History* 79 (September 1980): 40 lists the first three of these factors. The author adds the last.

7. Paul Dibb, "China's Strategic Situation and Defence Priorities in the 1980s," *Australian Journal of Chinese Affairs*, 5 (1981): 99.

8. These kinds of interchange were discussed in Point Two in Beijing's unification plan as enunicated by Marshal Ye Jian-ying. Press Release, Embassy of the People's Republic of China, Washington, D.C., 30 September 1981.

9. See, for example, U.S. International Communication Agency, Office of Research, "Japanese Perceptions of Defense Issues," prepared by Dr. Young C. Kim (Washington, D.C., 30 January 1981).

10. Ruth Benedict, *The Chrysanthemum and the Sword* (Boston: Houghton Mifflin, 1946).

11. U.S. International Communication Agency, Office of Research, "Current Japan-Soviet Relations and Soviet Channels of Influence in Japan: A Background Analysis," research memorandum International Communications Agency (Washington, D.C., 1 December 1981).

12. Isaac Shapiro, "The Risen Sun: Japanese Gaullism?" *Foreign Policy* 41(Winter 1980–1981): 63.

13. Ibid., p. 64.

14. This will remain difficult to accomplish so long as the antihegemony clause of the Sino-Japanese Peace and Friendship Treaty is taken seriously.

15. Shapiro, "Risen Sun," pp. 65–69.

16. Tong Whan Park, "The Korean Arms Race: Implications in the International Politics of Northeast Asia," *Asian Survey* 20 (June 1980): 649.

17. Morgan E. Clippinger, "Kim Chong-Il in the North Korean Mass Media: A Study of Semi-Esoteric Communication," *Asian Survey* 21 (March 1981): 289.

18. John Erickson, "The Soviet Strategic Emplacement in Asia," *Asian Affairs* 12 (February 1981): 9.

19. Ibid., p. 16.

20. U.S. International Communication Agency, Office of Research, "Soviet Elites: World View and Perceptions of the U.S.," prepared by Gregory Guroff and Steven Grant (Washington, D.C., 29 September 1981), pp. 32–33.

21. Ibid., p. ii.

22. Gerald Segal, "China and Afghanistan," *Asian Survey* 21 (November 1981): 1158–1173; also John W. Garver, "The Sino-Soviet Territorial Dispute in the Pamir Mountain Region," *China Quarterly* 85 (March 1981): 107–118.

23. Paul H. Nitze, "Strategy in the Decade of the 1980s," *Foreign Affairs* 59 (Fall 1980): 89.

24. Jane P. Shapiro, "The Soviet Leadership Enters the 1980's," *Current History* 79 (October 1980): 92–106.

25. Dr. Coit Blacker of the Center for Strategic and International Studies Soviet Project makes this point.

Scenario: Soviet Fishing in Waters Troubled by Systemic Tensions

In these kinds of futuristic scenarios, the caveats must be underscored even more vociferously than in a normal work. I begin with two.

First, what follows represents only an imaginative attempt to look through the kaleidoscope of future possibility. It is not necessarily what I think will happen, even less what I would want to happen. Nor is this a worst-case scenario. Rather, based on the rationale that the potentially most dangerous conflicts are those that have not been conceptualized, let alone anticipated, this scenario attempts to sketch the interactions of as many key variables—past, present, and future—in as many combinations as possible. The purpose is to pinpoint some of the pieces in the kaleidoscope rather than to detail the myriad of changing patterns into which they could evolve.

The second caveat is that what becomes true in actual fact will often be stranger than that which can be imagined. Regardless of our best efforts, we must be prepared to be surprised in the end. Who would have predicted Deng Xiaoping touring the United States wearing a ten-gallon hat and carrying a U.S. flag under his arm? This is a second reason, then, that the scenario spins some unlikely or preposterous future scenes from the present situation as well as from the situation as it may exist in the later 1980s.

It was a complex concatenation of events that led to crisis in East Asia, especially in China, in the summer and autumn of 1987. The immediate crisis was precipitated by the shooting, apparently accidental but possibly not, of a senior Chinese negotiator during a session of the Sino-Soviet border talks, which had dragged—on again, off again—through the early part of the 1980s. The story circulated that the Soviets had attempted to intimidate the Chinese plenipotentiaries in a kind of reverse Nerchinsk negotiation. Things had taken an unexpected turn when an unidentified person, apparently not in control of his senses, had begun shouting and brandishing what looked to be a gun. In the ensuing fracas someone had opened fire, although who he was and why he did it was wildly debated. Some blamed forces afraid of China of trying to disrupt the talks, others a single insane individual. Regardless, despite Soviet apologies and the sentencing of an obviously demented man claiming to have avenged the death of a relative who had died a Russian martyr while stemming the yellow tide, tension had mounted on both sides of the Sino-Soviet border.

To be sure, China's international situation had been difficult before the crisis. Although China had escaped much of the reverberation of the oil crunch—indeed, even the Daching oil fields threatened to show a profit that year—there had also been a major policy crisis when the United States, in the last years of the Reagan administration, had decided to sell advanced jet fighters to Taiwan. The political symbolism of the decision proved more significant than the fact that production rights to the all-weather F-5G were granted, not to sales of the F-16 as some had speculated. Washington's decision apparently undermined the assumption that it could always be cajoled into supporting a pro-Beijing policy and placed in jeopardy the orientation of the four modernizations, which had put industry, agriculture, and science and technology ahead of military in the blueprint for China's long-term growth.

Even more importantly, the strategic decision was made by the Second (Enlarged) Plenum of the Central Committee—apparently over the vigorous opposition of Deng and to the surprise of many—that the United States was more significantly a declining power and the Soviet Union more significantly an ascendent power than previously conjectured. Evidently U.S. military buildup in the early 1980s had proved disappointingly low when a basic continuity in real expenditures was discerned and the maximum of 6–8 percent of GNP spent on defense seemed to be an actual peacetime ceiling. The forecast that the United States would be unable to reverse the long-term trend was evidently the most salient point in the Chinese projection of the following twenty years.

After the U.S. decision to sell the advanced fighters to Taiwan, the Soviet Union had taken the diplomatic offensive—adopting a soft line on Japan and the surprising step of a toughened line against the P.R.C. Whereas many had expected an attempt by Moscow to woo the Chinese away from Washington, the Soviets had deliberately increased their pressure on the Sino-Soviet border. That had been the straw to break the back of the perception that the Soviet Union would threaten but essentially accept the status quo at least so far as the boundaries and territorial integrity of China were concerned.

Of course, the unsettled border dispute was only symptomatic of a more fundamental motivation for increased Soviet aggressiveness. The increasing accuracy of China's MIRVed CSS-X-5 missiles had taken many by surprise. Test flights of submarine launched intermediate range missiles in October 1982 argued that China was developing at least a rudimentary sea-land air strategic triad of its own. Indeed, the CIA's top-secret report had indicated that there was some truth to the Soviet perception that their window of vulnerability would widen somewhat in the period 1989–1991 as China deployed a road-mobile missile-launching system and hardened the silos around other of their ICBMs. The extent of China's second-strike capability was hotly debated in Moscow, Washington, and Beijing. Those who had maintained that China possessed at least "bee sting" second-strike capability during the previous decade found themselves at least partially vindicated.

So, sensing the potential for China's shift away from the United States and prone to a heavy-handed approach, the Soviet Union again floated—as always with deadly seriousness—the threat of surgical strikes against key Chinese nuclear and missile installations. Unable to use the U.S. nuclear umbrella as they had from 1964–1984, the P.R.C. was particularly sobered by the precedents of the successful Israeli attacks on nuclear installations in Iraq and Jordan and the mysterious destruction of the Brazilian nuclear-research facilities by an unknown group. The Soviets seemed ready to rationalize that world sentiment favored forcible self-preservation to escalating proliferation.

What made the Soviet threats more ominous were the unexpected Soviet successes on the diplomatic and military organizational fronts. Diplomatically, the Soviets had made gradual progress in their containment of China. Ties with India remained reasonable—at least the Sino-Indian attempts at reconciliation had proved abortive, despite the official fanfare. The issue of Sino-Indian borders remained highly controversial despite the efforts of both sides to develop other points of common interest. Soviet diplomats in India congratulated themselves on keeping the Chinese threat sufficiently real and the promise of Soviet assistance sufficiently sweet that, as one cable to Moscow read, "India was not fooled by China's lies."

The fact that Afghanistan remained an almost intractable problem had an unexpected boomerang effect on Sino-Soviet relations. In the early 1980s some Western analysts were arguing that the Soviet Union had decided to undertake what they knew would be a long-term engagement in Afghanistan, not so much out of a position of strength as out of a sense of vulnerability. According to such logic, the Soviets were afraid that, should they lose their protectorate in Afghanistan, the ring of encirclement running from Japan to Norway would snap shut.

By the mid-1980s, things were somewhat different. The partial containment of difficulties in Afghanistan meant that the Soviet force buildup along the Sino-Afghanistan border permitted the exertion of pressure not only on China but also on Pakistan. It was not specified which counter-revolutionaries the Soviet troops in the area were supposed to deter. China's concern over the situation in Afghanistan was best evidenced by the P.R.C.'s silence on the specific aspects of the subject from the time of the initial Soviet invasion. The possible opening of a major hostile front posed a seemingly insolvable problem for China's military strategists. In Pakistan the Soviets let it be known that the movement of over a million and a quarter Afghan refugees into Pakistan need not necessarily lead to the "spontaneous" provocations or to the exploitation of tribal differences. Pakistan got the message.

338   The Future of Conflict in the 1980s

Although tension on the Sino-Vietnamese border became an accepted political fact of life after the 1979 Sino-Vietnamese war, both countries were subsequently preoccupied with domestic construction. This did not prevent Vietnam from attempting to make inroads with the ASEAN countries, with hostilities in Kampuchea providing a barometer of tensions in the area. Still, Vietnam showed an expected wariness of Moscow and sought to balance its dependence on the Soviet Union with only partially successful efforts to integrate with the world community at large. For example, commentators in the United States criticized Hanoi's attempts to appeal directly to what the Vietnamese press called the "good will of the American people" as "anachronistic and cynical." Increasingly sensitive to the label of the "Cubans of the East," the Vietnamese had remained determined not to fall totally into Moscow's sphere, economically (which they eventually managed, partially through French assistance), politically (where they were less successful), or militarily (where the debate was not over guns or butter but over Soviet guns or domestically produced guns and self-reliance). At the same time, whenever Vietnam and/or the Soviet Union wanted to pressure the P.R.C., they revived the possibility of joint-staff talks with the thinly veiled threat of posing China with at least a two-front confrontation.

What gave the Soviet diplomatic successes teeth was the successful deployment of Soviet military forces for coordinated combat in specific theaters. Under the inspiration of Marshal Sokolov (who acted as the Commander/East) and Army General Petrov (an East Asian specialist), the Far Eastern TVD was surprisingly skillful in convincing skeptics both inside and outside the Soviet Union that the logistics of joint-command coordination were not insurmountable. Further, the increasing complexities of military operations meant that military professionals were gradually brought into Politburo-level decision making because of the need for their technical expertise. In Soviet East Asian operations this was especially the case. Senior military officials were persuasive in their claim to dual expertise in both East Asian politics and Soviet military doctrines.

Whatever its causes, the oil crunch—because it had come so unexpectedly—had paralyzed South Korea, Japan, and Singapore. The general tide of protectionism, which was sweeping the United States into a new kind of isolationism, and the lure of joint oil and trade ventures with the Soviet Union had increased the domestic pressure in Japan for a return to omnidirectional diplomacy. Playing on the Japanese frustration over the *Amai* relationship many supposed to exist with the United States, propagandists had skillfully whispered the refrain of long-term mutual misunderstanding by Asian and Western countries as a revival of culturalism swept around the Pacific rim. These forces were counterbalanced by the long-term relationship between Japan and the United States, which from the mid-1980s had been increasingly complemented by the dependence of the United States on the Japanese electronics industry for key aspects of its defense capability, particularly the complex software needed to monitor the trajectories of incoming ICBMs and the locations of on-station submarines.

Nevertheless, particularly in Japan, this undercurrent neonationalism polarized both public and elite opinion, and the moderate intermediate positions lost ground as the controversy became more heated. Led by a wing of the Liberal Democratic Party (LDP), one faction called for greater Japanese independence through incremental increases in defense spending. Even strict constructionists of the Japanese constitution increasingly agreed that Japan could legally assume the heavier defense responsibilties the United States had been urging for years. Where the strict constructionists differed with the emerging rich-country, strong-army (*fukoku kyohei*) group was on the speed and ultimate extent of rearmament.

Not unexpectedly, the latter group was adamant that Japan acquire nuclear weapons and the delivery system requisite for independent nuclear deterrence. The government's white paper on Japan's vulnerability to nuclear attack had increased the public outcry for accelerated construction of civil-defense networks and shelters. At the same time, opinion polls in the *Ashai Shimbun* also pointed to an increasing sense that any sacrifice would be endured.

Both the Chinese and Soviet press (the latter more stridently than the former) criticized the return of a "kamikaze great power jingoism." Senior officials from both the Chinese and Soviet foreign ministries privately explained that their primary fear for the stability of Northeast Asia lay in the destabilization of Japan's domestic polity. The uncertainty of Japan's direction was more worrisome than Japan's rearmament in itself.

Opposed to Japan's rearmament were those who wished to take a more neutral stand. Paralleling in some ways the underlying sentiments of European neutralism, Japan's emphasis on distancing itself from what was percieved as over-dependence on the United States took on a particularly Japanese flavor. It was unclear whether the carrot of promised joint Siberian exploration and exploitation or the stick of perceived Soviet military threat was ultimately more persuasive. Regardless, thousands joined in "peace demonstrations," while new adherents swelled the ranks of the leading pacifist Buddhist organizations.

Earlier in the decade, the names *Baoshan* and *Bohai* became synonymous with Sino-Japanese joint ventures that promised more than they delivered. Conflicts on the delimitation of the continental shelf and disputes over mineral and oil rights further depressed the initial Japanese ebullience over the possibilities of the China market. Although the dream of the China market lingered, the realists who demanded that Japan take a more even-handed approach became increasingly persuasive.

The Soviet Union made every effort to be accommodating. Placing high priority on the wooing of Japan, Moscow poured new money into the friendship and culture halls aimed at Hokkaido's fishermen, along with promises of more liberal fishing privileges; made greater efforts to develop contracts with binding clauses of agreement (to counter the common Japanese business complaint that terms were set only to be changed later); and with renewed determination continued to appeal to Japan's left, particularly the radical left-wing of the Japan Socialist Party (with whom Moscow had enjoyed better relations than the Japanese communists for years).

The situation in Korea had become increasingly unstable with the declining health of Kim Il-sung. Little was known about his son, Kim Chong-il, except that there was intense domestic competition for his father's position. The situation on the Korean peninsula remained an area where P.R.C. and U.S. interests diverged sharply, and the military faction in Beijing was reported to be vying with the Soviets in their efforts to support Kim Il-sung's avowed intentions to liberate South Korea within his lifetime. While Kim-Il-sung was in control of his senses, such talk was seen as primarily rhetoric, but as he gradually lost control of his senses, many feared that the fateful order might come. The discovery of two or more tunnels in the demilitarized zone prompted a full South Korean alert. It remained a mystery how they could have been dug, and high-level infiltration in the South Korean army remained an uncomfortable answer to a stubborn question.

Thus, with the Soviet Union threatening to play the so-called Japanese card by taking a soft approach—in contrast to the one they took toward China, including an offer to reopen talks with the tantalizing possibility of negotiations on the Kuriles and with China threatening to match any threats by Moscow to destabilize the Korean peninsula by keeping all possibilities open—including some kind of rapprochement with Seoul, the diplomatic situation involving the Soviet Union, the P.R.C. and Taiwan, the United States, Japan, North and South Korea, and other parts of East and Southeast Asia became increasingly fluid.

It was at this point that the fateful Sino-Soviet border talks had led to the shooting, the early attempts to localize the damage, the headlines blaring of "A Soviet Sarajevo," and finally the reports that Soviet armor and tactical air-support units, whether out of desperation or opportunism, were rolling to answer the call of Uighur and Kazakh national self-determination in Sinkiang.

17 Potential Conflict in Central America

Robert S. Leiken

Until recently, the tide of Central American affairs ebbed and flowed in obscurity. The Nicaraguan revolution, like lightning over a darkened sea, disclosed unsuspected turbulence in surrounding waters. In that previous darkness Central American society had undergone a "sea change" whose effect will be felt through and beyond the 1980s.

Conflict in Central America is hardly new, but the attention focused on the region and its attraction to extrahemispheric forces are. Central America is the newest zone of the third world to be converted into an arena of international conflict. This change in status largely derives from the Soviet global political and military offensive, which became the pivot of shifting world politics in the mid-1970s and which now has reached the Western Hemisphere. There the Soviets seek to exploit a crisis not of their making to advance their global and regional objectives in what they refer to as the U.S. "strategic rear."[1] Not unexpectedly, the Reagan administration has reacted sharply to the threat in the region, but to some extent this reaction has compounded rather than solved the problem. Focusing on a single aspect of the conflict, the East-West dimension, U.S. policy has depreciated its local causes and the regional instruments for its solution, fanning fears of unilateral U.S. intervention.

The factors contributing to the conflict atmosphere are multiple and complex. They include the world economic crisis, the regional economic crisis, the crisis in local political and ideological structures (the state, the military, the church), rising Central American nationalism, the entrance of new international actors to the region, the decline of U.S. hegemony and last, but hardly least, the hegemonic ambitions of the Soviet Union and its Cuban client. This chapter will analyze these factors in an effort to project their effects further into the decade of the 1980s. The very multiplicity of these factors makes a straight-line projection of tendencies hazardous, but one thing is clear: the status quo in Central America is gone forever.

The End of the Central American Status Quo

Struggles among tribes and tribal empires, political groupings, and economic factions, between peasants and landlords, and between military regimes and insurgents have been a constant feature of Central American society. Nonetheless, despite its rich history of conflict, until now the region has been geopolitically stable. No regime hostile to the United States or tied to a foreign power has been able to establish itself (forgetting the limited British presence in Belize and Bluefields) since independence from Spain and the Monroe Doctrine were mutually proclaimed in the third decade of the nineteenth century.

This status quo came to rest on the following pillars: a relatively immobile socioeconomic structure, authoritarian military governments monopolizing armed power, the allegiance of the Church, export dependency on the United States, and, in the last instance, recourse to U.S. power.

All these pillars have cracked in the last several years; some of them are crumbling. The sustained export-led economic growth and modernization has altered the social structure of large parts of Central America. The peasantry has reached an advanced state of decomposition, leaving in its wake landless laborers, an urban working class, a hypertrophic poor, and widespread internal migration.

Over the past twenty-five years the modernization of the export sector, the experiment in "import-substitution industrialization and the operation of the Central American Common Market brought a quickening of economic activity to the area." Over the last three decades the annual GNP grew at over 5 percent, the labor market expanded steadily, per capita income doubled, and exports increased sixteen fold.[2] Both the internal and external market widened, a manufacturing sector developed, and productivity and output grew steadily.[3] The index of urbanization increased from 16 percent in 1950 to 43 percent in 1980.[4]

Under Central American conditions economic growth has been a force not for stability but for its opposite. As the export sector modernized in response to rising prices for sugar, coffee, bananas, and so on, roads, electricity, and telephone lines were extended to previously isolated areas.[5] Irrigation made its appearance along with pesticides, improved seeds, fertilizers, and other new techniques.[6] But, although the medieval landscape of Central America acquired some of the appurtenances of the twentieth century and the old landlords and a small new rural bourgeoisie prospered, the direct producers suffered a dramatic deterioration in their living standards. The very success and expansion of the export sector created considerable pressure on generally scarce available land. Rents charged to peasants tripled or quadrupled during the 1960s.[7] According to the Secretariat for Central American Economic Integration, by the early 1970s about 70 percent of the region's rural holdings were minifundia of less than 10 acres. At the same time 6 percent of rural holdings comprised more than 70 percent of the total arable land.[8] Of the rural population of Central America, approximately one-half lives in minifundia. Rising rents withdrew the traditional option of the seasonal workers on the large export estates to rent land to subsist during their off-season. As productivity rose in the export sector, larger numbers of workers were forced to join the growing class of landless laborers. Currently less than one-half of the Central American rural population lives on minifundia, and more than a third are landless. Since the shrinking minifundia is unable to absorb even the natural growth of the population it supports, younger sons and daughters are constantly joining this new rural proletariat.

These workers migrate to rural towns and cities in search of work in the secondary and tertiary sectors. These sectors were able to absorb a portion of these workers (especially during the 1960s when economies were expanding rapidly), but this recourse was limited by the relatively capital-intensive technology employed in the process of import-substitution industrialization and by the restricted size of Central American markets.[9] This contradiction was sharpened by the effect of worldwide inflation. Real wages in Guatemala, for example, decreased by an estimated 25 percent between 1972 and 1977. Natural disasters like the earthquakes in Nicaragua and Guatemala and hurricane "Fifi" in Honduras took a toll paid mainly by the poor.[10] The latter occupy a disproportionate position in these economies, which are now to be counted among the most inequitable in Latin America.[11] In Guatemala, El Salvador, Nicaragua, and Honduras the poorest 20 percent of the population receive only between 3 and 4 percent of the national income, the poorest 30 percent between 16 and 18 percent. Correspondingly, the top 20 percent of the population receives about 60 percent of the national income, the richest 5 percent about 30 percent.[12] With the paralysis of the Central American Common Market in the mid-1970s, the pressures generated by this situation became intolerable.

In the late 1970s regional economic growth slowed to a standstill.[13] Inflation, which increased at an annual average of about 2 percent between 1961 and 1971, is now averaging over 10 times that figure.[14] The bulk of the Central American population lacks doctors (averaging one to more than 2,000 people), hospital beds, and clinics while chronically suffering from eye diseases, malnutrition, and epidemics of malaria, dengue, hepatitis, and typhoid fever. Its life expectancy is about 55 years,[15] one of ten children die as infants,[16] and only half of the survivors ever learn to read.[17] In Honduras only 46 percent of the population has access to safe drinking water; in El Salvador the portion rises to 53 percent.[18] Malnutrition is epidemic in the Central American countryside.[19] According to the United Nations, 96.6 percent of the rural homes in Honduras are without water; 89.4 percent have no toilet; 94.5 percent have no electricity. And all these conditions are getting worse.[20]

This panorama will almost certainly grow bleaker in the coming years. Central America is caught in the now typical price scissors of the non-petroleum underdeveloped. Prices for their exports have fallen while those of oil and manufacturing imports have skyrocketed. Monetary reserves are falling, and external debt is rising rapidly.[21] Thus even the present minimal medical, sanitary, and educational services will be cut back. This will thrive in a region whose population is increasing at an annual rate close to 3 percent. The Central American countryside, which several years ago the United Nations compared with the "poorest of the poor"—countries like Somalia, Bangladesh, and Haiti—is surrounding with its shantytowns of landless migrants, perilous cities where the wealthy seek sanctuary in armoured cars behind guarded, electrified walls.

The dependent nature of Central American economies make them highly subject to the influence of a stagnating world economy. As the latter lost impetus in the mid-1970s, the consequences for Central America were expressed in the economic decline we have been describing. Current assessment of the world economic future in the 1980s suggests that this loss of internal dynamics will be compounded by global factors. Two specific recent trends will have grave repercussions. High interest rates in the central economies will further shrink already scanty sources of capital. Combined with the tendency toward protectionism in the advanced countries, a tendency that will restrict the market for Central American products, we can expect plant closings, layoffs, and bankruptcies. This economic tendency will be accentuated by increasing risks resulting from the growing political instability of the region. Economic constriction and political radicalization will form a devastating spiral in the coming years.

With the partial exception of Costa Rica, whose singularity grows evermore precarious, the economic conditions of the countries of Central America are as proximate as their location. This is also true of their political history. Pressure for agrarian reform began to build throughout Nicaragua, Guatemala, El Salvador, and Honduras during the late 1960s and early 1970s. It constituted one of the demands common to the economic- and political-reform movements, which emerged almost simultaneously in each of these countries during the early 1970s. They suffered a similar fate. In 1972 the electoral coalition led by Napoleon Duarte and Guillermo Ungo was robbed of victory by fraud and a subsequent military coup. The populist reform movement led by young military officers that came to power in Honduras in the same year had been dispersed by 1975. In Guatemala the reform coalition led by General Efrain Rios Montt was deprived of victory by an electoral fraud in 1974.

From 1950 to 1970 the countries of Central America passed through a profound change. The economic experiences recounted (modernization of the export sector, import substitution in manufacturing, and so on) wrought major changes in the class structure. There was now a middle class, an urban working class, rural landless laborers, and masses of impoverished peasants. Moreover, the shock of earthquake and massive relief efforts caused a profound impact on social awareness at the local level. The poorest Indians in the remotest villages became aware that their welfare was now a matter not only of national but of international concern.[22] This awakening consciousness provided the necessary background for guerrilla groups, for the first time, to make major inroads among the Indian population. At the same time church and other socially concerned sectors were mobilized in relief efforts. The experience, combined with the strong internal pressure of the Medillin currents within the church, has changed the allegiance of large sectors of this traditionally conservative institution. They will not go back to the status quo ante.

The new activism in the Central American church reflects the emergence of a national middle class rooted in the industrial and tertiary sectors. It has been cosmopolitanized by international financial institutions, university education, and exposure to Western media. The church has been deeply permeated by new social forces and ideas. Central American armies have resisted the modernizing currents of young officers' movements. This has led to the rupturing of the century-old alliance in Central America between sword and church. Now the church is often the speaker of the opposition to the military, even as lower-level clergy have sometimes joined the guerrilla movements themselves. The latter too is a new phenomenon of the 1970s, at least in El Salvador and Honduras. In the remainder of the decade we can expect fissures in these two central pillars of Central American societies to deepen and to spread. It is quite possible, for example, that the populist military reform movement in Honduras will revive as economic conditions continue to deteriorate. As the war in El Salvador deepens, younger and middle-level officers in the Salvadoran army may well make a renewed bid for power as they did in 1979 under the leadership of Colonel Majano.

The economic, social, and ideological transformations we have been describing have not been followed by adjustments in the political apparatus or by the kind of democratic revolutions that took place in the West during the late eighteenth and nineteenth centuries after similar socioeconomic changes. Instead democratic political channels have been blocked. Agrarian reform has been stymied or paralyzed. Labor unions encompass only a small minority of the working population, and "labor is relatively unable to defend its interests in an organized way in most of Central America."[23] The result has been that in El Salvador, Guatemala, and Nicaragua the left-led popular organization and guerilla movements, with powerful Soviet and Cuban influence, have incorporated and directed popular discontent. Unless structural reforms permit Central America's new social forces to find political expression, such movements will gain wider support and will spread to neighboring countries in the 1980s.

In the past the sparks of such movements could be extinguished by U.S. police actions. In the twentieth century U.S. intervention became a periodic and structural fact of Central American political life. Intervention in Panama and Nicaragua in the first part of the century and in Guatemala in 1954—against the progressive middle-class government of Jacobo Arbenz— and U.S. support for unpopular military rule throughout the region have provoked deep-rooted anti-Yankee sentiment and powerful nationalist feelings in all sectors, especially in junior military officers.[24] Such feelings are now shared, in their fashion, even by the upper military establishment, particularly in Guatemala. This means that the U.S. capacity to control events through direct military force in Central America is severely limited and will continue to be in the foreseeable future. The day is past when the United States could expect to ward off political developments it considers antagonistic to its interests through police actions. The agonizing review of military options conducted by the Pentagon and the State Department in the fall of 1981 relected this change.[25] This appraisal of options led the United States to embark on a diplomatic and informational campaign to persuade the countries of the region of the necessity for a policy of "collective security."[26] A sine qua non for U.S. military action in Central America in the 1980s will be the requirement of first winning the countries of the region—beginning with Mexico and Venezuela—to support such actions. This is not an easy condition, but it is a necessary one. Collective security now requires collective will.

One legacy of a bitter history is that most Central Americans regard the U.S. reaction to Soviet-Cuban expansionism in the region as motivated by an exclusive concern for superpower competition with the Soviet Union. Countries of the region, drawing conclusions from the recent history of Africa, Southeast Asia, and the Middle East, express the fear that the area will be turned into another focus for East-West conflict. To them the new U.S. attention to the region looks for all the world like a repetition of Mexico and Nicaragua in the 1920s, Guatemala in 1954, and the Dominican Republic in 1965, when the so-called communist presence was used as a pretext for U.S. intervention. This means that collective security will be achieved with the greatest difficulty and that U.S. military assistance must be preceded by an effective campaign to expose Soviet and Cuban activities and objectives for what they are. This adds a new dimension to contingency planning for the 1980s.

Historically, U.S. intervention in Central America has been a viable but last resort. Central American dependence on the United States has rested first and foremost on more mundane relations. The bulk of the exports of the Central American one- or two-crop economies were sold primarily in U.S. markets. This fact shaped the economic development of Central America— characterized by a relatively modern export sector (based on rural sharecroppers), a backward internal economy, ruled by an oligarchy with close social and institutional ties to the United States. Anastasio Somoza, who spoke better English than Spanish, schooled from the age of ten in the United States, was an extreme example of the general type.[27]

Along with the changes in the internal relations of the Central American countries came changes in their external relations. Central American markets and sources of foreign capital began to diversify in the 1960s. In this they participated in a phenomenon general to Latin America, which in recent years has seen Western Europe displace the United States as its major trading partner. Similarly U.S. foreign investment in Latin America has declined as a portion of total foreign investment in the region, and Western European and Japanese equity has come to surpass that of the United States in major countries like Argentina and Brazil.[28] Central American political contacts with Western Europe, in particular, also have proliferated. The foundations of the Socialist International and the World Christian Democratic Federation have financed cooperatives, counselled trade unions, and assisted peasant organizations in Central America for over a decade. The Socialist International and the World Christian Democratic Federation themselves have established direct organizational links with the leading opposition parties of the region. Richard Feinberg notes that over the past decade

> Central America has become a battle ground where Social and Christian Democratic activists struggle over ideas whose edges have been dulled in the material prosperity of Western Europe. Under the influence of its West German and Nordic member parties, the Socialist International has become very deeply involved in Central America.[29]

The diversification of Central America's economic and political relations puts a further limitation on U.S. capacity to control events in the region. It conditions U.S. diplomacy and it gives Central American countries alternatives to U.S. influence. The Guatemalan government has been able to resist U.S. human-rights pressures because it can buy arms from Israel (to the tune of $20 million in the first six months of 1981.)[30] Given current U.S. economic weakness, its difficulty in meeting military exigencies in other parts of the world, and the U.S. public's lack of enthusiasm for hegemonic policies in Latin America, it is likely that the decline of U.S. influence in the area will not be arrested despite the current renewal of its interest. The decline of U.S. influence in Central America is not primarily a consequence of past policies of benign neglect but of changes in the region itself and in U.S. economic, political, and military power. In the future the United States will be obligated to consult more not only with major regional actors, with the Central American countries themselves, and with major regional actors like Mexico and Venezuela but also with its Western European and, perhaps, its Asian (Japan and China) allies. For an effective security policy, even in its own backyard, the United States will have to rely on the formation of a broad international strategic consensus.

The Soviet-Cuban Offensive in Central America

The diversification of Central American foreign relations has included the development of economic and political relations with the Soviet bloc. The Soviet Union, as in other third-world countries like India, Iraq, Egypt, and Argentina, has employed economic relations to develop influence in the area. From 1968 to 1970 it purchased $10.8 million worth of Costa Rican coffee at a time when the Costa Ricans were caught with a large surplus.[31] This led to closer diplomatic ties and considerable Soviet publicity of Costa Rican expressions of gratitude. Having gained some leverage as a vital outlet for Costa Rican coffee, the Soviets proceeded to tie their purchases of coffee to sales of Soviet equipment. Costa Rica agreed to purchase Soviet-made tractors (whose late and irregular delivery later caused recriminations in the Costa Rican press) and then two hydroelectric-power stations.[32] Czechoslovakia now assembles Skoda cars in Costa Rica in exchange for coffee.[33] The Soviet bloc has also developed commercial relations with Panama, El Salvador, and Nicaragua. In an era of economic crisis and falling prices for Central American primary products, increased Soviet bloc efforts to develop commercial ties can be anticipated for the 1980s. Jiri Valenta believes that

> The Soviets may calculate that in the long run Central America will offer a
> more lucrative opportunity for COMECON trade than do many of the
> much-courted African and Asian countries. . . . The Soviets view Cuba as
> a useful instrument in restructuring the economic base of the Caribbean
> basin by reducing the preponderance of [U.S. economic influence].[34]

Soviet bloc economic relations and the collaboration of its Cuban clients must be seen as a component in an integrated strategy to penetrate Central America and the Caribbean Basin region as a whole. Geopolitically Central America is part of the Caribbean Basin, a single region that embraces the littoral states as well as the islands. In this perspective the strategic significance of Central America and its potential for conflict can be better appreciated.

The Caribbean Basin is of manifold strategic importance. Stability in the region is essential to the North Atlantic Treaty Organization's (NATO) capacity to move ships, weapons, and troops to Western Europe in the event of a crisis. In World War II, over 50 percent of the U.S. supplies to Europe and Africa departed from Mexican gulf ports. In the early phase of the war German submarines destroyed considerable allied tonnage in the straits of

Florida even with a two-to-one allied submarine advantage. Today Soviet submarines have reversed that ratio. The thirteen Caribbean sea-lanes pass through four choke points vulnerable to interdiction from Cuba. It is clear that any conflict in Europe will impact on the Caribbean Basin in the 1980s.

The Panama Canal continues to increase the military and commercial value of the region. Although it is true that supertankers (at all events being abandoned for economic reasons) and large carriers have outgrown the Canal, its savings in fuel costs have grown more relevant in the last few years. Canal traffic and revenues are at record highs.[35] During the Korean War 22 percent of all U.S. troops and materials passed through the Canal. It remains as essential today as it was for the Cuban missile crisis and for troop movements in the Vietnam War. Only 13 of the Navy's 550 ships are too large for the Canal, which permits the United States to maintain a two-ocean navy presence with what is now only a so-called one-and-a-half-ocean navy.[36] Increasing political unrest and the appearance of terrorist networks in the region have alarming implications for the Canal and for the projected Panamanian oil pipeline. Once again as economic and political conditions continue to deteriorate in the region, we can expect the dangers of insurgencies and terrorism to mount and to force both the United States and Panama to fortify their security measures. On the other hand, to the extent that Panama continues to pursue a foreign policy of nonalignment, Soviet-Cuban directed efforts against the Canal will be complicated by the anticipated reaction of Latin America and the rest of the third world.

The Caribbean trade routes bear a steadily mounting cargo of strategic and other raw materials. As economic power grows more diffuse and resources scarcer, the strategic importance of these routes can only increase. The U.S. Commerce Department's "Peterson Report" projected that imported raw materials would rise from 20 percent of the total U.S. raw-material consumption to nearly 50 percent by the year 2000.[37]

The Caribbean serves as a transshipment point for raw materials flowing from the Middle East, Southern Asia, and Africa to the Western Hemisphere. Its high-density oil routes carry half of U.S. oil imports. About a quarter of U.S. imported oil is refined abroad, more than half of it in Caribbean refineries. Two of the main sources of imported oil share the Caribbean: Mexico and Venezuela. In the coming decade the aggregate strategic and economic significance of the Caribbean will come to rival that of the Persian Gulf. This point will become clearer after a brief review of Soviet global strategy.

Since 1965 the Soviet Union has carried out the greatest peacetime military buildup in history. This naturally has produced concrete changes in the military balance between the Soviet Union and the United States.[38] The Soviet Union has overtaken the United States in most categories of strategic nuclear power. It is worth recalling that it was the Soviet backdown, in the face of U.S. nuclear superiority, in the first Soviet attempt to penetrate the Caribbean strategically that spurred the Soviets to engage in their massive buildup in the years following 1962.

The Soviet Union has acquired the capacity to implement an offensive strategy by means of a global offensive navy, an aerial attack force, a leaping ability to air- and sea-lift troops and equipment over long distances, and a first-strike and counterforce nuclear capacity. These capabilities have been utilized to underwrite a Soviet strategic offensive in the Indian Ocean Basin. The Soviet deployment via the subversion of national-liberation movements, friendship treaties, the acquisition of bases, ports, moorings, and other naval facilities in the Indian Ocean Basin and around the coasts of Africa constitutes massive pressure on the raw-material life lines of Western Europe and Japan. This is the central military component of a strategy aimed at neutralizing Europe and Japan. It accompanies military pressure on the flanks of NATO (the buildup on the Kola Peninsula, persistent violations of Norwegian neutrality, the expansion of the Soviet Eastern Mediterranean fleet, and so on), the growth of Warsaw Pact forces, the theater nuclear threat to Europe, and the occupation and naval construction on Japan's Kurile Islands. All this has been supplemented by a sustained ideological, political, and diplomatic campaign seeking to encourage neutralist and pacifist sentiment in Western Europe and Japan.

The Soviet strategic deployment is the necessary background for understanding Soviet strategy in the Caribbean Basin. Soviet writers have recognized publicly that "in military strategic terms (the Caribbean) is a sort of hinterland on whose stability freedom of U.S. action in other parts of the globe depends."[39] As pointed out elsewhere, Soviet advances in the region "do not signify an independent threat to U.S. security (but) are more serious precisely because they are components of and subordinate to the USSR's global strategy."[40] From this perspective, the chief Soviet objective in the region is not the acquisition of Mexico's oil (as is frequently alleged) but to promote a state of turmoil that would divert U.S. resources and permit the Soviets a freer hand in the areas more central to their global strategy.[41] Thus the Soviets have backed low-cost Cuban harassment of the United States by funding and supporting Cuban intervention in the Caribbean and Central America.[42]

The second major Soviet objective in the region, closely related to the first, is the development of an offensive interdiction capability—the capacity to disrupt troop convoys leaving U.S. gulf ports or exiting through the Panama Canal. In pursuit of this objective the Soviets have established a significant naval presence, indirectly by building up the Cuban navy and directly by lengthening Soviet ship visits to the area. The latter has been described by Christopher Abel as a typical example of Soviet "incrementalism."[43] It is an approach which includes:

The elements of a gradual, purposeful buildup . . . as well as the strategic use of favorable opportunities when presented. . . . Inherently low-risk in nature, this strategy seeks steady success in the long run at the expense of larger triumphs. . . . Put simply, the plan calls for the setting of an initial precedent which is followed by desensitizing regional powers to that action's significance. Once accomplished, another precedent is set and the process begins over again.[44]

Having failed in their dramatic attempt to place strategic missiles and strike aircraft in Cuba, the Soviets began in 1962 to establish a low-level naval presence in Cuba. In the same year they signed an agreement to construct a fishing station on the island. At the same time less provocative elements of Soviet seapower were gradually introduced in the Caribbean, including oceanographic, merchant marine, and electronic-intelligence vessels.[45] This gave the Soviets access to Cuban ports for logistical purposes.[46] These first quiet measures were followed by the gradual deployment of warships in small but significant and carefully timed steps. On their ninth visit the Soviets quietly slipped a "Golf-II," conventionally powered, nuclear-ballistics-missile-equipped submarine and tender into the Cuban port of Nipe for servicing.[47] By 1975 more than a dozen separate Soviet naval deployments to the Caribbean had occurred and over thirty submarines had called at Cuban ports. These were coupled with Soviet "Bear-D" reconnaissance flights off the U.S. East coast, taking off and landing from Cuban airfields. By 1975 the Soviet and Cuban navies were routinely exercising together.[48] The visits gradually became longer and larger. The average of the first seventeen deployments were thirty days, and the two in 1978 lasted sixty-five and eighty-two days.[49] The most recent visit in April 1981 included two frigates, an oiler, and a cruiser armed with nuclear-tipped surface-to-surface missiles. None of these vessels is permanently based in Cuba, but their visits have rendered the Soviet naval presence a normal and persistent feature in the Caribbean. Moreover, this presence has been accompanied by a similarly incremental Soviet buildup of Cuba's own naval and air forces.

Again beginning in 1962, the Soviets have slowly but systematically transferred considerable naval craft to Cuba. This transfer has included twenty fast patrol boats armed with Styx missiles, four fast Turya-class hydrofoil boats, eighteen Komar class patrol boats, twelve OSA-class guided missile patrol boats, two conventional Foxtrot class submarines, a diesel-powered submarine, and, in August 1982, a 2,300 Koni-class frigate.[50]

The combination of the direct Soviet naval presence in the Caribbean with a burgeoning Soviet-supplied Cuban navy regularly participating together in naval exercises, has created a major coordinated and integrated offensive-interdiction capability for Soviet bloc power in the Caribbean.[51]

In addition Soviet Navy Fleet Admiral Sergei Gorshkov visited Grenada in 1980, and there were unconfirmed reports about Soviet intentions to build naval facilities there as well.[52]

This naval deployment also advances a third Soviet strategic objective. It is integral to an economic, diplomatic, political, and military strategy to hasten what Gorshkov calls "progressive changes" in the region.[53] Such changes are expected to deepen the Soviets' political and military foothold in the Caribbean Basin and eventually could lead to military facilities and bases.

The most important progressive change in the region, of course, has been the Nicaraguan revolution and its steady march toward the Soviet orbit. Although it would be hasty to affirm that Nicaragua has become or must become a Soviet vassal state, should present tendencies continue that will become its fate. Many of the characteristic features of such a relationship have already begun to emerge. Already elements of the Soviets' typical integrated coordinated approach can be discerned in Nicaragua.

In March 1980 the FSLN signed a mutual support agreement with the Soviet Communist Party. Such agreements were previously reserved for parties in regimes that Moscow regards as being of a socialist orientation. The agreements, coupled with the revised Soviet judgment that "military-political fronts of the July 26 Movement and the Sandinista Front of National Liberation . . . have shown . . . that they are capable . . . of substituting for the political parties of the proletariat" suggest Soviet expectations that the FSLN will, under Soviet guidance, become a Soviet-type vanguard party.[54]

The Soviet effort in Nicaragua is beginning to sport the characteristics of a now-familiar division of labor employed in places like Ethiopia, Angola, South Yemen, Kampuchea, Afghanistan, and Mozambique. As previously in Angola and Ethiopia, Cuba is acting as the Soviet stalking horse in Nicaragua. Cuban influence among the Sandinistas reaches back to the first years of the FSLN, for whom the Cuban revolution was a source of inspiration and emulation. Deep-rooted sympathy for the Cuban revolution among both the Nicaraguan people and the Sandinista leadership is one legacy of U.S. harassment of the Cuban revolution and its support for Somoza.

Cubans provide combat training for the growing Nicaraguan army, already the largest in Central America and projected to reach 50,000 by the end of the year (along with as many as 200,000 militia).[55] Cuba played a leading role in the literacy campaign as well as hosting more than 600 Nicaraguan students at their highly politicized educational facilities in the Isle of Youth. Cuban ideological influence is pervasive. *Barricada*, the official Sandinista organ, is modeled on *Granma*, and relies on *Prensa Latina*, the Cuban press agency. Like *Nuevo Diario*, the so-called independent progovernment paper, it routinely denounces U.S. efforts to destabilize Nicaragua and takes Cuban (and Soviet) positions on virtually all international issues from European theater nuclear modernization to Poland, Afghanistan, Libya, and China. Sandinista defense committees, imitations of the Cuban revolutionary defense committees, have FSLN party organs to erect a network of bosses and ward heelers to exercise vigilance over comings and goings at the grass roots. They are now being supplemented by a militia assisted by Cuban advisers.

Direct links with the Soviet Union have proliferated as well. In the fall of 1979 two studies prepared under government direction contemplated the replacing of Nicaragua's dependency on the U.S. market with ties with the Council for Mutual Economic Assistance (CMEA).[56] These have been revised, apparently in line with Soviet advice to preserve economic relations with the West. The Soviets advocate such relations in Angola and Ethiopia as well—preferring to let the West sustain the economic burden of these underdeveloped countries while they consolidate military and political ties. In late March 1980 the Nicaraguan and Soviet governments signed a series of agreements for "economic, technical, scientific and cultural cooperation," "cooperation in the area of planning," and air-transport linkage.[57]

The Soviets have provided some economic aid, but this has been minor compared with that of Western Europe, Mexico, and several Arab countries.[58] Of far greater importance from a strategic and political standpoint have been a series of military agreements between Nicaragua and the Soviet Union. The Soviets have loaned the Nicaraguans two HI8 helicopters and twelve pilot technicians.[59] Soviet T-55 tanks, tank-warfare courses from Soviet texts, and Soviet AK-47 rifles as standard issue now stud the Nicaraguan panoply.[60] Furthermore soft evidence strongly suggests that the Nicaraguans are preparing for the arrival of Soviet MIG fighters. Another agreement allows the Soviets to operate their floating workshop for ship repair off the Nicaraguan Pacific Coast.[61] Another agreement provides the Soviets fishing privileges off Nicaraguan waters. In other countries, concessions like these have permitted the Soviets to conduct naval surveillance and have led eventually to naval facilities and bases. Unconfirmed intelligence reports of the transfer of Soviet tankers from Cuba to Nicaragua suggest that the Soviets are taking in Nicaragua their customary incremental steps, coordinating economic, political, and security elements in an integrated strategy of penetration. As in such previous efforts East Germany, Bulgaria, Vietnam, and other Soviet bloc states are participating in the Nicaraguan buildup.

What is the significance of this all-round military buildup with Soviet bloc assistance? What does it hold for the future? Will Nicaragua become another "Soviet proxy" and a "platform for subversion" as the Reagan administration has charged?

Some believe that this is out of the question because the Soviets are "unwilling to pick up the tab for another Cuba." They cite the fact that Fidel Castro has urged the Nicaraguans not to break their economic ties with the West nor to expropriate the private sector.[62] Such optimistic forecasts ignore a major shift in Soviet tactics since the mid-1970s. Soviet writers have stated that as a result of the "changed correlation of forces on a world scale" new conditions prevail in which "material aid on the part of the socialist states has ceased to be a factor directly promoting the transition to a noncapitalist path." Instead "the main factors, favoring such an orientation, are the political, military-strategic and moral influence of the states of the socialist community."[63] Concretely in Nicaragua this involves in addition to Soviet bloc military assistance a predominant Cuban presence in the military, security, and intelligence apparati of the Nicaraguan government.[64] This presence is supplemented by the ascendence of Humberto Ortega to a position of preeminence in the Sandinista leadership. Comandante Ortega believes that the world is now divided "into two great camps: one side the camp of imperialism, the camp of capitalism, led by the United States . . . and on the other the socialist camp . . . with the Soviet Union in the vanguard."[65]

As the distinguished Nicaraguan ambassador to the United States Aturo Cruz has put it, the Sandinistas have yet "to make the transition from being soldiers to being political leaders."[66] Many fair-minded Latin Americans and U.S. Latin Americanists attribute this delay to the youthful pride of successful revolutionaries coupled with an understandable fear of U.S. intentions. Such a view is sensitive to the causes of third-world revolutions and the deep-rooted misery and oppression that spawns them but less sensitive to the dire consequences for the countries involved and their neighbors, when those revolutions become instruments of Soviet hegemonism. Deeply aware of the history of U.S. interference in the political processes of the third world, those who hold such views tend to overlook the systematic and strategic nature of current Soviet activities in the third world.

Recent disclosures of Cuban activities in Guatemala, El Salvador, Honduras, and Colombia indicate that this Soviet strategy is now being implemented in and around Central America.[67] Its incremental nature suggests that through the 1980s the region will be in for increased turbulence and that the present Soviet threat to Western shipping may be complemented by new Soviet bases. The United States has already responded by increasing ship visits to the region and by creating a special command for the Caribbean. Both the Soviet-Cuban and the U.S. military presence will increase in the coming decade. The United States will be obligated to seek the political and military cooperation of all those countries and political forces that can be united against Soviet-Cuban expansionism. The question of how to develop a strategic consensus, how to balance a military and

socioeconomic approach to the region, will increasingly occupy U.S. and
Latin American strategic planners. As the threat to NATO presented by
Soviet-Cuban expansionism in the Caribbean Basin becomes more apparent, Western European influence will be called in to redress the balance in
the new world. Central American issues will become internationalized.

Interregional Conflict

In his study of "Inter-State Conflict Behavior and Regional Potential for
Conflict in Latin America," Wolf Grabendorff finds that "most interstate
conflicts by far have occurred in the Central American and Caribbean
region."[68] This type of conflict has occurred regularly in Central America
since 1847. In more recent history they have been engendered by border and
terrritorial disputes (Nicaragua versus Honduras 1957, Honduras versus El
Salvador 1968–1980), ideological and political differences (Costa Rica versus Nicaragua 1948–1956, 1978–1979), colonial ambitions (Guatemala versus Great Britain, 1855–1979), conflicts over resources (Guatemala versus
Great Britain, Nicaragua versus Colombia, 1979–1981) and over interstate
migrations (Honduras versus El Salvador, 1969). As the peacekeeping role
of the OAS has declined and as the United States has lost its capacity to
"referee," regional conflicts have grown more intractable. With the decline
in U.S. influence a tendency has developed for Central American countries
to seek new extraregional associates. These now include Israel (Guatemala), Argentina (El Salvador), Libya and Algeria (Nicaragua and the
FMLN), Western Europe and Japan (throughout the region), and the Soviet
bloc. In some cases these forces have worked to reduce conflict in the region,
but in many others they have rendered them more refractory.[69]

Internal as well as international factors have been entangled with interstate conflicts. Ideological and political differences have stirred Costa
Rica and Nicaragua off and on for three decades. Today in the region
interstate-conflict potential of ideology and politics is at an unprecedented
level, fueling conflicts between Nicaragua and Honduras, Nicaragua and El
Salvador, Guatemala and Mexico and Belize, and so forth. As local ideological and political factors fuse with international ones the pressure on regional
stability will become intolerable.

This is all the more true when these variables interact with social and
economic factors, quite capable by themselves of generating interstate
conflict. The war between El Salvador and Honduras in 1969 derived solely
from socioeconomic factors. Land hunger led to a massive cross-border
migration that put unsupportable strains on Honduran economic and social
relations. The result was a territorial war unassisted by ideological or international factors. The deterioration of Central American economies has

created the preconditions for the reappearance of such conflicts in the 1980s—only this time supplemented by international, ideological, and strategic factors.

There is growing concern in the region that the Guatemalan government, which has consistently attributed internal guerrilla activities to intervention from Cuba and Nicaragua will choose to "go to the source."[70] The Guatemalan army of 18,000 has come to occupy a dominant place in Guatemalan politics. Government and military officials have characterized Belize as a potential haven for Central American guerrillas.[71] The Guatemalan government greeted Belizean independence in September 1981 by closing its borders with that country.[72] The Mexican government has stated that it would renew its claims to Belize should Guatemala invade.[73] A Guatemalan intervention in Belize, Nicaragua, or El Salvador would be predicated on possible U.S. support. Should that support be granted the zone would become an arena in which local conflicts were regionalized and regional hegemonist ambitions aligned with superpower objectives contending for supremacy.

This panorama threatens to unleash an arms race in the region. Governments throughout the region are beefing up their arsenals, spending an estimated $100 million in 1981.[74] Honduras and Guatemala are seeking to purchase jet fighters and tanks; El Salvador seeks to acquire as much as $150 million worth of U.S. military equipment; and Nicaragua has engaged in an unprecedented military buildup helping to fuel fires smoldering even before the Nicaraguan revolution. An expert witness before the Congress has testified that "the possibility of small scale war . . . in the 1980s cannot be dismissed."[75] Given international and regional pressures, the chances that small-scale war could become large-scale are excellent.

Increasing this possibility is a new diplomatic development in the region: the incipient formation of regional-solidarity blocs. Strong statements of mutual support from the governments of Nicaragua, Grenada, and Cuba suggest this. Were El Salvador to be added to the list, such a regional bloc, backed by Soviet political and military support, could develop into a powerful reality by the latter 1980s. The formation of a similar bloc this year among Libya, South Yemen, and Ethiopia and Soviet efforts to create a regional-security grouping in Southeast Asia will have claimed the attention of the Soviets and Cubans. As the decade wears on we should not discount the possibility that Guatemala (after a successful revolution) and Guyana (as a result of its contention with Venezuela) would join such a formation. In this case the security not only of the Caribbean Basin but also of Latin America will be endangered.

Were the United States to pursue a correct policy toward them, Venezuela and Mexico could provide part of a counterweight to these developments. Venezuela and Mexico have both been the object of charges of seeking regional hegemony, but such accusations fail to distinguish a concern with regional stability from a desire to impose one's will on one's neighbors. Over the last dozen years, beginning with the Social Christian government of President Rafael Caldera and his foreign minister Aristedes Calvani (1969–1973), Venezuela has sought a leadership role in the region.[76] Calvani comprehended that Caribbean Basin stability was critical to Venezuela's own economic and political development, if for no other reason than the fact that oil must transit the Caribbean to arrive at its chief market in the East Coast of the United States. Calvani was concerned also that the political instability of the poor and backward countries of the region was creating a potential security threat to Venezuela.[77] In Calvani's period the Venezuelan government began actively to expand its relations with its Caribbean neighbors. The succeeding Social-Democratic government of President Carlos Andres Perez deepened these relations by initiating Venezuela's policy of providing oil to its neighbors on concessional terms.[78]

A perfect illustration of Venezuela's ability to downplay adversarial relationships and to emphasize more positive aspects of cooperation was Venezuela's association with Mexico in the San Jose convention. These two countries agreed to provide oil on concessionary credit terms to Caribbean Basin countries over and above their own political differences and the differing policies of the recipients (which include Nicaragua as well as El Salvador). Other examples include Venezuela's championing of multilateral institutions like SELA (the Latin American Economic System), OLADE (the Latin American Energy Organization), the Andean Pact, the Caribbean Basin Plan, and OPEC.

Much of the same can be said for Mexico, even if the centrality and magnitude of its dealing with the United States obligates it to choose a bilateral and package format for managing a relationship so fundamental to Mexican economic and political development. Mexico's concern with the stability of the region and its conviction that social, economic, and political backwardness is the root cause of the region's unrest has led it to participate actively in regional politics. It continues to attribute to Cuba a wide margin of political independence. It seeks to use its leverage to moderate the foreign policies not only of Cuba but also of Sandinista Nicaragua and the FDR-FMLN in El Salvador. Whatever one may think of the Mexican analysis, its policies are not intended to dominate its neighbors but to promote their economic and political independence.[79]

Venezuelan and Mexican efforts to assist a peaceful outcome to the Central American crisis supplement Central American efforts in the same direction: most notably the meetings of Honduran, Guatemalan, Salvadoran, Nicaraguan, Costa Rican, and Panamanian representatives in Tegucigalpa in August 1981 and of those countries with the "Nassau Group" (Mexico, Venezuela, the United States, and Canada) later in Costa Rica.

These meetings made important progress toward a regional economic cooperation over and above ideological and political differences. Although the spiral of misperceptions, mutual recriminations, suspicions, and threats has created a situation reminiscent of the Balkan tinderbox before World War I, there is still hope that centripetal regional forces will prevail. One road in Central America leads to a peaceful resolution of its conflict and widening cooperation to resolve or at least to ameliorate its economic crisis. The other road leads to regional war with profound international implications. Much depends on the outcome of the conflict in El Salvador.

El Salvador

Both the military and the political situations in El Salvador deteriorated in 1981. The Salvadoran guerrillas established secure rearguard bases, learned to coordinate countrywide operations, and developed an effective strategy of so-called protracted people's war. The Salvadoran army, on the other hand, is being worn thin and is increasingly demoralized. The electoral plan backed by the United States is unlikely to bring about either an internal or an external legitimization of the government. Fissures among the pro-government forces are growing. Only two alternatives seem likely in El Salvador: an eventual guerrilla victory or a peaceful negotiated settlement. Should the guerrillas triumph, a government similar to Sandinista Nicaragua can be expected. A nonaligned and pluralistic government can only come about if a relative balance of forces emerges in El Salvador. This will be far more likely should the FDR-FMLN come to power in tandem with the official Christian Democratic Party and the moderate members of the Salvadoran army via a negotiated settlement. This is a lesson to be learned from the failed mediation efforts in Nicaragua, which allowed the Sandinistas to triumph with a monopoly of political and military power.

United States' military options to prevent such an outcome will be highly restricted in the coming decade. Like it or not the Nicaraguan buildup has changed the balance of power in Central America. An operation by a resurrected CONDECA (Central American Defense Council: Honduras, Guatemala, and El Salvador) would only be successful if supplemented by tens of thousands of U.S. troops. Such a project would jeopardize the precarious consensus in the United States for a revived U.S. defense posture and severely damage U.S. relations with its Latin American friends. The same holds for a major increase in U.S. military assistance to El Salvador. A blockade of Nicaragua would risk similar repercussions. It would be equally futile militarily without a massive deployment of U.S. naval resources already stretched to the limit in the face of the Soviet naval buildup in the Pacific and Indian oceans and in the Norwegian and Mediterranean seas. A blockade or invasion of Cuba would invite Soviet responses in West Berlin, Baluchistan, Pakistan, or Yugoslavia. Moreover such actions would restore the faded glory of the Cuban David resisting the U.S. Goliath. And all such options would fan the flames of Euroneutralism, weakening further the Western Alliance. Once again only such military actions as underwritten by Latin American consent based on an informed and collective Latin American opinion will be viable in the coming decade.

United States policy must seek to form a regional noninterventionist consensus in the 1980s. But the first step to the formation of such a consensus must be for the United States to foreswear unilateral military intervention in the region. Nonintervention is in the U.S. interest, particularly in view of the political-military situation in Central America.

Support for a negotiated settlement in El Salvador will go a long way toward creating the necessary conditions for such a consensus to form. As a by-product this will help to improve U.S. relations with Mexico, an indispensable regional collaborator. As the Guatemalan turmoil mounts, Mexican interest in such an arrangement will begin to surface.

Another factor that will assist the formation of a noninterventionist consensus in the region is the growing perception among third-world countries that Soviet imperialism has become the main danger to their national independence and their hopes for a tranquil international environment in which to develop their economies. The increasing self-assertion of the third world, which Central and Latin America certainly share, can in the 1980s become a positive factor in U.S. foreign policy. As Soviet expansionism becomes a perceived clear and present danger, a dramatic change of mood will occur in the third world. Latin America, with its increasing economic and political links to Africa, Asia, and the Middle East, cannot but feel the effect of this. Should the United States pursue such a strategy of indirect approach toward the region there will be real hope for the future of Central America.

Notes

1. See, for example, V. Vasilyev, "The United States' New Approach to Latin America," *International Affairs* (Moscow) 6 (June 1971): 43; S. Mishin, "Latin America: Two Trends of Development," *International Affairs* 6 (June 1976): 450.

2. William R. Cline and Enrique Delgado, eds., "Economic Integration in Central America" [study sponsored jointly by the Brookings Institution and the Secretariat of Economic Integration of Central America (SEICA)] (Washington, D.C.: Brookings Institution, 1978), pp. 196, 198, 323–327; Richard Feinberg, "No Easy Answers," *Foreign Affairs* vol. 59,

no. 5 (Summer 1981): 1121; Isaac Cohen and Gert Rosenthal, "The International Aspects of the Crisis in Central America" (Paper prepared for workshop on "The International Aspects of the Crisis in Central America," at Woodrow Wilson Center, Washington, D.C., 2–3 April 1981).

3. Monteforte Toledo Ms., *Centroamerica, subdesarrollo y dependencia*, (Mexico: Universidad Nacional Autonoma de Mexico, 1972).

4. Cohen and Rosenthal, "Crisis in Central America," p. 6.

5. Ibid.

6. Clark Reynolds, "Fissures in the Volcano? Central American Economic Prospects," *Latin America and World Economy: A Changing International Order*, vol. 2, ed. Joseph Grunwald (Beverly Hills: Sage, 1981), p. 203.

7. Ibid., p. 203.

8. Guillermo Molina Chocano, *Centroamerica: la crisis del viejo orden*, cuadro 3.0 (Tegucigalpa, Honduras: Editorial Guaymurat, 1981).

9. Cline and Delgado, "Economic Integration," pp. 198, 250.

10. Cohen and Rosenthal, "Crisis in Central America," p. 14.

11. Cline and Delgado, "Economic Integration," pp. 241–244.

12. Cohen and Rosenthal, "Crisis in Central America," pp. 11–12.

13. See Comisión Económica de los Paises de America Latina (CEPAL), "Preliminary Balance of the Latin American Economy in 1980," E/CEPAL.238, 30 December 1980, p. 5; International Bank for Reconstruction and Development (IBRD), *World Development Report 1980*, (New York: Oxford University Press, 1980) p. 112; U.S. Department of Commerce, "Costa Rica," *Foreign Economic Trends and Their Implications for the United States*, (Washington, D.C., June 1981), p. 2; U.S. Department of Commerce, "Guatemala," *Foreign Economic Trends and Their Implications for the United States* (Washington, D.C., August 1981), p. 3.

14. K. Ruddle and D. Oderman, *Statistical Abstract of Latin America*, (Los Angeles: Latin American Center, UCLA, December 1972), table 30; CEPAL, "Preliminary Balance," p. 7; Cline and Delgado, "Economic Integration," pp. 227–228.

15. IBRD, *World Development Report*, p. 150.

16. Population Reference Bureau, "1981 World Data Population Sheet," (Washington, D.C., 1981).

17. IBRD, *World Development Report*, p. 154.

18. Ibid.

19. Jorge Arturo Reina, *Que pasa hoy en Honduras?*, (Tegucigalpa, Honduras: 1981), p. 4.

20. United Nations, *Statistical Yearbook for 1978*, (New York, 1979), pp. 880–881; compare with Reina, *Que pasa hoy en Honduras?*, p. 4.

21. Compare with the following works by the World Bank, Latin American and Caribbean Regional Office: *Nicaragua: The Challenge of Recon-*

struction, Report no. 3524-NI (Washington, D.C., 9 October 1981), p. 73; *Costa Rica—Current Economic Position and Prospects*, Report no. 3193-CR (Washington, D.C., 3 November 1980), p. 44; *Guatemala: Country Economic Memorandum*, Report no. 2654-GU, (Washington, D.C., 4 February 1980), p. 48; *Current Economic Memorandum on Honduras* (Washington, D.C., 17 July 1981), pp. 57, 60.

22. Reynolds, *Latin America and World Economy*, p. 209.

23. Cline and Delgado, "Economic Integration," p. 189.

24. Compare with Richard Millett, "Central American Paralysis," *Foreign Policy* 39 (Summer 1980): 112.

25. "U.S. Policy for Nicaragua: No Force but Some Fleeing," *Miami Herald*, 26 November 1981.

26. Alexander Haig, Jr. "An Agenda for Cooperation," (address to the General Assembly of the Organization of American States, 26 April 1982), pp. 12–13; "Latin Policy: A New Plan," *New York Times*, 6 December 1981, p. 1.

27. Compare with Anastasio Somoza and Jack Cox, *Nicaragua Betrayed* (Belmont, Mass.: Western Islands, 1980), pp. xi, 342. Somoza told U.S. Ambassador Lawrence Pezzullo: "You know, you and I have the same background; I grew up in New York . . . since I was ten years old."

28. See Albert Fishlow, "The Mature Neighbor Policy," in *Latin America and World Economy: A Changing International Order*, ed. Joseph Grunwald (Beverly Hills, Calif.: Sage, 1978), p. 38.

29. Feinberg, "No Easy Answers," p. 1143.

30. "Growing Arms Race in Central America May Heat up Region," *Christian Science Monitor*, 28 October 1981.

31. Leon Goure and Morris Rothenberg, *Soviet Penetration of Latin America*, Institute for Advanced International Studies (IAIS), (Coral Gables: University of Miami Press, 1975).

32. L.A. Sobel, *Facts on File, Latin America* (New York: Facts on File, Inc., 1974), p. 234; "URSS: Boletin de la Embajada" (Soviet Embassy in Mexico City Information Bulletin), no. 17 (1 September 1973): 36.

33. UN Commission on Trade and Development, TD/243, supplement, 2: fn. 120: 33.

34. Jiri Valenta, "The USSR, Cuba, and the Crisis in Central America," *ORBIS*, vol. 25, no. 3 (Fall 1981): 728.

35. *Latin America Weekly Report*, 80–25, (27 June 1980), p. 8.

36. Compare with Testimony of Admiral Thomas B. Hayward, chief of Naval Operations, *Report to the Subcommittee on Seapower and Strategic and Critical Materials of the House Committee on Armed Services on Fiscal Year 1982 Military Posture* (Washington, D.C., 2 April 1981), p. 4.

37. Peter G. Peterson, *The U.S. in the Changing World Economy* 2 vols. (Washington, D.C.: U.S. Government Printing Office, 1971).

38. The International Institute for Strategic Studies, *The Military Balance, 1980–1981* (London, 1980), pp. 5–13.

39. *International Affairs* (Moscow) 2 (February 1967): 67.

40. Robert S. Leiken, "Eastern Winds in Latin America," *Foreign Policy* 42 (Spring 1981): 94.

41. For discussions of Soviet strategy in Latin America, see Leon Goure and Morris Rothenberg, *Soviet Penetration of Latin America*, Institute for Advanced International Studies (IAIS) (Coral Gables: University of Miami Press, 1975); James D. Theberge, *The Soviet Presence in Latin America* (New York: Crane Russak, 1974); Robert Moss, "Soviet Ambitions in Latin America," in *The Southern Oceans and the Security of the Free World*, ed. Patrick Wall (London: Stacey International, 1977); W. Raymond Duncan, "Moscow and Latin America: Objectives, Constraints and Implications," in *Soviet Policy in the Third World*, ed. W.R. Duncan, (New York: Pergamon Press, 1980), pp. 262–291.

42. Compare with Margaret Daly Hayes, "United States Security Interest in Central America in a Global Perspective" (Paper presented to the workshop of "International Aspects of the Crisis in Central America," Woodrow Wilson International Center for Scholars, Washington, D.C., (2–3 April 1981), p. 11.

43. Christopher Abel, "A Breach in the Ramparts," *U.S. Naval Institute Proceedings* (Annapolis, July 1980).

44. Ibid., p. 47.

45. Richard Sims and James Anderson, "The Caribbean Strategic Vacuum," *Conflict Studies* 121 (August 1980): 3.

46. James D. Theberge, *Russia in the Caribbean*, part 2 (Washington, D.C.: Center for Strategic and International Studies, Georgetown University, 1973), p. 80.

47. Abel, "Breach in Ramparts," p. 49; Barry Blechman and Stephanie Levinson, "Soviet Submarine Visits to Cuba," *U.S. Naval Institute Proceedings*, (Annapolis, September 1975), pp. 32, 33; Captain Leslie K. Fenton, "The Umpteenth Cuban Confrontation," *U.S. Naval Institute Proceedings* (Annapolis, July 1980), p. 44.

48. Abel, "Breach in Ramparts," p. 50: Micky Edwards, "Soviet Expansion and Control of the Sea Lanes," *U.S. Naval Institute Proceedings* (Annapolis, September 1980).

49. Jorge I. Dominguez, "The United States and Its Regional Security Interests: the Caribbean, Central and South America," *Daedalus*, vol. 9, no. 4 (Fall 1980): 119–120.

50. *Air Force Magazine*, 62 (December 1979): 118; *The Christian Science Monitor*, 11 October 1979, p. 9; David C. Jordan, "The Turbulent Caribbean," *Strategic Review* 8 (Fall 1980): 42; *Baltimore Sun*, 4 August 1981.

51. Paul Seidenman, "The Caribbean: A Sense of Urgency," *National Defense* 65 (March 1981): 50; F. Clifton Berky, "Cuba's Expanding Power," *Air Force* 63 (April 1980): 45–46.

52. Radio Paris, 21 January, 1981, Foreign Broadcast Information Service (FBIS), Latin America, 21 January 1981.

53. Valenta, "USSR, Cuba and Crisis," p. 18.

54. *Latinskaia Amerika* 3 (Moscow: March 1980): 36.

55. "Haig Says U.S. 'Watching' Flow of Arms to Nicaragua," *Washington Post*, 3 June 1981, p. A17; *Wall Street Journal*, 13 July 1981, p. 12.

56. Interview with Enrique Dreyfus, chairman of the Superior Council of the Private Sector in Nicaragua, 13 August 1981.

57. Compare with Leiken, "Eastern Winds," p. 101.

58. "Boletin de informacion de la embajada de la URSS" (Mexico), no. 4 (April 1980): 3; Managua Radio Domestic Service, 4 August 1981, FBIS, Latin America; ibid., 30 July 1981; *Diario Las Americas*, 6 August 1981; Christopher Dickey, "Arab States Help Nicaragua Avoid Ties to Superpowers," *Washington Post*, 19 July 1981.

59. *Diario Las Americas*, "2 Helicopteros prestara Rusia a Nicaragua," 25 April 1981; *Diario Las Americas*, "Asesores Sovieticos adiestran a Sandinistas en helicopteros," 6 June 1981; Ronald Richards, "Soviets 'Hinted' Copter Training in Nicaragua," *Providence Journal*, 9 June 1981.

60. "Nicaraguans Said to Get Soviet Tanks," *Washington Post*, 2 June 1981; "Les pays Arabes accroitraient leur aide militaire au gouvernement Sandiniste," *Le Monde*, 21 July 1981; Juan Vasquez, "Nicaragua Confirms It Has Been Given Some Soviet Tanks," *Los Angeles Times*, 15 July 1981; "Les dirigeants Nicaraguayens admettent avoir recu des Chars Sovietiques," *Le Monde*, 17 July 1981; "Tanques Rusos a Nicarauga," *Diario Las Americas*, 16 July 1981; *Washington Post*, 2 June 1981.

61. "Nicaraguans Said to Get Soviet Tanks," *Washington Post*, 2 June 1981; "The New Violence Brewing in Central America," *Business Week*, 8 June 1981, p. 74; "Nicaragua continua preparandose, para que?" *Diario Las Americas*, 14 June 1981.

62. Managua Radio, 27 March 1981 (FBIS-Latin America, 30 March 1981) as cited in Valenta, "USSR, Cuba, and Crisis."

63. N.I. Gavtilov, G.B. Starushenko, eds., *Africa: Problems of Socialist Orientation* (Moscow: Nauka, 1976), pp. 10–11.

64. Charles A. Krause, "Nicaraguan Defense Minister Sets off on Arms-Buying Trip," *Washington Post*, 1 September 1979.

65. Speech to military specialists, 25 August 1981.

66. *Boston Globe*, 17 April 1981.

67. "Cuba's Renewed Support for Violence in the Hemisphere," (Research paper presented to the Subcommittee on Western Hemisphere

Affairs, Senate Foreign Relations Committee, by the Department of State, Washington, D.C., 14 December 1981).

68. Wolf Grabendorff, "Inter-State Conflict Behavior and Regional Potential for Conflict in Latin America" (Paper presented at a colloquium 25 June 1981, sponsored by the Latin American Program, Woodrow Wilson Center, Smithsonian Institution, Washington, D.C., 25 June 1981), p. 14.

69. Grabendorff, "Inter-State Conflict Behavior," p. 15.

70. Compare with *Prensa Libre* (Guatemala City), 20 May 1981; *Diario Las Americas*, 7 March 1981.

71. *Diario Las Americas*, 22 August 1981; *Washington Post*, 4 October 1981.

72. *Miami Herald*, 9 September 1981.

73. *Miami Herald*, 31 August 1981.

74. "Growing Arms Race in Central America May Heat up Region," *Christian Science Monitor*, 28 October 1981.

75. Cesar D. Sereseres, statement before the Subcommittee on Inter-American Affairs and Subcommittee on International Security and Scientific Affairs, U.S. House of Representatives, Washington, D.C., 22 October 1981, p. 13.

76. For a historical account of Venezuela's Caribbean initiatives, see Demetrio Boernser, *Venezuela y el Caribe presencia cambiante* (Caracas: Monte Avila Editores, 1978).

77. Robert Bond, "Venezuela, the Caribbean Basin, and the Crisis in Central America," Latin American Program, The Wilson Center, Washington, D.C., Working Paper, April 1981; 94, p. 5.

78. Franklin Tugwell, "Venezuelan Foreign Policy" (Mimeograph of unpublished manuscript, 1976), p. 22, cited in ibid., p. 4.

79. Lorenzo Meyer, "Cambio politico y dependencia: Mexico en el siglo XX"; Ricardo Valero, "La politica exterior de Mexico: El proyecto de Echeverria"; Eugenio Anguiano, "Mexico y el Tercer Mundo: racional-izacion de una posicion"; Mario Ojeda, "Mexico ante los Estados Unidos en 1977"; Jorge Castaneda, "En busca de una posicion ante Estados Unidos"; in *Lecturas de politica exterior mexicana*, (Mexico: Centro de Estudios Internacionales, El Colegio de Mexico, 1979). Mario Ojeda, "El poder negociador del petroleo: el caso de Mexico," and Samuel Berkstein, "Mexico: estrategia petrolera y politica exterior," in *Foro Nacional 81*, 21 (El Colegio de Mexico, Julio–Septiembre 1980). Olga Pellicer de Brody, "Cambios recientes en la politica exterior mexicana," *Foro Internacional* 13 (El Colegio de Mexico, Octobre–Diciembre 1972).

Scenario: Caribbean Basin Conflict

Jack Child

The Broad Politicomilitary Panorama

In general, the politicomilitary alignment in the mid-1980s is the product of trends already evident in the late 1970s and early 1980s, with due allowances for a limited but significant set of new factors.

In Central America a tightly polarized situation has emerged, coalescing around two antagonistic political and military groupings, which have some of the features of a bipolar alliance structure. On the one hand a group of Marxist-Leninist anti-United States regimes have consolidated their revolutions, and have developed strong economic and diplomatic ties to Cuba, the Soviet Union, and radical Arab nations; the ties include covert and overt support to a variety of revolutionary insurgencies in the area. Confronting this quasi-alliance is a loose coalition of conservative regimes with strong ties to the United States and the military regimes of South America; this coalition has a number of covert and overt links to exile groups that are active in raids and continuing attempts at mounting and supporting insurgencies within the Marxist-Leninist states of the area.

In South America the conflict panorama is dominated by a delicately poised balance-of-power system. The system evolved in the Southern Cone as a result of the strongly geopolitical framework favored by the military regimes that have been in power since the 1960s and 1970s. The multination balance-of-power system is slowly being destabilized by the continuing emergence of Brazil as a dominant regional hegemonic power (a trend strongly resisted by Argentina). There also exists the possibility that a mistake, irrational act, or local breakdown of control at any one of several tension points might cause the balance-of-power system to break down and involve most of the South American nations in military hostilities.

A number of other factors have complicated Inter-American relations, have exacerbated these conflicts, and made other confrontations more likely:

1. There has been a continual decline in the ability of the United States to influence events and control conflict in the hemisphere. United States power has declined relative to the capabilities of other nations of the area, and there is a strong shift to multipolarity and diffusion of power.

2. There has been a parallel general loss of confidence in the Organization of American States (OAS) and its peacekeeping and mediatory mecha-

nisms. The old (and reasonably effective) methods of settling territorial and nonideological disputes of the past have proven almost impotent in the face of current ideological polarization, competition for resources, geopolitical doctrines, and the increasing military capabilities of a number of hemisphere nations.

3. A variety of unsettling economic events have made international cooperation more difficult. These events have included several national near-bankruptcies, defaults on loans from international banking institutions, oil-price shocks, various attempts at cartels, and competition for sea-bottom and ocean resources.

4. Economic and political unrest in Central America, the Caribbean, and Mexico has led to major migrations into the southwestern United States and Florida. This in turn has caused the U.S. government to try to seal the Mexican border with an expanded Immigration and Naturalization Service (supported by U.S. military units) and turn back all vessels carrying illegal immigrants. One result of these actions has been increasing tension between Anglo-America and Latin America in both international and internal terms.

5. The United States can count on few allies for help in facing this bewildering variety of problems. The Atlantic Alliance has weakened, and the European nations have taken stands generally critical of U.S. actions in Latin America. This criticism is echoed by most of the Latin American nations, although with a certain ambiguity stemming from concern over spreading Cuban influence in Central America and the Caribbean. The strongest hemisphere supporters of the United States tend to be the reactionary regimes in Central America, whose very existence depends on continued U.S. economic and military aid; despite this dependence, U.S. attempts to persuade these regimes to institute reforms have been largely ineffective.

Ideological Polarization, Interstate Conflict, and Guerrilla Warfare

The Actors

The Caribbean Basin conflict scene is dominated by an ideological polarization that has led to the formation of two loose politico-military alliances.

The Progressive Central American Self-Defense Organization (PROCASDO) is the first alliance, consisting of the Marxist-Leninist revolutionary states of Nicaragua, El Salvador, and Belize. PROCASDO has close ties to Cuba, the Soviet Union, and radical Arab nations and exerts strong pressure on Costa Rica and Panama to maintain their anti-United States neutrality. PROCASDO supports insurgencies in Guatemala and Honduras overtly through rhetoric, recognition, and safe havens and covertly through training, logistics, and access to the international arms markets. Direct Cuban involvement in these insurgencies has been long suspected, but little convincing proof has surfaced.

The remnants of the old Central American Defense Council (CONDECA) is the other alliance, consisting of Guatemala and Honduras, with close links to the United States and several of the military regimes of the Southern Cone. Like PROCASDO, CONDECA supports insurgencies at the overt and covert levels, making extensive use of the anti-Marxist exiles who came out of Cuba, Nicaragua, and El Salvador.

The other major actors involved include:

1. The Caribbean Falange, a loose network of exiled military officers, politicians, and supporters who left Nicaragua and El Salvador as those revolutionary regimes gradually lost their pluralistic nature and came under the control of Marxist-Leninist hard-liners. The Falange has close ties with the Cuban exile anti-Castro community, with CONDECA, with the U.S. government, and with insurgents within Nicaragua and El Salvador.

2. Several international liberation solidarity brigades, with varying degrees of dependency on PROCASDO. The brigades are made up of volunteers from Mexico, Costa Rica, Panama, Colombia, Venezuela, and the United States, and individual brigade members have appeared among the insurgents in Guatemala and Honduras.

3. Mercenaries and adventurers from Europe, Africa, and the United States.

4. The United States, which continues to support the CONDECA alliance (overtly) and the Caribbean Falange (covertly).

5. Cuba, which provides PROCASDO and the international liberation solidarity brigades with advice, training, arms, and leads to arms sources.

6. The Soviet Union, which continues to take advantage of a low-cost and low-risk opportunity to distract the United States from its NATO and European concerns and causes it to tie down major elements of its security assets in the western hemisphere.

7. Radical Arab nations and terrorist groups, which see in the Central American situation an opportunity to distract the United States from its historic support of Israel and moderate Arab states.

Other Considerations

A major by-product of the years of conflict in Central America has been the large numbers of refugees and dislocated persons who have sought to enter the United States, along with Caribbean refugees attempting to leave the economic chaos of their own countries. Mexican authorities have not been able to control entry of these refugees into southern Mexico and have tried to solve their own problem by transporting the refugees to northern Mexico and encouraging them to enter the United States illegally. Internal Mexican economic and political unrest has produced additional numbers of un-documenteds. The net result has been a quantum jump in illegal immigration into the United States via the Mexican-U.S. border and by sea to Florida and the Gulf Coast. The overwhelming flow of refugees has produced a strong backlash within the United States and has led to a sealing of the Mexican-U.S. border and a strengthening of U.S. Navy and Coast Guard patrols in the Gulf of Mexico and the Caribbean.

The Central American and Caribbean situation has had important repercussions within the United States. Key Hispanic-U.S. political organizations in the Southwest and Florida have protested alleged mistreatment of refugees at the border and have expressed solidarity with either PRO-CASDO or CONDECA forces, thus mirroring the Central American polarization within the U.S. Hispanic community. Important U.S. Catholic leaders have strongly supported progressive Catholic movements in Central America and have condemned U.S. government support to CONDECA. The need to reinstitute the draft has led to a wave of student protest movements on many U.S. campuses, a current that has found a lively issue in the question of possible U.S. military intervention in the area.

The OAS has not been capable of making a contribution to resolving these conflicts because of their complexity and the suspicion of the predominant (albeit diminished) U.S. role in the organization. Nevertheless, the United Nations, and especially a group of third-world nations in it, have made strong overtures to providing a mediatory effort linked to a neutral peacekeeping force to man a series of demilitarized zones between the PROCASDO and CONDECA countries.

New Variables

Historians eventually came to refer to the 1980s as the "decade of natural and unnatural disasters in the Caribbean Basin." The reference to unnatural disasters stemmed from the sharp PROCASDO-CONDECA polarization, and the natural-disaster-decade label came from a devastating series of hurricanes and volcanic eruptions that caused untold human dislocation and economic chaos. Private and international relief agencies were overwhelmed by the magnitude of the disasters and the relief-effort demands; as a result, military units of the United States and Cuba quickly became involved. Ironically, the disasters provided a rare opportunity for cooperation between the United States and Cuba.

Political and social instability in Mexico caused major concern in the mid-1980s; demographic pressures and a sense of frustrated rising expectation fueled the unrest. Astrologers and the superstitious waited for the "second Mexican revolution" to break out with the arrival of Halley's Comet in 1986 (it was remembered that the 1910 appearance of the comet was widely seen as an omen and augur of the Mexican revolution). Events in Mexico, the massive wave of undocumented immigrants, and reaction to the sealing of the border found an echo in the U.S. Hispanic community and in particular among a small group of political activists who began to press for greater political power and autonomy in the Southwest.

The seemingly interminable emergence of numerous weak and economically fragile ministates in the Eastern Caribbean was arrested in the 1980s as these vulnerable countries formed a series of modest but viable federations and became an important moderating force in the search for solutions to the Central American crisis. A similar role was played by Canada, which gradually established closer ties with the Caribbean Basin nations and applied its long-standing policy of acting as the "helpful fixer" to numerous conflict situations in this area.

An unexpected new factor in the conflict picture was the emergence of Pan-Mayan sentiment among the Indians of southern Mexico, Guatemala, Honduras, and Belize and a parallel Pan-Miskito sentiment among the Caribbean populations of Nicaragua and Honduras. These groups, which had for centuries been politically isolated and apathetic, went through a process of political-consciousness raising as a result of the CONDECA-PROCASDO polarization. Both groups attempted to gain their political and military support, with PROCASDO initially making the greater gains, especially in Guatemala. However, the end result of this process seemed to be a plague-on-both-your-houses sentiment, and in the mid-1980s transnational native movements became a major political force in their own right, separate from either one of the two major ideological groupings.

Interstate Tensions

The following interstate antagonisms have emerged from the politicomilitary scenario described.

Honduras–El Salvador. The strains between these two countries are deeply rooted in demographic problems, the 1969 war, conflicting territorial claims, and the general Central American polarization. The difficult terrain along the border provides ideal sites for base camps for the numerous groups of exiles and guerrillas operating in support of insurgents in both countries.

Honduras–Nicaragua. This situation is less tense than the previous one; it involves the presence of elements of the Caribbean Falange (mainly remnants of Somoza's Guardia Nacional and the prerevolutionary military of El Salvador). A significant portion of the Nicaraguan Ejército Popular Sandinista (the regular army) and supporting Sandinista militia has been moved to the Honduras-Nicaragua border in an attempt to control incursions into Nicaragua by the Falange.

Guatemala–Belize. The tensions here are rooted in strong nationalism, the historic Guatemalan claim to Belize, the belief that there are major oil deposits in the border area, and the presence of Cuban and Nicaraguan security advisors in revolutionary Belize. The Guatemalan military regime has requested increased U.S. military assistance on the grounds that these Cuban and Nicaraguan advisors are the spearhead of an invasion force.

Panama–United States. Panama's neutralism in Central America's polarization has always tended to tilt toward the PROCASDO side, especially whenever Panamanians and leftists and nationalists are able to exploit latent anti-U.S. sentiment. The most fertile ground for generating this deeply felt sentiment is a series of seemingly minor problems and irritants that stemmed from the process of implementing the 1977 treaties. The treaty-implementation process has been subject to constant strains and quibbling on both sides; incidents of harassment, sabotage, and terrorism (to include highjackings and the brief occupation of the U.S. embassy in late 1984) have been accompanied by frequent demonstrations by Panamanian labor unions and student groups. A reinforcement of U.S. military units in Panama has improved security (from the U.S. perspective), but it has also exacerbated Panamanian hostility and heightened the potential for continuing tensions and a further breakdown of the treaty-implementation process. Panama has been highly successful in obtaining Latin American and third-world support for an acceleration of the 1979–1999 transition timetable.

Insurgencies

As indicated, the principal insurgencies in the area are in: Nicaragua, along the Caribbean Miskito coast; Guatemala, in the Northeast Petén area; Mexico's Chiapas State (linked to the Petén and Pan-Mayan movements); Honduras, related to border conflicts with El Salvador and Nicaragua. In addition, the long-simmering insurgency in Colombia turned more serious in the 1980s, as economic malaise and the corruption of the drug trade increased public distrust of the government. The traditional culture of violence (*"La Violencia"*) provided fertile soil for diverse guerrilla groups, which unified under a single political-military front in 1984 and posed an increasingly grave threat to the shaky regime in Bogotá.

Other Tension Areas

A number of other situations of potential conflict which will not be discussed here in detail because of their lower tension level, should also be noted in passing: Colombia-Venezuela: the Gulf of Venezuela maritime-boundary dispute; Venezuela-Guyana: the Essequibo River claim; Guyana-Suriname: the New River Triangle claim; Haiti-Dominican Republic: migration and racial conflict; Puerto Rican independence movements, which became especially intense after the U.S. Congress rejected Puerto Rico's request for statehood on the grounds that no clear majority had been demonstrated in the referendum; Cuban-U.S. tensions over Guantánamo, including some limited Cuban incursions into the base; and the rise of transnational Rastafarian fundamentalism in the various Eastern Caribbean federations.

Conclusions

The scenarios developed here suggest that in the mid-1980s the United States might have to respond to a broad range of requirements within the hemisphere:

Military assistance to CONDECA (Guatemala and Honduras).

Support to exile insurgent groups operating in Nicaragua and El Salvador.

Sealing of the land border with Mexico; naval patrols to control illegal immigration to Florida and the Gulf Coast.

Responding to internal unrest in the United States, to include resistance to the draft and the emergency of radical anti-intervention movements.

Major disaster-relief operations.

Reacting to Guatemala's request for assistance to counter the Cuban-Nicaraguan presence in Belize.

Stepped-up defense of the Panama Canal, especially against threats of riots and sabotage.

Antiterrorist operations, to include responses to the seizing of U.S. embassies, aircraft, and ships.

Logistical and other support of peacekeeping operations.

Some fundamental caveats need to be stressed at this point. Several of these military responses involve intervention and unilateral action by the

United States. As such, they represent a regression to policies that have cost the United States a high price in the past, in terms of Latin American resentment and hostility. Many of these responses would probably also involve a political price of another sort in terms of internal opposition and domestic unrest in the United States.

Lastly, included among these responses are some that would in all likelihood be interpreted as confrontational and aggressive and would probably elicit an equally aggressive response and a spiraling of tensions. For these reasons, any consideration of these military responses must also include a careful analysis of the cost and dangers in spheres remote from normal military considerations.

18 African Crisis and Conflict in an Era of Unanticipated Sovereignty

Bruce E. Arlinghaus

A review of the political events of the past decade in Africa indicates clearly that Africans can look forward to increased crisis and conflict during the 1980s. Although this estimate to some extent is accurate, there have been significant changes in the African political environment that indicate that, although the levels of tension and violence in the region may continue, the forms that these events take may change significantly. This chapter analyzes the changing environment, identifies factors or variables most likely to influence crisis and conflict, and describes the most likely forms that will occur in this decade. At the same time, however, a tentative prediction is made: although conflict and crisis are likely to continue dominating the African political scene, the ongoing process of modernization and maturation will result in a pronounced tendency toward consolidation and stability in the region, at least internally, as Africans seek more conservative solutions to problems of social and economic change.

A New Era

Africa is entering a new era, one of unanticipated sovereignty. There are a number of reasons for this development (and indicators that it is in fact occurring), and the concept itself requires some definition and explanation.

A recurring element in African political thought since World War II has been the expressed desire for independence, or political, social, and economic autonomy for all Africans. But realistically, these goals could be achieved only gradually, not by fiat. What many Africans sought to express through participation in the nonaligned movement was a desire for sovereignty, the ability to design and control their individual and collective destinies free from neocolonial or superpower interference. Yet implicit in these statements, such as those demanding a new world economic order, was a tacit recognition that African nations were neither economically nor politically self-sufficient and would continue to be dependent on other nations for assistance, aid, and support as they made the gradual transition from colonial to sovereign status.

Because of changes in the world economy and the balance of strategic

373

power in recent years, this sovereignty has been either accelerated or thrust on African nations in ways that have been neither expected nor accepted. For good or bad, African nations rapidly are becoming freed from the burden of dependency, not because they no longer need or desire the assistance which such relations represent but simply because help is no longer available in the form, or to the degree, it was before. Thus, true African sovereignty has been unanticipated, and this change has had critical consequences for future political change.

The concept of sovereignty in this context also pertains to the nature of international-power dependence. For many developed nations, the fundamental interdependence of the world economy is an accepted fact, but for many Africans it is difficult to integrate such a concept with their own perceptions of independence. From their perspective, the North possesses, dominates, and controls world economic power, and Africans are required to submit to this dominance to be given even a subordinate role in the international marketplace. For them, the demands of the International Monetary Fund, for example, are not just a simple prerequisite for financial assistance; rather they are deliberate attempts to force Africa into an alien mold and thus an impingement of their rights as sovereign nations. Since they are resource-poor and dependent on the developed nations, African states must in many cases conform to the demands in order to survive economically. Their collective perceptions view the system as unfair and unjust, no matter how necessary.

Although it is difficult to generalize over such a broad and diverse region as Subsaharan Africa, several trends have emerged to demarcate clearly this era from those euphoric times immediately following independence in the late 1950s and early 1960s. First, and perhaps foremost, has been the passage of time and generations. The generation of Africans who wrested independence from the colonial powers is passing rapidly into eclipse as they retire, die, or are overwhelmed by a growing and increasingly younger population.[5] Although these leaders remain inspirational, unifying figures, they are being displaced by a new generation for whom the anticolonial struggle and experience are history, whose aspirations and world view are focused beyond the immediate, postindependence era. The new generation retains traditional African values regarding respect for their elders, admiring the persistence and courage demonstrated during the fight for freedom, but recognizing more urgent development and modernization problems, which they want resolved within their own lifetimes.[6] Lacking the perspective possessed by their elders, they simply will not accept freedom as sufficient in the face of rising expectations. Their elders may not be completely satisfied with the present situation, but many young Africans view them as complacent and, in fact, impotent in the face of serious economic and social issues. To say "be patient, see how far we have come" is not acceptable to the new generation.

Many might argue that recent coups in Liberia and elsewhere indicate that this generation is more prone to political violence. Although Southern Africa, which has lagged approximately fifteen years behind other African regions (Angola and Mozambique became independent in the mid-1970s), is characterized by liberation movements, elsewhere the dominant impression gained by talking to younger Africans is that the disruptive, counterproductive effects of violent regime change are to be avoided as much as possible.

As a result, the new generation represents a more pragmatic political element, retaining the idealism of their elders but not their romanticism. They realistically accept that former colonial nations and the superpowers have changed as well—that immediately following African independence, the Cold War, Vietnam, détente, and the world economic recession (brought on by the oil crisis) have reordered drastically their priorities and relationships with the developing world.

The policies of nations such as the United States have also matured, recognizing the strategic importance of Africa and appreciating the magnitude of its economic and social problems. The optimism of the early 1960s has evaporated as both African and developed countries realized that neither enthusiasm nor dollars alone work economic miracles. This has produced a curious contradiction: as the world has become more economically interdependent, Africans, because of investment and development-resource shortages, have in a sense become more independent, falling farther behind the developed nations in terms not only of real growth but also of their ability to meet basic human needs. In short, although some economic miracles have occurred elsewhere, they have not happened in Africa. The restructuring of world economic power represented by the steady rise in the cost of energy has devastated the fledgling economies of most African countries, at the same time causing their primary sources of aid to be reduced when needed most.

This economic crisis has served as a catalyst in transforming African countries from semisovereign to truly independent states in a radical and unanticipated manner. Immediately following independence, sovereignty was actively pursued and abstractly cherished, but it was certainly not expected to take such a shocking form. Africa's social and economic problems were to be solved through international cooperation and the assistance of developed nations, especially former colonial powers for whom it was a moral responsibility to somehow undo the inequities of imperialism. Such responsibility may remain, but it now constitutes a luxury that few developed countries perceive they can afford. Since both the will and means to assist Africa have eroded in real terms, Africans have finally achieved a sort of de facto economic independence created by the present inability or unwillingness of other countries to solve their problems. It is a status that Africans have both sought and feared for twenty or more years, reflected in the curious love-hate relations between former colonies and colonial powers that have characterized the past two decades.[12] This finally has caused some to question quietly, with hindsight, the wisdom of independence at the price of economic catastrophe.

Heightening the disillusionment that such economic conditions create has been the realization on the part of many young Africans that despite the idealism and rhetoric of the independence era, their leaders seemed destined to commit many of the same errors of pettiness, injustice, and corruption as their former colonial masters. Tribal and ethnic rivalries continue within African nations, unmoderated by any sense of public service or patriotism.[13] Although foreigners are often viewed with suspicion as potential neocolonialists, they are welcomed frequently as immune to institutionalized corruption, placing more value on ability rather than heredity.[14] This grates particularly on African sensibilities: to see members of a former colonial power behaving more sensitively and fairly toward fellow Africans than their own ethnic or economic elites.

Compounding these discords internally is the apparent rapid disintegration of intra-African solidarity.[15] Majority rule in South Africa seems the only cause that unites Africans today.[16] Irredentism, market competition, support of revolutionary movements in neighboring countries, and even armed conflicts otherwise characterize relations among African nations. Although such actions are typical of sovereign nations, there appeared at least initially a glimmer of hope that the newly independent African nations would rise above them to resolve disagreements peacefully in a spirit of solidarity and cooperation. Dismaying as this disintegration may be, it also has had the practical effect of weakening what political clout African nations could wield as a bloc, thus lessening their importance to the superpowers.[17] Those countries lacking either strategic resources or location have found themselves ignored further when existing aid is allocated, thus heightening their resentment. The perception that their more strategically blessed neighbors are somehow profiting at their expense weakens solidarity even more.

Finally, it appears that even nature has conspired against Africa. Just as the world economic crisis began to blossom and internal and external political conflict became a regular rather than occasional occurrence, a decade of drought has caused massive refugee populations, human suffering, and almost irreparable damage to the social, economic, and political fiber of African nations.[18] Heightening the retarding efforts natural catastrophes have had on economic progress has been the perception that most developed nations, compared with their concern for Cuban, Vietnamese, and Cambodian refugees, have more or less abandoned Africans to resolve their own problems and resources, at least until recently. The new generation recognizes, perhaps somewhat cynically, that they are now, more than ever, independent and must go it alone as sovereign nations.

Factors Influencing Crisis and Conflict

The new sense of political pragmatism engendered by unanticipated sovereignty constitutes a new environment for crisis and conflict in Africa. The recognition that rapid regime change creates instability, coupled with a desire to seek long-term solutions to social and economic problems, will bring about significant changes in the forms and levels of political violence. Africa has moved rapidly through an accelerated period similar to that experienced by Latin America in the last century—an initial period of violent military coups and eventually an era of imposed stability. To an extent, Africa has conformed to this model, with the exception that external international involvement has been much greater than it was in Latin America and that the final stage of stability, rather than being imposed by a military elite, is in fact emerging as a reaction to the excesses and instability of praetorianism.

Within this new environment a number of internal and external variables will affect crisis and conflict in Africa during the 1980s. Although several variables overlap and are manifest in a variety of forms, for discussion purposes they have been divided into two categories based on their origin: whether they are internal or external to individual African nations. They are not ranked by severity or probability; they are discussed as an interrelated set of factors in the African political milieu.

Internal Factors

One-Party States. The predominant form of political organization in Subsaharan Africa is the one-party state.[19] At first glance, it would appear that these parties serve as remarkably efficient groups for unifying the diverse ethnic and tribal populations that constitute the majority of African nations and provide an excellent basis for formulating and implementing development policy. With few exceptions, however, this has not been the case. While the single-party political organization was perhaps the most essential step for unifying and coordinating the independence movement, once this goal has been achieved only the illusion of unity remained.[20] One-party states, by limiting or even suppressing other political groups, stifle opposition and criticism and promote internal factionalism. This internal strife, exemplified in the process of resource allocation and the appointment of government officials, retards the process of orderly political and economic change in several ways.

Programs designed and supported by party elites, however inefficient or inappropriate, usually are jealously guarded from criticism. Any opposition to them is perceived as an attempt to either fragment the unity of the organization, and thus the nation, or to displace the elite that originally designed them. An example of this has been the persistent promotion of African socialism and the *ujamaa* ("brotherhood," a collectivization of villages) program in Tanzania despite its negative impact on economic growth and development in the country.[21] Party ideology has, in this case, stifled the flexibility necessary for any developing nation to survive in the current world economy. The need to discipline party members and control the media, and in so doing redefine reality to fit party ideology, can have perilous consequences for stability and growth over the long run. As the new generation emerges, they will increase pressure on their elders to change or adapt party programs. Unfortunately, those who have adhered to the party line will be most likely to succeed to elite positions, yet they lack precisely those qualities necessary to achieve the goals and desires of their peers. This may result in increased agitation for a more pluralistic system, promoting both crisis and conflict.

A second outgrowth of the one-party state is the pervasive politicization of all aspects of national life. Aside from the impact this has on individual freedom and the desire or ability of the public to participate in the political process, it stifles creativity and positive change. In Tanzania, excessive party involvement at the village level has resulted in alienation on the part of the masses and increased resentment toward the central government. This is manifested in noncooperation, black marketeering, and smuggling. Seen as criminal activities, they are often accompanied by violent resistance to police and paramilitary forces.[22]

Finally, although the one-party state may effectively subordinate the population in the short run, its inefficiency, lack of representation, and internal fragmentation will in the long run promote crisis and conflict. As new elites emerge, there will be an inevitable struggle for power and dominance. With the absence of a legal, recognized, and loyal opposition, the only recourse of the disenfranchised and frustrated will be extragovernmental and violent means to express themselves and effect change. Although some one-party states, notably Kenya and the Ivory Coast, have succeeded in achieving some of their economic, social, and political goals, this progress has been accompanied by liberal political and ideological constraints.[23] The question remains, however, whether other African nations will, in the absence of violent political change, effectively evolve more liberal and efficient political institutions that would reduce the causes of conflict.

Charismatic Leaders. Closely associated with one-party states and their evolution in Africa are a number of charismatic leaders who have demonstrated remarkable endurance and political astuteness. Comparable perhaps only to George Washington in the United States or Simon Bolivar in

Latin America, these men are treated with respect and reverence unequaled by other political leaders. They have, in many cases, succeeded in providing a focal point for both nation and party when internal rivalries and strife threatened unity or the development of a coherent plan for achieving national goals. To some extent, because of their influence, multiparty systems became impossible, since opposition to the leader and his party would somehow tarnish his popular image and detract from his status as the sole head of both country and political structure.[24]

Unfortunately, these leaders are rapidly approaching the end of their careers and the question is not whether they will be replaced but rather when and by whom.[25] At issue is peaceful transition and, in an environment in which party factions, including the military, have been carefully balanced to preclude their threatening the party leader, it is difficult to select and prepare a successor. Only two options exist to preclude the emergence of crisis and conflict on the death of a charismatic leader. The first is the Kenyatta option, in which a failing Jomo Kenyatta gradually transferred power to his vice-president, ensuring his acceptance as an interim leader and finally as the elected president.[26] When Daniel arap Moi ran for reelection he was unopposed, having already been elected to party leadership. The campaign he ran was designed to secure a popular mandate for his programs and cement his dominance within the party structure. The second option is the retirement option taken by Leopold Senghor in Senegal. He selected a successor prior to retirement, then used his considerable popular support and position as an elder statesman to guide and enforce the transition. Houphouët-Boigny of the Ivory Coast has apparently decided to follow this lead by creating a position of vice-president, to be filled in the 1983 elections.

While it can be assumed that leaders such as Nyerere of Tanzania, Banda of Malawi, Touré of Guinea, and Kaunda of Zambia have considered this problem, speculation remains regarding their succession, since no successors have been designated or plans for retirement announced. Some of these leaders may leave office for political reasons (for example, Mobutu of Zaire or Kaunda), but the chances of a premature demise make the probability of sudden and violent internal wars of succession very likely, especially where the charismatic leader so identifies with his programs as to make either option unlikely.

Military Regimes. Similar to the charismatic leaders are military strongmen or leaders who have emerged by their own seizure of power or by that of a ruling junta or council that had previously overthrown the civilian rule. Although it is appealing to view these men as power-hungry and corrupt despots who have sought only to establish their own authoritarian state, their motives and actions are exceedingly more complex. Although such military rulers as Amin of Uganda and Bokassa of the Central African Republic gained notoriety for ruthlessly consolidating control of their countries and promoting their own personal cult, they enjoyed, both initially and after their downfalls, a great deal of popular support.[27]

Western scholars and many Africans shared a perception that the military in developing countries is potentially the most efficient and unifying institution for nation building or political modernization.[28] Possessing a national consciousness, the military was expected to provide the coherence and organization lacking in civilian regimes subject to the tribal and ethnic rivalries that often underlie the factionalism of the one-party state. Public expectations were high, as the "man on horseback" was seen as perhaps the only means to purge bureaucratic corruption and reorient national goals. Given the tradition of strong charismatic leadership in African states, it is understandable that someone like Lieutenant Jerry Rawlins could seize power several times in Ghana, perceiving the need to serve his country and meeting with genuine popular support for his actions.[29]

Yet what has been so disappointing to some scholars and the public is the recognition that military leaders frequently decline to return power to civilians after it has been seized. In addition, as individuals or as a class, the military is as prone to factionalism, tribalism, corruption, and inefficiency as their predecessors. In only a few cases have military regimes successfully transferred power back to civilians (either by election or appointment), and more frequently they have acted only to consolidate their own power within the country.[30] Perceiving calls for civilian rule as threats and perpetuating the corrupt practices of the past, they have in turn made themselves vulnerable to countercoups.[31] Although some regimes—Sudan, Egypt, Ethiopia, Zaire, and others—have broadened to quasi-civilian status, they persist on a basis of military power.

In the numerous military regimes in Africa, the prospects for crisis and conflict are perhaps greatest of all because the tendency has been for coup to follow coup. Since the military possess a monopoly of coercive force and the training and propensity to use it, they and their opponents are more likely to engage in widespread and violent conflict. Insurgencies, support of governments in exile, cross-border military involvement by supporters (such as the Tanzanian support of Amin's overthrow), and escalation of the conflict involving regular forces from neighboring states are increasing in frequency and intensity, despite the success of the Organization of African Unity (OAU) so far to keep such intervention to a minimum.[32]

This propensity for military adventurism is especially alarming, since many military regimes have increased both the size and quality of their military forces. Not only are more men under arms, but their weapons have increased in sophistication and lethality. Whereas before, many African armies were clearly for internal-security purposes, they now possess or will soon possess the potential for cross-border force projections or simple coercive diplomacy toward their neighbors.

Tribalism, Corruption, and Separatism. Although issues of political succession, party structure, and military rule will remain the most likely sources of crisis and conflict in the 1980s, there are a number of residual factors that will continue to influence both the causes and forms of political violence throughout the decade. Perhaps the most insidious of these is tribalism. Although it is possible that wholesale massacres of ethnic groups will not reoccur elsewhere as they did in Rwanda, or that an ethnically based civil war will not begin such as in Nigeria/Biafra, the strong undercurrent of ethnic tension will continue to contribute to political factionalism, instability, and popular unrest.

Tribalism continues to manifest itself in two principal ways: through nepotism and through separatist movements. In the majority of African, as well as most other developing, nations corruption is both endemic and institutionalized. Extortion of bribes from local and expatriate businessmen for the performance of the simplest of governmental functions and open skimming of government revenues (to include foreign aid) are commonplace in many countries, to varying degrees. In itself a debilitating practice, it is intensified because family and ethnic ties cause corruption to reach staggering proportions. Positions in both the private and public sector are filled frequently on the basis of nepotism or to ensure the dominance of one tribe over others. Such favoritism breeds resentment on the part of other ethnic groups and leads frequently to civil disturbances. Even worse, in the long run, it fosters an avarice-oriented system in which rival factions seek economic power when opportunity arises, without care or reference to the future welfare of the country. This attitude has in many ways been a key factor leading to the inability of military regimes to foster nationalism and to halt the seemingly endless cycle of coup and countercoup.

The second way in which tribalism has been manifested is in the form of regional or separatist movements. To a certain extent these movements are prompted and supported by irredentist feelings in neighboring countries, but frequently they are caused by more basic economic factors. The natural resources of Africa are not evenly distributed among nations or even within them. Certain regions, such as Shaba Province in Zaire, possess high concentrations of mineral or other resources that are exported to the world market. The foreign exchange that these exports generate, and the benefits they purchase, are usually spread among the total population to varying degrees. Since most ethnic or tribal groups are homogeneous within national regions (with the exception of urban areas and where different groups live in a traditional symbiotic relationship), those groups whose region provided the natural resources frequently feel that other ethnic groups are exploiting them, cheating them of their birthright as it were. This is especially true where one tribal group dominates in the government bureaucracy and is totally distinct from the ethnic group or region from which the natural resources are exported (for example, oil discoveries in southern Sudan). The notion of a resource war has special relevance in many African nations as a source of renewed tribal tensions and competition. Even in southern Africa, competing revolutionary groups in Angola and Zimbabwe are more ethnically than ideologically homogeneous, and the ties to tradition are stronger than those to any political philosophy.[39]

Many cultural stereotypes persist regarding the roles of certain ethnic groups in their respective nations, but many of the charismatic leaders mentioned have been at least partially successful in overcoming or at least controlling tribalism. In Kenya, for example, many business and government officials attribute much of their economic success to Kenyatta's deliberate strategy of restraining ethnic rivalries, permitting each ethnic group to contribute to the overall development of the nation those qualities for which they are most commonly noted.[40] Yet resentment lingers, and despite the strategic move of appointing a successor from a minority tribe and thus precluding a major tribe from becoming too strong in national political and economic affairs, perceptions persist that the Luo, Kikuyu, or Somalis are becoming too influential, especially in education and commerce.

Many of the causes of corruption in African countries may be attributed to the colonial powers and their deliberate use of tribal and ethnic rivalries to subdue and govern colonial populations, but the roots of these perceptions and resentments are deep and they existed before colonization and exploitation.[41] Unfortunately, colonial government was designed for administration rather than local rule, and it resulted in the postindependence "soft state," an environment extremely vulnerable to continued exploitation by those groups or individuals who have become ruling elites by virtue of their dominance in modernizing institutions (as opposed to traditional institutions).[42] The pervasive influence of tribalism also affected the military, since recruitment of colonial military and police forces was often limited to one or a few ethnic groups, and tribal differences were reflected in the differential recruitment and education of officers, noncommissioned officers, enlisted men, and the various armed services.[43]

Tribalism, and the corruption and separatism that it has bred, places ruling elites in a perpetual state of crisis, giving a significant segment of the population traditional rather than ideological grounds for supporting violent overthrow of the government. This potential for conflict is further increased by reticence on the part of developed countries and investors to contribute to the economic growth of those countries where corruption and unrest are prevalent. This reduces available resources and limits the opportunities for equitable development. For many countries, the stability represented by a strongman is misleading. In Zaire, for example, Mobutu apparently cannot control corruption (many consider him the model of corruption) and the drain on economic resources that it represents. The economic obstacles to African development are enormous, and they will never be overcome until internal, ethnically based discord and corruption are eliminated.

Urbanization, Unemployment, and Economic Failure. The inequities and inefficiencies of tribalism and corruption would be tolerable, and in a sense controllable, if economic growth had followed independence. Although many African nations and leaders have attempted to blame this failure on external factors, there is increasing realization on the part of many Africans that fault lies closer to home, in their own inability to overcome elitism and tribalism to solve their own problems through efficiency in the allocation and conservation of resources. There also is recognition that elites are often urban-based and that, although tribalism is an important factor, immediate political demands are most often made by groups that are urbanized, acculturated, and politicized, groups that the government finds the most threatening. Although rural populations hold regional grievances against the government (because agricultural and mineral commodities are located in rural areas), they form a fragmented and therefore less coherent and visible political opposition. Unemployed urban dwellers, however, disgruntled over the absence of the opportunities that originally attracted them to the city and rising food prices, housing shortages, and the failure of social services, could be mobilized easily and manipulated by a rival faction to topple a government in a series of violent civil disturbances. In Liberia, the stage was set for the overthrow of the Tolbert regime by the rice riots that preceded it, giving Master Sergeant Doe both the motivation and means for his coup. In other instances, the political crises precipitated by urban discontent over economic failure may be used easily by Marxist or other groups as a basis for insurgent groups that offer more sweeping social and economic reforms.

A final internal factor that is growing in importance is the use of Islamic fundamentalism. Although externally stimulated by events in the Middle East, and perhaps capitalized on by leaders such as Qaddafi, the large populations in those African nations north of the equator are a vulnerable and volatile political element that cannot be ignored. Although religious differences have been important in some past conflicts (for example, Sudan), Islamic revivalism actually forms an added dimension to tribalism and resource conflict, since Islamic populations tend to be ethnically and religiously homogeneous.

External Factors

The variables influencing crisis and conflict in Subsaharan Africa that arise from sources external to individual nations fall roughly into two categories: those sources that are intra-African and those that are extra-African, dealing with superpowers, former colonial powers, and other nonaligned nations.

Intra-African Conflict. The factors that have shaped and will continue to shape crisis and conflict among African nations generally stem from the colonial era and the partition of Africa at the Berlin Conference of 1885. Although many of these issues can be traced directly to the unnatural and unrealistic borders imposed by the colonial powers, the changes described in internal African politics and in the general political environment of the new era have caused these issues to take on new dimensions.[49]

For example, the problem of irredentism is cited frequently as one of the most difficult for African nations. Tribalism has external aspects, since ethnolinguistic differences and similarities have created the desire on the part of many Africans to redraw the map of the region to achieve a degree of ethnolinguistic homogeneity. Whether these creations would constitute viable nations—since Africa contains over 800 distinctive ethnolinguistic groups—is a moot point and makes such proposals as unrealistic as they are improbable.[50] Yet, like the tribalism from which it originates, irredentism in contemporary Africa may be a disguise for deeper economic issues.

Somalia, for example, is one of the few African nations that is virtually ethnolinguistically homogeneous. Yet there are ethnic Somalis who reside in neighboring states such as Kenya and Ethiopia, and as such they are the basis for Somali claims to neighboring territory. The border dispute between Kenya and Somalia is considered by both sides to be more an emotional than political issue, and ethnic Somalis are being assimilated into Kenyan society.[51] The dispute between Somalia and Ethiopia, however, is much more severe because of the belief on the part of both parties that vast mineral resources lie below the surface of the Ogaden Desert, and ultimately access to these resources motivates continued irredentism of the Somalis.[52] Although not the principal cause of the conflict, resources may give it a new dimension that will increase in importance as the economic crisis heightens.

Border conflicts between neighboring states continue to flare up over more straightforward issues, such as access to and use of navigable bodies of water and control of marine resources (such as oil).[53] Nations possessing these resources guard them jealously—those who desire them can only hope to annex them after the provocations of their neighbors or on the pretext of establishing order in a border region. Perhaps the most common pretext is the intervention of military forces to assist incumbent neighboring governments or to support revolutionary groups.[54]

Senegalese forces were invited into the Gambia in 1981 to defuse a coup, and nations served as peacekeeping forces to assist their neighbors in time of instability and political unrest. More common, however, is that irredentism, or the desire to install a more cooperative regime, has caused many states to intervene militarily in their neighbors' affairs. Providing a base for governments in exile or sanctuaries for insurgent groups has led to conflicts where neighboring states' military forces in hot pursuit have violated the territory of the state harboring them, only to be confronted by regular forces of its neighbor poised for a counterstrike.

Recently, there have been as many as 73,000 South African troops in Namibia, 2,700 Senegalese in the Gambia, 11,000 Libyan and 900 Nigerian troops in Chad, and 1,000 Tanzanian troops remaining in Uganda. It is difficult in most cases to determine where forces are there by invitation, have stayed on beyond their welcome, or, in fact, are occupying the host country.

The support of Obote in Uganda by Tanzanian forces may be attributed to his long friendship with Nyerere, but, in this context, the less noble actions of individual leaders cannot be ignored. Colonel Qaddafi has exhibited tendencies to interfere in neighboring states for his own aggrandizement (to create a trans-Saharan, Islamic state), seeking directly through military confrontation and indirectly through the agitation of Islamic splinter groups to interfere in the domestic politics of neighbors and other states in the region. Since many African states are predominantly Muslim, the threat of Islamic revivalism is perceived as extremely threatening and may prompt an emerging regional power such as Nigeria to use its oil-based economic and military power to confront Libya directly.

Finally, wars of national liberation almost inevitably depend on the use and availability of sanctuaries in neighboring states or, at the very least, the inability of states to control the hinterlands bordering its neighbors. Most of these movements (Namibia, South Africa, Western Sahara, Eritrea, and Chad) are occurring in states and regions where independence or some form of recent regime change has occurred, and they should not be confused with more minor splinter groups or ideological factions such as the group that fomented the abortive 1981 coup in the Gambia. The former represent significant factors in the potential for conflict and instability in the 1980s. The latter, although certainly destabilizing, pose a less significant threat with which most African nations can cope.

Extra-African Conflict. Virtually all the factors described, important in themselves, indirectly promote the involvement of other non-African states in local conflicts and may lead to African involvement in international conflict as well.

Despite African preferences for nonalignment, and a sincere desire not to serve as a battleground between East and West, it is almost inevitable that

Africa will be drawn more directly into potential conflicts between the
superpowers, although both the Soviet Union and the United States remain
wary of being drawn into African conflicts. African dependence on the
superpowers for military and economic assistance and the dependence of
these powers on Africa for strategic resources and its strategic location make
such involvement likely.[59]

The Soviet Union, in an effort to gain influence in the third world and to
block U.S. access to strategic resources, actively supports guerrilla movements in southern Africa and those regimes more ideologically aligned to
it.[60] In addition, through the provision of military aid and Soviet, East
European, and Cuban advisors and troops, it has the opportunity to develop
African surrogate powers on the Cuban and Vietnamese models of the 1960s
and 1970s.[61] These regional surrogates will permit the Soviets to project
power locally without giving the impression of direct Soviet involvement,
and at the very least they will serve to destabilize the region to the detriment
of U.S. interests. This destabilization can be effected as much through the
intimidation of those states friendly to the United States as by actual military
conflict with them.

Yet, even the Soviets are vulnerable to miscalculations on their own
part and to the African desire for independence. The Ethiopians and
Angolans, although hostile to the United States, are becoming disenchanted
with Soviet paternalism.[62] Just as many West Africans are alarmed by the
actions of Libya (viewed by many as a Soviet puppet) as are Western
leaders. These events may produce a closer relationship between African
nations and our NATO allies, if not ourselves.[63] Few countries want development on a Soviet model. Even Angola, while host to Cuban troops,
continues its productive relationship with Gulf Oil and other Western
multinationals.[64] In this situation, most Africans would welcome nations
such as France, which are closely aligned with the West yet retain elements
of independence as well. The more successful developing countries such as
Brazil have greatly increased trade with Africa; although they are not yet
able to provide foreign aid such as that given on a selective basis by the
oil-producing countries, they at least offer Africans the chance to develop
on a neutral, although Western-oriented, course.[65]

The question remains, however, whether these countries will in turn
be able to replace both the United States and the Soviet Union as the
principal sources of development trade and aid that Africa so desperately
requires. France provides economic and military aid, and it also continues
to maintain a significant military presence on the continent and has intervened in its former colonies on several occasions.[66] Thus the price of French
aid may appear too high in terms of the loss of sovereignty that their forces
and their actions represent. The new generation of Africans may view these
sacrifices of their sovereignty more realistically and welcome such involve-

ment. They may in fact be more dismayed because François Mitterand's election may cause a significant retraction of that involvement.[67]

It is very likely that there will be no direct confrontation between U.S. and Soviet forces in the region, but there exists the continuing possibility that contending groups backed by the United States, or nations neighboring them, will offer opportunities for Soviet-supplied regional powers or surrogates to intimidate or subjugate their neighbors or support insurgencies against regimes friendly to U.S. interests. It is interesting to note that the highest concentration of Soviets and/or their surrogates are in precisely those nations for whom independence has come only recently (with the exception of Ethiopia, Africa's oldest independent state) and who are currently entering an era of euphoria similar to that experienced earlier by other nations.[68] Few if any of the more mature African nations would seek a comparable U.S. presence or ask for direct U.S. intervention in their affairs, since such involvement would cause a loss of nonaligned flexibility and possibly escalate conflict and instability in the region.

The Forms Conflict and Crisis Will Take

The factors previously described will persist during this decade to varying degrees throughout the region. The importance of the new era and of the new generation in African politics will be manifest more in the manner in which these influences are moderated and perhaps redirected. Although it is likely that one-party states will continue to predominate, to a certain extent political liberalization will occur in those states experiencing some success in economic development. This opening of the political process is, however, somewhat fragile, and the threat of civil disturbance or insurgency may retard it. As a result, actions should be taken by the United States and its allies to provide economic support that will alleviate many of the internal causes of such discord and to provide security assistance and international support to preclude either neighboring states or the Soviet Union and its surrogates from successfully destabilizing or intimidating nations whose indigenous difficulties are ripe for exploitation.

Ethnic and tribal factors will continue as before, always ready to surface during times of crisis and stress. However, the corruption that such rivalries promotes can be successfully controlled through more stringent requirements for performance in Agency for International Development (AID) projects and other assistance. Yet, such actions have their limitations and can easily run afoul of African sensibilities regarding sovereignty. Although the new generation can be expected to be somewhat less euphoric about independence, there is no reason to think they would permit it to be violated with impunity. In fact, there is reason to believe that their pragmatism would equip them to drive hard bargains with those nations seeking a quid pro quo for their aid—with the Soviets for military assistance, and with the United States for economic support.

The charismatic leaders of the independence generation will soon pass from the scene. Their absence, or perhaps more important their failure to provide for a well-organized and peaceful succession, will create the potential for crisis and conflict of a most serious nature. Their nations will be dealt a double blow—loss of their personal vision and strength and a wave of instability and dissension—as competing successors struggle to seize and consolidate power. The obvious candidates for victory in such a struggle are military men; there is a general disillusionment with them. Even in those states where leaders are blatantly inefficient and corrupt, there will be reticence to depose them, since no other viable leaders exist. Furthermore, few nations can afford to bear the massive costs associated with a coup, especially since there is no guarantee that a better leader would emerge.

Thus, the influence of the military in domestic politics is likely to diminish in Africa. That is not to say the coups will cease—rather their frequency should abate, and where they do occur will most likely be in those states where coups have occurred before and military regimes are already in place. However, the increased sophistication and quantity of weapons transferred to Africa, together with the desire on the part of Africans to jealously guard their sovereignty and interests (even within neighboring states), increases the likelihood of conventional war on the continent. Irredentism, tribalism, and other factors will be reduced to their barest economic terms, and the concept of an African resource war will take on special significance.

Although economic factors will permeate internal and external conflict within Africa, it is important that the increased strategic significance of the continent for both the United States and the Soviet Union be realized. The instability inherent in a region so rich and yet so poor, so united and yet so fragmented, makes it vulnerable to Soviet interference in U.S. interests there. Economically, the United States and its allies need Africa more than the Soviet Union, and Africans need assistance wherever they can get it—either the technology and capital of the West or the military aid of the East (although certainly the former much more than the latter). It is a situation ripe for Soviet exploitation, either by the encouragement of their surrogates to threaten their neighbors or by deliberate attempts to destabilize the internal political situation of key nations in the region.

It is in the area of South Africa that these factors and concerns coalesce to produce an infinitely complex situation. The Soviets back various insurgent groups and provide aid to some of the frontline states that give them shelter and support. In this case, the Soviets are actively promoting intra-African conflict in its most violent form, exploiting an unstable African situation for their own ends. The white minority of South Africa clings as tenaciously as their black counterparts to their perceived interests and independence.[69] They too find themselves sovereign in unanticipated ways, but it is only a faint hope that a new generation of South Africans will emerge to support a transition to majority rule.[70] The United States, on its part, has unsuccessfully tried to defuse this situation to protect its sizeable interests in the region, but some progress may be made by the Reagan administration pursuing a negotiated settlement in Namibia.[71]

The other African states, although morally supporting opposition to apartheid, often find themselves economically constrained to trade and cooperate with South Africa.[72] Their stagnating economies simply make them unable to afford the luxury of fully supporting a total isolation of South Africa. They may join in the criticism of the United States for its moderate stand on South Africa, but even this touchstone of African solidarity is illusory.

In addition to the conventional military threat that Libya poses to its southern neighbors, there remains the nagging issue of nuclear proliferation. Just as Libya and South Africa are geographical extremes, they also represent extremes as the only states suspected of being in possession of or seeking nuclear capability.[73] Crisis and conflict in Africa in the 1980s will center on limited conventional conflicts, but the possibility of these two states gaining and possibly using such an option is not unthinkable.

Thus the nature of conflict in Africa is changing, although its frequency may not be reduced. Intra-African conflict will rise as individual states become more stable and—willingly or not—more independent. As U.S. awareness of the strategic importance of Africa and its resources increases, competition with the Soviets will increase—first over more peripheral issues such as access to the Indian Ocean littoral and finally over the nature of political change in southern Africa. The 1980s will be a decade of conflict and a source of change as well. The new generation of Africans may, if supported adequately and with sensitivity to their independence, emerge as significant, although nonaligned, friends of the West.

Notes

1. Raymond W. Copson, "African International Politics: Underdevelopment and Conflict in the Seventies," *Orbis* 22 (Spring 1978): 227–245.

2. Dennis Austin, *Politics in Africa* (Hanover, N.H.: University Press of New England, 1978); Rupert Emerson, "Nations, Nationalism and the Third World," *African Review* 1 (September 1971): 1–2.

3. Basil Davidson, *Let Freedom Come* (Boston: Atlantic Monthly Press, 1978), pp. 283–285.

4. I.W. Zartman, "Europe and Africa: Decolonization or Dependency?" *Foreign Affairs* 54 (January 1976): 326–340.

5. This problem has two aspects—the age of leaders, which averages in the late 60s, and the incredibly high birth rates of African nations.

6. Harold K. Schneider, *The Africans: An Ethnological Account* (Englewood Cliffs, N.J.: Prentice Hall, 1981).

7. L.H. Gann and Peter Duignan, *Africa South of the Sahara: The Challenge to Western Security* (Stanford, Calif.: Hoover Institution Press, 1981).

8. William R. Cotter, "How AID Fails to Aid Africa," *Foreign Policy* 34 (Spring 1978): 109–117.

9. Wolfgang Sassin, "Energy," *Scientific American* 243 (October 1980): 118.

10. Richard Stryer, "Development Strategies," in *Africa*, ed. Phyllis M. Martin and Patrick O'Meara (Bloomington, Ind.: Indiana University Press, 1977), pp. 311–330.

11. "Haig Rebuffs Poor Nations' Program for More Aid, *New York Times*, 22 September 1981, p. A-1.

12. J.E. Goldthorpe, *The Sociology of the Third World: Disparity and Involvement* (London: Cambridge University Press, 1975).

13. Rene LeMarchand, "Political Clientelism and Ethnicity in Tropical Africa: Competing Solidarities in Nation Building," *American Political Science Review* 66 (1972): 68–90; M. Crawford Young, *The Politics of Cultural Pluralism* (Madison, Wis.: University of Wisconsin Press, 1976). Tribalism and ethnicity are used here interchangeably, since many ethnically homogenous groups suffer from internal and tribal conflict or competition.

14. Eli Ginzberg and Herbert A. Smith, *Manpower Strategy for Developing Countries* (New York: Columbia University Press, 1976).

15. Jon Woronoff, *Organizing African Unity* (Metuchen, N.J.: Scarecrow Press, 1970).

16. Ali A. Mazrui, *Africa's International Relations: The Diplomacy of Dependency and Change* (Boulder, Colo.: Westview, 1977), p. 234.

17. Jon Woronoff, "1980: Make or Break Decade for the OAU," *Africa Guide* (New York: Rand McNally, 1980), pp. 15–21.

18. Paul Hartling, "Refugees: An African Tragedy," *Africa Report* 25 (January–February 1981): 39–41; David Norman, "Progress or Catastrophe in Africa?," *Africa Report* 26 (July–August 1981): 4–8.

19. Ruth Berins Collier, "Political Change and Authoritarian Rule," in *Africa*, ed. Phyllis M. Martin and Patrick O'Meara (Bloomington, Ind.: Indiana University Press, 1977).

20. This has been most recently demonstrated in Zimbabwe, where

ZAPU and ZANU forces spent much of their time fighting each other. Once Mugabe emerged as the dominant leader, independence became a matter of time and negotiation.

21. Anthony H. Rweyemanu, "Some Reflections on Contemporary African Political Institutions and Their Capacity to Generate Socio-Economic Development," *Africa Review*, Vol. 1, No. 2 (September 1971), pp. 30–43.

22. Henry Bienen, *Tanzania: Party Transformation and Economic Development* (Princeton, N.J.: Princeton University Press, 1970); "Tanzania: The Cupboard Is Bare," *The Economist* (October 31, 1981): 80.

23. Astride Zolberg, *One-Party Government in the Ivory Coast* (Princeton, N.J.: Princeton University Press, 1969); Henry Bienen, *Kenya: The Politics of Participation and Control* (Princeton, N.J.: Princeton University Press, 1974).

24. Victor T. LeVine, "Problems of Political Succession in Independent Africa" in *Africa in World Affairs: The Next Thirty Years*, ed. Ali A. Mazrui and Hasu H. Patel (New York: Third Press, 1973), pp. 79–103.

25. The following are ages of some of the more prominent patriarchs of African politics: Nyerere (60), Touré (60), Senghor (76), Banda (76), Kaunda (58), Mobutu (52), Boigny (77).

26. "Kenya Special," *Africa* (July 1981): No. 119, pp. 95–118.

27. Kenneth W. Grundy, *Conflicting Images of the Military in Africa* (Nairobi: East African Publishing House, 1968). Many Ugandans, although they resented Amin's abuse of power, were at the same time proud of him in that he put Uganda on the map.

28. John J. Johnson, ed., *The Role of the Military in Underdeveloped Countries* (Princeton, N.J.: Princeton University Press, 1964).

29. Ali A. Mazrui, "The Lumpen Proletariat and the Lumpen Militariat: African Soldiers as a New Political Class," *Political Studies* 21 (March 1973): 1–12.

30. Claude E. Welch, "Cincinnatus in Africa: The Possibility of Military Withdrawal from Politics," in *The State of Nations: Constraints on Development in Independent Africa*, ed. M.F. Lofchie (Berkeley, Calif.: University of California Press, 1971).

31. Sabi H. Shabtai, "Army and Economy in Tropical Africa," *Economic Development and Cultural Change* 23 (July 1975): 687–702.

32. Just recently, for example, Libyan troops have moved into Chad, Senegalese into the Gambia, Tanzanians into Uganda, and of course on numerous occasions, the South Africans into Angola. Although Milton Obote did not throw out Amin, the fact that he and his family lived in Nyerere's home while in exile, together with their long-standing ideological and personal relations, cannot be discounted. Yet each intervention is

different: Both Libya and Chad intervened at the request of a recognized, sitting government, while Tanzanian and South African interventions were for different motives entirely.

33. Stockholm International Peace Research Institute, *Arms Trade Registers: The Arms Trade with the Third World* (London: MIT Press, 1975), pp. 72–92.

34. Paul Mercier, "On the Meaning of Tribalism in Black Africa," in *Africa: Social Problems of Change and Conflict*, ed. P. Van der Berghe (San Francisco: Chandler, 1965), pp. 438–501. See note 13.

35. Rene LeMarchand, "Ethnic Genocide," *Issue* 5 (Summer 1975): 9–16.

36. Charles W. Anderson, Fred R. Von der Mehden, and M. Crawford Young, *Issues of Political Development*, 2d ed. (Englewood Cliffs, N.J.: Prentice-Hall, 1974).

37. Joseph S. Nye, "Corruption and Political Development: A Cost-Benefit Analysis," *American Political Science Review* 61 (June 1967): 417–427.

38. Fred W. Riggs, *Administration in Developing Countries: The Theory of Prismatic Society* (Boston: Houghton Mifflin, 1964), pp. 201–206.

39. For example, in Zimbabwe, ZANU was predominantly Shona while ZAPU was composed of Ndebele.

40. Arthur Hazelwood, *The Economy of Kenya: The Kenyatta Era* (London: Oxford University Press, 1979).

41. L.H. Gann, and P. Duignan, eds., *Colonialism in Africa, 2 vols.* (Cambridge, England: Cambridge University Press, 1969–1970).

42. Gunnar Myrdal, *Asian Drama: An Inquiry into the Poverty of Nations* (New York: Pantheon, 1968).

43. Cynthia H. Enloe, *Police, Military and Ethnicity: Foundations of State Power* (New Brunswick, N.J.: Transaction Books, 1980), pp. 11–27.

44. Louis Kraar, "The Multinationals Get Smarter about Political Risks," *Fortune*, 24 March 1980, pp. 86–100.

45. Although it is well known that other nations suffer from similar problems, few if any suffer them to the same degree as Zaire and some other African states. The point is that their fragile economies simply cannot tolerate the waste and inefficiency such corruption generates.

46. Marc Howard Ross, *Grassroots in an African City: Political Behavior in Nairobi* (Cambridge, Mass.: MIT Press, 1975); Yohannis Abate, "Population Growth and Urbanization in Africa," *Current History* 78 (March 1980): 102–106, 132–133.

47. Gus Liebenow, "The Liberian Coup in Perspective," *Current History* 80 (March 1981): 101–105, 131–134.

48. Jon Kraus, "Islamic Affinities and International Politics in Sub-Saharan Africa," *Current History* 78 (April 1980): 154–158, 182–184.

49. Carol G. Widstrand, *African Boundary Problems* (Uppsala, Sweden: Scandinavian Institute of African Studies, 1969).

50. George P. Murdock, *Africa: Its Peoples and Their Culture History* (New York: McGraw-Hill, 1959).

51. See "Ethiopia: Is a Nod as Good as a Wink?," *The Economist*, 6 June 1981, pp. 51–52.

52. Gerard Chaliland, "The Horn of Africa's Dilemma," *Foreign Policy* 36 (Spring 1978): No. 30, 116–131.

53. Including, for example, recent conflicts between Nigeria and both Benin and Cameroon.

54. Most notable of these has been the Tanzanian support of Obote in Uganda, the Libyan activities in Chad, and the French interventions in CAR.

55. "Thank You and Goodbye—I Hope," *The Economist*, 8 August 1981, p. 27.

56. For example, Nigerian troops are reported to be guarding oil installations in Chad. See "New Scramble for Africa," *The Economist* (September 19, 1981), p. 44.

57. "Kaddafi's Dangerous Game," *Newsweek*, 20 July 1981, pp. 40–47.

58. Nigeria is quickly emerging as a regional power, largely because of its oil income. It has a large army, which it is modernizing, is expanding its industrial base, and, perhaps most important, has a common border with Chad, now occupied by Libya.

59. U.S. Arms Control and Disarmament Agency, *World Military Expenditures and Arms Transfers 1969–1978* (Washington, D.C.: U.S. Government Printing Office, 1980).

60. Gavriel D. Ra'anan, *The Evolution of the Soviet Use of Surrogates—Military Relations with the Third World, with Particular Emphasis on Cuban Participation in Africa* (Santa Monica, Calif.: Rand, December 1979).

61. Together with the stationing of advisors and surrogate troop units in African countries, the Soviets have also transferred massive amounts of military equipment, especially to Libya.

62. Gerald J. Bender, "Angola, the Cubans and American Anxieties," *Foreign Policy* 31 (Summer 1978): 3–31.

63. Ethiopia, for example, has increased its contacts and exchanges with Western nations. This does not imply an immediate rapprochement with the United States, but it does mean that the Ethiopians are seeking more economic aid and assistance in the West.

64. Even more dramatic, however, was the move on the part of Mugabe and Zimbabwe to actively seek and accept U.S. development aid.

65. "Brazil and Cuba Court Africa," *South* 1 (November 1980): 15–18.

66. James O. Goldsborough, "Dateline Paris: Africa's Policeman," *Foreign Policy* 33 (Winter 1978–79): 174–190; Pierre Lellouche and Dominique Moisi, "French Policy in Africa: A Lonely Battle against Destabilization," *International Security* 3 (Spring 1979): 108–133.

67. "France Seeks Closer African Ties," *New York Times*, 23 September 1981, p. A3; "France and Chad: Army v. Army v. Army," *The Economist*, 31 October 1981, p. 49; "Mitterand Tells Africans France Will Keep up its Aid," *New York Times*, 4 November 1981, p. A15.

68. Principally in Angola and Ethiopia. Although the latter has been independent for literally hundreds of years, it was only in 1975 that a popular revolution occurred.

69. "Botha the Biter," *The Economist*, 5 September 1981, p. 13.

70. John de St. Jorre, "South Africa: Is Change Coming?" *Foreign Affairs* 60 (Fall 1981): 106–122.

71. "Boomerang Diplomacy," *Africa* (July 1981): No. 119, pp. 90–92.

72. *South Africa: Time Running Out* (Berkeley, Calif.: University of California Press, 1981), p. 288.

73. "The Map Is Coloured Nuclear," *The Economist*, 13 June 1981, p. 71.

Scenario: Low-Intensity
Conflict in Ethiopia

David E. Albright

It is 1 November 1983. For months now, the economy of Ethiopia has been deteriorating. The government's unwillingness, or inability, to come up with pragmatic policies to replace the socialist principles guiding the economy has produced a severe food crunch in urban areas. Farmers, now relatively prosperous by local standards and able to feed themselves, have not been eager to part with their output except on terms highly advantageous to themselves, and the government has lacked both the power to extract it from them directly and the sort of goods, from either nationalized enterprises or imports, to entice them to engage in extensive trade.

In addition, the country has been running a major deficit in its balance of payments. As the cost of petroleum imports has continued to rise, the share of export earnings that has gone to pay for such imports has neared 100 percent. Even stringent controls on imports have failed to keep their total in line with exports. This situation, in turn, has caused a severe drain on Ethiopia's foreign-exchange reserves. Indeed, the country is nearing financial bankruptcy.

To make matters even worse, the number of men under arms has stayed at more than 250,000. Furnishing training, housing, clothing, and food for this massive military establishment has taken the lion's share of the state budget and diverted resources to military purposes that might have gone to education, health, and economic development.

These economic difficulties not only have stirred domestic unrest but also have fueled popular dissatisfaction with Ethiopia's ties with the USSR. Moscow is perceived as the source of an economic model that does not work. Moreover, the Soviet leadership is faulted for its niggardliness. Instead of providing petroleum on favorable terms from its own resources, the USSR has merely acted as a procurer for Ethiopia on the international market at essentially world prices. By the same token, the USSR has shied away from extending substantial amounts of economic aids to the Addis Ababa government. Finally, having done much to exacerbate the major threats that Ethiopia faces, the USSR has refused to provide any funds to cover the daily maintenance costs of an expanded military, even the local expenses of the roughly 13,000 troops that Cuba has deployed in the country since 1977–1978.

The military has not been immune from this discontent; the ferment is strongest among middle-level officers schooled under the prior imperial regime and among officers stationed outside the capital. Among the first group of officers, there have been elements of career frustration and Ethiopian nationalism mingled with the straightforward situational factors. These men have often found younger, less well-educated, but politically well connected officers leapfrogging them to high command; furthermore, they are imbued with a strong sense of Ethiopian military tradition and chafe at the idea of the need for foreign tutelage in the military realm. The second group of officers has worked closer to the grass roots of the country. Therefore, they have had a chance to observe the deficiencies of the economic system in considerable detail and to experience the impact of these with greater force than those at the center.

In the early morning of 1 November, a contingent of military officers assigned to the capital make their way to the residence of the head of state, Lieutenant Colonel Mengistu Haile Mariam, for the ostensible purpose of reporting on a plot against him. Once in his presence, however, they proceed to assassinate him. A gun battle between the officers and Mengistu's personal bodyguards ensues. Although a number of officers, as well as bodyguards, are killed, several escape and manage to rejoin their units.

Meanwhile, an allied group of conspirators has seized the national radio station. It proclaims a new government and its commitment to preserve the revolutionary gains of the people, but it indicates an intention to move toward an emphasis on private enterprise and material incentives in the economy and to ask Cuba and the USSR to withdraw their troops and advisers. Within a matter of hours, military units in most of the outlying areas declare their support of the new regime, although sporadic clashes occur in a few places.

In the wake of Mengistu's death, his intimates in Addis Ababa manage to rally sufficient forces, with the aid of East German advisers in the security and intelligence apparatus and Cuban and Soviet military advisers, to recapture control of the radio station and of the central area of the capital. They declare the formation of a successor government, under unspecified collective leadership, and they appeal for assistance from fraternal countries to thwart the "imperialist plot against the Ethiopian revolution."

Confronted with military resistance of uncertain dimensions in Addis Ababa, the original conspirators decide to set up headquarters temporarily in the nearby city of Nazret, even while military units loyal to them pursue the battle in the capital. By holding onto the airport outside Addis Ababa, moreover, they succeed in maintaining communication with other elements of the military around the country. In a matter of a short time, they mobilize backing from the commanders of forces in most of the major urban centers, including both Asmara and Diredawa. Thus, the Mengistu-successor forces appear to be on the ropes.

At this point, the situation is complicated further by an upsurge of activity on the part of separatist forces in Ethiopia. Taking advantage of the division among the Ethiopian military and the confusion of the moment, the Eritrean Popular Liberation Front and the Tigre Popular Liberation Front step up their attacks in the north. Guerrillas of the Western Somali Liberation Front commence to infiltrate back into the Ogaden toward Jijiga. At the same time, Somalia places its army on alert.

On 5 November, after considerable hesitation, Moscow and Havana issue a joint announcement that they are taking steps to protect their nationals in Ethiopia. Although they offer no specific details, it soon becomes apparent that some Soviet military vessels from the Dahlak Islands and Socotra are heading toward both Massawa and Assab; moreover, sources in Diredawa report that Cuban troops in the area have seized the local military facilities and that Cuban reinforcements from Aden are coming in by air. In Addis Ababa, Soviet military officers seem to have assumed direction of the forces loyal to the pro-Mengistu leadership.

The same day, Libya, in response to the appeal of Mengistu's former close associates, dispatches a number of fighter aircraft and transport planes loaded with troops to try to open up the airport at Addis Ababa. Although the effort fails and the anti-Mengistu forces shoot down or capture all the planes and personnel involved, Sudan protests vehemently at Libyan violation of its airspace. With the backing of Egypt, it seeks an emergency session of the Organization of African Unity to consider the crisis.

While the OAU machinery is at work to convene an emergency heads-of-state meeting, the anti-Mengistu regime in Nazret requests U.S. and French help to meet the Soviet and Cuban challenge. Before either Washington or Paris can react officially, however, there occurs an air confrontation near Berbera between U.S. planes on reconaissance patrol and Soviet fighter escorts for planes ferrying Cuban troops to Ethiopia from Aden.

After lengthy deliberation and mutual consultation, France decides to keep its forces confined to Djibouti, but the United States elects to commit some military units to try to stop further Soviet and Cuban deployments in Ethiopia. It sends a few elements of the Indian Ocean fleet that have recently arrived in the area to international waters off of Massawa and Assab and near the Soviet naval facilities in the Dahlak Islands. Moreover, it orders regular fighter patrols in the Gulf of Aden and the Strait of Bab el Mandeb. Moscow denounces these actions as provocative but refrains from challenging them.

On 10 November, the OAU heads of state finally convene to discuss the situation. They agree to hear representatives from the two internal parties to the conflict as well as complaints of Sudan against Libya. After long and stormy debate, however, the gathering divides along ideological lines, and the organization finds itself unable to take any decisive steps to resolve the conflict. Full-scale battle between the two internal sides resumes.

In the interim, the separatist forces in Ethiopia have capitalized on the divided Ethiopian military's preoccupation with its internecine struggle, and they have regained much of the momentum that they had lost as a result of Ethiopian pressure on them in the late 1970s and early 1980s. Their efforts have been facilitated by the increased willingness of Arab states such as Iraq and Syria to funnel arms to them in light of the chaotic circumstances in Ethiopia. Sensing growing prospects for the satisfaction of its claims in the Ogaden, Somalia now opts to dispatch its army into the region again.

As the disorder in Ethiopia mounts and as the rump government in Addis Ababa fails to do more than hold its own, Moscow gives notice that it is going to meet that government's request for additional assistance. Efforts to transfer to Ethiopia a portion of the Cuban contingent remaining in Angola get under way, and a Soviet naval task force that has been traveling from the Pacific fleet presses full steam toward the Horn.

Note

1. This scenario is only a plausible intensification of some trends evident in the Horn of Africa as of mid-1982. It does not necessarily set forth the most likely course of events, nor is it meant to suggest that there is anything inevitable about developments in the area.

19 A Fourth Decade of Peace in West Europe?

Paul M. Cole

Since World War II, the North Atlantic Treaty Organization (NATO) has successfully coordinated the defense and security interests of nations that have waged bitter, devastating wars against each other twice in this century. Stability was achieved and peace has prevailed because the West has been united by the threat of a common enemy. For the future the key issue is whether the West can sustain a cohesive, effective force that can deter the East throughout the decade of the 1980s and into the 1990s. In an era when war among the nations of West Europe is highly improbable, a major focus of international-security policy is on how the West's deterrent can remain credible as the consensus on the nature of the common threat erodes.

The two main issues for the 1980s are: (1) how the West can prevent the disintegration of its security arrangements, and (2) how the West can cope with a progressively damaging economic recession. This chapter addresses the security issue, but it is clear that import-export policies can have direct influence on the extent to which coordination occurs on national-security issues. The NATO framework is not capable of mediating every dispute among its members. There is reason to believe that NATO might "blow its circuits" if it becomes overextended into policy areas that it is not equipped to handle. One extreme result might be that the West will become a shell of military cooperation. NATO members will be reluctant to establish new coordinating structures because there is "too much danger in any kind of tampering lest something collapse."[1] Another extreme result might be that military cooperation will crack apart as neo-Gaullism emerges. More likely is the middle ground, where Europeans move closer to the United States and pursue common national-security interests at the same time that they diverge from specific U.S. economic policies designed by the United States in pursuit of those interests. A major example is U.S. policy on technology transfers to and financial credits for the USSR to construct the Siberian natural-gas pipeline.

United States interests in West Europe can be grouped in two broad categories. This is a brief list, stated in terms of the interests the United States will seek to preserve and the threats it will attempt to deter in West Europe over the course of the 1980s. It is in U.S. national interest to preserve:

1. The integrity of representative democracy.
2. Low trade barriers among Western nations.
3. Open travel, tourism, educational and scientific exchange.
4. A coordinated, effective political-military command structure in Europe.
5. A regional equilibrium in nuclear weapons.

It is in U.S. national interest to deter:

1. Soviet military aggression.
2. Overdependence on East bloc resources.
3. Unilateral, neutralist policies among the countries of West Europe.

This basket of political, security, and economic interests is not neatly layered in order of importance; each interest should be viewed as a strand of a rope intertwined and mutually supportive of other interests. The following sections indicate trends that will test the fibers of the lines that have tied U.S. and European interests together over the past three decades.

Central Europe in the 1980s

Economic recession, autonomous control of foreign policy, and the U.S. policy toward the USSR will continue to be the three major issues for central Europe (West Germany, France, Great Britain, and the Benelux group) during the 1980s.

In West Germany (FRG), the Social Democrats (SPD) will be forced to form a new coalition after the current partner, the Free Democratic Party (FPD), drops below the minimum 5 percent mandate required to seat a delegation in parliament. The likely replacement in the SPD-led government are the Greens, a collection of relatively small groups organized around environmental themes and nationalist foreign-policy issues. Consequently, moderate elements of the SPD will defect to the Christian Democrats (CDU) and the Christian Socialists (CSU). The product of this shift will be a distinct polarization of politics within West Germany. For the United States and NATO, West Germany will appear to be more Gaullist in terms of its foreign policy. The Greens will seek to assert German control over its foreign policy. The Greens and the left of the SPD will tend to define *control* as resistance to U.S./NATO political pressures, sometimes solely for psychological purposes. This can occur even when a U.S./NATO initiative would actually benefit West Germany. This is a trend toward a thorough reassessment of the FRG's role both in NATO and in the European Economic Community (EEC)—a trend that opens new doors for France. As Dominique Moïsi has observed, "Now that the Soviet Union seems to have a strategic edge and the Federal Republic of Germany, in its identity crisis, is flirting with Gaullism and pacifism, Mitterrand the realist is aware of France's new responsibilities."

A key development during the 1980s will be the reintegration of France into NATO's security policymaking. François Mitterrand recognizes that what appears to be the end of Helmut Schmidt's era as chancellor of the FRG gives France the opportunity to exert a leadership role as the European spearhead in an anti-Soviet coalition. The French will be prepared to take specific steps to keep the FRG solidly within NATO. This is a source of alliance cohesion that has the twin advantages of being viewed as "European," relatively immune from the vicissitudes of U.S. foreign policy, and serving to strengthen French-U.S. relations in a number of foreign-policy areas. These steps include: continued support for NATO Intermediate Range Nuclear Forces (INF) modernization, support for the U.S. defense program, removal of some overflight restrictions, and granting U.S. naval access to French ports and facilities.

In the Benelux countries, there will be a clear public consensus that U.S. presence in West Europe is critical to the military security of the West. But the governing coalitions in these countries will continue to be short-term constructs, which are vulnerable to economic fluctuations and cyclical turns in East-West tensions. The product could be a partial or complete reversal of the Belgian and Dutch decisions to accept deployment in their country of Pershing II missiles and ground-launched cruise missiles (GLCMs). The Dutch will continue to emphasize NATO's obligation to negotiate an INF agreement with the Soviets. Concentration on arms control and a reluctance to participate as a host for Pershing II and GLCMs will appear on the surface to weaken the U.S. bargaining position. But the United States can tolerate Dutch advocacy of negotiated alternatives because "it is NATO's intent to deploy the modern INF missiles which constitutes the most compelling, perhaps the only, blue chip on the table" for the U.S. negotiators in Geneva. If the United States can fulfill Belgian and Dutch expectations for negotiations, and should the Soviets prove to be unrealistic or intransigent, then the INF modernization will go through in a fashion reasonably similar to the original plan. But if U.S. policymakers reinforce anti-NATO, "no-nuke" political forces through a repetition of previously inconsistent leadership and impromptu statements about nuclear war, then it is difficult to imagine that the Belgian and Dutch governments will be able to accept new INF weapons in the face of widespread public resistance.

Great Britain will increase its defense spending over the next three or four years, but is unlikely to build carrier battle groups or even to postpone the sale of the *Invincible* to Australia. The extent to which Britain will devote defense spending to the Trident II submarine missile demonstrates that the nuclear deterrent will receive priority over general-purpose-force spending. The deficit created by the Trident II purchase will encourage British defense planners to specialize in certain capital-intensive military programs rather than support more costly, manpower-intensive alternatives. Antisubmarine warfare will stand out in this context.

Some developments in the 1980s will occur under any circumstances, but others may or may not occur depending on whether very high levels of unemployment swing European electorates to the left or the right. The following should occur in central Europe during the 1980s:

1. The so-called green parties will develop a significant parliamentary voice. The central issues will be ecology, antinuclear weapons, and greater autonomy from the consequences of U.S.-Soviet antagonisms.

2. Europeans will tend toward unilateralism to compensate for policy differences with the United States. This will be particularly true relative to trade restrictions.

3. France and the FRG will forge political bonds that are tighter than at any time since World War II. The two countries will also develop security policies that are by and large compatible with those of the United States. The FRG's relationship with France will tend to soften the impact of the greens on West German foreign policy and will help diminish the U.S. perception that NATO is drifting away from the United States.

4. Typical of the movement to exert European control over European national interests, the West Germans and others will resist U.S. initiatives that would restrict commerce and technology transfers with the Eastern bloc. The Europeans will reject the notion that East-West economic relations should be coordinated with U.S. political objectives.

5. Nuclear modernization will take precedence over general-purpose-force spending in the United Kingdom.

6. Defense spending in the NATO countries will stay relatively constant, probably declining in real terms.

The Nordic Region in the 1980s

Since World War II, the countries of the Nordic region (Sweden, Norway, Denmark, Iceland, and Finland) have managed to establish different yet compatible standards of national security. There has been a shared perception that the central security problem is how to deal with tensions created by the East-West conflict. Each nation designs its security policy so that its national interest, the Nordic balance, European security, and the East-West contest are served simultaneously (and in that order).

For Sweden and Denmark, the 1980s will represent a watershed. Sweden may be able to maintain the integrity of its policy of armed neutrality, but the most serious of many reevaluations of its defense ambitions will occur before 1990. The trade-offs will be high-cost perimeter defense versus social-welfare programs. For similar reasons, Denmark's status as a member of NATO could become more nominal than substantive. At issue for these two countries and the Nordic region as a whole in the 1980s are the continuity of their post–World War II security policies and the credibility of the Nordic balance.

Finland is coming into a new age. The strong traditions of Finland's Paasikivi-Kekkonen foreign-policy heritage have passed into the hands of a new generation that does not have the obligation to construct a Soviet policy; instead, they will manage it. Already the Finns are participating in a dialogue with their government that was not possible under Urho Kekkonen's firm leadership. The consequence of this new era should be a reevaluation of the validity of so-called finlandization. If the debate over foreign policy in Finland becomes more open and even more diffuse, the same U.S. analysts who fear the consequences in Europe of finlandization could begin to perceive positive elements in Finnish-Soviet relations. Whether the operative elements of Finnish security policy, such as the Treaty of Friendship with the USSR, will change drastically is not an issue. But a more open discussion will serve to question the validity of the popular conclusion (at least in the United States) that equates Finland's security policy with weakness and lack of self-determination.

Sweden's commander-in-chief, Lennart Ljung, summed up the task for the 1980s this way: "The 1982 defense budget is being decided against the background of unusually disturbing developments in the context of our national security. . . . In this type of environment we cannot deny that the risk that we may become involved in military conflict is increasing. It is my decided opinion that Swedish national security would be greatly served (if we can reverse the downward trend in our defense commitments)." For Sweden, therefore, the 1980s are a time when the government must increase spending to a level commensurate with its own threat perceptions or continue to justify the disparity by holding out hope for an improved security environment. If the Social Democrats (SD) return to power in 1982, the Swedish five-year defense budget will change little in real terms. The consequences of repeated Soviet submarine incidents will make it politically impossible to do otherwise. If the communists are replaced in parliament by a new party, perhaps an environmental or green party, the SDs might be forced to appease the greens by attempting to reverse, delay, or diminish the hard-fought decision over the replacement for the system thirty-seven aircraft. Should the nonsocialist coalition prevail, the resulting government will continue the traditional policies of modest modernization, lower defense ambitions, and high confidence in multinational solutions to East-West tensions.

More immediate than the long-term effects of diminishing defense expenditures will be the consequences of the peace movement against nuclear weapons in Scandinavia. The Scandinavian countries have provided leadership in the development of welfare policies and have been a source of pacifist and disarmament rhetoric that has received considerable amount of currency among Nordic governments. Ironically, the nuclear-weapon debate will receive greater attention in the nonnuclear Nordic countries than issues with more immediate impact on the economy and politics of these countries. Historically, attention to the atomic issue has been disproportionately focused on the United States. Scandinavians justify this by falling back on variations of the theme that it is easier to influence U.S. foreign policy than Soviet policy. Generally, however, it is understood that the nuclear threat to Sweden is indirect, that is, a product of a U.S.-Soviet war. But the nuclear-armed-submarine incidents that occurred in Sweden's eastern archipelago in 1981 and 1982 illustrate that Sweden will not necessarily remain outside any atomic war. In an attempt to establish credibility, therefore, the Nordic antinuclear protesters have made it a point to include the Soviet Union in their critique. The 15 May 1982 Nordic Peace Demonstration in Gothenburg, Sweden, proved, if nothing else, that there was a recognition that Soviet nuclear capabilities threaten West Europe. There was also a remarkable shortage of anti-U.S. sentiment. The 1980s might be characterized by an unprecedented level of awareness and debate in the Nordic countries over the magnitude and priority of the Soviet nuclear threat. At the very least, the Soviet Union will be the target of increased attention by the antinuclear groups in Scandinavia. Whether this attention will affect Soviet policies or behavior is problematic.

The probability of future conflict between members of the Nordic countries is near zero. The prospects for conflict between the northern countries and Warsaw Pact forces are also slim, particularly in the context of a military conflict that originates in the north. More likely is an accident, an airplane crash, or a successful depth-charge attack against a submarine of unknown origin that strays into territorial waters. This type of engagement would be brief and limited, but the consequences would be profound both in terms of NATO's commitment to the north flank and relative to the defense budget of each Nordic country.

In general, the Nordic region will not experience sudden changes, and the Nordic balance will be effective as a deterrent to direct, overt superpower involvement in the region's political-military affairs. The biggest change will be the rejection of empty discussions, such as the Soviet-inspired Nordic nuclear-weapons-free zone, in favor of a renewed examination of the role the Nordic nations will play in the East-West security equation throughout the decade and beyond. During the 1980s the fundamental question facing the Nordic countries (less so Norway, which has revenue-producing oil) will center on the degree to which they can escape the economic slump that has persisted since the mid-1970s. If the recession does not begin to abate by the mid-1980s, most Nordic countries will find it expedient to try to "stop the world and get off" rather than to pay the price to meet the challenges to Western security.

The following is likely to occur in the Nordic region during the 1980s:

1. The Soviets will continue to pursue a strategy aimed at diminishing Nordic cooperation with the United States. This strategy will seek to avoid military confrontation, relying on more subtle approaches, including: larger diplomatic presence, disinformation campaigns, cooperation with and covert support for anti-NATO interest groups, encroachment into disputed territories, such as the Barents Sea: and active identification with anti-nuclear-weapons movements.

2. The Danes will not conform to annual defense-spending targets as asked by the United States.

3. The disparity between Sweden's defense spending, force structure, and its threat assessment will grow.

4. Finland will continue to follow the post–World War II policies of friendship and restraint with the Soviet Union and will experiment with policies aimed toward achieving more autonomy from the Soviets.

Southern Europe in the 1980s

During the late 1980s, the Soviet Union will become accustomed to a reputation that they have an advantage over the West in the correlation of forces. As a result of such a perceived favorable position over the Western industrialized countries, the focus of Soviet policies will shift geographically. First, the Soviet Union will realize that a war with the West in Central Europe necessarily involves risks and costs disproportionate to any likely benefits. Such a confrontation would escalate almost inevitably to unacceptable levels of destruction for the USSR. Moreover, the Soviets will not consider military risks to be necessary. Soviet leaders will pursue a strategy against the Western countries that causes dependencies among elements of the industrial base and weakens the political resolve of the West to resist Soviet worldwide aspirations.

This changed focus will permit adjustments in priorities, and the Soviet Union will gradually increase political-military pressures in the Persian Gulf region and step up their efforts aimed at creating economic dissent among the Western allies and the other industrial democracies. Second, the USSR will seek to establish and expand proxy relationships with any country that potentially can weaken the military and political solidarity of the West.

The United States and the NATO alliance will reconsider their security interests according to the nature of this new threat from the USSR and slowly adjust their efforts and capabilities to counter it. The most important consequence of such a strategic reassessment of Western security interests probably will be an official shift of the NATO critical-defense area from Central Europe to Southern Europe, to the NATO Command that is closest to the Gulf region. Such a move would entail several major policy initiatives by the United States and the individual members of the alliance in a broad range of policy areas, including security assistance.

In order to sustain a credible defense in the region, the Turkish armed forces will have to undergo drastic modernization programs, financed mostly through foreign aid. Mobility and the fire power of the forces in eastern Turkey will have to be improved to counter a possible Soviet military move to the Persian Gulf area. This means an increased level of financial and technical assistance must go to Turkey from the United States and other industrial members of the NATO alliance.

Turkey will remain a loyal member in the North Atlantic alliance. The civilian centrist government in Turkey, made up of and supported by mostly former military officers, will enjoy an adequate level of political support from the Turkish people and will have the capability to control the legal political opposition in the country as well as the actions of possible underground opposition. The most significant source of opposition will emanate from concerns in the economic field. The ability of the government to capitalize on the economic-recovery program of the early 1980s will be tested severely in its efforts to determine the direction of new investments and to avoid previous errors. Foreign investments in Turkey will be a vital source of economic development, although they will depend largely on the encouragement of the Turkish government as well as of the governments of the other industrialized countries in the alliance. Improving trade and diplomatic relations between Turkey and her neighbors in the Middle East will provide Turkey an invaluable opportunity to act as a stabilizing factor in the region.

However, it is conceivable that the ratio of U.S. aid to Turkey will have to exceed the level that the United States has traditionally supplied. The ratio of 7 to 10 was originally introduced by the United States to avoid a military imbalance in the historic rivalry between Greece and Turkey on NATO's southern flank. As a result, obstacles that inhibit the resolution of political-military disputes between Greece and Turkey could grow as the aid mix shifts in Turkey's favor.

In the latter 1980s, foreign-policy decisions of the Greek government will not reflect the strong anti-U.S. rhetoric of the Papandreou government in the early 1980s. Because of Prime Minister Andreas Papandreou's failure to properly manage the favorable economic position of Greece, public support for the Socialist Party will erode, forcing the Greek government to compromise increasingly with the political opposition in the parliament on economic, political, and diplomatic issues. Thus, even though the Turkish threat will remain an important part of Greek foreign-policy thinking, modernization of the Turkish armed forces will never be openly accepted by the Greeks. Any reactions to U.S. and NATO positions in this respect necessarily will involve considerations of the threat from the north, that is, the USSR. Therefore, even if Greece denies Turkey access to Greek airspace, military installations in Greece used by the United States and NATO will not be affected greatly by the probable policies of the Greek government. However, NATO will have to cope with military command-and-control problems involving Greece and Turkey or be faced with an inability to maintain an efficient defense posture on the southern flank.

Greece could well change the disposition of its military forces to counter a potential attack on its eastern borders from Turkey. The consequences of such a move would be legion for Greece as well as for NATO. For Greece, the military threat to its borders from Bulgaria and possibly from Albania could increase. Increased Greek armaments on the Aegean Islands could create a serious possibility of a Turkish preemptive strike that would disarm those islands that lie closest to the Turkish mainland. For the alliance, these developments would be yet another test of the coherence of NATO and its ability to resolve internal conflicts. In the NATO context, weakening the northern defense of Greece could put heavy burdens on the Turkish First Army, which would have to be reinforced by additional U.S. military assistance.

Given these trends, the West European members of NATO will have to play a conciliatory role between Greece and the United States to maintain relative unity in NATO; the United States will have to assume a similar role between Turkey and the West Europeans. The result will be stronger political, diplomatic, and economic ties between Greece and Western Europe and weak political and economic ties between Turkey and Western Europe.

In the western portion of the southern flank, Spain and Portugal will continue to provide NATO with the full military benefits of the Mediterranean Gibraltar passage. United States and NATO bases in Spain will provide vital support for NATO naval forces in the region. However, any attempt to use these facilities for unilateral United States purposes will create serious problems. The Spanish socialists and communists will be a major force behind efforts to curtail U.S. (as opposed to NATO) facilities on the Spanish soil.

In Portugal, public support for NATO will decline considerably. The Portuguese Communist Party, which has remained closest to Moscow among European communist parties throughout the 1970s and the 1980s, will be instrumental in the establishment of a negative public attitude toward the alliance. Growing problems of inflation, unemployment, and balance-of-trade deficits will strengthen extreme political parties and make it increasingly difficult for the center parties to compromise on significant issues—one of which will be support for NATO.

Italy, at the center of the southern flank, is a critical link in any NATO scenario involving conflict in the Eastern Mediterranean. Italy will live up to its obligations because Italian governments will be consistently loyal to the principles and objectives of the Alliance. However, because of the influence of the Communist Party, Italy's foreign policy may appear cautious to the United States when the issue concerns taking strong, anti-Soviet positions. There is little doubt, however, that Italian communists will have more in common with other Italian political parties than they do with Moscow. Relations with Moscow will not become stronger even if Eurocommunism dies out completely.

Some of the events likely to occur in Southern Europe in the 1980 time frame are:

1. Soviet policy toward the Persian Gulf area will become more aggressive. Soviet military forces capable of projecting power into the Gulf region will become more formidable. During the 1980s, NATO will respond to these trends by improving the quality and size of southern-flank forces. These improvements will make NATO counterattack options more credible in the event of a Soviet assault on oil fields in the region.

2. France will continue its rapprochement with the Alliance in the field of military cooperation, which will eventually lead to a permanent joint NATO naval task force in the Western Mediterranean along with major British, U.S., and Italian naval units.

3. Bilateral relations with the United States will continue to be an important factor in the security relationship between Turkey and Greece. During the 1980s, both countries will count on the United States to provide substantial military assistance and to serve as a stabilizing force in continuing Turkish and Greek territorial disputes.

4. The Soviet Union will increase its conventional submarine forces in the Mediterranean to provide effective political and military support for the friendly Arab countries in the region in the likelihood of an Arab-Israeli confrontation.

5. The United States will reevaluate its aid formula to Turkey and Greece (presently 7:10) and shift toward a greater share for Turkey.

Notes

1. Flora Lewis, "Alarm Bells in the West," *Foreign Affairs, America and the World* 60 (1981):551.

2. Dominique Moïsi, "Mitterrand's Foreign Policy," *Foreign Affairs* 60 (Winter 1981–1982):349.

3. General Bernard W. Rogers, "The Atlantic Alliance: Prescriptions for a Difficult Decade," *Foreign Affairs* Vol. 60, No. 5, (Summer 1982):1150.

4. David Watt, "U.S. Interests in Europe," *The National Interests of the United States* (Washington, D.C.: Wilson Center, December 1980), p. 159.

5. Johan Holst, "Norway's Search for a Nordpolitik," *Foreign Affairs* 60 (Fall 1981):63–64.

6. "Finnish Professor Wants to Dismantle Treaty with U.S.S.R.," *Helsingin Sanomat*, 18 February 1982, translation available in Foreign Broadcast Information Service, Europe.

7. See Commander-in-Chief, Swedish Armed Forces, *Five Year Program for Military Defense* 1982–1987 (Stockholm: Swedish Ministry of Defense).

8. Walter Wicklund, "Whiskey on the Rocks," *Naval Forces* 3 (1982): 26–31; "Grounded 50 Meters from Land," *Dagens Nyheter*, 29 October 1981.

9. Peter Dükler, "Politicians Must Listen If Many Demand Peace," *Goteborgs Posten*, 25 April 1982.

10. See note 7; see also William J. Taylor, Jr., "The Defense Policy of Sweden," *The Defense Policies of Nations* (Baltimore: Johns Hopkins University Press, 1982), pp. 299–321.

11. William J. Taylor, Jr. and Steven A. Maaranen, eds., *The Future of Conflict in the 1980s* (Washington, D.C.: The Center for Strategic and International Studies, 1982), p. vi; see also Rodney W. Jones, "Southeast Asia," in Taylor and Maaranen, *Future of Conflict*, pp. 528–534.

12. As early as 1967, the NATO alliance started devoting greater attention to security needs in the Middle East and Southwest Asia. In December 1967, the final communiqué of the NATO ministerial council included in its annex the Harmel Report, a study of the "future tasks which face the Alliance." The report drew attention to the major problems arising in the relations between developed and developing countries. Also, it stressed the need for NATO to deal effectively with defense problems in the Middle East.

13. Duygu Bajoglu Seyer, *Turkey's Security Policies*, Adelphi Paper no. 164 (London: International Institute for Strategic Studies, 1981), pp. 30–41.

14. Michael Hardgor, *Portugal in Revolution*, Washington Paper no. 32 (London: Sage Publications, 1976), pp. 21–28.

15. Neil McInnes, *Euro-Communism*, Washington Paper no. 37 (London: Sage Publications, 1976), pp. 35–36.

Scenario: The Nordic Region in the 1980s

William J. Taylor, Jr.

The Nordic region encompasses the Kola Peninsula, Russian lands west of the White Sea and its southerly canal; Finland; Sweden; Norway; the Barents, Norwegian, North and Baltic seas; the Gulf of Bothnia, Jan Mayen Island, and the Svalbard Archipelago; Greenland, Iceland and the Greenland, Iceland, and United Kingdom passages to the North Atlantic. Increasingly important to strategists during the 1970s, the Nordic region (also known as the Northern theatre or NATO's northern flank) became a cockpit in the 1980s where the clear, vital national interests of the East and West converged.

The Legacy of the 1980s

The Nordic region was nominally the quiet corner of the world after World War II, based largely on a Nordic balance that functioned as a kind of buffer to reduce the prospects of direct superpower confrontation in the region. The early 1980s witnessed political-military trends that did not auger well for U.S. vital national interests for the rest of the decade. First, the heightened tensions in superpower relations had the political effect of driving Central European nations, led in this respect by the Federal Republic of Germany (FRG), toward a mediating and neutral position between the United States and the Soviet Union. Periodic attempts by the Reagan administration to regain NATO leadership served only as minor interruptions in this general secular trend. Suspicious initially that they had been promised too much by U.S. zero-base (INF) proposals and convinced by the mid-1980s that lack of progress in INF negotiations was based on U.S. bad faith, the antinuclear movement in Central and Northern Europe came on with a vengeance in the mid-1980s. Various proposals with historical antecedents for a Nordic nuclear-free zone consolidated into a movement with a broad-based, Northern European, international constituency, bringing increasing pressure on governments in the region. The apparent recalcitrance in arms negotiations of successive Republican administrations in the United States reinforced sentiments about U.S. lack of sincerity.

Second, the United States' massive rearmament in the early 1980s, designed to close the window of vulnerability, matched by continued Soviet defense spending to ensure that the window remained open, led to increased

411

Nordic predispositions, led and shaped by the Stockholm International Peace Research Institute, to blame the United States for an ever-accelerating arms race worldwide.

Third, the return of the Social Democrats to power in most of the Nordic countries in the mid-1980s, combined with the failure of most of those nations [like most Organization for Economic Cooperation and Development (OECD) countries] to achieve an annual 3.5 percent annual gross-national-product (GNP) growth rate, led to continued, but accelerated efforts to shore up social-welfare programs by cutting defense spending.

Fourth, and partially in reaction to the three changes mentioned, a predictable (and predicted) backlash in the mood of the U.S. public occurred. Increasingly by the mid-1980s the U.S. public was asking (in view of continued low levels of U.S. social-welfare spending): "Why should the U.S. working-class poor be forced to pay for the security of the European, middle-class rich?" A strong movement vaguely reminiscent of the Mansfield Amendment had begun in the mid-1980s to slowly withdraw U.S. troops from Europe. Part of the underlying rationale in this respect was the increasing capability of U.S. strategic nuclear forces, U.S. naval capabilities, and the need to release U.S. conventional ground forces for deployment in contingencies viewed as increasingly dangerous in Central and South America, Africa and Southwest Asia. Tired of its international burdens, the U.S. polity clearly had entered a new isolationist phase by the mid-1980s.

Finally, a new period of détente began to set in by the mid-1980s. The U.S. and West Europe became inured to Polish-style repressions of increasingly unstable situations in Eastern Europe, an area that, after all, clearly was in the Soviet sphere of influence. United States boredom and European wishful thinking converged with a Soviet interest in a period of détente so that its energies could be focussed on its East Europe satellite problems and a consolidation of gains in the third world.

The Late 1980s

The Soviets sought to exploit in the Nordic region the vulnerabilities of the West implied by these conditions. Soviet policy focused on three policy dimensions.

The Military-Strategic Dimension

There was renewed Soviet stress on the importance of the region to its defense interests in general access to world seas, in preservation and protection of its Submarine Launched Ballistic Missile (SLBM) strategic retaliatory capability, and in exiting as well as protecting the exits for its attack submarines to deny U.S. reinforcements for a NATO attack into Eastern Europe. Modernization of the Soviet Northern fleet, begun in the late 1960s, accelerated in the 1980s. Soviet naval exercises in the Norwegian, North, and Baltic seas increased in frequency and expanded in scope. Violations of the territorial waters of neutral Sweden and NATO's Norway and Denmark became commonplace and, the Swedish reaction to the 1981 Soviet submarine incident notwithstanding, diplomatic complaints from all three became weaker and weaker—each finding restraint in these Soviet acts in view of what the Soviets could do.

The number of Category (CAT) I Soviet naval-infantry requirements in the region was increased and the expansion of Roll-on Roll-off (RO-RO) amphibious capabilities continued apace. Backfire bombers, largely unknown in the region prior to the mid-1980s, began to operate regularly from bases both in the Leningrad Military District and Kola and to patrol regularly south into the Greenland-Iceland-U.K. gap. By 1986, the two CAT I motorized rifle divisions on Kola had received a full complement of T-72 tanks. Both units had received the latest Nuclear, Biological and Chemical (NBC) equipment, with which they trained regularly.

The Political-Ideological Dimension

Soviet policies manifested gains toward three principal objectives. First, emphasis on continued neutrality for Sweden and Finland and their use as crucial bridge builders in Europe, westward into Norway, and south into Denmark and Central Europe apparently met with success (single-factor analysis properly caveated) as more and more Europeans spoke in the latter 1980s of NATO's lack of utility or disutility, proposing that each nation should look to its own defense according to the Swedish model or through bilateral European defense arrangements as more appropriate in doing first things first—that is, looking foremost to differing defense needs among different European countries.

Second, the Soviets intensified their traditional policy aimed at prying Norway, Denmark, and Iceland away from the NATO alliance. In Iceland, where the first concern always was economic security, there was a renewal in the latter 1980s of the dormant movement to get rid of the U.S. presence at Keflavik Base and, more worrisome, to withdraw from NATO entirely. Soviet disinformation programs perfected during the 1970s focused on renewed U.S. belligerence and the dangers of nuclear war. Disinformation began to take a heavy toll, judging by the frequency of anti-NATO articles appearing in the Icelandic, Swedish, Norwegian, Danish, and West German presses.

Third, by 1988, it was clear that the Soviets had been successful in increasing the role of the domestic Left in all the Nordic countries. As partial evidence, the local communist parties in Denmark, Norway, and Sweden, which had never gained more than 6 percent of votes cast in parliamentary elections and which lost ground in the early 1980s in each country, increased its percentage above 10 percent. More important in the late 1980s, the combined Left in most of the Nordic nations appeared much more conciliatory toward positions advanced by the USSR. Paradoxically, Soviet-U.S. arms-control negotiations were now mediated largely by the FRG, whose coalition government has shifted to the Right, and by the French socialist government headed by François Mitterand's successor—a leadership acquiesced in by the combined Left in other West European states.

The Economic Dimension

The Soviets expanded enormously their economic ties with Northern Europe, seeking in this vein not only economic advantages but political-military and ideological gains as well. Their pipeline to Europe fully in operation, the Soviets sought principally in the north to import the technology, machinery, and finished goods of Norway, Sweden, and Denmark and to export raw materials, mainly oil, to the Nordic countries. Whereas in 1978, Norway, Sweden, and Denmark sent no more than 1 percent of all their exports to the USSR, by 1988 this figure had risen to 5 percent. Over the same time frame, total imports from the USSR by the three nations rose from less than 3 percent to 6 percent. Although Iceland imported over 80 percent of its oil from the USSR until 1979, the Icelandic government reacted to high Soviet spot-market prices in 1980 by diversifying its oil imports. However, Icelandic trade with the Soviet Union increased significantly in other raw materials and imports, and the percentage of its main export, fish, increased to the USSR also.

The significance of these economic relations resided in political and ideological areas as much as in trade figures. Ostensibly to manage all these increases, the Soviets enlarged their already oversized embassy staffs, mainly with KGB agents.

Soviet interest in access to the fishing and mineral resources of the Barents/Norwegian seas and to mineral rights and intelligence-gathering sites on the Svalbard had led to increasing tensions with Norway in the 1980s. Maintaining its international legal position over contested "grey zone" fishing rights, the USSR began to dominate the region relative to these issues in the late 1980s. Soviet fishing ships, increasingly escorted by nearby surface combatants, dropped anchor at will and took whatever catches were available and without regard to quotas. Despite the provisions of the 1921 treaty, USSR personnel on Svalbard had doubled by 1988, and helicopter-landing and maintenance facilities proliferated. Rumors of oil reserves under the Barents Sea were confirmed, and six major oil rigs were under construction. In brief, the Soviets dared anyone to contest their dominance in this sphere of influence, and no one dared.

By the late 1980s, the U.S. leadership could see the handwriting on the wall. Just as the Soviets had made significant advances in the correlation of forces in the Nordic and Central European regions, so they had used another period of détente in the late 1980s to undermine NATO, encourage the finlandization (or "Swedenization") of Europe, and to make further inroads in Africa, Southwest Asia, the Caribbean Basin, and the Pacific Basin through the use of surrogate or proxy forces. All this had taken place during a period of resurgence in neoisolationism in the United States—a period when critical decisions on U.S. conventional-force structure and weapons acquisition were not made because of domestic political reasons. The U.S. leadership reacted sharply to these events in 1990 with diplomatic rhetoric, just as the Reagan administration had attempted almost ten years earlier. It was difficult to get European allies aboard diplomatically in 1980–1981, and the situation was far worse in 1990.

United States conventional forces had largely atrophied in the interim. Although naval shipbuilding programs had increased significantly in the early and mid-1980s, they began to languish in appropriations after fiscal year 1984. Despite all the warnings of the early 1980s, the all-volunteer force was in serious trouble by 1990, when the predicted drop of draft-eligible males and a series of congressional cuts in funding for manpower programs had taken effect. This, coupled with decisions in the middle to late 1980s driving the U.S. armed services increasingly toward a capital-intensive, highly sophisticated force structure (the weapons systems for which were not available by 1990)—meant that U.S. military capability as a backdrop for diplomacy was not effective. Threats by the United States to resort to force in checking Soviet Union expansionism were credible neither to the Soviet Union nor to the Nordic countries.

For their part, spiralling defense costs had led Finland, Sweden, Norway, and Denmark in the latter 1980s to reduce manpower costs by reducing conscription, by shrinking their already small active forces, and, much worse for nations relying on large, quickly mobilizable resources, by cutting reserve training and other reserve support drastically. Conscription had been considered the backbone of the Nordic defense establishment, and many considered its erosion critical in undercutting psychological defense. Simultaneously, spending on high-technology weapons systems was reduced also. Sweden, for example, which had one of the world's most potent air forces in the late 1960s and early 1970s and which had delayed its decision on a follow-on to the Viggen aircraft far too long (a decision that should have been made in 1975), ran into production difficulties. Too, the government was confronted by a series of parliamentary decisions to reduce the number of JAS (Jakt Attack Spaning) fighters scheduled to be in the inventory in the mid-1990s.

The great concern in relation to the Nordic region among U.S. national-security planners was not so much that the Soviets would attack directly to seize the airfields of North Norway and the Danish Straits littorals but that events elsewhere would trigger a Soviet response in those same areas. Soviet successes in Southwest Asia—final consolidation, at great cost, of Afghanistan in the late 1980s; a presence in the Iranian province of Azerbaijan following Soviet military support for a 1984 separatist movement there (for which the U.S. rapid-deployment force (RDF) was alerted but not deployed); and increased Soviet naval maneuvers in the Indian Ocean—had led to increasing strategic tension in the region. The worst fear in 1990 was that a contingency requiring commitment of the RDF in this area where U.S. vital national interests were clear would be met by a Soviet horizontal escalation in a region where its vital national interests were equally clear—the Nordic region. Here, NATO and neutral-nation defenses were weak, and political resolve had been undermined by a prolonged period of "living with the bear in the woods."

20 Space Scenarios

Space Mines   *Thomas H. Johnson*

Let us suppose that it is late in the decade, say 1988, and that the Soviet Union has just delivered us a shock with the unveiling of a new military capability. This is not so implausible, regardless of what date we might choose.

The history leading up to this event may be constructed to suit our dramatic predilections. Say that by 1985 both the United States and the USSR have completed secret testing and are engaged in the deployment of conventional antisatellite (ASAT) systems. By "conventional" I mean ASAT systems in which satellites are destroyed by small nonnuclear rockets that either strike the satellites or at least approach very close to them. Although each nation is aware, fairly precisely, of the capabilities of the other's system, the public has received only rumors—although well-publicized rumors—about them.

We can imagine several other important developments in space during this period. For instance, free-world commercial enterprises in space expand from a few million dollars annually at the beginning of the decade to a multibillion dollar enterprise by mid-decade. Thus, moderately large civilian assets would seem to be at stake, in addition to the military ones, in even a low-intensity conflict confined to space.

By mid-decade, the United States has decided to adopt a moderate open-skies policy. Of course, some space-based intelligence information remains protected, but the United States releases to the world massive amounts of pictorial data. Geographical and meteorological data are offered for sale cheap, partly to gain us third-world friendships. More importantly, a great deal of intelligence data are released to demonstrate to the world the justice of U.S. claims concerning Soviet aggression and Soviet strategic buildup. (One may postulate here future Afghanistans we might wish to publicize.)

One of the things that comes out during this unprecedented campaign in world public relations is the Soviet ASAT capability. The Soviets, we hasten to point out, are threatening this beneficent aid to our third-world buddies. The Soviet response, of course, is to release details of U.S. ASAT systems, exaggerating their capabilities and claiming that a Soviet satellite has actually been destroyed by our tests. The unavoidable implication is that we are now in the midst of an undeclared space war.

For three years, undeclared space war rages, primarily in the pages of certain U.S. technocratic news magazines. Heavy security has descended over all U.S. and Soviet military activities related to space. The U.S.-directed energy-weapons program is accelerated to $2 billion per year, with the prospect of larger increases next year and possibly even some small advance in the technology. Both the United States and the USSR seem to be concentrating, however, on ways to protect their satellites.

The U.S. program has three principal thrusts: first, to harden space systems against attack; second, to develop some workable satellite-defense (DSAT) capabilities (naturally, shuttle-based); and third, most immediately, to proliferate U.S. satellite assets, putting as many of them as possible at synchronous altitude or beyond.

Space-war intelligence involves of course a large amount of surveying of the sky, to locate both Soviet targets and Soviet threats. It is in the course of this project that, in the spring of 1988, we receive a surprise. We discover numerous small Soviet satellites traveling on the same orbits as many of our own, particularly the synchronous ones, and only a few hundred kilometers distant from those satellites. These Soviet satellites must be presumed to contain, and in fact do contain, nuclear weapons—in direct violation of treaty. However, at this point do we wish to charge the Soviets with violation of the treaty, thus exposing our own weakness?

Such nuclear-armed satellites are commonly referred to as space mines. They are mines because they rest peacefully in their medium—space—rather than dirt or water, to be exploded on command. Thus, the Soviets have the capability to destroy instantaneously all or any portion of our satellite resources. This is particularly easy for them to do, because of the proverbial softness of satellites to attack. Even moderate-sized nuclear weapons can destroy them from great distances. Soviets can track the launches of our new satellites sufficiently well to place space mines within these large kill radii. The secret technological war turns toward satellites that can change their own orbits and toward the protection and detection of orbit-changing propulsion.

The most compelling thing about the hypothesis of space mines is that it does not depend on any other speculation. The discovery we postulated for the spring of 1988 might be made tomorrow. No technological advance stands between them (or us) in the deployment of space mines. So the questions are two: First, do we do anything about it now, such as developing our own fleet of space mines? Second, if we discover that the Soviets have in fact deployed large numbers of space mines, what do we do about that? Complain to the U.N.? Exercise our own ASAT? Put yet more money into directed-energy weapons? Or give up any military reliance on space systems and assure the commercial community that they really have nothing to worry about?

Space war, like most aspects of our space enterprises, is especially provocative of millennial speculation. Advocates of space projects would regard the scenario we sketched—with slow progress on beam-weapon development—as hopelessly retarded; critics would view the same projections, with rapid increases in commercial space applications, as flamboyantly optimistic. But we need not engage in such speculation to wonder seriously about what we should be doing. The potential destructiveness of nuclear weapons in space presents policy problems that require attention now.

The heart of the matter is precisely what premium we wish to put on our survivable military space systems. On one extreme is the claim that whoever controls space will dominate any conceivable strategic conflict. That claim rests on some presumption of technological advances. On the other extreme is the attitude that says that those advances will not produce significant offensive or active-defensive capabilities and that all our intelligence and communications activities in space can be regarded as luxuries during a shooting war. In the former case, space mines could prove a dominant consideration; in the latter one, they are no consideration at all. But, at most points in between, they represent an eventuality we should be prepared to deal with, even if that dealing is but a matter of changing, or refusing to change, our attitude toward nuclear weapons in space.

ASATs in the 1990s   *Jeffrey R. Cooper*

The time is 7 December 1991; the place is the Korean demilitarized zone (DMZ). Food riots have taken place during the summer of 1991 in both Rostock and East Berlin, and the increasingly anti-Soviet Polish Peoples government announces that it will aid the people of the German Democratic Republic (GDR) with emergency food relief—much of it obtained from the United States. The Group of Soviet Forces Germany (GSFG) has been put on alert and moved to border positions, east and west, in the GDR to close the East German borders and free the Soviet equivalent of the U.S. Military Airlift Command (VTA) for internal security duties.

Following a left-wing Iranian Air Force mutiny against the Islamic Republic of Iran (IRI) on 5 November 1991, procommunist elements seize Tabriz and Kermanshah and proclaim a Free Provisional Democratic Republic of Iran (FPDRI). The Soviet Union, answering calls from the FPDRI to safeguard the new procommunist government, lands two divisions of airborne troops at Tabriz, followed by an army from the Trans-Caucusus military district. The militant but nonaligned IRI requests U.S. assistance to defend Tehran and Kuhzistan. The United States responds quickly with airborne elements of the Rapid Deployment Joint Task Force (RDJTF) and follows with amphibious elements of the Fifth Fleet to secure oil fields, Abadan, Ahwaz, and Tehran and moves two carrier battle groups from the Indian Ocean to the Persian Gulf approaches.

On 25 November, Chairman Andropov announces that in response to "aggressive U.S. actions against the fraternal government of the FDRI," the USSR "will once and for all end the problem of NATO use of West Berlin as an outpost of capitalist, neo-fascist aggression against the peace-loving peoples of the German Democratic Republic" and proceeds to close the three air corridors and all land routes to Berlin from the Federal Republic of Germany (FRG). On 26 November, Andropov announces that "Western revanchist" elements will have two weeks to vacate Berlin and that Group of Soviet Forces Germany (GSFG) units will allow only westbound traffic out of Berlin in accordance with this decision. The United States, United Kingdom, and France lodge strong protests with the Soviet government but are told that the only communication that will be accepted is an evacuation plan.

On 2 December, the president of the Republic of Korea (ROK), General Lee, is assassinated, and riots break out in Seoul, Pusan, and Taegu. By the night of 5 December, it is apparent that pro-DPRK (Democratic People's Republic of Korea) elements are leading the riots and are in control of sensitive facilities in several major cities. From the early morning of the 6th on, a concerted series of attacks are being made on U.S./ROK facilities by North Korean commando units, slowing movement to forward defense positions and disrupting logistics and communications links.

On 7 December 1991, units of the DPRK cross the Korean DMZ in force at two invasion points, at 0200 local time. The U.S./ROK ground-air integrated-surveillance system identifies two major invasion axes but cannot detail the extent of DPRK commitment nor order of battle of follow-on invasion elements because of disruption by North Korean special-operations units.

By 0600 local time, leading elements of reinforcements from the Twenty-Fifth Division in Hawaii and the First Marine Division in Okinawa are loading on C-141s. Pacific Air Force (PACAF) assets are being readied for ferry flights to Japan, Okinawa, and Korea, and two carrier battle groups are sailing at flank-speed toward Korean waters.

United States Commander–U.S. Forces Korea (USFORKOR) requests, via Commander in Chief, Pacific (CINCPAC), collection-tasking priority on U.S. national-intelligence assets, to provide detailed coverage of second and third echelons of North Korean force, in addition to overall surveillance of DPRK. The collection-tasking request is accepted only as priority three because of required coverage of ongoing situations in northwestern Iran and Berlin.

At 0700, CINCPAC orders launch of its own dedicated surveillance satellite from converted Lafayette-class (Navy designation for Nuclear Submarine) SSBN. During the early part of its second orbit, the satellite is destroyed by what appears to be Soviet ASAT.

At 1000, CINCPAC requests National Command Authority (NCA) to reposition and retask a national-intelligence collector for Korean situation; NCA agrees and begins to change orbital plane of satellite. Within minutes after commencing plane change, satellite detects high-energy laser radiation and alerts ground station; forty-five seconds later all signals are lost from satellite.

At 1400, Soviet government announces that any space platform directly supporting military forces hostile to the Soviet Union will be considered legitimate targets for Soviet Air Defense Command (PVO) Strany. Soviets also begin operating (PVO) air Combat Air Patrol (CAP) over northern Iran to "prevent unintentional violation of Soviet airspace by foreign aircraft operating in disputed territory." Soviets also place all four fleets on alert and begin moving ballistic-missile submarines out to sea. There is increased naval activity in the Mediterranean and Indian oceans. The Soviets launch a series of reconnaissance satellites over Iran and ocean-surveillance satellites over the Indian Ocean.

On 8 December 1991, at 0900, the United States responds to attacks on support satellites, with declaration that "because of the threat to U.S. national security" it is taking measures to ensure the survivability of its critical space-based warning assets. The United States launches laser Defensive Satellites (DSATs) into a low Earth orbit and declares that it is establishing a keep-out zone around the DSAT and the protected satellites. Any uninspected foreign satellites launched into the keep-out zone will be attacked. Any attack on a DSAT will be considered tantamount to an attack on U.S. terrestrial forces and will be met with appropriate retaliation. Any attack on national-warning assets will be considered an attack on the United States.

At 1030, NCA informs CINCPAC that COMMA (name of satellite) 12 has been lost to assumed hostile action and that additional Soviet Radar Ocean Reconnaissance Satellite (RORSAT)/Electronic Reconnaisance Satellite (EORSAT) birds are being readied for immediate launch; CINCPAC receives permission to destroy Soviet satellites that could threaten fleet assets as a demonstration of proportional retaliation.

By 1045, F-14Bs from Subic Bay and F-15s from Hickam Air Force Base

(AFB) are flying toward their launch points, with MHV-2s (Miniature Homing Vehicle) ready for use. By 1120, three Soviet low-altitude oceans-surveillance satellites have been destroyed.

At 1200, U.S. commander Fifth Fleet resorts to launch of dedicated assets to observe Soviet naval movements in Indian Ocean to support initiation of U.S. naval air operations in Iran. Information indicates movement of Soviet fleet assets into attack position.

At 1500, U.S. DSAT detects Soviet ASAT maneuvering for intercept against U.S. low-altitude reconnaissance satellite operating over Indian Ocean. When the Soviet ASAT enters the keep-out zone, the U.S. DSAT fires and destroys incoming ASAT.

At 1600, in the face of renewed space conflict and growing Soviet maritime threat in both western Pacific and Indian oceans, U.S. NCA directs CINCPAC to continue attacks on Soviet oceans-reconnaissance assets and to eliminate capability to target U.S. naval forces from space; CINCPAC orders the Seventh and Fifth fleets to resume ASAT attacks on Soviet satellites. F-14s and F-15s, armed with MHV-2s, begin a new series of attacks, which eliminate four remaining Soviet satellites by 1800.

At 1800, Moscow announces that further attacks on Soviet satellites will be met with attacks directed against the bases of U.S. ASAT-carrying aircraft. Soviets also increase preparations at Tyuratam for launches of what appear to be additional ASAT vehicles.

At 2000, the United States responds with warning that attacks by Soviet ground-based or space-based ASATs on U.S. strategic-support satellites or U.S. bases, anywhere, will result in direct attacks against Soviet space-launch centers. This is followed by the launch of additional DSATs to increase coverage of U.S. satellites. The United States warns that it will use its space-based laser weapons, if need be, against Soviet air forces operating in Iranian airspace and over the seas, if there are attacks on U.S. forces.

At 2400, activity at Tyuratam suddenly subsides. Soviet naval forces remain on alert. There are no additional launches of ocean-surveillance satellites.

Beam Warfare in Space   *Lowell Wood*

It is late 1985, and the worst fears of the disarmament crowd have been realized. In the brief span of fifty years, the arms race has gone a full lap, and all the shibboleths, jargon, and proposals pertinent to the old arms race have become hopelessly passé; the scramble to remain reasonably current has taken on an ever-more-frantic character, and the rhetoric of many of the less mentally nimble so-called "grand old men" of the field is now considered just a trifle embarrassing.

The era of space warfare has arrived, long before even its proponents predicted. Despite their several-year head start in most of the relevant technologies, the Soviets have succeeded in branding the United States as the originator of this latest arms-race spiral, a stunt greatly facilitated by the usual U.S. mad-scramble-in-public to catch up.

Two technologies presently dominate the scene. The Soviets have emphasized the throwing of beams of unobtainium hydrochloride at space objects whose existence they wish to terminate. Space battle systems flinging such beams have the somewhat disconcerting habit of destroying themselves as they are used; they have the compensating virtue of generating essentially as many independently aimable beams of unobtainium as one desires, so that one station going to glory can clear at least half the sky of targets.

Although the Soviets started early in this technology and proceeded with a large team from many institutes led by top-quality people, the United States made a frantic, well-publicized, and highly successful effort to overtake them. In the heyday of the U.S. effort, the required unobtainium was distilled with a fantastically low yield from its only known U.S. source, elementary school lunches—so many of which were needed that a dedicated trucking line was set up to transport the lunches to the U.S. weapons factories from the Office of Management and Budget's main school-lunch repository.

However, as is usually the case, the United States soon becomes infatuated with another even more exotic technology, leaving its now well developed and extensively leaked unobtainium technology to be picked up and weaponized by the Soviets. This the Soviets did characteristically well and uncharacteristically rapidly, to the usual surprise and chagrin of the U.S. intelligence community, the consternation of the U.S. right wing, and the quickly growing concern of the U.S. Congress. [The Department of Defense (DOD) bureaucracy even now is in the latter phases of its usual sequence of denying that the Soviets have done anything at all, followed by insistence that the development has no military significance, on through stipulating that it is indeed significant but is being followed closely and countermeasures are being considered, to blind panic and drenching in funds of any beltway bandit offering to document in detail that the incipient Soviet mastery of space is the fault of the previous DOD management and/or administration.]

The technology on which the United States has now staked all its hopes for control of the space environment can most aptly be described as magic and is widely believed to be such, even by many senior U.S. leaders who have had its admittedly arcane physical principles explained many times in private. By vigorous, synergic exploitation of several previously known effects, the United States has acquired the capability to effectively cast spells of nonfunctionality on all types of war machines within a given space-time locus—and to do so faster than any possible countermeasure or defense can act.

Not only is all military machinery knocked out by the U.S. magic beams, but gear so enchanted stays knocked out—it is essentially impossible to restore to working condition quickly or under wartime conditions and must be completely rebuilt from unbewitched components to escape the broken-ness spells cast on it by the magic beams. Like the unobtainium beams, many magic beams heading in very different directions can be created by a given generator; however, the magic beams are of much larger size than the unobtainium ones, so that they either can be aimed less precisely or can sweep out larger sections of the sky.

Most wonderful of all, these beams enchant equipment in subtle, difficult-to-detect ways and leave people completely unharmed—indeed unaware that they have been beamed. (The Soviet propaganda machine, although frothing with indignation at U.S. possession of these magic-beam generators, has not yet been able to get a really convincing line going against this ultrahumane weapons technology, even though it has been created by the same people who brought the human race the neutron bomb.) Indeed, the only substantial drawback of the magic beams is that they must be originated in vacuum.

Even more so than with most strategic-weapons systems, the unobtainium and magic beams have been developed in exceedingly strict and semistrict secrecy by the USSR and the United States, respectively. The U.S. effort suffers from the chronic problem that many of their most talented scientists will not deign to work on weapons development and continue to express skepticism that any system developed by those they consider their intellectual inferiors could possibly function with as devastatingly great effectiveness as the magic beams are reputed to have. The Soviets, although they are not laboring under these handicaps, have their usual difficulties in conscripting highly capable technical effort into professional black holes, whose cultural and geographical amenities are barren even by Soviet standards, and in motivating most of those who are impressed into such service. The technically incompetent political-leadership groups on both sides thus continue to wonder whether their respective efforts have sufficient intrinsic quality to match the competition and whether the cadres they do have are overclaiming as to the capabilities of their systems. The USSR is particularly worried that the United States has walked away from the unobtainium-beam technology, and the U.S. leaders fret continually that they have exchanged a blow-it-to-smithereens technology (admittedly of relatively limited scope) for one of far greater scope that merely lays a brokenness spell on all enemy systems on which it is directed.

The comparatively revolutionary nature of these beam-weapons systems has also caused unusually severe strains within the military institutions on each side. The ballistic-missile crowds on both sides of the planet are faced with the imminent prospect of dozens to hundreds of their expensive little toys being simultaneously slaughtered in flight by a single unobtainium or magic-beam generator and are understandably distraught; the military-satellite people on both the Soviet and U.S. sides are little more pleased with the recent developments. Since both groups are very solidly entrenched and have a twenty-five-years worth of massive wealth-conducting pipelines installed into their respective national treasuries, they constitute very formidable opposition to the advance of beam-weapons technologies in their own countries. Indeed, it is only the inability of their shared interests to transcend national boundaries that is undoing both crowds, and rapidly so. Attempts by their representatives in their respective national political leaderships to ban the beam technologies have been effectively checked by the beam politicians on the other side, using by-now very standard arguments.

The United States in particular has put a large number of national-security eggs in the space basket, and the very recent demonstration-in-principle of a capability to neutralize them all with a ridiculously small number of inexpensive magic-beam generators has caused pandemonium in the Pentagon—pandemonium much greater than even that caused by the intelligence estimates that the Soviets are attaining the same capability with the unobtainium technology, albeit with the requirement of many more generators.

The Soviets, who only during the last decade have started to seriously emulate the United States with respect to the fraction of communications, surveillance and, most recently, war-fighting capability that they have committed to the space environment, have been feeling particularly desperate, since the anxiety as to the security of space assets that the United States has endured incrementally for two decades has been compressed into a few years for them. (Indeed, the United States somewhat unfeelingly exploited the atmosphere of recrimination in the Soviet military-in-space program by risking one of their few well-placed double agents to put out the word that the whole U.S. military surge into space had been an elaborate play to stimulate Soviet reliance on assets in the space environment, where these assets could then be readily compromised by the magic-beam technology; the U.S. reputation for ineptness at disinformation and Soviet paranoia about being played for technological fools were both so great that this well-timed rumor triggered a major purge in the Soviet program, which set back its progress by nearly two years, according to U.S. estimates.)

Ironically, the race for military supremacy in space is being fought out almost entirely on and under the surface of the Earth. Because assets predeployed in space have positions at future times that can be dithered only slightly relative to the sweep of the beam weaponry now entering deployment by both sides, putting an asset into space merely targets it for early, certain liquidation in the first few minutes of strategic war. Military space stations of all flavors—those bearing beam generators of various types, manned observation stations, and so on—thus have been the first major casualties of the new beam-weapons technologies. All the techniques dreamed up during the preceding quarter-century of the space age for maintaining military capability in space are now being exploited on a crash basis.

Both the unobtainium and the magic-beam generators are planned for use in a "pop-up" mode and will be launched from the Earth's surface. Because so little energy is required to rapidly position these very compact systems into operating positions above the atmosphere—relative to what would be required to insert them into even low Earth orbits—semicold launch techniques are being exploited, so as to emit minimum signatures and give negligible warning of the impending use of the formidable sky-clearing capability that they represent. Both sides have also found this ground-based-deployment mode to be a convenient way to side-step the treaty prohibition against the deployment of weapons of mass destruction in space—the beam generators stay underground until they are to be used, just as do Inter-Continental Ballistic Missile (ICBMs) and Submarine Launched Ballistic Missile (SLBMs), even though they can operate only in space.

The enormous investments that each side has in the military status quo have spawned massive countermeasures-development efforts on both sides. However, the extremely robust nature of an unobtainium-beam attack and the subtly but comprehensively ruinous character of an assault with magic beams has thus far frustrated really effective countermeasures creation, even at the conceptual level. Hardening against either type of attack, in the memorable phrasing of a senior member of the U.S. technological community, has all the intrinsic practicality of hardening a city against a large hydrogen bomb exploded at optimum altitude—doing so is not physically impossible, it is merely incomprehensibly expensive. The ability of either type of beam generator to create many simultaneously operating, independently aimable beams shifts the cost-exchange ratio so far in favor of the beam-generator owner as to severely depress the morale of the countermeasures community, a condition from which both sides' defensive efforts have yet to recover.

The so-called mad momentum of the peace race has continued to constrain both Soviet and U.S. weaponeers to test their space-mastery beams-weapon systems in environments that both consider to be grossly unrepresentative of the space environment. Pressure from the military-technology crowd to test their respective types of beam generators in space—possibly far from the Earth—continues to build on the political leaders of both sides but has thus far been resisted successfully by a variety of forces. Amusingly enough, these force combinations have thus far carried the day not through their own political strengths but through hesitancy on both sides to publicly resolve how well their own and the other side's systems actually work—the leadership on each side would be very pleased to have demonstrated that it has clear mastery over the space environment through the demonstrated success of its own system and the failure of the other side's, but the risk that the definitive shakedown testing in space would have the opposite result has thus far been considered too great by both sides. However, the temptation to realistically test the beam technology covertly—or at least in a fashion whose results will be obscure to the other side—is rapidly growing to the point that it soon will be overwhelming to at least the Soviets, in the opinion of many observers.

Moreover, as it becomes ever more clear that control of the space environment is tantamount to mastery of Earth, the pressure to demonstrate such control continues to build. Since either side could at any time undertake such demonstration of capability—perhaps after a covert test in space had virtually guaranteed the success of such an open demonstration—and thereafter be able to exercise it fully, each side has felt constrained to commence deployment of its most advanced technology in these areas, albeit untested in its operating environment (as far as is presently known).

The more technologically exuberant on each side are currently pushing to develop versions of their respective beam-generator systems that could project beams down to ground level from generators in space far above the Earth. Although the physical mechanisms behind the attempt of each side to advance its beam-weapons technology through this quantum leap in capability are very different, they have the common property of being exotic and subject to intense secret debate on each side: the cautious old timers maintain that doing so is utterly impossible, and the young and reckless insist that it is reasonably straightforward to accomplish. *Aviation Week* reports that the Soviets will definitely succeed in mastering the required physics and technology before the next cycle of defense authorization and appropriation hearings commences in the U.S. Congress.

The highly touted Soviet effort in this direction is presently putting emphasis on simulations of the actual space-and-atmospheric environment in testing—which take away even the United States' breath for elaborateness, scale, and cost—and the United States is putting its hopes behind physical simulation, using computer modeling of completely unprecedented scale and completeness. The appetite for reliable success in these developments is sharpened on both sides by the universal realization that this arms race is being run for the prize of a planet. Since it is machines, not cities or armies, that these weapons uniquely attack, and since effective countermeasures presently seem hopeless, neither side has any illusions as to the hesitancy of the other to use such capabilities—once they are developed, tested successfully (by fair means or foul), and sufficiently deployed. The race for supremacy in space via beam weaponry has, therefore, taken on a quality of utterly determined desperation not experienced by either side since the darkest days of World War II, and the *Bulletin of Atomic Scientists* has advanced the hands of its clock to thirty seconds before midnight.

The major issues and questions facing the United States in this situation are:

1. Whether it erred in abandoning the unobtainium technology for the magic beam and, if so, whether the situation can now be retrieved.
2. How to break the intellectual/conceptual logjam presently surrounding effective countermeasures to unobtainium-beam-weapons systems.
3. How to test the magic-beam technology in a realistic fashion and how to resolve the present huge uncertainty as to the workability of the Soviet unobtainium technology (for which the details of implementation are exceedingly uncertain).
4. How to cope with the possibility that the Soviets will be able to covertly test their unobtainium-beam technology and convince themselves that they have thus gained reliable mastery of space.
5. How to resolve the intertwined issues of whether unobtainium and magic beams can be propagated from generators in space, down through the atmosphere to target systems at or near the Earth's surface—and what to do thereafter.
6. Whether it is either possible or desirable to move back to the situation of a half-decade earlier, when the offense, rather than the defense, dominated the strategic scene.
7. Whether the unprecedented rapid shifting of the strategic-warfare posture at the present time offers opportunities for arms limitations or reduction that have not been apparent previously and how to productively bring any such opportunities to the attention of the Soviets (who are currently more suspicious of U.S. motives and intentions than at any time in the past two decades, if such be possible).

The Little Shuttle That Couldn't   *Richard L. Garwin*

This is a brief fantasy sketch of how low-intensity conflict in space was prevented by the assertion of the self-interest of the United States and the Soviet Union. In 1980 and 1981, the Soviet Union made ridiculous claims in the press that the NASA space shuttle was contributing to the militarization of space and, in particular, had an antisatellite role. The United States explained that the space shuttle obviously could not touch an uncooperative satellite because that satellite could readily be equipped with a small amount of explosive and pellets, arranged so that any acceleration of the satellite except in response to its own thrusters would set off the explosive and destroy not only the satellite but especially anything that was disturbing it.

As for inspection from a distance of objects in space, NASA explained that could be done much more readily with a special-purpose unmanned spacecraft, which would use television techniques to radio pictures back to earth. The Soviet Union equips a few of its satellites with these booby traps and rests easy.

The United States considers both the cost of developing laser battle stations and satellites bearing directed-energy weapons such as hydrogen-atom beams and their effectiveness and vulnerability. It decides that such satellites would provoke the launch by the Soviet Union of small nonnuclear space mines arranged to follow the satellite at a distance of 1 km or less and to be exploded by radio control. The United States develops such space mines in the event that the Soviets deploy satellite-bearing weapons and holds them in readiness after testing them in low-earth orbit.

The United States and the Soviet Union, noting the possible (but noncompetitive) utility of laser battle stations against satellites, noting both the potential (clear-air) utility against aircraft and the enormous development and deployment effort required to obtain a space defense against ICBMs and reckoning the vulnerability of these satellites, decide to move early in 1982 to the negotiation of a treaty banning antisatellite (ASAT) activities and tests. Specifically, this treaty bans throughout space the deployment of vehicles capable of projecting damaging levels of radiation, vehicles that have the intent or capability to damage other satellites, and the test in space of such vehicles and mechanisms.

The United States assesses soberly the great increase in military capability it achieves by surveillance, communication, and navigation satellites. This is typified by the ability of vehicles equipped to receive Navstar—a global positioning system (GPS)—signals to know their position to 10 meters in three dimensions, anywhere on earth, and their velocity to 1 cm/sec or less. Tests of an aircraft delivering ordinary high-explosive bombs, straight from inventory, will have shown Circular Error Probable (CEP) of 10 m or less, increasing the point-target kill capability by a factor of 100 above that from the next most accurate means of delivering this inexpensive inventory weapon. This accuracy is obtained equally well from level flight or in toss bombing, the latter keeping the fighter bomber entirely away from terminal defenses and so allowing it to operate with lower losses and to extend the period of effective manned-weapon delivery in conventional war. Coldly assessing the benefits to be derived from U.S. ASAT activities versus the loss of U.S. satellite capability, the United States judges that it did right to sign the international treaty banning ASAT but worries that, during a high-intensity conventional war, the Soviet Union may opt for denouncing that treaty to destroy U.S. navigation satellites (and others) to reduce that U.S. military capability.

Remembering the reluctance of military and regulated users to take advantage of satellite-based capabilities, being led by civil competitive users of communication satellites with their enormous impact on the reduction of cost of communication, including that of competitive cable, the United States decides to ensure the continued availability of the benefits of satellites to U.S. and allied military. It does this paradoxically by investing in backup systems that provide the same effectiveness in a limited theater as do the satellites worldwide. Since it is not worldwide capability that is defeating the Soviet Union but theater capability, and since the Soviet Union gains some marginal effectiveness from use of some of the U.S. satellite systems in civil-user mode, the cost of the Soviet Union to destroy U.S. satellites (and thereby lose both its own and the use of the U.S. satellites) is too great; so the United States does not, in fact, need to undertake the continuing expenditure of the backup systems. However, it is glad it has made the investment.

These backup systems were developed and purchased by the United States after consideration of stockpiling of pure replacement satellites and launch facilities, but this proved excessively expensive because they were to replace worldwide, long-lived capabilities and would have required an enormous investment in peak-load launch facilities. With the European theater as an example, the backup facilities consist of the following.

Navstar Backup

Since the Navstar receivers require four transmitters in view at any time, some fifty ground-beacon-system (GBS) transmitters are placed on high ground in the European theater, five more are carried actively transmitting on AWACS and other aircraft airborne for other purposes in the theater, and four per day are launched as short-lived battery-operated payloads on looping orbits. These payloads are simple relays containing quartz clocks rather than atomic clocks, and they confine their radiation to the European theater, thereby providing a signal level 20 dB higher than that from Navstar. NATO Navstar receiver-computers have been provided with the capability to work with transmitter ephemeris information suitable for airborne as well as space-borne systems. A stock of several hundred such submarine-launched or aircraft-launched missiles have cost the United States $300 million and would involve an expenditure rate of $3 million per day, but whether or not they need to be used, NATO continues to obtain the effectiveness in its logistic and attack operations to which it has become accustomed by the use of Navstar in training.

Meteorological Satellite

The Meteorological Satellite (METSAT) that provides worldwide meteorological information by direct transmission from its polar orbit contributes substantially to NATO capability. It is backed up by a small rocket launched twice a day to an altitude of 1,000 km, which returns to earth in a reentry vehicle a few frames of high-resolution 70-mm film. NATO commanders find this more useful than the METSAT data and regret somewhat that they are not allowed to launch this METSAT replacement while the METSAT is still surviving in orbit.

Communication Satellites

NATO vehicles have long been equipped with steerable antennae to allow them to communicate with Communication Satellites (COMSATS) in synchronous orbit, on which they rely heavily. These are backed up by comparable equipment carried on aircraft airborne at all times for other purposes, which serve as relays in communication with mm wave links to ground stations. Maintaining high-data-rate communications with COMSATS during wartime has always been considered a problem, since the Soviets are known to have invested large resources in high-power ground-based jammers for jamming the uplink to the COMSATS. In expectation of this jamming, NATO has installed and practiced spread-spectrum communications, but its wartime capability is reduced by about a factor 100 beyond that available in peacetime. NATO has thus deployed an auxiliary communication system consisting of high-flying helicopters lifting a special communications package consisting of a phased-array antenna, which is scheduled to look in turn at each NATO communicator requiring service.

This is used with conventionally armed cruise missiles at cryptographically determined intervals, to provide high peak-power communications in burst mode so that neither the link to the cruise missile nor that from the cruise missile can be jammed effectively by the Soviets. This has been used to implement a terminal-correction maneuver by arranging for the cruise missile to attack targets essentially by navigation with an accuracy of 200 ft; five seconds before expected impact, the cruise missile is scheduled to transmit via the relay in the sky a single television picture of a 500-ft diameter circle including the expected impact point. Back in a control station, an individual target designator (person) sees the picture, compares it with a predistorted reconnaissance picture, and identifies immediately the desired impact point. An automatic command generator then commands the maneuver of the cruise missile to correct its path to strike the desired impact point with an accuracy of 10 ft.

Imaging Satellites

By the 1990s, NATO commanders have available a photographic satellite in a 400-km altitude polar orbit, equipped with a 1-m diameter optical system. Diffraction-limited performance of the system is 0.5 microradians, which would correspond to best ground resolution of 20 cm—very useful for counting vehicles, distinguishing tanks from armored personnel carriers, and the like. It provides once a day the opportunity of photographing any spot in the theater, which NATO commanders find reassuring. They provide against the potential loss of this satellite by investing in hypersonic drones, capable of flying at Mach 5 at 40-km altitude. Using these at the same observation angles from the vertical, diffraction-limited performance equal to that from the imaging satellites can be obtained with a lens 10 times smaller in diameter (10-cm diameter), which the commanders find very useful. In fact, for the expenditure of $10 million per day from the inventory of these ram-jet-propelled drones, NATO receives vastly more imagery than they can obtain from the imaging satellite. Laser data links are used for direct transmission of the pictures.

Pipeline and Factories

These low-unit-cost, high-launch-rate backup systems are stockpiled in numbers sufficient to continue fighting until the factory can produce more. An analysis has shown that obsolescence is best avoided by a modest stockpile corresponding to sixty-day expenditure, with an investment in short-lead-time factory production to take over from then.

Bombs That Squeak

Concerned with the gross inefficiency represented by a military requirement to obtain 95 percent probability of target destruction with weapons that are 85 percent reliable, requiring the assignment of two weapons per target, with the result that the second weapon has an expected destruction capability of only 15 percent of the first, NATO has implemented real-time reconnaissance for keeping track of the point of explosion of its more expensive weapons—nuclear cruise missiles, Pershing II, and the like. This is achieved by providing in each weapon a high-explosive-powered radio transmitter, which radios a coded impulse at extremely high frequency to be picked up by specialized satellites at super synchronous orbit and retransmitted to control stations on Earth. The time difference of arrival of the pulse by the various satellite links can be used, as in the case of Navstar, to provide location of the burst point to an accuracy of 10 m or less.

   Thus NATO targeting now assigns only one weapon against a target, with a small fraction of the weapons having a rapid retargeting capability so that they can be used to replace those that failed en route. The merits of this scheme have not been lost on the Soviets who realize that the United States now needs only 1.2—not 2.0—accurate Re-entry Vehicles (RVs) to destroy a Soviet missile silo with 98 percent reliability, thereby suddenly increasing the force effectiveness and imperiling (according to Soviet worst-case calculations) the survival of the Soviet ICBM force, even if preferentially defended. In addition to installing the same system aboard her nuclear weapons, the Soviet Union has put her ICBMs on launch-under-attack (LUA) status, thereby ensuring that only silos (and not missiles) would be destroyed by such an attack. Unknown to the Soviet Union, the United States no longer targets Soviet missiles because the Soviet ICBMs are on LUA. However, the United States has put its ICBMs on LUA as well.

Conclusion

It has taken the United States a long time to cut through a fog of supersalesmanship and lack of understanding. It uses satellites in peace and in war, protecting them by treaty and by backup systems. It uses the cheaper and more flexible expendable boosters instead of the prestigious shuttle, which is relegated to ceremonial occasions. Lasers are used for designation and data transmission and greatly increase U.S. and NATO capabilities.

21 National Oceanic Policy as a Counter to Confrontation and Crisis

Gilven M. Slonim

Our plans miscarry, because we have no aim. When a man does not know what harbor he is making for, no wind is the right wind. —Seneca

Edmund A. Walsh, the Jesuit priest who established the Foreign Service School at Georgetown, observed nearly a half-century ago: "In major policy it is not speed but direction that counts."[1]

The year was 1934, when he published his catechism of oceanic policy, a sixty-four page treatise titled *Ships and the National Safety*. No longer in print, the work is now a collectors' item. It must be dusted off and brought into the emerging dialogue on national policy. The Vinson-Trammel Act, which laid the keel for the two-ocean navy, was enacted that same year. Two years later, Franklin Roosevelt's "Magna Charta of the American Merchant Marine," the 1936 Act, became law. With this maritime philosophy, and these legislative actions to forge oceanic policy, policy at the national level should have been well on its way. As a matter of fact, in their wake the United States did become the greatest maritime power the world had ever beheld by war's end. The policy lesson is evident; there was policy provision—more significantly, policy incentives—in advance of the crisis!

Unfortunately, from this pinnacle of maritime preeminence the United States has plummeted to eleventh place as a world trade-carrying power; today, the U.S. fleet encounters a mounting confrontation on the seas, as the Soviets move with relentless drive to control the world ocean. Despite the burgeoning oceanic challenge, most U.S. citizens are oblivious to the disparity in vitality of oceanic policy of the two superpowers. But, the unfortunate fact remains: the force levels in both U.S. fleets, naval and mercantile, have dwindled to pre–Pearl Harbor posture. Oceanic policy has proven frustratingly elusive over the forty years since the Japanese struck Pearl Harbor. Despite the demands of the postwar world for the wisdom of policy, even today policy remains foreign to the U.S. way; historically, we have been conditioned to reaction to crisis. Yet, there are daily reminders stressing that seat-of-the-trousers reaction is a luxury we can no longer afford.

The modern world has become too compressed strategically; twenty-first-century weapons are too long-range, too accurate, too powerful; world events move too swiftly, the stakes are too high, and the power struggle too pervasive to permit moving after the fact. In a world of instantaneous communications, no longer is there time to think through our countering moves after the fact. We continue to pay the price for hesitancy, for uncertainty in power moves in the Indian Ocean, where the need for an insertion of fleet forces was foreseen thirty years ago. The premium must be placed on a long-glass policy process that dictates a national competence in futuristic planning, with well-considered courses of action to meet the crises likely to be encountered. This nation requires a process that provides direction toward realization of the future national objectives it establishes. Nor can we look to international policy arrangements to crystallize our national-policy thinking or our actions—to do so merely curtails our capabilities, forecloses our options, and fails to serve the national interest. Look to the Law of the Sea, and how without substantive decision by any of the parties through creeping jurisdiction, freedom of global oceanic research has been curtailed.

Hardly a week passes without serious incident spelling new logic for reorientation to a policy mode in the conduct of national affairs, in the provision for a secure, a prosperous, a well-respected future. Whether on the high seas or in Sweden, in Namibia or Taiwan, Poland, Saudi Arabia or Cambodia, the staccato of world events dictate a global wisdom and, even beyond, sheer strength—a prime requirement for vision in the international arena. Viewing the Camp David Accord—as it served to antagonize most of the Arab world—and the Ball mission to Iran, untempered by considerations of leadership alternatives as it finally affected U.S. vital interest, one is given pause to question how this nation has been handling issues central to its future. At the outset of the 1980s Derek Bok, president of Harvard University, expressed these concerns as he asked were we, indeed, educating our children for the world of the future: "In the United States we are becoming isolated and separated from one another, just when we are losing our control of essential resources and our economic and military dominance, and therefore need a new spirit of national cooperation, national purpose and unity." Within his plea, the evident quest is seen as one of unifying policy. Here the stress becomes one of constituency— enlightened citizens as participants with the Congress and the executive in the formulation of far-reaching policy.

Policy capable of dealing with the recurrent challenges and crises that continue to plague the nation can be created only when U.S. citizens gain a grasp of the world beyond their shores. For we as a people require bona fide understanding of the peoples of the world. Our citizens must comprehend global oceanic geography, since it serves as the matrix to bind the modern world. This knowledge must be reinforced by far wider linguistic ability to communicate truly the essence of U.S. leadership to peoples throughout the world. The stimulation of world trade and trade carrying encourages this competence through the cooperation in direct working relationships between trading partners. Here is also seen the significant peace-preserving spin-off that is found in the carrying of world commerce. Development of these major factors of oceanic contribution to the long-range welfare of the nation will flow within the national policy projected. They must be part of compelling competence in future plans of global reach mandated by a viable policy process.

Observing this swiftly moving world scene, a highly tantalizing fact emerges: The seeds of this new national policy can best be sown and nurtured on the world ocean. Beyond the vast physical dimensions of oceanic space, affording room for maneuver and attenuation, the thinking of the seafarer offers a pattern of precious policy thought. Man's thought in sailing the sea is disciplined to global perspective. He deals with the sea as a global entity—as it provides his weather, as it poses threats to his safety, as it affords worldwide opportunity for productive, profitable enterprise. There on the seas comprehensive, conceptual, and creative thought is central to survival. Anticipatory planning becomes a way of maritime life in this unnatural, hostile environment. When Buckminster Fuller suggests that an individual, just as a people, must think at least twenty-five years ahead to accomplish anything really worthwhile, his eye is searching to seaward. For the Navy, he emphasizes, thinks in a characteristically different manner from the landed majority of our people. What he stresses is here on the vast ocean, where man projects a tiny dot; it is mind, not muscle, that can manage this powerful environment. And it is here, he goes on to say, "the foundations of a creative future can be forged" in the long-term national interest. To confirm his thesis, he looks back to the tremendous contribution that has come out of the sea, through the more-with-less philosophy of the seafarer that "has changed our world!"

If, as Alvin Toffler contends, the U.S. future is being stolen, dribbled, and bumbled away by a government that does not plan for the long range—does not know how to plan—and is therefore outplanned at every step by major corporations who are staking out pieces of the future for themselves as well as by foreign nations who are doing the same on a global scale; if, as he suggests, failure to look at the United States' current economic and political crisis in terms of the next twenty-five to fifty years is costing us unmeasurable billions in lost economic and social opportunities, the United States must begin now to develop very long-range strategies. The United States must invent wholly new forms of planning that involve not merely a handful of technocratic experts but millions of ordinary citizens—then we must turn to the seas with unprecedented vigor both intellectually and operationally. The United States must learn to ride the fourth policy wave toward regaining productivity and competitive global drives; for it is within our understanding of the seas, our uses of the global ocean, that the policy process the nation needs desperately can be found.

We are obliged to understand national policy; we must gain competence in the policy process. Above all, we as a people must grasp the critical nature of the reorientation dictated.

There is policy, and there is policy. Everybody has a different perception as to what constitutes policy. No two citizens see policy in the same light, nor at the same level. This may be merely a matter of convenience, sheer indolence, or our failure to think through what national policy must mean. But, generally, we are prone to place the entire burden of national policy on one man's shoulders. Obviously, the wisdom of Solomon, the strength of Atlas, the vision of Pericles is rarely combined within one human. Few can be found, therefore, with the competence to entrust the future of the nation for the centuries that lie ahead. Yet, offhandedly we continue to state, "It is Jimmy Carter's Middle East policy" that failed, "Al Haig's foreign policy" is too hard on the Soviets, "Cap Weinberger's defense policy" is too costly or, previously, Elliot Richardson's "Law of the Sea policy" requires rethinking. Patently, where national policy should serve to integrate all the functions and functioning—all enterprise that affects the national interest—we continue to accept fragmented concepts of policy.

Whereas all the resources of the United States should be brought to bear within a well-defined and well-directed policy process that musters the concerted action necessary to the attainment of the long-term national objectives policy establishes, our oceanic assets remain disquietingly fragmented. We play musical chairs organizationally within the government and call the process policy. This was seen at National Oceanographic and Atmospheric Administration (NOAA) several years ago. Strangely, the *New York Times* bold-faced its headline "New National Oceanic Policy," but the article merely reported organizational changes made by the new administrator; for he too claimed he was instituting new policy. And there we are, with little sense of purpose and no direction, because our concept of policy does not deal directly with the potential, the promise, the prospect to be realized.

These symptoms show why some are led to accept the nonsense that the United States is a wounded giant, incapable of realizing its full measure of power. Policy must deal with more than the immediate solution of short-term problems, day-to-day crises, however perplexing; the central thrust of policy perforce is toward realization of long-term potential.

The first order of policy business is to think through what the process must provide in the context of the long-term welfare, the future well-being of the nation—to discern what are the major elements of contribution that must be considered. To accomplish this end, certain glaring deficiencies within the U.S. educational process require rectification. First, there must be emphasis accorded to students as well as educators gaining competence in conceptual thought. Ambassador Harlan Cleveland makes this point with convincing clarity in his "What's Higher about Higher Education?" presentation. Nowhere within our billion-dollar educational system is this emphasis to be found. Of equal significance, education within the United States must be brought into balance—at all levels, between land and sea. Once having established the broad conceptual framework for policy at the national level, the next step becomes one of making the determination as to wherein the national interest reposes. This sounds simple; in reality, this becomes intensely complex. Some suggest this can never be done; you can never get there from here. But you must fix national interest if policy is to gain the direction Father Walsh emphasizes.

Here a consensus of all major elements of U.S enterprise must be forged. For how is the direction of policy stressed to be gained, if there is no clear-cut criteria as to the direction of the nation's interest? The fact is, to date none of the false starts in oceanic-policy formulation first endeavored to fix its departure point in the national interest. This oversight, in itself, may well account for the failure to structure national policy. For, lacking this departure point, there has never been a national commitment calling for fuller, comprehensive, and enlightened utilization of the world ocean to reenforce the national economy, encourage investment, stimulate U.S. productivity and competitive drives in the world market, and elevate the U.S. standard of life.

To make Lane Kirkland responsible to what is perceived as the consensus-held view as to wherein this elusive national interest reposes in the long range, he must serve as a participant, a contributor in the formulation of this critical departure point of policy. Otherwise, what will happen is what has been happening. Everybody in and out of government interprets the national interest in the image of his own self-enlightened interest. "What's good for General Motors, is good for the country" as Charlie Wilson put it when he was secretary of defense. But is it? The American Petroleum Institute and the multinational corporations, CBS and the farmers, the yachtsmen and educators—just as sailor Kirkland—must participate in the process. Kirkland, as a matter of fact as an ex-sea captain, understands this better than most. For the thought pattern that he gained in sailing the seas adheres to the policy pattern that must evolve within a conceptual framework, which derives its substance and drive from the leaders of the major segments of U.S. endeavor.

In a U.S. technological turn to the sea in the 1960s, the national-policy thrust was recognized as central to the realization of the potential of the world ocean. President Johnson realized the importance of the oceans, and attempted to spur the development of ocean resources.

What the president failed to provide, unfortunately, was the twin oceanic imperative: public education and national policy. Both are critical to the attainment of his lofty oceanic aim. The thrust of the 1960s, instead, was narrowly confined to the oceanographic-scientific-resource segment of oceanic potential through legislative action. Nonetheless, a fleeting moment of maritime euphoria was gained with the passage of the Marine Resources and Engineering Development Act of 1966. Conceivably, a consensus about the national scene considered that comprehensive national oceanic policy has been formulated. Some still cling to that illusion. But the regrettable fact remains that the United States, to this day, remains rudderless without the guidance of national policy.

We continue to talk of policy as though each of the elements were a policy unto itself. I recall, during the last administration, the president would allocate either a Monday or a Tuesday for the purpose of preparing his "water policy." The next week he was busy on his energy policy. A month later he got around to his defense policy, according to the White House press. We had a policy for everything in those days, and Meg Greenfield blasted the president for his inability to bring them all into confluence in her perceptive profile title, "Jimmy the Engineer." I daresay had she analyzed Carter's predecessors along the lines she would have pinpointed the same critical deficiency in their policy functioning, or absence thereof. For the concept of policy generally held has been one of fragmentation rather than concerted action by government and, in turn, the nation; the integrative function of bringing all the nation's strength together in a well-orchestrated, concerted national effort is lost. At the same time, we equate governmental policy to national policy. As a consequence, all elements of our government are dancing to different tunes—each jockeying for position, power, and prestige. Athelstan Spilhaus, father of the Sea Grant College Program, quips, "As to Law of the Sea, our U.S. position is closer to that of the Soviet Union, than that of the Department of State is to Commerce." As humorous as this may sound, the overtones are sorrowful, since there is more than a modicum of truth in what the jolly oceanographer has to say.

Henry Kissinger made the more serious point in his *White House Years*, in reporting his first interview for assignment as national-security advisor. Asked "what direction should our diplomacy take?" Kissinger was quick to reply, "Our policy should be freed of its violent fluctuations from euphoric actions to those of profound despair dependent upon the emotions of the policymakers. And it must extend beyond the changing of Presidents." The genius of policy obviously reposes in its ability to bring all its elements within a synergistic interplay, with central purpose providing the dynamics and direction of drive.

How clearly his policy point has been confirmed throughout the continuing crisis in the Middle East! At no point in U.S. history has the compelling need for policy, and continuity of policy, been driven home with more dramatic directness than in the aftermath of the abdication of the shah of Iran. This critical need for national policy to guide our reaction to crises—

better still to forestall crises—was seen with comparable intensity at the time of Anwar Sadat's assassination. Ad hoc actions, after the fact, remain singularly unconvincing. Whether they result in an overreaction or an underreaction, such tend to convey weakness and anything but resolution; credibility, just as leadership, is inevitably lost. From the seething turmoil in the Middle East another major policy lesson is gleaned. In focusing on U.S. vital interests within the Persian Gulf, one readily observes the inseparability of the major elements of comprehensive policy in the real world. At no time, from the outset could defense policy—the strategic measures to be taken—disregard the implication of maritime policy. The flow had to be direct, for the criticality of sea lift proved the Achilles' heel in any reinforcement of the U.S. fleet presence. This relationship, in turn, brought implications vis-á-vis economic and energy policy to the fore, as all elements required splicing to so-called foreign policy. Cultural-policy overtones remain inherent, requiring concurrent emphasis on both educational and scientific policy if a mastery of world affairs is to be realized through the orchestration of the nation's global oceanic policy.

This brings us to Senate Resolution 222 of February 1974. With its unanimous passage the U.S. Senate clearly signaled its policy concern. More significant, perhaps, than its unanimous passage was the fact the sixty senators of every political stripe, representing every geographical sector, cosponsored the resolution. This called for a complete investigation and study, incident to the formulation of national oceanic policy. This would include analysis of all the elements of national interest, incident to foregoing the policy seen as a critical national need. Beyond this first step, the comprehension and support of the administration, industry, academia, and the public would be required to formulate and guide its implementation. The study was assigned a core staff, which has since disappeared. A number of publications were printed by the National Ocean Policy Study (NOPS), one of which concluded that ocean policy was adequate—based on the legislation passed—but the fact remains that NOPS failed to initiate action toward a determination of wherein the national interest resides as a departure point. Actually, the focus of their thrust finally was at the level of governmental policy. Frankly, I was not surprised to learn from the secretary of the Navy that seven years after the Senate's original policy initiative, this administration was revitalizing NOPS under the chairmanship of Senator Bob Packwood.

What then, is this policy that has remained elusive to the U.S. view through these many years? United States citizens must answer this question in moving to chart the future of the nation. Simply stated, policy may be defined as the process whereby a nation establishes long-term goals and provides incentives to accomplish those aims, seeking what it perceives as long-range potential and moving toward what it envisions as its national objectives framed in the public interest. The formulation and implementation of national oceanic policy entails an orchestrated effort of the executive, congressional, and public sectors. This becomes the iron triangle that fosters the dynamics of the entire process.

The major elements of long-term policy span the full spectrum of oceanic endeavor:

1. A competitive posture on the seas is a cardinal element; it requires both regaining a competitive trade-carrying posture on the global seas to spearhead a vibrant seafaring industry as well as U.S. foreign policy with fleet built and manned by competent, able-bodied U.S. citizens—and an ongoing shipbuilding industry to stimulate the economy to promote productivity and job opportunities.

2. A strategic posture (nuclear and nonnuclear) and doctrine is needed to meet the variety of threats to U.S. citizens and interests worldwide, within the mounting confrontation developing on the seas. The United States must exploit the strategic potential of oceanic space toward attainment of international stability and the preservation of world peace.

3. The United States must probe the total geoeconomic potential of the oceans to stimulate the economy, to stabilize the dollar, to reverse a critical trade balance, to provide long-term prosperity in a revitalization of its competitive drives in the world market. This encompasses the full range of oceanic use and the resources reposing within the sea.

4. The United States should launch a multidisciplinary public oceanic education program throughout U.S. schools at all levels, to achieve citizen comprehension of the human stake in oceanic advancement, thus providing the potential of enlightenment within the requisite constituiency to participate within the policy process, to support the magnitude of the oceanic program in the national interest indicated.

5. The nation can ensure, through resolute oceanic research, gaining both the fullest portent of the oceanic frontier of the future and the means for solving crucial national and international problems, the incidents and crises arising on the seas.

6. United States policy provision that moves to tap the full energy sources prospectively held within the sea can enable the United States to realize a posture of self-sufficiency. Beyond meeting fossil-fuel requirements, exotic-fuel development and innovative propulsion will enable U.S. forces and fleets to sustain the preeminence operationally that nuclear power afforded.

7. In regard to the law of the sea, policy provision is essential if the United States is to assume a role of leadership to ensure that negotiations are conducted on the basic principles established within national policy and adhering to the seafaring requirement of optimum utilization of the global sea—both commercially and strategically.

8. The dominant portion of the U.S. people are engaged enjoyably in

water-based recreation, highlighting the economic and societal significance of so-called seacreation. Small boats are big business—$8 billion each year. National policy should encourage the activity, for here the prospect of a major constituency is to be created through education of the sea.

Comprehensive knowledge and policy provision for fuller uses of the global seas afford new oceanic solutions to problems and crises, just as to the fulfillment of mounting human needs: water for human use, energy from sources invulnerable to arbitrary interruption and price manipulation, medicine, food, and oceanic space. Dynamic policy can counter a burgeoning adverse balance of trade, mounting welfare rolls, and reinforce a faltering inflated economy.

The concept of a U.S. assumption of oceanic leadership entails first and foremost a public educational imperative—for the seas remain distant to the thinking of most people. The finest U.S. minds, honed through the centuries-long vigil of seafaring experience, must mold this enlightened policy. The United States's future will be inextricably tied to the oceanic world. How well the nation rises to this challenge of the seas will depend ultimately on the enlightenment, the determination, and the direction of its policy drive, and this is a function of how well its people understand the sea—every substantive aspect of the global sea's influence on the human condition. For the United States must invest its energies and ingenuities as well as additional educative resources in multicultural, multidisciplinary oceanic education, to sharpen its citizens' understanding of the world ocean. This new knowledge will enrich their sense of the nation's future.

Notes

1. See Edmund A. Walsh, *Ships and the National Safety* (Washington, D.C., Georgetown School of Foreign Service, 1934): 7.

2. Speech to Harvard University Alumni, Cambridge, Mass., 7 June 1979.

3. Keynote address by Buckminster Fuller at the "Wealth and World Ocean Symposium," Washington, D.C., 4 February 1970.

4. Testimony before the U.S. Senate Subcommittee on Environmental Pollution, Senate Committee on Public Works, 94th Cong., 15 December 1975, 94–431: 3; and "America's Future," in *Parade* 8 (February 1976): 24.

5. Ibid.

6. Meg Greenfield, "Jimmy the Engineer?," in *Newsweek* 25 (April 1979) 89: 17, p. 104.

7. In conversation with Athelstan Spilhaus.

8. Henry Kissinger, *White House Years* (Boston and Toronto: Little, Brown and Co., 1979): 12.

Scenario I:
The Impact
of a New Law
of the Sea

James H. Doyle, Jr.

There are a number of potential crises at sea associated with the law of the sea, such as confrontations over the breadth of the territorial sea, passage through and over straits, high-seas freedoms, coastal-state rights and duties within the exclusive economic zone, exploitation of deep-seabed resources, pollution zones, military-exercise areas, restrictions on scientific research, and fishing rights. These confrontations take place between allies, friends, and potential enemies. They can involve warships and military aircraft, commercial shipping, fishing trawlers, research vessels, and exploitation equipment such as oil rigs and deep-seabed-mining gear. They can occur in territorial waters, straits, exclusive economic zones, and the high seas, or the ocean floor below and the airspace above. They can occur in time of peace or limited conflict or perhaps some situations in general war, although in this latter case the laws of land, aerial, and naval warfare and the Geneva Conventions for the protection of war victims would probably govern.

Before discussing potential crisis at sea in more detail, it would be well to review the current state of oceans law and its impact on the U.S. strategy. This is important because debate on law-of-the-sea issues has largely been focused on U.S. interests in deep-seabed resources—an important issue but by no means the only important issue.

The fundamental objective of U.S. national security is to preserve the United States as a free nation, with all its democratic institutions and values intact. To meet this objective we must maintain:

A political and military posture adequate to counter the threat or use of force against the United States, our allies, and our friends.

Access to and an uninterrupted supply of petroleum and critical raw materials.

An ability to protect our economic interests and citizens overseas.

It is quite clear that the Soviet Union is the predominant external threat to our national security. This threat is characterized by a massive Soviet buildup of conventional and strategic arms and the systematic use of diplomacy, military aid, and proxies throughout the world to further Soviet designs.

It is also clear that the new administration is taking steps to align U.S. military strategy, forces, and resources to match the Soviet threat and also to deal effectively with other threats to world peace.

For too many years, U.S. military strategy has been narrowly focused on the central front in Western Europe; our armed forces have been allowed to deteriorate in readiness, capability, and numbers to the extent that today the U.S. Navy is trying to carry out a three-ocean commitment with a one-and-one-half-ocean navy.

The new U.S. strategy that has emerged under the Reagan administration is global in nature and relies on sea power in a comprehensive and integral way: sea power to overcome the great distances separating the United States from its allies and friends in Europe, Asia, and South America; to offset the preponderance of power on and around the Eurasian continent; to forge economic ties between the United States, its allies, and third-world resource markets; to ensure an uninterrupted supply of petroleum for civil, industrial, and military uses; to provide trained forces ready for quick deployment to trouble spots; and to reinforce and resupply U.S. allied forces in a crisis.

Sea power means strong naval and air forces with maximum operational mobility through, over, and under the world's oceans. It means naval forces able to back up our friends, warn potential enemies, exert influence in ambiguous situations, demonstrate resolve, and deter or prevent actual conflicts. It means a strong merchant marine and free-and-open sea lines of communication, which bring in 50 percent of our oil, and 50 to 100 percent of our 20 most critical minerals (amounting to over 500 million tons of goods unloaded annually). Remember as well that without these sea routes for petroleum, Western Europe and Japan could not survive.

Naval and commercial mobility are paramount in the implementation of the new global sea-power strategy and must operate within the framework of the law of the sea. The fundamental foreign-policy objective of the U.S. law-of-the-sea policy is to achieve a stable, predictable, and harmonious regime of the oceans that protects and fosters U.S. interests.

The current state of oceans law is characterized by rapidly expanding coastal-state claims of ocean space, including those of the United States, which affect traditional freedoms of maritime travel and the movement of peacekeeping forces. It is clear that the combined effort of rapid technological advances in the exploitation of ocean resources and the increasingly assertive claims of coastal states to the benefits of such exploitation demand some new accommodation between coastal-state jurisdiction and high-seas freedoms. Neither the first UN Conference on Law of the Sea in 1958 nor a second conference in 1960 were able to reach agreement on the seaward limit of coastal-state claims, whether 3 miles or beyond.

Approximately one hundred countries claim territorial seas ranging from 12 to 200 miles, and several of these claims contain significant restrictions on the right of innocent passage through the territorial sea, such as the subjective criteria as to innocence. Also, a number of island countries have asserted the equivalent of sovereignty over waters embraced by their islands, for example, Indonesia and Fiji.

In addition, more than one hundred straits around the world are more than 6 but less than 24 miles wide. An extension of the territorial sea on both sides to 12 miles would eliminate the high-seas corridor. The bordering states would then be able to contend that the straits remain subject only to a right of innocent passage, with no right of overflight or submerged transit by submarines, and, moveover, with varying (and often unpredictable) interpretations of what is innocent. Indeed, all the world's major straits would be subject to these restrictions: the Strait of Gibraltar separating the Atlantic Ocean from the Mediterranean Sea; the links between the Pacific and Indian Oceans, including the straits of Malacca and Singapore as well as the Gateway Straits to the Indonesian Archipelago; the Strait of Hormuz at the entrance of the Persian Gulf; and the Bab el Mandeb Strait connecting the Indian Ocean to the Red Sea and Suez. The result could seriously impair the flexibility and survivability of our conventional and strategic forces and the reliability of our commercial shipping—all of which depend on freedom of navigation and unimpeded passage through international straits.

Finally, by prior action or relying on the consensus in favor of exclusive economic zones that emerged in 1975, a number of states now claim resource jurisdiction beyond the territorial sea out to 200 miles. A few purport to restrict navigation and overflight, and these claims may be difficult to distinguish from some of the more extensive territorial sea claims. Roughly 40 percent of the entire surface of the world's oceans lie within 200 miles from the shore. All the strategically important seas—the Mediterranean, the Caribbean, the Black Sea, the Red Sea, the Persian Gulf, and the Sea of Japan—would be decimated by coastal zones less than 200 miles in width if these vast areas ever became restricted as to navigation, overflight, and related activities.

Such was, and still is, the chaotic state of the law of the sea. One can legitimately ask whether the existing legal framework assists in implementing our new global sea-power strategy, encourages naval and commercial mobility, and is in consonance with our basic objectives associated with oceans law. The existing law of the sea has adverse political effects as well. First, the present instability of the oceans regime strains relations with our allies and friends, at a time when we can do without unnecessary confrontations.

Second, a challenge by a coastal state to our right of passage poses a very real dilemma. Should we ignore it, proceed ahead, and thus generate hostility and expose ourselves to political and economic costs? Remember, we do not have the military resources to fritter away; we must use our forces selectively and only in those instances that affect our vital interests. Or should we hold back, hamstring our forces, and call into question our credibility and resolve? This latter solution is always a loser and is inconsistent with our role as a world leader.

Third, legal rules of the sea that are not compatible with the routine peacetime deployments of our ships and planes do not assist in their primary role—that of deterring or controlling conflicts. The trick is to be in position before a crisis heats up to a shooting match and to attempt to prevent the escalation rather than arriving with too little, too late.

Fourth, it is important for our democratic government to gain maximum support for its policies and actions. We want to be and need to be on the side of international law. Any serious question about the legality of our actions can undermine our capacity to act and the ability of our allies and friends to support us.

Keeping in mind these problems and constraints in the current law of the sea, let us examine the draft of the law-of-the-sea treaty in relation to our national-security interests. Basically, the Draft Convention creates a common understanding and acceptance of rules compatible with global deployments of U.S. air and naval forces and seaborne commerce, and it maximizes the operational mobility and flexibility of our forces. Specifically:

1. The text establishes a 12-mile maximum limit for territorial sea and will result in a rollback of existing claims of jurisdiction beyond 12 miles. In addition, a more objective criterion for innocent passage is established.

2. The draft provides for unimpeded passage through straits used for international navigation not dependent on the destination, flag, type of vessel, or cargo. This so-called transit passage includes the right of overflight and submerged transit. The legitimate interests of the coastal state are protected in that it may enforce internationally approved maritime safety and pollution-control measures.

3. The draft guarantees freedom of navigation and overflight through archipelagos on terms equivalent to transit passage through straits, but in specified sea-lanes. Subject to this transit right, an archipelago state would have rights over waters embraced by baselines joining the outermost points of its outermost islands, equivalent to the rights of a coastal state over its territorial waters.

4. The text, in giving coastal states sovereign rights over living and nonliving resources in a 200-mile exclusive economic zone, preserves the traditional high-seas freedoms of navigation and overflight and other international lawful uses of the seas related to these freedoms, such as those associated with the operation of ships, aircraft, and submarine cables and pipelines.

5. Under the draft, the United States would have the right to bring suit

against a state that interferes with navigation or overflight.

In view of the chaotic state of existing oceans law, the alternative of having no treaty is very likely to be harmful to U.S. national-security interests and could seriously hamper implementation of our new global sea-power strategy.

As to bilateral agreements with coastal states on navigation and over-flight, anyone familiar with the political, military, and economic complications of base-rights negotiations would avoid this alternative like the plague. The bargain is often fragile and temporary: witness the history of bases throughout the world. Moreover, the concessions and costs are generally high. Further, U.S. interests in global mobility are worldwide and not limited to particular ocean areas. Finally, adoption of a bilateral or regional approach would undermine support for a comprehensive ocean regime.

As to deep-seabed minerals, there is certainly an important U.S. interest in preserving our access rights and developing and producing critical minerals. However, this interest must be kept in perspective. First, we require access to about twenty critical minerals, not just the four in the deep seabed. Second, access to deep-seabed minerals in no way reduces our dependence on the sea lines of communication. We still have to transport these minerals, from wherever mined, through economic zones and territorial seas. Third, the U.S. requirement in a year for any one seabed metal pales in comparison to the annual amount of seaborne commerce unloaded in the United States. For example, in the case of manganese we are talking less than one-half of 1 percent of our seaborne trade. Fourth, access to seabed minerals cannot be equated to the requirement of global and naval air mobility to deter and prevent conflict. This is not to say that serious obstacles in the seabeds portion of the draft treaty should not be removed.

Based on a consideration of U.S. maritime strategy and foreign-policy objectives, the disarray and uncertainty in existing international law of the sea, and the provisions of the draft treaty affecting our national-security interests, the new law-of-the-sea (LOS) treaty is a plus in reducing or controlling crisis. In other words, under the new treaty there is less chance of a confrontation with our allies or potential enemies and, if such a confrontation develops, the United States is in a better position to employ either diplomatic or military means to resolve the crisis. A few examples follow.

Suppose, as in the past, we need to provide military support to a friend, and our only access is to overfly an international strait, since other nations, for varying reasons, have denied overflight and landing rights in their territory. There is no question that the straits article provides that right to overfly, whereas without a treaty a legitimate basis for an opposite view arises because of disagreements over the breadth of the territorial sea and the traditional rule against overflights.

Or suppose, as in the past, a friendly nation demands advance clearance before the United States can operate air and naval forces within 200 miles of her shore. Again, the draft treaty restricts sovereign rights to no more than 12 miles and preserves traditional high-seas rights of navigation and over-flight within the 200-mile exclusive economic zone.

Suppose a potential enemy attempts by decree to seal off a portion of the high seas and then attempts to enforce that claim by an armed-inter-ceptor attack on U.S. aircraft entering this zone. Further, the United States opposes this action by force and shoots down the interceptors. It is abun-dantly clear that, under the new treaty, the decree is illegal and the United States has acted in legitimate self-defense and exercise of its rights over the high seas under international law. The international-law lesson from the Gulf of Sidra incident is that the international community represented at a LOS negotiating session in Geneva at the time raised no issue as to U.S. actions. They knew very well what the draft treaty said about unilateral attempts to annex parts of the high seas and privately felt that Libya de-served what she got from such illegal action. In the absence of the draft treaty, the international repercussions might have been different. This is not to say that U.S. actions would or should have been different. But it is always a plus to have U.S. actions aligned with international law.

Suppose that a U.S. commercial tanker, or any flags-of-convenience tanker carrying oil for the United States or its allies is detained, searched, or otherwise harassed while transiting through the territorial sea or exclusive economic zone. The draft treaty carefully sets forth the right of innocent passage through the territorial sea and high-seas passage through the exclu-sive economic zone. The interests of the coastal state are carefully spelled out to include protecting only legitimate interests according to objective standards. Thus, if the vessel is in legitimate transit and has complied with international standards regarding pollution, there is no basis for interfer-ence with the voyage. Because of the uncertainty in existing law and varying coastal state claims and regulations, there have been a number of incidents of harassment of commercial shipping.

Finally, assume that one state seizes the exploitation equipment of another, such as an oil rig or seabed bucket (the controversy might have been generated by a dispute over who owns the continental shelf). The draft treaty attempts to establish uniform rules of delimitation. Or the issue might be over rights to exploit a particular area of the deep seabeds. Again, the draft treaty establishes uniform rules as to access. In this particular case, the draft treaty does not attempt to lay down rules as to the naked use of force. One would necessarily fall back on traditional international law governing self-help and self-defense.

There are, no doubt, other examples of crisis at sea that could be postulated. They would cover the spectrum from pure use of force to a mild diplomatic protest. The point is that the new law-of-the-sea treaty, if adopted, provides a consistent and predictable framework of oceans law that would cover many situations short of general war. This treaty is needed because existing oceans law, particularly that affecting our navigation rights, is uncertain and could become less clear. The United States—in attempting to control or resolve a crisis—is in a much stronger position politically and internationally if it can be said that its actions—diplomatic or military—are in accordance with international law; U.S. policy is affected by domestic and world opinion, and it is always well to have the law on our side. Insofar as our vital national-security interests are concerned, the draft law-of-the-sea treaty appears to be on our side.

Scenario II: Potential Naval Hostilities in the Bab el Mandeb

Donald B. Disney, Jr.

Setting and Conflict

It is 0630 on 10 May 1982. Amphibious readiness group (ARG) 3-82, consisting of USS *Inchon* (LPH-12), USS *Raleigh* (LPD-1), USS *Spiegel Grove* (LSD-32), and USS *Harlan County* (LST-1196), is conducting a southbound transit of the Red Sea approximately 20 nm north of the Bab el Mandeb Strait. After an uneventful Suez Canal transit on 3 and 4 May, the ARG [still under Commander in Chief U.S. Navy Europe Operational Control (CINCUSNAVEUR OPCON)] is on a periodic deployment of about six weeks in the Indian Ocean. The 2,000-man, 32 marine amphibious unit (MAU) is embarked in the ARG shipping.

USS *Harlan County* has just rejoined the formation after visiting the Yemen Arab Republic. The visit was cut short, however, because of rumors of saboteur teams targeted against *Harlan County*. Because of this information, the ARG is at condition-III readiness. During its Indian Ocean deployment, the ARG/MAU is scheduled for several training exercises in the region. Various port visits will also be conducted to demonstrate U.S. presence and resolve.

Commander Amphibious Squadron (COMPHIBRON Four), in USS *Inchon*, has signalled his intention to transit the large strait of the Bab el Mandeb to the west of Perim Island. Intelligence reports from the last month indicate that the People's Democratic Republic of Yemen (PDRY) has reinforced its positions on Perim by adding surface-to-surface missile batteries. In the last week, Ethiopia and the PDRY have restated their territorial sea claims and, in notices to mariners, warned that foreign warships may be subject to escort, boarding, and search while in claimed territorial waters. A strident anti–United States propaganda campaign has also been initiated.

At 0700, ARG 3-82 has just been overflown by a flight of four MIG-21s showing PDRY markings. *Inchon* visually has two unidentified high-speed surface craft approaching at a range of 15 miles, fine on the port bow. Shortly after the sighting of the surface craft, four large flashes of light are observed from the direction of Perim Island.

Events Leading to Conflict

In August 1981, during a tour of Middle East and Persian Gulf countries, Libya's Colonel Qaddafi convinced the leaders of Steadfastness Front Countries (SFC)—Ethiopia and the PDRY—to cooperate more closely in mutual defense. This agreement was widely viewed as Qaddafi's attempt to form a group of Arab states that would actively resist efforts of the Gulf Cooperation Council (GCC), which had been created as the result of Saudi and Omani efforts. Reactions among Gulf States, notably Kuwait and the United Arab Emirates (UAE), to Qaddafi's visit were cool. Sultan Qabus of Oman, facing some evidence of renewed insurgence on the PDRY border near the Dhofar region, was noticeably concerned over Qaddafi's visit.

Libya, the PDRY, and Ethiopia pledged to resist all imperialist efforts of the United States. It was also rumored that in return for their support, Ethiopia and the PDRY would receive substantial Libyan financial aid. Moderate countries in the region, led by Oman, Somalia, and Egypt, felt that Libyan support for terrorist activities would become more of a threat. Shortly after the agreement was concluded, Western governments determined that there was a possible threat to shipping in the Red Sea and Gulf of Aden. This was especially worrisome in view of the 12-nm territorial sea claimed by the PDRY and Ethiopia, and the PDRY's 24-nm security zone. Astute observers noted that this claim narrowed the safe-transit area from the Gulf of Aden to the Bab el Mandeb Strait and that Ethiopian and PDRY claims effectively covered most of the Strait. Special warning notices to mariners were issued advising all shipping to exercise caution while in the vicinity of Ethiopian and PDRY territorial waters.

As a corollary to these developments, Egypt's late president, Anwar Sadat, warned the United States of increased efforts by Libya and the USSR to encircle Egypt and the Sudan. He repeatedly asserted that the 20,000 Cuban troops in the region, coupled with large stocks of modern Soviet weapons, notably in Libya, in effect added up to Moscow's own Southwest Asian rapid-deployment force.

The United States was concerned by Sadat's prognosis and responded by initiating the planning of several military options, including B-52s, AWACS, and fighter deployments, as well as increased military aid to Egypt. This U.S. effort was greatly accelerated with Sadat's assassination. Egypt's primary worry was that Libya might attempt a back-door victory through overthrowing Sudan's President Nimieri. In Egyptian eyes, Qaddafi's actions in Chad, coupled with insurgent infiltrations into Sudan from Ethiopia, posed a grave threat to the Sudan, which controls the headwaters of the Nile and, therefore, ultimately to Egypt.

Washington hoped to accomplish several objectives in the area: guarantee access to Persian Gulf oil, resolve the Lebanese crisis, continue progress toward Middle East peace within the framework of the Camp David Accords, bolster the morale of regional friends, and achieve access and support for the RDJTF. It was felt that the morale of U.S. partners could be raised by a strong show of U.S. strength (largely naval), coupled with increased arms sales and efforts to form a regional-defense network led by key states. The first and last of the U.S. objectives were hampered by the continued reluctance of most Gulf states to allow RDJTF forces on their soil. These states, including Saudi Arabia, were concerned that an overt, prominent U.S. ground presence could draw in Moscow and could also weaken their internal strength because of lack of progress on reaching a peace settlement with Israel. They reminded the United States that Israel was still widely perceived in the region as a U.S. client. Doubts about the RDJTF's true purpose (for example, seizure of oil fields) were still prevalent throughout most of the Gulf states. Yet there was fear that the Soviets or Iran could destroy them. The United States was, therefore, not criticized too vocally by moderate Arabs as long as an over-the-horizon presence was maintained.

Resolution of the Lebanese crisis and progress toward peace proved to be extremely difficult. At best, a situation of no peace but no war continued to prevail. Israeli actions, partially designed to prevent Washington from moving closer to the Arabs, continued to reinforce Arab perceptions that the main threat to the region was Israel, not the Soviet Union.

Sadat's death cast several immediate doubts on the overall peace process and the stability of Egypt. The new Egyptian President Hosni Mubarak's rapid and controlled accession to power served to alleviate most of these doubts, as did Egypt's reconfirmed intention to abide by the provisions of the Camp David Accords. Egypt had little choice in this matter, since U.S. support was required to face a perceived threat from Libya to the west and economic problems at home. Israel certainly would not return the remaining portion of the Sinai (seized in 1967) unless the Camp David Accords were adhered to. Failure to obtain full sovereignty over the Sinai could greatly endanger the rule of Hosni Mubarak, since it had become a political cause célèbre in Egypt and a main justification for peace with Israel.

Following U.S. approval for the AWACS sale to Saudi Arabia in October, several policy lines appeared to be converging—U.S.-Israeli strategic cooperation was moving along, the Saudis and other pro-Western Arabs were pleased by the sale, and the United States was successful in bringing off the latest in a series of RDJTF exercises in the area. These exercises, however, were accompanied by extensive radical Arab (and Iranian) propaganda against traitorous support for a U.S. invasion of the Arab homelands. Libya, Ethiopia, and the PDRY were the primary leaders in this effort, with some of the most pointed and hostile anti-U.S. rhetoric.

Unfortunately, in November, Crown Price Fahd chose to press for Arab acceptance of his eight-point Middle East peace program. Unguarded U.S. comments favorable to the plan, as well as the approval of the AWACS sale, served to increase Israeli alarm at a perceived U.S. tilt toward the Arab world.

By the end of 1981, the United States faced a hard-line Israeli government that was becoming increasingly intransigent on autonomy negotiations and much more assertive in threatening moderate Arab states. Meanwhile, Tel Aviv pressed Cairo to be more forthcoming in the areas of normalization and an autonomy framework and hinted that the return of the Sinai could depend on progress in bilateral talks. West Bank occupation policy, which had appeared to be loosening up under Israeli Defense Minister Sharon, suddenly reverted to a stronger stance, as widespread Palestinian Arab riots took place. The moderate Arabs, led by Saudi Arabia and Jordan, pressed the United States to control Israeli actions or face the consequences of renewed Arab hostility.

In mid-February 1982, two key developments occurred: Saudi Arabia, with a majority Arab consensus, presented Fahd's plan to the UN Security Council for approval; and the United States decided to consult with its closest allies and encourage all U.S. citizens residing in Libya to leave. The Saudi UN campaign presented the United States with a difficult and delicate problem.

If the plan passed without a U.S. veto, Arab support for regional-security policies would be maintained, probably at the cost of a strong Israeli reaction. There was considerable concern in the West that the fragile cease-fire in Lebanon, in effect since July of 1981, could be destroyed if Prime Minister Begin displayed his pique by attacking Syrian missile sites in the Biqa Valley or by smashing reinforced Palestinian Liberation Organization (PLO) positions in the south. On the other hand, a U.S. veto of the resolution would severely damage ties with Saudi Arabia and could lead to increased Arab links, as advocated by Kuwait, to the USSR. An abstention would be viewed by either side as an attempt to avoid the issue and would also have adverse results for U.S. southwest Asian policy.

It was decided to pursue delaying tactics in the UN. U.S. Ambassador Kirkpatrick embarked on a fairly successful attempt to stall a vote while Secretary Haig attempted to work with Crown Prince Fahd toward a modified plan that would clearly recognize Israel's legitimacy as a state.

In late March, the U.S. ambassadors to Rome and Paris were assassinated by Libyan commando squads. In a worldwide broadcast, Colonel Qaddafi claimed that the assassinations were acts of retaliation in defense of the great Jumhuriya for U.S. aggressive actions in shooting down two Libyan SU-22s in August 1981.

An economic embargo of Libya was declared. Two U.S. carrier battle groups and ARG 3-82 were immediately stationed off the coast of Libya for approximately three weeks, and diplomatic efforts were pursued to seek international condemnation of Libya for its terrorist acts. Shortly after their arrival on station, the Carrier Battle Group (CVBGs) were ordered to conduct a retaliatory strike on Benghazi Airfield. The strike was conducted with minimal damage to U.S. forces, and Qaddafi was warned that unless an immediate apology and restitution were made for the assassinations, Libya would be punished further.

The UN Security Council resolution condemning Libya was vetoed by the Soviet Union. In its Security Council statement, the USSR asserted that it would stand by its SFC friends in the region and warned of military action if necessary. A Soviet airlift of weapons and advisors was immediately initiated, and IL-38 and TU-16 Badger wings were moved to Tripoli.

Following the UN veto, President Reagan directed that steps be undertaken to weaken Colonel Qaddafi's hold on Libya. One U.S. CVBG and ARG 3-82 was ordered to resume normal operations one week later. The second CVBG was ordered to remain within forty-eight hours of Libyan waters.

At the end of April, the Sinai was returned to Egypt, and a multinational force and observers were in place. Hosni Mubarak, faced with no success in achieving Palestinian autonomy and on the receiving end of Arab world criticism for selling out the Palestinians, openly endorsed the Saudi peace plan, which was finally back on the UN Security Council agenda for debate. The GCC on 3 May announced a formal defense agreement, accompanied by a sharply worded statement that was critical of superpower presence in the Red Sea and Persian Gulf. Bahrain notified the U.S. ambassador that Middle East Force (MIDEASTFOR's) status would have to be reviewed and could likely hinge on U.S. approval of the Fahd plan. In a personal communiqué, Prime Minister Menachim Begin notified President Reagan of Israel's extreme opposition to the Fahd plan and warned of possible forceful moves to ensure Israeli security should the plan be approved by the UN Security Council.

Colonel Qaddafi was warned by Cuban security advisors on 4 May of a possible U.S. assassination attempt. He immediately contacted the Soviet Union and asked for protection. The Ethiopian and PDRY ambassadors were notified of the need for an urgent appointment. The Soviet chargé d'affaires informed Qaddafi on 6 May that a crack security detachment was en route and the Soviet *Medrom*, augmented by the *Kiev*, had been placed on increased alert, as had Soviet units in the Indian Ocean, including the *Minsk*.

The U.S. CVBG commander in the Indian Ocean at Gonzo station, on 6 May reported to the NCA that Soviet submarine activity was growing and requested an increase in P-3 surveillance flights operating from Seeb, Oman, and Berbera, Somalia. Late in the day on 8 May, a P-3 en route to Djibouti for normal refueling reported that evasive action had been taken after a probable missile firing in the vicinity of Perim Island.

On 9 May, Soviet units at Dahalak Island, Assab, Massawa, and Socotra sortied and proceeded to a rendezvous in the Indian Ocean some 200 miles east of Socotra. Late in the day on 9 May, COMPHIBRON Four reported an Ethiopian patrol craft shadowing at 10 miles for approximately two hours. The patrol craft broke off and returned toward Ethiopia at sunset.

Conclusion: Thinking about Strategy

William J. Taylor, Jr., and
Steven A. Maaranen

The level of interstate and intrastate conflict in the world will be high in the 1980s. Much of it will occur in the regions occupied by the developing states, either generated by conditions and concerns internal to those states or eventuating from their sovereign relations with other states. Some will be stimulated or exploited by major world powers—in particular the Soviet Union—for their own ends. The United States will be required to discern among these conflicts the ones that pose genuine threats to U.S. interests, identify the nature of the threat, and formulate appropriate responses. To protect its own interests, the United States should have the ability to apply diplomacy or force at whatever level is required for each situation, whether before or after a crisis has risen. This capability implies a military strategy and force posture that prepare and allow for the use or nonuse of military force as appropriate and necessary.

We focus here on low-intensity conflict because it will pose the most common threat to U.S. interests in the 1980s. This focus does not mean that other threats to U.S. interests should be ignored; it does mean that they should not be addressed to the exclusion of the more common problem. The probability of central war between the United States and the Soviet Union will be small, as will the probability of large-scale conventional war between NATO and the Warsaw Pact countries (although the consequences of such conflicts would be so great that they must always take first place in defense planning). Similarly, large-scale war between the Soviet Union and the Peoples' Republic of China is unlikely.

As the regional discussions and scenarios in this book have indicated, we must expect conflicts in the developing world to be numerous, although the causes and circumstances of each conflict will be unique. Still, certain generalizations should apply. Internal conflicts will arise chiefly from problems associated with institutional development, just as they did in cases of the French and Russian revolutions, in the German and Italian wars of unification, and so on. But development may be even more difficult and disrupting in the 1980s because of the special problems arising from shortages of natural resources essential for development—particularly energy resources. Even resource-rich states with enlightened leadership prob-

---

For some passages in this chapter, we are indebted to Colonel George K. Osborn III, Department of Social Sciences, U.S. Military Academy.

459

ably will not escape problems in building durable political institutions in the coming decade. Mid-range states with moderate resources will face more serious challenges, and those without any natural resources, particularly energy resources, will face almost insurmountable obstacles and may in consequence fall victim to internal violence flowing from frustration and despair. In many developing states internal violence will also continue to flow from tribal differences and hostilities and from differing views about the proper regime, motivated by clashing ideologies, religions, and other differences.

External conflict for the developing nations will arise from problems of jurisdiction over or access to scarce resources, because of the great importance of natural resources for development. Other issues will concern irredentist claims to populations or territories, whether resulting from previous wars or from colonial divisions of territory.

Other factors are likely to contribute in new ways to intrastate and interstate conflict. Among these are the ready and increasing availability of sophisticated weaponry on world markets and the relative ineffectiveness of supernational organizations. The first factor may intensify conflicts and broaden their geographical scope, and the second may reduce the ability of outside states to contain conflicts. The peculiar capability of nuclear-weapon proliferation to affect both regional balances and the potential intensity and outcome of conflicts will be another complicating factor in conflicts in the 1980s.

Conflicts within and among developing nations will be troublesome enough even if all outside states observe the general rule of noninterference in the internal affairs of others. But agreement not to intervene, even if feasible theoretically, probably would not be effective in most cases—for reasons to be outlined. In addition, although leaders in developing states might agree in principle to nonintervention by outsiders, in practice their governments or other factions are likely to seek assistance in advancing their causes when and where they can find it. Outside powers will often have powerful motives to intervene when the opportunity arises.

Low-Intensity Conflict and U.S. Interests

Political violence in the developing world will not always involve interests that are vital or even important to the United States. Preeminently the United States seeks to live in peace and security at home. Abroad the United States seeks to retain the international status quo, which has been favorable to the protection of domestic security, and it favors the development of wider prosperity among nations, national self-determination, and the advancement of the world's states toward democracy. Yet the United States, despite what some have charged, has not sought the role of international gendarme, and has not consciously sought to impose a pax Americana.

It is equally clear, however, that the "detached and distant situation" described by George Washington in his farewell address has not applied for a long time. Indeed, Washington himself went on to say that "the period is not far off . . . when we may choose peace or war, as our interest, guided by justice, shall counsel." In Washington's day, our interests could be protected or advanced through our contacts in London, Paris, the Hague, and Lisbon. During the acknowledged bipolar era, the distinction between the so-called free world and the communist world was clear-cut, and the determination of our interests in relation to these distinctions was relatively straightforward.

Today U.S. interests have become worldwide. It is often said these days that we no longer live in a bipolar world and that political and military power have diffused (it certainly is true that U.S. power has declined relative to U.S. interests.) That does not necessarily mean that U.S. interests abroad have contracted or that the resources needed to protect them are necessarily any less. Our interests have only become more complex.

Today, U.S. interests are nowhere more difficult to clarify and protect than in the developing world. Our struggle to identify the best policy toward El Salvador and the rest of Central America is but one very visible example of this. Our need to protect our interests in these circumstances, at a time when the United States is less powerful relative to its industrialized friends (and enemies), calls for continuing critical analysis of interests and consultation with other states to determine when and how those interests should be defended. Prestigious U.S. and European councils now advocate joint preparations. Where there is a congruence of well-understood vital or important Western (plus Japanese) interests in areas where challenges to those interests are likely, joint contingency plans appear both desirable and feasible.

The Role of the Soviet Union in Low-Intensity Conflict

Few subjects can generate as much heat as the debate over the intentions behind Soviet foreign policy. With allowances for variants and combinations, there are three fundamental views: (1) the USSR remains a state in the service of an international revolutionary ideology, seeking every feasible opportunity to advance the cause of world revolution, accepting tactical retreat as a momentary necessity without ever altering revolutionary goals; (2) the USSR is a status quo power, dedicated to holding onto what it has, suspicious of external threats, willing to exploit weakness in the enemy camp, but basically unwilling to risk much outside its own sphere of influence; (3) the USSR has become an imperialist power, using ideology (like any other tool of foreign policy) for what it is worth, but basically using flexible tactics to pursue a strategy of world dominion, not in the interest of some transnational ideology but for the absolute security of the Soviet state and perpetuation of its unique political system.

Unfortunately, the heat generated by argument among these divergent views sheds little light. Until (if ever) more concrete evidence is available to judge Soviet intentions and motivations, and until much more is known about the process of making decisions in the USSR, it is prudent to base our judgment and action on the record of Soviet conduct. Here matters are somewhat clearer. There can be no doubt of the quantitative and qualitative buildup in Soviet military capacity across the board, at least since the early 1960s. Given events in Hungary (1956), Poland (1959), Czechoslovakia (1968), and Poland again (1982), no one should doubt Soviet capability or willingness if necessary to intervene directly or indirectly in the affairs of its Eastern European satellites, with military force if necessary. Nor can there be any doubt of Soviet willingness to intervene militarily in the developing states, when and where opportunities arise to extend Soviet influence and establish Soviet base facilities. There can be little doubt of Soviet willingness to use proxies where it is feasible to do so and to exploit its own friends and allies when they can contribute. And finally, there can be little doubt of Soviet willingness to probe on a global scale for opportunities that might be exploited more intensively.

When considering prospective U.S. intervention in the developing world, account must be taken of specific developments in Soviet military capabilities. The Soviet Navy has a global reach today that it lacked a generation ago. It is true this navy may have only limited staying power (although very impressive initial striking power) in the event of major conventional or nuclear war involving the Warsaw Pact countries and NATO, but its peacetime deployments and the constant search for basing facilities in the developing world give it an impressive and growing intervention capability in local conflicts. Recent increases in naval infantry with associated amphibious craft, as well as construction of Kiev-class carriers and Kirov-class cruisers add to Soviet intervention capability. Soviet strategic airlift also has improved steadily in recent years, and there is no sign that this will flag.

Soviet military personnel have gained some experience in supplying and training local forces in overseas areas. With the notable exception of Afghanistan, the USSR has not deployed ground force units in large quantities outside the Warsaw Pact countries, but it has sent Soviet advisors and technicians, and trained, equipped, transported, and supplied proxies in many places. The role of the Cubans in Angola and Ethiopia is well known, and reports of an airborne force in Yemen (Aden) composed of Ethiopians, Palestinians, and Yemenis may indicate willingness to experiment further with proxies in the Middle East. Evidence of Soviet-sponsored Cuban activities in Nicaragua and El Salvador coupled with a greater Soviet naval presence in the Caribbean may connote a major Soviet proxy initiative in the United States' backyard. The Soviets have been building up a capability to intervene in the developing world. They have demonstrated a willingness to intervene when attractive opportunities appear, and this has led to access to facilities that may permit future intervention.

United States Forces for the 1980s

Overall Mission Requirements

During the 1970s U.S. military-posture requirements declined from a demand to be able to fight simultaneously "2.5 wars," then "1.5 wars," then to the swing strategy for one war plus a minor contingency. In every case, it has been assumed that forces designated for the major contingency in Europe could be earmarked for other contingencies. This assumption probably is no longer valid. Conventional forces committed to the crucial role of deterring a Soviet attack in central Europe must remain in place and on call in Europe, in the United States, and elsewhere, readily available for commitment to the European battle. One lesson we should have learned from Vietnam was that our current level of armed forces is not adequate for 1.5 wars, even with the draft. With a Vietnam War high of 3.5 million people in uniform, U.S. policymakers were forced to draw down to dangerous levels the personnel and equipment committed to or designated for reinforcement of Central Europe and to use Europe as a rotation base for Vietnam.

Since Vietnam, challenges to the security of the United States and its allies have grown. The Reagan administration apparently intends to augment the missions assigned to U.S. armed forces. The forces needed to counteract the most important threat over the next five years—Soviet strategic nuclear superiority that could enable the USSR to coerce the West or that could cover a nuclear or conventional attack in Europe—will be expanded. Only the means for doing so (for example, missiles, basing modes, bombers, and ballistic-missile defense) remain in doubt. More to the point, the deterrence and war-fighting missions of the U.S. armed forces are being expanded significantly, with implications not only for conventional-force strategy and doctrine but also for the size of the total force required for the future.

Official opinion now appears to be that the best counter to Soviet conventional capabilities (backed up as they are by tactical nuclear- and chemical-weapon systems) is an integrated U.S./allied doctrine and force structure for conventional, chemical, and battlefield nuclear-war fighting. The first signs of movement in this direction were the Carter administration's decision (with NATO concurrence) to deploy long-range (or intermediate) theater nuclear weapons (Pershing II and Cruise missiles) and the aborted decision to deploy enhanced radiation (neutron) weapons in Europe. A more recent signal was the July 1981 neutron-reversal decision, in which Secretary of Defense Weinberger decided to manufacture neutron projectiles but not deploy them to Europe.

Evidence also suggests that the growing concern with Soviet military expansion may lead the United States to increase its conventional-force capabilities by: (1) altering the structure of the U.S. armed forces; (2) augmenting U.S. capabilities to deploy military forces rapidly to disparate locations around the world and sustain them in combat; and (3) expanding the number and types of roles that U.S. armed forces must be prepared to execute. At the strategic-policy level, this may call for a capability for horizontal escalation (as opposed to vertical escalation to tactical and then strategic nuclear exchanges) of any conflict initiated by the Soviet Union. This is not to say that vertical escalation has been ruled out. Secretary of Defense Weinberger reaffirmed in his Senate confirmation testimony that the United States retains that option. Horizontal escalation appears to mean that, if the Soviets initiate military conflict in a theater where they hold a strategic military advantage, the United States will consider deploying military forces rapidly to other theaters where the United States, in tandem with its allies, holds comparative strategic military advantage.

Such a strategic concept has two theoretical advantages. First, the United States might be able to threaten Soviet vital interests, without resorting to the risky and perhaps self-deterring threat of vertical escalation, perhaps without even directly confronting Soviet forces. Second, if U.S. armed forces can be placed rapidly in another theater where the Soviets have vital national interests, but where they have not deployed military forces, the awful psychological burden of initiating a direct military confrontation between the superpowers, or opting for vertical escalation, will be placed on the shoulders of the Soviet leadership. However, horizontal escalation requires that the Soviets are not able successfully to threaten vertical escalation. This will be far from assumed as the 1980s proceed. This concept explains in part the rationale for forward basing in the Indian Ocean/Persian Gulf region as well as pre-positioning equipment (but not basing U.S. military personnel) in central Norway.

Beyond seeking a capability for horizontal escalation, there appears to be a shift of U.S. strategy away from older concepts that underlie the 1.5-wars and swing strategies. Both these strategies envisioned NATO-designated forces being temporarily diverted to participate in a brief lesser war. The new direction appears to be toward developing forces capable of rapid deployment anywhere, without derogation of deterrent or conventional war-fighting capabilities in NATO Europe. This would be a significant change. Either U.S. conventional forces would have to be expanded to allow for extended, simultaneous, non-NATO contingencies or European nations would have to expand their military forces, releasing U.S. units for such missions.

The expanded mission requirements of the Reagan administration's ". . . more global approach toward the employment of force" are especially important for the Army. The Army chief of staff indicated he will require manpower levels that he doubts can be acquired without a return to the draft. The Navy appears to be moving from sea denial to sea-control missions with emphasis on protecting sea lines of communication. It is possible to overstate the doctrinal significance of this change; however, significant numbers of new ships will be required. This is especially so in the areas of: (1) sealift for reinforcement and supply in longer-war scenarios in the European theater; (2) support for larger numbers of amphibious landings in defended or undefended areas, for example, Marines in the Persian Gulf; and (3) supplying and supporting local land-combat operations in far-flung regions of the world.

The expanded missions of the Army and Navy will demand expanded air forces both to project forces and to support combat operations in distant areas. In the European theater there will be a need to expand counterair, air-superiority, and battlefield-interdiction operations. The new emphasis on rapid deployment of Army and Marine forces implies greater Air Force responsibilities to defend lines of communication as well as the need for rapidly supporting over-the-shore joint-force operations. In addition to requiring more equipment and a larger infrastructure, all these new missions will demand many more U.S. soldiers in uniform.

To meet these new mission requirements and to fill the other defense gaps that have been detected, the Reagan administration introduced an amended five-year defense-budget plan for fiscal years 1982–1986, calling for: (1) $32.6 billion in surge spending to accelerate force modernization and sustainability to a level in 1982 that would not have been reached until 1984 under the Carter budget and (2) an annual increase in defense appropriations at a rate of 7 percent, rather than the 5 percent proposed by the Carter program.

Overall Force Requirements

One of the purposes of the Reagan defense program is to develop combat forces adequate to meet expanded threats to U.S. interests worldwide, including low-intensity conflicts in the developing world. But just how many forces of what types are going to be required? This depends on a number of assumptions. For example, will third-world contingencies be carried out without the threat of Soviet involvement?

When there is a possibility of Soviet involvement, how much warning time will there be of Soviet attack; how quickly can Soviet units be mobilized and brought to combat-ready status; how long can the Soviets sustain units in combat; and how will NATO use the warning time available? One must assume in the worst case that any calculated Soviet attack in central Europe would not be a geographically isolated event. Understanding current inadequacies in U.S. airlift and sealift and manpower-mobilization capabilities, Soviet planners almost certainly would tie down U.S. and NATO forces in Asia, the Caribbean, Africa, and the Middle East either by initiating hostilities there or by raising the level of alert sufficiently to preclude the shifting of allied forces to the European theater. Allied forces in the European theater might similarly be tied down during Soviet operations elsewhere (for example, in the Persian Gulf).

Any U.S.-Soviet confrontation might quickly become a worst-case, global military operation where shortfalls in U.S. force structure and manpower would quickly constrain U.S. options. In such a high-threat situation, Army problems would be the most serious. It would take months to mobilize current U.S. Army Reserve units; the immediate shortfall in Army requirements would be substantial. Of some thirty-one Army divisions that might be required worldwide, only sixteen would be readily available. For the Army alone the shortfall would be at least 1 million people, and some analysts would add another 235,000 for the Navy, Marine Corps, and Air Force.[6]

On the other hand, one might assume a long period of international crisis and longer warning times, so that war would be slow in developing and would be sustained over a long period. In this scenario, U.S. reserves could be mobilized, additional inductees could be trained, and the picture could change significantly. About twenty-nine Army divisions might be required worldwide, and up to twenty-four might be made available. The additional Army manpower requirements would total at least 250,000 but could come to 500,000 depending on the extent to which the current shortfall in the trained manpower pool had been overcome.

A final scenario would assume long warning times, Soviet objectives in Western Europe only, and greater limitations on Soviet conventional land forces. Requirements would be on the order of twenty-six Army divisions, with up to twenty-four made available.

Reagan administration planning for the five-year defense program for 1982–1987 envisioned an increase in active-duty manpower and strength of over 200,000 by 1987 (of which about 90,000 would have been for the Army). There appeared to be little doubt that all the armed services except the Army could meet their active duty and reserve quotas by 1987. But the Army chief of staff doubted that the Army could meet a 90,000 increase without conscription.[7] Unless extraordinary manpower actions are approved by Congress, the Army almost certainly will continue to have a serious shortfall in both active-duty forces and the reserves—especially if so-called Reaganomics works and the economy improves.

Beyond manpower issues, which have been covered by press reports, the new mission requirements will demand modified training of considerable import, for example in joint special-forces operations.[8] All the services have been involved in a massive effort to rethink strategy, doctrine, training, and weapons acquisition. For example, the Army is in the midst of a major overhaul of its basic "How to Fight" manual, partly at Army initiative, partly under the assaults of Robert W. Komer (former under secretary of defense for plans) and partly from the initiatives of the "Reform Movements" led by analysts such as James Woolsey, Edward Luttwak, Jeffrey Record, Steven Canby, Pierre Sprey, and John Boyd, joined now by the expanding Congressional Reform Caucus and by strategists in uniform who routinely remain nameless.[9]

Whatever the results of current efforts to change strategy and doctrine, we can be relatively certain that, given bureaucratic processes, there will be a long delay between studies, proposals, and decisions on training requirements and the implementation of training changes that reflect those decisions in the professional military-education system, at training facilities and in active-duty-unit training programs worldwide. The delay for National Guard and selected reserve units will be even greater. In the meantime, U.S. conventional forces will be inadequate to accomplish missions indicated by plausible scenarios for the 1980s.

Forces for Low-Intensity Conflicts

The conclusion of active U.S. military participation in Southeast Asia permitted our military leaders to focus on serious problems that had developed with our central-war forces and forces committed to NATO. Soviet attainment of strategic nuclear parity in the 1960s, the impressive upgrading of Soviet air and ground forces, especially in Central Europe, and increased Soviet capabilities to deny vital North Atlantic shipping lanes demanded a U.S. response if the viability of NATO were to be ensured. The U.S. public and policymakers were thoroughly disenchanted with projection forces and low-intensity, limited-risk military operations, identifying them with the Vietnam experience. As détente lost its savor in the mid-1970s, and information on the impact of relative shifts in the balance of power in favor of the USSR penetrated public and congressional consciousness, interest intensified in rehabilitating the U.S. central strategic forces and NATO forces.

In many ways, the change in emphasis was a reversion to pre-1965. The

Air Force concentrated on manned bombers and on missiles critical to deter (and wage) central war and to fight the possible air battle in NATO. The Army concentrated on forces to meet the demands of forward defense in Europe in the critical early days of hostilities (or mobilization preceding imminent hostilities). The Navy concentrated on providing its contribution to the central-war triad and to the sea control of the North Atlantic. Even the Marine Corps began to turn from more traditional projection-force concerns to beefing up its division to carry out a greater role in a NATO/ Warsaw Pact war. The argument was advanced that, although the so-called general-purpose forces could be employed anywhere, they had to be trained and equipped to fight in the highest-intensity combat environment envisioned, that is, the central sector of Europe.

But later in the 1970s it became clearer that the USSR was also developing a significant capability (via new fleet capabilities, proxy forces, and so on) and an inclination (first in Angola, then in Ethiopia) to intervene militarily in the developing world. The possibility emerged that political violence in the developing world might have serious impact on the interests of the United States, its allies, and its friends. And it became obvious that U.S. capabilities for intervention were severely limited and declining. Very recently, attention has begun to shift again to what might be done to meet these contingencies. In this climate, Secretary of Defense Brown first advanced the concept of the rapid-deployment force.

Although almost three years have elapsed since its formation, it is not entirely clear just what threats the current rapid-deployment joint task force (RDJTF) is designed to counter, where or how it will be deployed, or what weapons systems it will use. Due to become a unified command in January 1983, the RDJTF will have responsibility for eighteen countries of Southwest Asia between the European Command and the Pacific Command. The force mix will include eleven tactical fighter squadrons from the 7th Air Force, the 18th Airborne Corps, Navy elements including up to three aircraft-carrier battle groups, one Marine division and a Marine amphibious force (with thirteen pre-positioning ships in the Indian Ocean) and a large shopping list of support forces. Current inadequacies in airlift and sealift and pre-positioning ships are well-known and addressed in the five-year defense program.

In light of our need to address contingencies in the developing world in the 1980s, the development of the RDJTF concept is welcome. However, there are a number of issues that need to be resolved. Most important, there is a qualitative issue concerning strategy, to be treated later. Also of immediate concern are the following: (1) whether adequate forces would ever be made available for an RDJTF outside Europe at a time of high tension in Europe; (2) whether the United States is about to forge a sledgehammer to swat flies; and (3) whether sufficient attention is being paid to the kinds of specialized forces that might be needed and used at very low levels of intervention.

The U.S. armed forces, since the advent of Secretary Robert Mc-Namara, have been divided into the two broad categories of strategic forces and general-purpose forces. Strategic forces are the central-war forces of ICBMs, SLBMs, and manned bombers and their supporting infrastructures that make up the triad. All other forces, including some dually capable ones (conventional or nuclear, such as carrier-borne attack aircraft) are general-purpose forces. General-purpose forces tend to be equipped and trained to fight and survive in the environment of a general war (nuclear or nonnuclear) between NATO and the Warsaw Pact countries. Because of the extremely high demands for (and on) such forces in the early days of a NATO mobilization or NATO/Warsaw Pact war, the services have been reluctant to build up special-purpose forces for non-NATO commitments. Service leaders have insisted that forces that are able to survive in the NATO/Warsaw Pact war environment are obviously capable of carrying out any mission in a less intense one. The dispersion of sophisticated technology (air-defense systems, antiarmor weapons, and the like) throughout the developing world has reinforced their desire to provide projection forces with the fullest possible military capabilities.

In light of these built-in tendencies, and the emerging needs for projection forces, it is necessary to address two fundamental questions. What missions must U.S. forces be prepared to accomplish in the 1980s, and what force structure and doctrine would best enable us to accomplish these missions? We need to consider whether U.S. military interventions or counterinterventions in the developing world in the 1980s will always call for forces of the type and scale used by the United States in Vietnam in the 1960s and by the USSR in Afghanistan in 1979–1980. Will they also call for forces along the lines the French and Belgians used in Shaba I and II (roughly 2,500), the French used in the Central African Republic in 1979 (one company), and the British Commonwealth used in Zimbabwe-Rhodesia in 1979–1980 (approximately 1,200). Two factors merit special consideration in this connection: (1) the decisive impact of even relatively small, disciplined forces in a chaotic political environment where local forces may be disorganized and ill-disciplined; (2) the very great lethality the small combat unit has at its disposal today, compared with a generation ago, and will have at hand increasingly in the 1980s. Properly timed commitment of small formations with high mobility and firepower support at hand (armed helicopters, close support aircraft, naval gunfire) could in some cases be decisive without setting in motion the ponderous (and inevitably slow) deployment of two or three divisions.

Thus, there is a need to focus on the kinds of missions rapid-deployment forces might have. It is possible that for many operations small special-purpose forces may be of greater utility than larger general-purpose units. Some attention has been paid to the development of special-purpose forces recently. A so-called delta force has been developed for hostage seizures and similar operations. However, current forces (including appropriate intelligence capabilities) to deter or defeat either sophisticated operations by professional terrorists or for larger-scale, unconventional-warfare operations, are inadequate.

One approach to meeting some of these needs would be to develop a corps of political-military technicians to provide expertise on local conditions as well as general language competence and cultural knowledge to assist intervention forces in carrying out their missions. Such individuals and units exist in some form in all the services today (Army special forces, rangers, and foreign-area officers; Navy SEAL teams; Air Force special-operations units; Marine force-reconnaissance forces). But, there are not enough of them; joint service capabilities are not adequately exercised; psychological-warfare capabilities are inadequate; and there is a real shortage of language skills. Perhaps even the Foreign Service could contribute in this regard.

Tailoring or organizing, equipping, and training existing forces and acquiring new hardware is another possible approach, but it would require changes and decisions fraught with pitfalls. Each agency involved almost inevitably would make the case that its own role should be expanded, and Congress would be inclined to advocate programs that contribute to the vitality of individual constituencies.

A third approach sure to be suggested would be to configure the RDJTF within existing defense-budget and force-structure ceilings. This familiar approach would earmark units with other principal missions for deployment with the RDJTF under various contingencies. The net result would be to add training responsibilities to military units that are already overburdened by diverse mission requirements. Consequently, more missions would be accomplished less well. Nor would this approach address the prospect that serious contingencies in the developing world will probably coincide with events that will demand these earmarked units for their principal missions.

Consideration must be given to some scheme to coordinate the diverse and dispersed assets of the Department of Defense so that the president and his advisors have some options in selecting forces appropriate for meeting a wide range of threats to U.S. interests—in other words to make sure that the punishment fits the crime.

Strategy for Low-Intensity Conflict

Missing from the public discussion of U.S. projection forces until very recently has been the critical question of strategy. Military leaders will state frankly in private that it is all but impossible to develop capabilities without political-military guidance and that such guidance is woefully lacking. Simply put, the generals and admirals want to know what they are supposed to be preparing U.S. armed forces to do.

The role of strategy is to transform the total capabilities of a state into instruments of policy and to apply them to accomplishing the state's goals. Strategy must tell military planners what it is they must create capabilities for and how they should plan to use them. Strategy is not abstract; at the highest level it may start with an abstract statement of policy, but strategy must apply the policy in the concrete environment of the world as it is today and as it is envisioned for the future. Strategy must be refined and stated with increased specificity at each planning level, until it is stated most explicitly in the missions assigned to specific forces.

In the absence of strategy and the guidance it supplies, planners must turn to ad hoc substitutes. On the one hand, this usually leads to preparation of contingency plans based on best guesses about what the services might be asked to accomplish. On the other hand, in the absence of policy guidance, strategy tends to be inferred from tactics. Strategy at the highest level then becomes a restatement of successive aggregations of tactical goals. In the extreme, national decision makers responsible for setting policy can become prisoners of events. There is an old saw in public policy analysis: "Show me your programs and I'll tell you your policies." There is a certain element of truth in it. We are indeed constrained by the capability we provide ourselves. But, if this is in fact true, it will sometimes mean that program goals and procurement decisions will come to substitute for policy goals, and policy will be dictated from bottom to top.

Enunciating policy and strategy with sufficient clarity to provide guidance to those who must translate them into programs is not simple. The elaborate national-security-policy apparatus of the United States has undergone a number of modifications since its creation early in the post–World War II era as successive presidents have sought to develop ways of carrying out national-security tasks. Looking back at the experience, it is fair to conclude that one of the most successful efforts in this area also is one of the earliest, NSC-68, National Security Council Memorandum Number 68, written in early 1950. There is no little irony in the fact that NSC-68 never was approved at the highest level. Yet despite its difficulty, the development and promulgation of clear and adequately detailed policy guidance is the sine qua non of an effective national-security posture.

General Considerations for Low-Intensity Conflict

For the foreseeable future, U.S. national-security planners, like Soviet planners, will be preoccupied with central strategic nuclear and large-scale theater issues. The tenuous situation that exists for the United States at these levels will continue through most of the 1980s, even if the Reagan defense program continues as planned. It will profoundly affect our planning for and willingness to engage in low-intensity conflicts. The need to keep adequate forces immediately available to deter or defeat Soviet attacks in decisive theaters will inhibit our deployment of significant military assets to conflicts in peripheral areas such as the developing world. And the possibility of coming into battle against Soviet forces, or forces that the Soviet Union might be inclined to support as its own, will entail risks of escalation to the theater nuclear or central strategic levels, which we will be extremely reluctant to undertake, given the overall military balance. These facts of the correlation of world forces will color our approach to low-intensity conflict in the 1980s and will importantly shape our strategy. Bearing these facts in mind, we suggest some guidelines for U.S. strategy to deal with low-intensity conflict in the 1980s.

First, we have to become better at evaluating the developing world, to be sure we understand where U.S. interests reside and to appreciate which developments may pose threats to important U.S. interests. Given the centrality of Soviet actions in the formulation of U.S. strategy, we should evaluate likely Soviet involvement in conflicts as well as the prospects that proposed U.S.-sponsored measures will actually result in changes to our liking. Historically, we have suffered from a lack of foresight in attempts to predict soft spots in the third world where it appears that U.S. interests are vulnerable and potentially threatened. Why was the United States caught off guard so readily by the Iranian crisis in 1980, the fall of Ethiopia in 1977, the Cyprus crisis in 1974, the Arab-Israeli war in 1973, the Cuban missile crisis in 1962, and the Chinese revolution in 1949? Why was the United States not more aware of the innumerable variables involved in Vietnam and Korea?

A partial answer is inadequacy in U.S. gathering, processing, analysis, and assimilation of intelligence into decision making. Specifically, the U.S. intelligence community may be incapable of monitoring constantly every area of expressed U.S. interest. More important, regional assessments often cannot be incorporated optimally into the U.S. foreign-policy decision-making process. This defeats even the most sophisticated intelligence-gathering system.

Intelligence analysts cannot be expected to predict the future of a rapidly changing international system, especially given the fragmented and disputable data they often receive. However, analysts should be able to illustrate, judging from trends in political systems, options available to U.S. policymakers and to indicate the probabilities of various outcomes. They should also be able to identify and give prominence to those areas and developments most likely to affect U.S. interests and see their assessments transmitted to policymakers. Some intelligence experts have argued that the centralization of all collection and analysis operations would improve our record; a number of events have illuminated that healthy competition and even duplication of effort can safeguard against unforeseen variables and institutional biases.

Next, we must be sure that any set of policies that we develop for low-intensity conflict and for specific intervention is fully explained to the U.S. public and is capable of gaining their approval. A major information campaign should elaborate the U.S. interests that are involved in prospective conflict areas and the purposes and intended results of any actions. Historically the U.S. public (and allied publics as well) has been unwilling to sacrifice lives and other resources unless clearly defined, vital national interests are defined by U.S. national leaders.

If, as will often be the case, there is current or probable Soviet involvement in a conflict, the first task of the information program should be to highlight the strategic implications of Soviet and Soviet-sponsored activity. It should depict the advantages the Soviet Union would gain from acquisition of bases along sea lines of communication, the protection of which are vital to the long-term security of the Western world; the link between the health of Western economies (or the principal economies of the North) and the future development of the nations of the South; and the geopolitical advantages that can be gained by certain Soviet military and political successes, for example, on the southern and northern flanks of NATO. The recent history of Soviet efforts to foment instabilities or capitalize on unstable situations to undermine pro-Western governments, and how the efforts relate to geopolitical considerations, should be documented and explained. Patterns should be developed that infer Soviet intentions clearly.

The current administration attempted to explain its perception of Central American geopolitical realities in its White Paper on El Salvador. The long-term impact of this continuing information effort remains to be seen. The initial impact was diminished by several alleged inadequacies in documentation, which surfaced in the U.S. press. The continuing efforts of the Reagan administration to document the nature and extent of Soviet and Soviet proxy interventions in Central America hold some promise of success in preparing public opinion for U.S. responses.

Third, the United States needs to rely on the support and forces of its allies and friends who may have mutual interests in specified conflicts in the developing world. In a given conflict we may act either alone, in concert with allies, or through the forces of our allies or friends acting either overtly or covertly on behalf of the United States. There are several principal reasons why the United States should rely increasingly on allies and friends. For one thing, depending on the conflict, the United States may not have the capability to act alone. Simultaneous, worst-case conflicts, perhaps involving Soviet proxy military interventions (for instance, South Yemen attacks into Saudi Arabia; Cuban regular units, introduced through Nicaragua, move into El Salvador; and Libyan attacks into Chad) occurring during a period of high tension in U.S.-Soviet relations (pinning down NATO-Warsaw Pact forces in Europe as well as U.S./NATO units designated for reinforcement of NATO) would constitute requirements beyond the capability of U.S. active-duty military units. In less stressful situations, introducing U.S. troops where the Soviet military might be involved might create risks U.S. decision makers would be unwilling to take. In some of these cases, U.S. allies or friends may have interests involved for which they should and will spontaneously assume responsibility. And as a final consideration, as a matter of economy of effort, U.S. allies or friends often might have capabilities more efficient that those of the United States. For all of these reasons, the United States should work in closer cooperation with its friends and allies in resolving the challenges of low-intensity conflicts.

Given these general strategic considerations, we turn to the specific strategies that may be applied to low-intensity conflicts at the successive stages of their development.

Deterrence

Making the link between Soviet initiatives and potential proxy operations is important in deterrence. If the Soviet link is clear, the United States might threaten Moscow directly, at least on a nonmilitary level, through existing control mechanisms on technology exports. The United States could threaten to exert leverage over the Soviet Union by linking the quantity and quality of U.S. technology exports to the USSR to Soviet proxy behavior in the third world. Similarly, despite well-known domestic pressures, the United States has the capacity to threaten restrictions on grain and other food shipments. Also we might threaten important but not vital Soviet interests in areas noncontiguous to the original conflict, the increasingly popular theory of horizontal escalation.

There may be a number of options for deterring proxy forces themselves, both inside and outside the area of potential or actual intervention. In this case, the political-military instruments available to the United States are broader. Propaganda might be effective in deterring proxy incursions by emphasizing cultural and ideological differences between the USSR and the proxy or between the proxy and the nation in which it operates. Diplomatic exchanges and psychological operations might develop several themes: (1) the long-range inability of the Soviets to deliver little other than sales of conventional military equipment to proxy states; (2) weaknesses in Soviet economic-assistance programs, including the failure to promote technological and industrial growth in developing nations; (3) lack of support from other nations and in international fora for Soviet-sponsored ventures; and (4) the absence of Soviet security guarantees for its proxies. But the U.S. threat to the Soviet proxy or ally would have to contain all the elements of credibility outlined.

Preemption

Preemption is, of course, intervention unless the United States is invited in by a generally recognized government of a sovereign nation. The consequences of intervention under international law are problematic, especially in the case of intervention by a superpower.

The objects of preemption may be the same as those of deterrence. However, unlike deterrence, preemption requires an actual commitment of resources (rather than a stated intention to do so). Preemption may take place in the country where U.S. interests reside, between that country and sources of outside support, or directly against the supporting country's homeland. For obvious reasons, the last option would be highly problematic against a Soviet "ally" like the German Democratic Republic.

Possible modes of preemption by the United States and/or its allies are legion (and somewhat dependent on the time available). Some important preemptive options in the country where U.S. national interests reside are:

Psychological operations to induce the government and/or population to resist Soviet or Soviet proxy intervention or psychological operations to undercut support of an undesirable government.

Economic assistance to shore up the economy and provide the population with stakes to defend.

Military or paramilitary assistance (including weapons and advisors) to provide for defense of a status quo or to support a revolutionary force. If time is short (as it often will be), the weapons could be drawn from a U.S. quick-reaction stockpile of munitions ranging from simple rifles, mortars, and antitank weapons to more sophisticated systems.

Deploying non-U.S. military forces (allies or friends) with specific missions in defense of mutual interests.

Special-forces and ranger units, for training local forces in special operations or unconventional warfare.

Deployment of U.S. combat units with specific missions and doctrine, training, and weapons tailored to meet the threat of particular conflicts.

Preemption of the last type carries heavy risks, because most U.S. Army forces are structured to engage in attrition warfare on the plains of Central Europe—although the Army may be moving as fast as it can to develop doctrine applicable for maneuver warfare. With heavy units, there is a proclivity for digging in and reducing maneuver-warfare capability. Such a practice, if it leads to an extended commitment, would risk losing the support of the U.S. public.

A number of preemptive options are also available for imposing forces between the subject country and support forces:

Visible air surveillance of borders or coastlines.

Where relevant, border or sea surveillance by armed patrols.

Mining of harbors and key coastal areas.

Enforced blockade or quarantine to inspect and deny access.

Warning shots.

Disabling strikes to deny access.

Such actions up the ante by placing visible hurdles in the path of the supporting country, which it may not decide to test. They have some increased deterrent value by shifting the burden of risk taking or escalation onto the supporting country.

Finally, there are several preemptive actions that can be taken directly against the homeland of a supporting country:

Psychological operations to subvert the cause or the indigenous base of support.

Mining of ports and harbors.

Blockade of borders, coastlines, or territorial waters by military force or implantation of chemical or radiological agents.

Clandestine provision of arms, advice, or training for revolutionary groups.

Special operations in support of an indigenous coup d'e´tat or an outright military operation to seize, abduct, or neutralize government leaders.

Clandestine use of chemical or biological agents.

Unconventional warfare by special forces.

Armed demonstration air or sea attacks against selected targets.

Conventional military invasion by the military forces of U.S. friends or allies, with or without U.S. support.

Conventional invasion by specifically tailored U.S. military units, based on thorough intelligence and with specific missions.

The object in this mode is to destroy the supporting country's will or military capability to intervene contrary to U.S. interests. Operations should be controlled by adaptive command structures and should be designed insofar as possible for quick, local decisions. Occupation generally should not be envisioned; if land forces are committed, withdrawal should be quick.

Preemptive actions will entail risk. Although sound intelligence should be able to help determine the level of risk, Soviet troops or advisors may be in the country and avoiding them might be difficult or impossible. Such actions also will be inherently questionable to the U.S. Congress and public at large and so will entail a different sort of risk and cost. And the requirement for timely and secret action may not provide an opportunity to explain in advance and gain acceptance for preemptive armed force, which might take on the appearance, if not the legal form, of intervention. A quick, successful operation might find greater ex post facto acceptance.

Reaction

This mode assumes far greater political, military, and psychological burdens and military risks. Reaction generally will require that military forces already in place withdraw or be defeated. The initiative already is with the enemy. He and his possible supporters will have made an overt commitment already and probably will have the momentum of his population behind him.

Given the traditional assumption that the defender has the advantage and that the attacker would require a three-to-one advantage to dislodge him, the magnitude of U.S., allied or friendly military efforts required would be greater than for preemption. As indicated, U.S. conventional forces might not be adequate for such contingencies, leading to a need for new unconventional weapons, forces, and even for new forms of unconventional warfare.

Conclusion

In a recent presentation centering on the generic problem of the decline of U.S. power and worldwide perceptions of that decline, James R. Schlesinger stated:

> The Third World will continue to be the source of low-intensity conflicts, none of which is likely to bring about a serious alteration in the overall

balance of power, in contrast to major conflicts in the Middle East or in Europe. Included in the Third World is Central America, an area of renewed American interests. The war in El Salvador is not going well. Further, the attempt to compel or to induce a change in policy on the part of Nicaragua and Cuba has, to this point, been a failure.

Unless we are able to improve our capacity to act very rapidly, in all likelihood, one can look forward to a further deterioration of our position in Central America.

Clearly, our planning needs to proceed and be governed by strategic guidance, and that guidance must be based on careful thinking about the environment of the 1980s. That environment will abound with conflicts requiring responses quite unconventional for U.S. planners. Yet we must be able to help shape the environment in ways that will advance and protect concrete U.S. interests.

Planning for conflict in disparate areas of the developing world is not an insuperable task. A useful step would be to set up a forum where academics and others with specific country and regional knowledge could come together with government officials to assess the current state of thinking and planning for low-intensity conflict. This would include evaluating probable trends and the instrumentalities the United States and its allies might have available for affecting them. Allied foreign-policy planners should be brought in to assess our mutual interests and capabilities and discuss possibilities for combined unconventional operations.

The initial study could be followed by annual reviews that would re-evaluate the trends and provide near-term (say, 1–2-year) details for planners. Such a forum would not be a substitute for the formal planning machinery within the national-security system, either at the top or in the several departments. But it would provide for an approach to this problem that would routinely integrate thinking and planning about policy with more detailed thinking and planning for execution.Such arrangements, while complex and cumbersome, are no more complex than the world in which the United States must make its way during the 1980s.

Notes

1. A fourth possibility, that the Soviet Union builds military forces because of some internal dynamic and that this results in capabilities employed tactically in search of a strategy, is fascinating intellectually but is not widely held (to say nothing of its credibility).

2. Indeed, it is fair to ask how much more really is known than George

Kennan gave us in "The Sources of Soviet Conduct" first published in *Foreign Affairs*, 25 (July 1947).

3. See, for example, Caspar W. Weinberger, *Soviet Military Power* (Washington, D.C.: U.S. Government Printing Office, 1981), p. 1.

4. General Edward C. Meyer, quoted in Charles W. Corddry, "Army Seeks to Move East in Germany," *Baltimore Sun*, 16 August 1981.

5. Ibid.

6. The Army general-planning figure for the total personnel to support an Army division of 16–18,000 is approximately 50,000, although this figure varies by theater to which divisions are deployed. In addition to a 750,000 shortfall in required division strength, one must add a shortfall of 250,000 in reserve strength and at least another 100,000 for overhead. The figure for the Navy, Marine Corps, and Air Force is from William W. Kaufman, "US Defense Needs in the 1980s," in Lt. Gen. Brent C. Scowcroft, ed., *Military Service in the United States* (New York: the American Assembly, 1981), p. I-31.

7. Charles W. Corddry, "Army Seeks to Move East in Germany," *Baltimore Sun*, 16 August 1981.

8. The latter is in the light of the failed rescue mission in Iran.

9. For the reasons why military strategists remain nameless, see William Taylor, " 'Clearance' Muzzles Military Strategists," *Washington Star*, 14 July 1981.

10. Some of these recommendations were articulated by Robert W. Komer at the Georgetown University Center for Strategic and International Studies Conference on the Future of Conflict, Washington, D.C., 23–24 November 1981.

11. See Amos A. Jordan, William J. Taylor, Jr., and Associates, *American National Security: Policy and Process* (Baltimore: Johns Hopkins University Press, 1981), pp. 127–150.

12. For example, note the different estimates of production costs and logistical backup for Soviet combat forces during the 1960s and early 1970s and the different estimates of Soviet strategic forces during the same period, ibid., p. 149. Also, the CIA and DIA recently have used similar information to arrive at far different predictions for the future of Soviet energy policy.

13. Actually these are among the lessons that should have been learned in the Korean War. They were elaborated on early in Robert E. Osgood, *Limited War: The Challenge to American Strategy* (Chicago: University of Chicago Press, 1957). See also Jordan, Taylor, and Associates, *American National Security*, pp. 42–57.

14. See Samuel P. Huntington, "Trade, Technology, and Leverage: Economic Diplomacy," *Foreign Policy*, (Fall 1978): 67–70 and J. Frederick

Bucy, "Technology Transfer and East-West Trade: A Reappraisal," *International Security* (Winter 1980–1981): 132–151.

13. James R. Schlesinger (Presentation at the Georgetown University Center for Strategic and International Studies Conference on The Future of Conflict, Washington, D.C., 23–24 November 1981).

Index

92, 131–132, 282, 283, 347, 359, 366,
399–408 *passim*, 412, 461, 473–474;
World War II, 125, 129
U.S. Aid for International Development
(AID), 387
U.S. Air Force, 21, 190, 212, 465, 466,
468, 470; Pacific Command
(PACOM), 295, 310
U.S. Army, 114, 465, 466–467, 468, 470,
475–476, 479 n.6; delta force, 470;
Green Berets, 21, 180; special forces,
125–127, 180, 470
U.S. Commerce Department: "Peter-
son Report," 349
U.S. Congress, 17–18; Congressional
Reform Caucus, 467
U.S. Immigration and Naturalization
Service, 366
U.S. International Communication
Agency, 113
U.S. Joint Chiefs of Staff (JCS), 21, 114
U.S. Marines, 175, 206, 466, 468, 470
U.S. National Security Council, 126
U.S. Navy, 36, 40, 128, 181, 446, 453,
465, 466, 468; SEAL, 470; Under-
water Units, 21
U.S. Office of Technology Assessment,
29
U.S. Presidency, 17, 125
U.S. Senate: Foreign Relations Com-
mittee, 135; Resolution 222 (1974),
441; Subcommittee on Security and
Terrorism, 141
Upper Volta, 35
Uruguay, 146
Urutu LMV (Brazil), 61
Uzi submachine gun (Israel), 65

Valenta, Jiri, 348
Van Creveld, Martin, 70
Vance, Cyrus, 123
Velindaba reactor (South Africa), 99
Venezuela, 146; and Guyana, 37, 356,
371; oil resources, 349, 357; and
U.S., 61, 346, 347, 356–357
Vietnam, 142, 183–191 *passim*, 293–318
passim; and China, 35, 37, 172, 183,
184, 190–191, 293, 296, 297, 305,
308–309, 316, 317, 318, 338; and
USSR, 23, 169, 172, 177, 183, 296,

297, 304, 305, 306, 308, 314, 318, 329,
338
Vietnam War, 19–20, 21, 23, 125, 145,
178, 293, 302, 303, 304, 306; and
television, 117, 121–122
Vietnamese refugees, 155, 296
Viggen aircraft (Sweden), 415
Vinson-Trammel Act (1936), 435
Voice of America, 113

Walsh, Edmund A., 435
Waltz, Kenneth, 82, 85–86
War of Attrition (1970), 174, 240, 248
Washington, George, 461
Washington Energy Conference (1974),
38, 39
Washington Post, The, 164
Weather Underground, 165
Weathermen, 117
Webster-Ashburton Treaty (1942), 36
Weinberger, Caspar, 464
West Bank (Jordan), 159, 456
West Berlin, 420
West Central Asia, 294
West Germany, 40, 101, 113, 196, 400–
401, 402; and Nordic conflict sce-
nario, 411, 414; and psychological
warfare scenario, 131–134; terrorism,
135, 145, 147, 157–158
Western Europe, 46, 51, 399–408; arms
transfers, 76–77; and Central
America, 347, 355; defense spending,
412, 415; and Middle East oil, 13–14,
38, 39, 88, 92, 102, 238, 244, 263, 350;
military interventions, 189–190; and
NATO, 399–408 *passim*; nuclear
policy, 87, 101–102; psychological
warfare, 113, 120, 131–132; Scandinavia and Nordic conflict scenario,
102, 113, 402–405, 411–416; and
U.S., 12, 15, 16, 88, 92, 131–132,
282, 283, 347, 359, 366, 399–408
passim, 412; and USSR, 12, 40, 88,
102, 143, 146, 148, 399, 400, 412, 414
Western Sahara, 241, 385
Wheeler, Earl, 229
White Guard émigrés, 144
Wilson, Charles, 439
Witte, Sergei, 328
Wohlstellter, Albert, 82, 84, 107 n.10

About the Contributors

David E. Albright is currently professor of national-security affairs at the Air War College, Maxwell Air Force Base, Alabama. He was formerly senior text editor of the journal *Problems of Communism* and earlier research associate and editor for the project on the United States and China in world affairs at the Council on Foreign Relations, New York City. He has written extensively on the policies of the Communist states toward Africa. His publications include *Communism in Africa* and the forthcoming *The Communist States and Africa*.

Yonah Alexander is professor of international studies and director of the Institute for Studies in International Terrorism, State University of New York; Fellow, Institute for Social and Behavioral Pathology, University of Chicago; and a senior staff member at The Center for Strategic and International Studies, Georgetown University. Educated at Columbia University and the University of Chicago, Professor Alexander is editor-in-chief of *Terrorism: An International Journal* and *Political Communication and Persuasion: An International Journal*. His most recent publications include *Political Terrorism and Energy* (1982), *Business and the Middle East* (1982), and *Terrorism in Europe* (1982).

Bruce E. Arlinghaus, Captain, U.S. Army, is assistant professor of anthropology in the Department of Social Sciences at the United States Military Academy. After commissioning through ROTC at The Ohio State University, he was named a university Fellow at Indiana University, receiving the M.A. (1973) and Ph.D. (1983) in anthropology and African studies. He is currently engaged in research on the impact of high-technology arms transfers on economic development and political stability in Subsaharan Africa and is the editor of *Arms for Africa* (Lexington Books, forthcoming).

Jack Child is currently an associate professor for language and foreign studies at The American University. He is a retired lieutenant colonel of the U.S. Army and has taught Spanish and Latin American Studies at the United States Military Academy, the Inter-American Defense College, and The American University. His research interest and publications have focused on the Latin American military, the Inter-American Military/Security System, international relations of Latin America, geopolitical thinking in Latin America, and conflict and peacekeeping in the Western Hemisphere. He received the Ph.D. from The American University.

499

Paul M. Cole is a graduate of the Georgetown University Graduate School of Foreign Service. He is currently a research associate in political-military studies at The Center for Strategic and International Studies, Georgetown University. Mr. Cole was previously assistant editor of *Arms Control Today*.

Jeffrey R. Cooper is the founder and president of Jeffrey Cooper Associates, Inc., which conducts specialized policy research for the national-security community in the areas of nuclear-weapons modernization, military applications of space, and East–West trade and technology transfer. Prior to forming his own company, Mr. Cooper created and managed the Department of Policy Studies at R&D Associates. From 1977 to 1979, he was assistant to Secretary of Energy James R. Schlesinger. Previously, he held positions at the U.S. Arms Control and Disarmament Agency, the Federal Energy Administration, and the U.S. Senate.

M. Thomas Davis, Captain, U.S. Army, is currently assigned to the Department of Social Sciences at the United States Military Academy. He received the B.S. from West Point and the M.A. from Harvard University's Center for Middle Eastern Studies. His military service includes five years with the U.S. Army in Europe.

Donald B. Disney, Jr., is a commander in the U.S. Navy. He received the B.S. in foreign affairs from the U.S. Naval Academy and was awarded the M.A. in national-security affairs from the Naval Postgraduate School. He has submitted articles for publication to both the U.S. Naval Institute *Proceedings* and Naval College *Review*. A command-qualified surface-warfare officer with experience in minesweepers, destroyers, and amphibious ships, Lieutenant Commander Disney has served as Middle East Plans Officer at the Office of the Chief of Naval Operations since 1981.

James H. Doyle, Jr., Vice-Admiral, U.S. Navy (Ret.), graduated from the U.S. Naval Academy in 1946. He received the J.D. in 1953 from the George Washington University Law School. When he retired in 1980, he was deputy chief of naval operations. He is now a consultant on defense matters, executive vice-president of the Naval Historical Foundation, and on the faculty of the George Washington University Law School. He is a member of the bar in the District of Columbia and the State of California.

Richard L. Garwin is IBM Fellow at the Thomas J. Watson Research Center, adjunct professor of physics at Columbia University, and has been professor of public policy at Harvard University, member of the president's Science Advisory Committee, member of the Defense Science Board, and a consultant to the Defense Department and other agencies of the U.S.

government, including the Los Alamos Scientific Laboratory. His contributions to the development, analysis, and choice of weapons systems extend from 1950 to the present and include technologies of communications, surveillance, navigation, and propulsion.

Gerrit W. Gong, a former Rhodes scholar, is currently a research associate at The Center for Strategic and International Studies, Georgetown University. He received the Ph.D. and the M.A. in international relations from Oxford University, where his postdoctoral research focused on the evolution of the international political system with special reference to the ramifications brought by the entry of culturally diverse non-European countries, for example, China and Japan.

Thomas H. Johnson, Lieutenant Colonel, U.S. Army, is currently special assistant to the president's science advisor and executive director of the White House Science Council. He received the Ph.D. in theoretical physics from the University of California . He is in Washington, D.C., on leave from the United States Military Academy, where he is director of the Science Research Laboratory.

Rodney W. Jones is senior Fellow and director of the Proliferation of Small Nuclear Forces project at The Center for Strategic and International Studies, Georgetown University. He received the B.A. from Juyatia College and the M.A. in international relations and the Ph.D. in political science from Columbia University. He is the author of several books and articles, including *Nuclear Proliferation: Islam, the Bomb and South Asia* (1981).

Richard J. Kessler is deputy director of the Project on Energy and National Security and program director for the Energy Emergency Planning Program at The Center for Strategic and International Studies, Georgetown University. He is coauthor of *The Critical Link: Energy and National Security in the 1980s* (1982) and a contributor to *Political Terrorism and Energy, The Threat and Response* (1982). He received the B.A. from Colgate University and the M.A. and M.A.L.D. from The Fletcher School of Law and Diplomacy, Tufts University. He is currently preparing his doctorate.

Robert A. Kilmarx is a former special advisor to Headquarters U.S. Air Force. He has served as an advisor to the United Nations as well as to international corporations and foreign governments. Dr. Kilmarx is the author of *A History of Soviet Air Power* (1962) and numerous Georgetown University Center for Strategic and International Studies publications on economic and defense issues including *America's Maritime Legacy*, an analysis of merchant shipping and shipbuilding under sovereign U.S. jurisdiction from precolonial times to the present. Dr. Kilmarx is currently the senior consultant in the international division of Fraser Associates.

Robert W. Komer has had a distinguished career in the U.S. national-security community. He served in the U.S. Army stationed in Europe during World War II. He became deputy special assistant to the president for National Security Council affairs in 1965 and special assistant to President Johnson in 1966. He went to Vietnam from 1967 to 1968 as chief pacification advisor, with the rank of ambassador. From 1968 to 1969 he served as U.S. ambassador to Turkey. He was advisor to the secretary of defense on NATO affairs from 1977 to 1979 and under secretary of defense for policy from 1979 to 1981.

Christopher Lamb is currently on leave from Georgetown University to serve as a research Fellow at the North Atlantic Assembly in Belgium. His research there concerns NATO manpower problems and the military technology of outer space. His recent publications have focused on diplomacy and U.S. foreign policy and on public opinion and nuclear weapons in Europe.

Robert S. Leiken is director of the Soviet-Latin American Project at The Center for Strategic and International Studies, Georgetown University. He received the B.A. (1961) and the M.A. (1964) from Harvard University. Mr. Leiken has contributed to a variety of magazines and newspapers and published a widely discussed article in *Foreign Policy* (Spring 1981). Mr. Leiken's most recent publication was *Soviet Strategy in Latin America* (1982).

Michael Moodie is director of program analysis at The Center for Strategic and International Studies (CSIS), Georgetown University, with responsibility for developing, integrating, and monitoring CSIS programs. He is also an associate editor for the Center's *Washington Quarterly* as well as executive secretary of the CSIS Maritime Policy Study Group. He has published articles on a variety of international-security issues and on naval policy. Mr. Moodie is a graduate of The Fletcher School of Law and Diplomacy, Tufts University.

John Norton Moore received the A.B. in economics from Drew University in 1958, the LL.B. from Duke Law School in 1962, and the LL.M. from the University of Illinois in 1965. He has been a Fellow at the University of California and at the Yale Law School. From 1973 to 1976 Mr. Moore was the U.S. ambassador to the Law of the Sea Conference. He is currently the director of the Center for Ocean Law and Policy at the University of Virginia

Law School and the chairman of the National Security Council Interagency Task Force on the Law of the Sea.

Kenneth A. Myers is currently a professiorial lecturer in European politics at Georgetown University. He was formerly a staff member of the Research Analysis Corporation and of the Washington Center of Foreign Policy Research. From 1975 to 1976 he held the Chair of Strategic Studies at Carleton University in Ottawa. He is the author of Georgetown University Center for Strategic International Studies (CSIS) monograph *German Ostpolitik and American Security Interests in Europe* and a CSIS Washington Paper (1979), *North Atlantic Security: The Forgotten Flank?* He also headed the CSIS study on *Soviet Decision Making and SALT*. He was coordinator of the NATO Conference in 1979.

Michael C. Ryan, Major, U.S. Army, is currently assigned to the United States Military Academy as an instructor of international relations and national-security studies. He has served in a variety of training, staff, and command assignments in Europe and the United States. He received the S.M. in political science from the Massachusetts Institute of Technology and is also an MIT Ph.D. candidate, writing his dissertation on national-defense issues.

James R. Schlesinger is currently a senior advisor at The Center for Strategic and International Studies, Georgetown University, as well as a senior advisor to Lehman Brothers Kuhn Loeb, Inc. He has served as the first secretary of energy, secretary of defense, director of Central Intelligence, chairman of the Atomic Energy Commission, and as assistant and acting director of the Bureau of the Budget. He received the A.B., A.M., and Ph.D. in economics from Harvard University.

Gilven M. Slonim currently serves as president of the Oceanic Educational Foundation, established in 1970. His publications include "Humanities of the Sea—Antidote to Future Shock," "Oceanic Education—Pathway to the Frontier of the Future," "A Flagship View of Command Decisions," "Sea-creation Wave of the Future," "Have We Learned the Lesson of Pearl Harbor?" "The Oceanic Contribution to Future Quality of Living," "Oceanic Policy—Prelude to Opportunity," and "Oceanic Education—The Policy Imperative."

W. Scott Thompson graduated from Stanford University in 1963, where he was awarded a Rhodes scholarship. He is a founding member of the Committee on the Present Danger and a member of the Council on Foreign Relations and the International Institute for Strategic Studies. Dr. Thompson served as senior Fellow in political-military affairs at The Center for Strategic and International Studies, Georgetown University. He is the editor of the recently published *From Weakness to Strength: National Strategy in the 1980s* and coauthor of *Fulcrum of Power: The Third World Between Moscow and Washington.*

Lowell Wood leads the Special Studies Group at the Lawrence Livermore Laboratories of the University of California at Berkeley. The members of this group do research on the technological aspects of national-security problems, with present emphasis on ensuring the survival of the United States through the course of serious, large-scale conflict with absolutely minimal collateral loss of human life. Dr. Wood received the B.S. and Ph.D. in math, chemistry, and astrophysics from the University of California at Los Angeles.

About the Editors

William J. Taylor, Jr., is director of Political-Military Studies and Deputy Chief Operating Officer at the Georgetown University Center for Strategic and International Studies. From 1970 to 1981 he was professor of social sciences, director of national-security studies, and director of the Debate Council and Forum at the United States Military Academy. From 1975 to 1976 he was a visiting professor at the National War College. Dr. Taylor is the author of numerous publications on national- and international-security affairs.

Steven A. Maaranen is a member of the staff of the Office of Planning and Analysis, Los Alamos National Laboratory. He received the Ph.D. in government from Claremont Graduate School. Dr. Maaranen's publications include *Strategic Trends and Critical Choices* (1981) and *Illusions of Peace and the Coming of War: The British Parliamentary Defense Debate, 1932–1939* (forthcoming).